Nonparametric Econometrics

This book systematically and thoroughly covers a vast literature on the non-parametric and semiparametric statistics and econometrics that has evolved over the past five decades. Within this framework this is the first book to discuss the principles of the nonparametric approach to the topics covered in a first-year graduate course in econometrics, for example, regression function, heteroskedasticity, simultaneous equations models, logit-probit, and censored models. Nonparametric and semiparametric methods potentially offer considerable reward to applied researchers, owing to the methods' ability to adapt to many unknown features of the data. Professors Pagan and Ullah provide intuitive explanations of difficult concepts, heuristic developments of theory, and empirical examples emphasizing the usefulness of the modern nonparametric approach. The book should provide a new perspective on teaching and research in applied subjects in general and econometrics and statistics in particular.

Adrian Pagan is a Professor of Economics at the Institute of Advanced Studies, Australian National University. A Fellow of the Econometric Society, Australian Academy of Social Sciences, and Journal of Econometrics, he is the coauthor or author of several books and numerous articles in economics, econometrics, and public policy. Professor Pagan has been coeditor of the *Journal of Applied Econometrics and Econometric Theory* and associate editor of *Econometrica* and *Journal of Econometrics*. He is currently a member of the editorial boards of *Economic Record, Advances in Computational Economics*, and *Econometric Reviews* and is coeditor of the *Themes in Modern Econometrics* series for Cambridge University Press. He has also served as a visiting professor or scholar at UCLA, Johns Hopkins University, University of Rochester, Princeton and Yale Universities, and Institute of Advanced Studies, Vienna. Professor Pagan is also a member of the Board of Governors of the Reserve Bank of Australia.

Aman Ullah is a Professor and Chair in the Department of Economics at the University of California, Riverside. A Fellow of the National Academy of Sciences (India), he is the coauthor, editor, or coeditor of six books and over ninety professional papers in economics, econometrics, and statistics. Professor Ullah is a coeditor of the journal *Econometric Reviews* and associate editor of *Journal of Nonparametric Statistics, Journal of Quantitative Economics*, and *Empirical Economics*, among others. He has taught at the University of Western Ontario, Canada, for several years and has served as a visiting professor or scholar at Southern Methodist University, UCLA, Stanford University, University of Illinois, Bilkent University, Turkey, Australian National University, Monash University, Tinbergen Institute, Holland, and CORE, Belgium, among others.

Themes in Modern Econometrics

Managing editor
PETER C.B. PHILLIPS, *Yale University*

Series editors
ADRIAN PAGAN, *Australian National University*
CHRISTIAN GOURIEROUX, *CREST and CEPREMAP, Paris*
MICHAEL WICKENS, *University of York*

Themes in Modern Econometrics is designed to service the large and growing need for explicit teaching tools in econometrics. It will provide an organised sequence of textbooks in econometrics aimed squarely at the student population, and will be the first series in the discipline to have this as its express aim. Written at a level accessible to students with an introductory course in econometrics behind them, each book will address topics or themes that students and researchers encounter daily. While each book will be designed to stand alone as an authoritative survey in its own right, the distinct emphasis throughout will be on pedagogic excellence.

Titles in the series

Statistics and Econometric Models: Volumes 1 and 2
CHRISTIAN GOURIEROUX and ALAIN MONFORT
Translated by QUANG VUONG

Time Series and Dynamic Models
CHRISTIAN GOURIEROUX and ALAIN MONFORT
Translated and edited by GIAMPIERO GALLO

Unit Roots, Cointegration, and Structural Change
G.S. MADDALA and IN-MOO KIM

Generalized Method of Moments Estimation
Edited by LASZLO MATYAS

NONPARAMETRIC ECONOMETRICS

ADRIAN PAGAN

Australian National
University

AMAN ULLAH

University of California,
Riverside

CAMBRIDGE
UNIVERSITY PRESS

PUBLISHED BY THE PRESS SYNDICATE OF THE UNIVERSITY OF CAMBRIDGE
The Pitt Building, Trumpington Street, Cambridge, United Kingdom

CAMBRIDGE UNIVERSITY PRESS
The Edinburgh Building, Cambridge CB2 2RU, UK   http://www.cup.cam.ac.uk
40 West 20th Street, New York, NY 10011-4211, USA   http://www.cup.org
10 Stamford Road, Oakleigh, Melbourne 3166, Australia

First published 1999

Printed in the United States of America

Typeset in Times Roman 10/12 pt. in LaTeX 2_ε [TB]

*A catalog record for this book is available from
the British Library.*

Library of Congress Cataloging-in-Publication Data
Pagan, Adrian.
    Nonparametric econometrics / Adrian Pagan, Aman Ullah.
        p.   cm. – (Themes in Modern Econometrics)
    Includes bibliographical references (p.   ).
    ISBN 0-521-35564-8 (hardbound)
    1. Econometrics.   2. Mathematical statistics.   3. Economics –
Statistical methods.   I. Ullah, Aman.   II. Title.
HB139.P34   1999
330'.01'5195 – dc21   98-37218
                                                                CIP

ISBN 0 521 35564 8 hardback
ISBN 0 521 58611 9 paperback

To my parents, Razia Begum and Ataullah Khan

Contents

Contents

Contents

Preface

It took almost a decade to complete the work on this book. During this period Pagan moved from the University of Rochester to the Australian National University while Ullah moved to the University of California, Riverside from the University of Western Ontario. Such moves are always difficult and are made more so when the protagonists were trying to write about a field that at time seemed to be growing at an exponential rate. All of this disruption caused the book to be typed and retyped several times on two continents as well as ensured that the idea of completing it died and was reborn more than once. In the end our desire to see a completed text won out.

As anyone who performs applied work knows, many assumptions are made in coming up with answers. Mostly these involve assertions about the distributional features of variables and functional relations among them. It is not unusual for one to feel a little uncomfortable with some of these assumptions and to wonder what would happen if they could be relaxed. We were therefore rather intrigued to come across a literature in mathematical statistics that provided tools for doing some of the applied work with a minimal number of assumptions. This "nonparametrics" literature was found to be very useful in some of our early work on the risk premium, and that experience suggested that these methods could be quite useful more generally and that they should be more widely known to econometricians. Hence our objective became one of bringing this literature together in a systematic and integrated way within a single source. In the back of our mind was the idea that we might produce a book that paralleled traditional econometrics texts in the sense of explaining how one might perform the same analyses as was done parametrically in those books but in a nonparametric way. Principally, the idea was to provide a nonparametric treatment for the regression model along with its extensions to handle complications like heteroskedasticity and censoring. To some extent this vision faded under the weight of the rapidly expanding literature that we needed to cover, although traces of it are still evident in the selection of topics that are studied.

The book is designed for those who might be beginning research in the area as well as those who are interested in appreciating some of the statistical theory that underlies the methods. Many of these techniques have seen increasing application as they have become more readily available in various computer packages. Generally the audience will be those taking graduate courses in econometrics and statistics, but the book may also be useful for students in other applied sciences, such as engineering, medicine, psychology, and sociology. Many techniques are discussed in the book. If it has a bias it is toward kernel-based methods of nonparametric estimation. The emphasis in the book is upon a discussion of the methods and the theory that underlies them. Some empirical examples and/or a summary of the empirical literature are presented to illustrate certain points, although the book is not an applied one in any sense.

It is a pleasure to express our appreciation toward those who have influenced this work. Michael Parkin was especially encouraging regarding this project. Joel Horowitz read the complete manuscript and made many valuable comments upon it. Given that we have sometimes not incorporated what he said he should not be blamed for it in any way. Many others have also made their mark on it. In particular, N. Roy, C. Chiu, J. Racine, P. Rilstone, Y. Fan, Q. Li, R. Breunig, M. Brenner, S. Kumar, K. Mundra, and S. Thompson have read and commented on several chapters. On the production side, B. Chatman and K. Lowney typed early drafts with skill and patience. Finally, as those closest to you are the ones who bear the greatest cost, we want to record our tremendous debt to our families who suffered through it all. For Aman this means his wife, Shobha, and daughter, Sushana. For Adrian it is Janet, Becky, and Mandy.

1   Introduction

In the past fifty years since it first came to prominence, econometrics has broadened, both in the nature of the data being worked with and in the range of issues that it addresses. Initially econometricians were primarily interested in relations between two or more series, but today they find themselves concerned with measuring volatility of financial returns, durations of events, and the conditional probabilities of decisions, *inter alia*. A textbook such as Greene's (1997) captures this expansion extremely well. The same textbook also shows that there is still an underlying unity in the way analysis proceeds, in that the method of linear regression and maximum likelihood form the tool kit of an applied econometrician.

In one area of quantitative economics, namely that concerned with the analysis of observed choices made by economic agents in the sphere of consumption and production, it has long been felt that the investigation of questions such as consistency of the data with the maximization principle, homotheticity, and separability of preferences should not be constrained by the need to make precise assumptions about the nature of preferences or production relations. Probably the earliest manifestation of this concern was Samuelson's (1938) development of the revealed preference theory, and since that time there has been a series of contributions aiming to develop a nonparametric approach to the economics of production and consumption, for example, Afriat (1967), Hanoch and Rothschild (1972), Diewert and Parkan (1978), and Varian (1984). These papers deal with nonparametric tests of the predictions of economic theory without specifying particular functional forms for underlying demand and production relations, something that would be required if one proceeded to test the predictions in the traditional framework (e.g., Greene 1997, Chapter 15). Perhaps the major limitation to these methods has been the fact that the stochastic nature of the data is ignored, although the recent work of Varian (1985) and Epstein and Yatchew (1985) attempts to remove some of these difficulties.

A different approach, more in line with traditional work, has been to locate the source of unease in particular assumptions being made during the application of the classic techniques. In the case of linear regression, a particular concern has been with the linearity of the functional form connecting the variables appearing in it. This concern initially spawned an interest in transformations of the dependent and independent variables, leading to the use of flexible functional forms, such as those of Diewert (1971), Berndt and Khaled (1979) and Christensen et al. (1973), to approximate the unknown relation. A drawback of this literature was that it only provided local Taylor series approximations. Consequently, it is not surprising that interest arose in improving on such approximations.

To do this it was important to realize that, in many instances, one was attempting to estimate an expectation of one variable, Y, conditional upon others, X. This identification directs attention to the need to be able to estimate the density of Y conditional upon X, as the knowledge of that quantity would enable one to extract the conditional mean. Accordingly, Chapter 2 reviews the procedures that have been advocated for doing that. This is a surprisingly long chapter, partly because there are many different strategies, and partly because all of the techniques involve "tuning parameters" whose determination has been the subject of an enormous literature, which has only now settled down to reflect a consensus view.

Having determined ways of nonparametrically estimating a conditional density, the conditional mean at a point x readily follows as a weighted average $\sum_{i=1}^{n} w(x_i; x) y_i$ of the n data points $\{x_i, y_i\}$; here y_i are observations on the dependent variable and x_i on the independent variable, and $w(x_i; x)$ are a set of weights that depend upon x_i and the point x at which the conditional expectation is to be evaluated. Of course there turn out to be many weighting functions $w(x_i; x)$ that work, and some of the popular ones are detailed in Chapter 3. Broadly these correspond to whether one wishes to have a local (to the point x) or a global approximation. This chapter also shows how the procedures extend to the estimation of any higher order moment, whereas Chapter 4 considers the modification needed if interest centers upon the derivatives of the function linking Y and X, either at a point or as the average over an interval.

Perhaps the major complication in a purely nonparametric (*NP*) approach to estimation is the "curse of dimensionality." Every method has some cost associated with it and, in the instance of nonparametrics, it is the need for very large samples if an accurate measurement of the function is to be made. Moreover, the size of sample required increases rapidly with the number of variables involved in any relation. Such a feature leads to the proposition that one might well prefer to restrict some variables to have a linear impact while allowing a much smaller number to have a nonlinear one. A well-known example of this phenomenon occurs in studies of the wage paid to an individual. The wage is regarded as being influenced by the individual's personal characteristics as well as the number of years of job experience, but, whereas the impact of the personal characteristics is taken to be linear, that for experience is nonlinear. Accordingly, the first part of Chapter 5 deals with such models, allowing the nonlinearity to be located either in the conditional mean or the conditional variance. Effectively, estimation involves a combination of parametric and nonparametric methods, leading to the estimators being described as *semiparametric* (SP).

In the second part of Chapter 5 the nature of the conditional mean is taken to be known up to a finite number of parameters, and attention switches to the distributional properties of the error term left over after the conditional mean has been extracted. Regression analysis either explicitly or implicitly treats this error as normally distributed, except for those instances in which the dependent variable involves "count" or duration data, whereupon densities such as the negative binomial or Weibull are invoked. Consequently, it is of interest to study the estimation of the parameters of the conditional mean when the error density is unknown. This scenario also falls into the class of semiparametric problems, and a range of concepts have been introduced to categorize the properties of such SP estimators. In parametric models being estimated by maximum likelihood, questions relating to the efficiency of an estimator and its dependence on nuisance parameters are most usefully analyzed with the Cramer–Rao bound and Fisher's information matrix. There are analogous concepts in the SP literature, such as the SP efficiency bound, and the definition and construction of such quantities is laid out in Chapter 5 within the context of the simplest possible environment. Once done, it is natural to seek to design a fully efficient estimator in the face of an unknown density. It is shown that the crucial step in performing such a task is the ability to estimate the "score" of the unknown density – the ratio of the first derivative of the density to the density itself. Hence, the techniques of Chapter 2 are called upon to estimate this unknown variable.

Chapter 6 represents an excursion into the estimation of the parameters of nonlinear simultaneous equations. It has been known for many years that the optimal instruments are related to the expectation of the endogenous variables conditional upon the exogenous ones, but when the system is nonlinear there is no closed form expression for this. Nonparametric techniques therefore appeal as a way of generating the optimal instruments for later use in estimating the unknown parameters. A number of such SP estimators exist in the literature and the sections of this chapter are devoted to an enumeration of them.

The following three chapters concentrate upon some important models in econometrics where semiparametric methods are likely to be popular – binary choices (Chapter 7), censored regression (Chapter 8), and selectivity models (Chapter 9). Mostly, the unknown parameters of these models have been estimated by maximum likelihood. We therefore seek to describe estimators that do not make assumptions about the density of the observations, with particular emphasis being given to the construction of an estimator that attains the SP efficiency bound. It is not always possible to find the latter, and that leads to the development of a range of alternatives that might be expected to produce good results without necessarily being optimal. Throughout these chapters a common strategy, first used in Chapter 5, is employed. This involves describing what a parametric estimator would look like, and then seeking to replace the unknown quantities in such an expression with nonparametric estimates. Our experience has shown this to be a valuable discipline when considering nonparametric issues. In many instances it is worth enquiring into the limitations of parametric models before engaging in the more general problems that arise with a nonparametric orientation. Finally, for the benefit of the readers, we have included an Appendix which contains basic concepts, definitions and results of Statistics and Probability which have been used in the book.

It is useful to close this introduction with a word about the scope of the book. Our primary objective is to present a survey of the NP and SP literature that practitioners might find useful. It is not our intention to provide an account of the theoretical tools that one would need to conduct research in this area. A book that did that would treat the subject with much more rigor than we have tried to do. Indeed, to specialists in the area the degree of rigor of this book may be distressingly low, but we feel that it is more important to isolate the essentials in some of the theory than to worry about it being completely rigorous. Moreover, it is our belief that, when the theory is made rigorous, it becomes almost impossible to see the "wood for the trees."

Nevertheless, the theoretical material in the book is not insignificant, being at the level of complexity of a second-year graduate econometrics course. This raises the issue of why we spend time on these matters rather than just providing a "cook book" that would describe the different approaches – as for example the excellent book on nonparametrics by Härdle (1990). Essentially, this is because we feel that something important is lost with such an orientation. There are issues raised in the NP and SP literatures that we do not come across in parametric literature and, unless one grasps these, it is hard to fully comprehend the nature of NP and SP methods. As an example, one might cite the "bias" problem of NP estimators that recurs throughout the book. In the parametric estimation context, we are used to the idea that, when suitably normalized by some function of the sample size, estimators are asymptotically normally distributed around the true value of the parameters. This is not true for NP estimators, and strategies to eliminate the bias end up accounting for many of the choices made in both the SP and NP literature. Consequently, understanding the theory can be important if one wishes to use the methods, although we feel that this can be done by capturing the flavor of the arguments rather than presenting their rigorous underpinnings.

2   Methods of Density Estimation

2.1   Introduction

This chapter describes various methods of estimating the univariate density function of a random variable, closing with extensions to the multivariate case. Some motivation needs to be given for why we should be interested in density estimation at all. An important reason is that the techniques used in, and the complications arising from, the nonparametric estimation of densities recur many times in later chapters, and it pays to study them in a simplified setting first. But, apart from this pragmatic purpose, the need to estimate densities does arise in practice sufficiently often to make a study of this literature of interest in its own right.

Broadly, one can distinguish three areas in which the need to estimate densities arises. First, density estimates can be important in capturing the stylized facts that need explanation and for judging how well a potential model is likely to fit the data. For example, if it is known that the variable being examined has a density with fat tails, or strong peaks, any model of data corresponding to such a variable needs to be capable of generating a density with this characteristic. In other instances, one can efficiently learn about interrelationships between variables in large data sets from joint density estimates – a feature well illustrated in Deaton's (1989) work on rice subsidies in Thailand, in Marron and Schmitz's (1992) work on the U.K. income distribution, in Dinardo et al.'s (1996) study on the U.S. distribution of wages conditional on labor market institutions, and in Quah's (1997) cross-country analysis of the growth and convergence of economies.

Second, it is often desirable to perform a Monte Carlo analysis of a particular estimator being used in a study. Traditionally, only a few moments of this estimator are recorded or a test statistic such as Kolmogorov–Smirnov's is provided to assess departures from normality. Nonparametric density estimates, however, enable a complete picture of the distribution of the estimator and therefore seem a preferable way of summarizing the outcome of a Monte

Carlo experiment. An illustration of this point is given as an example in the concluding section of the chapter.

Finally, it is sometimes the case that parametric estimators have an asymptotic distribution that depends on a density evaluated at a specific point. For example, the median of X has variance $.25\,n^{-1}f^{-2}(0)$, where $f(0)$ is the density of X evaluated at $x = 0$. Hence, any test statistic involving the median demands an estimate of $f(0)$. Section 5.9 presents other estimators for which a density estimate at a point is required.

As before, $f = f(x)$ denotes the continuous density function of a random variable X at a point x, and $x_1, \ldots, x_n$ are the observations drawn from f. Two general methods have been advanced for the estimation of f.[1]

(i) **Parametric Estimators:** Parametric methods specify a form for f, say, the normal density,

$$ f(x) = \frac{1}{\sigma \sqrt{2\pi}} \exp\left[-\frac{1}{2} \left(\frac{x - \mu}{\sigma} \right)^2 \right], $$

where the mean μ and the variance σ^2 are the parameters of f. An estimator of f can be written as

$$ \hat{f}(x) = \frac{1}{\hat{\sigma} \sqrt{2\pi}} \exp\left[-\frac{1}{2} \left(\frac{x - \hat{\mu}}{\hat{\sigma}} \right)^2 \right], $$

where μ and σ are estimated consistently from data as

$$ \hat{\mu} = \overline{p}x = \frac{1}{n} \sum_{i=1}^{n} x_i \quad \text{and} \quad \hat{\sigma}^2 = \frac{1}{n-1} \sum_{i=1}^{n} (x_i - \overline{p}x)^2, $$

respectively.

(ii) **Nonparametric Estimators:** A disadvantage of the parametric method is the need to stipulate the true parametric density of f. In the nonparametric alternative $f(x)$ is directly estimated without assuming its form. The histogram is one such estimator, and it is one of the oldest methods of density estimation (Van Ryzin (1973) and Scott (1979) among others). But, although the histogram is a useful method of density estimation, it has the drawbacks of being discontinuous and too "rough." Further, it is extremely complicated to use for two or more variables. In view of these disadvantages, in the past three decades several nonparametric estimators have been developed with the aim of producing "smooth" estimates of $f(x)$.

---

[1] There have been suggestions to combine the two (e.g., Olkin and Spiegelman, 1987).

Section 2.2 of the chapter sets out a variety of ways of nonparametrically computing a density estimate; Section 2.3 concentrates upon the modifications needed if it is a derivative of the density which is of interest. An example of the need for the latter arises when estimating the "score" of the density, $f^{-1}(u)\partial f/\partial u$, a quantity that appears many times in later chapters, making it important to discuss its estimation at an early stage. Sections 2.4–2.6 deal with the sampling properties of the most widely used nonparametric estimator, the *kernel* method. Many of the complications that arise in describing the distributions of nonparametric estimators occur in this simple problem, so that some time is spent studying them. As these sections demonstrate, the important elements in nonparametrics are the need to choose a smoothing function – the kernel – and a parameter – the window width – and Section 2.7 discusses the extensive literature on how to make these choices in practice. Section 2.8 outlines extensions of the ideas to multivariate density estimation, and Section 2.9 looks at the techniques that have developed for testing whether a nonparametrically estimated density has a specified parametric form or whether two estimated densities are close; that is, it focuses upon measures of the affinity of densities. Finally, Section 2.10 provides a few examples.

2.2 Nonparametric Density Estimation

There is no unique way to perform nonparametric density estimation, and some eight approaches are described in this section. Despite this variety it is possible to achieve a degree of unification by placing each estimator in a common format, namely as the sample mean of certain functions of the data.

2.2.1 A "Local" Histogram Approach

To understand some of the density estimation techniques discussed later we begin with the situation when X is a discrete random variable. Let one of the values it can assume be x and our purpose is to estimate $f(x)$ from the data x_i, $i = 1, \ldots n$. Estimation of $f(x)$ in the discrete case is essentially the estimation of the proportion of x values in the population of X. From the data $x_1, \ldots, x_n$ an obvious and well-known consistent estimator of this is the sample proportion $\hat{f}_1(x) = n^*/n$, where n^* is the number of $x_1, \ldots, x_n$ equal to x. Alternatively, $\hat{f}_1(x) = n^{-1} \sum_{i=1}^n I(x_i = x)$, with $I(x_i = x)$ being an indicator function taking the value 1 if $x_i = x$ and zero otherwise.

Now, considering the case where X is a continuous random variable, the probability that x_i is equal to x is zero, and $f(x)$ will need to be estimated by averaging those x_i that are in an interval around x, say, $x \pm h/2$, where h is the width of the interval. Thus the empirical density estimator $\hat{f}(x)$ can be written as $\hat{f}_1(x) = (nh)^{-1} \sum_{i=1}^{n} I(x - \frac{h}{2} \le x_i \le x + \frac{h}{2})$, where $I(\mathcal{A}) = 1$ if $\mathcal{A}$ is true and zero otherwise. Alternatively, we can write

$$\hat{f}_1(x) = \frac{1}{nh} \sum_{i=1}^{n} I\left(-1/2 \le \frac{x_i - x}{h} \le 1/2\right)$$

$$= \frac{1}{nh} \sum_{i=1}^{n} I(-1/2 \le \psi_i \le 1/2), \tag{2.1}$$

where $\psi_i = (x_i - x)/h$.

Notice that $\hat{f}_1(x)$ in (2.1) is the per unit relative frequency in the interval $(x - h/2, x + h/2)$ whose midpoint is x. In this sense it is exactly the ordinate of the histogram at x. Thus the estimator (2.1) can be seen to be an attempt to construct a histogram that is based on the observations "local" to x, and where every point x is the center of a sampling interval. The width of the interval h controls the amount by which the data are smoothed (averaged) to produce the estimate (2.1). The $\hat{f}_1$ is also known as the "naive" estimator, following Fix and Hodges (1951).

Clearly the indicator or weight function $I(-1/2 < \psi_i < 1/2)$ in (2.1) depends upon the distance of x_i from x. If this absolute distance is less than or equal to $1/2$ the weight is 1; otherwise it is zero. Furthermore, the weight function $I(\psi) = I(-1/2 < \psi < 1/2)$ is such that

$$\int_{-\infty}^{\infty} I(\psi) \, d\psi = \int_{-\infty}^{-1/2} I(\psi) \, d\psi + \int_{-1/2}^{1/2} I(\psi) \, d\psi + \int_{1/2}^{\infty} I(\psi) \, d\psi$$

$$= \int_{-1/2}^{1/2} I(\psi) \, d\psi = \int_{-1/2}^{1/2} d\psi = 1. \tag{2.2}$$

Thus

$$\int_{-\infty}^{\infty} \hat{f}_1(x) \, dx = \frac{1}{nh} \sum_{i=1}^{n} \int_{-\infty}^{\infty} I\left(-\frac{1}{2} < \frac{x_i - x}{h} < \frac{1}{2}\right) dx$$

$$= \frac{1}{n} \sum_{i=1}^{n} \int_{-\infty}^{\infty} I\left(-\frac{1}{2} < \psi_i < \frac{1}{2}\right) d\psi_i = 1, \tag{2.3}$$

and the density estimate is proper in that it is nonnegative and integrates to unity. A feature of (2.3) is that the integral was taken over x since it can assume values over the whole range of X.

2.2.2 A Formal Derivation of $\hat{f}_1(x)$

Let $F(x) = P(X \le x)$ denote the cumulative probability distribution function of X. Then the density function $f(x)$ is defined by

$$f(x) = \frac{d}{dx}F(x) = \lim_{h \to 0} \frac{F\left(x + \frac{h}{2}\right) - F\left(x - \frac{h}{2}\right)}{h}$$

$$= \lim_{h \to 0} \frac{P\left(x - \frac{h}{2} < X < x + \frac{h}{2}\right)}{h}. \tag{2.4}$$

Our problem is to estimate $f(x)$ based on $x_1, \ldots, x_n$. For this we consider h to be a positive function of n that goes to zero as $n \to \infty$, and estimate $P(x - \frac{h}{2} < X < x + \frac{h}{2})$ by the proportion of sample observations $x_1, \ldots, x_n$ falling in $(x - \frac{h}{2}, x + \frac{h}{2})$. Then an obvious consistent estimator of $f(x)$ in (2.4) is

$$\hat{f}_2(x) = \frac{1}{nh}\left[\text{number of } x_1, \ldots, x_n \text{ in } \left(x - \frac{h}{2}, \ x + \frac{h}{2}\right)\right]$$

$$= \frac{1}{nh}\left[\text{number of } \frac{x_1 - x}{h}, \ldots, \frac{x_n - x}{h} \text{ in } (-1/2, \ 1/2)\right]$$

$$= \hat{f}_1(x), \tag{2.5}$$

which is the same as (2.1). The estimator in (2.5) was first proposed by Fix and Hodges (1951).

2.2.3 Rosenblatt–Parzen Kernel Estimator

The density estimator produced by the indicator function in (2.1) has the property that it integrates to unity, but has the disadvantage of being "rough." Also, $\hat{f}_1(x)$ is not a continuous function but has jumps at the points $x_i \pm h/2$ with zero derivative elsewhere. This gives estimates a stepwise nature, and one might prefer a smoother set of weights. Rosenblatt (1956b) addressed this issue by replacing the indicator function in (2.1) with a real positive kernel function K satisfying

$$\int_{-\infty}^{\infty} K(\psi)\,d\psi = 1. \tag{2.6}$$

His general "kernel" estimator is

$$\hat{f}(x) = \hat{f}_3(x) = \frac{1}{nh}\sum_{i=1}^{n} K\left(\frac{x_i - x}{h}\right) = \frac{1}{nh}\sum_{i=1}^{n} K(\psi_i), \tag{2.7}$$

where $\psi_i = h^{-1}(x_i - x)$ as in (2.1) and h, the window-width (also called the smoothing parameter or band width), is a function of the sample size n and goes to zero as $n \to \infty$.

A number of features that a kernel should possess can be inferred from the nature of the indicator function. First, for large values of $|\psi_i|$ (i.e., x_i lies far from x) $K(\psi_i)$ should be small, as very small weights need to be assigned to such data points in constructing the density estimate. In particular, because $h \to 0$ when $n \to \infty$, it follows that $|\psi_i| \to \infty$ for any $x_i \neq x$, and therefore $K(-\infty) = K(\infty) = 0$, which is implied by the requirement (2.6). This feature reproduces the "zero" property of the indicator function, whereas the "unity" part is exhibited by having $\int_{-\infty}^{\infty} K(\psi)\,d\psi = 1$. This amounts to replacing a square centered on x with length of unity by a smooth curve, also centered on x with the same area but no longer necessarily having bounded support. Moreover, because these features are those of a density function, kernels are frequently chosen to be well-known density functions, for example, the standard normal $K(\psi) = (2\pi)^{-1/2} \exp(-.5\psi^2)$. In this vein the indicator function could be thought of as a kernel estimator with $K(\cdot)$ being the uniform density over $[-1/2, \ 1/2]$. Parzen (1962) pointed out that allowing $K(\cdot)$ to be negative could reduce the bias of the estimator $\hat{f}$, a theme taken up in Section 2.4.3. A disadvantage with allowing the kernel to be negative is that $\hat{f}_3(x)$ may now be negative, and this may be unsatisfactory for some purposes. There is a vast literature on kernels. Silverman (1986) and Härdle (1990) are very good guides to this. Mostly the nature of K is not critical to analysis, and the "optimal" kernel, discussed in Section 2.4.2, will be found to yield only modest improvements in the performance of $\hat{f}(x)$ over selections such as the standard normal.

Suppose that $K(\cdot)$ is restricted to be the standard normal. Then it is well known that $K(\psi) \approx 0$ for $|\psi| \geq 3$, and it is apparent that the weights used in (2.7) depend vitally upon the window width h. For an $x_i \neq x$, whether $\psi_i = (x_i - x)/h$ is less than or greater than 3 will depend solely upon h. Although it is true that $h \to 0$ as $n \to \infty$, in practice this still leaves the problem of determining exactly how h should vary with n. Section 2.4 contains an extensive analysis of this issue.

Usually, but not always, K will be a symmetric density function (e.g., the standard normal density). Moreover, as long as it is everywhere nonnegative and satisfies $\int K(\psi)\,d\psi = 1$, $\hat{f}_3$, like $\hat{f}_1$, will be a probability density in that $\int \hat{f}_3(x)\,dx = 1$. The kernel estimator $\hat{f}_3$ also possesses all the continuity and differentiability properties of the kernel K. This is unlike $\hat{f}_1$, which has jumps at $x_i \pm h/2$ and zero derivatives everywhere else. It is the fact that it produces a smooth function out of a discontinuous one that makes the kernel attractive, and a number of times in later chapters it will prove to be advantageous to replace indicator functions by appropriate kernels, even when the context is not specifically density estimation.

2.2.4 The Nearest Neighborhood Estimator

The naive estimator in (2.1) or (2.5) is essentially the proportion of $x_1, \ldots, x_n$ in the interval $(x - \frac{h}{2},\ x + \frac{h}{2})$ divided by a fixed window width (smoothing parameter) h. Ideally, however, one would expect that the window width should be larger when trying to estimate the tails of a density than in its center, since there will be fewer observations available in the former situation. Moreover, since $f(x)$ will be small and flat in the tails, it will not matter much that observations distant from x are employed. In contrast, when it is varying rapidly, as in the central part of the density, incorrect estimates are likely unless observations close to x are used. Attempts to estimate with a fixed window width are likely to lead to undersmoothing in some part of the range and oversmoothing in another. A procedure that responds to this observation is the nearest neighborhood estimator, first suggested by Fix and Hodges, which is another naive estimator, but one where h is defined in terms of distances of the data points from x. For example, let $d(x_1, x)$ represent the distance of point x_1 from the point x, and for each x denote $d_k(x)$ as the distance of x from its kth nearest neighbor (k-NN) among $x_1, \ldots, x_n$. Then, taking $h = 2d_k(x)$, and applying the logic of (2.5), the estimator can be written as[2]

$$\hat{f}_4(x) = \frac{\#(x_1 \ldots x_n) \text{ in } [(x - d_k(x)),\ (x + d_k(x))]}{2nd_k(x)}$$

$$= \frac{k}{2nd_k(x)} = \frac{1}{2nd_k(x)} \sum_{i=1}^{n} I\left(\frac{x_i - x}{2d_k(x)}\right). \tag{2.8}$$

Thus the degree of smoothing (h) is controlled by an integer k; typically $k \approx n^{1/2}$. In the tails of the distribution, the distance $d_k(x)$, and hence h, will be larger than in the middle part of the distribution, since there will be fewer observations in any given sample from the tail. This corrects a potential problem with the kernel estimator arising in the tails of the density. There few observations will be encountered in the range $x \pm (h/2)$, and therefore the estimate will tend to be undersmoothed. By effectively increasing h in the tails a smoother estimate is likely. As $n \to \infty$ and $k \to \infty$, $d_k(x)$ will tend to zero as more and more observations will be encountered that are close to x.

As an illustrative example, consider the four data points 5, 5.5, 9, and 4; let $x = 6$ be the point at which the density is to be estimated; and choose the distance measure $d(x_1, x)$ as $|x - x_1|$. For this example $k \simeq \sqrt{4} = 2$, and $d_2(x) = |6 - 5| = 1$ because the data point 5 is the second nearest neighbor of 6. Hence $\hat{f}_4(x = 6) = 1/4$. For multivariate problems more complex distance

---

[2] Throughout the remainder of the book #($\mathcal{A}$) will designate the operation "number of elements in $\mathcal{A}$."

measures are needed and they would need to be made unit free. A simple way to ensure this is to standardize the data by dividing each observation by its estimated standard deviation.

Obviously the nearest neighbor estimator shares some of the disadvantages of the naive estimator: It is continuous but has discontinuous derivatives at the same points as d_k. Moreover, it will generally not integrate to unity. Indeed, as Silverman (1986) observes, for points x less than or greater than the minima and maxima of x_i, the window width dies away like x^{-1}, and so the integral of the density is actually infinite. He concludes that the nearest neighbor estimate is unlikely to be appropriate if an estimate of the entire density is required. One way to circumvent these problems is to generalize the nearest neighbor estimator $\hat{f}_4(x)$ by replacing the indicator function in (2.8) by the kernel function (Loftsgaarden and Quesenberry, 1965):

$$\hat{f}_4(x) = \frac{1}{2nd_k(x)} \sum_{i=1}^{n} K\left(\frac{x_i - x}{2d_k(x)}\right). \tag{2.9}$$

2.2.5   Variable Window-Width Estimators

Rather than allowing the window width to be selected by how close x is to other points in the data, it might be made to vary directly with each data point according to some prescribed rule. Such an estimator could take the form

$$\hat{f}_5(x) = \frac{1}{n} \sum_{i=1}^{n} \frac{1}{h_{ni}} K\left(\frac{x_i - x}{h_{ni}}\right), \tag{2.10}$$

where $h_{ni} = d_k(x_i)$ is the distance of x_i from its kth (a positive integer) nearest neighbor among the remaining $n - 1$ data points. The parameter k of local smoothness is as in the nearest neighbor estimator (2.8). Varying h_{ni} in this way ensures that the regions where there are fewer observations will have flatter kernels. The estimator $\hat{f}_5(x)$ is known as the *variable kernel estimator* (see, e.g., Breiman et al., 1977). Note that, whereas in the k-NN estimator the window widths depend on the point x at which the density is estimated, in the variable kernel estimator the window widths are independent of the point x. Furthermore, although the variable kernel estimator will itself be a probability density function, this is not true for the nearest neighbor estimator.

As described earlier it is plausible that the window width should vary inversely with the density and this leads to the *adaptive two-stage estimator* (A2SE) considered by Breiman et al. (1977) and Abramson (1982). The A2SE is essentially (2.10) with $h_{ni} = h\delta_{ni}$, $\delta_{ni} = \left[\tilde{f}(x_i)/G\right]^{-\lambda}$, where G is the geometric mean of some preliminary estimator of the density $\tilde{f}(x_i)$ over all x_i, $0 < \lambda \leq 1$ is a sensitivity parameter, and $\tilde{f}(x_i)$ is any convenient initial estimator.[3] The numerical results of Abramson (1982) and others suggest that $\lambda = .5$ gives good results, for reasons explained in Section 2.4.3. It is not clear why the scaling factor is taken to be the geometric mean. Presumably it would be desirable to have $\delta_{ni} \approx 1$ in the region of the mode of the density and $\delta_{ni} > 1$ elsewhere. To explore the likely magnitude of δ_{ni} with the selection rule above, suppose that X_i is $\mathcal{N}(0, 1)$ and that the *true density* is used to form G, that is, $G = \left[\Pi_{i=1}^{n} (2\pi)^{-1/2} \exp(-.5x_i^2) \right]^{1/n}$. Taking logs and rearranging, we get $G = (2\pi)^{-1/2} \exp \left\{ -(2n)^{-1} \sum x_i^2 \right\}$ and $G \to (2\pi)^{-1/2} e^{-1/2}$ as $n \to \infty$. Consequently, the ratio $[f(x)/G]^{-1/2} = e^{-.25(1-x^2)}$ and δ_{ni} will be .77 for $x = 0$, 1 for $x = 1$, and 7.34 for $x = 3$. Because the mode of the normal density is at $x = 0$, it suggests that the value of δ_{ni} at $x = 0$ is smaller than desirable and needs to be multiplied by the factor 1.3. Of course the true adjustment factor will vary with the true density, but it might be used as a rough guide. As will be seen in Section 2.10.1 problems can emerge with the use of an adaptive estimator if δ_{ni} does not equal unity around the mode.

When h_{ni} in (2.10) is replaced by positive smoothing factors h_i that do not depend on n, $\hat{f}_5(x)$ can be thought of as a *recursive estimator* (RE). It is recursive in the sense that, when an additional data point becomes available, it can be updated according to (writing $\hat{f}_{5,n+1}(x) = \hat{f}_{n+1}(x)$)

$$\hat{f}_{n+1}(x) = (n+1)^{-1} \left[n\hat{f}_n(x) + h_{n+1}^{-1} K \left(\frac{x_{n+1} - x}{h_{n+1}} \right) \right]. \qquad (2.11)$$

The estimator (2.11) was first introduced by Wolverton and Wagner (1969) and independently by Yamato (1971).

2.2.6 Series Estimators

The orthogonal series method was first suggested by Cencov (1962) and is defined below. Suppose X is a random variable with density f on the unit interval $[0,1]$. Under these circumstances it can be expressed as the Fourier series

$$f(x) = \sum_{j=0}^{\infty} a_j \zeta_j(x), \qquad (2.12)$$

where, for each $j \geq 0$, the coefficients

$$a_j = \int_0^1 f(x)\zeta_j(x)\,dx = E\zeta_j(x), \qquad (2.13)$$

---

[3] h is the window width used in forming $\tilde{f}(x_i)$.

and the sequence $\zeta_j(x)$ is given by $\zeta_0(x) = 1$ and $\zeta_j(x) = \sqrt{2}\cos \pi(j+1)x$ when j is odd and $\sqrt{2}\sin \pi jx$ when j is even.

Using $\hat{a}_j = n^{-1}\sum_{i=1}^{n}\zeta_j(x_i)$ as an estimator of a_j, the orthogonal series estimator is defined as

$$\hat{f}_6(x) = \sum_{j=0}^{m} \hat{a}_j\zeta_j(x), \tag{2.14}$$

where m is the cutoff point in the infinite sum and determines the amount of smoothing. The m corresponds to the h of the kernel-type estimator, and $\zeta_j(x)$ correspond to kernels. Rather than truncating at a fixed number of m, an alternative is to set m to ∞ and to weight the elements in the summation of (2.14) by weights λ_j. This alternative has the form

$$\hat{f}_6(x) = \sum_{j=0}^{\infty} \lambda_j\hat{a}_j\zeta_j(x). \tag{2.15}$$

Various other orthogonal series estimators of f (not necessarily defined on a finite interval) can be obtained by using different orthogonal sequences of functions. For example, if $b(x)$ is a weighting function, say, $b(x) = \exp(-\frac{1}{2}x^2)$, then H_j can be chosen as Hermite polynomials, which are distinguished by the property

$$\int_{-\infty}^{\infty} H_j(x)H_{j'}(x)b(x)\,dx = \begin{cases} 1 & \text{for } j = j', \\ 0 & \text{otherwise.} \end{cases} \tag{2.16}$$

The orthogonal series estimator then becomes

$$\hat{f}_6(x) = \sum_{j=0}^{m} \hat{a}_j H_j(x), \tag{2.17}$$

where

$$\hat{a}_j = \frac{1}{n}\sum_{i=1}^{n} H_j(x_i)b(x_i). \tag{2.18}$$

Alternatively, once again m might be set to ∞ and weights would be applied to the terms in the summation to get

$$\hat{f}_6(x) = \sum_{j=0}^{\infty} \lambda_j\hat{a}_j H_j(x). \tag{2.19}$$

There are several variations of this idea in the literature. A classical approach was to approximate the unknown density as the product of a normal density and a linear combination of Hermite polynomials; see Spanos (1986). The coefficients of the polynomials are estimated from the sample moments of x_i. Generally, it would seem sensible to transform x_i to z_i as $z_i = (x_i - \overline{p}x)/\hat{\sigma}_x$, where $\overline{p}x$ and $\hat{\sigma}_x$ are the sample mean and standard deviation of x_i; apply the Hermite approximation to estimate the density of z, $\hat{f}_z(z)$; and to then transform back to recover $\hat{f}(x) = \hat{\sigma}_x^{-1} \hat{f}_z (\hat{\sigma}_x^{-1}(x_i - \overline{p}x))$. A nonparametric analogue of this procedure might be to allow the degree of approximating polynomial to tend to infinity as $n \to \infty$. A related approach is that used by Gallant and his coworkers – see Gallant and Tauchen (1989), Gallant, Hsieh, and Tauchen (1991), and Gallant and Tauchen (1992) for example. Their idea is to write $f(z) = \phi(z)P^2(z)$, where $\phi(z)$ is a standard normal density and $P(z) = 1 + b_1 z + \cdots + b_R z^R$ is a polynomial of degree R in z, and to then maximize $\sum_{i=1}^n \log f_z(z_i)$ with respect to $b_1, \ldots, b_R$, subject to the constraints that the estimated density is nonnegative and integrates to unity. It is generally easy to impose these restrictions; for example, $\int f(z)\,dz = 1$ requires $\int \phi(z)P^2(z)\,dz = 1$ and, when $P(z) = 1 + b_1 z$ (say), this becomes $\int \phi(z)(1 + 2b_1 z + b_1^2 z^2)\,dz = 1 + b_1^2$ from the properties of the $\mathcal{N}(0, 1)$ density. This procedure is frequently referred to as the *seminonparametric method* (SNP) of density estimation. Because most of the applications of this idea are not specifically aimed at density estimation per se, but rather at the determination of conditional moments or regression parameters in the presence of unknown error density, discussion of this approach is deferred until later chapters.

2.2.7 Penalized Likelihood Estimators

The empirical density estimators discussed so far are essentially derived or motivated from the definition of a density. Another possibility is to treat $f(x)$ as an unknown "parameter" and to try to employ likelihood methods for estimating the unknown quantity. By definition the likelihood of the unknown "parameter," here the function f, given the data is

$$L = L(f|x_1, \ldots, x_n) = \prod_{i=1}^n f(x_i), \tag{2.20}$$

and

$$\log L = \sum_{i=1}^n \log f(x_i). \tag{2.21}$$

Unfortunately, $\log L$ has no *finite* maximum over the class of *all* densities. To see this, consider the lower bound to the estimated density (provided by the naive estimator)

$$\hat{f}_1(x) = \frac{1}{nh} \sum_{i=1}^n I\left(-\frac{1}{2} < \frac{x_i - x}{h} < \frac{1}{2}\right) > \frac{1}{nh}.$$

Substituting this trial solution into (2.21), we get

$$\log L = \sum_{i=1}^{n} \log \hat{f}_1(x_i) \geq \sum_{i=1}^{n} \log \frac{1}{nh} = -n \log nh, \tag{2.22}$$

which tends to ∞ as $h \to 0$. Thus, unless restrictions are placed on the class of densities, the method of maximum likelihood breaks down. In fact, the above example shows that the likelihood is effectively maximized by the density

$$g_n(x) = \frac{1}{n} \sum_{i=1}^{n} \delta(x_i - x), \tag{2.23}$$

where δ is the Dirac delta function.

As observed above $\log L$ has no finite maximum over the class of all densities. However, it is possible to obtain the maximum likelihood estimator of f if we are willing to impose a smoothness condition on the density to be estimated. To implement this proposal, let $R(f)$ represent a measure of roughness for f. For example, Good and Gaskins (1971, 1980) considered the following two functions:

$$R(f) = \frac{1}{4} \int \frac{\left(f^{(1)}(x)\right)^2}{f(x)} dx \tag{2.24}$$

and

$$R(f) = \int \left(f^{(2)}(x)\right)^2 dx, \tag{2.25}$$

where $f^{(s)}$ represents the sth derivative of $f(x)$ with respect to x; $s = 1, 2, \ldots$. Whereas the $R(f)$ in (2.24) measures roughness in the slope of the density, the $R(f)$ in (2.25) measures the roughness in the curvature, having a high value if f contains a large amount of local curvature (variation) but the value zero if f is a straight line.

Incorporating the roughness term $R(f)$ into the likelihood, we can define the penalized log likelihood as

$$\ell(f) = \sum_{i=1}^{n} \log f(x_i) - \alpha R(f), \tag{2.26}$$

where the positive number α is the smoothing parameter (corresponding to h). Notice that the value of R depends on f. The penalized likelihood takes into account the fact that there are often two conflicting aims in density estimation. One is to choose an f that fits the data well, with the goodness of fit determined by the log likelihood $\sum \log f(x_i)$, while the other is to avoid densities that have too much roughness or variation, and this is represented by $R(f)$. The choice of α controls the balance between these conflicting aims of smoothness and goodness of fit. The estimated probability density $\hat{f}$ is said to be a penalized maximum likelihood estimator if it maximizes $\ell(f)$ over the class of all curves f that satisfy $\int f(x)\,dx = 1$, $f(x) \geq 0$ for all x, and $R(f) < \infty$. We note, however, that this maximization problem does not provide an explicit expression for $\hat{f}$. The computational aspects of the optimization under alternative $R(f)$ are discussed in Good and Gaskins (1971, 1980) and Ghorai and Rubin (1979); also see Silverman (1982, 1984) for alternative $R(f)$ and the connection between kernel and penalized likelihood estimators. Silverman's paper is particularly interesting as he shows that the penalized likelihood estimator can be regarded as a kernel estimator with kernel $K(\psi) = .5\exp(-|\psi|/\sqrt{2})\sin(|\psi|/\sqrt{2}+\pi/4)$ and window width proportional to $f(x)^{-1/4}$. Hence the procedure effectively yields an adaptive kernel estimator. Scott, Tapia, and Thompson (1980) suggested replacing the integrals in $R(f)$ (see (2.24) and (2.25)) by their discrete approximations. They have argued that this is useful for the computation and provides a good approximation to exact results.

2.2.8   *The Local Log-Likelihood Estimators*

We observe that the maximization of the log-likelihood in (2.21) is the same as the maximization of the average log-likelihood

$$\log L_n = \frac{1}{n}\sum_{i=1}^{n}\log f(x_i) = \int \log f(x)\,d\hat{F}(x),$$

where $\hat{F}(x) = n^{-1}\sum^{n} I(x_i \leq x)$ is the empirical (naive) distribution function. Recently, Loader (1993) has argued that the log-likelihood is actually

$$\log L_n = \int \log f(x)\,d\hat{F}(x) - \int f(x)\,dx$$

$$= \frac{1}{n}\sum^{n}\log f(x_i) - \int f(x)\,dx,$$

but the second term on the right-hand side is usually dropped since its value is unity. Written in this way, the maximization of $\log L_n$ is also the maximization of Shannon's entropy or minimization of a Kullback–Leibler-type distance function of the density $f(x)$ from a uniform density. This is because

$$\log L_n \rightarrow \int f(x)\log f(x)\,dx - \int f(x)\,dx$$

$$= \int f(x)\log f(x)\,dx - 1.$$

The log L_n above can be called the global log-likelihood function, which, as noted in Section 2.2.7, has no finite maximum. In view of this, let us consider the *local log-likelihood* or local kernel smoothed log-likelihood at a point x. This can be written as

$$\log L_n(x) = \int \frac{1}{h} K\left(\frac{t-x}{h}\right) \left[\log f(t) \, d\hat{F}(t) - f(t)\right] dt$$

$$= \frac{1}{nh} \sum_{i=1}^{n} K\left(\frac{x_i - x}{h}\right) \log f(x_i)$$

$$- \int \frac{1}{h} K\left(\frac{t-x}{h}\right) f(t) \, dt, \tag{2.27}$$

where the domain of the random variable t is the same as that of X. This local log-likelihood is essentially the log-likelihood weighted by the kernel function.

When h is large, $\log L_n(x) \simeq h^{-1} K(0) \log L_n$, and so the maximization of the local likelihood is the same as the usual likelihood. However, when h is small or moderate, then the maximization of $\log L_n(x)$ will provide the best local estimate of f. In fact, considering $f(t) = a$ as a parameter in $\log L_n(x)$, and maximizing this with respect to a, gives

$$\frac{\partial \log L_n(x)}{\partial a} = \frac{1}{a} \left[\frac{1}{nh} \sum_{i=1}^{n} K\left(\frac{x_i - x}{h}\right) \right] - 1 = 0$$

or

$$\hat{a} = \hat{f}(x) = \frac{1}{nh} \sum_{i=1}^{n} K\left(\frac{x_i - x}{h}\right),$$

which is Rosenblatt's kernel density estimator given in (2.7). In this sense Rosenblatt's estimator is a local likelihood estimator.

A natural extension of this idea is to obtain the local linear estimator of a by fitting a line, $a + b(t - x)$, locally to x. This amounts to replacing $f(t) \simeq f(x) + f^{(1)}(x)(t - x) = a + b(t - x)$ and maximizing with respect to a and b. Since $\int K(t - x)(t - x) \, dt = 0$, it will be the case that $\hat{a}$ will again be identical to $\hat{f}(x)$. A further extension is to consider local polynomials, which is analogous to local polynomial fitting for regressions, described later in Chapter 3. Loader (1993) has considered using local exponential functions of the form $a \exp(b(t - x))$. Most of these local polynomial estimators have the advantage, compared to the kernel estimator, that they perform better in the tails. Rather than use a polynomial, Hjort and Jones (1996) estimate the parameter vector θ of an assumed parametric density $f(\cdot, \theta)$ by the maximization of its log-likelihood function, local to the point x as in (2.27), with respect to θ. The resulting estimator of f, at x, is given by

$$\tilde{f}_1(x) = f(x, \tilde{\theta}(x)).$$

A density estimator similar to $\tilde{f}_1$ has also been developed in Copas (1995). Hjort and Glad (1995) provide an estimator that is the parametric density multiplied by a kernel-estimated correction factor. Finally, some local density estimators based on Bayesian methods are developed in Hjort (1996).

2.2.9 Summary

Various methods of density estimation have been discussed above. Among them the kernel estimator is the best known estimator, and it is better developed than many of the others, both with respect to its numerical calculation and known analytical properties. Moreover, several estimates of densities are almost invariably created with it. For this reason, much of the theory outlined in the succeeding sections pertains to the kernel estimator. However, when appropriate, relevant results for other estimators will be mentioned.

In using the kernel estimator described above, choices need to be made for the kernel and the window width h. As described later in Section 2.4.2 it is now well known that the choice of kernel is a minor issue, with any kernel being close to an optimal kernel for large samples. In contrast the selection of the window width h is crucial. On the one hand, a very large h would be expected to result in an oversmoothed density and little noise, because a large number of points will effectively be used in forming an estimate. Effectively, oversmoothing distorts the shape of the density, and this may lead to bias. On the other hand, a very small h may give a noisy and wiggly density estimate, involving an increased variance but producing less bias. Thus great caution is required in selecting h, and Sections 2.7.1 and 2.7.3 are devoted to this issue.

2.3   Estimation of Derivatives of a Density

Estimation of the derivatives of a density may be required in various situations, for example, for the evaluation of modes and inflection points, for estimation of the derivatives of a regression function (Chapter 4), and for the evaluation of density scores, particularly when engaging in semiparametric estimation, as set out in Chapters 5 onwards. Provided f is s times differentiable there are various ways in which the sth-order derivative $f^{(s)}$ with respect to x could be estimated. The first method is straightforward: Estimate $f^{(s)}$ by the sth-order derivative of the kernel estimator given in (2.7). This is

$$\hat{f}^{(s)}(x) = \frac{(-1)^s}{nh^{s+1}} \sum_{i=1}^{n} K^{(s)}\left(\frac{x_i - x}{h}\right) \tag{2.28}$$

and is advocated by Bhattacharya (1967) and Schuster (1969).

Another method is the finite difference approach. The first derivative could be formulated as

$$f^{(1)}(x) = \frac{d}{dx}f(x) = \lim_{h \to 0}\left[\frac{f\left(x + \frac{h}{2}\right) - f\left(x - \frac{h}{2}\right)}{h}\right]$$

$$= \lim_{h \to 0}\left[\frac{1}{h}\sum_{j=0}^{1}(-1)^j f\left(x + (1 - 2j)h/2\right)\right],$$

$$(2.29)$$

with the straightforward extension to the sth derivative as

$$f^{(s)}(x) = \lim_{h \to 0}\left[\frac{1}{h^s}\sum_{j=0}^{s}(-1)^j\binom{s}{j}f\left(x + (s - 2j)h/2\right)\right]. \qquad (2.30)$$

Then the estimator of the sth-order derivative will be

$$\hat{f}^{(s)}(x) = \frac{1}{h^s}\sum_{j=0}^{s}(-1)^j\binom{s}{j}\hat{f}\left(x + (s - 2j)h/2\right). \qquad (2.31)$$

Expression (2.31) throws up a variety of estimators of sth-order derivatives merely by employing different density estimators. Maltz (1974) and Mustafi (1978) considered (2.31) for the case where $\hat{f}(x)$ is the empirical density estimator whilst Rilstone (1987) adopted the kernel estimator (when $s = 1$). The choice of h for density derivatives is discussed in Section 2.7.3.

2.4   Finite-Sample Properties of the Kernel Estimator

Let $f = f(x)$ denote the continuous density function of a random variable X at a point x, and let $x_1, \ldots, x_n$ be the observations from f. Following (2.7) the kernel density estimator $\hat{f}(x)$ of f can be rewritten as

$$\hat{f} = \hat{f}(x) = \frac{1}{nh}\sum_{i=1}^{n}K\left(\frac{x_i - x}{h}\right) = \frac{1}{n}\sum_{i=1}^{n}w_i;$$

$$w_i = w_{ni}(x) = \frac{1}{h}K\left(\frac{x_i - x}{h}\right), \qquad (2.32)$$

where K is the kernel function, h is the window width, and $w_{ni}(x)$ is the weight function, which depends on the distance of x_i from x and the sample size through h. We make the following assumptions:

(A1) The observations $x_1, x_2, \ldots, x_n$ are independent and identically distributed (i.i.d.).

(A2) The kernel K is a symmetric function around zero satisfying
  (i) $\int K(\psi) \, d\psi = 1$,
  (ii) $\int \psi^2 K(\psi) \, d\psi = \mu_2 \neq 0$,
  (iii) $\int K^2(\psi) \, d\psi < \infty$.

(A3) The second-order derivatives of f are continuous and bounded in some neighborhood of x.

(A4) $h = h_n \to 0$ as $n \to \infty$.

(A5) $nh_n \to \infty$ as $n \to \infty$.

Some comments on the assumptions are in order. Assumption 1 is considered here for the sake of simplicity in the derivation of analytical results. In practice, economic data may not be i.i.d., and Section 2.6 relaxes this assumption by allowing for certain types of dependence appropriate to time series data. Assumption (A2) is satisfied by a large class of functions, for example,

(i) standard normal:

$$K(\psi) = (2\pi)^{-1/2} \exp\left[-\frac{1}{2}(\psi)^2\right] \tag{2.33}$$

and

(ii) uniform:

$$K(\psi) = (2c)^{-1}, \quad -c < \psi < c \text{ and } 0 \text{ otherwise.}$$

Assumption (A3) is required when evaluating the bias and MSE of $\hat{f}(x)$, while Assumptions (A4) and (A5) imply that, as n increases, h should decrease at a slower speed than n^{-1}. An explanation for this latter restriction will become apparent in the context of the asymptotic properties of the kernel estimator.

2.4.1 The Exact Bias and Variance of the Estimator $\hat{f}$

Notice from (2.32) that $\hat{f}$ is the simple average of $w_1, \ldots, w_n$. According to Assumption (A1) $x_1, \ldots, x_n$ and, hence, $w_1, \ldots, w_n$, are i.i.d., resulting in the mean and variance of w_i being the same for all i and the covariance being zero, that is,[4]

$$E(w_i) = E(w_1), \quad V(w_i) = V(w_1), \quad \text{cov}(w_i, w_j) = 0, \quad i \neq j. \tag{2.34}$$

---

[4] It is convenient in what follows to treat x_i as both data and a random variable, allowing the context to make it clear which usage is current.

Independence of w_i enables an easy derivation of the exact bias and variance of $\hat{f}$, and this is provided in Theorem 2.1.

Theorem 2.1: Under Assumptions (A1) and (A2(i)) the exact bias and the variance of the estimator $\hat{f}$ in (2.32) are, respectively,

$$\text{Bias}(\hat{f}) = E\hat{f} - f = \int K(\psi)[f(h\psi + x) - f(x)]\,d\psi \qquad (2.35)$$

and

$$V(\hat{f}) = (nh)^{-1} \int K^2(\psi) f(h\psi + x)\,d\psi$$
$$- n^{-1} \left[\int K(\psi) f(h\psi + x)\,d\psi\right]^2. \qquad (2.36)$$

Proof: From (2.32) and (2.34), the exact mean and variance $\hat{f}$ are

$$E\hat{f} = \frac{1}{n}\sum_{i=1}^{n} Ew_i = \frac{1}{n}(Ew_1 + \cdots + Ew_n) = \frac{n}{n} Ew_1 = Ew_1 \qquad (2.37)$$

and

$$V(\hat{f}) = \frac{1}{n^2}\left[\sum_{i=1}^{n} V(w_i) + \sum_{i \neq j}\sum \text{cov}(w_i, w_j)\right]$$
$$= \frac{1}{n^2}\sum_{i=1}^{n} V(w_i) = n^{-1} V(w_1). \qquad (2.38)$$

Now, using $\psi = \psi_1 = h^{-1}(x_1 - x)$, we obtain

$$Ew_1 = h^{-1} E\left[K\left(\frac{x_1 - x}{h}\right)\right] = h^{-1} \int K\left(\frac{x_1 - x}{h}\right) f(x_1)\,dx_1$$
$$= \int K(\psi) f(h\psi + x)\,d\psi \qquad (2.39)$$

and

$$Ew_1^2 = h^{-2} E K^2\left(\frac{x_1 - x}{h}\right) = h^{-2} \int K^2\left(\frac{x_1 - x}{h}\right) f(x_1)\,dx_1$$
$$= h^{-1} \int K^2(\psi) f(h\psi + x)\,d\psi, \qquad (2.40)$$

where the second equalities in (2.39) and (2.40) follow by noting that $Eg(x_1) = \int g(x_1) f(x_1) dx_1$.   Q.E.D.

The expressions for exact bias and variance given above are in terms of integrals that, in the absence of unknown f, cannot be simplified any further. Perhaps the only information that can be deduced is that the bias depends on the sample size only through the window width h. In general both bias and variance will depend on the kernel K and the shape of the density and these expressions may not be of much use for analysis, although the following subsection provides some discussion on the choice of h based on the exact expressions.

The expressions for exact bias and variance for the density derivative estimators can also be written in a similar way. It has been pointed out by Stoker (1993) that a generic feature of smoothed density estimation is that the estimated derivative $\hat{f}^{(1)}$ and the score function, $-\hat{f}^{(1)}/\hat{f}$, will be systematically downward biased. The reasoning for this is that, by Jensen's inequality, $E\hat{f} \leq f$ in ranges where f is concave and $E\hat{f} > f$ in ranges where f is convex. Thus the pointwise $E[\hat{f}^{(1)}]$ will typically be smaller in absolute value than $f^{(1)}$.

2.4.2   Approximations to the Bias and Variance and Choices of h and K

In order to get some useful results we now turn to approximations for the bias and variance. For the derivations and discussion of these results we use the concepts of small o and big O given in the appendix, Section A.4.

Theorem 2.2: Under assumptions (A1)–(A5) the bias, up to $O(h^2)$, and the variance, up to $O(nh)^{-1}$, of the estimator $\hat{f}$ are given by

$$\text{Bias } (\hat{f}) = \frac{h^2}{2} \mu_2 f^{(2)}(x) \qquad\qquad (2.41)$$

and

$$V(\hat{f}) = (nh)^{-1} f(x) \int K^2(\psi) d\psi, \qquad\qquad (2.42)$$

where $\mu_2 = \int \psi^2 K(\psi) d\psi$.

Proof: First a Taylor series expansion of $f(h\psi + x)$ around the point x, for small h, gives

$$f(h\psi + x) = f(x) + h\psi f^{(1)}(x) + \frac{h^2}{2} \psi^2 f^{(2)}(x) + \cdots . \qquad (2.43)$$

Substituting this into (2.35) we get

$$\text{Bias}(\hat{f}) = \int K(\psi) \left[h\psi f^{(1)}(x) + \frac{h^2\psi^2}{2} f^{(2)}(x) + \cdots \right] d\psi. \quad (2.44)$$

Applying (A2) and (A3) and retaining terms up to $O(h^2)$ only produces (2.41). Similarly, substituting (2.43) into (2.36) makes the variance

$$V(\hat{f}) = (nh)^{-1} \int K^2(\psi) \left\{ f(x) + h\psi f^{(1)}(x) \right.$$
$$\left. + \frac{h^2\psi^2}{2} f^{(2)}(x) + \cdots \right\} d\psi$$
$$- n^{-1} \left(\int K(\psi) \left\{ f(x) + h\psi f^{(1)}(x) \right. \right.$$
$$\left. \left. + \frac{h^2\psi^2}{2} f^{(2)}(x) + \cdots \right\} d\psi \right)^2, \quad (2.45)$$

which, after applying (A2) to (A5) and collecting terms up to $O(nh)^{-1}$, gives the result in (2.42). Q.E.D.

To make a choice of h or K it is necessary to have some criterion. By far the most popular strategies have been to either minimize $\int [(\hat{f}(x) - f(x)]^2 dx$, the *Integrated Squared Error (ISE)*, or minimize $E\{ \int [\hat{f}(x) - f(x)]^2 dx \}$, the *Integrated Mean Squared Error*, generally referred to as *MISE* (the Mean Integrated Squared Error). These correspond to *loss* and *risk* respectively. Clearly, the first criterion depends upon the data whereas the second should not (see Jones (1991) for further comparison of *ISE* and *MISE*). Focusing upon risk, and defining the value of h that minimizes *MISE* as h_{opt}, the problem facing investigators is how to compute an estimator of this quantity, since the expression for exact *MISE* is difficult to obtain. This generally leads to some approximation to *MISE*, *AMISE* of which the simplest is to use the approximate formulas for bias and variance given in (2.41) and (2.42), respectively. Following this strategy we get

$$MISE = \int \left[(\text{Bias } \hat{f})^2 + V(\hat{f}) \right] dx,$$

$$AMISE = \frac{h^4}{4} \mu_2^2 \int (f^{(2)}(x))^2 dx + (nh)^{-1} \int f(x) dx \int K^2(\psi) d\psi$$

$$= \frac{1}{4} \lambda_1 h^4 + \lambda_2 (nh)^{-1}, \quad (2.46)$$

where

$$\lambda_1 = \mu_2^2 \int \left(f^{(2)}(x) \right)^2 dx, \qquad \lambda_2 = \int K^2(\psi) \, d\psi. \qquad (2.47)$$

Notice that the use of *MISE* was motivated by the idea that one wished to estimate the density over a wide range of values of x rather than at a single point. Nevertheless, sometimes it is the latter which is of interest, in which case the *MISE* would be replaced by the *MSE* at the point x. Operationally this just means dropping the integrals appearing in (2.46). Consequently, the difference is between a "local" measure, the *MSE* at a point x, and a "global" one, the average *MSE* over the domain of X.

It is clear from the expressions (2.41) and (2.42) that, if we choose a very small h, the bias in the density estimate is small but the variance (noise) is large. On the one hand, a very small h means that there may not be enough points for averaging or smoothing and thus we may get an undersmoothed density estimate exhibiting wiggles. On the other hand, if we choose a very large h, the bias will be large but the variance (noise) is small, resulting in an oversmoothed density estimate and a distortion of the true picture of the density. An extreme example might be when a bimodal density is incorrectly estimated as unimodal. Thus, in practice, h must be set to achieve the "best" possible trade-off between bias and variance, and that necessitates some sort of criterion. One possibility is to focus upon the *AMISE*. Notice that $(\text{Bias})^2 = O(h^4)$ and variance $= O(nh)^{-1}$, meaning that the *AMISE* is $\max\{O(h^4), O(nh)^{-1}\}$. Thus the *only* value of h for which the bias and variance are of the same order of magnitude is

$$h \propto n^{-1/5}, \qquad (2.48)$$

because then the *AMISE* $= O(n^{-4/5})$.

Although (2.48) was arrived at heuristically, it is in fact an optimal selection rule, in the sense that it minimizes *AMISE*. To see this, take the *AMISE* in (2.46), differentiate it with respect to h, and equate the outcome to zero, thereby obtaining

$$h^3 \lambda_1 - \frac{1}{nh^2} \lambda_2 = 0,$$

or

$$h = cn^{-1/5}, \qquad (2.49)$$

where $c = (\lambda_2/\lambda_1)^{1/5}$ depends on both the kernel and the second derivative (curvature) of the density. A closer examination of $\lambda_1 = \mu_2^2 \int \left(f^{(2)}(x) \right)^2 dx$ is therefore warranted. By inspection, λ_1 depends on the variance of the kernel density and $\int \left(f^{(2)}(x) \right)^2 dx$; the latter indicates the degree of variability in the density. Thus, for example, if the true density is flat, then $\lambda_1 \to 0$ and $c \to \infty$

(large window width). In contrast, if the density is highly variable, $\lambda_1 \to \infty$ and $c \to 0$ (small window width). Thus, care should be taken when choosing c in practice. To get some perspective on the magnitude of c, suppose that K is the standard normal density and $f(x) \sim \mathcal{N}(\mu, \sigma^2)$. Direct calculation then shows that $c \sim 1.06\sigma$ and

$$h = 1.06\sigma\, n^{-1/5}. \tag{2.50}$$

Silverman (1986) considers a number of possible alternatives for c in (2.49). He compares the formula in (2.50) with the optimal h if the unknown density is really a mixture of normals or heavily skewed, finding that (2.50) does fairly well unless the density is bimodal or very strongly skewed. A simple improvement is to replace σ by a robust estimator of spread and he specifies two alternatives that seem to work well:

$$h = .79\, Rn^{-1/5} \tag{2.51}$$

and

$$h = .9\, An^{-1/5}, \tag{2.52}$$

where R is the interquartile range and $A = \min(\sigma, (R/1.34))$.

Exactly how to select c is a major concern in the determination of window width, and many suggestions have been made. Some attempt to estimate the components of c and then to "plug-in" such estimates into (2.49). Others try to determine c by reference to criteria such as predictive ability. A more extensive discussion of these proposals is contained in Section 2.7.1. Obviously, the difficulties in estimating a window width are bound up with the ability to estimate $\int \left(f^{(2)}(x)\right)^2 dx$. Using the theory of semiparametric efficiency bounds discussed in Chapter 5, Fan and Marron (1992) determine how well this "parameter" can be estimated, in the sense of the lowest variance that is attainable. In turn this leads to a minimal asymptotic variance for estimators of h of $B^2(f)n^{-1}$, where

$$B^2(f) = \frac{4}{25}\left(\frac{\int_{-\infty}^{\infty} \left(f^{(4)}(x)\right)^2 f(x)\, dx}{\left(\int_{-\infty}^{\infty} \left(f^{(2)}(x)\right)^2 dx\right)^2} - 1 \right).$$

Fan and Marron use this as an index of how difficult it is to select a window width for a given density. For a normal density $B(f) = 1.3$, whereas for density no. 4 in Marron and Wand (1992), a kurtotic unimodal density, $B(f) = 2.638$, making the ratio of the corresponding $B^2(f)s$ equal to 4.1. That is, it is 4.1 times more difficult to estimate this leptokurtotic density than it is to estimate a normal density. Expressed another way, the sample size needs to be four times larger if one is to estimate the optimal window width for the leptokurtotic density with the same accuracy as can be done for a normal density.

Finally, the criterion used in identifying h was an approximation to *MISE*. If higher order terms in the bias or variance expansions (2.44) and (2.46) were retained, then a different formula for h can result. In the above analysis *MISE* was approximated by a polynomial in h, with h^4 being the maximal order retained. If, instead, the expansion is taken to h^6, Hall et al. (1991) show that the resulting optimal window width is

$$h = cn^{-1/5} + \mu_2 \lambda_4 \lambda_1^{-8/5} \lambda_3 n^{-3/5}, \tag{2.53}$$

where $\lambda_4 = \frac{1}{20} \left(\int K^2 \right)^{3/5} \mu_2^{-1/5} \int \psi^4 K(\psi) \, d\psi$ and $\lambda_3 = \int \left(f^{(3)}(x) \right)^2 dx$. This estimator has the property that it will converge to the h minimizing *MISE* at the rate $n^{-\frac{1}{2}}$.[5]

The *MISE* of (2.46) is affected not only by h but also by the kernel through the terms μ_2 and $\int K^2(\psi) \, d\psi$. An optimal K might be found by substituting the optimal h from (2.49) into the expression (2.46) and then minimizing it with respect to K subject to the constraints in (A2). To do this we first write (2.46), using (2.49), the definitions of λ_1, λ_2 in (2.47), and $c = (\lambda_2/\lambda_1)^{1/5}$, as

$$MISE \left(\hat{f}(x) \right) = \lambda_4 \left(\int \mu_2^{1/2} K^2(\psi) \, d\psi \right)^{4/5}, \tag{2.54}$$

where $\mu_2 = \int \psi^2 K(\psi) \, d\psi$ as before, and $\lambda_4 = (5/4) n^{-4/5} \left[\int \left(f^{(2)}(x) \right)^2 dx \right]^{1/5}$ does not depend on K. Replacing $K(\psi)$ by the rescaled version $\mu_2^{-1/2} K(\mu_2^{-1/2} \psi)$, we find that the minimization of (2.54) subject to (A2) is the same as the minimization of $\int K^2(\psi) \, d\psi$ subject to the constraints that $\int K(\psi) \, d\psi$ and $\int \psi^2 K(\psi) \, d\psi$ are both equal to one. That is, determine K, δ_1, and δ_2 (Lagrange multipliers) such that, using symmetry of $K(\psi)$, the Lagrangean

$$L = \int_0^\infty K^2(\psi) \, d\psi + \delta_1 \left[\int_0^\infty K(\psi) \, d\psi - \frac{1}{2} \right]$$

$$+ \delta_2 \left[\int_0^\infty \psi^2 K(\psi) \, d\psi - \frac{1}{2} \right] \tag{2.55}$$

is a minimum.

To solve this problem let ΔK represent a small change and apply the method of calculus of variations to give

$$\Delta L = \int_0^\infty [2K(\psi) + \delta_1 + \delta_2 \psi^2] \Delta K(\psi) \, d\psi = 0, \tag{2.56}$$

---

[5] Since this is the typical rate of convergence in parametric estimation problems it is not surprising that it is the best possible rate; see Hall and Marron (1991).

or

$$2K(\psi) + \delta_1 + \delta_2\psi^2 = 0. \tag{2.57}$$

The first-order conditions for the multipliers are $\partial L/\partial \delta_1 = 0$ and $\partial L/\partial \delta_2 = 0$, or

$$\int_0^\infty K(\psi)\,d\psi = 1/2, \qquad \int_0^\infty \psi^2 K(\psi)\,d\psi = 1/2. \tag{2.58}$$

We now solve (2.57). Note that $K(\psi) = -2^{-1}(\delta_1 + \delta_2\psi^2)$ is symmetric, and it is zero at $\psi = \pm(-\delta_1/\delta_2)^{1/2}$. Thus we can take

$$K_0(\psi) = \begin{cases} -2^{-1}(\delta_1 + \delta_2\psi^2), & |\psi| \le (-\delta_1/\delta_2)^{1/2}, \\ 0, & \text{otherwise.} \end{cases} \tag{2.59}$$

The kernel in (2.59) is optimal if δ_1 and δ_2 are determined by (2.58) with K replaced by K_0. It can be verified that $\delta_1 = -(3/2)5^{-1/2}$ and $\delta_2 = (3/10)5^{-1/2}$, making the optimal kernel

$$K_0(\psi) = \begin{cases} \frac{3}{4}5^{-1/2}\left(1 - \frac{\psi^2}{5}\right), & |\psi| \le 5^{1/2}, \\ 0, & \text{otherwise,} \end{cases} \tag{2.60}$$

or simply

$$K_0(\psi) = \begin{cases} \frac{3}{4}\left(1 - \psi^2\right), & |\psi| \le 1, \\ 0, & \text{otherwise.} \end{cases} \tag{2.61}$$

This kernel (2.61) is commonly known in the literature as the Epanechnikov (1969) kernel, although Bartlett (1963) seems to have obtained it before him.

The optimal kernel is nonnegative everywhere and it is a parabola. There is an extensive literature comparing the *MISE* of the optimal kernel with the *MISE* of other possible kernels. These results indicate that the difference between the values of *MISE* attained by most kernels and the optimal kernel is small (see Silverman, 1986, Table 3.1, p. 43). Consequently, the computational cost, simplicity, and the speed of convergence of the density estimator may largely determine the choice of a kernel. The last aspect is considered in Section 2.4.3. Perhaps the main disadvantage of Epanechnikov's kernel is that its Fourier transform is not absolutely integrable, a condition used in proving the uniform consistency of $\hat{f}(x)$ in Section 2.5.2.

It has been found by Marron and Wand (1992) and Rahman et al. (1994) that the optimal h for normal densities, based on the exact *MISE*, does not differ much from the approximate optimal values described above. However, they show that this result may not be true for other densities such as mixtures of normal and skewed densities. According to their results the approximate optimal h may provide serious underestimation of the exact optimal h.

2.4.3 Reduction of Bias

The bias in the density estimator was given in Theorem 2.2 to be of $O(h^2)$. This was for the case of kernels that satisfy (A2), usually being symmetric probability density functions. However, if the kernels are allowed to take negative as well as positive values it is possible to reduce the bias. A particular class of such kernels is useful for this task and (A6) below summarizes its characteristics.

(A6) Let K be the class of symmetric kernels such that

$$\int \psi^j K(\psi)\, d\psi = 1 \text{ if } j = 0,$$

$$= 0 \text{ if } j = 1, \ldots r - 1, \ r \geq 2,$$

$$< \infty \text{ if } j = r.$$

To allow the use of such kernels, the following requirement on the density is needed.

(A7) The rth-order derivatives of the density are continuous.

Assumption (A6) implies that only those kernel functions whose first $(r - 1)$th-order moments are zero and whose rth moment is finite are being considered. These kernels will be said to be *higher order* kernels, with the order determined by the largest nonzero moment. Assumption (A2) is the special case when $r = 2$. For $r \geq 3$ condition (A6) may not be satisfied for positive kernels. Expressions for kernels that satisfy (A6) are given in Section 2.7.2. For the moment it is assumed that such kernels may be constructed and Theorem 2.3 demonstrates why their use can reduce the bias of a density estimator.

Theorem 2.3: Under Assumptions (A1) and (A4)–(A7), the bias, up to $O(h^r)$, and the variance, up to $O(nh)^{-1}$, of the estimator $\hat{f}$ are given by

$$\text{Bias}(\hat{f}) = \frac{h^r}{r!}\mu_r f^{(r)}(x), \qquad \mu_r = \int \psi^r K(\psi)\, d\psi \qquad (2.62)$$

and

$$V(\hat{f}) = (nh)^{-1} f(x) \int K^2(\psi)\, d\psi. \qquad (2.63)$$

Proof: From (2.43) we have

$$f(x + h\psi) = f(x) + h\psi f^{(1)}(x) + \cdots$$

$$+ \frac{h^{r-1}\psi^{r-1}f^{(r-1)}(x)}{(r-1)!} + \frac{h^r \psi^r f^{(r)}(x)}{r!} + \cdots.$$

The results (2.62) and (2.63) then follow from using the proof of Theorem 2.2 and exploiting the fact that the kernel has zero moments up to rth order.   Q.E.D.

Comparing (2.62) and (2.41), we see that the use of the kernel in (A6) has reduced the bias from $O(h^2)$ to $O(h^r)$(h^r, $r > 2$, is smaller than h^2 for large n). The expression for the approximate variance is, however, not affected by assumption (A6). Thus the approximate *MISE* in this case is

$$AMISE = \left(\frac{1}{r!}\right)^2 h^{2r}\lambda_{1r} + \frac{1}{nh}\lambda_2, \tag{2.64}$$

where $\lambda_{1r} = \mu_r^2 \int \left(f^{(r)}(x)\right)^2 dx$ and λ_2 is as given in (2.47). The optimal h (differentiating *AMISE* in (2.64) with respect to h) becomes

$$h^* = \left(\frac{\lambda_2(r!)^2}{2r\lambda_{1r}}\right)^{1/(2r+1)} n^{-1/(2r+1)}$$

$$\propto n^{-1/(2r+1)}. \tag{2.65}$$

Substituting h^* in (2.64), we obtain

$$AMISE = O\left(n^{-2r/2r+1}\right). \tag{2.66}$$

Equation (2.66) implies that, if the density function has r continuous derivatives, by picking higher order kernels satisfying (A6), the speed of convergence can be improved over that of $O(n^{-4/5})$ found for $r = 2$. For example, when $r = 3$, the *AMISE* converges at rate $O(n^{-6/7})$, which is better than $O(n^{-4/5})$. It is tempting to make r very large so as to force the *AMISE* to be close to $O(n^{-1})$, which would be the best possible rate and which is attained by parametric estimators. However, the inescapable concomitant of a large r is the need for $f^{(r)}$ to exist and to specify kernels whose higher order moments are zero. For example, the case of $r = 10$ would require kernels whose first nine moments are zero. Such kernels may not always be easy to find, although in Section 2.7.2, a general approach to finding such kernels is provided. Perhaps the main argument against choosing r very high is that a negative density estimate is almost inevitable.

A number of other methods for bias reduction have been put forward. An approach analogous to choosing a higher order kernel is to consider local likelihood estimators described in Section 2.2.8. The bias of the estimators of that section is the same as that of the regular kernel estimator with $f^{(2)}(x)$ replaced by a function $g(x)$ related to but different from $f^{(2)}$. The nature of $g(x)$ depends on the characteristics of the parametric density and it would generally be smaller in size than $f^{(2)}$. Hjort and Jones (1996) also show that the variance of the local density estimator is the same as that of the kernel estimator $\hat{f}$ in (2.32), at least to the order of approximation $(nh)^{-1}$.

The variable-window kernel estimator, when $h_{ni} = [\tilde{f}(x_i)/G]^{-1/2}h$, is also known to have reduced bias. To see this suppose that $h_i = h\alpha(x_i)$; for the two-stage estimator $\alpha(x_i)$ is $[f(x_i)/G]^{-1/2}$. Then, following the same steps as above, we find that $E[\hat{f}(x)] = \int \alpha(x + h\psi) f(x + h\psi) K\{\psi\alpha(x + h\psi)\} d\psi$ and the bias to any order depends upon the nature of the function $\alpha(\cdot)$. When $\alpha(x_i) = 1$, $E(\hat{f}(x)) = \int f(x+h\psi) K(\psi) d\psi$, as established in (2.39). For general $\alpha(\cdot)$, and the application of an rth-order kernel, Hall (1990) finds the bias to $O(h^r)$ to be $\mu_r C_r\{\alpha(x + h\psi)^{-r} f(x + h\psi)\}$, where C_r is the coefficient of h^r in the expansion of the bias. By inspection of this formula, the bias can be made zero if $\alpha(x + h\psi)$ is proportional to $f(x + h\psi)^{-1/r}$, as then C_r is proportional to $\int K(\psi) d\psi = 0$. Thus, if $\alpha(x_i)$ is proportional to $f(x_i)^{-1/2}$, as was the case with the adaptive two-stage estimator, the term involving h^2 will be zero and bias will only appear at $O(h^4)$ (assuming a symmetric kernel eliminates the h^3 term). In theory, a combination of a higher order kernel and a variable window width can be very effective in reducing small-sample bias.

Another suggestion, made by Schucany and Summers (1977), is to "jackknife." In this procedure $\overline{pf}(x) = (\hat{f}(x) - c^{-2}\tilde{f}(x))/(1 - c^{-2})$, where c is a constant exceeding unity and $\tilde{f}(x)$ is a kernel estimator using window width ch. To see why this works observe from (2.41) that, to $O(h^2)$, $E \hat{f}(x) = f(x) + .5h^2\mu_2 f^{(2)}(x)$, whereas $\tilde{f}(x) = f(x) + .5c^2h^2\mu_2 f^{(2)}(x)$. Consequently, to $O(h^2)$, $E \overline{pf}(x) = f(x)(1 - c^{-2})/(1 - c^{-2}) = f(x)$. Values of c have to be assigned, but experience suggests a range of $1 < c < 1.1$ is adequate. Reduction of bias to higher order than $O(h^2)$ is possible; for example, to remove terms like h^4 one would combine together two estimators with window widths h and ch with weights c^{-4} rather than c^{-2}. Of course, removing bias terms of $O(h^4)$ does not remove those involving $O(h^2)$ and one would need to utilize convolutions of different jackknife estimators to remove all terms up to a specified order. Generally, it will be easier to employ a higher order kernel, although one might combine the two approaches, for example, eliminate terms involving h^2 with a higher order kernel and terms with h^4 with the jackknife. It should be noted however that, although the higher order kernel and jackknifing approaches are capable of reducing the bias to zero for any predetermined order, in practice this seems uncertain, at least for small n (see Hong and Pagan, 1988).[6]

It is interesting to note that substituting (2.65) into the *MISE* and optimizing with respect to K may not give the optimal K previously described in (2.61). Because (2.61) could be found by minimizing $\int K^2(\psi)\,d\psi$ subject to (A2), an alternative is to optimize the asymptotic variance subject to the restriction given in Assumption (A6) for $r = 4$. After doing so an Epanechnikov-type kernel

$$K(\psi) = \begin{cases} \frac{3}{8}(3 - 5\psi^2), & |\psi| < 1, \\ 0, & \text{otherwise} \end{cases} \tag{2.67}$$

again emerges. The kernel is discontinuous at ± 1 and the implied density estimate would also exhibit such a discontinuity.

It should be said that the number of applications using higher order kernels is very small. Fan and Marron (1992) argue that there are two important reasons for this. The first is simply the difficulty of understanding the logic of negative weights in averaging the data while the second is that the gains in terms of a lower *MISE* seem to be either nonexistent or very small with realistic sample sizes. Perhaps the major reason for interest in this topic is the fact that theoretical work with semiparametric estimators recounted in later chapters frequently invoke this device in their proofs of the asymptotic properties of proposed estimators.

2.5   Asymptotic Properties of the Kernel Density Estimator $\hat{f}$ with Independent Observations

This section turns to a consideration of the asymptotic properties of the kernel density estimator. Definitions of the various modes of convergence employed are given in the appendix. Our proofs will tend to be heuristic; for rigorous proofs, see Prakasa-Rao (1983), Devroye and Györfi (1985), and Devroye (1983). Assumptions (A1), (A4), and (A5), as detailed in Section 2.4, are retained for the derivation of asymptotic results, but (A2) and (A3) are replaced by (A8) and (A9) respectively:

(A8) Let K be the class of all Borel measurable bounded real-valued functions $K(\psi)$ such that
   (i) $\int K(\psi)\,d\psi = 1$,
   (ii) $\int |K(\psi)|\,d\psi < \infty$,

---

[6] Silverman (1986, p. 68) observes that $\overline{f}(x)$ can be interpreted as a kernel estimator with kernel $(1 - c^{-2})^{-1}[K(\psi) - c^{-3}K(c^{-1}\psi)]$ and then the limit of this as $c \to 1$ is the higher order kernel $1.5K(\psi) + .5\psi K^{(1)}(\psi)$.

(iii) $|\psi| |K(\psi)| \to 0$ as $|\psi| \to \infty$,

(iv) $\sup |K(\psi)| < \infty$,

(v) $\int K^2(\psi) \, d\psi < \infty$.

(A9) $f(x)$ is continuous at any point x_0 and $\int |f(x)| \, dx < \infty$.

Before proceeding to the derivation of asymptotic results we recall the lemma on bounded convergence (Lemma 1 in the appendix, Section A.2.6) and relate it to the rth moment of the kernel.

Lemma 2.1: Under Assumptions (A1), (A4), (A8), and (A9) we have

$$\frac{1}{h} E K^r \left(\frac{x_1 - x}{h} \right) = \int K^r(\psi) f(h\psi + x) \, d\psi$$

$$\to f(x) \int K^r(\psi) \, d\psi, \qquad (2.68)$$

as $n \to \infty$.

Proof: See (A.55) in the appendix. Q.E.D.

A simpler way to see that $\int K^r(\psi) f(h\psi + x) \, d\psi$ converges to $f(x) \int K^r(\psi) \, d\psi$ is to note that, when $n \to \infty$, $h \to 0$ and $f(h\psi + x) \to f(x)$. We observe that Assumption (A8) is satisfied by a large class of functions such as those given in (2.33).

2.5.1 Asymptotic Unbiasedness

In Theorem 2.1 it was found that the kernel density estimator was biased in finite samples, and this leads to an examination of whether the bias disappears asymptotically. To answer that question the behavior of $E\hat{f}(x)$ as $n \to \infty$ is investigated.

Theorem 2.4: Under Assumptions (A1), (A4), (A8), and (A9) the estimator $\hat{f}$ is asymptotically unbiased, that is,

$$\lim_{n \to \infty} E\hat{f} = f \qquad (2.69)$$

and $\sup_x |E\hat{f} - f| = 0$ as $n \to \infty$.

Proof: From (2.35), and using Lemma 2.1, for $r = 1$, we get

$$E(\hat{f} - f) = \int K(\psi) f(h\psi + x) \, d\psi - f \to f - f = 0 \qquad (2.70)$$

as $n \to \infty$. Hence the result in (2.69) follows. The second result comes from (2.70) and (A9) as $n \to \infty$, making $\hat{f}$ asymptotically unbiased uniformly for all x.   Q.E.D.

2.5.2   Consistency

Consistency of an estimator is normally a more desirable property for an estimator than asymptotic unbiasedness, and this section considers the possibility of convergence of $\hat{f}$ to f. Results will be exhibited for a variety of modes of convergence.

Theorem 2.5: Suppose the assumptions of Theorem 2.4 and (A5) hold. Then the estimator $\hat{f}$ is MSE consistent (converges in mean square to f), that is, MSE $(\hat{f}) \to 0$ as $n \to \infty$.

Proof: By definition $MSE(\hat{f}) = (\text{Bias } \hat{f})^2 + V(\hat{f})$. From Theorem 2.4 the Bias$(\hat{f}) \to 0$ as $n \to \infty$. Starting with the expression for $V(\hat{f})$ in (2.36), and invoking Lemma 2.1 for $r = 1, 2$, as well as (A5) ($nh \to \infty$ as $n \to \infty$), we get

$$V(\hat{f}) = (nh)^{-1} \int K^2(\psi) f(h\psi + x) \, d\psi$$

$$- n^{-1} \left[\int K(\psi) f(h\psi + x) \, d\psi \right]^2$$

$$\to 0 \cdot \left(f(x) \int K^2(\psi) \, d\psi \right) - 0 \cdot f^2(x) = 0 \quad \text{as } n \to \infty.$$

Hence the $MSE \to 0$ and Theorem 2.5 holds.   Q.E.D.

From the proof of Theorem 2.5 it follows that

$$AV[(nh)^{1/2}\hat{f}] = \lim_{n \to \infty} \left[(nh)V(\hat{f}) \right] = f(x) \int K^2(\psi) \, d\psi, \qquad (2.71)$$

where AV represents the asymptotic variance. It follows that the AV of $\hat{f}$ will be $(nh)^{-1} f(x) \int K^2(\psi) \, d\psi$.

Theorem 2.6: Suppose the assumptions of Theorem 2.5 hold. Then $\hat{f}$ is weakly consistent, that is,

$$p \lim_{n \to \infty} \hat{f} = f \quad \text{or} \quad \hat{f} - f = o_p(1). \tag{2.72}$$

Proof: From Theorem 2.5, $MSE(\hat{f}) \to 0$ as $n \to \infty$. Thus, using Chebychev's inequality (see the appendix), $P\left[|\hat{f} - f| < \epsilon\right] \to 1$ as $n \to \infty$, and hence (2.72) holds.   Q.E.D.

Strong consistency of the estimator requires an additional assumption:

(A10) $\sum_{n=1}^{\infty} \exp(-\alpha n h) < \infty$ for all $\alpha > 0$,

for which a sufficient condition is

(A11) $nh(\log n)^{-1} \to \infty$ as $n \to \infty$.

Theorem 2.7: Suppose the assumptions of Theorem 2.6 hold. Then $\hat{f}$ is strongly consistent, that is,

$$\hat{f} \overset{a.s.}{\to} f, \tag{2.73}$$

if (A10) holds.

Proof: Adding and subtracting $E\hat{f}$ from $\hat{f} - f$, we get

$$\hat{f} - f = \hat{f} - E\hat{f} + E\hat{f} - f = a_n + b_n, \tag{2.74}$$

where $a_n = \hat{f} - E\hat{f}$ and $b_n = E\hat{f} - f$. From (2.37) we have

$$a_n = \hat{f} - E\hat{f} = \frac{1}{n}\sum_{i=1}^{n}(w_i - Ew_i), \tag{2.75}$$

with $w_i = h^{-1}K((x_i - x)/h)$. Note that $w_i - Ew_i$ are i.i.d. random variables with $|w_1 - Ew_1| \le 2h^{-1}M$, where $M = \sup_{\psi}|K(\psi)|$. Furthermore, from (2.38) and (2.40)

$$nV(\hat{f}) = V(w_1) < Ew_1^2$$

$$= \frac{1}{h}\int K^2(\psi)f(h\psi + x)\,d\psi \le h^{-1}c\lambda_2, \tag{2.76}$$

with $\lambda_2 = \int K^2(\psi)\,d\psi$ and c being a constant. Applying Bennett's (1962) inequality in the appendix to (2.75) produces

$$P\left[|\hat{f} - E\hat{f}| > \epsilon\right] = P\left[\frac{1}{n}\left|\sum_{i=1}^{n}(w_i - Ew_i)\right| > \epsilon\right]$$

$$\leq 2\,\exp\left[-n\epsilon^2/(2V(w_1) + 2h^{-1}M\epsilon)\right]$$

$$= 2\,\exp[-\alpha nh], \tag{2.77}$$

where $\alpha = \epsilon^2/2(c\lambda_2 + M\epsilon) > 0$. Thus for every $\epsilon > 0$

$$\sum_{n=1}^{\infty} P\left[|\hat{f} - E\hat{f}| > \epsilon\right] < \infty \tag{2.78}$$

if (A10) holds. Therefore, by the Borel–Cantelli lemma $|\hat{f} - E\hat{f}| = |a_n| \to 0$ *a.s.* (almost surely) as $n \to \infty$. Combining this fact with asymptotic unbiasedness, that is, $b_n \to 0$ as $n \to \infty$, gives $\hat{f} - f \to 0$ *a.s.* as $n \to \infty$, establishing the strong consistency of $\hat{f}$.   Q.E.D.

An alternative proof of weak consistency is available from the inequality in (2.77), which implies that

$$P\left[|\hat{f} - E\hat{f}| > \epsilon\right] \leq 2\,\exp[-\alpha nh] \to 0 \tag{2.79}$$

as $n \to \infty$ if (A5) holds $(nh \to \infty)$. Thus $\hat{f} - E\hat{f} \to 0$ in probability. This, along with asymptotic unbiasedness, immediately leads to the weak consistency conclusion in (2.72).

Finally, it is of interest to establish the uniform consistency of $\hat{f}$; again a strengthening of assumptions is needed, summarized in the following triplet:

(A12) The characteristic function $\phi(t)$ of K is absolutely integrable.
(A13) f is uniformly continuous in R^1.
(A14) $nh^2 \to \infty$ as $n \to \infty$.

Theorem 2.8: Suppose the assumptions of Theorem 2.4 as well as (A12)–(A14) hold. Then $\hat{f}$ is uniformly weak consistent, that is,

$$p\lim_{n \to \infty}\left[\sup_x |\hat{f} - f|\right] = 0. \tag{2.80}$$

Proof: Under Assumption (A12) the inversion theorem of Fourier transforms means that

$$K(\psi) = \frac{1}{2\pi}\int \exp\{-it\psi\}\phi(t)\,dt. \tag{2.81}$$

To prove the uniform consistency of $\hat{f}$, first rewrite the kernel estimator using (2.32) and (2.81) as

$$\hat{f} = \frac{1}{nh} \sum_{j=1}^{n} K \left(\frac{x_j - x}{h} \right)$$

$$= \frac{1}{nh} \sum_{j=1}^{n} \frac{1}{2\pi} \int \exp \left\{ -is \left(\frac{x - x_j}{h} \right) \right\} \phi(s) \, ds$$

$$= \frac{1}{2\pi} \int \left[\left(\sum_{j=1}^{n} \frac{1}{nh} \exp \left\{ \frac{isx_j}{h} \right\} \right) \exp \left\{ \frac{-isx}{h} \right\} \phi(s) \, ds \right]$$

$$= \frac{1}{2\pi} \left[\int \left(\sum_{j=1}^{n} \frac{1}{n} \exp \left\{ itx_j \right\} \right) \exp \left\{ -itx \right\} \phi(ht) \, dt \right]. \qquad (2.82)$$

After making the change of variable $t = s/h$, we get

$$\hat{f} = \frac{1}{2\pi} \left[\int \exp \left\{ -itx \right\} \hat{\phi}(t) \phi(ht) \, dt \right],$$

where

$$\hat{\phi}(t) = \frac{1}{n} \sum_{j=1}^{n} \exp \left\{ itx_j \right\} \qquad (2.83)$$

is the empirical characteristic function, which is an unbiased estimator of $\phi(t)$ because the x_js are i.i.d. It is thus true that

$$E\hat{f} = \frac{1}{2\pi} \int \exp \left\{ -itx \right\} \left(E(\hat{\phi}(t)) \right) \phi(ht) \, dt$$

$$= \frac{1}{2\pi} \int \exp \left\{ -itx \right\} \phi(t) \phi(ht) \, dt, \qquad (2.84)$$

making

$$|\hat{f} - E\hat{f}| = \left| \frac{1}{2\pi} \int \left\{ \hat{\phi}(t) - \phi(t) \right\} \phi(ht) \exp \left\{ -itx \right\} dt \right|. \qquad (2.85)$$

But $|\exp \{-itx\}| = |\cos tx - i \sin tx| = (\cos^2 tx + \sin^2 tx)^{\frac{1}{2}} = 1$. Therefore

$$\sup_{x} |\hat{f} - E\hat{f}| \leq \frac{1}{2\pi} \int |\hat{\phi}(t) - \phi(t)| \, |\phi(ht)| \, dt, \qquad (2.86)$$

with no sup on the right-hand side because it does not depend on x. It follows from Lemma 2.1 of Jennrich (1969) that $\sup |\cdot|$ is measurable, its expectation is well defined, and

$$E \sup_x |\hat{f} - E\hat{f}| \le \frac{1}{2\pi} \int E\,|\hat{\phi}(t) - \phi(t)|\,|\phi(ht)|\,dt. \qquad (2.87)$$

Now,

$$E\,|\hat{\phi}(t) - \phi(t)| = E\left|\frac{1}{n}\sum_{j=1}^{n}(\exp\{itx_j\} - E\exp\{itx_j\})\right|$$

$$= E\left|\frac{1}{n}\sum_{j=1}^{n}(\cos tx_j - E\cos tx_j)\right.$$

$$\left.+i\frac{1}{n}\sum_{j=1}^{n}(\sin tx_j - E\sin tx_j)\right|$$

$$= E\,|X_1 + iX_2| = E\,[(X_1 + iX_2)(X_1 - iX_2)]^{1/2}$$

$$= E\left(X_1^2 + X_2^2\right)^{1/2} \le \left(EX_1^2 + EX_2^2\right)^{1/2}$$

$$= \left[V\left(\frac{1}{n}\sum_{j=1}^{n}\cos tx_j\right) + V\left(\frac{1}{n}\sum_{j=1}^{n}\sin tx_j\right)\right]^{1/2},$$

$$(2.88)$$

where

$$X_1 = \frac{1}{n}\sum_{j=1}^{n}(\cos\,tx_j - E\cos\,tx_j),$$

$$X_2 = \frac{1}{n}\sum_{j=1}^{n}(\sin\,tx_j - E\sin\,tx_j) \qquad (2.89)$$

are such that $EX_1 = 0 = EX_2$, $V(X_1) = EX_1^2$, and $V(X_2) = EX_2^2$. Also note that $E(X_1^2 + X_2^2)^{1/2} \le (EX_1^2 + EX_2^2)^{1/2}$ follows by substituting $Z^2 = X_1^2 + X_2^2$.
Using the i.i.d. assumption we note that

$$V\left(\frac{1}{n}\sum_{j=1}^{n}\cos tx_j\right) + V\left(\frac{1}{n}\sum_{j=1}^{n}\sin tx_j\right)$$

$$= \frac{1}{n}[V(\cos tx_1) + V(\sin tx_1)]$$

$$\leq \frac{1}{n} \left[E \cos^2 tx_1 + E \sin^2 (tx_1) \right]$$

$$= \frac{1}{n}. \tag{2.90}$$

Thus, substituting (2.90) into (2.88), we obtain

$$E \left| \hat{\phi}(t) - \phi(t) \right| \leq \left(\frac{1}{n} \right)^{1/2}. \tag{2.91}$$

Substituting (2.91) into (2.87) yields

$$E \left[\sup \left| \hat{f} - E \hat{f} \right| \right] \leq \frac{1}{2\pi \sqrt{n}} \int |\phi(ht)| \, dt$$

$$= \frac{1}{2\pi \sqrt{nh}} \int |\phi(s)| \, ds, \tag{2.92}$$

which tends to zero as $n \to \infty$ under Assumption (A14) $(nh^2 \to \infty)$. Furthermore, using the Markov inequality in the appendix, we get

$$P \left[\sup \left| \hat{f} - E \hat{f} \right| > \epsilon \right] \to 0 \quad \text{as } n \to \infty, \tag{2.93}$$

implying that $\sup \left| \hat{f} - E \hat{f} \right| \to 0$.
  Finally, because

$$\sup \left| \hat{f} - f \right| < \sup \left| \hat{f} - E \hat{f} \right| + \sup \left| E \hat{f} - f \right|, \tag{2.94}$$

the second term tends to zero from Theorem 2.4, and the first term is $o_p(1)$ from (2.93). Thus $\hat{f}$ is uniformly consistent. Q.E.D.

2.5.3 Asymptotic Normality

Consistency is a desirable property of an estimator but it is also valuable to be able to make some inferences regarding the magnitude of a density at a particular point. To do that demands a distributional theory, which is the concern of Theorem 2.9.

  Theorem 2.9: Suppose the assumptions of Theorem 2.5 hold and that there exists some δ such that $\int K(\psi)^{2+\delta} d\psi < \infty$. Then

$$(nh)^{1/2}(\hat{f} - E \hat{f}) \xrightarrow{d} \mathcal{N} \left(0, \; f(x) \int K^2(\psi) \, d\psi \right) \quad \text{as } n \to \infty.$$

$$\tag{2.95}$$

Proof: Normalizing $\hat{f} - E\hat{f}$ by its standard deviation leaves the expression

$$S_n = \frac{\hat{f} - E\hat{f}}{(V(\hat{f}))^{1/2}} = \sum_{i=1}^{n} \frac{w_i - Ew_i}{(nV(w_1))^{1/2}} = \sum_{i=1}^{n} L_{ni},$$

where $w_i = h^{-1}K((x_i - x)/h)$ is defined in (2.32).

Now L_{ni} is a triangular array of n i.i.d. random variables such that $EL_{ni} = 0$, $V(L_{ni}) = n^{-1} < \infty$, and $V(S_n) = 1$. Thus two of the conditions of Liapounov's central limit theorem (see the appendix) are satisfied. To check the third condition we need to show that, for some $\delta > 0$, $\sum E|L_{ni}|^{2+\delta} \to 0$ as $n \to \infty$. Verification proceeds by observing that

$$\sum_{i=1}^{n} E|L_{ni}|^{2+\delta} = (nV(w_1))^{-(1+\delta/2)} \sum_{i=1}^{n} E|w_i - Ew_i|^{2+\delta}$$

$$= (V(w_1))^{-(1+\delta/2)} n^{-\delta/2} E|w_1 - Ew_1|^{2+\delta}$$

$$\leq (hV(w_1))^{-(1+\delta/2)} 2^{(1+\delta)}(nh)^{-\delta/2}$$

$$\times E\frac{1}{h}\left|K\left(\frac{x_1 - x}{h}\right)\right|^{2+\delta}, \qquad (2.96)$$

where we have used $E|w_1 - Ew_1|^{2+\delta} \leq 2^{1+\delta}E|w_1|^{2+\delta}$ from the c_r inequality in the appendix. Now, from (2.38) and (2.71), $hV(w_1) = nhV(\hat{f}) \to f \int K^2(\psi)\,d\psi$ as $n \to \infty$, and, from Lemma 2.1, $Eh^{-1}|K((x_1 - x)/h)|^{2+\delta} \to \int |K(\psi)|^{2+\delta}\,d\psi$ as $n \to \infty$. These give

$$\lim_{n \to \infty} \sum_{i=1}^{n} E|L_{ni}|^{2+\delta} = 0 \qquad (2.97)$$

by using (A5). Hence, using Liapounov's central limit theorem, we have $S_n \sim \mathcal{N}(0, 1)$. The result in (2.95) then follows by observing that $(\hat{f} - E\hat{f})/(AV(\hat{f}))^{1/2}$ will be equal to $S_n(V(\hat{f}))^{1/2}/(AV(\hat{f}))^{1/2}$ and so has the same limiting distribution as S_n because $V(\hat{f})/AV(\hat{f}) \to 1$ as $n \to \infty$ (using (2.71)). Q.E.D.

In practice one is much more interested in the distribution of $(nh)^{1/2}(\hat{f} - f)$ instead of $(nh)^{1/2}(\hat{f} - E\hat{f})$, owing to the fact that $E\hat{f}$ is unknown and a confidence interval needs to be placed around f, not $E\hat{f}$. Because

$$(nh)^{1/2}(\hat{f} - f) = (nh)^{1/2}(\hat{f} - E\hat{f}) + (nh)^{1/2}(E\hat{f} - f),$$

the quantity $(nh)^{1/2}(\hat{f} - f)$ will only be asymptotically normally distributed and centered at zero if the second term on the right of the equality, the "normalized bias," tends to zero as $n \to \infty$. There is no certainty that this is so; a sufficient condition derives from Theorem 2.2, namely that

(A15) $(nh)^{1/2}h^2 \to 0$ as $n \to \infty$.

Exploiting (A15) enables us to state the following theorem concerning the distribution of $(nh)^{1/2}(\hat{f} - f)$.[7] Note that a sufficient condition for (A15) to be true is that $nh^3 \to 0$ as $n \to \infty$.

Theorem 2.10: Suppose the assumptions of Theorem 2.5 hold. In addition if (A3) and (A15) hold, then

$$(nh)^{1/2}(\hat{f} - f) \sim N\left(0, \ f \int K^2(\psi)\,d\psi\right). \qquad (2.98)$$

Proof: The proof follows from the arguments advanced above.
Q.E.D.

From (2.98) a pointwise 95% confidence interval for f can be written as

$$\hat{f} \pm 1.96(nh)^{-1/2}\left[f(x)\int K^2(\psi)\,d\psi\right]^{1/2}.$$

In practice f and $\int K^2(\psi)\,d\psi$ might be replaced by consistent estimators. The integral of the squared kernel may be found analytically for some kernels but numerical procedures may be needed for others (see footnote 18 in Section 2.10.1 for more details). It is important to observe that the optimal h, given in (2.49), does not satisfy (A15). In fact, if we consider three window width selections of the form $cn^{-\frac{1}{5}+k}$, where k is greater than, equal to, or less than zero, these three cases correspond to instances of over, optimal, and undersmoothing of the data. In turn, if one substitutes the value of $h = n^{-\frac{1}{5}+k}$ into $(nh)^{1/2}h^2$, it is apparent that this term tends to infinity, a constant, and zero respectively for the three cases. Consequently, with undersmoothing the bias disappears; with optimal smoothing it causes a centering problem in the limiting distribution; and in oversmoothing the bias dominates the stochastic part $(nh)^{1/2}(\hat{f}(x) - E(\hat{f}(x)))$, which has a limiting distribution. This same behavior persists when a bias-reducing kernel is adopted, but now the optimal window width is that

---

[7] An alternative proof would be to use the Lindberg–Feller theorem given in the appendix, Section A.2.4.

in (2.65) and the lead term in the Taylor series expansion of $E(\hat{f}(x))$ around $f(x)$ will be $(nh)^{1/2}h^r$. Substituting the optimal window width of $cn^{-\frac{1}{(2r+1)}}$ produces the same outcomes as just discussed (where $r = 2$). Undersmoothing is therefore likely to appear in many guises as a way of removing the bias from the kernel, although the cost is that of failing to use an optimal window width. Alternatively, if an optimal window width is to be employed some allowance may be made for the bias. Effectively such methods exploit the bias-reduction capabilities of the higher order kernels introduced in Section 2.4.3.

2.5.4 Small-Sample Confidence Intervals

Rather than rely upon asymptotic normality for the construction of confidence intervals, increasing attention has been paid to the use of the bootstrap for this purpose (Hall, 1992). Defining $x_1^j, \ldots, x_n^j$ as the jth resample of the original data $x_1, \ldots, x_n$ drawn randomly with replacement, we define the resampled density estimate as

$$\hat{f}^j(x) = \frac{1}{nh} \sum_{i=1}^{n} K\left(\frac{x - x_i^j}{h}\right), \tag{2.99}$$

and, following (2.36), the variance $v\left(\hat{f}^j\right)$ will be replaced by

$$v\left(\hat{f}^j\right) = (nh)^{-1}\left[(nh)^{-1} \sum_{i=1}^{n} K^2\left(\frac{x - x_i^j}{h}\right) - h\hat{f}^j(x)^2\right]. \tag{2.100}$$

Now, $E\left(\hat{f}^j(x) \mid x_1, \ldots, x_n\right) = \hat{f}(x)$ since we have simply rearranged the data and, conditional upon them, this just defines the estimator $\hat{f}(x)$ itself.[8] Since the bootstrap is performed conditional upon the observed data, the quantity $\delta^j(x) = v^{-1/2}(\hat{f}^j)(\hat{f}^j(x) - \hat{f}(x))$ is equal to $v^{-1/2}(\hat{f}^j)(\hat{f}^j(x) - E(\hat{f}^j(x) \mid x_1 \ldots x_n))$, and therefore confidence intervals constructed using $\delta^j(x)$ will approximate the distribution of $\hat{f}(x)$ around $E(\hat{f}(x))$ and not around $f(x)$. To correct for the bias in $\hat{f}(x)$, two approaches might be followed. One is to directly estimate it, that is, the terms in (2.41) can be estimated from the data. Estimating a second derivative $f^{(2)}$ is not easy however, particularly if the sample is small, which is the motivation for employing the bootstrap rather than asymptotic theory. A second alternative is to eliminate the bias by use of higher order kernels and a window width that is small, to undersmooth the data. The motivation for undersmoothing is that it is likely to be less critical when we are constructing a confidence interval than when a good point estimate is desired. Hall (1992) provides a theoretical analysis of this issue, and his work favors the latter strategy in

---

[8] Note that we require that the kernel used not depend upon i.

the sense that the coverage error of a two-sided bias-corrected bootstrap interval is smaller. To get this result, however, he needs to use a fourth-order kernel.[9]

2.6 Sampling Properties of the Kernel Density Estimator with Dependent Observations

Section 2.5 considered the properties of the kernel estimator when observations were independent, and this section generalizes that material to allow for some forms of dependence. Throughout it is assumed that

(A16) $\{x_i, i = 0, \pm 1 \ldots\}$ is a strictly stationary real-valued stochastic process.

This stipulation also implies the stationarity of the kernel $K((x_i - x)/h)$, because it is a Borel-measurable function on R^1; see Ibragimov and Linnik (1971, Section 18.b).

2.6.1 Unbiasedness

Since K is stationary, $E\hat{f} = Ew_1$ as in (2.37). Thus the exact, approximate, and asymptotic biases on $\hat{f}$ are as in the i.i.d. case given in Theorems 2.1, 2.2, and 2.4, respectively. Under stationarity, therefore, the mean of $\hat{f}$ remains the same as in the i.i.d. case.

2.6.2 Consistency

To establish pointwise *MSE* consistency we first consider the expression for the exact variance of $\hat{f}$ when observations are dependent, $V_d(\hat{f})$. This is given in the following theorem.

Theorem 2.11: Under Assumption (A16) the exact variance of the estimator $\hat{f}$ in (2.32) is

$$V_d(\hat{f}) = V(\hat{f}) + \gamma_n, \tag{2.101}$$

where $V(\hat{f})$ is as in (2.36) and

$$\gamma_n = 2n^{-2} \sum_{i=1}^{n-1} (n - i)\text{cov}(w_1, w_{i+1}). \tag{2.102}$$

---

[9] In simulations he sets $K(\psi) = (15/32)(7\psi^4 - 10\psi^2 + 3)$ if $|\psi| < 1$ and $K(\psi) = 0$ otherwise, which is an optimal fourth-order kernel. The window width is taken to be $5.05c\hat{\sigma}_x n^{-1/9}$. This is an optimal window width when used with this kernel and the data are normal ($c = 1$).

Proof: From (2.32) and (2.38), and under (A16), we have

$$V_d(\hat{f}) = n^{-1}V(w_1) + n^{-2}\sum_{i \neq j}\sum \mathrm{cov}(w_i,\ w_j)$$

$$= V(\hat{f}) + 2n^{-2}\sum_{i=1}^{n-1}\sum_{j=1}^{n-i}\mathrm{cov}(w_j,\ w_{i+j})$$

$$= V(\hat{f}) + 2n^{-2}\sum_{i=1}^{n-1}(n-i)\mathrm{cov}(w_1,\ w_{i+1}). \tag{2.103}$$

$$\text{Q.E.D.}$$

The result in (2.101) shows that the variance of $\hat{f}$ in the dependent case is equal to its variance in the i.i.d. case plus a term that depends on the covariance γ_n. If this covariance is positive/negative the variance in the dependent case will be accordingly more/less than that in the i.i.d. case.

We observe that, although under the assumptions of Theorem 2.5 $V(\hat{f}) \to 0$ as $n \to \infty$, this may not be true for γ_n, and MSE consistency of the estimator will be dependent upon the behavior of γ_n. To determine if γ_n tends to zero, recourse will be made to the bounds on γ_n under the various measures of weak dependence described in the appendix.

Lemma 2.2: Suppose the sequence $\{x_i\}$ satisfies (A16). Then under weak dependence measures β_n, ϕ-mixing, and α-mixing of x_i,

$$|\gamma_n| \leq \frac{2\beta_n}{n}\left(\int |K(\psi)|\,d\psi\right)^2, \tag{2.104}$$

$$|\gamma_n| \leq 4M\left(\frac{1}{nh}\sum_{i=1}^{n}\phi_i\right)\left(\int |K(\psi)|\,d\psi\right), \tag{2.105}$$

and

$$|\gamma_n| \leq 8M^2\left(\frac{1}{nh^2}\sum_{i=1}^{n}\alpha_i\right), \tag{2.106}$$

respectively, where $M = \sup|K(\psi)|$.

Proof: From (2.102) and (2.32) we get

$$|\gamma_n| \leq \frac{2}{n}\sum_{i=1}^{n-1}|\mathrm{cov}(w_1,\ w_{i+1})|$$

$$= \frac{2}{nh^2} \sum_{i=1}^{n-1} \left| E\left\{ K\left(\frac{x_1 - x}{h}\right) K\left(\frac{x_{i+1} - x}{h}\right) \right\} \right.$$

$$\left. - EK\left(\frac{x_1 - x}{h}\right) EK\left(\frac{x_{i+1} - x}{h}\right) \right|$$

$$\leq \frac{2}{nh^2} \sum_{i=1}^{n} \int \int \left| K\left(\frac{y - x}{h}\right) K\left(\frac{z - x}{h}\right) \right|$$

$$\times |f_i(y, z) - f(y) f(z)| \, dy \, dz, \tag{2.107}$$

where $f_i(y, z)$ is the joint density of (x_1, x_{i+1}) at the points y, z. Now using the definition of the weak dependence in the appendix we get

$$|\gamma_n| \leq \frac{2\beta_n}{nh^2} \int \left| K\left(\frac{y - x}{h}\right) \right| dy \int \left| K\left(\frac{z - x}{h}\right) \right| dz,$$

which is (2.104).

Turning to (2.105) and (2.106), K is a Borel measurable function and so it has the same mixing coefficient as x_i. Invoking the inequality in the appendix on ϕ-mixing processes, we get

$$\left| \mathrm{cov}\left\{ K\left(\frac{x_1 - x}{h}\right), K\left(\frac{x_{i+1} - x}{h}\right) \right\} \right| \leq 2M\phi_i E \left| K\left(\frac{x_1 - x}{h}\right) \right|$$

for ϕ-mixing and $\leq 4M^2 \alpha_i$ for α-mixing. Inserting these results in the first inequality on the right of (2.107) delivers (2.105) and (2.106).   Q.E.D.

From Lemma 2.2 it is apparent that $|\gamma_n| \to 0$ as $n \to \infty$ if

(A17) $\frac{\beta_n}{n} = \frac{1}{nh}\theta_n = o(1)$

or

(A18) $\frac{1}{nh}\theta_n' = o(1)$

or

(A19) $\frac{1}{nh^2} \sum_{i=1}^{n} \alpha_i = \frac{1}{nh}\theta_n'' = o(1),$

where $\theta_n = h\beta_n$, $\theta_n' = \sum_{i=1}^{n} \phi_i$, and $\theta_n'' = h^{-1} \sum_{i=1}^{n} \alpha_i$. Notice that (A17), (A18), and (A19) hold if $\theta_n = O(1)$, $\theta_n' = O(1)$ and $\theta_n'' = O(1)$, respectively.

Theorem 2.12: Under the assumptions of Theorem 2.5 and (A16) the estimator $\hat{f}$ is *MSE* consistent if one of (A17), (A18), or (A19) holds.

Proof: $MSE_d(\hat{f}) = MSE(\hat{f}) + \gamma_n$, where $MSE_d(\hat{f}) = V_d(\hat{f}) + (\text{Bias}(\hat{f}))^2$ represents the *MSE* under dependent observations, while $V_d(\hat{f})$ and γ_n are described in (2.101) and (2.102) respectively. But $MSE(\hat{f}) \to 0$ as $n \to \infty$ from Theorem 2.5, and $\gamma_n \to 0$ as $n \to \infty$ if one of (A17), (A18), or (A19) holds.   Q.E.D.

From (2.101) we have

$$(nh)V_d(\hat{f}) = nhV(\hat{f}) + nh\gamma_n, \tag{2.108}$$

and, as $n \to \infty$,

$$(nh)V_d(\hat{f}) \to nhV(\hat{f}) \tag{2.109}$$

if

(A20) θ_n or θ'_n or $\theta''_n = o(1)$,

that is, the asymptotic variance of $\hat{f}$ for dependent observations is the same as that for the i.i.d. case. For the approximate variance we notice that approximate $V_d(\hat{f}) = $ approximate $V(\hat{f}) + $ approximate γ_n, where approximate $V(\hat{f})$ is as given in (2.42), and approximate γ_n has one of the following orders: $O\left((nh)^{-1}\theta_n\right), O\left((nh)^{-1}\theta'_n\right),$ or $O\left((nh)^{-1}\theta''_n\right)$, according to whether it is (A17), (A18), or (A19) that pertains. In general, therefore, $V_d(\hat{f})$ will depend upon the correlation structure of the x_is. Moreover, the optimal h corresponding to (2.46) will become $h_d = c_d n^{-1/5}$, where $c_d = (\lambda_{2d}/\lambda_1)^{1/5}$, and λ_{2d} will also depend on the correlation structure of the x_is.

Following a sequence such as that used when discussing consistency of estimators in the presence of i.i.d. data, Theorems 2.13 and 2.14 deal with the weak and uniform consistency of $\hat{f}$.

Theorem 2.13: When the assumptions of Theorem 2.12 hold, $\hat{f}$ is a weakly consistent estimator of f.

Proof: The proof proceeds as for that of Theorem 2.6.   Q.E.D.

Theorem 2.14: Under the assumptions of Theorem 2.8, (A16), and

(A21) β_n or $\sum_{i=1}^{n} \phi_i$ or $\sum_{i=1}^{n} \alpha_i$ is $O(1)$,

$\hat{f}$ is a uniformly consistent estimator of f.

Proof: From (2.87) and (2.88) we know that

$$E \sup_x \left| \hat{f} - E\hat{f} \right| \leq \frac{1}{2\pi} \int E \left| \hat{\phi}(t) - \phi(t) \right| |\phi(ht)| \, dt,$$

where

$$E \left| \hat{\phi}(t) - \phi(t) \right|$$

$$\leq \left[V \left(n^{-1} \sum_{j=1}^{n} \cos tx_j \right) + V \left(n^{-1} \sum_{j=1}^{n} \sin tx_j \right) \right]^{1/2}.$$

Using stationarity and the equivalent of (2.90) when there is dependence, we find

$$V \left[\frac{1}{n} \sum_{j=1}^{n} \cos tx_j \right] + V \left[\frac{1}{n} \sum_{j=1}^{n} \sin tx_j \right] \leq \frac{1}{n} + |\gamma_n^*|, \tag{2.110}$$

where $|\gamma_n^*| = 2n^{-1} \sum_{i=1}^{n-1} |\text{cov}(\cos tx_1, \cos tx_{i+1}) + \text{cov}(\sin tx_1, \sin tx_{i+1})|$. But, following the proof in Lemma 2.2,

$$|\gamma_n^*| \leq 2n^{-1}\beta_n \left[\left(\int \cos |u| \, du \right)^2 + \left(\int \sin |u| \, du \right)^2 \right]$$

or

$$|\gamma_n^*| \leq 4Mn^{-1} \left(\sum_{i=1}^{n} \phi_i \right) \left[\left(\int \cos |u| \, du \right)^2 + \left(\int \sin |u| \, du \right)^2 \right]$$

or

$$|\gamma_n^*| \leq 8M^2 n^{-1} \sum_{i=1}^{n} \alpha_i.$$

Using these results in (2.110), and noting that $\int |\phi(ht)| \, dt = h^{-1} \int |\phi(t)| \, dt$, it can be verified that

$$E \sup_x \left| \hat{f} - E\hat{f} \right| = 0 \left(\frac{1}{\sqrt{nh}} \right) \tag{2.111}$$

under (A21). The uniform consistency of $\hat{f}$ then follows by arguments similar to those in the proof of Theorem 2.8 (in particular those subsequent to (2.92)). Q.E.D.

Note that the rate of uniform consistency, $(\sqrt{nh})^{-1}$, is the same as in the i.i.d. case, so that dependence does not affect this asymptotic property. However, given the fact that the approximate variance does rely upon the degree of correlation in the $x_i s$, it is to be expected that the small-sample performance of the estimator will be different in the two situations.

2.6.3 Asymptotic Normality

The asymptotic normality results of Theorems 2.9 and 2.10 go through for the dependence case provided (A20) holds. For detailed proofs, see Robinson (1983) for the α-mixing case and Castellana and Leadbetter (1986) for the β-dependence case.

2.6.4 Bibliographical Summary (Approximate and Asymptotic Results)

The exact bias and variance results of Section 2.4.1 can be found in Rosenblatt (1956b) and Bartlett (1963). The approximate results in Section 2.4.2 are due to Parzen (1962). Section 2.4.3 is essentially based on Bartlett's (1963) results. For the comparison of the rates of decline of the *MSE* and *MISE* of various density estimators, see Nadaraya (1970), Davis (1975, 1977), Deheuvels (1977), and Watson and Leadbetter (1963).

  In Sections 2.5.1 and 2.5.2 the results on pointwise asymptotic unbiasedness and weak consistency are from Parzen (1962) and Cacoullos (1966), with the strong consistency result being due to Devroye and Wagner (1979). It is important to note, however, that Assumptions (A8) and (A9) can be relaxed considerably. For example, instead of (A8), if it is assumed that the kernel K is a bounded density with compact support while, instead of (A9), we assume that every point is taken to be a Lebesgue point for f, then under (A4) and (A5) the weak consistency of $\hat{f}$ follows; see Deheuvels (1974) and Devroye and Györfi (1985, Chapter 6). Devroye and Györfi (1985) also discuss the pointwise consistency (weak and strong) of $\hat{f}$ when the window width h depends on n as well as the data. The uniform weak consistency result is based on the work of Schuster (1969, 1970) and Nadaraya (1965). The weakest possible conditions for uniform strong consistency available to date are by Bertrand-Retali (1978). These are (A4), (A11), and (A13) with K almost everywhere a continuous bounded kernel with compact support. Another very similar condition was independently obtained by Devroye and Wagner (1980a), whereas the results of Van Ryzin (1969) and Silverman (1978) are under restrictive assumptions on the kernel K; see Devroye and Wagner (1980c, p. 61). Silverman (1978) found the best possible rate of $nh/\log n$ for uniform consistency. Devroye and Wagner (1980a) and Deheuvels (1979) have also obtained uniform consistency results for many practical situations where h is a function of n as well as the data. For further details, see Devroye and Györfi (1985, Chapter 6).

  The conditions for the various types of consistency described above are merely the sufficient conditions for occurrence in the L_2 norm. Convergence under the global L_1 criterion, that is, $\int |\hat{f} - f| \, dx \to 0$ in probability or almost surely as $n \to \infty$, is discussed in the work of Devroye and Wagner (1979) and Devroye (1983) among others. For an excellent treatment of the L_1 criterion, see Devroye and Györfi (1985). The main results of Devroye (1983) are that, under the L_1 criterion, various types of consistency are equivalent, with (A4) and (A5) being the necessary and sufficient conditions for consistency. In general, the L_1 criterion is well defined and provides somewhat weaker conditions for consistency. More recently Bai and Chen (1987) have given the necessary and sufficient conditions for consistency under the L_p criterion, that is, conditions under which $\left[\int |f_n - f|^p \, dz \right]^{1/p} \to 0$ as $n \to \infty$. Note that, except for $p = 1$, the L_p criterion is not scale invariant. The L_2 criterion is easier to work with and it has been used extensively in the literature, and this accounts for our emphasis upon it in this chapter.

For the case of dependent observations, under the weak dependence measure β_n, the unbiasedness, weak consistency, and asymptotic normality results are given in Castellana and Leadbetter (1986). Robinson (1983) gives a normality result under α-mixing. Abdulal (1984) provides asymptotic normality and uniform weak consistency results under ϕ-mixing; also see Bierens (1983) for uniform weak consistency. Uniform weak consistency under α-mixing reflects the corrected version of Singh and Ullah (1985, Theorem 3). For asymptotic results on the orthogonal series estimator and nearest neighbor estimators, see Ahmad (1979) and Boente and Fraiman (1988).

2.7 Choices of Window Width and Kernel: Further Discussion

When implementing density estimates the choice of the kernel (K) and the smoothing parameter (h) are essential. Some discussion about this was provided in Section 2.4.2. However, in view of the importance of this issue it is taken up again here, and several possibilities are canvassed, beginning with the selection of the window width h and moving on to the kernel.

2.7.1 Choice of h

A crude way of choosing h is by a trial and error approach consisting of looking at several different plots of $\hat{f}(x)$ against x, when $\hat{f}(x)$ is computed from different values of h. With the good graphical facilities available on PCs today, this method can be very effective, although it would seem advantageous to be able to select a value for h by means that are more "objective" or "automatic." To this end, the current section will consider some of the more popular proposals for the automatic determination of h.

Any automatic selection procedure inevitably involves a criterion to be optimized. Popular choices have been the integrated squared error (*ISE*) or its expected value *(MISE)*(L^2 norm); the integrated absolute error (L^1 norm), or its expected value *(MIAE)*; the supremum norm; as well as other distance measures. In general squared error criteria are much easier to work with than the absolute error criteria and hence have received more attention. A decision between the ISE, loss, and the MISE, risk, is more complex; in small samples the value of *h* minimizing each may be far apart, though asymptotically both would give the same value (Hall and Marron, 1987). Given this discrepancy, it is not clear as to which should be preferred in practice. One advantage of the *ISE* is that it gives the optimal *h* for a given data set. At the same time, because it is random, two data sets realized from the same density will typically yield different *h* values. Many of the issues raised by this choice are canvassed in Grund et al. (1994). Their theoretical work points to the likelihood of substantial differences in conclusions when evaluating the merits of various candidate window widths. However, simulations performed in their paper lead them to conclude, "This indicates that for $n = 100$, or even $n = 1000$, it is not really important whether we assess the performance of bandwidth selectors by loss or by risk, despite the major philosophical differences and contrary to the asymptotical theory."

The use of *MISE* as a criterion is hampered by the need to evaluate an expectation with respect to the true unknown density. For this reason it is frequently approximated by a polynomial in *h*, to produce the *AMISE* criterion. Two examples are when this approximation uses terms to either order h^4 or h^6:

$$AMISE_1 = n^{-1}h^{-1}R(K) + \frac{1}{4}h^4\mu_2^2 R(f^{(2)}),$$ (2.112)

$$AMISE_2 = n^{-1}h^{-1}R(K) + \frac{1}{4}h^4\mu_2^2 R(f^{(2)}) - \frac{1}{24}h^6\mu_2\mu_4 R(f^{(3)}),$$ (2.113)

where $R(g) = \int_{-\infty}^{\infty} g(x)^2\,dx$ and $\mu_j = \int_{-\infty}^{\infty} \psi^j K(\psi)\,d\psi$. Even when a criterion has been selected there are still two alternative ways to proceed. In the first, unknown terms in the criterion function are replaced by sample estimates and then minimization is performed with respect to *h*. In the second, the criterion function is minimized analytically and a solution for *h* is found, after which any population quantities are replaced by sample estimates. The latter is commonly referred to as producing a "plug-in" estimate.

Given this general orientation we now turn to some of the proposals in the literature.

Least Squares Cross Validation

The basic idea behind this cross-validation (CV) procedure, due to Rudemo (1982) and Bowman (1984), is to choose *h* by minimizing the *ISE*.

Consider

$$ISE(h) = \int \left(\hat{f}(x) - f(x)\right)^2 dx$$

$$= \int \hat{f}^2 \, dx + \int f^2 dx - 2 \int \hat{f} f \, dx, \tag{2.114}$$

where $\hat{f}$ is an estimator of f, and $\int f^2 dx$ does not depend on h. Thus the minimization of $ISE(h)$ with respect to h is the same as the minimization of $ISE(h)_0 = \int \hat{f}^2 dx - 2 \int \hat{f} f \, dx$. Now, because $\int \hat{f} f \, dx$ is $E(\hat{f})$ it might be estimated unbiasedly by $n^{-1} \sum_{i=1}^{n} \hat{f}_{-i}(x_i)$, where $\hat{f}_{-i}$ is the "leave-one-out" estimator omitting the ith observation.[10] By change of variable to $t = (x - x_j)/h$ it can be shown that

$$\int \hat{f}^2 dx = n^{-2} h^{-2} \sum_{i=1}^{n} \sum_{j=1}^{n} \int_x K\left(\frac{x_i - x}{h}\right) K\left(\frac{x_j - x}{h}\right) dx$$

$$= n^{-2} h^{-1} \sum_{i=1}^{n} \sum_{j=1}^{n} \int_t K\left(\frac{x_i - x_j}{h} - t\right) K(t) \, dt,$$

leading to the estimate $n^{-2} h^{-1} \sum_{i=1}^{n} \sum_{j=1}^{n} (K \circ K)\left(\frac{x_i - x_j}{h}\right)$, where $K \circ K$ is the convolution of the kernel with itself, that is, $\int K(u - t) K(t) \, dt$. If K is an $\mathcal{N}(0, 1)$ density, then $K \circ K$ is $\mathcal{N}(0, 2)$. Thereupon the actual criterion minimized is

$$ISE(h)_1 = n^{-2} h^{-1} \sum_{i=1}^{n} \sum_{j=1}^{n} K \circ K\left(\frac{x_i - x_j}{h}\right) - 2n^{-1} \sum_{i=1}^{n} \hat{f}_{-i}(x_i).$$

$$\tag{2.115}$$

In the least squares CV principle, h is set to $\hat{h}_{cvls}$, which minimizes $ISE(h)_1$.

Hall (1983, 1985), Stone (1984), and Nolan and Pollard (1987) among others have shown that, under various assumptions, $\hat{h}_{cvls}$ asymptotically converges to h_{opt} in (2.49), the window width minimizing *MISE*. However, the rate of convergence is extremely slow, being of the order of $n^{-1/10}$. If, instead, we take the reference point to be the value of h minimizing the true *ISE*, h^*, then the convergence of $\hat{h}_{cvls}$ to h^* occurs at rate $n^{-3/10}$. Apart from this slow rate of convergence, and associated variability, its principal disadvantages are that $ISE(h)_1$ may have several local minima, and quite different values for $\hat{h}_{cvls}$ may

---

[10] Think of X as a random variable and form $\hat{f}(X)$. Then $E[\hat{f}(X)] = \int \hat{f}(x) f(x) \, dx$ and so we need to form an estimate of $E[\hat{f}(X)]$ using the data.

be derived for data sets coming from the same distribution (see Hall and Marron, 1987), and it can be expensive to compute. Aids in reducing computational cost are the fast Fourier transform approximation mentioned in Silverman (1986, Section 3.5), the average shifted histogram technique in Scott, and the "binning" technique recommended in Härdle (1990) and used extensively in the XPLORE program.

Hall and Johnstone (1992) point to the possibility of reducing the variability of the cross-validated estimator of h by improving the empirical approximation to the term $\int f \hat{f}$. They expand it as a polynomial in h giving $\int f \hat{f} \approx \int f^2(x) - c_2 R(f^{(1)})h^2 - c_3 R(f^{(2)})h^4$, where c_j are constants, substitute this approximation into ISE, and then minimize with respect to h. The resulting estimator has the same rate of convergence as $\hat{h}_{cvls}$ but a smaller asymptotic variance.

Other Variants of Cross Validation

Scott and Terrell (1987) observe that $E(ISE(h)_1) = AMISE_1 - R(f)$, and they concentrated upon finding a good estimator of $AMISE_1$. It is natural to replace $R(f^{(2)})$ by $R(\hat{f}^{(2)})$, but they observe that this is a biased estimator if window widths such as $n^{-1/5}$ are used. Specifically, $E(R(\hat{f}^{(2)})) = R(f^{(2)}) + n^{-1}h^{-(2p+1)}R(K^{(2)})$, and so the estimator may be improved upon by subtracting the last term from $E(R(\hat{f}^{(2)}))$ before substituting it into $AMISE_1$. Thereafter, the resulting criterion can be minimized to produce an estimator of h. Scott and Terrell (1987) show that the rate of convergence of the sample variance of this "biased CV" estimator of h is the same as that of the "unbiased CV" estimator, although a smaller constant of proportionality means better performance for the former. In Park and Marron's (1990) Monte Carlo study its performance was greatly superior to the unbiased CV estimator but still exhibited considerable variability and tended to have a bias toward oversmoothing. Drawbacks of the biased CV are that its effective performance requires much stronger smoothness assumptions than those required for the unbiased CV, while for very small samples (say $n = 20$) one may not get any minimum at all. The latter may not be as serious as the spurious local minima in the unbiased CV, particularly since the problem seems to disappear for large samples.

The criterion minimized by Scott and Terrell is

$$BCV = (nh)^{-1}R(K)$$
$$+ n^{-1}(n-1)^{-1}\sum_{i \neq j}\sum (K \circ K - 2K)(x_i - x_j). \qquad (2.116)$$

An extension to this idea is to presmooth the variable $(x_i - x_j)$ before entry into the kernels. This smoothed cross-validation idea replaces $K \circ K - 2K$ by

$(K \circ K - 2K) \circ L \circ L$, where L may differ from K and a different window width may be used as well. This method does not seem to have had much application.

Plug-In Methods

From (2.49) the optimal h that minimizes $AMISE_1$ is $h = cn^{-1/5}$. Because this h depends on the unknown $R(f^{(2)})$ it is not operational. The basic idea behind the plug-in method is to replace the unknown $\int (f^{(2)}(x))^2 dx$ with its estimate, $\int (\hat{f}(2)(x))^2 dx$, where $\hat{f}^{(2)}(x)$ is an estimate of $f^{(2)}(x)$ found with some initial value of h. This approach was first suggested by Woodroofe (1970) and later studied by Scott and Factor (1981, Equation 2.11). Obviously, the "biased" CV approach described above is effectively a plug-in method. If $AMISE_2$ is the selected criterion then even more elements need to be estimated.

Park and Marron (1990) pointed out that improvements may be had by choosing a different window width α to estimate $R(\hat{f}^{(2)})$ than that used to estimate the density. They find that the asymptotically optimal estimate of α is $\alpha_{MSE} = c_3 c_4 h_{AMISE}^{10/13}$, where

$$c_3 = \{18R(K^{(4)})\sigma_K^8/\sigma_{K \circ K}^4 R(K)^2\}^{1/13},$$

$$c_4 = \{R(f)R(f^{(2)})^2/R(f^{(3)})^2\}^{1/13},$$

and $\sigma_g^2 = \int z^2 g(z)dz$. When this is used in the criterion, the resulting estimator of h converges to h_{opt} at rate $n^{-8/13}$, so that it improves on cross validation. A popular extension of the idea, proposed by Sheather and Jones (1991), is to estimate $R(f^{(2)})$ by a "diagonals in" formula in which the i, j summations used to form estimates of $R(f^{(2)})$ evident in criteria such as BCV do not delete the $i = j$ terms. This changes the optimal choice of α as the introduction of the "diagonals" creates a bias in the resulting estimator of $R(f^{(2)})$, but, as this bias is of the opposite sign to that caused from h, they select α so as to make the net bias zero. An exact algorithm for doing this is presented in their paper (p. 689). The Sheather–Jones method of determining h has become a very popular one in recent years and seems to give good performance in simulation studies.

Hall et al. (1991) have concentrated upon the possibility of finding an h that converges to h_{opt} at the fastest possible rate of $n^{-1/2}$. They point out that this is not attainable by any methods that use $AMISE_1$, regardless of how well $R(f^{(2)})$ is estimated, and that it is necessary to utilize $AMISE_2$ to get the requisite rate of convergence. The disadvantage of this procedure is the need to estimate $R(f^{(3)})$, and this may well negate the asymptotic benefits in small samples. Complete details on how to implement the method are available in the article.

Likelihood Cross Validation

The basic idea behind this method is to choose an h that maximizes the likelihood. Consider the log likelihood in (2.21), $\log L = \sum_{i=1}^{n} \log f(x_i)$.

An estimated log likelihood or pseudo log likelihood can be written as

$$\log L = \sum_{i=1}^{n} \log \hat{f}(x_i) = \log L(h),$$

where $\hat{f}(x_i)$ is a density estimator of f and it depends on h. However, maximizing $\log L$ with respect to h just produces a trivial maximum at $h = 0$. To overcome this problem, the cross-validation principle might be adopted, in which $\hat{f}(x_i)$ is replaced by $\hat{f}_{-i}(x)$, the density estimator at $x = x_i$ excluding the ith observation. In the context of kernel estimation, this "leave one out" version of the estimator can be written as

$$\hat{f}_{-i}(x_i) = ((n-1)h)^{-1} \sum_{\substack{j=1 \\ j \neq i}}^{n} K\left(\frac{x_j - x_i}{h}\right). \tag{2.117}$$

Thus the likelihood CV principle is to choose h such that $\log L(h) = \sum_{i=1}^{n} \log \hat{f}_{-i}(x_i)$ is a maximum. This procedure was suggested by Duin (1976), among others. The procedure is also known as Kullback–Leibler cross validation in the sense that it gives an h for which the Kullback–Leibler distance measure between two densities f and $\hat{f}$, $I(f, \hat{f})$, is a minimum, where

$$I(f, \hat{f}) = \int f(x) \log \left\{ \frac{f(x)}{\hat{f}(x)} \right\} dx; \tag{2.118}$$

see Hall (1987a,b).

A disadvantage of the h obtained by likelihood CV is that it can be severely affected by the tail behavior of f. Furthermore, Hall (1987a,b) has indicated that although selecting h by minimizing the Kulback–Leibler measure may be useful for the statistical discrimination problem it is not for curve estimation. Thus the likelihood CV procedure has not proven to be of much current interest in the literature.

2.7.2 *Choice of Higher Order Kernels*

As mentioned in earlier sections, higher order kernels may need to be adopted to either reduce the small-sample bias in density estimators or to ensure that the asymptotic distribution of $(nh)^{1/2}(\hat{f} - f)$ is centered at zero. Consequently, it is important to be able to generate kernels with the properties described in assumption (A6) of Section 2.4.3, that is, kernels whose first $r - 1$ moments are zero. To illustrate how to find such kernels we first take, say, $r = 3$, and consider $K(\psi) = (a_0 + a_1\psi + a_2\psi^2)\phi(\psi)$, where $\phi(\psi)$ is an $\mathcal{N}(0, 1)$ density and a_0, a_1, and a_2 are to be determined such that $\int K(\psi) \, d\psi = 1$ and $\int \psi K(\psi) \, d\psi =$

$0 = \int \psi^2 K(\psi) \, d\psi$. From the fact that the odd-order moments of an $\mathcal{N}(0, 1)$ random variable are zero and the even-order moments are

$$E\psi^{2j} = \frac{2^j}{\sqrt{\pi}} \Gamma\left(\frac{2j+1}{2}\right), \qquad (2.119)$$

we get

$$\int K(\psi) \, d\psi = 1 \Rightarrow a_0 + a_2 = 1,$$
$$\int \psi K(\psi) \, d\psi = 0 \Rightarrow a_1 = 0, \qquad (2.120)$$
$$\int \psi^2 K(\psi) \, d\psi = 0 \Rightarrow a_0 + 3a_2 = 0,$$

leading to the solutions $a_0 = 3/2$, $a_1 = 0$, and $a_2 = -1/2$. Substituting back into $K(\psi) = (a_0 + a_1\psi + a_2\psi^2)\phi(\psi)$ culminates in a kernel $K(\psi) = 2^{-1}(3 - \psi^2)\phi(\psi)$ whose first two moments are zero. This kernel comprises a mixture of a polynomial of degree 2 and a normal density and it can take positive as well as negative values.

The above process can be generalized to obtain kernels whose first $r - 1$ moments are zero, that is,

$$K_r(\psi) = \left(a_0 + a_1\psi + a_2\psi + \cdots + a_{r-1}\psi^{r-1}\right)\phi(\psi), \qquad (2.121)$$

where $a_0, a_1, \ldots, a_{r-1}$ are determined such that (A6) is satisfied. Using (2.119) it can easily be verified that for $r = 1, \ldots, 7$

$$K_1(\psi) = K_2(\psi) = \phi(\psi),$$
$$K_3(\psi) = K_4(\psi) = \frac{1}{2}(3 - \psi^2)\phi(\psi),$$
$$\qquad (2.122)$$
$$K_5(\psi) = K_6(\psi) = \frac{1}{8}(15 - 10\psi^2 + \psi^4)\phi(\psi),$$
$$K_7(\psi) = K_8(\psi) = \frac{1}{48}(105 - 105\psi^2 + 21\psi^4 - \psi^6)\phi(\psi).$$

Other base kernels could replace the standard normal in (2.121). If, for example, $\phi(\psi)$ is a uniform density instead of normal ($|\psi| < 1$), then it can be verified that $K(\psi) = 2^{-1}$ for $r = 0, 1, 2$ and $8^{-1}(9 - 15\psi^2)$ for $r = 3$. Moreover, the restriction of $K_r(\psi)$ to be the product of a base kernel with a polynomial in ψ is not necessary to find a kernel satisfying (A6). For example, $K(\psi) = \left[2\phi(\psi) - 2^{-1}\pi^{-1/2}e^{-\psi^2}/4\right]$ is such that its first three moments are zero. Rather than use a Gaussian density as the base kernel it might be desirable to find the optimal higher order kernels in the same way as was done for Epanechnikov's kernel in Section 2.4.2. Of interest is the optimal fourth-order kernel that has $K(\psi) = 15/32(7\psi^4 - 10\psi^2 + 3)$ for $|\psi| \leq 1$ and zero otherwise.

A Recurrence Relationship

Although the kernels described in (2.122) can be found directly, it may be useful to express them in terms of a recurrence relationship, particularly if higher order kernels with large r are needed in practice. To see such a relation rewrite (2.122) generically as (for $r \geq 1$)

$$K_{2r}(\psi) = P_{2r-2}\phi(\psi), \tag{2.123}$$

where $P_{2r} = P_{2r-2} + (-1)^r H_{2r}(2^r r!)^{-1}$ and $H_r(\psi) = \psi H_{r-1} - (r-1)H_{r-2}$ is the rth Hermite polynomial with $H_0 = 1$ (see Spanos, 1986, p. 204). Alternatively, one can calculate higher order kernels in (2.123) by noting the following recurrence relationship, for $r \geq 1$:

$$\begin{aligned} K_{2r}(\psi) = {} & K_{2(r-1)}(\psi) \\ & + (-1)^{r-1} H_{2(r-1)}(\psi)(2^{r-1}(r-1)!)^{-1}\phi(\psi). \end{aligned} \tag{2.124}$$

2.7.3 Choice of h for Density Derivatives

We discussed above two basic procedures for choosing h in the case of density estimation. First, minimizing the *AMISE* with respect to h gave $h \propto n^{-1/5}$. The *AMISE* was obtained by observing that, under certain conditions on the kernel, the bias of $\hat{f}$ is of $O(h^2)$ and its variance is of $O(1/nh)$. This procedure for choosing h can easily be extended to the sth-order derivative estimate $\hat{f}^{(s)}$ in Section 2.3. For this we merely need to note that, under the following conditions on kernels,

$$\int K^{(s)}(\psi)\psi^j d\psi = \begin{cases} 0 & \text{for } j = 0, \ldots, s-1; \\ (-1)^s s! & \text{for } j = s; \\ 0 & \text{for } j = s+1; \\ \text{a finite constant} & \text{for } j = s+2, \end{cases}$$

and, using similar derivations as in the case of $\hat{f}$, the approximate Bias $(\hat{f}^{(s)})$ is of $O(h^2)$ and the $V(\hat{f}^{(s)})$ is of $O(1/nh^{2s+1})$. This implies that the *AMISE* of $\hat{f}^{(s)}$ is $O(h^4) + O\left(1/nh^{(2s+1)}\right)$ and thus the optimal $h \propto n^{-1/(2s+5)}$. For $s = 0$ we get $h \propto n^{-1/5}$ as for the density case. For more details, see Stone (1980). We also note that, following the derivations as in the density case, it can be verified that

$$\left(nh^{2s+1}\right)^{1/2}\left(\hat{f}^{(s)} - f^{(s)}\right) \sim \mathcal{N}\left(0, f\int K^{(s)}(\psi)^2 d\psi\right),$$

provided $nh^{(2s+1)} \to \infty$ and $nh^{(2s+1)}h^2 \to 0$ as $n \to \infty$. The latter condition is satisfied if $nh^3 \to 0$ as $n \to \infty$. For an alternative proof, see Aït-Sahalia (1994).

The second method of choosing h, in the case of density estimation, was based on the cross-validation principle, which minimizes the estimate of $ISE(h) = \int (\hat{f} - f)^2 dx$ given by $ISE(h)_1$ in (2.115). This idea can be extended to the selection of h for the estimation of derivatives of the density (Härdle and Marron, 1988) by observing that the estimate of

$$ISE^{(s)}(h) = \int (\hat{f}^{(s)} - f^{(s)})^2 dx = \int (\hat{f}^{(s)})^2 - 2 \int \hat{f}^{(s)} f^{(s)} dx$$

(dropping the third term since it does not depend on h) is

$$ISE^{(s)}(h)_1 = (-1)^s n^{-2} h^{-(2s+1)} \sum_i \sum_j (K \circ K)^{(2s)} \left(\frac{x_i - x_j}{h} \right)$$

$$- 2n^{-1}(-1)^s \sum_{i=1}^{n} \hat{f}_{-i}^{(2s)},$$

where

$$\hat{f}_{-i}^{(2s)}(x_i) = (n - 1)^{-1} \sum_{j \neq i=1}^{n} h^{-(2s+1)} K^{(2s)} \left(\frac{x_i - x_j}{h} \right).$$

Thus the bandwidth h_s, which minimizes $ISE^{(s)}(h)_1$, is the least squares cross-validation value for the estimate $\hat{f}^{(s)}$. This value can be determined by calculating $ISE^{(s)}(h)_1$ directly or by using the fast Fourier transform approximation given in Silverman (1986, Section 3.5). Härdle and Marron (1988) report good results for the selection of h for $\hat{f}^{(1)}$, especially with Gaussian kernels. It was also found that the estimate of h from density cross validation is usually smaller than that for derivative cross validation. This is not surprising since, as indicated above, the derivative's bandwidth is of $O(n^{-1/(2s+5)})$, which increases in s.

Regarding an optimality property of the cross-validated h_s Härdle and Marron report a similar result as in the density case given above. More specifically, under the conditions that there are $2s$ bounded derivatives of the kernel and $2s + 2$ continuous bounded derivatives of f, they show that the cross-validated bandwidth h_s is asymptotically the same as the optimal bandwidth that minimizes the $AMISE$. That is, the $ISE^{(s)}(h)_1$ is asymptotically the same for h replaced by the cross-validated value and the optimal $MISE$ value.

2.8 Multivariate Density Estimation

The kernel estimator $\hat{f}$ in (2.7) was first extended to the multivariate case by Cacoullos (1966). Let $Z = (Y, X_1, \ldots, X_q) = (Y, X)$ be a vector of $q + 1$ random variables, where Y is a scalar and X is a $1 \times q$ vector. Then the kernel estimator of the density of Z is the following straightforward generalization of (2.7):

$$\hat{f}(y, x) = \hat{f}(z) = \frac{1}{nh^{q+1}} \sum_{i=1}^{n} K_1 \left(\frac{z_i - z}{h} \right),$$ (2.125)

where z_i is the ith sample observation (y_i, x_i) and $z = (y, x)$ is a fixed point. Furthermore, the kernel estimator of the marginal density $f_1(x)$ of X is

$$\hat{f}_1(x) = \int \hat{f}(y, x) \, dy = \frac{1}{nh^{q+1}} \sum_{i=1}^{n} \int K_1 \left(\frac{y_i - y}{h}, \frac{x_i - x}{h} \right) dy$$

$$= \frac{1}{nh^q} \sum_{i=1}^{n} K \left(\frac{x_i - x}{h} \right),$$ (2.126)

where $K(x) = \int K_1(y, x) \, dy$ is such that $\int K(x) \, dx = 1$. The estimator of the conditional density of Y given X can then be written as

$$\hat{f}(y|x) = \frac{\hat{f}(y, x)}{\hat{f}_1(x)}.$$ (2.127)

Similarly, the extensions of other estimators in Section 2.2 are straightforward.

The use of a single h for all the $q + 1$ variables in z may not be appropriate if the variation in one of the zs is much greater than in the others. In these situations it may be more appropriate to use a vector or matrix of window width parameters. An attractive practical approach is to linearly transform the data to have a unit covariance matrix, apply (2.125) to the transformed data, and finally transform back to the original metric.

Almost all the results in the previous sections go through for the multivariate density estimator $\hat{f}(z)$ by replacing nh with $nh^{q+1} = nh^d$. Such analysis is straightforward and hence not given. For precise details, the reader could see the papers referred to in Section 2.6.4. A result worth noting here is the format of the optimal h that minimizes the approximate *MISE*. Substituting nh^d for n in the *MISE* expression in (2.46) and minimizing with respect to h leaves

$$h = cn^{-1/(4+d)},$$ (2.128)

and, for this h, $AMISE = O(n^{-4/(4+d)})$. The constant c in (2.128) is the same as in (2.49), except that the integral with respect to x is now over a d-dimensional space. Silverman (1986, Table 4.1) computes c for various kernels when the unknown density is multivariate normal. Thus, when the kernel is multivariate standard normal, $c = \{4/(2d + 1)\}^{1/(d+4)}$. It is clear from this result that the higher the dimension d, the slower will be the speed of convergence of $\hat{f}$ to f.

Thus one may need a large data size to estimate the multivariate density in high dimensions.

Appropriate kernels in the multidimensional context would be multivariate density functions. Examples are the standard multivariate normal density, $K(\psi) = (2\pi)^{-d/2} \exp(-\frac{1}{2}\psi'\psi)$ where $d = \dim(\psi)$, and the multivariate Epanechnikov kernel, $K_c(\psi) = .5\, c_d^{-1}(d+2)(1 - \psi'\psi)$ if $\psi'\psi < 1$ and equaling 0 otherwise, where c_d is the volume of the unit d-dimensional sphere ($c_1 = 2$, $c_2 = \pi$, $c_3 = 4\pi/3$). Silverman (1986, p. 76) also mentions a set of other kernels of the form $K_j(\psi) = j\pi^{-1}(1 - \psi'\psi)^j$ if $\psi'\psi < 1$ and equaling zero otherwise; these are particularly useful if higher order derivatives of the density are needed. One disadvantage with direct application of the kernels above is that the variables may exhibit disparate variation. To overcome this problem it is good practice to work with standardized data, that is, data normalized by the standard deviation or some measure of scale. Then each of the elements in ψ will have unit variance and application of a kernel such as the multivariate standard normal is appropriate. Another popular class of kernels are "product kernels," which are the product of d univariate kernels, that is, if $k_j(\psi_{ij})$ is a kernel with entry ψ_{ij}, the product kernel would be $K(\psi) = \Pi_{j=1}^{d} k_j(\psi_{ij})$. Of course, the multivariate standard normal is a product kernel, and Epanechnikov (1969) showed that this was the kernel that minimized the *MISE* over the class of product kernels.[11] These kernels have the advantage that higher order multivariate kernels can be easily generated. Suppressing the i subscript for ψ_{ij}, we define such a kernel as $K(\psi) = \Pi_{j=1}^{d}(a_{0j} + a_{1j}\psi_j + a_{2j}\psi_j^2 + \cdots)k_j(\psi_j)$, where $k_j(\psi_j)$ are base kernels. Clearly $\int K(\psi)\, d\psi = 1$, $\int \psi K(\psi)\, d\psi = 0$, etc. if $\int (a_{0j}+a_{1j}\psi_j+a_{2j}\psi_j+\cdots)k_j(\psi_j)\, d\psi_j = 1$, $\int (a_{0j}+ a_{1j}\psi_j + a_{2j}\psi_j + \cdots)\psi_j k_j(\psi_j) = 0$, etc. But this just means that the higher order product kernel is just the product of the univariate higher order kernels. For product kernels, each of the window widths h_j occurring in $\psi_{ij} = h_j^{-1}(x_{ij} - x_j)$ could be set with (2.50) and (2.51).

Perhaps the major difficulty with multidimensional estimation is that very large sample sizes will be needed to get accurate estimates of a density. Common sense indicates that there will have to be many empty cells when constructing (say) a six-variate histogram from only 1,000 data points, and that would be an extremely large sample for many economic series. Sometimes, intuition developed in the univariate case is also faulty; Silverman (1986; pp. 92–3) describes the *empty-space phenomenon* where very few points are around the origin when

---

[11] A general form of (2.125) can be written as $\hat{f}_1(x) = (n \det(H))^{-1} \sum_{i=1}^{n} K(H^{-1}(x_i - x))$ where H is a nonsingular window-width matrix and $K(\cdot)$ is the multivariate kernel function. For the ease of product kernels and a scalar $H = hI$, $\psi_{ij} = h^{-1}(x_{ij} - x_j)$, whereas for the diagonal H with elements h_j, $\psi_{ij} = h_j^{-1}(x_{ij} - x_j)$.

d is large, in contrast to the case when $d = 1$. In fact, for a ten-dimensional standard normal, some 99% of the mass of the distribution lies at points whose distance from the origin is greater than 1.6, versus only 10% in the scalar case. Estimating $f(0)$ in a multidimensional context then becomes enormously difficult and Table 4.2 of Silverman (1986) vividly illustrates this, with required sample sizes to estimate $f(0)$ to a given degree of accuracy expanding from $n = 4 (d = 1)$ to $n = 842,000 (d = 10)$. These considerations point to the fact that we might be content to estimate only certain characteristics of the conditional density, in particular, estimation of either the conditional mean or conditional quantiles. The first of these is studied in the next chapter and a restricted version of the second in Section 5.9.

2.9 Testing Hypotheses about Densities

Suppose F and G are two possible candidates for the distribution of the random variable X with probability density functions $f(x)$ and $g(x)$ respectively. One might like to test several types of hypotheses regarding these densities, each of which can be formulated as testing for $H_0 : f(x) = g(x)$ against $H_1 : f(x) \neq g(x)$. A number of examples can be given. First, it is sometimes desirable to be able to test whether a nonparametrically estimated density has a particular form, for example, $\mathcal{N}(0, 1)$. That is, one wishes to test $H_0 : f(x) = g(x)$ against $H_1 : f(x) \neq g(x)$ where $g(x)$ is $\mathcal{N}(0, 1)$. In general $g(x)$ can be any fully specified parametric density $g(x) = g(x, \theta)$, where θ is a vector of known or unknown parameters. Second, another test of interest may be that of symmetry around zero, $g(x) = f(-x)$, an issue that has arisen in the analysis of business cycles. Third, we might be interested in testing whether the densities $f(x)$ and $g(x)$ differ for two different regions (rural and urban), groups (male and female), or time periods. Finally, testing for independence between two economic variables X, Y involves testing $H_0 : f(y, x) = f(y)f(x)$, which is equivalent to testing $H_0 : f(z) = g(z)$, where $z = (y, x)$ and $g(z) = f(y)f(x)$.

The above testing problems can be tackled by considering a widely accepted measure of global distance (closeness) between two densities $f(x)$ and $g(x)$, for example, the integrated squared error

$$I = I(f(x), g(x)) = \int_x (f(x) - g(x))^2 dx$$
$$= \int_x \left[f^2(x) + g^2(x) - 2f(x)g(x) \right] dx$$
$$= \int_x \left[f(x) dF(x) + g(x) dG(x) - 2g(x) dF(x) \right]. \tag{2.129}$$

This measure is nonnegative and equals zero if and only if $H_0 : f(x) = g(x)$ is true, which makes it a proper candidate for testing H_0. It might also be expressed as

$$I = (1 - \phi_1) \left(\int f^2(x)\,dx + \int g^2(x)\,dx \right), \qquad (2.130)$$

where

$$0 \le \phi_1 = \frac{2\int f(x)g(x)\,dx}{\int f^2(x)\,dx + \int g^2(x)\,dx} \le 1 \qquad (2.131)$$

captures the *affinity* between f and g and was proposed for that purpose by Ahmad and Van Belle (1974) and Ahmad (1980). Note that, under H_0, $\phi_1 = 1$, implying that $I = 0$, which led Ahmad and Van Belle (1974) to develop tests based on $1 - \phi_1$.

Just as an optimal window width was chosen based on either the integrated squared error or its average one might also consider a closeness criterion that is the expected value of I above, that is,

$$M = E(I) = \int (f(x) - g(x))^2 f(x)\,dx,$$

which could be estimated by

$$\hat{M} = n^{-1} \sum_{i=1}^{n} ((\hat{f}(x_i) - g(x_i))^2.$$

Ait-Sahalia (1996a,b) works with this measure when comparing parametric interest rate models to the data.

An alternative measure of distance (affinity) between f and g is the well-known Kullback–Liebler information measure, defined by

$$I^* = \int_x g(x) \log \left\{ \frac{f(x)}{g(x)} \right\} dx. \qquad (2.132)$$

Again $I^* = 0$ under H_0. Such a basis for tests of affinity was entertained by Ullah and Singh (1989) and by Robinson (1991b). For a broader class of distance measures for testing $H_0 : f(x) = g(x)$, see Ullah (1996).

2.9.1 Comparison with a Known Density Function

Now consider the problem of testing $H_0 : f(x) = g(x)$ where $g(x) = g(x, \theta)$ is a fully specified (known) density. Let x_i be the i.i.d. sample and $\hat{f}$ be the nonparametric kernel estimator of f. Then a suitable estimator of I would be

$$
\begin{aligned}
\hat{I} = \hat{I}(\hat{f}, g) &= \int_x \left(\hat{f}(x) - g(x)\right)^2 dx = \int_x \left(\hat{f} - E\hat{f} + E\hat{f} - g\right)^2 dx \\
&= \int_x \left(\hat{f} - E\hat{f}\right)^2 dx + 2\int_x \left(\hat{f} - E\hat{f}\right)\left(E\hat{f} - g\right) dx \\
&\quad + \int_x \left(E\hat{f} - g\right)^2 dx \\
&= \left(n^2 h^2\right)^{-1} \sum_{i=1}^{n}\sum_{j=1}^{n} H_n\left(x_i, x_j\right) + 2\int_x \left(\hat{f} - E\hat{f}\right)\left(E\hat{f} - g\right) dx \\
&\quad + \int_x \left(E\hat{f} - g\right)^2 dx \\
&= \left(n^2 h^2\right)^{-1} \sum_i \sum_{j\neq i} H_n(x_i, x_j) + \left(n^2 h^2\right)^{-1} \sum_i H_n(x_i, x_i) \\
&\quad + 2\int_x \left(\hat{f} - E\hat{f}\right)\left(E\hat{f} - g\right) dx + \int_x \left(E\hat{f} - g\right)^2 dx \\
&= \hat{I}_1 + \hat{I}_2 + \hat{I}_3 + \hat{I}_4,
\end{aligned}
\tag{2.133}
$$

where

$$
H_n(x_i, x_j) = \int_x \Delta_i(x)\Delta_j(x)\, dx,
$$

$$
\Delta_i(x) = K\left(\frac{x_i - x}{h}\right) - EK\left(\frac{x_i - x}{h}\right),
$$

and $\hat{I}_1$, $\hat{I}_2$, $\hat{I}_3$, and $\hat{I}_4$ are the first, second, third, and fourth term, respectively, on the right-hand side of the fourth equality in (2.133).

The asymptotic distribution of $\hat{I}$, for testing H_0, has been studied by Bickel and Rosenblatt (1973), Rosenblatt (1975), and Hall (1984). Under our earlier assumptions (A1) to (A5), allied with $nh^5 \to 0$ as $n \to \infty$, they show that, under H_0,

$$
nh^{1/2}\left(\hat{I} - c^*(n)\right) \sim \mathcal{N}(0, \sigma^2),
\tag{2.134}
$$

where the center term

$$
c^*(n) = c(n) + \int \left(E\hat{f} - f\right)^2 dx,
$$

with

$$
c(n) = (nh)^{-1} \int K^2(\psi)\, d\psi,
$$

and $\sigma^2 = 2 \left[\int f^2(x) \, dx \right] \left[\int \left\{ \int K(\psi) K(\psi + t) d\psi \right\}^2 dt \right]$. This result follows by verifying a number of facts. First, $nh^{1/2} \hat{I}_2 = nh^{1/2} c_n + O_p(h^{1/2})$ from Lemma 2.1. Next, $nh^{1/2} \hat{I}_3 = nh^{1/2} O_p \left(h^2 n^{-1/2} \right) = O_p \left(n^{1/2} h^{5/2} \right)$ from Fan (1994, pp. 344–5). The intuition for this is that $\hat{I}_3 = \int (\hat{f} - E(\hat{f}))(E(\hat{f}) - f + f - g)$ becomes, under $H_0 : f = g$, the integrated (averaged) value of the bias part $E\hat{f} - f$ and is $O(h^2)$, whereas the stochastic part $\hat{f} - E\hat{f}$ is $O_p \left((nh)^{-1/2} \right)$. Thus $nh^{1/2} \hat{I}_3$ is $o_p(1)$ if $nh^5 \to 0$. This leaves the limiting distribution of $nh^{1/2} \left(\hat{I} - c^*(n) \right)$, under $nh^5 \to 0$, as the limiting distribution of $nh^{1/2} \hat{I}_1$, which is $\mathcal{N}(0, \sigma^2)$ due to Hall's (1984) central limit theorem for U-statistics given in the appendix. A consistent estimator of σ^2, $\hat{\sigma}^2$, is obtained by replacing $Ef(x) = \int f^2(x) \, dx$ by

$$\int \hat{f}^2(x) \, dx = (n^2 h)^{-1} \sum_{i=1}^{n} \sum_{j=1}^{n} K \circ K \left(\frac{x_i - x_j}{h} \right)$$

as in (2.115).[12] Consequently, the test statistic and its distribution, under H_0, will be

$$T^* = nh^{1/2} \frac{\left(\hat{I} - c^*(n) \right)}{\hat{\sigma}} \sim \mathcal{N}(0, 1); \qquad (2.135)$$

see Fan (1994, p. 321).

If, instead of $nh^5 \to 0$, we undersmoothed by using a window width such that $nh^{4.5} \to 0$, then

$$nh^{1/2} c^*(n) = nh^{1/2} c(n) + nh^{1/2} \int \left(E\hat{f} - f \right)^2 dx$$

$$= nh^{1/2} c(n) + O(nh^{4.5}),$$

because $(E\hat{f} - f)^2 = (\text{Bias} \hat{f})^2 = O(h^4)$ and the second term in $c^*(n)$ disappears asymptotically. Accordingly, we would get the test statistic

$$T = \frac{nh^{1/2}(\hat{I} - c(n))}{\hat{\sigma}} \sim \mathcal{N}(0, 1); \qquad (2.136)$$

see Fan (1994, p. 324).

The test statistic T still has a center term $c(n)$ that may contribute to some finite sample bias. This stems from the inclusion of the "diagonals" terms $(i = j)$ $\hat{I}_2$ in $\hat{I}$. To eliminate such an effect we can introduce a modified test statistic based on $nh^{1/2}(\hat{I} - \hat{I}_2)$, which will be centred at zero. Such a statistic,

---

[12] A simple alternative is to estimate $Ef(x)$ by $n^{-1} \sum \hat{f}(x_i)$.

under H_0 and an undersmoothed window width such that $nh^{4.5} \to 0$, is

$$T_1 = \frac{nh^{1/2}\tilde{I}_1}{\hat{\sigma}} \sim \mathcal{N}(0, 1), \qquad (2.137)$$

where

$$\tilde{I}_1 = (n^2 h^2)^{-1} \sum_i \sum_{j \neq i} \int K\left(\frac{x_i - x}{h}\right) K\left(\frac{x_j - x}{h}\right) dx$$

$$+ \int g^2(x)\, dx - 2 \int \hat{f}(x) g(x)\, dx.^{13}$$

The asymptotic normality of T_1 follows by noting that

$$nh^{1/2}(\hat{I} - \hat{I}_2) = nh^{1/2}(\hat{I}_1 + \hat{I}_3 + \hat{I}_4)$$

$$= nh^{1/2}\hat{I}_1 + O_p\left(n^{1/2}h^{5/2}\right) + O_p(nh^{4.5})$$

$$= nh^{1/2}\tilde{I}_1 + o_p(1),$$

where $nh^{1/2}\tilde{I}_1 = nh^{1/2}\tilde{I}_1 + o_p(1)$ and we use the condition $nh^{4.5} \to 0$.

A very similar analysis can be provided for tests based on the mean integrated squared distance between the densities. Ait-Sahalia (1996b) shows that

$$nh^{1/2}(\hat{M} - E(\hat{M})) \sim \mathcal{N}(0, V_m),$$

where $E(\hat{M}) = \int K^2(x)\, dx \int g^2(x)\, dx$ and

$$V_m = 2\left[\int_{-\infty}^{\infty} \left\{\int_{-\infty}^{\infty} K(u) K(u + x)\, du\right\}^2 dx\right]\left[\int g^4(x)\, dx\right].^{14}$$

Note that there is an asymptotic bias in the limiting distribution, whose elimination has been a major source of concern with the tests adopting I as their criterion of closeness.

Fan (1994) shows that the T tests given above (T^*, T, and T_1) are consistent in the sense that the power goes to 1 as $n \to \infty$. They also have local power in the sense that they can detect Pitman alternatives, $f(x) = g(x, \theta) + \gamma_n \Delta$, that differ from the null by $O\left(n^{-1/2}h^{-1/4}\right)$, where $\int \Delta(x)\, dx = 0$ and $\gamma_n = n^{-1/2}h^{-1/4}$. In fact the T tests cannot detect local alternatives that differ from the null by $O(n^{-1/2})$, and in this sense they are less powerful than the Kolmogrov–Smirnov test for the affinity of densities. Rosenblatt (1975), however, introduced a new class of local alternatives, $f(x) = g(x, \theta) + \alpha_n \Delta_n(x)$, where $\int \Delta_n(x)\, dx = 0$, $\int \Delta^2(x)\, dx \to 0$, and $\alpha_n \to 0$ as $n \to \infty$, and showed that tests based on $\hat{I}$

---

[13] $\tilde{I}_1$ is also $\tilde{I} - \tilde{I}_2$ where $\tilde{I} = \int \left(\hat{f} - g\right)^2 dx = \int \hat{f}^2\, dx + \int g^2\, dx - 2 \int \hat{f}g\, dx$ and $\tilde{I}_2$ is $\int \hat{f}^2\, dx$ for $j = i$.

[14] In fact Ait-Sahalia has the range of integration over x restricted since interest rates must be nonnegative.

are more powerful than the Kolmogrov–Smirnov test, because they can detect local alternatives that differ from the null by $o(n^{-1/2})$. For further details on T tests, see Bickel and Rosenblatt (1973), Rosenblatt (1975), and Fan (1994); Li (1997) deals with T and T_1.

We note that, under H_0, T tests based on $\hat{I}$ converge to normality at the rate of $nh^{1/2}$, that is, $\hat{I} = O_p\left(1/nh^{1/2}\right)$. Accordingly, the asymptotic distribution of $\sqrt{n}\hat{I}$, under H_0, becomes degenerate, and the $h^{1/2}$ term that appears in the normalizing factor is there to offset the degeneracy. The same problem was indicated by Fan and Gencay (1993) when considering the test first proposed by Ahmad and Van Belle (1974) and Ahmad (1980), which was based on the affinity measure ϕ_1 described above.

Other tests appear in the literature. Robinson (1991b) began with the Kullback–Leibler information criterion but, upon noting its degeneracy, actually worked with the statistic

$$\hat{\phi}_2 = n_\gamma^{-1} \sum_{i=1}^{n} c_i(\gamma) \log\left[\hat{f}(x_i)/g(x_i)\right],$$

where

$$c_i(\gamma) = \begin{cases} 1+\gamma & \text{for } i \text{ odd,} \\ 1-\gamma & \text{for } i \text{ even} \end{cases}, \qquad n_\gamma = \begin{cases} n & \text{for } n \text{ even,} \\ n+\gamma & \text{for } n \text{ odd} \end{cases},$$

and γ is a parameter that needs to be specified. Robinson indicates that the effect of nonparametric estimation is negligible under the null hypothesis, so that the distribution of $n^{1/2}\hat{\phi}_2$ is $\mathcal{N}\left(0, 2\gamma^2 E\left[\log\left(f(x_1)/g(x_1)\right)\right]^2\right)$. When $\gamma = 0$ (i.e., no weighting is done) the distribution is degenerate. Fan and Gencay (1993) show that $\hat{\phi}_1$ can also be modified by the use of a weighting function to ensure that it is not degenerate. The tests due to Robinson and Fan and Gencay are consistent for a given weight function and feature convergence to the asymptotic distribution at the rate of $\sqrt{n}$ rather than $nh^{1/2}$ as happens with the T tests. The latter rate should not be misinterpreted as implying that one can find a nonparametric test whose convergence rate is faster than that of a parametric test; in this context parametric test statistics based on the integrated squared difference have convergence rates of n rather than $\sqrt{n}$. The power of the test also depends on the choice of the weight function. Fan (1994, p. 318) indicates that these tests can only detect Pitman alternatives that differ from the null by $O(n^{-1/4})$. Thus, since $n^{-1/2}h^{-1/4}/n^{-1/4} = n^{-1/4}h^{-1/4} = o(1)$, the T tests based on $\hat{I}$ are more powerful. One difficulty with the T tests that has been noted in the simulation results of Fan (1994) is that a big difference existed between the true and nominal sizes of the test in small samples. In view of this Fan (1995) has proposed a bootstrap approximation to the distribution of T that works very well in small samples and is robust to the choice of h. Pritsker (1998) finds a similar result for Ait-Sahalia's test based on $\hat{M}$, although he attributes this to the fact that, in his simulations, x_i are highly persistent rather than i.i.d. Some nonmonotonicity is observed in test size as the degree of persistence varies due to effects upon the optimal window width.

Various extensions of tests based on the integrated square distance $\hat{I}$ are available in the literature. First, Li (1997) considers the case where the data x_i are not observed but are a product of prior estimation, as could happen if the x_i were regression residuals. He has shown that both the T and T_1 tests remain valid with the indicated distributions. Second, Fan (1994) generalizes the T statistic to the case of a multivariate density of q random variables X. In this instance $nh^{1/2}$ is simply replaced by $nh^{q/2}$ and $nh^5 \to 0$ by $nh^{q+4} \to 0$, while K is now a multivariate kernel. In the same paper, Fan considers the case where $g(x)$ involves a set of estimated parameters, $\hat{\theta}$, that is, $g(x) = g(x, \hat{\theta})$, where $\hat{\theta}$ is a $\sqrt{n}$ consistent estimator of θ. Under such a scenario she and Bickel and Rosenblatt (1973) (for $q = 1$) show that, as long as $nh^{q+4} \to 0$, the test statistic T has the same properties. The assumption $nh^{q+4} \to 0$ implies undersmoothing of the data, and it results in both a suboptimal choice of h, say $h \propto n^{-[\frac{1}{(q+4)} - \epsilon]}$ for some negative ϵ. Fan (1994) also considers the cases where h is oversmoothed and optimally smoothed ($h \propto n^{-1/(q+4)}$), with $g(x, \theta)$ being either fully specified or estimated by $g(x, \hat{\theta})$. Instead of using variations of T tests depending on undersmoothness, optimal smoothness, and oversmoothness, Fan (1994) proposes a test whose asymptotic distribution is the same regardless of the degree of smoothing, basing it on the squared distance of $\hat{f}(x)$ from the estimated $\hat{E}\hat{f}(x) = \frac{1}{h} \int K\left(\frac{x-u}{h}\right) g(u, \hat{\theta}) \, du$ under H_0. Essentially she compares the kernel density estimator with the kernel-smoothed parametric estimator to avoid bias effects. The resulting test statistic is

$$T^{**} = nh^{1/2} \frac{[I^{**} - c(n)]}{\hat{\sigma}_0} \sim \mathcal{N}(0, 1), \tag{2.138}$$

where $I^{**} = \int \left(\hat{f}(x) - \hat{E}\hat{f}(x)\right)^2 dx$. The behavior of the T^{**} test is found to be very similar to that of T. A center-free test statistic is available by removing the $i = j$ terms from T^{**}. The resulting test statistic, $nh^{1/2}\hat{\sigma}_0^{-1}\overline{p}T$, where

$$\overline{p}T = T^{**} - (nh)^{-2} \int \left\{ \sum_i \left[K\left(\frac{x_i - x}{h}\right) - \hat{E}\hat{f}(x) \right]^2 \right\} dx,$$

is asymptotically $\mathcal{N}(0, 1)$; see Fan and Ullah (1999). The latter paper also contains proofs of the asymptotic normality of the tests given above and below when there are weakly dependent observations.

2.9.2 Testing for Symmetry

The T tests can also be extended to other comparisons that one might like to effect: testing symmetry, independence of two random variables, and closeness between two unknown distribution functions. For the purpose of testing symmetry, the null and alternative hypotheses will be $H_0 : f(x) = f(-x)$ and $H_1 : f(x) \neq f(-x)$ respectively. Imposing symmetry, Ahmad and Li (1997a) proposed

$$I = \frac{1}{2} \int [f(x) - f(-x)]^2 dx = \int [f(x) - f(-x)] dF(x)$$

for such a test and estimated it by

$$\begin{aligned}
\tilde{I} &= \int_x [\hat{f}(x) - \hat{f}(-x)] \, d\hat{F}(x) \\
&= \frac{1}{n^2 h} \sum_{i=1}^{n} \sum_{j=1}^{n} \left[K\left(\frac{x_i - x_j}{h}\right) - K\left(\frac{x_i + x_j}{h}\right) \right] \\
&= \frac{1}{n^2 h} \sum_{i=1}^{n} \sum_{i \neq j=1}^{n} \left[K\left(\frac{x_i - x_j}{h}\right) - K\left(\frac{x_i + x_j}{h}\right) \right] \\
&\quad + \frac{1}{n^2 h} \sum_{i=1}^{n} \left[K(0) - K\left(\frac{2x_i}{h}\right) \right] \\
&= \tilde{I}_1 + \tilde{I}_2,
\end{aligned} \tag{2.139}$$

where $\tilde{I}_1$ is the first term in the third equality and

$$\tilde{I}_2 = (n^2 h)^{-1} \sum_{i=1}^{n} \left[K(0) - K\left(\frac{2x_i}{h}\right) \right] = c_1(n) + O_p\left((nh^{1/2})^{-1}\right),$$

where $c_1(n) = K(0)/nh$. Then, under the standard assumption of $h \to 0$ and $nh \to \infty$, Ahmad and Li (1997a) show that, under H_0,

$$T = nh^{1/2} \frac{(\tilde{I} - c_1(n))}{\hat{\sigma}_1} \sim \mathcal{N}(0, 1), \tag{2.140}$$

and

$$T_1 = \frac{nh^{1/2} \tilde{I}_1}{\hat{\sigma}_1} \sim \mathcal{N}(0, 1), \tag{2.141}$$

where $\hat{\sigma}_1^2 = n^{-1} \sum_{i=1}^{n} \hat{f}(x_i) \int K^2(\psi) \, d\psi$. This outcome holds with under-, over-, or optimally smoothed h. Ahmad and Li also extend their results to the case where the x_i are regression residuals. The statistics in (2.140) and (2.141) are simpler than those suggested by Fan and Gencay (1993, 1995) in the same context. The latter use the affinity measure $\hat{\phi}_1$ and weighting of observations. Ahmad and Li also extend their results to testing bivariate symmetry.

2.9.3 Comparison of Unknown Densities

Now we turn to the problem of testing $H_0 : f(x) = g(x)$ against $H_0 : f(x) \neq g(x)$, a situation that can arise when we are interested in testing whether, for example, income distributions across two regions, groups, or time are the same. In what follows $\{x_i\}$ and $\{y_i\}$ are taken to be two equally sized samples of size n from f and g respectively. Li (1996) claims that the tests below are valid when x_i and y_i are either independent, as may be the case for cross-sectioned data from two different groups, or dependent, as in the case of a panel of n individuals over two periods.

The obvious test statistic, based on $\tilde{I} = \int (\hat{f} - \hat{g})^2 \, dx$, can be written as

$$\tilde{I} = \int \hat{f}^2(x) \, dx + \int \hat{g}^2(x) \, dx - 2 \int \hat{f}(x) \hat{g}(x) \, dx$$

$$= \int \hat{f}(x) \, d\hat{F}(x) + \int \hat{g}(x) \, d\hat{G}(x) - 2 \int \hat{g}(x) \, d\hat{F}(x)$$

$$= \frac{1}{n^2 h} \sum_{i=1}^{n} \sum_{j=1}^{n} \left[K\left(\frac{x_i - x_j}{h}\right) + K\left(\frac{y_i - y_j}{h}\right) - 2K\left(\frac{y_i - x_j}{h}\right) \right]$$

$$= \frac{1}{n^2 h} \sum_{i=1}^{n} \sum_{j=1, j \neq i}^{n} \left[K\left(\frac{x_i - x_j}{h}\right) + K\left(\frac{y_i - y_j}{h}\right) \right.$$

$$\left. - K\left(\frac{y_i - x_j}{h}\right) - K\left(\frac{x_i - y_j}{h}\right) \right]$$

$$+ \frac{1}{n^2 h} \sum_{i=1}^{n} \left[2K(0) - 2K\left(\frac{x_i - y_i}{h}\right) \right]$$

$$= \tilde{I}_1 + \tilde{I}_2, \tag{2.142}$$

where $\tilde{I}_1$ is the first term in the fourth equality and

$$\tilde{I}_2 = 2(n^2 h)^{-1} \sum_{i=1}^{n} \left[K(0) - K\left(\frac{x_i - y_i}{h}\right) \right]$$

$$= c_2(n) + O_p(n^{-1}),$$

where $c_2(n) = 2K(0)/nh = 2c_1(n)$. Then, applying a central limit theorem for degenerate U statistics proposed by Hall (1984) (see the appendix), Li (1996) has shown that, under H_0, $h \to 0$, and $nh \to \infty$,

$$T = nh^{1/2}\frac{(\tilde{I} - c_2(n))}{\hat{\sigma}_2} \sim \mathcal{N}(0, 1),$$ (2.143)

and

$$T_1 = \frac{nh^{1/2}\tilde{I}_1}{\hat{\sigma}_2} \sim \mathcal{N}(0, 1),$$ (2.144)

where

$$\hat{\sigma}_2^2 = \frac{2}{n^2 h}\sum_{i=1}^{n}\sum_{j=1}^{n}\left[K\left(\frac{x_i - x_j}{h}\right) + K\left(\frac{y_i - y_j}{h}\right)\right.$$
$$\left. + 2K\left(\frac{x_i - y_j}{h}\right)\right]\int K^2(\psi)\,d\psi.$$

Earlier, Mammen (1992) had put forth a test statistic related to T that required the computation of the convolution of kernels, something that generally involves numerical integration.[15] Anderson, Hall, and Titterington (1994) also gave a variant of the T statistic, where h was considered fixed, leading to their test statistic failing to have an asymptotic normal distribution. As was true of the previous comparisons we might also make use of a test based on the Ahmad and Van Belle affinity measure, that is, $\sqrt{n}\,(\hat{\phi}_1 - 1)$, where $\hat{\phi}_1$ is as before with $g(x)$ replaced by $\hat{g}(x)$ and some weighting scheme to avoid any degeneracy. Although both the T and $\hat{\phi}_1$ tests are consistent, since $nh^{1/2}/\sqrt{n} \to \infty$ as $n \to \infty$, the T tests are expected to be asymptotically more powerful than the $\hat{\phi}_1$ test. Moreover, there is a well-developed theory for them which allows for window widths that under-, over-, or optimally smooth the data. Finally, the T tests can also be extended for the case of different sample sizes and to q-dimensional X; see Li (1996).

2.9.4 Testing for Independence

Ahmad and Li (1997b) concentrate upon testing for independence between two random vectors, X and Y, with the hypotheses being $H_0 : f(y, x) = f(y)f(x)$

[15] Mammen (1992) uses, for example, $\int \hat{f}^2(x)\,dx = (n^2 h^2)^{-1}\sum\sum K \circ K\left(\frac{x_i - x_j}{h}\right)$ with similar expressions for $\int \hat{g}^2(x)\,dx$ and $\int \hat{f}(x)\hat{g}(x)\,dx$.

against $H_1 : f(y, x) \neq f(y)f(x)$. Their test involves

$$I = \int \int [f(y, x) - f(y)f(x)]^2 \, dy \, dx$$

$$= \int \int f(y, x) \, dF(y, x) + \int f(y) \, dF(y) \int f(x) \, dF(x)$$

$$- 2 \int \int f(y)f(x) \, dF(y, x)$$

and its estimator (where a product kernel $K^x(\psi)K^y(\psi)$ is adopted)

$$\tilde{I} = \int \int \hat{f}(y, x) \, d\hat{F}(y, x) + \int \hat{f}(y) \, d\hat{F}(y) \int \hat{f}(x) \, d\hat{F}(x)$$

$$- 2 \int \int \hat{f}(y)\hat{f}(x) \, d\hat{F}(y, x)$$

$$= (n^2 h^2)^{-1} \sum_i \sum_j K_{ij}^x K_{ij}^y + (n^4 h^2)^{-1} \sum_i \sum_j K_{ij}^x \sum_k \sum_l K_{kl}^y$$

$$- 2 (n^3 h^2)^{-1} \sum_i \sum_j \sum_k K_{ij}^x K_{jk}^y$$

$$= \tilde{I}_1 + \tilde{I}_2, \tag{2.145}$$

where

$$K_{ij}^x = K \left(\frac{x_i - x_j}{h} \right), \qquad K_{kl}^y = K \left(\frac{y_k - y_l}{h} \right),$$

$\tilde{I}_1$ is $\tilde{I}$ retaining only those elements for which $i \neq j$, and $\tilde{I}_2$ is $\tilde{I}$ with $i = j$. Then, under H_0, and if $h \to 0$ and $nh^2 \to \infty$, Ahmad and Li show that

$$T = \frac{nh(\tilde{I} - \hat{c}_3(n))}{\hat{\sigma}_3} \sim \mathcal{N}(0, 1), \tag{2.146}$$

$$T_1 = \frac{nh\tilde{I}_1}{\hat{\sigma}_3} \sim \mathcal{N}(0, 1), \tag{2.147}$$

where

$$\hat{c}_3(n) = (nh^2)^{-1} K^x(0) K^y(0)$$

$$- (nh)^{-1} \left\{ K^y(0)\hat{E} f(X) + K^x(0)\hat{E} f(Y) \right\}^3,$$

$$\hat{E} f(X) = n^{-1} \sum_i f(x_i),$$

and

$$\hat{\sigma}_3^2 = n^{-2} \left(\left(\sum \hat{f}(x_i) \right) \left(\sum \hat{f}(y_i) \right) \right)$$
$$\times \int (K^x(\psi))^2 d\psi \int (K^y(\psi))^2 d\psi.$$

The T tests above were first proposed by Rosenblatt (1975) and Rosenblatt and Wahlen (1992). Ahmad and Li (1997b) generalize them to handle multivariate y and x and to allow the window widths for y_i and x_i to be different. The test T_1 was first set out in Ahmad and Li (1997b). They report Monte Carlo experiments indicating that T_1 has better sampling performance than the T test, owing to the need to estimate the "mean" of the latter. They also detail an alternative estimator of σ_3 that improves the performance of the T_1 test.[16]

2.10   Examples

2.10.1   Density of Stock Market Returns

Some of the earliest work on density estimation was concerned with returns of financial assets or commodities and it is of interest to estimate the density of monthly stock market returns from 1834 to 1925, yielding a sample of 1,104 observations on x_i. The data are the same as those used in Pagan and Schwert (1990), and they have been adjusted for calendar effects by regressing out twelve monthly dummies.

After determining the minimum and maximum of the data a grid of 100 points was selected to lie between this range. Figure 2.1 presents density estimates at these 100 points using the Gaussian, $K(\psi) = (2\pi)^{-1/2} \exp -\frac{1}{2}\psi^2$, and Epanechnikov (Eq. (2.61)) kernels, with $\psi = ((x_i - x)/h)$ and $h = n^{-1/5}\hat{\sigma}_x$ (or $.246\hat{\sigma}_x$ given that $n = 1104$).[17] There are clearly only trivial differences between the two estimates, emphasizing that the kernel is relatively unimportant. Figure 2.2 contrasts the estimated density with what the normal density of a variable with the same sample variance would look like; also presented is the lower band of the 95% confidence interval, computed as $(nh)^{-1}(.2821\hat{f}(x))$

---

[16] An alternative test of independence in the time series context was proposed by Robinson (1991b) based on the Kullback–Leibler divergence measure with a weighting scheme to avoid degeneracy. See also Andrews (1997).

[17] The estimates are very similar if any of the alternatives in (2.50)–(2.52) are taken, e.g., $\hat{\sigma}_x = .0313$, $A = .0353$. A referee also notes that one might make the comparison with a normal density with variance $\hat{\sigma}_x^2 + h$. As this produces a larger variance it would depress the peak of the normal density even further, and so the contrast would be stronger.

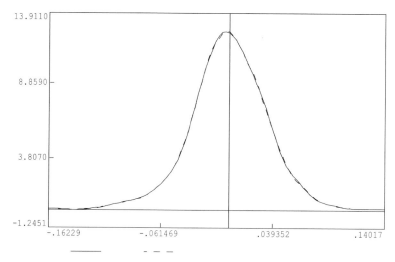

Figure 2.1. Density of monthly stock returns, 1834–1925: Gaussian and Epanechnikov kernels.

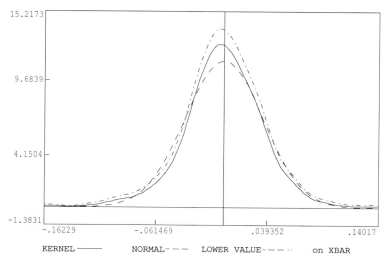

Figure 2.2. Stock returns, kernel estimates, normal distribution, and lower value of 95% confidence interval.

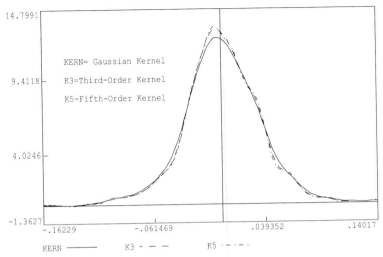

Figure 2.3. Estimates of density of stock returns: regular and higher order kernels.

(see (2.95)).[18] There is no doubt that the density departs significantly from a normal density, and its striking characteristics are the fat tails and sharp peak around zero, that is, there are too many large and very small returns to be consistent with a normal density. It also appears that there are more large positive returns, suggesting some asymmetry in the density. From the confidence interval it seems to be less clear whether the peak at zero is as pronounced as the point estimate suggests. Moreover, because $\hat{f}(x)$ is only asymptotically normally distributed around $f(x)$ if $(nh)^{1/2}h^2 \to 0$ as $n \to \infty$ (Theorem 2.10) and $h = n^{-1/5}\hat{\sigma}_x$ does not satisfy this requirement, it is desirable to assess the impact of the asymptotic bias. One way to eliminate the bias was with higher order kernels (Section 2.4.3), and the kernels $K_3(\psi)$ and $K_5(\psi)$ in (2.122) were therefore applied. Figure 2.3 compares these two estimates with the regular Gaussian one; the higher order kernels are very close to one another and both indicate a higher peak around the origin than that determined in Figure 2.1. It is noticeable that the higher order kernels tend to give more ragged density estimates.

---

[18] $\int K^2(\psi)\,d\psi$ for a normal density equals .2821. For other densities $\int K^2(\psi)\,d\psi = \int K^2(\psi)f_\psi^{-1}(\psi)f_\psi(\psi)\,d\psi = E[K^2(\psi)f^{-1}(\psi)]$, which may be estimated by $n^{-1}\sum K^2 (\psi_i)f_\psi^{-1}(\psi_i)$. Since ψ_i comes from a density f_ψ and this is arbitrary, it might be taken as $\mathcal{N}(0,1)$, after which n numbers for ψ_i may be generated and used in the average. Other densities for f_ψ could be used, but this seems the most convenient. When $K(\psi)$ is the Gaussian kernal $K^2(\psi)f^{-1}(\psi) = K(\psi)$.

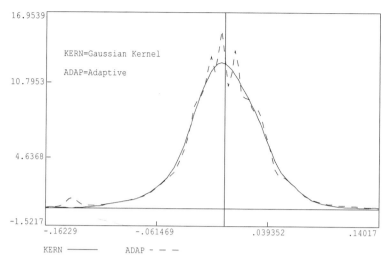

16.9539

KERN=Gaussian Kernel

ADAP=Adaptive

10.7953

4.6368

-1.5217

    -.16229   -.061469   .039352   .14017

KERN ————   ADAP - — —

Figure 2.4. Estimates of density of stock returns: Gaussian kernel and adaptive estimators.

Because there are few observations in the tails, there is an argument for the application of an adaptive estimator. The two-stage version due to Breiman (Section 2.2.5) computes the density with (2.10) and with the window width at each point $h_{n_i} = h[\hat{f}(x_i)/G]^{-1/2}$, where h equals the window width chosen earlier while G is the geometric mean of the density estimates. Figure 2.4 gives these estimates. The resulting density is very poorly estimated. Apparently the reason for this is the use of the geometric mean as a normalizing factor. There would seem to be a good argument that the ratio $\hat{f}(x)/G$ should be close to unity near the mode of the density, whereas in this case it is only .3082, so that a much smaller window width is being applied at this point than in Figures 2.1–2.4. Thus the selection of G is not trivial and it makes the adaptive estimator problematical.

2.10.2   *Estimating the Dickey–Fuller Density*

As mentioned earlier, the output from Monte Carlo experiments can usefully be subject to nonparametric analysis, particularly when it is desirable to have a complete picture of the density of the estimator. One instance in which the latter obtains is for the estimator of the first-order autoregressive parameter when the true value of the parameter is unity, that is,

$$y_t = \rho y_{t-1} + e_t, \tag{2.148}$$

where $\rho = 1$. Fuller (1976) provides tables for the density of $n(\hat{\rho}_{OLS} - 1)$,

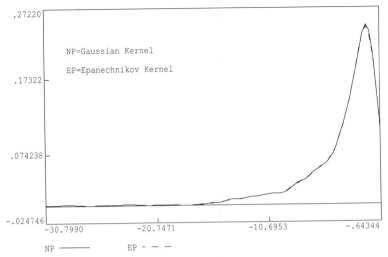

Figure 2.5. Estimates of Dickey–Fuller density: Gaussian and Epanechnikov kernels.

where $\hat{\rho}_{OLS}$ is the OLS estimator of ρ, and these tables are extensively used in the literature involving the determination of the order of integration of a series – see Pagan and Wickens (1989) for a summary of this literature.

For pedagogic purposes there would seem to be advantages to having a picture of the density of $n(\hat{\rho} - 1)$. To this end data on $n = 1,000$ series for y_t, $t = 1, \ldots, 1,000$, were generated by setting $y_0 = 0$ and drawing e_t from an $\mathcal{N}(0, 1)$ density. Designate each of these y_t series by $\{y_t^{(i)}\}_{i=1}^{1000}$. Then

$$\hat{\rho}^{(i)} = \left[\sum_{t=1}^{1000} \left(y_{t-1}^{(i)} \right)^2 \right]^{-1} \sum_{t=1}^{1000} y_{t-1}^{(i)} \, y_t^{(i)}, \qquad x_i = 1000 \left(\hat{\rho}^{(i)} - 1 \right),$$

and the unknown density will be estimated nonparametrically employing $\{x_i\}_{i=1}^{1000}$. Of course a greater number of replications could have been employed to provide more x_i, and a large number of y_t could also have been constructed. However, this estimate seems accurate enough for pedagogic purposes, although perhaps not if precise estimates of the distribution function are needed.

Figure 2.5 presents estimates of the density of $n(\hat{\rho}_{OLS} - 1)$, when $\rho = 1$, made with Gaussian and Epanechnikov kernels and window width computed as in (2.52).[19] The factor A in (2.52) was 2.31, whereas $\hat{\sigma}_x = 3.47$, reflecting

---

[19] Just as for the stock return data 100 equispaced points over the range of $\min(x_i)$ to $\max(x_i)$ are selected to evaluate the density. We will not repeat much of the discussion regarding kernels, etc., merely highlighting differences that emerged for this data set.

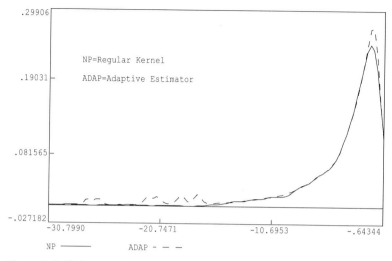

Figure 2.6. Estimates of Dickey–Fuller density: regular kernel and adaptive estimators.

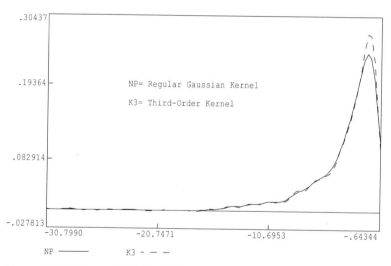

Figure 2.7. Estimates of Dickey–Fuller density: regular and third-order kernel.

the asymmetry in the density. There is no discernible difference between the estimates. Figure 2.6 compares the adaptive and Gaussian kernel estimates, with the geometric mean as scaling factor. Unlike the case with stock return data the adaptive estimator is well behaved around the mode of the density, although it

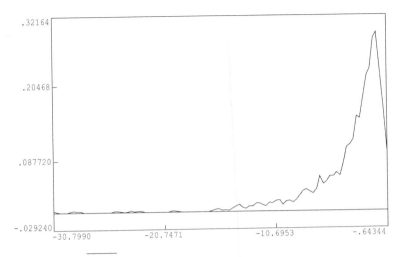

Figure 2.8. Dickey–Fuller density, kernel estimator; cross-validated window width.

tends to be fairly ragged in the tails. One striking similarity to the stock returns analysis is that the Gaussian kernel tends to understate the mode. As this might be a consequence of bias, the two higher order kernels $K_3(\psi)$ and $K_5(\psi)$ of (2.122) were again applied, and Figure 2.7 plots the Gaussian and K_3 estimates (K_5 results are virtually identical). There does appear to be evidence of a bias in the Gaussian case.

An experiment was made in selecting h by least squares cross validation, that is, h was chosen to minimize (2.115), using a Gaussian kernel. In this formula the convolution of kernels equals K_2, the Gaussian density with variance 2. Cross validation for the window width was performed, producing a window width of $h = .182$, substantially below the values used to this point. Figure 2.8 graphs the estimated density using this window width and a normal kernel. What is noticeable is the extremely ragged shape, generally a sign that the window width is too small. Hence, the utility of cross validation as a selection device is questionable, even here where there is a very large sample of observations.

3   Conditional Moment Estimation

3.1   Introduction

Perhaps the main use of econometric analysis is for counterfactual purposes. Economists are regularly asked to advise on what the impact upon employment or sales in an industry would be if a tax was imposed or lifted; what the likely effect upon unemployment would be if employment subsidies were introduced; or what might have happened if a different policy had been followed in some historical episode. Steps toward answering such questions involve the formulation of some theoretical relationship that is presumed to exist between the impacted and policy variables, the choice of some specific functional form relating these variables and any others needed for "control purposes," and the selection of a formula that will provide the requisite information "accurately."

Cast at this level of generality it is not clear how one should proceed, and in practice extra restrictions are placed upon the problem. Historically, the most prevalent has been that the relationship is a linear one, or that it be linear after some suitable transformation. Johnston (1984, pp. 61–74) for example discusses simple transformations such as logarithms or the inverse of a variable that might be employed. If y_i is the target and x_i the policy variable and $E|y_i| < \infty$, the relation among them might be expressed in terms of the conditional moment $E(y_i|x_i) = m(x_i)$, where the dependence upon x_i is made explicit. Now the central issue becomes the determination of the function $m(\cdot)$. The two functions mentioned above would sustain $m(x_i) = \alpha + x_i\beta$ or perhaps $m(x_i) = \alpha + \beta \log x_i$. In particular areas of econometrics a variety of more complex transformations have been exploited; for example, in demand theory the Rotterdam system has relations between quantities and prices that are linear in first differenced data, whereas in production function theory the transcendental logarithmic production function is a quadratic form in the logs of factor supplies. Interest in this question of estimating an unknown functional form extends out of the range of just estimating a conditional mean to higher order moments. Thus, in many models emphasizing uncertainty, a conditional variance, σ_i^2,

78

needs to be estimated. That task is easily subsumed into the determination of a conditional expectation by noting that the variance of a variable z_i conditional upon x_i would be

$$E\left[(z_i - E(z_i \mid x_i))^2 \mid x_i\right] = E\left(z_i^2 \mid x_i\right) - (E(z_i \mid x_i))^2,$$

which would involve estimating two conditional expectations with y_i in turn set to z_i^2 and z_i. Present approaches to the estimation of conditional variances almost always make the $\sigma_i^2 = m(x_i)$ function a quadratic in x_i (e.g., Engle, 1982).

Approximations such as those described above have served econometrics well, but there has always been a residual doubt that the functional form $m(\cdot)$ might be more complex than the set allowed for and that the approximation is seriously deficient. For this reason it is of interest to explore what might be learned about $m(x_i)$ without recourse to parametric models. The following sections of this chapter therefore outline two procedures that have been rec-ommended for this task. First, there is the kernel regression estimator set out in Nadaraya (1964) and Watson (1964), which derives from the nonparamet-ric density estimators analyzed in the preceding chapter. Second, there are the proposals by Gallant (1981) and Geman and Hwang (1982) that $m(x_i)$ be ap-proximated by a series expansion in which the number of terms is allowed to grow with the sample size. The following sections set out these estimators and discuss difficulties encountered in implementation as well as what is known about their statistical properties in large and small samples. We also describe a general class of nonparametric estimators that includes the Priestly and Chao (1972) kernel estimator, k-nearest neighbor, spline smoothing estimators, and locally linear regression smoothers; some of the properties of these alterna-tive estimators are presented and compared with the Nadaraya–Watson kernel estimator.

3.2   Estimating Conditional Moments by Kernel Methods

Let us consider $q + 1 = p$ economic variables (Y, X'), where Y is the dependent variable and X is a $(q \times 1)$ vector of regressors; these p variables are taken to be completely characterized by their unknown joint density $f(y, x_1, \ldots, x_q) = f(y, x)$, at the points y, x. As noted in the introduction interest frequently centers upon the conditional mean $m(x) = E(Y | X = x)$, where x is some fixed value of X, for instance, a tax rate of a prescribed magnitude.

Now suppose that we have data $(y_i, x_i')(i = 1, \ldots, n)$ upon the random vari-ables Y and X, where x_i is a $(q \times 1)$ vector of variables and y_i is a scalar. By definition, the model is

$$Y = E(Y|X = x) + u = m(x) + u, \tag{3.1}$$

where the error term u has the properties $E(u|x) = 0$ and $E(u^2|x) = \sigma^2(x)$. Although uppercase letters Y, X, etc. represent population random variables, and y_i, x_i will be sample (data) random variables, it will generally be more convenient to allow y_i and x_i to represent both a random variable and data points. The context should make it clear about which definition is being used in any instance. Small y, x will be fixed points whose range of values are those of Y and X, respectively. Major emphasis will be placed, in this chapter, on the kernel and series approximation methods of estimation, although some results on other estimation procedures will be mentioned. In the derivation of the properties of the kernel estimator, analysis is provided both when x_i is stochastic and when it is nonstochastic, whereas that for series estimators is done when x_i is nonstochastic. Most of the results are obtained by assuming that y_i, x_i, and u_i are independently and identically distributed (i.i.d). After deriving the results under a set of simplified conditions, mention will be made of extensions, particularly to the case where the random variables are dependent. In some proofs it is also easier to make the conditional and unconditional variance of u_i coincide, and it will then be written as σ^2.

We turn now to the problem of finding a nonparametric estimator of $m = m(x)$ that is at least consistent and which might be used for inferences about m. Because it is a theme of this book that many nonparametric methods represent extensions of standard parametric approaches, it is useful to review parametric estimation of m before embarking upon the nonparametric procedures in Section 3.2.2 and succeeding sections.

3.2.1   Parametric Estimation

Parametric methods specify a form of $m(x_i)$, say, that it is linear in the variables x_i. In this case, Equation (3.1) can be written as (for $q = 1$)

$$y_i = \alpha + x_i \beta + u_i, \tag{3.2}$$

where α and β are scalar parameters. The least squares estimators of α and β are $\alpha^* = \bar{y} - \bar{x}\beta^*$ and $\beta^* = \left(\sum_{i=1}^{n}(x_i - \bar{x})^2\right)^{-1}\left(\sum_{i=1}^{n}(x_i - \bar{x})y_i\right)$, respectively, where $\bar{y} = n^{-1}\sum y_i$ and $\bar{x} = n^{-1}\sum x_i$. The best unbiased parametric estimator of $m(x) = \alpha + x\beta$ is

$$m^*(x) = \alpha^* + x\beta^* = \sum_{i=1}^{n} a_{ni}(x)y_i, \tag{3.3}$$

where $a_{ni}(x) = n^{-1} + (x - \bar{x})(x_i - \bar{x})\left(\sum_{i=1}^{n}(x_i - \bar{x})^2\right)^{-1}$. The m^* in (3.3) is the weighted sum of y_i, where the weights a_{ni} are linear in x and depend on the distance of $\bar{x}$ from x.

The assumption that $m(x_i) = \alpha + x_i\beta$ implies certain assumption, about the data generating process (joint density). For example, if (y_i, x_i) is a bivariate normal density then it can be shown that the mean of the conditional density of y_i given x_i is $E(y_i|x_i) = \alpha + x_i\beta$, where $\alpha = Ey_i - (Ex_i)\beta$ and $\beta = (var(x_i))^{-1}cov\{(x_i, y_i)\}$. This implies that the assumption of linear specification for $m(x)$ holds if the data come from the normal distribution. However, if the true distribution is not normal then the linear specification for the conditional expectation may be invalid, and so the least squares estimator of $m(x)$ will become biased and inconsistent. This discussion is related to the well-known problem of bias due to misspecification in the functional form. That is, if the true relationship is, say, $y_i = \alpha + x_i\beta + x_i^2\gamma + u_i$, then the "parameter of interest" is $\beta + 2\gamma x_i = \partial y_i/\partial x_i$. However, if a linear approximation is taken, $\partial y_i/\partial x_i$ is being estimated under the false restriction that $\gamma = 0$. Typically, the exact functional form connecting $m(x)$ with x is unknown. Because of the possibility that forcing the function to be linear or quadratic may affect the accuracy of estimation of $m(x)$, it is worthwhile considering nonparametric estimation of the unknown function, and this task is taken up in the following sections.

3.2.2 Nonparametric Estimation: A "Local" Regression Approach

The basic idea behind nonparametric estimation is to approximate $m(x)$ arbitrarily closely, given a large enough sample. To understand later developments it is useful to begin with the situation when x_i is a discrete random variable. Let one of the values it can assume be x and let the observations corresponding to these values of x_i be arranged as the first n^*. Then a sensible way to estimate $m(x)$ would be to average the y_i corresponding to all x_is that equal x, that is, to form $\hat{m} = (n^*)^{-1}\sum_{i=1}^{n^*} y_i$. Because $\hat{m} = m + (n^*)^{-1}\sum_{i=1}^{n^*} u_i$, and $E(u_i) = 0$, application of a law of large numbers shows that $\hat{m}$ is a consistent estimator of m provided $n^* \to \infty$ as $n \to \infty$.

Now let h be a *window width* that is smaller than the distance between the discrete values taken by x_i. Then

$$\sum_{i=1}^{n} I(x - .5h < x_i < x + .5h) = \sum_{i=1}^{n} I_i = n^*,$$

since h is such that the indicator function I_i can equal unity only if $x_i = x$, otherwise I_i is zero. Similarly, $\sum_{i=1}^{n^*} y_i = \sum_{i=1}^{n} I_i y_i$. Combining these alternative expressions allows $\hat{m}$ to be rewritten as

$$\hat{m} = \sum_{i=1}^{n} I(-.5 < \psi_i < .5)y_i \bigg/ \sum_{i=1}^{n} I(-.5 < \psi_i < .5), \qquad (3.4)$$

where $\psi_i = (x_i - x)/h$. Simply put, $\hat{m}$ is the sample average of those y_i values which correspond to $x_i = x$. This is an obvious estimator of m, the population average of Y when $X = x$.

Moving to the case where x_i is a continuous random variable, the exact value x will occur in the data with probability zero, and m will need to be estimated by averaging the y_i corresponding to x_i in an interval around x. In density estimation this transition was solved by replacing the indicator function $I(\psi)$ over the range $(-.5,.5)$ by a kernel $K(\psi)$ over (possibly) $(-\infty, \infty)$; by direct analogy $m(x)$ should be estimated by

$$\hat{m} = \sum_{i=1}^{n} K(\psi_i) y_i \Big/ \sum_{i=1}^{n} K(\psi_i), \tag{3.5}$$

where $K(\psi_i) = K((x_i - x)/h)$ and h will be a window width that determines how many of the x_is around x are to be used in forming the average. When $h = \infty$ we get $\hat{m} = \sum y_i/n$ and when $h = 0$ we get $\hat{m}(x_i) = y_i$. However, when the value of h is small $\hat{m}$ provides the best local estimate of m.

The local averaging description of the estimation of m is a useful one, highlighting the fact that observations are weighted by the kernel K_i. For values of x_i that lie far from x, and with any given window width h, ψ_i will be large and so K_i will be small. Hence, these observations get low weight in the determination of $\hat{m}$, as we would want. This perspective also proves helpful in understanding a number of issues that arise in estimation. First, it will be necessary for h to tend to zero as n increases so as to effectively delete all observations not close to x as the sample expands. Second, the *shape* of the kernel is not going to be very important provided it gives a low value to those observations x_i that lie far from x. Third, the dual requirements for getting a good estimator of m by this technique are that a law of large numbers can be applied to the u_i and that, as $n \to \infty$, there is an increasing number of values of x_i close to x. What is particularly important about this observation is that u_i need not be a continuous random variable, provided that its average converges to zero. Because the dependent variable in some econometric models is in fact discrete, for example in discrete choice models, this fact significantly extends the range of application of the approach.

A final benefit of conceiving of kernel estimators as local averaging is the warning provided about the impact of outliers in the data. If x lies a long way from all observed data, with the exception of a single point, that point will effectively determine $\hat{m}$, since the weights applied to all other observations will be small. In fact, in the limit one would merely recover that observation, y_s, as the numerator would be approximately $y_s K_s$ and the denominator K_s. This is a warning not to evaluate conditional expectations outside the range of the bulk of the data, and it might not be too important in many applications. However, later we will be using kernel estimators in contexts where x is a point x_J in the data set. If the x_J happens to be an outlier, then $\hat{m} \simeq y_J$, and this can have very serious consequences. In these situations, and in some other situations pointed out later, it is common for researchers to employ the "leave-one-out" estimator in which (3.5) becomes

$$\hat{m}(x = x_J) = \left[\sum_{\substack{i=1 \\ i \neq J}}^{n} K(\psi_i) y_i \bigg/ \sum_{\substack{i=1 \\ i \neq J}}^{n} K(\psi_i) \right]. \tag{3.6}$$

3.2.3 Kernel-Based Estimation: A Formal Derivation

Suppose that the x_i are i.i.d. random variables. Because $m(x_i)$ is the mean of the conditional density $f(y_i|x_i) = f(Y|X = x_i)$, there is a potential to employ the methods of density estimation provided in Chapter 2 to estimate $m(x) = E(Y|X = x)$, the conditional expectation at the point $X = x$. By definition the conditional mean is

$$m = \int_{-\infty}^{\infty} (yf(y, x)/f_1(x)) \, dy, \tag{3.7}$$

where $f_1(x)$ is the marginal density of X at x. Nadaraya (1964) and Watson (1964) therefore proposed that m be estimated by replacing $f(y, x)$ by $\hat{f}(y, x)$ and $f_1(x)$ by $\hat{f}_1(x)$, where these density estimators were the kernel estimators discussed in Chapter 2. A restriction that they placed upon the kernels was that they be *symmetric*, for reasons that will shortly become apparent.

The expressions for $\hat{f}(y, x)$ and $\hat{f}_1(x)$ in (2.125) and (2.126) may be substituted into (3.7) to give

$$\hat{m} = \int_{-\infty}^{\infty} y \left[\frac{(nh^p)^{-1} \sum_{i=1}^{n} K_1\left(\frac{y_i-y}{h}, \frac{x_i-x}{h}\right)}{(nh^q)^{-1} \sum_{i=1}^{n} K\left(\frac{x_i-x}{h}\right)} \right] dy, \tag{3.8}$$

where $p = q + 1$ and h is the window width. Our aim is to simplify (3.8). Consider first the numerator, defining $v_i = h^{-1}(y_i - y)$ so that $y = y_i - hv_i$ and the Jacobian of transformation between v and y as h. Therefore the numerator becomes

$$\int_{-\infty}^{\infty} (nh^p)^{-1} \sum_{i=1}^{n} (y_i - hv) K_1\left(v, \left(\frac{x_i-x}{h}\right)\right) h \, dv \tag{3.9}$$

$$= n^{-1} \sum_{i=1}^{n} y_i \int_{-\infty}^{\infty} K_1\left(v, \left(\frac{x_i-x}{h}\right)\right) h^{-q} \, dv$$

$$- n^{-1} \sum_{i=1}^{n} \int_{-\infty}^{\infty} vh^{-p+2} K_1\left(v, \left(\frac{x_i-x}{h}\right)\right) dv. \tag{3.10}$$

The last term in (3.10) is zero when K_1 is a symmetric kernel in v, reducing the numerator to

$$= n^{-1} \sum_{i=1}^{n} y_i h^{-q} \int_{-\infty}^{\infty} K_1 \left(v, \left(\frac{x_i - x}{h} \right) \right) dv \qquad (3.11)$$

$$= n^{-1} \sum_{i=1}^{n} y_i h^{-q} K \left(\frac{x_i - x}{h} \right) \qquad (3.12)$$

from the relation between the kernels used to estimate the joint (K_1) and marginal (K) densities (i.e., $\int K_1(y, x) \, dy = K(x)$). Replacing the numerator in (3.8) by (3.12) gives the estimator of m:

$$\hat{m} = \left[(nh^q)^{-1} \sum_{i=1}^{n} y_i K \left(\frac{x_i - x}{h} \right) \right] \bigg/ \left[(nh^q)^{-1} \sum_{i=1}^{n} K \left(\frac{x_i - x}{h} \right) \right]$$
$$\qquad (3.13)$$

$$= \sum_{i=1}^{n} K \left(\frac{x_i - x}{h} \right) y_i \bigg/ \sum_{i=1}^{n} K \left(\frac{x_i - x}{h} \right), \qquad (3.14)$$

which is the same as that derived from the local regression approach of the preceding section.

In the analysis above the quantity of interest was presumed to be $m(x)$. But, paralleling the debate in macroeconomics over rules versus discretion, it may be that a more realistic way of treating a "change in policy" is as a shift in the *distribution* of the policy variables. This viewpoint seems particularly appropriate when data are upon individuals. For example, if x_i was the tax levied on the ith individual, tax reform (say) is probably best represented as affecting *all* the x_i rather than any individual one, and it is the change in the *unconditional* expectation of y induced by the distributional shift that needs to be estimated. This expectation is $E(y) = E[m(X)] = E[m(x_i)]$, where the expectation is being taken over the density function for the x_i, and this connection points to the possibility of estimating $E(y)$ as $n^{-1} \sum_{i=1}^{n} \hat{m}_i$. Any effects upon $E(y)$ originating from a policy rule change leading to values $\{x_i^*\}$ and $\{x_i^{**}\}$ can therefore be estimated by $n^{-1} \sum \hat{m}_i^{**} - n^{-1} \sum \hat{m}_i^*$. Stock (1989) uses this idea for assessing the impact of environmental policy.

3.2.4   *A General Nonparametric Estimator of $m(x)$*

A feature of the Nadaraya–Watson estimator is that it is a weighted sum of those y_is that correspond to x_i in a neighborhood of x. The weights are low for x_is far away from x and high for x_is closer to x. With this motivation, a *general class* of nonparametric estimators of $m(x)$ can be written as

$$\tilde{m} = \tilde{m}(x) = \sum_{i=1}^{n} w_{ni}(x) y_i, \qquad (3.15)$$

where $w_{ni}(x) = w_n(x_i, x)$ represents the weight assigned to the ith observation y_i, and it depends on the distance of x_i from the point x. Usually, the weight is high if the distance is small and low if the distance is large. If the weights are such that $w_{ni}(x) \geq 0$ and $\sum w_{ni}(x) = 1$ then they may be called "probability weights." The estimators (3.4) and (3.5) are special cases of (3.15), both having probability weights. Note that the parametric estimator in (3.3) is also a special case of (3.15) with linear weights $w_{ni}(x) = a_{ni}(x)$ such that $\sum w_{ni}(x) = 1$, but $w_{ni}(x) \geq 0$ is not necessarily true.

An implicit assumption in nonparametric estimation is that $m(x)$ is smooth over x, implying that y_i contains information about $m(x)$ whenever x_i is near to x. The estimator $\tilde{m}(x)$ is a smoothed estimator in the sense that it is constructed, at every point, by local averaging of the observations y_is corresponding to those x_is close to x in some sense. The graph of the smoothed estimator $\tilde{m}$ (smoother) is referred to as the smooth (Tukey, 1977). We show below that a large class of smoothed estimators of $m(x)$ belong to $\tilde{m}(x)$, but, before doing so, some alternative interpretations of $\tilde{m}(x)$ are provided.

In parametric regression, a functional form is specified for the conditional mean $m(x)$. This functional form, say $m(x, \beta)$, depends on a finite number of unknown parameters β. The least squares estimate of $m = m(x)$ is $m(x, \hat{\beta})$, where $\hat{\beta}$ is chosen to minimize

$$\sum_{i=1}^{n} \left(y_i - m(x_i, \hat{\beta}) \right)^2. \tag{3.16}$$

Compare (3.16) with the following weighted least squares criterion for the nonparametric estimation of $m(x)$:

$$\sum_{i=1}^{n} w_{ni}^*(x) \left[y_i - m(x) \right]^2. \tag{3.17}$$

In (3.17), $m(x)$ replaces the $m(x, \beta)$ that appears in (3.16). If $m(x)$ is regarded as a single unknown parameter m, it may be estimated by minimizing

$$\sum_{i=1}^{n} w_{ni}^*(x) [y_i - m]^2. \tag{3.18}$$

The resulting estimate, $\tilde{m}$, of $m(x)$ is precisely (3.15), after writing $w_{ni}(x) = w_{ni}^*(x) / \sum_{i=1}^{n} w_{ni}^*(x)$. Thus the kernel estimator $\hat{m}$ in (3.5) is also a least squares estimator, with $w_{ni}^*(x) = K((x_i - x)/h)$.

One might also think of $\tilde{m}(x)$ as a method of moments estimator. Since $E(u_i|x_i) = 0$ in (3.1),

$$E w_{ni}^*(x) (y_i - m(x_i)) = 0, \tag{3.19}$$

or

$$E\left[w_{ni}^*(x)(y_i - m) + w_{ni}^*(x)(m - m(x_i))\right] = 0. \tag{3.20}$$

If the second term in (3.20) is ignored and a sample estimate of the first, $n^{-1}\sum_{i=1}^{n} w_{ni}^*(x)(y_i - m)$, is used, the value of m for which this is zero is just $\tilde{m}$ in (3.15). Whether the second term can be ignored depends upon the weights $w_{ni}^*(x)$. If the weights were the indicator functions of (3.4) it will be identically zero, whereas with kernel weights it is only asymptotically zero. Because the orthogonality relation only holds as $n \to \infty$, the situation is out of the normal framework described by Hansen (1982), but it is close to work reported in Powell (1986a), in that the expected value of the function the parameter solves changes with the sample size (through h) and so its large-sample limit has to be used instead.

3.2.5 Unifying Nonparametric Estimators

Various nonparametric estimators are special cases of (3.15), differing mainly with respect to the choice of w_{ni}. What follows is a listing of some of the better known estimators of $m(x)$. Each estimator has the format of (3.15) but is distinguished by the weights w_{ni} adopted.

Nadaraya–Watson Kernel Estimator
Substituting

$$w_{ni}^1(x) = K\left(\frac{x_i - x}{h}\right) \bigg/ \sum_{i=1}^{n} K\left(\frac{x_i - x}{h}\right)$$

in (3.15) gives $\tilde{m}^1(x) = \hat{m}(x)$ as in (3.5).

Recursive Kernel Estimators
In the Nadaraya–Watson regression estimator $\hat{m}$, the window width h is the same for all the data points. An alternative is

$$w_{ni}^2(x) = h_i^{-p} K\left(\frac{x_i - x}{h_i}\right) \bigg/ \sum_{i=1}^{n} h_i^{-p} K\left(\frac{x_i - x}{h_i}\right), \tag{3.21}$$

where h_i denotes a sequence of positive numbers. Substituting $w_{ni}^2(x)$ in (3.15) leaves

$$\tilde{m}^2(x) = \sum_{i=1}^{n} w_{ni}^2(x)\, y_i, \tag{3.22}$$

which is known as the recursive regression estimator. The h_i are assumed to satisfy $\sum_1^n h_i^p \to \infty$ as $n \to \infty$. This estimator was first examined by Ahmad and Lin (1976) and later by Greblicki and Krzyzak (1980), Devroye and Wagner (1980a), Gyorfi (1981c), and Singh and Ullah (1986).

An alternative estimator, which suppresses h_i^{-p} from (3.21), is

$$\tilde{m}^3(x) = \frac{\sum_{i=1}^n y_i K\left(\frac{x_i - x}{h_i}\right)}{\sum_{i=1}^n K\left(\frac{x_i - x}{h_i}\right)} = \sum_{i=1}^n w_{ni}^3(x)\, y_i. \tag{3.23}$$

This estimator has been studied by Devroye and Wagner (1980a) and Greblicki and Pawlak (1987). Note that this estimator is obtained by simply replacing h by h_i in (3.5). Rutkowski (1985a,b) considered an estimator very similar to $\tilde{m}^3(x)$ that asymptotically located the regression functions even under some unbounded $m(x_n)$.

The estimators $\tilde{m}^2(x)$ and $\tilde{m}^3(x)$ are recursive in the sense that, when an additional data point becomes available, they can be updated according to

$$\tilde{m}_n^2(x) = \tilde{m}_{n-1}^2(x) + \frac{y_n - \tilde{m}_{n-1}^2(x)}{1 + \hat{f}_{n-1}(x)/h_n^{-p} K\left(\frac{x_n - x}{h_n}\right)},$$

$$\tilde{m}_n^3(x) = \tilde{m}_{n-1}^3(x) + \gamma_n^{-1}\left(y_n - \tilde{m}_{n-1}^3(x)\right) K\left(\frac{x_n - x}{h_n}\right), \tag{3.24}$$

where $\gamma_n = \gamma_{n-1} + K\left(\frac{x_n - x}{h_n}\right)$ and $\gamma_0 = 0$. When γ_n in (3.24) is replaced by nh^p the estimator $\tilde{m}_n^3$ becomes very similar to the recursive estimator obtained by the method of stochastic approximation (see Revesz, 1977). An interesting feature of the recursive estimator $\tilde{m}_n^3(x)$ is that $\tilde{u}_n = y_n - \tilde{m}_{n-1}^3(x)$ on the right-hand side of $\tilde{m}_n^3(x)$ can be considered as a one-step-ahead prediction error; the new information at time n comes in the form of $\tilde{u}_n$ and m is estimated by updating $\tilde{m}_{n-1}^3$.

Kernel Estimators with Known $f_1(x)$

In some situations the marginal density of x, $f_1(x)$, may be known, allowing the kernel estimator to be written as (from (3.7) and (3.8))

$$\tilde{m}^4(x) = \frac{1}{f_1(x)} \int y \hat{f}(y, x)\, dy$$

$$= \frac{1}{nh^q f_1(x)} \sum_{i=1}^n K\left(\frac{x_i - x}{h}\right) y_i$$

$$= \sum_{i=1}^n w_{ni}^4(x)\, y_i, \tag{3.25}$$

where

$$w_{ni}^4(x) = (nh^q)^{-1} K\left(\frac{x_i - x}{h}\right) \Big/ f_1(x). \tag{3.26}$$

This estimator has been considered by Johnston (1979, 1982) and is appropriate when the density $f_1(x)$ is known. In Monte Carlo experiments this will be true. It may also be a realistic presumption if the data on x are at regularly spaced intervals; such data sets can often be transferred to the unit interval [0,1] and one might then assume that $f_1(x)$ in (3.25) is the uniform density on [0,1]. An important point to be noted is that the variance of $\tilde{m}_4$ is strictly higher than when f_1 is estimated, and the bias is also different; see Lemma 3.1 and Theorem 3.2.

Fixed Design Estimators
    When there is a univariate ($q = 1$) fixed "design" regressor on [0, 1], Priestly and Chao (1972) and Benedetti (1977) considered the regression estimator $\tilde{m}^5$ of the form (3.15) with

$$w_{ni}^5(x) = \frac{1}{h}(x_i - x_{i-1}) K\left(\frac{x_i - x}{h}\right), \qquad x_0 = 0. \tag{3.27}$$

In the same set of circumstances Gasser and Muller (1979) proposed the estimator $\tilde{m}$ having the form (3.15) with weights

$$w_{ni}^6(x) = \frac{1}{h}\int_{s_{i-1}}^{s_i} K\left(\frac{t - x}{h}\right) dt, \tag{3.28}$$

where $x_{i-1} \le s_{i-1} \le x_i$. For the special case $s_i = x_i$, see Cheng and Lin (1981). Using the mean value theorem it can be shown that $w_{ni}^5(x)$ is asymptotically equivalent to $w_{ni}^6(x)$. In fact the theoretical properties (Cheng and Lin, 1981) and finite sample results for both estimators (Gasser et al., 1985) are almost indistinguishable. A minor advantage of (3.28) is that the weights always add to unity. Weights similar to $w_{ni}^6(x)$ are considered in Ahmad and Lin (1984) for the q-variate "fixed design" regressors on $[0, 1]^q$, $q \ge 1$, and their paper also deals with the consistent estimation of the unconditional variance of u.

    Moreover, although data on x_i are sometimes of the "fixed design" type, mostly this will not be true; whilst economic variables X are usually nonexperimental they are not nonstochastic. There are a number of advantages if x_i can be regarded as fixed. First, the weights applied are not the ratio of random variables as in the case of the Nadaraya–Watson estimator and this makes the derivation of small-sample and asymptotic properties of estimators much simpler. Second, the task of estimating higher order derivatives is easier compared to the Nadaraya–Watson estimator. However, there are a number of reasons why the estimators (3.27) and (3.28) may not be useful in practice. Foremost among these is that the Gasser–Muller estimator is hard to implement in high dimensions without some regular shape to the design. Even when implemented it has a poor rate of convergence for dimension greater than two and its unconditional variance is higher than that for the Nadaraya–Watson estimator.

Nearest Neighbor (NN) Estimates

The kernel estimator $\hat{m}(x)$ was defined in (3.5) and (3.14) as a weighted average of y_i values in a fixed symmetric neighborhood around x values, with the property that values of i where x_i is close to x get higher weights than those that are far from x. The kth nearest neighbor (k-NN) estimator is also a weighted average with the weight sequence having a similar property. Such a weight sequence has been discussed in Chapter 2 in the context of density estimation. For the regression case considered here the first general presentation seems to be in Royall (1966), although Watson (1964) may be interpreted as mentioning uniform nearest neighbors.

The k-NN estimator is (3.15) with $w_{ni}^7(x) = k^{-1} I_{ki}(x)$, yielding

$$\tilde{m}^7(x) = \sum_{i=1}^{n} w_{ni}^7(x) y_i = k^{-1} \sum_{i=1}^{n} I_{ki}(x) y_i. \tag{3.29}$$

In (3.29) $I_{ki}(x) = 1$ if x_i is one of the k nearest observations to x and 0 otherwise, and k is the preassigned number of nearest neighbors of x, which depends upon the sample size. Thus, for example, if there are 9 observations $\{y_i, x_i\}$, $i = 1, \ldots, 9$ and $k = n^{1/2} = \sqrt{9} = 3$, the k-NN estimator can be calculated by following the steps below:

(a) Out of 9 values of x_i, pick the set of $k = 3$ x_is that are nearest to the point x.
(b) Take the mean of the y_i values corresponding to the x_is chosen in (a).

In view of the above observations the k-NN estimator can be rewritten as

$$\tilde{m}^7(x) = \frac{1}{k} \sum_{j=1}^{k} y_j^*(x), \tag{3.30}$$

where y_j^* are the y_is *ordered* according to the distance measure employed. Thus y_1^* is the y_i whose x_i is closest to x, y_2^* is the second closest, etc. In a multivariate context "closeness" would need to be measured by some norm, say the Euclidean norm. The parameter k regulates the degree of smoothness of $\tilde{m}^7$ and, in this respect, it is the analogue of the window width for the kernel estimator.

The estimator in (3.30) is actually a k-NN estimator with uniform weights. Stone (1977) proposed k-NN estimators of the form $\sum_{j=1}^{n} w_{nj} y_j^*(x)$ with the triangular (T) or quadratic (Q) weights in (3.31),[1]

$$w_{nj}^T = 2(k - j + 1)/(k(k + 1)),$$
$$w_{nj}^Q = 6(k^2 - (j - 1)^2)/(k(k + 1)(4k - 1)), \quad \text{for } k > j, \quad (3.31)$$
$$w_{nj}^T = w_{nj}^Q = 0 \quad \text{for } k \leq j.$$

More general nearest neighbor $(G\text{-}NN)$ estimators with weights analogous to kernel functions with unbounded support may also be of interest. These are

$$\tilde{m}^8(x) = \sum_{i=1}^n w_{ni}^8(x) y_i, \quad (3.32)$$

where

$$w_{ni}^8(x) = K\left(\frac{x_i - x}{d}\right) \bigg/ \sum_{i=1}^n K\left(\frac{x_i - x}{d}\right), \quad (3.33)$$

with $d = d_n$ being the distance between x and its kth nearest neighbor. Note that the above estimator is similar to the Nadaraya–Watson kernel estimator in (3.5) with $h = d_n$. Also, k-NN is a special case of (3.32); see (3.35) below. Suppose we wish to compute the k-NN estimate at all points in the sample $x_1, \ldots, x_n$. Let x_J be one of these points. Provided we define the k-NN estimate as the average of the y_i that lie $k/2$ on the left and those that lie $k/2$ to the right of y_J^*, Härdle (1990) observes that a nice recursive formula exists to compute $\tilde{m}^8$, namely $\tilde{m}^8(x_{i+1}) = \tilde{m}^8(x_i) + k^{-1}\left(y_{i+[k/2]+1}^* - y_{i-[k/2]}^*\right)$.

We now investigate some aspects of kernel, k-NN, and G-NN estimators. As indicated before, the general estimator $\tilde{m}$ is essentially a weighted average of observations in a neighborhood of the point under consideration. In the kernel method, a deterministic region $\mathcal{A}$, based on h_n, is located around x, and those sample points falling inside $\mathcal{A}$ are averaged; the k-NN method assigns a sequence of integers $k = k(n)$ with $k \to \infty$, $k/n \to 0$ as $n \to \infty$, determines the smallest sphere S containing the k nearest neighbors of x among the observations, and averages these k points. In each method the estimators are obtained by the volume of the appropriate region ($\mathcal{A}$ in the kernel case and S for k-NN). In this respect kernel and k-NN estimators have a similar *modus operandi*. To be more precise let $\zeta_i = x_i - x$ and define

$$K(\zeta) = \frac{1}{2h} I_{\mathcal{A}}[|\zeta| \leq h] \quad (3.34)$$

---

[1] Modifications are needed to these formulae if there are ties in the data. See Stone for further details, also see Carroll and Härdle (1988).

for the kernel estimator, whereas *k-NN* can be written as

$$\left(\sum_{i=1}^{n} K_i^* \right)^{-1} \sum_{i=1}^{n} K_i^* y_i, \tag{3.35}$$

where

$$K^*(\zeta) = \frac{1}{2d_n} I_S \left[|\zeta| \leq d_n \right], \tag{3.36}$$

and I_A is an indicator function on the set $\mathcal{A}$.

One advantage of the *k-NN* method is that it is locally adaptive; that is, if $f(x)$ is small, then S is large, and vice versa. This is not true for the kernel method since $\mathcal{A}$ remains the same for all x. Another disadvantage with the kernel method is that it need not be invariant under a scale change on the x variable; however, this problem could be avoided by standardizing the data before entry into the kernel, and, in practice, this is commonly done.

In the special case where the x_i values are equispaced or follow a uniform distribution, the *k-NN* estimator, for $k = 2nh$, reduces to the Priestly–Chao kernel in (3.27) with uniform kernel $K(\psi) = 1/2$, $|\psi| \leq 1$. The *G-NN* estimator in (3.32) incorporates features of both the kernel and the *k-NN* methods, and the weights are a function of not only the distance but also the direction of the data from x. Stone (1977) provides general conditions on w_{ni} under which the estimates are globally consistent. Royall (1966) derives the MSE and MISE of the *k-NN* estimator and proves its asymptotic normality; see also Owen (1987) and Bhattacharya and Mack (1987). The bias is $(24f^3)^{-1} \left[m^{(2)} f + 2m^{(1)} f^{(1)} \right] (k/n)^2$. Mack (1981) analyzes the bias, MSE, and asymptotic normality of the *G-NN* estimator. He suggests that the window width in kernel estimation, h, and the parameter k are linked by $k = nh^{4/(4+q)}$, making $k_{opt} \propto n^{4/5}$ when $h_{opt} \propto n^{-1/5}$.

Spline Smoothing

The smoothing spline estimator of $m(x)$ is found from the function $g(x)$ that minimizes

$$\frac{1}{n} \sum_{i=1}^{n} (y_i - g(x_i))^2 + \lambda \int \left(g^{(r)}(x) \right)^2 dx, \tag{3.37}$$

where $\lambda > 0$ is a smoothing parameter and $g^{(r)}$ is the rth derivative of $g(x)$. The first term penalizes lack of goodness of fit of the function to the data, and the second penalizes lack of smoothness of the approximating function, in the sense of having a large rth derivative. Since the second term (for $\lambda \neq 0$) tends to zero if and only if $g(x)$ is a polynomial of order $r - 1$, the criterion described above can be viewed as penalizing any estimator of m that departs too much from the

rth-order polynomial. For other techniques of quantifying local variation see Good and Gaskins (1971) and Boneva et al. (1970).

Usually, $r = 2$ has been considered in the literature and in this case $\int \left(g^{(2)}(x) \right)^2 dx$ can be treated as a measure of local variation of $m(x)$. The functional minimizer of (3.37) is then a unique, smooth, piecewise cubic polynomial (spline) in $(x - x_i)$, $\hat{m}(x) = \hat{g}(x)$, where x belongs to $[x_i, x_{i+1}]$, $i = 1, ..., n-1$ (see Reinsch, 1967). At the point x_i, the curve $\hat{m}(x)$ and its first two derivatives are continuous but the third derivative may be discontinuous. At the boundary points the second derivative is zero.

After r has been chosen, the choice of λ needs to reflect the degree of confidence in the value of r selected. Large values of λ reflect consistency with the assumed r or the polynomial in x. In the extreme cases, when λ goes to infinity, the function is forced to be linear over the whole range of x values, and it is then the best least squares line through the data. When $\lambda \to 0$, y tends to be an interpolating function for the data, fitting every data point exactly, making the first term zero for any function $m(x)$. The spline smoothing approach therefore seeks a trade-off between goodness of fit and too much local variation. Quite often λ and r are made data dependent, being selected by procedures such as generalized cross validation (Craven and Wahba, 1979; Rice, 1984a; Wahba, 1985).

Smoothing splines were originally proposed by Whittaker (1923), Schoenberg (1964), and Reinsch (1967). For recent developments on this, see Eubank (1988). A drawback with the smoothing spline method is that the function minimizing (3.37) becomes quite complicated for $r > 2$ and $q > 1$. When $r = 2$, the function solution can be written in the format of (3.15), but explicit determination and computation of the weights is difficult, although see Reinsch's (1967) algorithm for $q = 1$. Silverman (1984) develops an asymptotic approximation to the solution $\tilde{m}$ in terms of a variable kernel, which is

$$\tilde{m}^9 = \sum_{i=1}^{n} w_{ni}^9(x) y_i, \tag{3.38}$$

where

$$w_{ni}^9(x) = (nh(x_i))^{-1} K \left(\frac{x_i - x}{h(x_i)} \right) \tag{3.39}$$

and $h(x_i) = \lambda^{1/4}(f(x_i))^{-1/4}$.[2]

---

[2] Jennen-Steinmetz and Gasser (1988) provide an analytical comparison among kernel, spline, and k-NN estimators. This is done by considering the Gasser and Muller–type kernel estimator in (3.28) with variable window width proportional to $(f(x))^{-\alpha}$, $0 \le \alpha \le 1$. Their work encompassed the spline estimator ($\alpha = 1/4$), the G-NN estimator ($\alpha = 1$), and the kernel estimator ($\alpha = 0$). They show that the kernel estimator ($\alpha = 0$) is minimax optimal in the sense of minimizing maximum integrated MSE over all $m(x)$.

In a recent study Koenker, Ng, and Portnoy (1994) developed quantile spline estimators by using the objective function in (3.37), with the first term replaced by $\sum \varsigma_\alpha (y_i - g(x_i))$, where $\varsigma_\alpha (z) = z\{\alpha - I(z < 0)\}$. These estimators aim to be robust to extreme observations. Ng (1995) develops an algorithm for quantile smoothing splines, and Ng and Smith (1995) apply the median spline estimator to the price elasticity for gasoline.

The Local Linear and Polynomial Regression Estimators

The Nadaraya–Watson estimator of $m(x) = m$ minimizes $\Sigma_{i=1}^n \{y_i - m\}^2 K\left(\frac{x_i - x}{h}\right)$ with respect to m, giving the normal equation $\sum y_i K_i = \sum K_i m$ and hence the solution of m as $\hat{m}(x) = (\sum K_i)^{-1} \sum K_i y_i = \bar{y}_K$ where $K_i = K\left(\frac{x_i - x}{h}\right)$ and $\bar{y}_K$ is the weighted average of y_i values. Alternatively, $\hat{m}(x)$ is the least squares estimator of the parameter in the weighted regression of y_i on unity with weights $K_i^{1/2}$. Stone (1977) and Cleveland (1979) suggested that instead one minimize

$$\sum_{i=1}^n \{y_i - m - (x_i - x)\beta\}^2 K\left(\frac{x_i - x}{h}\right),$$

with respect to m and β. This estimate can be found by performing a weighted least squares regression of y_i against $z_i' = (1, (x_i - x))$ with weights $K_i^{1/2}$. Thus, whereas the Nadaraya–Watson estimator fits a constant to the data close to x, the local linear approximation fits a straight line. This local linear smoothing estimator has been extensively investigated in recent years by Fan (1992, 1993), Fan and Gijbels (1992), and Ruppert and Wand (1994). Obviously the resulting estimator has the form

$$\tilde{m}^{10}(x) = \sum_{i=1}^n w_{ni}^{10}(x) y_i,$$

with weights $w_{ni}^{10} = e_1' (\sum z_i K_i z_i')^{-1} z_i K_i$, where e_1 is a column vector of dimension the same as z_i with unity as first element and zero elsewhere. Fan (1992) suggested adding a small quantity, declining with n, such as n^{-2}, to $\sum z_i K_i z_i'$, so as to ensure that it is bounded away from zero. Inverting the matrix $\sum z_i K_i z_i'$ one can verify that

$$\tilde{m}^{10}(x) = \bar{y}_K - \hat{\beta}(\bar{x}_K - x), \quad \hat{\beta} = \hat{\beta}(x) = \frac{\sum (y_i - \bar{y}_K)(x_i - \bar{x}_K) K_i}{\sum (x_i - \bar{x}_K) K_i}$$

where $\bar{x}_K = \sum x_i K_i / \sum K_i$. These expressions are the familiar standard regression estimators except for the weights K_i.

One advantage of the local linear estimator is that it can be analyzed with standard regression techniques. It also has the same first-order statistical properties irrespective of whether the x_i are stochastic or nonstochastic. Various extensions of the idea are available: Either a polynomial in $(x_i - x)$ or even more general functions suggested by theory such as the exponential (see Gozalo and Linton, 1994) can replace the linear function if it is felt that $m(x)$ has bounded higher order derivatives, while x_i can be made a vector. Fan and Gijbels (1992) work with a variable window width $h(x_i) = h\alpha^{-1}(x_i)$, showing that $\alpha(x_i) = f^{1/5}(x_i)$ is the optimal choice in the sense of minimizing the MISE. Hall et al. (1995) also find an expression for the optimal window width when estimating $m(x)$ on the boundaries of the support of x_i. The optimal window width is proportional to $n^{-1/5}$ within the support but changes near the boundaries. They provide an algorithm for finding the optimal value of h. In their experiments the choice of h was not a particularly sensitive issue in the middle of the support, but the window width needed to be made much larger near the boundary.

Applications of this idea in econometrics include: McManus (1994a,b) to estimation of cost functions, Gourieroux and Scaillet (1994) to the term structure, Lin and Shu (1994) to estimation of a disequilibrium transition model, Bossaerts and Hillion (1997) to options prices and their determinants, and Ullah and Roy (1998) for a nutrition/income relation. Implementation and computations are discussed in Cleveland (1979) and Cleveland et al. (1988). Hastie and Loader (1993) provide an excellent account of the history and potential of the method.

The logic of linear local regression smoothing can be seen by expanding $m(x_i)$ around x to get

$$m(x_i) = m(x) + \frac{\partial m}{\partial x}(x^*)(x_i - x), \qquad (3.40)$$

where x^* lies between x_i and x. This may be expressed as

$$m(x_i) = m + \beta(x^*)(x_i - x). \qquad (3.41)$$

Now, since $E(y_i|x_i) = m(x_i)$, the objective function

$$\Sigma(y_i - m(x_i))^2 K_i = \Sigma(y_i - m - \beta(x^*)(x_i - x))^2 K_i$$

is essentially the residual sum of squares from a regression using only observations close to $x_i = x$. Notice that this means that $\beta(x^*)$ will be very close to constant as x^* must lie between x_i and x. This also points to the fact that improvements might be available from expanding $m(x_i)$ as a jth-order polynomial in $(x_i - x)$, but doing so requires the derivatives $m^{(j)}$ to exist. The analogous results for density estimators were discussed in Section 2.2.8.

3.2.6 Estimation of Higher Order Conditional Moments

Repeated use of (3.15) enables the computation of any moment for y_i and any covariance of it with other variables. For example, the second moment is defined as $\sigma^2(x) = E(y_i^2|x) - (m(x))^2$ and the first term can be estimated by replacing y_i with y_i^2 in (3.15). Thus $\tilde{\sigma}^2(x) = \sum w_{ni}(x)y_i^2 - (\tilde{m}(x))^2$. Quite often, one is interested in estimating $\sigma_u^2(x) = E(u_i^2|x)$, where $y_i = m(x_i) + u_i$. The natural estimator would be $\tilde{\sigma}_u^2(x) = \sum w_{ni}(x)u_i^2$. In practice, u_i needs to be replaced by $\tilde{u}_i = y_i - \tilde{m}(x_i)$, giving $\tilde{\sigma}_u^2(x) = \sum w_{ni}(x)\tilde{u}_i^2$, and this will constitute the more general formula for estimating the conditional variance of u_i. For the Nadaraya–Watson case, $w_{ni}(x) = K(\psi_i)/\sum K(\psi_i)$, and thus

$$\hat{\sigma}_u^2(x) = \sum K(\psi_i)\hat{u}_i^2 \Big/ \sum K(\psi_i), \tag{3.42}$$

where $\hat{u}_i = y_i - \hat{m}(x_i)$. In fact $\tilde{\sigma}_u^2(x)$ is identical to $\tilde{\sigma}^2(x)$ provided $\tilde{m}(x) = \sum w_{ni}(x)y_i$. This equivalence can be seen by substituting for $\tilde{u}_i^2 = y_i^2 - 2\tilde{m}(x)$ $y_i + \tilde{m}^2$ and observing that $\sum w_{ni}(x)\tilde{m}(x)y_i = \tilde{m}(x)^2$. It is not always the case however that the same weights would be used in computing the conditional mean and variance, since the conditioning variables may differ. Also, the conditional mean might be taken to be linear and the least squares weights used instead of kernel weights in forming $\tilde{m}(x)$. It is also the case that one can apply the local linear regression estimator. Bossaerts et al. (1996) do this, putting $y_i = \hat{u}_i^2$ and $x_i = y_{i-1}$.

As in the case of $\sigma^2(x)$, the Jth conditional moment of y_i can always be written in terms of the Jth moment around the origin, $E(y_i^J|x)$, and lower order moments, so that J applications of (3.15) with $y_i, y_i^2, \ldots, y_i^J$ successively substituting for y_i will give all the requisite information. Similarly, the estimate of the covariance between y_i and z_i will be formed by nonparametrically estimating the components of $E(y_iz_i|x) - E(z_i|x)E(y_i|x)$. That is,

$$\tilde{cov}[y_i, z_i|x] = \sum w_{ni}(x)y_iz_i - \left(\sum w_{ni}(x)y_i\right)\left(\sum w_{ni}(x)z_i\right).$$

This result is also the basis of the nonparametric estimation of conditional autocovariance and autocorrelation functions in the time series context. For the properties of the nonparametric estimators of the higher order moments see Singh and Tracy (1970) and Singh et al. (1987). Their variances can also be obtained by using (3.77) below.

3.3 Finite-Sample Properties

Let us rewrite the general class of nonparametric estimators $\tilde{m}(x)$ in (3.15) in the abbreviated form

$$\tilde{m} = \sum_{i=1}^{n} w_i y_i. \tag{3.43}$$

Frequently it will be helpful to write $m = m(x)$ and $m_i = m(x_i)$. As noted in Section 3.2.5, $\tilde{m}$ incorporates the k-NN, kernel, spline, and other estimators as special cases. In the case of the Nadaraya–Watson kernel estimator

$$w_i = K\left((x_i - x)/h\right) \bigg/ \sum_{i=1}^{n} K\left(\frac{x_i - x}{h}\right).$$

When analyzing the properties of $\tilde{m}$ two scenarios can be distinguished: when X is nonstochastic (fixed) and when X is random. The sampling distribution of $\tilde{m}$ is relatively easy to determine when the X is fixed since it is just a weighted average of y_i with fixed weights; Georgiev (1988) has an extensive analysis. Roussas (1989) extends Goergiev's work to allow for dependent but strictly stationary u_is and Fan (1990a) allows for both dependence and heterogeneity. For example, under the assumptions

(A1) the vector X is nonstochastic,
(A2) u_i in (3.1) is i.i.d $(0; \sigma^2)$,

it can easily be verified that $E\tilde{m} - m = \sum w_i (m_i - m)$ and $V(\tilde{m}) = \sigma^2 \sum w_i^2$ for w_is such that $\sum w_i = 1$. For the distribution of $\tilde{m}$, under (A2), see Ullah (1992).

Because the situation of fixed X is of limited interest when working with economic data, we now turn to the stochastic case. However, because results are not available here for general weights, analysis is restricted to particular choices of weights such as the Nadaraya–Watson estimator.

3.3.1 Approximate Results: Stochastic x

The Nadaraya–Watson Estimator

This section studies approximations to the bias and MSE of the estimators. Approximate results for the general class of estimators $\tilde{m}$ are not known in the literature. In view of this only the Nadaraya–Watson kernel estimator $\hat{m}$ in (3.5) is explicitly considered, although results will be described for other estimators.

In what follows attention is restricted to the univariate $(q = 1)$ case with the additional assumptions:

(A3) m and f are twice continuously differentiable in a neighborhood of the point x.
(A4) The kernel K is a symmetric function satisfying

$$(i)\ \int K(\psi)\,d\psi = 1, \qquad (ii)\ \int \psi K(\psi)\,d\psi = 0,$$

(iii) $\int \psi^2 K(\psi)\, d\psi = \mu_2 < \infty.$

(A5) $h = h_n \to 0$ and $nh \to \infty$ as $n \to \infty.$

(A6) x_i in (3.1) is i.i.d. and independent of the u_is.

(A7) The second-order derivatives of the marginal density f of x_i are continuous and bounded in a neighborhood of x, and x is a point in the interior of the support of x_i.[3]

The derivation of exact expressions is rather difficult in the stochastic case, and perhaps no meaningful results could be obtained. A major difficulty arises when the weights w_i are the ratio of random variables, such as happens with the Nadaraya–Watson estimator $\hat{m}$. In view of this we explore asymptotic approximations in Section 3.4. Before proceeding in this section we briefly consider the question of the existence of moments of $\tilde{m} = \sum w_i y_i$ in (3.15) or (3.43). The notation E_X below represents the expectation conditional on $x_i, i = 1, \ldots, n.$

Theorem 3.1: If w_i are strictly positive such that $\sum |w_i| = a < \infty$ and $m(x_i)$ is bounded, then $E\tilde{m}$ exists.

Proof: From (3.43), taking the expectation conditional upon $x_1, \ldots, x_n$, we get

$$|E_X(\tilde{m})| = \left| \sum_{i=1}^{n} w_i m(x_i) \right| < \sum_{i=1}^{n} |w_i|\, |m(x_i)| \le ca,$$

where $|m(x_i)| < c.$ Now

$$|E\tilde{m}| = |E\, (E_X(\tilde{m}))| < |E_X(\tilde{m})| < ca. \quad \text{Q.E.D.}$$

A similar argument demonstrates that the variance $V(\tilde{m})$ exists if $E(u_i^2 | x_i) = \sigma^2(x_i)$ is bounded, which is satisfied for the homoskedastic case $\sigma^2(x_i) = \sigma^2 < \infty.$ However, if the w_i could be zero, as in the case of kernels with bounded support, or the higher order kernels described in Section 2.7.2, the mean and variance of $\tilde{m}$ may not exist. See Härdle and Marron (1983).

---

[3] The properties of the estimator are different on the boundary as there are fewer observations and only negative values of $((x_i - x)/h)$ are available, so that the effective kernel is asymmetric. "Boundary kernels" have been advocated to overcome this problem–see Rice (1984b). Other suggestions are outlined in Härdle (1990).

To obtain an approximation to the bias and variance of $\hat{m}$ in (3.5), we first rewrite it as[4]

$$\hat{m} = \sum w_i y_i = \frac{(nh)^{-1} \sum_{i=1}^n K\left(\frac{x_i-x}{h}\right) y_i}{(nh)^{-1} \sum_{i=1}^n K\left(\frac{x_i-x}{h}\right)} = \frac{\hat{g}(x)}{\hat{f}(x)}$$

$$= \frac{E\hat{g} + \hat{g} - E\hat{g}}{E\hat{f} + \hat{f} - E\hat{f}} = \frac{E\hat{g} + \hat{g} - E\hat{g}}{E\hat{f}}\left[1 + \frac{\hat{f} - E\hat{f}}{E\hat{f}}\right]^{-1} \qquad (3.44)$$

$$= \frac{E\hat{g}}{E\hat{f}} + \frac{1}{E\hat{f}}(\hat{g} - E\hat{g}) - \frac{E\hat{g}}{(E\hat{f})^2}(\hat{f} - E\hat{f})$$

$$+ O\left[\left(\hat{f} - E\hat{f}\right)^2 + (\hat{g} - E\hat{g})\left(\hat{f} - E\hat{f}\right)\right] \qquad (3.45)$$

provided $\left|(\hat{f} - E\hat{f})/E\hat{f}\right| < 1$ and $E\hat{f} \neq 0$.

Each of the terms in (3.45) will need to be evaluated to form the approximate moments and the following lemma is useful for that purpose:

Lemma 3.1: Suppose Assumptions (A2)–(A6) hold. Then

$$E\hat{g} = mf + \frac{h^2}{2}\left(m^{(2)}f + f^{(2)}m + 2m^{(1)}f^{(1)}\right)\mu_2 + o(h^2), \qquad (3.46)$$

$$V(\hat{g}) = \frac{(m^2 + \sigma^2)f}{nh}\int K^2(\psi)\,d\psi + O\left(\frac{1}{n}\right), \qquad (3.47)$$

and

$$\text{cov}(\hat{g}, \hat{f}) = \frac{mf}{nh}\int K^2(\psi)\,d\psi + O\left(\frac{1}{n}\right). \qquad (3.48)$$

Proof: From (3.44) and (3.1), and denoting E_X as the expectation conditional upon $\{x_1 \ldots x_n\}$, we get

$$E\hat{g} = E\left[\frac{1}{nh}\sum_{i=1}^n K\left(\frac{x_i-x}{h}\right)y_i\right]$$

$$= E\left[E_X\left(\frac{1}{nh}\sum_{i=1}^n K\left(\frac{x_i-x}{h}\right)y_i\right)\right]$$

---

[4] A different way of getting the result is to think of $\hat{m}$ as the ratio of two random variables W/Z and to take a Taylor series expansion around the points W^*, Z^* to get (to a linear approximation) $\frac{W^*}{Z^*} + \frac{1}{Z^*}(W - W^*) - \frac{W^*}{(Z^*)^2}(Z - Z^*)$. Setting $W = \hat{g}$, $Z = \hat{f}$, $W^* = E\hat{g}$, and $Z^* = E\hat{f}$ gives (3.45). The approximations here would be meaningful if the mean and variance of the estimator existed; otherwise one might think of them as relating to the asymptotic moments.

$$= E \left[\frac{1}{nh} \sum_{i=1}^{n} K \left(\frac{x_i - x}{h} \right) m(x_i) \right]$$

$$= \frac{1}{h} \int K \left(\frac{x_1 - x}{h} \right) m(x_1) f(x_1) \, dx_1$$

$$= \int K(\psi) m(x + h\psi) f(x + h\psi) \, d\psi$$

$$= mf + \frac{h^2}{2} \left(m^{(2)}(\tau) f + f^{(2)}(\tau) m + 2m^{(1)} f^{(1)} \right) \mu_2, \qquad (3.49)$$

where we use (A3), (A4), and $m(x + h\psi) = m + h\psi m^{(1)} + h^2\psi^2 m^{(2)}(\tau)/2$, with $\tau = \tau_n(x, \psi)$ being between x and $x + h\psi$.

Next, denoting V_X as the variance conditional on x_i, and using (A2) and $\hat{g} - E_X(\hat{g}) = (nh)^{-1} \sum K_i u_i$, leaves

$$V(\hat{g}) = E(V_X(\hat{g})) + V(E_X(\hat{g}))$$

$$= \sigma^2 \frac{1}{n^2 h^2} E \sum_{i=1}^{n} K^2 \left(\frac{x_i - x}{h} \right)$$

$$+ V \left[\frac{1}{nh} \sum_{i=1}^{n} K \left(\frac{x_i - x}{h} \right) m(x_i) \right]. \qquad (3.50)$$

Following the same steps as in (3.49), the first term of (3.50) is

$$\frac{\sigma^2}{n^2 h^2} E \sum_{i=1}^{n} K^2 \left(\frac{x_i - x}{h} \right) = \frac{\sigma^2}{nh} \int K^2(\psi) f(x + h\psi) \, d\psi$$

$$= \frac{f\sigma^2}{nh} \int K^2(\psi) \, d\psi + O \left(\frac{1}{n} \right). \qquad (3.51)$$

Similarly, the second term of (3.50) is

$$V \left[\frac{1}{nh} \sum_{i=1}^{n} K \left(\frac{x_i - x}{h} \right) m(x_i) \right]$$

$$= \frac{1}{n^2 h^2} E \left(\sum_{i=1}^{n} K \left(\frac{x_i - x}{h} \right) m(x_i) \right)^2$$

$$-\left(E\left\{ \frac{1}{nh} \sum_{i=1}^{n} K\left(\frac{x_i - x}{h} \right) m(x_i) \right\} \right)^2$$

$$= \frac{1}{nh} \int K^2(\psi) m^2(x + h\psi) f(x + h\psi) \, d\psi$$

$$+ \frac{n(n-1)}{n^2} \left(\int K(\psi) m(x + h\psi) f(x + h\psi) \, d\psi \right)^2$$

$$- \left(\int K(\psi) m(x + h\psi) f(x + h\psi) \, d\psi \right)^2$$

$$= \frac{m^2 f}{nh} \int K^2(\psi) d\psi + O\left(\frac{1}{n} \right). \tag{3.52}$$

Substituting (3.51) and (3.52) into (3.50) yields (3.47).

Finally, we can write

$$\text{cov}(\hat{g}, \hat{f}) = E\hat{g}\hat{f} - E\hat{g}E\hat{f}$$

$$= \frac{1}{n^2 h^2} E\left[\sum_{i=1}^{n} K^2\left(\frac{x_i - x}{h} \right) m(x_i) \right] + \frac{n(n-1)}{n^2 h^2}$$

$$\times EK\left(\frac{x_1 - x}{h} \right) m(x_1) EK\left(\frac{x_1 - x}{h} \right) - E\hat{g}E\hat{f}$$

$$= \frac{1}{nh} \int K^2(\psi) m(x + h\psi) f(x + h\psi) \, d\psi$$

$$+ \frac{n(n-1)}{n^2} \left(\int K(\psi) m(x + h\psi) f(x + h\psi) \, d\psi \right)$$

$$\times \left(\int K(\psi) f(x + h\psi) \, d\psi \right)$$

$$- \left(\int K(\psi) m(x + h\psi) f(x + h\psi) \, d\psi \right)$$

$$\times \left(\int K(\psi) f(x + h\psi) \, d\psi \right)$$

$$= \frac{mf}{nh} \int K^2(\psi) \, d\psi + O\left(\frac{1}{n} \right). \tag{3.53}$$

Q.E.D.

Theorem 3.2: When Assumptions (A2)–(A7) hold and $f > 0$,

$$\text{Bias}(\hat{m}) = \frac{h^2}{2f}\mu_2 \left(m^{(2)} f + 2f^{(1)}m^{(1)}\right) + O(nh)^{-1} + o(h^2) \quad (3.54)$$

$$V(\hat{m}) = \frac{\sigma^2}{nhf(x)} \int K^2(\psi)\,d\psi + o\left(n^{-1}h^{-1}\right). \quad (3.55)$$

Proof: Taking the expectation on both sides of (3.45) and using (2.41), (2.42), (3.46), (3.47), and (3.48) we obtain

$$
\begin{aligned}
E\hat{m} &= \frac{E\hat{g}}{E\hat{f}} + O\left(E(\hat{f} - E\hat{f})^2 + E(\hat{f} - E\hat{f})(\hat{g} - E\hat{g})\right) \\
&= \frac{mf + h^2\xi\mu_2/2}{f + h^2 f^{(2)}\mu_2/2} + O\left(V(\hat{f}) + \text{cov}(\hat{g}, \hat{f})\right) \\
&= \frac{mf + h^2\xi\mu_2/2}{f}\left[1 + \frac{h^2 f^{(2)}\mu_2}{2f}\right]^{-1} + O\left(\frac{1}{nh}\right), \quad (3.56)
\end{aligned}
$$

where $\xi = m^{(2)} f + f^{(2)}m + 2m^{(1)} f^{(1)}$. Expanding $\left[1 + h^2 f^{(2)}\mu_2(2f)^{-1}\right]^{-1}$ for large n (small h) and collecting terms up to $O(h^2)$ in (3.56) gives (3.54).
Now, from (3.44), dropping the fourth term, which is $O_p\left((nh)^{-1}\right)$, we find

$$\hat{m} - E\hat{m} = \frac{1}{E\hat{f}}(\hat{g} - E\hat{g}) - \frac{E\hat{g}}{\left(E\hat{f}\right)^2}\left(\hat{f} - E\hat{f}\right) \quad (3.57)$$

and

$$V(\hat{m}) = \frac{1}{(E\hat{f})^2}V(\hat{g}) + \frac{(E\hat{g})^2}{(E\hat{f})^4}V(\hat{f}) - \frac{2E\hat{g}}{(E\hat{f})^3}\text{cov}(\hat{g}, \hat{f}). \quad (3.58)$$

Substituting (2.41), (2.42), (3.46), (3.47) and (3.48) into (3.58) and retaining terms up to $O((nh)^{-1})$ we get (3.55). Q.E.D.

An alternative way to derive the bias and variance of $\hat{m}$ is to write

$$\hat{m} - m = \frac{\hat{g} - m\hat{f}}{\hat{f}} = \frac{(\hat{g} - m\hat{f})}{f}\left[1 - \frac{\hat{f} - f}{\hat{f}}\right]$$

and note that the term $(\hat{f} - f)/\hat{f}$ is $o_p(1)$ and hence it can be dropped. Thus $\hat{m} - m \simeq (\hat{g} - m\hat{f})/f$, which gives

$$E(\hat{m} - m) \simeq f^{-1}\left(E\hat{g} - mE\hat{f}\right)$$

and

$$V(\hat{m}) \simeq f^{-2} V \left[\hat{g} - m \hat{f} \right] = f^{-2} \left[V(\hat{g}) + m^2 V(\hat{f}) - 2m \, \mathrm{cov}(\hat{g}, \hat{f}) \right].$$

Using the results from Lemma 3.1 we then get Theorem 3.2.

Another alternative is to first find the approximate bias and variance of $\hat{m}$ conditional on x_i and to then obtain the unconditional results. In our context, this approach is useful because the approximate conditional bias and variance are free from x_i, making them identical to the unconditional approximate bias and variance. This approach will also be used in analyzing the bias and variance of the local linear estimator in Section 3.3.2.

To obtain the bias, up to $O(h^2)$, we approximate

$$y_i = m(x_i) + u_i \simeq m(x) + (x_i - x)m^{(1)}(x) + \frac{1}{2}(x_i - x)^2 m^{(2)}(x) + u_i$$

$$= m + h\psi_i m^{(1)} + \frac{h^2}{2}\psi_i^2 m^{(2)} + u_i.$$

In fact the error term contains u_i plus the terms of higher order of smallness than h^2. However since the results, to the order of approximations considered, are not affected by these additional terms, only u_i has been retained. Substituting this approximation into (3.5) we get

$$\hat{m}(x) - m(x) = \frac{m^{(1)}}{\hat{f}}\frac{1}{n}\sum_{i=1}^{n} K(\psi_i)\psi_i + \frac{hm^{(2)}}{2\hat{f}}\frac{1}{n}\sum_{i=1}^{n} K(\psi_i)\psi_i^2$$

$$+ \frac{1}{\hat{f}}\frac{1}{nh}\sum_{i=1}^{n} K(\psi_i)u_i.$$

Thus, conditional on x_i, the bias and variance are

$$E_X\left(\hat{m}(x) - m(x)\right) = \frac{m^{(1)}}{\hat{f}}\frac{1}{n}\sum_{i=1}^{n} K(\psi_i)\psi_i + \frac{hm^{(2)}}{2\hat{f}}\frac{1}{n}\sum_{i=1}^{n} K(\psi_i)\psi_i^2,$$

$$V_X\left(\hat{m}(x)\right) = \frac{\sigma^2}{\hat{f}^2}\frac{1}{n^2h^2}\sum_{i=1}^{n} K^2(\psi_i).$$

(3.59)

Now, from the results in Chapter 2, it can be verified that, for large n,

$$\hat{f} = f + o_p(1),$$

$$\frac{1}{n}\sum_{i=1}^{n} K(\psi_i)\psi_i = h^2\mu_2 f^{(1)} + o_p(h^2),$$

$$\frac{h}{n}\sum_{i=1}^{n} K(\psi_i)\psi_i^2 = h^2\mu_2 f + o_p(h^2),$$

$$\frac{1}{nh} \sum_{i=1}^{n} K^2(\psi_i) = f \int K^2(\psi) \, d\psi + o_p(1).$$

Substituting into the expressions in (3.59) produces the approximate bias and variance as

$$E_X\big(\hat{m}(x) - m(x)\big) = \frac{h^2}{2f} \mu_2\big(m^{(2)} f + 2f^{(1)} m^{(1)}\big),$$

$$V_X(\hat{m}(x)) = \frac{\sigma^2}{nhf} \int K^2(\psi) \, d\psi.$$

(3.60)

Since the right-hand sides of these expressions are free from x_i, they become the approximate unconditional bias and variance as given in Theorem 3.2.

The expressions for approximate bias and variance in Theorem 3.2 can be found in Collomb (1981), Mack (1981), Jennen-Steinmetz and Gasser (1988), and Chu and Marron (1991).[5] Chu (1989) obtained the results of Theorem 3.2 by relaxing the differentiability condition on m and f and replacing it with Holder continuity of K, m, and f. Jennen-Steinmetz and Gasser (1988) provide analogous results for the k-NN estimator (also Mack, 1981), the Gasser and Muller kernel estimator, and the spline smoothing estimator. A comparative study of these estimators would be a useful topic for future research.

The optimal h can be found by minimizing $MISE = \lambda_0 n^{-1} h^{-1} + \lambda_1 h^4$, where the values taken by λ_0 and λ_1 can easily be determined from (3.54) and (3.55). The calculations, similar to the density case in Chapter 2, show that the mean integrated squared error is minimized by

$$h_{opt} = \left(\frac{\lambda_0}{4\lambda_1}\right) n^{-1/5}.$$

(3.61)

The results extend to the multivariate context with q elements in x_i simply by replacing nh by nh^q. Other modifications needed when $q > 1$ are that h_{opt} in (3.61) will be proportional to $n^{-1/(q+4)}$, and the term $\mu_2 m^{(2)}$ in (3.54) will now be replaced by $(\operatorname{tr} G m^{(2)})$, where $G = \int \psi \psi' K(\psi) \, d\psi$. Reduction of bias by higher order kernels is done exactly as described in Section 2.4.3.

The results in Lemma 3.1 and Theorem 3.2 rely upon the assumption of homoskedasticity of $u_i (V(u_i) = \sigma^2)$, but they can be extended to allow for heteroskedasticity, where $V(u_i \mid x_i) = \sigma^2(x_i)$, provided the variance exists and is continuous, simply by replacing σ^2 with $\sigma^2(x)$. This change occurs because, in the heteroskedastic case, the first term of (3.50), and hence (3.51), changes

---

[5] The main derivation of the proof of Theorem 3.2 follows that of Mack (1981). The conditioning approach is that of Ruppert and Wand (1994). If the x_i were nonstochastic the bias and variance of $\hat{m}$ are the same as those conditional on x_i.

to

$$\frac{1}{n^2 h^2} E \sum_{i=1}^{n} \sigma^2(x_i) K^2 \left(\frac{x_i - x}{h}\right)$$

$$= \frac{1}{nh} \int K^2(\psi) \sigma^2(x + h\psi) f(x + h\psi) \, d\psi$$

$$= \frac{f\sigma^2(x)}{nh} \int K^2(\psi) \, d\psi + O\left(\frac{1}{n}\right).$$

Other expressions in the derivation of Lemma 3.1 and Theorem 3.2 are not altered due to heteroskedasticity.

Just as for density estimation one could also work with "plug-in" estimators of h. However, as Theorem 3.2 shows, the number of unknowns requiring estimation is quite extensive and can become quite cumbersome if there is more than one conditioning variable. Härdle, Hall, and Marron (1992) provide a theoretical analysis of this procedure.

3.3.2   The Local Linear Regression Estimator

The local linear regression estimator performs a weighted regression of y_i against $z_i' = (1, (x_i - x))$ using weights $w_i^{1/2} = \left[K\left(\frac{x_i - x}{h}\right)\right]^{1/2}$. Because it may be that elements of w_i are zero (e.g., if $K(\cdot)$ is a kernel with compact support there may well be observations at the boundary), the resulting estimator may have no moments. For this reason the analysis is either done conditional upon x_i or a small amount that tends to zero as $n \to \infty$ is added to w_i. Ruppert and Wand (1994) follow the first strategy whereas Fan (1993) pursues the latter. We will utilize Ruppert and Wand's treatment.

As described earlier the estimator of $m(x)$ is

$$\hat{m}(x) = e_1' \left(\Sigma z_i w_i z_i'\right)^{-1} \Sigma z_i w_i y_i, \tag{3.62}$$

where e_1 is a vector with unity in the first place. Since

$$y_i = m(x_i) + u_i$$
$$\simeq m(x) + (x_i - x) \beta(x) + (x_i - x)^2 \gamma(x^*) + u_i$$
$$= z_i' \delta + (x_i - x)^2 \gamma(x^*) + u_i, \tag{3.63}$$

where $\beta(x) = m^{(1)}(x)$, $\gamma(x^*) = m^{(2)}(x^*)$, and $\delta(x)' = \delta' = (m(x) \beta(x))$, one can find an alternative expression for $\hat{m}(x)$ by substituting for y_i from (3.63):

$$\hat{m}(x) = e_1' \delta(x) + e_1' \left(\Sigma z_i w_i z_i'\right)^{-1} \Sigma z_i w_i (x_i - x)^2 \gamma(x^*)$$
$$+ e_1' \left(\Sigma z_i w_i z_i'\right)^{-1} \Sigma z_i w_i u_i. \tag{3.64}$$

Because $e_1' \delta(x) = m(x)$, the conditional bias and variance are

$$Ex\left(\hat{m}(x) - m(x)\right) = e_1' \left(\Sigma z_i w_i z_i'\right)^{-1} \Sigma z_i w_i (x_i - x)^2 \gamma(x^*)$$

and

$$Vx\left(\hat{m}(x)\right) = \sigma^2 e_1' \left(\Sigma z_i w_i z_i'\right)^{-1} \left(\Sigma z_i w_i^2 z_i'\right) \left(\Sigma z_i w_i z_i'\right)^{-1} e_1.$$

For large n, following Ruppert and Wand, we can evaluate this expression by using the asymptotic results in Section 3.3.1 to get

$$\left((nh)^{-1} \Sigma z_i w_i z_i'\right)^{-1} \xrightarrow{p} \begin{bmatrix} f^{-1}(x) & -f^{(1)}(x) f(x)^{-2} \\ -f^{(1)} f(x)^{-2} & \{\mu_2 f(x) h^2\}^{-1} \end{bmatrix},$$

$$\left((nh)^{-1} \Sigma z_i w_i^2 z_i'\right) \xrightarrow{p}$$
$$\begin{bmatrix} f(x) \int K^2(\psi) d\psi & hf(x) \int K^2(\psi) \psi d\psi \\ hf(x) \int K^2(\psi) \psi d\psi & h^2 f(x) \int K^2(\psi) \psi^2 d\psi \end{bmatrix},$$

where $\mu_2 = \int \psi^2 K(\psi) d\psi$ and we have used

$$(nh)^{-1} \sum_{i=1}^{n} K^2(\psi_i) \psi_i^2 = f \int K^2(\psi) \psi^2 d\psi + o_p(1).$$

Using these results gives the asymptotic bias and variance of $\hat{m}$. Being free of x_i these are also the unconditional quantities. Such reasoning leads to the following theorem.

Theorem 3.3: The approximate bias and variance of the local linear regression estimator of $m(x)$ are

$$\text{Bias}(\hat{m}(x)) = \frac{1}{2} \mu_2 h^2 m^{(2)}(x), \tag{3.65}$$

$$V(\hat{m}(x)) = \sigma^2 \frac{(nh)^{-1}}{f(x)} \int K^2(\psi) d\psi. \tag{3.66}$$

It is interesting to compare the moments of this estimator to that of the Nadaraya–Watson estimator in Theorem 3.2. First, notice that the variance is the same but that the bias is different. In particular, the latter does not depend upon the density of x_i, making it "design adaptive" in the sense of Fan (1992). Second, unlike the Nadaraya–Watson kernel estimator, Fan and Gijbels (1992) show that its bias and variance are of the same order of magnitude in both the interior and near the boundary of the support of f. Third, the fact that the bias is of order h^2 does not derive from the symmetry of the kernel as it does with the Nadaraya–Watson estimator. Fourth, the bias of the latter estimator is large if either $|m^{(1)}|$ or $|f^{(1)}/f|$ are large, but neither term appears in (3.65). Fifth, when $m(x)$ is linear, the bias in the local linear estimator vanishes but the bias in the Nadaraya–Watson estimator does not vanish. Finally, Fan's work suggests that it is generally the case that the local linear regression estimator has smaller MSE than the kernel estimator; this turns out to be particularly true around the boundary points.

It is interesting to observe that the expressions for bias and variance are similar to those for the density estimator in Section 2.4.2 (see (2.41) and (2.42)) and so the discussion on window width choice provided there will not be repeated. The derivation of the bias above also points to ways of removing it. Suppose that z_i' was defined as $[1, (x_i - x), (x_i - x)^2]$ (i.e., a quadratic polynomial was used). Then, the expansion of $m(x_i)$ around x will now give

$$m(x_i) = z_i'\delta_1 + (x_i - x)^3 \gamma_1(x^*),$$

and hence the lead term in the bias will involve h^3 rather than h^2. Accordingly, expanding the order of the polynomial in the regression is the equivalent of using a higher order kernel to perform bias reduction. Such results imbue the local linear regression estimator with a good deal of flexibility and account for its favorable reception in recent years.

3.3.3 Combining Parametric and Nonparametric Estimators

We note that whereas the Nadaraya–Watson estimator is obtained by deriving the weighted least squares estimator of the intercept $\alpha = m(x)$ in the regression

$$y_i = \alpha + u_i,$$

the local linear estimator is the weighted least squares estimator of α in the regression

$$y_i = \alpha + (x_i - x)\beta + u_i.$$

Thus if the latter regression is a closer approximation of $y_i = m(x_i) + u_i$, then the Nadaraya–Watson regression is misspecified and we have the standard "omitted" variable regression problem. It is then the case that the Nadaraya–Watson estimator is biased in small samples due to omission of $(x_i - x) = h\psi_i$, especially for a "fixed" h. This bias however vanishes for large samples if $h \to 0$.

The Nadaraya–Watson estimator is unbiased when the function m being estimated is a constant. Similarly, local polynomial estimators are unbiased when m is a polynomial. As indicated above, for unknown m the bias behavior of the local polynomial estimators is better than that of the Nadaraya–Watson estimator. This is especially true in the tails and wherever the density is changing rapidly. Several other bias reduction estimators have been proposed in the literature.

One such procedure, which is a generalization of the local polynomial estimators, is discussed in Gozalo and Linton (1995) and in Hjort and Jones (1996); Tibshirani (1984) is an early reference. Gozalo and Linton (1995) propose a nonparametric estimator procedure in which the parameters of a parametric model $m(x) = m(x, \theta)$ are estimated from the data in the neighborhood of the point of interest. Specifically, $\hat{\theta} = \hat{\theta}(x)$ is obtained by minimizing

$$\sum_{i=1}^{n} [y_i - m(x_i, \theta)]^2 K \left(\frac{x_i - x}{h} \right),$$

producing $\hat{m}(x) = m(x, \hat{\theta}(x))$. This is analogous to the local likelihood estimator of a density as discussed in Chapter 2, and therefore we refer to it as a local least squares estimator. In the special case of $m(x_i, \theta) = \alpha$, $\hat{m}(x) = \hat{\alpha}(x)$ is the Nadaraya–Watson estimator. When $m(x_i, \theta) = \alpha + x_i \beta$ then $\hat{m}(x) = \hat{\alpha}(x) + x\hat{\beta}(x)$ is the local linear estimator. Notice that the local linear estimator described in Sections 3.2.5 and 3.3.2 minimizes $\sum[y_i - (m(x) + (x_i - x)\beta(x))]^2 K \left(\frac{x_i-x}{h} \right)$, which can be reparameterized as $\sum[y_i - \alpha(x) - x_i \beta(x)]^2 K \left(\frac{x_i-x}{h} \right)$, where $\alpha(x) = m(x) - x\beta(x)$, see Section 3.2.5 for the local linear estimators of $m(x)$ and $\beta(x)$. Gozalo and Linton (1995) have shown that the asymptotic variance of $\hat{m}(x) = \hat{m}(x, \hat{\theta}(x))$ is independent of the parametric model $m(x, \theta)$ used, and hence it is the same as the Nadaraya–Watson and local linear estimators. Furthermore, the asymptotic bias is

$$\text{Bias } \hat{m}(x) = \text{Bias } \hat{m}(x, \hat{\theta}(x)) = \frac{1}{2}\mu_2 h^2 \left(m^{(2)}(x) - m^{(2)}(x, \theta(x)) \right),$$

which does not depend on f. Thus $m(x, \hat{\theta}(x))$ is design adaptive. Also, the behavior of the bias depends on the distance of the parametric model $m(x, \theta)$ from the nonparametric model $m(x)$. If $m(x) = m(x, \theta)$ for all x, then $\hat{m}(x, \hat{\theta}(x))$ is unbiased. However, if $m(x)$ is close to $m(x, \theta)$ in the sense that $\left| m^{(2)} - m^{(2)}(x, \theta) \right| \leq \left| m^{(2)} \right|$, then the bias of $\hat{m}(x, \hat{\theta}(x))$ will be smaller than that of the Nadaraya–Watson and local linear estimators, both of which have $m^{(2)}(x, \theta) = 0$. Thus, if the true function was closer to the exponential function, local estimation with the exponential function may have better bias performance.

Gozalo and Linton's procedure can be considered as a way of utilizing parametric information in nonparametric estimation. Other approaches that combine parametric and nonparametric estimators are in Hjort and Glad (1995) for density estimation and Glad (1998) for regression estimation. Glad (1998) writes $m(x) = m(x, \theta)r(x)$, where $r(x)/m(x, \theta)$ is called the correction factor. The combined estimator of $m(x)$ is then $\hat{m}(x) = m(x, \hat{\theta})\hat{r}(x)$, where $m(x, \hat{\theta})$ is a parametric estimator of $m(x, \theta)$ and

$$\hat{r}(x) = \sum_{i=1}^{n} y_i^* K(\psi_i) \Bigg/ \sum_{i=1}^{n} K(\psi_i)$$

is the Nadaraya–Watson kernel estimator with $y_i^* = y_i / m(x_i, \hat{\theta})$. He also considered a local linear estimator of $r(x)$.

Another way of combining parametric and nonparametric estimators is proposed in Ullah and Vinod (1993) and Fan and Ullah (1996). The Fan and Ullah (1996) version is

$$\hat{m}(x) = \hat{\lambda} m(x, \hat{\theta}) + (1 - \hat{\lambda}) \hat{g}(x),$$

where $m(x, \hat{\theta})$ is the parametric estimator, $\hat{g}(x)$ is the Nadaraya–Watson kernel estimator, and $\hat{\lambda}$ is the least squares estimator of λ in the density-weighted combined model

$$\hat{f}_{-i} y_i = \hat{f}_{-i} \left[\lambda m(x_i, \hat{\theta}) + (1 - \lambda) \hat{g}_{-i} \right] + \hat{f}_{-i} u_i,$$

with $\hat{f}_{-i}$ and $\hat{g}_{-i}$ being the leave-one-out density and regression estimators respectively.

It follows from the above papers that the combined estimators just discussed share two properties. (i) Although they have the same variance, at least to the order of approximation considered here, they often have smaller bias compared to the Nadaraya–Watson kernel estimator. (ii) If the parametric model is incorrect, then the combined estimators have similar asymptotic behavior to that of the Nadaraya–Watson kernel estimator.

One advantage of Fan and Ullah's estimator is that it automatically adapts to the data through $\hat{\lambda}$. If the parametric model accurately describes the data, then $\hat{m}(x)$ puts all the weight on the parametric estimate; otherwise, it puts all the weight on the kernel estimate. The estimator $\hat{\lambda}$ can also be used for testing the null hypothesis of $m(x) = m(x, \theta)$ (see Section 3.13). For the other combined estimators above, this role is played by the smoothing parameter and there is, as yet, no way for choosing this parameter such that the estimates adapt to the data in the above sense.

3.4   Asymptotic Properties

3.4.1   Asymptotic Properties of the Kernel Estimator
with Independent Observations

This section takes up the question of the asymptotic properties of the Nadaraya–Watson estimator $\hat{m}$. As for the treatment of approximate moments, only the situation for stochastic x_i is analyzed, with qualifications presented for when the variable is nonstochastic. Our proofs will be heuristic. Definitions of the various modes of convergence are provided in the appendix. It is shown that the kernel estimator is weakly consistent and has a limiting normal distribution. The proof follows Rosenblatt (1969) and Bierens (1987a). To simplify it we adopt a much stronger set of assumptions than is strictly necessary. Throughout this section we make the following assumption, as well as maintaining a number of those presented earlier:

(A8) Let K be the class of all Borel measurable, bounded, real-valued functions $K(\psi)$ such that (i) $\int K(\psi)\,d\psi = 1$, (ii) $\int |K(\psi)|\,d\psi < \infty$, (iii) $|\psi||K(\psi)| \to 0$ as $|\psi| \to \infty$, (iv) $\sup |K(\psi)| < \infty$, and (v) $\int K^2(\psi)\,d\psi < \infty$.

Assumption (A8) is the same as assumption (A8) used in Chapter 2 for density estimation. For the results below we note that Assumptions (A3) and (A7) imply that m and f are continuous at x. Throughout, $f > 0$, $m(x) < \infty$, and $Eu_i^2 = \sigma^2 < \infty$ are maintained; together these imply $\int y^k f(y, x)\,dy < \infty$ for $k = 1, 2$. Theorem 3.4 deals with the weak consistency of $\hat{m}$.[6]

Theorem 3.4: When Assumptions (A5), (A6), and (A8) hold, $\hat{m}$ is weakly consistent, that is,

$$p \lim_{n\to\infty} \hat{m} = m. \tag{3.67}$$

Proof: Notice that $\hat{m} = \hat{g}/\hat{f}$ from (3.44) while, from (3.49),

$$E\hat{g} = \int K(\psi)m(x + h\psi)f(x + h\psi)\,d\psi$$

$$= \int K(\psi)g(x + h\psi)\,d\psi,$$

and this converges to g using Lemma 2.1 in Chapter 2. Similarly, from (3.47),

$$(nh)V(\hat{g}) = (\sigma^2 + m^2)f \int K^2(\psi)\,d\psi + o(h).$$

Thus $V(\hat{g}) \to 0$ as $n \to \infty$. These results, along with Chebychev's inequality, mean that $p \lim \hat{g} = g$ as $n \to \infty$. Further, from Theorem 2.6 of Chapter 2, $p \lim \hat{f} = f$. Thus $p \lim \hat{m} = (p \lim \hat{f})^{-1}(p \lim \hat{g}) = g/f = m$.   Q.E.D.

It is useful to derive the limiting distribution in two stages, as this approach isolates the main issues in a proof and can also be applied to the series estimator discussed in later sections. For the kernel estimator the normalizing factor will be $(nh)^{1/2}$ and we will work with the decomposition

$$(nh)^{1/2}(\hat{m} - m) = (nh)^{1/2}(\hat{m} - E_X(\hat{m})) + (nh)^{1/2}(E_X(\hat{m}) - m),$$

---

[6] The weak consistency of $\hat{m}$, under strong conditions, also follows from the asymptotic normality result given later.

where E_X denotes the expectation conditional upon $x_1, \ldots, x_n$. Theorem 3.5 shows that the first term is asymptotically normal, whereas the second, the normalized "bias," converges to zero in probability provided the set of assumptions is strengthened. Throughout our demonstration it is convenient to make x_i a scalar, that is, $q = 1$, although the proofs go through for the more general case. The centering of the estimator at $E_X(\hat{m})$ is unconventional but arises because $\hat{m}$ is the ratio of two random variables, making it very hard to find its exact expectation. It is readily apparent that $E_X(\hat{m}) = (\hat{f})^{-1}(nh)^{-1}\Sigma K_i m_i$, where $\hat{f} = (nh)^{-1}\Sigma K_i$ is a consistent estimator of $f(x)$. The proof parallels that for the density estimator (Theorem 2.9) and so some details are omitted.

Theorem 3.5: Suppose Assumptions (A5), (A6), (A8) and

(A9) $E |u_i|^{2+\delta} < \infty$ and $\int |K(\psi)|^{2+\delta} \, d\psi < \infty$ for some $\delta > 0$

hold. Then $(nh)^{1/2} (\hat{m} - E_X(\hat{m}))$ is asymptotically distributed as

$$\mathcal{N}\left(0, \ f(x)^{-1}\sigma^2 \int K(\psi)^2 \, d\psi\right).$$

Proof: From the definition of the estimator

$$\hat{m} = (\hat{f})^{-1} \left[(nh)^{-1}\Sigma K_i(m_i + u_i)\right], \tag{3.68}$$

and therefore

$$(nh)^{1/2} (\hat{m} - E_X(\hat{m})) = \hat{f}^{-1} \left[(nh)^{-1/2}\Sigma K_i u_i\right]. \tag{3.69}$$

The function $\hat{f}$ converges to $f(x)$ from Chapter 2 so that it is the distribution of the numerator that is of concern. Since $K_i u_i$ is i.i.d. by assumption, $h^{-1/2}K_i u_i$ depends upon n only through h and is therefore a triangular array of random variables; for each row where n is fixed the $h^{-1/2}u_i K_i$ are i.i.d. Applying Liapunov's central limit theorem for i.i.d. random variables in arrays (Chung 1974, p. 209) gives

$$n^{-1/2} \sum h^{-1/2} K_i u_i \xrightarrow{d} \mathcal{N}\left(0, \ \lim_{n\to\infty} E\left(K_i^2 u_i^2 h^{-1}\right)\right)$$

provided that

$$\sum_{i=1}^{n} E \left|n^{-1/2} K_i u_i h^{-1/2}\right|^{2+\delta} \to 0 \text{ as } n \to \infty$$

or if

$$(nh)^{-\delta/2} E |u_i|^{2+\delta} E |K_i|^{2+\delta} h^{-1} \to 0 \text{ as } n \to \infty.$$

But

$$(nh)^{-\delta/2} E |u_i|^{2+\delta} E |K_i|^{2+\delta} h^{-1} \leq (nh)^{-\delta/2} C_1 E \left(K_i^{2+\delta}\right) h^{-1},$$

(3.70)

where $C_1 = E |u_i|^{2+\delta} < \infty$. After making the change of variable $\psi = h^{-1}(x_i - x)$, (3.70) becomes

$$\leq (nh)^{-\delta/2} C_1 \int |K(\psi)|^{2+\delta} f(x + h\psi) \, d\psi.$$

(3.71)

But, by the bounded convergence result of Lemma 2.1,

$$\int |K(\psi)|^{2+\delta} f(x + h\psi) \, d\psi \to f(x) \int |K(\psi)|^{2+\delta} \, d\psi.$$

Thus (3.71) converges to zero since $nh \to \infty$ as $n \to \infty$. In a similar way

$$\lim_{n \to \infty} E \left(K_i^2 h^{-1} u_i^2\right) = \sigma^2 f(x) \int K(\psi)^2 \, d\psi,$$

from which the asymptotic variance follows.   Q.E.D.

An alternative proof of Theorem 3.5 can be given by using the Lindberg–Feller Theorem in the appendix, Section A.2.4. In this case one needs $E u_i^2 < \infty$ instead of the "$2 + \delta$ condition" in assumption A9 (see Gozalo and Linton, 1995). When the possibility that the variance of u_i conditional upon x_i is not a constant is allowed for, the variance of the limiting distribution will be $f(x)^{-1} \sigma^2(x) \int K(\psi)^2 \, d\psi$, where $\sigma^2(x) = E(u_i^2 \mid x_i = x) < \infty$ and is continuous. The simplest way to see why this is so is to think back to the situation when x_i assumed only discrete values. Then the u_i making up $\hat{m}$ would only be those corresponding to $x_i = x$, and the variance of these is $\sigma^2(x)$, so that the central limit theorem will provide $\sigma^2(x)$ as the scale factor. A formal demonstration would involve evaluating

$$E \left(K_i^2 h^{-1} u_i^2\right) = \int K^2(\psi) \sigma^2(x + h\psi) f(x + h\psi) \, d\psi,$$

which tends to $\sigma^2(x) f(x) \int K^2(\psi) \, d\psi$ by bounded convergence.

To eliminate asymptotic bias in the limiting distribution of the estimator we need an additional assumption:

(A10) $(nh)^{1/2} h^2 \to 0$ as $n \to \infty$.

Theorem 3.6 shows that the second term in the decomposition is then asymptotically irrelevant.

Theorem 3.6: Under Assumptions (A3)–(A8) and (A10), $(nh)^{1/2}(E_X(\hat{m}) - m) \to 0$ as $n \to \infty$.

Proof: By substitution

$$(nh)^{1/2}(E_X(\hat{m}) - m) = \hat{f}^{-1}(nh)^{1/2}\left[(nh)^{-1}\sum_{i=1}^{n}(m_i - m)K_i\right]$$

$$= \hat{f}^{-1}(nh)^{-1/2}\sum_{i=1}^{n}\epsilon_i$$

$$= \hat{f}^{-1}d_n,\tag{3.72}$$

where $d_n = (nh)^{-1/2}\sum\epsilon_i$, $\epsilon_i = K_i(m_i - m)$, and the probability limit of each of these terms will be determined. Owing to the consistency of $\hat{f}$ (see Theorem 2.6 in Chapter 2) we only need to show that d_n converges to zero in probability. For this we show that $Ed_n \to 0$ and $V(d_n) \to 0$ as $n \to \infty$.

First,

$$Ed_n = (nh)^{-1/2}\sum E(\epsilon_i) = (nh)^{1/2}\left[h^{-1}E(\epsilon_i)\right]$$

$$= (nh)^{1/2}\left[\int (m(x + h\psi) - m(x))K(\psi)f(x + h\psi)\,d\psi\right]$$

$$= (nh)^{1/2}\left[h^2\mu_2\left(m^{(1)}f^{(1)} + \frac{1}{2}m^{(2)}f\right)\right] + O(h^4),$$

and this converges to zero if $(nh)^{1/2}h^2 \to 0$. Now, because the ϵ_is are i.i.d. we have

$$V(d_n) = Ed_n^2 - (Ed_n)^2$$

$$= \frac{1}{nh}\sum_{i=1}^{n}E\epsilon_i^2 - \frac{1}{nh}\left(\sum_{i=1}^{n}E\epsilon_i\right)^2$$

$$= \frac{1}{h}E\epsilon_1^2 - \frac{n}{h}(E\epsilon_1)^2.\tag{3.73}$$

But

$$h^{-1}E\epsilon_1^2 = h^{-1}E\left(K_1^2(m_1 - m)^2\right)$$

$$= \int (m(x + h\psi) - m(x))^2 K^2(\psi)f(x + h\psi)\,d\psi \to 0$$

as $n \to \infty$ by using the bounded convergence result of Lemma 2.1. Similarly,

$$nh^{-1}(E\epsilon_1)^2 = nh\left[\int (m(x + h\psi) - m(x))K(\psi)f(x + h\psi)\,d\psi\right]^2$$

$$\to 0 \text{ as } n \to \infty.$$

Thus $V(d_n) \to 0$ as $n \to \infty$. Consequently, the $\text{MSE}(d_n) \to 0$ implying that d_n is $o_p(1)$, making (3.72) tend to zero in probability as $n \to \infty$.   Q.E.D.

Consistency follows directly from the fact that $(nh)^{1/2}(\hat{m} - m)$ has a limiting distribution, but it is apparent from the proof of Theorem 3.3 that many of the assumptions made in Theorems 3.4 and 3.5 are not needed if only consistency needed to be established. Moreover, the assumptions are possibly stronger than required to ensure that $(nh)^{1/2}(\hat{m} - m)$ has a limiting distribution. In particular, the boundedness restrictions might be replaced by assumptions about the tail behavior of the functions as $x \to \infty$. The second-order differentiability of m and f may also be relaxed by considering Hölder continuity of K, m, and f. Nevertheless, the proofs are instructive as they show that some smoothness conditions upon the function and the density for x_i are needed. They also highlight a central problem for any kernel estimator that its distribution need not be centered at the true quantity being estimated. Theorem 3.6 removed this potential bias by choice of window width, but this is rarely an efficient means of accomplishing that objective, slowing convergence, as is evident from a comparison of the window widths in (A5) and (A10). As mentioned in the analysis of density estimation (Section 2.4.3) an alternative strategy to eliminate the bias is to construct a kernel with enough higher order moments equal to zero in order to eradicate the $O(h^2)$ terms in $E(d_n)$ and $V(d_n)$ that give rise to the asymptotic bias in Theorem 3.6. Accordingly, (A4) might be replaced by:

(A4)′ The kernel must be of the higher order variety with all moments up to order $(r - 1)$ set to zero and finite rth moment while (A10) is modified to $(nh)^{1/2}h^r \to 0$.

Just as for density estimators it is possible to strengthen the mode of convergence.[7] In many practical applications of the kernel estimator it may be desirable that $\hat{m}$ be a uniformly consistent estimator of m. Theorem 3.7 records the conditions under which $\hat{m}$ has this property (see Bierens, 1987a, p. 114–15). It should be observed that, unlike for the density estimator, uniform convergence of $\hat{m}$ is only over a compact set.

Theorem 3.7: Under the assumptions (A8); $h \to 0$ and $nh^2 \to \infty$ as $n \to \infty$; $f(x)$ is continuous and bounded away from zero uniformly over its support; m is uniformly continuous; and that the characteristic function of

---

[7] As in the earlier sections, we note here that the results and proofs of Theorems 3.5 to 3.7 generalize to q regressors by replacing nh everywhere with nh^q.

$K(\psi)$ is absolutely integrable, that is,

$$\int \left| \int \exp(it\psi) K(\psi)\, d\psi \right| dt \le \infty,$$

$$\sup_x |\hat{m} - m| \to 0 \; a.s. \text{ as } n \to \infty. \tag{3.74}$$

Proof: The outcome described in (3.74) follows by applying the proof of Theorem 2.8.   Q.E.D.

Another issue concerns the rate of convergence to normality for the limiting distribution. Theorem 3.5 (replacing nh by nh^q) emphasizes that this rate depends upon the number of conditioning elements (q) in x_i, and it can be very slow if q is large. For this reason it seems unlikely that a $q > 4$ will be feasible unless very large numbers of observations are available. There are, however, situations when the rate of convergence does not depend upon q, and in fact the standard rate associated with parametric models, $n^{1/2}$, can be attained. One of these is when x_i consists only of discrete random variables. To appreciate why, observe that the kernel estimator can be written as $\hat{m} = \Sigma w_i y_i$, where $w_i = K\big((h^{-1}(x_i - x))/\Sigma K\big(h^{-1}(x_i - x)\big)$. Now, for a discrete random variable, x_i is either equal to x or distant from it by an amount dependent upon the spacing of the possible values the random variable can take. Since the size of this gap is independent of n, $|h^{-1}(x_i - x)|$ must either be zero $(x_i = x)$ or ∞ $(x_i \ne x)$ as n grows (h shrinks), making the corresponding w_i either unity or zero. Ultimately then the kernel estimator behaves like the simple average discussed earlier and must have standard convergence properties. In fact, if x_i consists of q discrete regressors we get $n^{1/2}(\hat{m}(x) - m(x)) \sim \mathcal{N}(0, \sigma^2(x)/f(x))$ as $n \to \infty$. Bierens (1987a) has a rigorous proof of this proposition. Delgado and Mora (1995) report better performance of an estimator that uses the indicator function rather than a kernel when the underlying function being estimated is not smooth and x_i is discrete. In the event that both q_1-dimensional continuous (x_{i1}) and q_2-dimensional discrete (x_{i2}) random variables are present, one might use as kernel a product like $K(\frac{x_{i1}-x_1}{h}) \cdot I(x_{i2} = x_2)$. In this case, we get $(nh^{q_1})^{1/2}(\hat{m}(x) - m(x)) \sim \mathcal{N}(0, \frac{\sigma^2(x)}{f(x)} \int K^2(\psi_1, 0) d\psi_1)$ as $n \to \infty$. Finally, we note that, under suitable assumptions, the asymptotic distributions of the local least squares estimator is identical to that of the Nadaraya–Watson estimator given by Theorems 3.5 and 3.6; see Härdle and Linton (1994), Kneisner and Li (1996), and Gozalo and Linton (1995).

3.4.2 Asymptotic Properties of the Kernel Estimator
with Dependent Observations

There are two ways in which observations might be dependent. One possibility is that u_i is dependent and so y_i will also be dependent, irrespective of x_i. A second is when x_i involves lagged values of y_i and u_i may actually be i.i.d.. In the latter case it is not possible to find the properties of the kernel estimator in the same way as set out in Theorems 3.5 and 3.6; the problem is that one cannot sensibly condition upon x_i. However, some insight can be gained by recognizing that the conditioning was performed to fix the denominator; once this was done the expectation of the ratio in the kernel estimator could be found by just taking the expectation of the numerator. This suggests that we try a similar trick in the dependent observation case. After writing $(nh^q)^{1/2}(\hat{m} - m)$ as $\hat{f}^{-1}(nh^q)^{-1/2}\Sigma K_i(y_i - m)$ and using the notation of Theorem 3.5, we find that replacing $\hat{f}$ by f does not affect the limiting distribution due to the consistency of the estimator of f. Consequently, the asymptotic distribution of the kernel estimator will depend upon that of

$$(nh^q)^{-1/2}\Sigma K_i(y_i - m) = (nh^q)^{-1/2}\sum K_i(y_i - m_i + m_i - m)$$

$$= (nh^q)^{-1/2}\Sigma u_i K_i + (nh^q)^{-1/2}\Sigma K_i(m_i - m);$$

the first part of this expression corresponds to the part investigated in Theorem 3.5, and the second is analogous to the term dealt with in Theorem 3.6. Bias is eliminated under the same conditions as in Theorem 3.6, whilst the distributional result in Theorem 3.5 demands a central limit theorem for $(nh^q)^{-1/2}\sum K_i u_i$.

Traditionally the literature has proceeded to make y_i, x_i stationary random variables obeying some mixing conditions, as K_i will inherit the same mixing properties due to the nature of the kernel. Bierens (1983) proved that the estimator of m was uniformly consistent if conditions similar to those of Theorem 3.7 held, (y_i, x_i) was φ-mixing with $\rho_n = n^{-1}\sum_{k=0}^{n}\varphi(k)^{1/2}$, and the window width satisfied $\lim_{n\to\infty} h^q \rho_n^{-1/2} = \infty$. Robinson's (1983) important work demonstrates that the consistency and asymptotic normality results of the i.i.d. case continue to hold when the series was α-mixing with mixing coefficients $\alpha(k)$ that obeyed the condition $n \sum_n^{\infty} \alpha(k)^{1-2/\delta} = O(1)$ and $E|y|^{\delta} < \infty$, $\delta > 2$. Thus, the asymptotic theory of kernel estimators in the presence of stationary dependent observations is reasonably well developed. The restrictions on the mixing coefficients noted above are the most important limitation of existing theory, but it seems likely that they will be relaxed to some extent in future work.

Little work is available when series are integrated. An exception is that of Hoogstrate (1994) who considered the estimation of $m(x_i)$ in (3.1) under the assumption that $m(x_i)$ is of degree one and $x_i = x_{i-1} + v_i$ is integrated of order one. Using the homogeneity restriction he transforms the data to $y_i^* = n^{-1/2} y_i$, $x_i^* = n^{-1/2} x_i$ and uses these in place of y_i and x_i in forming the kernel estimator. He then shows the consistency of the kernel estimator by using functional central limit theory. Phillips and Park (1998) develop the asymptotic theory of kernel autoregression in the special case of a random walk. They show that the kernel estimator of the regression function is consistent, as in the case of a stationary autoregression. However, the asymptotic distribution of the estimator in the unit root case is mixed normal instead of normal, and that the rate of convergence is slower than that in the stationary case. These important results of Phillips and Park open a new dimension of research in the time series context.

3.5   Bibliographical Summary (Asymptotic Results)

The weak consistency of $\hat{m}$ has been treated in Watson (1964), Rosenblatt (1969), and Noda (1976) for $q = 1$ and by Greblicki and Krzyzak (1980) for $q > 1$. In econometrics this result is discussed in Bierens (1987a) and Singh et al. (1987). Nadaraya (1964) and Noda (1976) give a strong consistency proof, that is, $\hat{m} \to m$ with probability one (almost surely) for $q = 1$. What is interesting is how weak the assumptions can be and yet the asymptotic theory still applies. Much of the theoretical literature on nonparametric estimation concentrates on this question, and some of that work will now be described, see also Benedetti (1977).

A rigorous proof of pointwise consistency (weak as well as strong) was first given by Devroye (1981). Based on that paper weak consistency follows if $E|y| < \infty$, (A5) holds, and there exists a, c_1, and c_2 such that

$$c_1 I(\|\psi\| < a) < K(\psi) < c_2 I(\|\psi\| < a). \tag{3.75}$$

Moreover, if $|y| < \infty$ a.s. and (A9) holds then $\hat{m} \to m$ a.s. for almost all x. Devroye's (1981) weak consistency condition on K is weaker than (A8). Also, his results hold for continuous as well as discrete distributions $F(x)$ of x. However, Devroye's kernels are effectively confined to the "window" class of kernels (i.e., kernels that equal 1 for $\|\psi\| < 1$ and 0 otherwise), a limitation overcome in Greblicki et al. (1984) and Krzyzak and Pawlak (1984) who provide consistency results by replacing $I(x)$ with a nonnegative, nonincreasing function $H(\|x\|)$ having bounded support with a positive radius and $0 < H(0) < \infty$. Kernels satisfying this latter restriction are

$$K(\psi) = \left(1 - \|\psi\|^\delta\right) I(\|\psi\| < a), \quad 0 < \delta < \infty,$$

where $a = 1$. Other types of kernels are also accounted for in Greblicki and Krzyzak (1980), such as those with unbounded support, for example, for $q = 1$,

$K(\psi) = e^{-1}$ for $|x| < e$ and $(|\psi| \log |\psi|)^{-1}$ otherwise. For the proof of strong consistency, also see Zhao and Fang (1985).

Uniform weak consistency of $\hat{m}$ is treated in Bierens (1987a). Uniform strong consistency of $\hat{m}$, that is, $\sup_{a \leq x \leq b} |\hat{m} - m| \rightarrow 0$ $a.s.$, if (A8) holds with K having bounded variation on $a < \psi < b$, f is continuous with $\min_{a \leq x \leq b} f(x) > 0$, m is continuous on R^q, $|y| < c < \infty$ $a.s.$, and

$$\sum_{n=1}^{\infty} \exp(-\alpha n h^{2q}) < \infty. \qquad (3.76)$$

This result was also given by Nadaraya (1964, 1970) for $q = 1$. Devroye (1978) proves uniform strong consistency under a weaker set of conditions than those used by Nadaraya and Bierens; in particular his proof avoids the necessity of bounded variation of K, does not require that X or Y have densities, and K needs only to be of the radial type. In place of (3.76), (A9) holds. Mack and Silverman (1982) determine that the rate of weak and strong (uniform) consistency is $O\big((nh)^{-1} \log h^{-1}\big)^{1/2}$ under a moment condition on y and with K uniformly continuous and of bounded variation.

Although convergence is largely discussed in the L_2 norm there are exceptions to this rule. Devroye and Wagner (1980a) discuss conditions for consistency under the global L_1 criterion, that is, conditions under which $L_1 = \int |\hat{m} - m| F(dx) \rightarrow 0$ in probability or almost surely, where $F(dx)$ represents a probability measure for x. Distribution-free consistency results were first established by Stone (1977) when he showed that a large class of weighted regression estimators (e.g., (3.15)) satisfy $EL_1 \rightarrow 0$ for *all* possible distributions of (y, x) having $E|y| < \infty$. Similar results were developed for the kernel estimator by Devroye and Wagner (1980b). Stone (1977) and Devroye and Wagner (1980b) established that $E \int |\hat{m} - m|^p F(dx) \rightarrow 0$ as $n \rightarrow \infty$ under the same conditions as for $p = 1$, but with $E|y|^p < \infty$.

The joint asymptotic normality of $\hat{m}(x_1), \ldots, \hat{m}(x_L)$ at the L fixed points $x_1, \ldots, x_L$ was first shown by Schuster (1972) for $q = 1$ and later by Bierens (1987a), Singh et al. (1987), and Rilstone (1987) for $q > 1$. These papers also point to the fact that the asymptotic covariance matrix of $\hat{m}(x_1), \ldots, \hat{m}(x_L)$ is diagonal.

For the recursive estimators $\tilde{m}^2$ and $\tilde{m}^3$ given in (3.22) and (3.23), Ahmad and Lin (1976) treated consistency for $\tilde{m}^3$; Greblicki and Krzyzak (1980) considered weak consistency of both $\tilde{m}^2$ and $\tilde{m}^3$. Essentially, weak consistency of these estimators is obtained under the same set of circumstances as for $\hat{m}$ but with $\sum h_i^q \rightarrow \infty$ substituted for (A5).

When observations are dependent, consistency and asymptotic normality results are given in Robinson (1983) and Bierens (1983, 1987a). Both of these papers allow x_i to be lagged values of y_i, whereas Roussas (1989) and Fan

(1990a, 1990c) treat the case when x_i is strongly exogenous. For the nonstationary time series case, see Phillips and Park (1998).

3.6   Implementing the Kernel Estimator

The kernel estimator is very easy to implement. Once a window width and kernel are selected, $K\left(h^{-1}(x_i - x)\right)$ is computed for each value of the x_i in the sample and the numerator and denominator of (3.14) are then found by summation. Although the point x is set by the investigator, many applications of kernel estimators require x to be a point in the sample, x_J, and in that case the summations should probably delete the Jth observation, for reasons discussed in connection with local averaging. Confidence intervals can be attached to the estimate of the nonparametric mean using Theorem 3.5, and that for the variance could be found from (3.77) given later. When evaluating the variance of $(nh)^{1/2}(\hat{m} - m)$, $f(x)^{-1}\sigma^2(x) \int K(\psi)^2 \, d\psi$ needs to be determined. For a standard normal kernel $\int K(\psi)^2 \, d\psi = (4\pi)^{-1/2} = .2821$, found by expressing $K(\psi)^2$ as the product of a constant and an $\mathcal{N}(0, 1/2)$ random variable, $f(x)$ can be estimated as described in Chapter 2. The term $\sigma^2(x)$ will be replaced by $\hat{\sigma}^2(x) = \sum \hat{u}_i^2 K(\psi_i)/\sum K(\psi_i)$, where $\hat{u}_i = y_i - \hat{m}(x_i)$ is the nonparametric residual and $\hat{m}(x_i)$ estimates $E(y_i \mid x = x_i)$.

3.6.1   Choice of Window Width

The key questions about kernel estimators therefore devolve to selection of kernel and window width. Because we are effectively computing a density, all the kernels set out in Chapter 2 can be utilized again. In fact, all the points made about kernels and window widths in connection with density estimation apply forthwith. This material will not be repeated. Readers are merely reminded that it is believed that the choice of kernel is not crucial, that there are a number of ways to eliminate the asymptotic bias problem, and that data should be transformed to standardized form before entry into kernels.

A key way of eliminating bias in density estimators was to use higher order kernels. When estimating moments an alternative sometimes suggested is a procedure known as "twicing."[8] Define the residual $\hat{u}_i = y_i - \hat{m}(x_i)$ and define a modified estimator of $m(x)$ as $\hat{m}(x) + (nh)^{-1} \sum K((x_i - x)/h)(y_i - \hat{m}(x_i))$. From the formula for $\hat{m}(x_i)$, it is evident that the "twicing" estimator could be approximately regarded as a kernel estimator with kernel $2K(\psi) - \int_{-\infty}^{\infty} K(\psi - v)K(v) \, dv$. Comparisons of the efficiency of twicing versus other methods of bias adjustment could therefore be made directly. An obvious

8 Due originally to Tukey and studied in this context by Stützle and Mittal (1979).

disadvantage of twicing is the need to compute $\hat{m}(x_i)$, that is, we will need to compute $n + 1$ conditional moments to correct a single one.

The determination of a window width for moment estimation does have some twists that merit mention. As well as trying to choose h to minimize a number of mean square error criteria, for example $\int (\hat{m} - m)^2$, $E(\int (\hat{m} - m)^2)$, it has been suggested that the Average Squared Error (ASE), $n^{-1} \sum_{i=1}^{n} (\hat{m}(x_i) - m(x_i))^2$, or its expectation (MASE) could be suitable candidates. Alternatively, one might work with the mean integrated squared error

$$\text{MISE} = E\left[\int_{-\infty}^{\infty} (\hat{m}(x) - m(x))^2 \, dx \right].$$

Cross validation is frequently performed in this case by minimizing the estimated prediction error EPE, $n^{-1} \Sigma (y_i - \hat{m}(x_i))^2$, with respect to h, where $\hat{m}_i = \hat{m}(x_i)$ is computed as the "leave-one-out" estimator deleting the ith observation in the sums. To appreciate why minimizing EPE is sensible notice that, when the "leave-one-out" estimator is employed and observations are independent, $\hat{m}_i$ is independent of y_i, meaning that $E(\hat{m}_i (y_i - m_i)) = 0$, and so $E(\text{EPE}) = \sigma^2 + E(n^{-1} \Sigma (\hat{m}_i - m_i)^2) = \sigma^2 + \text{MASE}$. Minimizing $E(\text{EPE})$ with respect to h is therefore equivalent to minimizing MASE with respect to h. Unfortunately, minimizing the *sample* EPE tends to produce an estimator of h that converges only extremely slowly to the value of h minimizing $E(\text{EPE})$, of order $n^{-1/10}$ (Härdle, Hall, and Marron, 1988). Marron (1988) has further discussion of the difficulties associated with this estimator, also see Clark (1980) for more on cross validation.

An alternative line of attack that seems promising is to recognize the close connection between the window width and the choice of the number of parameters in any regression aiming to approximate the unknown function. The idea is to penalize the "goodness of fit function" for too many parameters. If EPE is taken to define the function some penalty should be attached to h.[9] The principle is a direct descendent from the solution to selecting the order of an autoregression in time series analysis formulated by Akaike (1974). Many penalty functions have been derived for time series models (see Chow (1983) for a survey), and Rice (1984a) adapted these penalty functions to bandwidth selection, that is, he chose h to minimize the product of EPE and $\zeta(h)$, where $\zeta(h)$ is the penalty term. Examples of $\zeta(h)$ are $\exp(2n^{-1}h^{-1}K(0))$ (corresponding to Akaike's criterion), $\zeta(h) = (1 + 2n^{-1}h^{-1}K(0))$ (Shibata's criterion), and $\zeta(h) = (1 - 2n^{-1}h^{-1}K(0))^{-1}$ (Rice's T). Rice showed that the estimators of h obtained in this way converge to the h minimizing MASE. In a simulation study Härdle et al. (1988) found that Rice's T was best, but this may be misleading

---

[9] It is necessary to use all observations when forming $\hat{m}(x_i)$ for use in these criteria; that is, one penalizes $n^{-1} \sum (y_i - \hat{m}_i)^2$, where $\hat{m}_i$ is the regular kernel estimator.

as their experiment featured fixed and equally spaced x_i, and criteria other than Rice's tended to give global minima that implied no smoothing. The idea of a penalty function is an attractive one, however, since it opens up the possibility of adapting the "model selection" literature to window width determination. As an example, Mallows (1973) formulated a criterion C_p by examining the ability of a regression model to predict a hypothetical set of n observations in the future. Application of this idea here results in the criterion n^{-1} EPE $+ (2\sigma^2 K(0)/nh)$. Li (1987) has analyzed this approach and Marron (1988) claims that the C_p method has the advantage that it is good for handling cases where h is close to zero, whereas cross validation is very poor in that context. Andrews (1991c) considers modifications of these criteria when the u_i are heteroskedastic. One advantage that the penalty criteria possess is that they are easily applied to the selection of any unknown parameter. Thus, the number of nearest neighbors, the smoothing parameter in splines, etc. could all be chosen in this way.

In principle, "plug-in" estimators of h can be constructed, but there has not been a great deal of enthusiasm for this approach, unlike the situation with density estimation. A recent treatment is by Härdle, Hall, and Marron (1992). Another interesting recent solution advanced by Härdle and Bowman (1988) is to estimate MASE by bootstrapping and to then minimize the simulated MASE with respect to h. At least for the scalar x_i case that they deal with the method seemed to be quite successful, judged by the complex functions estimated. Moreover, they observe that a by-product of the approach is a confidence interval for $\hat{m}$ that may well be superior to the predictions of the asymptotic theory.

Despite all these endeavors, in some ways it is still unclear whether automatic bandwidth selection is preferable to "eye-balling." If the expectation is to be evaluated at only a limited number of points x, and x is of no more than two dimensions, there is much to be said for selecting h by graphical methods. But, with higher dimensional x, and evaluation at a large number of points, some automatic method of selection may be necessary. At this stage cross validation seems to be the preferred method, although its unpredictability means that one cannot be entirely comfortable with its use.[10]

In principle the move from independent to dependent observations should not change the way window width selection is done. However, the fact that

---

[10] Don Andrews has pointed out to us that another disadvantage of automatic window width procedures is that they determine an h that violates the restrictions placed on it when proving asymptotic normality. The reason is that automatic methods work by forcing the ratio of bias and variance to tend to a constant, whereas one wishes the ratio to tend to zero so as to center the limiting distribution for $\hat{m}$ at m (Theorem 3.6). Of course one might always define h as a weighted average of a window width satisfying Theorems 3.5 and 3.6 and an automatic choice, where the weight on the latter shrinks to zero as $n \to \infty$. That is, in practice investigators could presumably switch from data-dependent to deterministic rules for h as their sample size becomes very large.

theorems establishing consistency and asymptotic normality of the estimator frequently feature restrictions involving both the window width and the sum of mixing coefficients, for example Bierens (1983) and Robinson (1986a), hints that a larger window width might be needed for good sample performance as the degree of serial correlation increases. That is, although the bias of the estimator does not depend on the extent of serial correlation in the errors $y_i - E(y_i \mid x_i)$, the variance does, so that the optimal choice of h must depend on this feature. Robinson (1986a) makes this contention, although his analytic work only weakly supports it. Nevertheless, he does mention some Monte Carlo experiments where he has found this to be the case, and the point needs further attention. Altman (1990), working with (3.1), a fixed regressor over $(0,1)$, and serial correlation in the u_i, and using the Priestly–Chao estimator, found that the optimal window width was larger (smaller) relative to the situation when u_i was independent with the same variance, if the sum of the autocorrelations of the u_i process was positive (negative). Herrmann et al. (1992), using the same configuration of assumptions, except that the kernel estimator was that of Gasser and Müller (1979) instead of Priestly–Chao, showed that the optimal window width has σ_u^2 replaced by the "long-run variance" of u_i, the spectral density of u_i at zero, $\phi = \sigma_u^2 + \sum_{j=2}^{\infty} \text{cov}(u_1, u_j)$. Hence, whether the window width is too large or too narrow depends upon the ratio of σ_u^2 to ϕ. For most economic time series this is likely to be less than unity as the serial correlations are positive, and therefore the window width needs to be widened. When the x_i are not from an equally spaced design the situation is more complex. Conditioning upon the x_i, it is clear from (3.69) that the variance will now be $\hat{f}^{-2}(nh)^{-1}\left(\text{var}(K_1u_1) + 2\sum_{j=2}^{\infty} \text{cov}(K_1u_1, K_ju_j)\right)$ and the extent of over- or underprediction depends upon the sign of $2\sum_{j=2}^{\infty} \text{cov}(K_1u_1, K_ju_j)$.

The discussion above was focused upon short-range dependence in u_i, whereas increasingly attention has been paid to long-range dependence in which the kth autocorrelation coefficient dies away like $c_3 k^{-\alpha}$ rather than geometrically. Hall and Hart (1990) found the value of h minimizing the asymptotic MISE in such circumstances to be of the form $(c_3 \alpha c_4 / [n^\alpha c_2^2 \int_0^1 f(x)(m^{(2)}(x))^2 dx])^{\frac{1}{2p+\alpha}}$, where $f(x)$ is p times differentiable, $m(x)$ is a function over $(0, 1)$ with x_i equispaced, and c_j are constants depending upon α and the kernel used. Ray and Tsay (1997) provide an iterative algorithm for estimating the unknown values in this formula.

Much of the discussion above has been very similar to that presented in density estimation. There is however an important difference between the two. Because $\hat{f}(x)$ appears in the denominator of the expression for $\hat{m}$, a very small value of $\hat{f}(x)$ can result in a very large estimate for m. Such an event is merely a warning that x should not be taken from the tails of the density of x_i, and it is unlikely to occur when conditional moments are being evaluated at a point chosen by the investigator. However, there exist circumstances when it is necessary to compute $\hat{m}_i$ for all x_i values in the sample, and some of these might well be in the tails. For this reason, it is a standard procedure to trim the estimator of m_i to safeguard against a very large estimate for $\hat{m}_i$ that could seriously distort the average.

Trimming can be done in a number of ways. Robinson (1986a) eliminates all observations from the average that have $\hat{f}(x_i)$ lying below a number b_n, and this is probably the simplest strategy. The trimming parameter, b_n, depends upon the sample size and should converge to zero as $n \rightarrow \infty$. Because of this dependence upon n it interacts with the window width in statement of theorems. For example, Robinson requires $nh^{2q}b_n^4 \rightarrow \infty$, as well as some other restrictions. In his simulation work he set b_n to .01, 0.005, and .001, corresponding to $n = 25$, 50, and 200 respectively.

3.7   Robust Nonparametric Estimation of Moments

As mentioned in Section 3.2.4 one way to think of the origin of the Nadaraya–Watson estimator of m is as the solution to a set of first-order conditions $[\Sigma (y_i - \hat{m})K_i] = 0$. The role of K_i is to only give weight to observations that are close to x; when K_i was an indicator function, solving the first-order conditions made the nonparametric estimator $\hat{m}$ the sample mean of the corresponding y_i. It is well known that the mean is only an efficient estimator of m if the errors u_i are normally distributed, a theme we will return to in Chapter 5. When errors are not normal it has been suggested that m be estimated from a different set of first-order conditions that have zero expectation but which tend to down-weight observations even more. Take the case when x_i assumes only discrete values as an example. Rather than finding m by solving the sample analogue of $E[(y_i - m)I(x_i = x)] = 0$, one might instead solve $E[\rho(y_i - m)I(x_i = x)] = 0$, where $\rho(\cdot)$ is a bounded, nondecreasing, odd function of its argument. Examples of such functions are $\rho(\psi) = \text{sgn}(\psi)$ or $\rho(\psi) = \max[-c, \min(\psi, c)]$ for some constant c. The sample analogue of the first of these functions will be $n^{-1}\Sigma \, \text{sgn}(y_i - m)I_i$, and the estimator of m that sets this sample moment to zero is the *median* of the observations that correspond to x.

When one moves to the situation when x_i is a continuous random variable the sample moment to be equated to zero will be $n^{-1}\Sigma\rho(y_i - m)K_i$, where K_i is the kernel. This idea seems to have initially been suggested by Stone (1977) and has been extended by Tsybakov (1982), Härdle (1984), Robinson (1984), and Härdle and Tsybakov (1988). The first three papers deal with the estimation of the conditional mean whereas the last also deals with the conditional variance, or, as it is known in the robust estimation literature, the joint estimation of location and scale. It is necessary to differentiate the two as the $\rho(\cdot)$ function that is appropriate varies. When estimating a conditional variance an even function is needed and Härdle and Tsybakov propose $\rho(\cdot) = \min(c^2, \psi^2) - \beta$, where $0 < \beta < c^2$.

Robinson (1984) and Härdle and Tsybakov (1988) discuss the assumptions needed for the estimator of the conditional mean to be asymptotically normal with covariance matrix

$$\left(\int K(\psi)^2 \, d\psi\right) \left(\int \rho^2(y-m) f(y\,|\,x) dy\right) \Big/ \{(\partial v/\partial m)'(\partial v/\partial m)\} f(x),$$

(3.77)

where $v = E(\rho(y-m)) = \int \rho(y-m) f(y\,|\,x)\,dy$. The same formula holds when estimating the standard deviation σ except that the argument in $\rho(\cdot)$ will be $\sigma^{-1}(y-m)$. Moreover, asymptotically, the estimators of m and σ will be uncorrelated, just as is true for generalized least squares estimators. It is instructive to observe that, when $\rho = y - m$, the variance of $(nh)^{1/2}(\hat{m} - m)$ reduces to that given in Theorem 3.5 earlier, whereas if $\rho = (y-m)^2/\sigma^2$, one would get the kernel estimator of the conditional variance. Equation (3.77) therefore gives the asymptotic variance of the kernel-conditional variance estimator just by this substitution. Note also that the robust procedure will also exhibit an asymptotic bias unless steps are taken to remove it by one of the procedures set out in Chapter 2.

3.8 Estimating Conditional Moments by Series Methods

Early methods for estimating (3.1) in the context of production and demand functions, such as flexible functional forms, took their inspiration from the idea that $m(x_i)$ could be approximated by a polynomial series in x_i, although only a fixed number of terms in this series representation were actually retained in estimation. Gallant (1982) and Geman and Huang (1982) extended this approach by proposing instead that the number of terms, M, be allowed to expand with the sample size, thereby approximating (3.1) with

$$y_i = \sum_{k=1}^{M} z_{ik}\theta_k + v_i = z_i'\theta + v_i.$$

(3.78)

A "series" or "sieve" estimator of m is then $\hat{m}^s = \sum_{k=1}^{M} z_{ik}\hat{\theta}_k$, where $\hat{\theta}$ was obtained by regressing y_i against z_i. The basic idea is therefore to *globally* approximate $m(x_i)$ by the linear series $z_i'\theta$, and subsequently to get a local approximation by replacing z_i by z, the values of the approximating variables corresponding to x. It only remains to select z_i. Geman and Huang (1982) set the z_{ik} to the trigonometric terms $\sin(kx_i)$, $\cos(kx_i)$, $k = 1, \ldots, (M/2)$ (assuming for the moment that x_i is a scalar). Gallant's modification of this was to define the *flexible Fourier form* that augments the trigonometric terms with a quadratic polynomial in x_i, making his regressors x_i, x_i^2, $\cos(x_i)$, $\sin(x_i)$, $\cos(2x_i)$, $\sin(2x_i)$, etc. Candidates for z_i, other than the trigonometric forms mentioned above, have been the class of Muntz–Satz polynomials (Barnett and Yue, 1988), spline polynomials (Wahba, 1986), logistic functions as in neural networks, and Bernstein or Chebyshev polynomials. As will be seen later, what is a good choice for z_i is determined by the need for the approximation of $m(x_i)$ by $z_i'\theta$ to improve at a certain rate as the sample size tends to infinity. Series estimators such as these have been described by Gallant (1987) as "seminonparametric" (SNP); their orientation is nonparametric but their *modus operandi* is parametric. It is this last characteristic that makes them especially attractive, as estimation is performed in a familiar environment.

As seen above the concept is a very simple one when x_i is a scalar, but it is not immediately apparent what the generalization is to higher dimensions (i.e., when x_i is $(q \times 1)$). The desired extension is achieved with the device of treating k in the trigonometric terms as a $q \times 1$ vector, rather than a scalar, whose elements are integers with *absolute* values summing to a number (k^*) less than a prescribed value (K^*). After that the Fourier series is in terms of $k'x_i$, and M is determined as a function of q and K^*. These vectors, k, are referred to as *multi-indices*. Examples of multi-indices for $q = 3$ would be $k' = (0, 1, -1)$, $k' = (1, 0, -1)$, $k' = (1, 1, -1)$, giving $k^* = 2$, 2, and 3 respectively. The rules for construction of the k vectors are as follows (Gallant, 1981, p. 215), and a FORTRAN program for generating the multi-indices is available in Monahan (1981).

(i) Delete from $\mathcal{H} = \{k : k^* \leq K^*\}$ the zero vector and any k whose first nonzero element is negative, i.e., $(0, -1, 1)$ would be deleted but $(0, 1, -1)$ would remain.
(ii) Delete any k whose components have a common integral divisor, i.e., $(0, 2, 4)$ would be deleted but $(0, 2, 3)$ would remain.
(iii) Arrange the k that remain into a sequence $\{k_\ell; \ell = 1, 2, \ldots, L\}$ such that k_ℓ is nondecreasing in ℓ and such that the first q of the k_ℓs, $k_1, k_2, \ldots, k_q$, are the elementary vectors. For $q = 3$, $K^* = 3$, the sequence is displayed in Table 3.1.

Using these ideas, the multivariate extension for the Fourier approximation has the format

$$y_i = \sum_{\ell=1}^{L} \sum_{j=1}^{J} \left(\gamma_{j\ell} \cos\left(jk_\ell'x_i \right) + \delta_{j\ell} \sin\left(jk_\ell'x_i \right) \right). \tag{3.79}$$

Table 3.1. *Multi-indices* $\{k_l\}$ *for* $q = 3$, $K^* = 3$.

k^*	1	2	3
	$(1, 0, 0)$	$(1, 1, 0)$	$(1, 1, 1)$
	$(0, 1, 0)$	$(1, 0, 1)$	$(1, -1, 1)$
	$(0, 0, 1)$	$(0, 1, 1)$	$(1, 1, -1)$
		$(1, -1, 0)$	$(1, -1, -1)$
		$(1, 0, -1)$	$(0, 1, 2)$
		$(0, 1, -1)$	$(0, 2, 1)$
			$(1, 2, 0)$
			$(1, 0, 2)$
			$(2, 1, 0)$
			$(2, 0, 1)$
			$(0, 1, -2)$
			$(0, 2, -1)$
			$(1, -2, 0)$
			$(1, 0, -2)$
			$(2, -1, 0)$
			$(2, 0, -1)$

It might be asked why there is a double summation here rather than the single summation in (3.78). The reason is that many of the multi-indices appearing in the definition of a generalized Fourier representation are multiples of the minimal set defined by the three rules above. Thus the summation over j is designed to account for the fact that the sequence $\{k_\ell\}$, as defined by the rules, does not contain terms such as $(0,2,4)$, which would appear in a Fourier expansion. Clearly $(0,2,4)$ is twice $(0,1,2)$ and the latter is in the class of $\{k_\ell\}$ defined above (see Table 3.1). When $q = 1$, K^* would be unity, $k = 1$, and $J = M/2$, making (3.79) agree with (3.78) if z_{ik} is either $\cos(kx_i)$ or $\sin(kx_i)$ (note that a constant term would normally appear in both (3.78) and (3.79) but this has been suppressed).

In a similar fashion to kernel estimation (see Section 3.2.6) it is possible to utilize SNP methods to estimate a number of conditional moments. Taking the variance of y_i, conditional on $X = x$, as the example, it could be estimated either from the formula $E(y_i^2 \mid X = x) - m^2$ or from the fact that $E\left(w_i^2 \mid X = x\right) = \sigma^2(x)$, where $w_i = y_i - m_i$. In the first formulation each of the conditional expectations is estimated separately and then combined. In the second the residuals $\hat{w}_i = y_i - \hat{m}_i$ are formed, where $\hat{m}_i$ is the estimate of the conditional mean of y_i when x takes the value observed for it at the ith point in the sample. After that $\hat{w}_i^2$ is regressed against z_i and $\sigma^2(x)$ is estimated as $z'\hat{\theta}$.

Because $E\left(y_i^2 \mid X = x\right)$ involves the square of the conditional mean, the terms in z_i to approximate this term must be more extensive than needed to capture m alone. By itself that makes the second procedure appealing, but its attraction is heightened by the feature that, when m_i is linear in the x_i, the procedure is the same as used in diagnosing heteroskedasticity (Amemiya, 1977; Pagan and Hall, 1983), leaving aside the fact that an approximation to the true function is now being attempted.

It is not always the case that the conditional expectation is taken to involve a completely unknown mapping with x_i. There are instances in which $m(x_i)$ is a linear function of some variables (x_{1i}) but a nonlinear function of the remaining variables x_{2i}. For example, Engle et al. (1986) explain electricity demand by a series of variables but only time of day affects demand nonlinearly. Another instance potentially arises from the sample selectivity literature in which the x_{2i} represent variables that determine whether an individual is self-selected into or out of a sample, since then it is known that the mean of y_i is influenced by x_{1i} and x_{2i}. In Heckman's (1976) two-step method of estimation, a precise form for $m_1(x_{2i})$ is found by making some strong distributional assumptions, but one may not be willing to do this. Despite such a connection, treating the selectivity model in this way would not be very efficient as it ignores the fact that m_1 is actually a function of a linear combination of the x_{2i}, and so only a scalar rather than a vector of variables enters nonlinearly into the relation. Such models are termed single-index models and will be studied more intensively in Chapters 7 and 8.

3.9   Asymptotic Properties of Series Estimators with Independent Observations

Intuitively it seems reasonable to argue that the prediction from the series representation (3.78), $\hat{m}^s$, will be a consistent estimator of m provided $M \to \infty$ as $n \to \infty$. But it might also be supposed that some restrictions need to be placed upon the quality of the approximation in that any associated error will be absorbed into v_i in (3.78), and this may affect the statistical properties of the estimator. Normality of the estimator is more problematical and the conditions upon approximations and data are likely to be much more stringent. Below, convergence of the estimator to normality is analyzed. As is common in the asymptotic theory of estimators, once asymptotic normality has been established weak consistency follows directly, and for this reason we concentrate solely upon the former property. Obviously, consistency could be proven under a much weaker set of assumptions than laid out below, but it is hard to imagine why one would be interested in just a point estimate. The proof given below is not complete, being adapted from a more general statement by Andrews (1991a), but it aims to highlight the requirements upon M, the number of terms in the approximation, and the quality of the approximation needed to ensure desirable limiting properties for $\hat{m}^S$.

Define Z as the $(n \times M)$ matrix with z_i' as the ith row, z as the values of the approximating variables corresponding to x, $\hat{\theta} = (Z'Z)^{-1}Z'y$, and $\hat{m}^s = z'\hat{\theta}$. The following assumptions will be used in various parts of the proof.

(B1) u_i in (3.1) is i.i.d. with the mean 0 and variance σ^2, $\sigma^2 < \infty$.

(B2) The x_i are fixed.

(B3) For some $0 < r < 1$, $M = C_1 n^r$, where C_1 is a finite positive constant.

(B4) The elements in z, z_i, the approximating function $z_i'\theta_{(n)}$, and the function $m(x)$ are uniformly bounded by a constant C_4 for all $i \geq 1$.

(B5) $\lambda_{\min}(Z'Z)/M \to \infty$ as $n \to \infty$, where $\lambda(\cdot)$ indicates an eigenvalue.

(B6) There exists $\theta_{(n)}$ such that $M^{(1/2r)} \sup_x |z'\theta_{(n)} - m(x)| \to 0$ as $n \to \infty$, where z is defined as the vector corresponding to any value of x.

(B7) $v = \sigma^2(z'(Z'Z)^{-1}z) \geq C_3/n$ for all large n.

The assumptions above are labeled "B" to differentiate them from the earlier ones "A" for the kernel estimator. Assumptions (B1) and (B2) can be relaxed. Indeed, Andrews proves the limiting properties with heteroskedastic errors, although the conditional variance σ_i^2 needs to be bounded for proofs. Furthermore, he observes that, since these properties do not depend upon the x_i when it is strongly exogenous, treating x_i as fixed can be done without loss of generality. Assumption (B4), might also be relaxed in a way that will be evident from the proofs. Assumption (B5) cannot be changed much but is likely to be fairly weak. It is (B6) that is very important. It could be interpreted in either of two ways: first, as a constraint on the smoothness of the underlying function $m(x)$ – if the function is not smooth enough it will be hard to get an approximation satisfying (B6); second, as a restriction upon the type of approximation being employed – the global linear approximation $z'\theta_{(n)}$ to $m(x)$ that improves in a specific way as $n \to \infty$. Fourier series approximations possess this property (Edmunds and Moscatelli, 1977, Corollary 1), provided that the data are *restricted to lie between* $(0, 2\pi)$ $((0, 2\pi)^q$ in the multivariate case). Therefore, if the Fourier series approximation is to be employed, care must be taken to ensure that data have been appropriately scaled. Obviously, if one can find other approximations that obey (B6), these could also provide alternative series expansions; for example, the Muntz–Satz expansion has been shown to have the requisite property as have power series and splines (with fixed knots) – see Newey (1997). Assumption (B6) plays the same role in the asymptotic theory of series estimators that (A3)–(A5) performed for kernel estimators, forcing the approximation error to zero and implicitly imposing some smoothness conditions upon the underlying function being estimated.

If (3.78) were exact $v = \sigma^2 z'(Z'Z)^{-1}z$ would be the variance of $\hat{m}^s$, leading us to consider the properties of $v^{-1/2}(\hat{m}^s - m)$. To emphasize the common problems that arise with nonparametric estimators, it is again useful to employ the decomposition

$$v^{-1/2}(\hat{m}^s - m) = v^{-1/2}(\hat{m}^s - E(\hat{m}^s)) + v^{-1/2}(E(\hat{m}^s) - m),$$

and the proof parallels that of the kernel estimator. Theorem 3.8 demonstrates that the first term is asymptotically normal under assumptions (B1)–(B5), and this replicates Theorem 3.5 for the series estimator, whereas Theorem 3.9 corresponds to Theorem 3.6 in showing that the second term is $o_p(1)$. Assumption (B6) is only needed for Theorem 3.9. If the second term does not go to zero the limiting distribution would not be centered at zero and would exhibit an "asymptotic bias," a problem encountered earlier when discussing density and moment estimation by the kernel method. However, unlike that estimator it is very hard to give a closed-form expression for the bias.

As a prelude to Theorems 3.8 and 3.9 we state and prove a result on inequalities for quadratic forms that is used later.

Lemma 3.2: If $d = v^{-1/2}z'(Z'Z)^{-1}Z'\varphi$, where φ is an $n \times 1$ vector and $v = \sigma^2 z'(Z'Z)^{-1}z$,

$$|d| \leq \sigma^{-1}\left[\varphi' Z(Z'Z)^{-1}Z'\varphi\right]^{1/2}, \tag{3.80}$$

$$|d| \leq \sigma^{-1}\left[\varphi' Z Z'\varphi \, \lambda_{\min}^{-1}(Z'Z)\right]^{1/2}, \tag{3.81}$$

$$|d| \leq \sigma^{-1}[\varphi'\varphi]^{1/2}. \tag{3.82}$$

Proof: d can be written as

$$d = \left\{v^{-1/2}z'(Z'Z)^{-1/2}\right\}\left\{(Z'Z)^{-1/2}Z'\varphi\right\}, \tag{3.83}$$

to which the Cauchy–Schwartz inequality can be applied to produce

$$|d| \leq \left\{v^{-1}z'(Z'Z)^{-1}z\right\}^{1/2}\left\{\varphi' Z(Z'Z)^{-1}Z'\varphi\right\}^{1/2} \tag{3.84}$$

$$= \sigma^{-1}\left[\varphi' Z(Z'Z)^{-1}Z'\varphi\right]^{1/2} \tag{3.85}$$

as the first term in (3.84) is σ^{-1} by the definition of v. Then

$$|d| \leq \sigma^{-1}\left[\varphi' Z Z'\varphi \, \lambda_{\min}^{-1}(Z'Z)\right]^{1/2} \tag{3.86}$$

because

$$\lambda_{\min}\left[(Z'Z)^{-1}\right] I_M \leq (Z'Z)^{-1} \leq \lambda_{\max}\left[(Z'Z)^{-1}\right] I_M$$

and

$$\lambda_{\max}\left[(Z'Z)^{-1}\right] = \lambda_{\min}^{-1}[Z'Z].$$

Finally,

$$|d| \le \sigma^{-1}[\varphi'\varphi]^{1/2} \tag{3.87}$$

from (3.85) by the fact that $\varphi'Z(Z'Z)^{-1}Z'\varphi \le \lambda_{\max}[Z(Z'Z)^{-1}Z]\varphi'\varphi$ and $Z(Z'Z)^{-1}Z'$ is idempotent. Q.E.D.

Theorem 3.8 will be concerned with the distribution of $\hat{m}^s$ centered at its expected value. Since the x_i are being taken as fixed there is no difference between the conditional and unconditional expectations, and therefore the centering is exactly the same as employed in Theorem 3.5 dealing with the kernel estimator. To appreciate the significance of the centering note that $\hat{\theta} = (Z'Z)^{-1}Z'y$, making

$$\hat{m}^s = z'\hat{\theta} = z'(Z'Z)^{-1}Z'\left[Z\theta_{(n)} + \left(m - Z\theta_{(n)} + u\right)\right] \tag{3.88}$$
$$= z'\theta_{(n)} + z'(Z'Z)^{-1}Z'u + z'(Z'Z)^{-1}Z'\left(m - Z\theta_{(n)}\right), \tag{3.89}$$

where m is the $n \times 1$ vector containing m_i as ith element. Subtracting m from both sides of (3.89) gives

$$\hat{m}^s - m = \left[z'\theta_{(n)} - m\right] + \left[z'(Z'Z)^{-1}Z'\left(m - Z\theta_{(n)}\right)\right] + z'(Z'Z)^{-1}Z'u. \tag{3.90}$$

Looking at (3.90) it is apparent that the first two terms in square brackets constitute $E(\hat{m}^s - m)$ as the last term has zero expectation. Consequently, unless the approximation improves as $n \to \infty$, there will be a bias in the series estimator of m. Ignoring the case when $m(x)$ is linear in z, there will always be a small sample bias since these two terms will never be zero. Centering $\hat{m}^s$ at $E(\hat{m}^s)$ therefore means that the asymptotic distribution depends only upon $z'(Z'Z)^{-1}Z'u$. Theorem 3.8 establishes the distribution of $v^{-1/2}(\hat{m}^s - E(\hat{m}^s))$ using this fact.

Theorem 3.8: Under Assumptions (B1)–(B5), $v^{-1/2}(\hat{m}^s - E(\hat{m}^s)) \xrightarrow{d} \mathcal{N}(0, 1)$.

Proof: As shown above $\hat{m}^s - E(\hat{m}^s) = z'(Z'Z)^{-1}Z'u$ and $v^{-1/2}(\hat{m}^s - E(\hat{m}^s)) = v^{-1/2}z'(Z'Z)^{-1}Z'u = D'u$. From Huber (1973) $D'u \to \mathcal{N}(0, 1)$ if $\max_i |d_i| \to 0$ and $\lim_{n\to\infty} D'D > 0$. By definition $D'D = \sigma^{-2} > 0$ and $d_i = v^{-1/2}z'(Z'Z)^{-1}Z'e_i$, where e_i is an $n \times 1$ vector with unity in the ith place and zeros elsewhere. Applying Lemma 3.2, inequality (3.86), to d_i gives

$$\max_i |d_i| \leq \sigma^{-1} \left[\left(\max_i e_i' Z Z' e_i \right) \lambda_{\min}^{-1}(Z'Z) \right]^{1/2}$$

$$\leq \sigma^{-1} \left[M C_4^2 \lambda_{\min}^{-1}(Z'Z) \right]^{1/2}$$

by (B4), and this tends to zero by (B5), so that Huber's condition on $|d_i|$ holds. Q.E.D.

It is apparent from the proof of Theorem 3.8 that the main difficulty in getting asymptotic normality for the series around m lies in proving that $v^{-1/2}(E(\hat{m}^s) - m^s)$ converges in probability to zero. Once this is done normality follows directly from Theorem 3.8. Intuitively it is clear that the desired result only follows if the quality of the approximation improves fast enough and Theorem 3.9 shows that the rate stipulated in Assumption (B6) is the critical one.

Theorem 3.9: Under Assumptions (B1)–(B7), $v^{-1/2}(E(\hat{m}^s) - m^s) \to 0$ as $n \to \infty$.

Proof: From (3.90), $v^{-1/2}(E(\hat{m}^s) - m^s)$ is

$$v^{-1/2} \left[z'(Z'Z)^{-1} Z' \left(\underline{m} - Z\theta_{(n)} \right) + \left(z'\theta_{(n)} - m \right) \right] = Q_1 + Q_2. \tag{3.91}$$

Applying Lemma 3.2, inequality (3.87), to Q_1 we get

$$|Q_1| \leq \sigma^{-1} \left[\left(\underline{m} - Z\theta_{(n)} \right)' \left(\underline{m} - Z\theta_{(n)} \right) \right]^{1/2} \tag{3.92}$$

$$\leq \sigma^{-1} n^{1/2} \left[\max_i |m_i - z_i'\theta_{(n)}| \right] \tag{3.93}$$

$$\leq \sigma^{-1} n^{1/2} M^{-1/2r} \left[M^{1/2r} \max_i |m_i - z_i'\theta_{(n)}| \right], \tag{3.94}$$

and this converges to zero by (B3) and (B6). Now

$$|Q_2| \leq v^{-1/2} \sup |z'\theta_{(n)} - m(x)| \tag{3.95}$$

$$\leq C_3^{-1/2} n^{1/2} \sup |z'\theta_{(n)} - m(x)| \tag{3.96}$$

from (B7), and thus

$$|Q_2| \leq C_3^{-1/2} \left(n/M^{1/r} \right)^{1/2} M^{1/2r} \sup |z'\theta_{(n)} - m(x)|, \tag{3.97}$$

and this tends to zero by applying (B3) and (B6).   Q.E.D.

The proof highlights the restrictions on the nature of the underlying and approximating functions and the degree of freedom available in choosing r. As can be seen, the restriction on r from (B1)–(B6) is not a major one, essentially only that r be such that $M/n \to 0$ as $n \to \infty$. This interpretation arises from the role of (B4) in bounding $\lambda_{\min}(Z'Z)$ by $C_4^2 n$. But it is really (B7) that tightens the bound, particularly when the x_i are stochastic. Andrews (1991a) does a number of examples and finds that M could take values between $C_1 n^{1/5}$ and $C_1 n^{1/3}$. Generally, it seems very hard to find the appropriate rate without a good deal of mathematical skill and knowledge of the properties of various series approximations. It might also be observed that Assumptions (B5) and (B6) are stronger than are needed, in that inequality (3.85) could have delivered the desired result in situations where (3.86) and (3.87) were invoked. In particular, for the proof of Theorem 3.9, rather than using a bound on how fast the approximation converges to zero in terms of n, it would have been possible to restate it as $(\underline{m} - Z\theta_{(n)})'Z(Z'Z)^{-1}Z'(\underline{m} - Z\theta_{(n)}) \overset{p}{\to} 0$, and this quantity constitutes the residual sum of squares from the regression of $\underline{m}$ against Z, allowing a nice interpretation to the sufficient conditions.

Unfortunately, the fact that $v^{-1/2}(\hat{m}^s - m)$ is asymptotically $\mathcal{N}(0, 1)$ is of limited interest unless $v^{-1/2}$ can be consistently estimated. Within the context of (3.1) and fixed regressors, this necessitates the consistent estimation of σ^2. Theorem 3.10 gives a sufficient condition to achieve that goal.

Theorem 3.10: $\hat{\sigma}^2 = n^{-1} \sum_{i=1}^{n}(y_i - \hat{m}_i^s)^2$ is a consistent estimator of σ^2 under the conditions of (B1)–(B6) if $\hat{m}_i^s$ is a uniformly consistent estimator of m_i, that is, $\sup_x |\hat{m}^s(x) - m(x)| \overset{p}{\to} 0$ as $n \to \infty$, where $\hat{m}^s(x)$ indicates the estimator of the conditional mean for an arbitrary x.

Proof:

$$\hat{\sigma}^2 = n^{-1} \sum (y_i - m_i)^2 + 2n^{-1} \sum (\hat{m}_i^s - m_i)(y_i - m_i)$$
$$+ n^{-1} \sum (\hat{m}_i^s - m_i)^2 \tag{3.98}$$
$$\leq n^{-1} \sum u_i^2 + 2 \sup |\hat{m}_i^s - m_i| \left(n^{-1} \sum |u_i|\right)$$
$$+ \left(\sup |\hat{m}_i^s - m_i|\right)^2. \tag{3.99}$$

For the first two terms $n^{-1} \sum u_i^2 \overset{p}{\to} \sigma^2$ and $n^{-1} \sum |u_i| \overset{p}{\to} E(|u_i|) < \infty$ by an application of Khinchin's Theorem (Spanos, 1986, p. 169), utilizing Assumption (B1). Uniform consistency of $\hat{m}_i$ then ensures that the last two terms in (3.99) converge to zero so that $\hat{\sigma}^2 \overset{p}{\to} \sigma^2$. Q.E.D.

From Theorem 3.10 it becomes desirable to strengthen the mode of convergence of $\hat{m}_i^s$ to uniform consistency. It should be stressed that requiring uniform consistency of $\hat{m}_i^s$ may well be too strong, but it has the advantage of allowing for a simple proof of the consistency of $\hat{\sigma}^2$. To get uniform consistency for $\hat{m}_i$ an additional assumption needs to be imposed:

(B8) $\lambda_{\min}(Z'Z)/M^2 \rightarrow \infty$ as $n \rightarrow \infty$.

Theorem 3.11 illustrates how the need for (B8) arises.[11]

Theorem 3.11: Under Assumptions (B1)–(B8) with (B4) restated to provide an upper bound upon x

$$E \sup_x (\hat{m}^s(x) - m(x))^2 \rightarrow 0 \quad \text{as } n \rightarrow \infty.$$

Proof: By the triangle and Cauchy–Schwartz inequalities the theorem will be true if $\sup_x |E(\hat{m}^s(x)) - m(x)|^2 \rightarrow 0$ and $E \sup_x [\hat{m}^s(x) - E\hat{m}^s(x)]^2 \rightarrow 0$. The first of these can be established from the proof of Theorem 3.9, treating x as arbitrary. The second is shown through the following sequence of inequalities:

$$E \sup_x [\hat{m}^s(x) - E(\hat{m}^s(x))]^2 = E \sup_x \left[z'(Z'Z)^{-1} Z'u \right]^2, \qquad (3.100)$$

where z corresponds to the arbitrary value of x. Then

$$E \sup_x \left[z'(Z'Z)^{-1} Z'u \right]^2 \leq \sup_x \left\{ z'(Z'Z)^{-1} z E \left[u'Z(Z'Z)^{-1} Z'u \right] \right\}$$
$$\qquad (3.101)$$

$$\leq \sigma^2 \left[\sup(z'z)/\lambda_{\min}(Z'Z) \right] tr \left[Z(Z'Z)^{-1} Z' \right] \qquad (3.102)$$

$$\leq \sigma^2 \left[C_4^2 M/\lambda_{\min}(Z'Z) \right] M, \qquad (3.103)$$

which tends to zero under (B8).   Q.E.D.

Andrews deals with the case that the u_i are heteroskedastic and also allows for the estimation of derivatives and integrals. The existence of heterogeneity in the error terms makes the proofs more complex but, provided the conditional moments of y_i are bounded up to sufficient order (generally four would suffice), the results in Theorems 3.8–3.11 continue to hold. Of course it is no longer just σ^2 that must be estimated for inferences, and Andrews shows that the heteroskedastic-consistent standard errors introduced by White (1980b)

---

[11] Eastwood and Gallant (1991) also deal with the consistent estimation of σ^2 in a special model in which $\lambda_{\min}(Z'Z) = (n/2) \sigma^2$ and conclude the (B8) should be $M^3/n \xrightarrow{p} 0$, which is stronger than the corresponding implication of (B8) in this situation that $M^2/n \xrightarrow{p} 0$. It appears that the discrepency arises as their condition is sufficient but not necessary; the inequalities utilized in their proofs can be strengthened along Andrews's lines.

into econometrics will be consistent estimators of the true standard deviations. Consequently, once the number and type of approximating terms are selected, estimation and inference can proceed as if the model was a finite parameter one.

3.10 Asymptotic Properties of Series Estimators with Dependent Observations

The basic idea of a series estimator, that the unknown function be globally approximated, does not depend in any way upon the nature of the data, other than that the function is invariant over time. What has proven to be difficult though is the derivation of the properties of series estimators when observations are dependent. If the x_i are exogenous then the proofs given earlier would continue to apply with suitable limit theorems for dependent processes being applied to the sums involving u_i. But, if the x_i contain lagged values of y_i, it is not possible to condition upon the x_i as was done in the proofs. White and Wooldridge (1991) and Newey (1997) have looked at the broader question. White and Wooldridge present some general theorems for analyzing the consistency of estimators when there is dependence in the data, essentially generalizations of the approach set out in Amemiya (1985). They then apply these results to estimate the moments of y_i conditional upon $y_{i-1}, y_{i-2}, \ldots, y_{i-p}$. Consistency is shown whenever y_i is a stationary mixing process with mixing coefficients declining geometrically as $\varphi(k) = \varphi_0 \rho^k$ (φ-mixing) or $\alpha(k) = \alpha_0 \rho^k$ (α-mixing) ($k > 0$), where $\varphi_0, \alpha_0 > 0$, $0 < \rho < 1$, the sum of the elements in $\theta_{(n)}$, Δ_n, is $o(n^{1/4})$, while M is $o(n^{1/2}/\Delta_n^2 \log \Delta_n)$. The latter conditions interact in various ways. For example, if $\Delta_n = O(\log n)$, M would be $O(n^{1/2-\epsilon})$ for $\epsilon > 0$, which enables a fast expansion in the number of regressors. Alternatively, if the restrictions on the growth in $\theta_{(n)}$ are tightened, for example to $M \log n$, then M would have to be $O(n^{1/6-\epsilon})$. Newey makes the process stationary and α-mixing with mixing coefficients $\alpha(k) = \alpha_0 k^{-\mu} (\mu > 2)$. He establishes consistency and asymptotic normality. With only one lag in y_i as conditioning variable, the support of y_i being bounded, and restrictions upon the nature of the density, he establishes that M would be $o(n^{1/4})$. Clearly, there is a strong trade-off between the strength of dependence and the nature of convergence. In Newey's case dependence dies off very rapidly and this enables him to establish stronger results.

3.11 Implementing the Estimator

There are a number of issues that must be addressed when implementing series estimators. A major problem resides in the selection of M in (3.78) (or J and L in (3.79) if the series expansion is Fourier). As mentioned earlier Andrews (1991a) finds that M should grow at various rates depending upon the nature of x_i and z_i. Even when a rate is found, however, it is not terribly helpful, being only an order of magnitude with the "constant factor" C_1 unknown. Unfortunately, series estimators can be very demanding in the number of z_i needed to approximate the unknown moment. In a pure Fourier expansion terms multiply rapidly when the number of elements in x_i is even of moderate size; as seen from Table 3.1, when $q = 3$, taking $K^* = 3$ requires $M = 50$ if *all* the k_ℓ compatible with this (q, K^*) configuration are used (the twenty-five combinations come in both a cosine and sine version) and J in (3.79) is unity. Extremely large amounts of data would therefore be needed to estimate $m(x)$ well if x_i has dimension above three. In practice, Gallant has tended to set M at less than its potential maximum value and to employ the approximation as part of a system, such as a set of consumer demand equations, so that the same parameters appear in each equation. Furthermore, typically in these systems the number of free parameters is much lower still, because of the possibility of incorporating restrictions upon the total set by appealing to the tenets of consumer or producer theory. Moving to a system and incorporating restrictions effectively increases the number of observations.

One suggestion to minimize this "curse of dimensionality" has been made by Hastie and Tibshirani (1986, 1990) and Buja, Hastie, and Tibshirami (1989). They assume that the underlying function exhibits some separability in the arguments. Using Andrews and Whang's (1990) terminology, an "order one additive interactive regression model" would be the sum of nonlinear functions of each element in x_i alone, whereas an "order-two" version augments this with nonlinear functions of the elements of x_i taken two at a time. Since Leontief (1947) separability has been an important feature in economic theory, both in production and demand relations. Such theory might therefore be invoked to indicate how $m(x_i)$ might be partitioned. Moreover, in some cases researchers could be prepared to assume that $m(x_i)$ is linear in (say) $q - 1$ of the xs and that the nonlinearity applies only to the qth variable. Then the Fourier approximation needs only to be applied to determine this last term. There would seem to be a number of applications of this type available; for example, in many household budget studies in which expenditure is related to income it is the form of this relationship that is primarily of interest and believed to be nonlinear. Yet there are also many other variables used to control for age, family size, etc., and the investigator may be prepared to assume that these are linearly related to expenditure or to introduce a degree of nonlinearity via dummy variables. In these situations the series approach has a strong appeal, as it merely involves the addition of variables to the basic linear regression model. Estimation of additive models need not be done by series methods and we discuss in the next section the literature that has grown up under the heading of "generalized additive models."

Experience with series estimators has not been extensive. In Gallant (1982) the flexible Fourier form was applied to the estimation of production relations; Gallant and Tauchen (1989) model asset price relationships taking the basis functions z_i as rational polynomials in x_i. Strictly this makes the estimation problem one of a nonlinear regression, and in fact they attempt to model the complete density of y_i rather than just some moments. For this reason the technique is discussed more fully in Chapter 5. Another paper by Pagan and Hong (1991) employs the flexible Fourier form to model the conditional moments of a number of financial series. In their paper $q = 2$ and separability between the two variables is imposed so that the underlying model was assumed to have the first-order additive format, $m(x_i) = m_1(x_{1i}) + m_2(x_{2i})$, with each of the $m_j(\cdot)(j = 1, 2)$ being approximated separately. In this situation k' is either $(1\ 0)$ or $(0\ 1)$ as there are no cross-terms between x_{1i} and x_{2i}. The Fourier procedure worked quite well and gave answers that were much the same as the kernel method discussed earlier. It is noticeable that all these applications have been to time series, and we have already indicated that the theory for nonparametric series estimators in such a context is not well developed.

Gallant and Tauchen (1987) refer to the ratio M/n as the "saturation ratio." In many applications that Gallant has made with the flexible Fourier form, Gallant (1982) and Gallant and Golub (1984) for example, the saturation ratio is very high and can come up to one half. Chalfant and Gallant (1985) constructed a Monte Carlo study of the ability of the Fourier expansion to estimate an elasticity of substitution from cost function data. Data was simulated from the first-order conditions of an optimizing producer faced with a variety of production functions, with the sample size (n) set to 25 (although there were two equations giving an effective size of 50). Their saturation ratio (measured relative to effective sample size) ranged from about one quarter to one half, and they argue that good estimates are obtained. The conclusions of the study are clouded however by the existence of bias in the estimator arising from an "errors in variables" problem and not due to the approximation. They interpret the fact that bias does not change much as the underlying production relations are modified as evidence that the bias due to approximation is small. Hong and Pagan (1988) tried to estimate a constant elasticity of substitution (C.E.S.) production function from simulated data with low saturation ratios of around .1 to .3. They also found that the Fourier approximation was a good one, in that the bias in the estimators was small even for samples as low as $n = 30$.

Both of these studies looked only at bias. Eastwood and Gallant (1991) instead concentrated upon the coverage probabilities of the estimator, relative to those predicted by asymptotic normality, when the true model followed beta, truncated quadratic, and truncated exponential functions. Initially they set $r = 1/5.5$, but they found important differences between the nominal and actual probabilities, even for samples in excess of one thousand. Setting r at such a low value seems a little unrealistic as it yielded a saturation ratio that was never greater than .11 ($M = 7$, $n = 60$), and this is below any value that Gallant has chosen in practice.

Nevertheless, the marked nonnormality of the distributions led them to investigate the possibility of adaptive rather than deterministic rules for the selection of r, that is, rules for choosing M that are data dependent. For their Monte Carlo design u_i was normal, allowing the inference (from $\hat{m}^s - E(\hat{m}^s) = (Z(Z'Z)^{-1}Z'u)$) that any failure of the estimators to give coverage probabilities predicted by normality must be due to the presence of bias (and this fact would point to a larger value of r being desirable). Their suggestion was to set two deterministic truncation rules M_1^* and M_2^* that satisfy the restraints on r needed to get asymptotic normality, and to then add extra trigonometric terms above M_1^* (up to a maximum of M_2^*) if they are "significant." To do this a critical value for the F-statistic for added regressors must be set and the question of how many terms should be added at any one time also needs to be determined. In their Monte Carlo work a critical value of 2 was applied and the number of extra approximating variables when testing upwards was 10% of the previous aggregate. With these modifications they found that estimators seemed to be normally distributed. Some of the problems encountered by Eastwood and Gallant may originate from the complexity of the functions examined; the exponential is very smooth over much of $(0, 2\pi)$ but has a very sharp downturn after $x = 4.9$. To model such behavior at the end of the range of x is almost certainly going to demand large values of M. Nevertheless, the idea that M should be selected in a data-dependent way is a natural one for applied workers, and it is very interesting that the movement from a fixed rule to an adaptive one did not affect the limiting distribution of the estimators provided the random choice of M essentially converges to a deterministic rule as $n \to \infty$. Andrews (1991a) shows that the asymptotic theory of the estimators obtained with adaptive rules is the same as with deterministic ones. He also considers a number of alternative ways of choosing M in a data-dependent way.[12] Newey's (1994c) proofs also allow for data-based choice of M, although only if observations are independent.

There are other ways in which the number of z_{ij} can be controlled. Gallant argues that the leading terms in the expansion should be a quadratic form in x_i (more precisely in $k'x_i$) as the addition of low order polynomials might be expected to be beneficial in smaller samples. Our experience has been that doing this is worthwhile. Economic theory may also indicate some simplifications. For example, if an additivity condition upon the coefficients of an equation has to be satisfied the elementary multi-indices would be made to have elements summing to zero rather than unity (see Chalfant and Gallant, 1985, p. 212).

Mention of the way in which theoretical information could determine the nature of k also brings up the query of whether the Fourier expansion is the

---

[12] In fact the criteria used for automatic window-width selection could all be directly applied to finding a suitable value for M. However, again the limiting distribution would no longer be centered upon m.

most useful for economic problems. Barnett and Yue (1988) argue in favor of the Muntz–Satz expansion when modeling producer and consumer behavior. This expansion is in terms of $x_i^{1/2j}$ ($j = 1, 2, \ldots$), satisfies (B6), and is attractive because the monotonicity and curvature constraints needed for neoclassical optimization are easily imposed upon such functions. Other proposals have been surveyed by McFadden (1985) and include Bernstein and orthogonal polynomials. One might expect that rational polynomials could well be the best way of performing the approximation as they tend to converge to the true function at a much faster rate than the Fourier series does. A disadvantage of their use however is that the approximating function is now nonlinear in the z_i and $\theta_{(n)}$, owing to the ratio format. Obviously a study comparing the ability of different basis functions to estimate conditional moments would be useful.

Apart from the dimensionality problem the major difficulty a practitioner has with the Fourier method is the need to *scale the data so that it lies between* $(0, 2\pi)$. Failure to do this can mean very poor results, and in some cases the cosine and sine terms show such little variation that they are highly correlated with the intercept, x_i, and x_i^2 terms, making the regressor matrix very near to singular. The data transformation needed to translate the observations in x_i to $(0, 2\pi)$ is very simple and generally involves adding on a constant followed by a scale change. If all observations are positive a scale transformation is all that is needed. When data can be negative we have found it useful to first add on a number that is slightly larger than the minimum of the raw series and to then apply a scale change. Notice that the trigonometric terms in transformed variables $w_i = c + bx_i$ are multiples of the originals but with $\cos(kx_i)$ replaced by $\cos(akx_i)$ etc., where a is a constant. Hence the nature of the trigonometric terms employed adapts to the data.

3.12   Imposing Structure on the Conditional Moments

When discussing the dimensionality problem of series estimators in the preceding section it was argued that there were advantages to having some structure placed upon the nature of the conditional mean. Three important proposals are: the generalized additive models of Hastie and Tibshirani (1986, 1990), the projection pursuit regression (PPR) method of Friedman and Tukey (1974), Breiman and Friedman (1985), and Friedman and Stuetzle (1981), and the neural networks procedures outlined in Kuan and White (1994).

3.12.1   *Generalized Additive Models*

To illustrate the methodology consider a separable nonparametric regression with q regressors,

$$y_i = m(x_{i1}, \dots, x_{iq}) + u_i$$

$$= \sum_{j=1}^{q} m_j(x_{ij}) + u_i,$$

where m_j are functions of single variables with $Em_j(x_j) = 0$ for identification. Hastie and Tibshirani (1990) call this a generalized additive model and they proposed an algorithm to obtain estimates of m_j, but the statistical properties are complicated. Tjøstheim and Auestad (1994), Newey (1994b), Linton and Nielsen (1995), and Chen et al. (1996) have considered alternative methods of estimating m_j. Here we illustrate the ideas with the case $q = 2$, whereupon

$$m(x_1, x_2) = m_1(x_1) + m_2(x_2).$$

The basic equality exploited by the methods is that

$$m_1(x_1) = \int m(x_1, x_2) f(x_2) \, dx_2, \tag{3.104}$$

since $\int m(x_2) f(x_2) = 0$ due to the assumption $E(m_2(x_2)) = 0$. One can then estimate $m(x_1, x_2)$ nonparametrically with some estimator $\hat{m}(x_1, x_2) = \sum_{j=1}^{n} w_j (x_1, x_2) y_j$, leaving one with the problem of what to do about $f(x_2)$. Linton and Nielsen (1995) replace $f(x_2)$ by some known deterministic function $f(x_2)$ that integrates to unity. Then the estimator of $m_1(x_1)$ is

$$\hat{m}_1(x_1) = \int \hat{m}(x_1, x_2) f(x_2) \, dx_2$$

$$= \sum_{j=1}^{n} y_j \int w_j(x_1, x_2) \, dF(x_2)$$

$$= \sum_{j=1}^{n} w_j(x_1) y_j,$$

where $w_j(x_1) = \int w_j(x_1, x_2) f(x_2) dx_2$. An alternative method, used by Chen et al. (1996), is to note that (3.104) can be written as $E(m(x_1, X_2))$ and therefore $m_1(x_1)$ might be estimated by $n^{-1} \sum_{i=1}^{n} \hat{m}(x_1, x_{i2})$. Essentially they replace $F(x_2)$ by the empirical distribution function. In some ways this seems a better choice as it avoids difficulties in choosing what $f(x_2)$ should be.

Following Wand and Jones (1993), Linton and Nielsen consider different bandwidths, h_1 and h_2, for x_1 and x_2 respectively, in the estimator $\hat{m}_1(x_1)$. Under the assumptions that $\{y_i, x_{i1}, x_{i2}\}$ are i.i.d.; $h_1, h_2 \to 0$; $nh_1 h_2^2 \to \infty$; and $nh_1^5 \to 0$, $nh_1 h_2^4 \to 0$, they show that

$$(nh_1)^{1/2} [\hat{m}_1(x_1) - m_1(x_1)] \sim \mathcal{N}(0, V(x_1))$$

as $n \to \infty$, where

$$V(x_1) = \sigma^2 \left(\int K^2(\psi)\, d\psi \right) \int f^2(x_2) f^{-1}(x_1, x_2)\, dx_2.$$

When $h_1, h_2 \propto n^{-1/5}$ the estimator is biased and $m_1(x_1)$ is replaced by $E\hat{m}_1(x_1)$ when stating the limiting distribution result. A higher order kernel would be needed to eliminate the bias. With this choice of window width $\hat{m}_1(x_1)$ converges to $m_1(x_1)$ at rate $n^{2/5}$, a rate result earlier established by Stone (1985), and which equals that attainable when there is a single conditioning variable in the conditional mean m.

For the extension to q-dimensional x, how to discriminate between the additive and multiplicative specifications of $m(x)$, and how to test for the additive specification of m, see Linton and Härdle (1996), Linton and Nielsen (1995), Linton and Gozalo (1996), and Chen et al. (1996). The latter also estimate a production function featuring additive separability in five inputs.

3.12.2 Projection Pursuit Regression

Projection pursuit regression (PPR) makes the assumption that $m(x_i)$ can be decomposed as the sum of $r < q$ nonlinear functions in scalars $z_{ij} = x_i' \beta_j$, that is,

$$y_i = \sum_{j=1}^{r} g_j \left(x_i' \beta_j \right) + \epsilon_i. \tag{3.105}$$

If the g_j were known we could conceive of this as a series approximation to $m(x_i)$, but PPR works on the principle of jointly determining g_j and β_j. To this end consider the estimation of β_1 in $z_{i1} = x_i' \beta_1$. Taking the expectation of (3.105) with respect to z_{i1} gives

$$E(y_i \mid z_{i1}) = \sum_{j=1}^{r} E[g_j(z_{ij}) \mid z_{i1}], \tag{3.106}$$

and, after subtracting (3.106) from (3.105), we find

$$y_i = E(y_i \mid z_{i1}) + v_i, \tag{3.107}$$

where

$$v_i = \sum_{j=2}^{r} \left\{ g_j \left(x_i' \beta_j \right) - E[g_j(z_{ij}) \mid z_{i1}] \right\} + \epsilon_i$$

and $E(v_i \mid z_{i1}) = 0$ by construction. Hence we have

$$y_i = \phi(z_{i1}) + v_i, \tag{3.108}$$

and, if $\phi(\cdot)$ were known, β_1 could be estimated by performing nonlinear least squares on (3.108).

PPR uses this idea. An initial guess of the value of β_1 is made, z_{i1} is formed, nonparametric methods are employed to estimate $E(y_i \mid z_{i1})$, and the sum of squared residuals $\sum_{i=1}^{n} (y_i - \hat{E}(y_i \mid z_{i1}))^2$ is then minimized with respect to β_1 to produce a new estimate of β_1. The method is iterated to convergence to produce a value $\hat{\beta}_1$. Having therefore estimated $g_1(z_{i1})$, the quantity $w_i = y_i - \hat{g}_1(z_{i1})$ is formed and the process described above is repeated by obtaining $\hat{g}_2(z_{i2})$, etc. Hall (1989) deals with the properties of these estimators.

PPR is an interesting approach. There are a number of models in econometrics in which the conditional expectation of y_i is a function of a number of indices z_{ij}; examples include the discrete choice, selectivity, and limited dependent variable models treated in later chapters. Moreover, there has been a recent revival of interest in the use of "factors" as explanatory variables, particularly in the context of time series analysis. For this reason PPR has some appeal when working with economic data, and its use of the nonparametric methods discussed in this chapter make it natural to treat it here. Because z_{ij} is a scalar, both the kernel and series estimators should be easily applied, although the need to compute the conditional expectation at all n observations does suggest that series methods may be numerically the most efficient.

3.12.3   Neural Networks

Neural networks can be regarded as a series approximation of the form

$$y_i = \sum_{j=1}^{M} \gamma_j g_j \left(x_i' \beta_j \right) + \epsilon_i,$$

where g_j are some *known* basis functions, most commonly the logistic function $g(z) = (1 + e^{-z})^{-1}$. There are clear similarities to projection pursuit, but there are also significant differences. Foremost among these is that the β_j are not estimated from the data. Rather, ranges of values for β are decided upon and values are then selected randomly from these spaces. Once M values of β are selected, β_j^*, the indices $z_{ji} = x_i' \beta_j^*$ can be computed and a regression run of y_i against $g_j(z_{ji})$. Predictions from this regression would then be taken as the conditional mean. Of course a very large number of values for β can be found, far more than the number of regressors we would want to include in a regression, so that some way of choosing between the various models (indexed by their z_j sets) is needed. Typically, this is done via a model selection procedure, as the models are nonnested. In practice, the M functions, $g_j \left(x_i' \beta_j \right)$, are sometimes replaced by a few principal components (e.g., in Lee et al. (1993), $M = 10$ or 20 but these are replaced by two and three components respectively).

3.13 Measuring the Affinity of Parametric and Nonparametric Models

In many instances it is desirable to assess the correspondence of an estimated parametric regression model with the data. Mostly this is done by the addition of variables to the maintained regression model. These variables function as indicators of the likely misspecification. Rather than do this, however, one might seek to evaluate the parametric model by comparing its fit to that of a nonparametric one, and there have been a number of proposals along these lines.

Designate the nonparametric estimator of the conditional mean by $\hat{m}^{NP}$ and the parametric one by $\hat{m}^P$ and consider evaluating these at the points $\{x_j^*\}_{j=1}^d$. Under the null hypothesis both $\hat{m}^{NP}(x_j^*)$ and $\hat{m}^P(x_j^*)$ are consistent estimators of $m(x_j^*)$. Under the alternative, however, the parametric estimator converges to $\bar{m}(x_j^*)$, which differs from $m(x_j^*)$. In general, $(nh)^{1/2}(\hat{m}^{NP}(x_j^*) - m(x_j^*))$ and $n^{1/2}(\hat{m}^P(x_j^*) - \bar{m}(x_j^*))$ are both asymptotically normal; the first follows from Theorem 3.5 and the second from standard analysis of misspecified parametric models (e.g., see White, 1992). Hence, using the decomposition

$$(nh)^{1/2}(\hat{m}^{NP}(x_j^*) - \hat{m}^P(x_j^*))$$
$$= (nh)^{1/2}(\hat{m}^{NP}(x_j^*) - m(x_j^*))$$
$$- (nh)^{1/2} n^{-1/2}\{n^{1/2}(\hat{m}^P(x_j^*) - \bar{m}(x_j^*))\}$$
$$+ (nh)^{1/2}(m(x_j^*) - \bar{m}(x_j^*)),$$

it is clear that the distribution of $(nh)^{1/2}(\hat{m}^{NP}(x_j^*) - \hat{m}^P(x_j))$ will be

$$\mathcal{N}\left(\lim_{n\to\infty}(nh)^{1/2}(m(x_j^*) - \bar{m}(x_j^*)), v_1\right),$$

since the second term converges to zero as $n \to \infty$. The expression for $\lim_{n\to\infty}(nh)^{1/2}(m(x_j^*) - \bar{m}(x_j^*))$ determines the magnitude of any noncentrality parameters, whereas $v_1 = f(x_j^*)^{-1}\sigma^2 \int K(\psi)^2 d\psi$, from Theorem 3.5. Under the null hypothesis, $m(x_j^*) = \bar{m}(x_j^*)$, so that the statistic

$$\hat{T}_j = (nh)^{1/2} v_1^{-1/2}(\hat{m}^{NP}(x_j^*) - \hat{m}^P(x_j^*))$$

will be asymptotically $\mathcal{N}(0,1)$.

Gozalo (1997) proposes the above test. One difficulty is that there are many possible values that can be used for x_j^*. He suggests doing a random selection over the range of X, being careful to avoid choosing values for which $\hat{f}(x_j^*)$ is very small, and for which the kernel estimator would be ill defined. Since asymptotically $\hat{m}^{NP}(x_j^*)$ and $\hat{m}^{NP}(x_k^*)$ ($j \neq k$) are independently distributed, the statistic $G = \sum_{j=1}^d \hat{T}_j^2$ will be a $\chi^2(d)$ under the null hypothesis. Obviously, one has to be careful when choosing the magnitude of d; if it is allowed to change with n it must rise at a slower rate than $(nh)^{1/2}$ to ensure convergence of T_j. His recommendation is to select a single point, chosen as $\max_j \hat{T}_j$, and to test this against an $\mathcal{N}(0, 1)$ random variable. Gozalo constructs a simulation experiment in which the true model is a quadratic expenditure system while the estimated model is either a Working–Leser model or a quadratic expenditure model. His results point to good size for the test provided x_j^* was not near the boundary of the variable space; in this instance the size of the test could be .93 rather than the .05 predicted by the asymptotic theory (when $n = 1,000$).

Recently Gozalo (1995) proposed a generalization of his test as

$$G^* = \frac{nh^{\frac{1}{2}} \left(\bar{T} - E\bar{T} \right)}{v_2^{1/2}},$$

where

$$\bar{T} = d^{-1} \sum_{j=1}^{d} \left(\hat{m}^{NP}(x_j^*) - \hat{m}^{P}(x_j) \right)^2 w(x_j),$$

$E\bar{T}$ is the expectation of $\bar{T}$ under $H_0 : m(x) = m^P(x)$, $v_2 = V(nh^{\frac{1}{2}}\bar{T})$, and $w(x_i)$ is a prespecified nonnegative weighting function used to eliminate boundary problems. The statistic $G^* \sim \mathcal{N}(0, 1)$ for $d \to \infty$ as $n \to \infty$. The fact that G^* depends on unknown parameters through $E\bar{T}$ reduces its attractiveness. Related tests are those of González-Manteiga and Cao-Abad (1993), Härdle and Mammen (1993), and Staniswalis and Severini (1991).

It would be useful if the tests did not depend upon the need to select the points x_j^*, and this has led to interest in devising tests that are "automatic." One test for model inadequacy that has received attention has been Ullah's (1985) suggestion that the residual variance from a parametric model be compared to the residual variance estimate after a nonparametric regression has been fitted. That is, using tilde to denote parametric residuals and hats for the nonparametric residuals, the test is based upon $\hat{c} = n^{-1}\Sigma\tilde{u}_i^2 - n^{-1}\Sigma\hat{u}_i^2$. Unfortunately, $n^{1/2}\hat{c}$ has a degenerate distribution as n tends to infinity, since $n^{-1/2}[\Sigma_{i=1}^{n}\{\hat{u}_i^2 - \tilde{u}_i^2\}]$ is $o_p(1)$ under the null hypothesis. Early procedures that avoid the degeneracy problem are found in Yatchew (1992) and Lee (1992, 1994). The former splits the sample, using parametric residuals to construct a sum of squares on one part of it and nonparametric residuals on the other. Then $n_1^{-1/2}\left\{\sum_{i=1}^{n_1}\tilde{u}_i^2 - \sum_{i=n_1}^{n_2}\hat{u}_i^2\right\}$ is no longer $o_p(1)$. Lee suggests a weighting procedure, reminiscent of that used to break a similar degeneracy problem arising with estimated affinity measures of densities. He compares $\bar{w}^{-1}\Sigma w_i\tilde{u}_i^2$ to $\Sigma\hat{u}_i^2$, where w_i are weights depending upon x_i and $\bar{w}$ is their sample mean. Provided $E\left(u_i^2\right) = \sigma^2$, the mean of this test statistic would be zero under the null, but the presence of any heteroskedasticity creates a bias, as $E\left(\Sigma w_i u_i^2\right)$ does not equal a multiple of $E(w_i)$. Thus the test may not be a very powerful one for functional form in the mean and Lee (1992) actually uses it as a test for heteroskedasticity.

A different set of solutions is to change the normalizing factor. Fan and Li (1996a) do this by employing Hall's (1984) central limit theorem for degenerate U-statistics (see appendix), as they show that the distance between the nonparametric and parametric sum of squares of suitably weighted residuals can be treated as a degenerate U-statistic. Specifically, their consistent test statistic, for $n \to \infty$, is

$$FL = \frac{nh^{1/2}[\tilde{c} - c_1 - c_2]}{\hat{\sigma}} \sim \mathcal{N}(0, 1),$$

where $\tilde{c}$ is the $\hat{c}$ above but with the residuals weighted by the kernel density $f(x_i)$, that is, $\tilde{u}_i$ and $\hat{u}_i$ are replaced by $\tilde{u}_i \hat{f}(x_i)$ and $\hat{u}_i \hat{f}(x_i)$, respectively. The other component in the test statistic is the center term $c_1 + c_2$ which appears for the reasons similar to those in Section 2.9 on testing hypotheses about densities. The elements of this center term are

$$c_1 = \frac{1}{n^2(n-1)h^2} \sum_i \sum_{j \neq i} \tilde{u}_i^2 K^2\left(\frac{x_i - x_j}{h}\right),$$

$$c_2 = \frac{1}{n^2(n-1)h^2} \sum_i \sum_{j \neq i} \left[\hat{m}^P(x_i) - \hat{m}^P(x_j)\right]^2 K^2\left(\frac{x_i - x_j}{h}\right),$$

where

$$\hat{\sigma}^2 = 2n^{-1} \sum_{i=1}^n \hat{\sigma}^4(x_i)\hat{f}^3(x_i)$$

$$\times \int_v \left[\int_u K(u)K(u+v)\,du - 2K(v)\right]^2 dv.$$

Since a test for linearity, a special case of the parametric specification, is essentially a test of whether extra terms in a series expansion are needed after the linear ones, Wooldridge (1992) has considered how one might implement such an idea. One possibility would be to choose z_i in (3.78) as terms in a series expansion. Unfortunately, as the number of terms grows, $z_i'\theta$ will approximate the null hypothesis of a linear model as well (i.e., the degeneracy mentioned above operates). Hence, there is a tension between adding on enough terms to get a good approximation to any nonlinearity but yet not enough to capture the linear part. Wooldridge establishes the rate of increase of the terms that will permit a consistent test of the null hypothesis of linearity. It is *very* slow, and his simulation experiments throw some doubt on the usefulness of this approach. Similar simulation findings have been observed in Gokhale et al. (1997) where they also propose to test for parametric specificaton

$H_0 : m(x) = m(x, \theta)$ against the nonparametric alternative by testing for $\lambda = 0$ in the regression $y = m(x, \hat{\theta})(1 - \lambda) + \lambda \hat{m}(x) + u$, where $\hat{\theta}$ is the estimator of the parameter vector θ. Essentially this amounts to doing an artificial regression of the parametric residuals on $(\hat{m}(x) - m(x, \hat{\theta}))$. Gokhale et al. also consider testing $\lambda = 0$ in the regression of the parametric residual on $\hat{m}(x)$. Fan and Ullah (1996) multiply both sides of the artificial regression by $\hat{f}_{-i}(x_i)$, the leave-one-out kernel density estimator $f(x)$, and then perform a weighted least squares regression. They establish asymptotic normality of this estimator.

Hong (1993) and Horowitz and Härdle (1994) consider a conditional moment test of the form

$$\hat{\rho} = n^{-1} \sum_{i=1}^{n} w_i \left(\hat{m}_i^{NP} - \hat{m}_i^{P} \right) \left(y_i - \hat{m}_i^{P} \right),$$

where w_i is a weight function.[13] For simplicity, set w_i to unity and replace $(y_i - \hat{m}_i^{P})$ by $(y_i - m_i)$. Although m_i is estimated parametrically, we will ignore this complication and set $\hat{m}_i^{P} = m_i$, in order to better understand the nature of the solution to the degeneracy problem.

Using the simplifications described above we get

$$\hat{\rho} = n^{-1} \sum_{i=1}^{n} \left(\hat{m}_i^{NP} - m_i \right) (y_i - m_i).$$

Accordingly,

$$n^{1/2}\hat{\rho} = n^{-1/2} \sum_{i=1}^{n} \left(\hat{m}_i^{NP} - m_i \right) (y_i - m_i). \tag{3.109}$$

Now, writing $\hat{m}_i^{NP} - m_i = \hat{m}_i^{NP} - E_X(\hat{m}_i^{NP}) + E_X(\hat{m}_i^{NP}) - m_i$ and using Theorem 3.2, we would have

$$\hat{m}_i^{NP} - m_i \approx (nh)^{-1}\eta_i + h^2 \xi_i, \tag{3.110}$$

where

$$\eta_i = f(x_i)^{-1} \sum_{i \neq j, j=1}^{n} K(h^{-1}(x_i - x_j))u_j$$

---

[13] Horowitz and Härdle actually replace $\hat{m}_i^{NP}$ by $E(y_i \mid \hat{m}_i^{P})$. This makes $\hat{m}_i^{NP}$ a function of a single random variable and that may make the sampling distribution closer to its asymptotic prediction. As this estimator is particularly useful for checking the adequacy of the specification of single index models we discuss it in Chapter 7.

and

$$\xi_i = 1/2 \left(\int K^2(\psi)\psi^2 \, d\psi \right) \left[m_i^{(2)} f(x_i) + 2 f_i^{(1)} m_i^{(1)} \right] / f(x_i),$$

if the leave-one-out kernel estimator is employed. Substituting (3.110) into (3.109) gives

$$n^{1/2} \hat{\rho} = n^{-1/2} \sum_{i=1}^{n} u_i \left\{ (nh)^{-1} \eta_i + h^2 \xi_i \right\}$$

$$= n^{-1/2} \sum_{i=1}^{n} v_i.$$

Examining v_i, we see that its MSE is approximately

$$f(x_i)^{-1} (nh)^{-1} \sigma^4 \int K^2(\psi) \, d\psi + h^4 E(\xi_i^2) \sigma^2 = S_1 + S_2,$$

due to the independence of η_i and u_i, and this points to using $(S_1 + S_2)^{-1/2} n^{1/2} \hat{\rho}$ as the basis of a test statistic, as this will involve a central limit theorem being applied to the random variables $(S_1 + S_2)^{-1/2} v_i$, which have variance of unity. Consequently, the test statistic should be asymptotically $\mathcal{N}(0, 1)$, thereby overcoming the degeneracy problem. Expressions for S_1 and S_2 are considerably more complex in Hong's paper as he allows for nonunit weights, the fact that m_i has to be estimated, and the possibility of heteroskedasticity in u_i, but the essentials of his derivation are preserved in the description above. In one respect his formulae are simpler, as his chosen weights are a multiple of $\hat{f}(x_i)$, and so ξ_i does not involve $f(x_i)$ or its derivative.

Li and Wang (1998), Fan and Li (1996a), and Zheng (1996) proposed a conditional moment test of the form

$$\tilde{\rho} = n^{-1} \sum_{i=1}^{n} \hat{f}(x_i) \hat{m}_{\tilde{u}_i}^{NP} \left(y_i - \hat{m}_i^P \right)$$

for testing $H_0 : y_i = m(x_i, \theta) + u_i$ against $H_1 : y_i = m(x_i) + v_i$ or $H_0 : m(x_i) = m(x_i, \theta) = m_i^P$ against $H_1 : m(x_i) \neq m(x_i, \theta)$; $\hat{m}_{\tilde{u}_i}^{NP} = E(\tilde{u}_i | x_i)$ and $\tilde{u}_i = y_i - \hat{m}_i^P$. This test statistic is based on the fact that $m_u(x_i) = E(u_i | x_i) = 0$ if and only if the null hypothesis is true. Thus one can construct a test based on whether $E(u_i m_u(x_i)) = E(m_u^2(x_i))$ is zero. Since it is also true that $E(f(x_i) u_i m_u(x_i))$ would be zero under H_0, one might base a test upon this equality as that avoids any problems with small values of the denominator in constructing $E(\tilde{u}_i | x_i)$.

Such a test is a conditional moment test (Newey, 1985; Tauchen, 1985). Eubank and Spielgelman (1990) test the equivalent condition that $E\left[m_u^2(x_i) \right]$

is zero using a series-type estimation method for $m_u(x_i)$ and assuming normally distributed random error terms. To derive Li and Wang's (1998) $\tilde{\rho}$ test statistic from the moment condition first replace $E\left(u_i m_u(x_i) f(x_i)\right)$ by its sample analogue to get $n^{-1} \sum_{i=1}^{n} u_i m_u(x_i) f(x_i)$, and then substitute the parametric residual for u_i and kernel estimators for $m_u(x_i)$ and $f(x_i)$. Using the expressions for $\hat{m}^{NP}$ and $\hat{f}$, an alternative form for $\tilde{\rho}$, which may be useful computationally, is

$$\tilde{\rho} = \frac{1}{n(n-1)h} \sum_{i=1}^{n} \sum_{j=1, j \neq i}^{n} \tilde{u}_i \tilde{u}_j K\left(\frac{x_i - x_j}{h}\right).$$

Li and Wang (1998) have shown that

$$nh^{1/2}\tilde{\rho} \sim \mathcal{N}(0, \upsilon_4),$$

where $\upsilon_4 = 2[\int K^2(\psi)d\psi] \int f^2(X)\sigma^4(X)\,dX$. In practice υ_4 can be consistently estimated by

$$\hat{\upsilon}_4 = 2\left(n(n-1)h\right)^{-1} \sum_i \sum_{j \neq i} \hat{u}_i^2 \hat{u}_j^2 K^2\left(\frac{x_i - x_j}{h}\right).$$

For the q-dimensional X we need to replace nh with nh^q.

The test statistic $\tilde{\rho}$ is closely related to Hong's $\hat{\rho}$ above and Fan and Ullah's (1996). Since the parametric residual is $\tilde{u}_i = y_i - \hat{m}_i^P$ and $E\left(\tilde{u}_i | x_i\right) = m_i - E\left(\hat{m}_i^P | x_i\right)$, this could be estimated by $\hat{m}_i^{NP} - \tilde{m}_i^P$ where $\tilde{m}_i^P = \hat{E}\left(\hat{m}_i^P | x_i\right) = (nh)^{-1} \sum_j \hat{f}(x_i)^{-1} K\left(\frac{x_j - x_i}{h}\right) \hat{m}_j^P$, which is a "kernel-smoothed" estimator of m_i^P. Setting $w_i = \hat{f}(x_i)$ in the $\hat{\rho}$ statistic, the only difference between $\hat{\rho}$ and $\tilde{\rho}$ will be that $\hat{m}_i^{NP} - \hat{m}_i^P$ in the $\hat{\rho}$ test is replaced by $\hat{m}_i^{NP} - \tilde{m}_i^P$ in the $\tilde{\rho}$ test. In $\hat{\lambda}_N$ the weight is $f^2(x_i)$ instead of $f(x_i)$. Consequently, the distribution of $\tilde{\rho}$ is the same as that of $\hat{\lambda}_N$, with $f(X)$ replaced by $f^2(X)$ in υ_4. Both the statistics $\hat{\lambda}_N$ and $\tilde{\rho}$ are invariant to the variances of u_i.

Härdle and Mammen (1993) suggested a weighted integrated square difference between the kernel estimator $\hat{m}^{NP}$ and the kernel-smoothed parametric estimator $\tilde{m}^P$, that is,

$$\tilde{\rho}_1 = \int_x \left[\hat{m}^{NP}(x) - \tilde{m}^P(x)\right]^2 w(x)\,dx = \int_x \left(\hat{E}(\tilde{u}|x)\right)^2 w(x)\,dx,$$

where $w(x)$ is a smooth weighting function. The asymptotic properties of $\tilde{\rho}_1$ are similar to those for $\tilde{\rho}$. Li and Wang (1998) used a "wild bootstrap" procedure to compare the size and power of the tests $\tilde{\rho}$ and $\tilde{\rho}_1$ and found them to be similar. However, the simplicity and computational ease of $\tilde{\rho}$ may make it more appealing.

Most of the proposals for checking on the fit of parametric models just mentioned involve seeking to add variables to it. The conditional moment test Hong works with adds $\hat{m}_i^{NP} - \hat{m}_i^P$ to the parametric model, whereas the $\tilde{\rho}$ test tries to add on $\hat{m}_i^{NP} - \tilde{m}_i^P$. Viewed in this light, one might query whether one gains much from such endeavors over what could be had by just augmenting the parametric model with a finite number of variables such as polynomials in x_i and then testing the significance of such variables. Such tests are much easier to implement and feature parametric rates of convergence. As an example of these qualms, Hong finds that the power of his test to detect an inadequate parametric model ranges between .533 and .923 (depending on how h is selected) for a Monte Carlo experiment in which the term $.5(3x_i^2 - 2x_i^3)\exp(-x_i^2/2)$ is omitted from a parametric model. The fitted model is a quadratic in x_i and one might add in a cubic term as a test of specification. Doing this the power comes out to .883, which is comparable with Hong's test. Alternatively, the regression specification test that seeks to add on the squared predictions from the parametric model would give a power of .86 as well. Given the dependence of the power of the nonparametric test upon the window width, it is not entirely clear whether these procedures currently provide significant advantages over the range of specification tests for functional form that are currently available to us.

All the above nonparametric tests are consistent model specification tests and they employ some nonparametric estimator of $m(x)$, mainly the kernel estimator. One advantage of these tests is that they are consistent in the sense that their power goes to one as $n \to \infty$ against all the alternatives. The usual parametric specification tests are however consistent only against a specified alternative. An approach to developing consistent model specification tests, without using any nonparametric estimator of m, is due to Bierens (1982, 1990), Bierens and Ploberger (1997), Ploberger and Bierens (1995), and Stinchcombe and White (1998). These tests are called integrated conditional moment tests (ICM), and they can be viewed as extensions of the class of the conditional moment tests proposed by Newey (1985) and Tauchen (1985). The test statistics of Bierens (1982) and Bierens and Ploberger (1997) are

$$\rho^* = \int \left| \frac{1}{n} \sum_j \hat{u}_j w_j(\xi) \right|^2 d\mu(\xi),$$

where $\mu(\xi)$ is some probability measure and $w_j(\xi)$ is a weight function chosen such that the test statistic is consistent. In Bierens (1982), $w_j(\xi) = \exp(i\xi\Phi(x_j))$, $i = \sqrt{-1}$, and $\Phi()$ is a bounded Borel measurable function. Although the statistics $\tilde{\rho}$, $\tilde{\rho}_1$, and ρ^* look quite different, in that they are developed from different principles, Fan and Li (1996b) have shown that $\tilde{\rho}$ and ρ^* are quite closely related. In particular, they show that, if $w_j(\xi) = \exp(i\xi x_j)\bar{K}(\xi h)$, where $\bar{K}$ is the Fourier transform of K for fixed h, then ρ^* is the same as the Härdle and Mammen (1993) test $\tilde{\rho}_1$ with $w(x) = \hat{f}^2(x)$. The only difference is that $h = h_n \to 0$ as $n \to \infty$ in $\tilde{\rho}_1$, whereas h is fixed in ρ^*. Fan and Li also demonstrate the similarity between Li and Wang's and Bierens and Ploberger's (1997) test. Although Bierens-type tests, ρ^*, are similar to the tests $\tilde{\rho}$ and $\tilde{\rho}_1$, their treatment of h as fixed contrasts with the declining value of h (as $n \to \infty$) in $\tilde{\rho}$ and $\tilde{\rho}_1$ and this leads to completely different asymptotic distributions under H_0 as well as H_1. In fact the existing results indicate that the tests under a fixed h approach nonnormal distributions under H_0. Further, the available results indicate that fixing h improves the power of the tests, since Bierens's type ρ^* tests can detect Pitman local alternatives that approach the null at the rate $O(n^{-1/2})$, whereas the $\tilde{\rho}$ and $\tilde{\rho}_1$ tests can only detect such local alternatives at the rate $O\left((nh^{1/2})^{-1/2}\right)$, that is, slower than $n^{-1/2}$. However, Fan and Li show that, under high frequency (Rosenblatt (1975) type local alternatives (see Chapter 2)) the tests with vanishing h will be more powerful than tests based on a fixed h.

Another related problem of testing involves selecting variables in the non-parametric regression framework. Ullah and Vinod (1993) discuss this and other hypothesis testing problems of interest to econometricians. The problem is to test $H_0 : m(x) = m_1(x_1)$ against $H_1 : m(x) = m_2(x_2)$, where x_1 is a vector of regressors in the null model and x_2 are the vector of regressors in the alternative model. Again one can use Gozalo's (1993, 1995) tests. The alternative is to compare the nonparametric residual sum of squares from the null model, $n^{-1/2} \sum^n \hat{u}_{i1}^2$, with the nonparametric residual sum of squares under the alternative, $n^{-1/2} \sum^n \hat{u}_{i2}^2$, where $\hat{u}_{i1} = y_i - \hat{m}_1(x_{i1})$ and $\hat{u}_{i2} = y_i - \hat{m}_2(x_{i2})$. This comparison, suggested in Ullah (1985) and Hidalgo (1992), implies that we are testing $H_0 : Eu_2^2 - Eu_1^2 = 0$ against $H_1 : Eu_2^2 - Eu_1^2 > 0$, $H_2 : Eu_2^2 - Eu_1^2 < 0$. The rejection of H_0 in favor of either H_1 or H_2 indicates which model's residual variance dominates. In the nested case, however, where $x_2 = (x_1, z)$ H_0 is identical to $H_0 \cup H_1$. We also note that under the nested situation $H_0 : m(x) = m_1(x_1) = m_2(x_2)$ is equivalent to $H_0 : Eu_2^2 - Eu_1^2 = 0$.

For details see Lavergne and Vuong (1996) where they also show that, under H_0, the test statistic

$$T = \frac{n^{-1/2} \left[\sum_{i}^{n} \hat{u}_{i2}^2 w_{i2} - \sum_{i}^{n} \hat{u}_{i1}^2 w_{i1} \right]}{\hat{\sigma}} \sim \mathcal{N}(0, 1)$$

asymptotically, where $w_{ij} = I(\hat{f}_j(x_{ji}) > b_j)$ for $j = 1, 2$; b_j is a trimming parameter; and

$$\hat{\sigma}^2 = n^{-1} \sum_{i=1}^{n} \left[\hat{u}_{i2}^2 w_{i2} - \hat{u}_{i1}^2 w_{i1} \right]^2.$$

This result goes through provided $m_1(x_1) = m(x^*)$ or $m_2(x_2) = m(x^*)$ does not hold, where x^* are the regressors common to x_1 and x_2. Lavergne and

Vuong (1996) refer to this situation as being a generalized nested regression and indicate that under this situation T will have a degenerate distribution. We observe that the weights w_{ij} are stochastic weights and depend on the trimming and bandwidth parameters. The size and power performances of T are reported to be good.

Fan and Li (1996a) considered the nested case where $x_{2i} = (x_{1i}, z_i)$ and developed a consistent $\tilde{f}$ type conditional moment test for the significance of the subset of regressors z_i. Observing that $E[u_{i1}|x_{i2}] = m_2(x_{i1}, z_i) - m_1(x_{i1}) = 0$ under H_0 and $E(u_{i1}|x_{i2}) \neq 0$ under H_1, so that $E(u_{i1}|x_{i2})$, being a function of x_{i2}, should be uncorrelated with u_{1i}, they proposed a test for H_0 : $E[u_{i1}E(u_{i1}|x_{i2})] = 0$. Their test statistic is based on the density-weighted version of the sample analogue of this moment condition (e.g. $n^{-1}\sum_{i=1}^{n} u_{i1} E(u_{i1}|x_{i2})$) and is given by

$$\bar{\rho} = \frac{1}{n}\sum_{i=1}^{n}\left[\hat{u}_{i1}\hat{f}(x_{i1})\right] E\left[\hat{u}_{i1}\hat{f}(x_{i1})|x_{i2}\right]\hat{f}(x_{i2})$$

$$= \frac{1}{n(n-1)h}\sum_{i}\sum_{j\neq i}\left[\hat{u}_{i1}\hat{f}(x_{i1})\right]\left[\hat{u}_{j1}\hat{f}(x_{j1})\right] K\left(\frac{x_{i2}-x_{j2}}{h}\right),$$

where $\hat{u}_{i1} = y_i - \hat{m}_1(x_{i1})$ is the nonparametric residual. Fan and Li (1996a) show that

$$nh^{1/2}\bar{\rho} \sim \mathcal{N}(0, \upsilon_5),$$

where $\upsilon_5 = 2\int K^2(\psi)d\psi\, E\left[f(x_2)f^4(x_1)\sigma^4(x_2)\right]$. A consistent estimator of υ_5 is

$$\hat{\upsilon}_5 = (n(n-1)h)^{-1}\int K^2(\psi)d\psi$$

$$\times \sum_{i}\sum_{j\neq i}\left[\hat{u}_{i1}\hat{f}(x_{i1})\right]^2\left[\hat{u}_{j1}\hat{f}(x_{j1})\right]^2 K\left(\frac{x_i-x_j}{h}\right).$$

In parametric regression analysis there are several methods of selecting regressors, most of which can essentially be written as the residual variance multiplied by a penalty factor. Similar methods have been used for selecting h in the nonparametric literature, and these were described previously. They can also be used for variable selection; see Vieu (1994) where the CV score function of Härdle et al. (1988) has been advocated.

The statistic T above can also be used for testing nonnested models where x_1 and x_2 have no common variables. An alternative is again to do an artificial regression of the nonparametric residual under H_0 on the nonparametric mean

$\hat{m}_2(x_2)$ and test that the latter's coefficient is zero. This can be implemented by writing $y_i = (1 - \lambda)\hat{m}_1(x_{i1}) + \lambda\hat{m}_2(x_{i2}) + \epsilon_i$ or $y_i - \hat{m}_1(x_{i1}) = \lambda\,[\hat{m}_2(x_{i2}) - \hat{m}_1(x_{i1})] + \epsilon_i$ and testing for $\lambda = 0$. Delgado and Stengos (1994) establish the asymptotic normality of such a test. Alternatively, one can write $y_i = \theta(x_{i1}) + \lambda\hat{m}_2(x_{i2}) + \epsilon_i$, where $\theta(x_{i1}) = (1 - \lambda)m_1(x_{i1})$ is an unknown function of x_{i1}. In this case a semiparametric estimator of λ can be obtained by using Robinson's (1988a) method; see Section 5.21. Essentially, this is the least squares estimator, $\bar{\lambda}$, of the parameter in the regression of $y_i - \hat{E}(y_i|x_{i1})$ on $\hat{m}_2(x_{i2}) - \hat{E}(\hat{m}_2(x_{i2})|x_{i1})$, where $\hat{E}(\cdot)$ is obtained by the kernel method. Delgado et al. (1996) consider the numerator of $\bar{\lambda}$, weighted by the density, $\tilde{\lambda}_N$, as a test for $\lambda = 0$. The test therefore is based on

$$\tilde{\lambda}_N = \frac{1}{n}\sum_{i=1}^{n}\left[(y_i - \hat{E}(y_i|x_{i1}))\right]\left[\hat{y}_i - \hat{E}(\hat{y}_i|x_{i1})\right]\hat{f}^2(x_{i1}),$$

where $\hat{y}_i = \hat{m}_2(x_{i2})\hat{f}(x_{i2})$. They have shown that

$$n^{1/2}\tilde{\lambda}_N \sim \mathcal{N}(0, \upsilon_6)$$

as $n \to \infty$, where

$$\upsilon_6 = E\left[(m(x_{i2}) - Em(x_{i2}|x_{i1}))^2\,f^4(x_{i1})u_{i1}^2\right].$$

A consistent estimator of υ_6 is

$$\hat{\upsilon}_6 = n^{-1}\sum_{i=1}^{n}\left[(y_i - \hat{E}(y_i\,|\,x_{i1}))^2\,(\hat{y}_i - \hat{E}(\hat{y}_i\,|\,x_{i1}))^2\,\hat{f}^4(x_{i1})\right].$$

For the application of nonnested tests to the specification of Engle curves, see Delgado and Mora (1998).

3.14 Examples

3.14.1 A Model of Strike Duration

Kennan (1985) investigated the influence of cyclical activity upon strike duration. His variable to be explained was the completed duration of a strike (in weeks) as a function of a cyclical index. Horowitz and Neumann (1989a) find that a strike beginning in February has a different duration to other months, leading them to propose that y_i (duration) be related to the cyclical index (x_{1i}) and a dummy variable (x_{2i}) taking the value unity if the ith observation corresponds to a February strike, but zero otherwise. There were 566 observations in Kennan's sample and he fitted a high order polynomial in x_{1i} to find the relation between y_i and x_{1i}.

Our interest is in computing $E(y_i | x_{1i} = x_1, x_{2i} = x_2 = 0)$, the average completed duration (ACD) of non-February strikes when the activity index takes a value x_1. One possible estimator is the kernel estimator based on a product Gaussian kernel, that is,

$$K(\psi) = \Pi_{j=1}^2 (2\pi)^{-1/2} \exp\left(-\frac{1}{2}\psi_j^2\right),$$

where $\psi_j = (x_{ji} - x_j)/h$, with window width determined from Sections 2.7.1 and 3.6.1 after substituting x_{1i} for x_i. The latter choice results in $h = .316$, meaning that the entry $h^{-1}(x_{2i} - x_2) = h^{-1}(x_{2i} - 0)$ is either zero (for all non-February observations) or $h^{-1} = 3.1646$.[14] Consequently, it follows that the weight attached to any observation that has $x_{2i} = 1$ is close to zero because

$$K(\psi) = (2\pi)^{-1} \exp\left[-.5\left((x_{1i} - x_1)/h\right)^2 - .5h^{-2}\right] \simeq 0.$$

In turn this implies that the conditional expectation is being formed by deleting all February observations. Because of this reasoning it can be argued that the effective sample is lower (by about 10%) and one might want to adjust n to reflect this fact. Such an adjustment is not performed here; it would have a minor effect owing to the relatively large number of observations being employed.

Figure 3.1 gives a plot of the conditional mean, estimated by the kernel method, for fifty values of x_1 over the range of values observed in the sample for x_{1i}.[15] It is interesting to observe that the ACD appears to possess a complex relation with cyclical activity; the average completed duration of strikes would seem to peak for both large and small contractions in activity ($x_{1i} = 3.4$ corresponds to a zero value of the cyclical index before transformation). To further examine how robust this conclusion is to the choice of nonparametric estimator, it was decided to fit a flexible Fourier form, yielding the regression equation

$$y_i = \beta_0 + \beta_1 x_{1i} + \beta_2 x_{1i}^2$$

$$+ \sum_{j=1}^L \gamma_j \cos(j x_{1i}) + \sum_{j=1}^L \delta_j \sin(j x_{1i}) + x_{2i}\alpha + v_i. \tag{3.111}$$

Following the principles of Eastwood and Gallant (1991) outlined in Section 3.11, an upward testing strategy was used to select L. The F statistics for

---

[14] Data on x_{1i} was transformed to lie in $(0, 2\pi)$ for later use with the Fourier estimator. The transformation adopted was $25(x_{1i} + .14)$.

[15] If $\min_i\{x_{1i}\}$ or $\max_i\{x_{1i}\} = \bar{x}$, modifications of the kernel estimator are needed for values of x_1 within one window width of $\bar{x}$ to prevent bias. Rice (1984b) proposes a reflection method based on Richardson extrapolation. Here, it may be more sensible to focus on values of the conditional mean that have x_1 ranging between $.001 + .316$ and $5.528 - .316$ only. This would not change our discussion in any way.

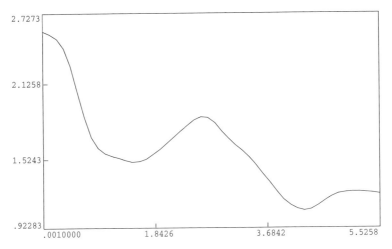

Figure 3.1. Average duration of strikes conditional on activity: Gaussian kernel estimator.

the addition of two trigonometric terms at a time, corresponding to $L = 1, 2, 3$, were 3.79, 2.92, and .4486 respectively, pointing to $L = 2$ as being a reasonable choice. Figure 3.2 therefore plots the estimates made of the conditional mean at x_1 from (3.111) by replacing x_{1i} by x_1, x_{2i} by zero, and β_j, γ_j, α by the ordinary least squares (OLS) estimates. It is striking that there is good agreement between the kernel and Fourier estimators, and both point to a peak at both low and high levels of contraction. However, the 95% confidence intervals associated with the Fourier estimator, presented in Figure 3.3, cast doubt on this feature, as the intervals are very wide for a large contraction. Partly, this could reflect the "boundary value" problem alluded to earlier, but it also reflects the paucity of observations on large contractions.[16] One fact that should be emphasized is that, despite the detection of a relation between strike duration and activity, only a very small fraction of the variation in strike activity is actually explained; the R^2 from the regression (3.111) when $L = 3$ is only .058. Hence, a good model for the duration series really requires a much wider set of determining variables.

3.14.2   Earnings–Age Profiles

In the example here we consider the specification of relationships between mean earnings and age (a proxy for experience) and the variability in earnings

---

[16] Note that the model fitted by Horowitz and Neumann implies that duration declines exponentially with activity; this is a common assumption in the duration literature.

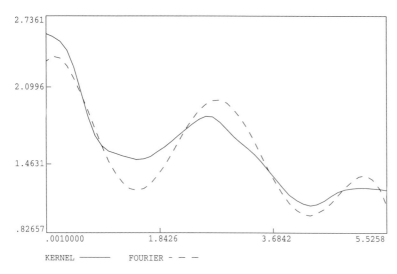

Figure 3.2. Average duration of strikes conditional on activity: kernel and flexible Fourier estimates.

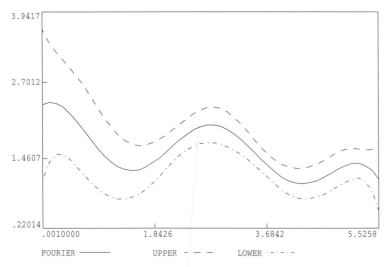

Figure 3.3. Average duration of strikes conditional on activity: flexible Fourier form estimates with upper and lower 95% confidence.

with age. There is an extensive parametric literature in labor economics, where earnings are generally modeled as

$$y_i = \alpha + \beta z_i + \gamma_o x_i + \gamma_1 x_i^2 + u_i,$$

where y_i is logarithm of earnings, z_i is education, and x_i is age (see Mincer, 1974 and Heckman and Polachek, 1974). Mincer finds that earnings increase with age through much of the working life but the rate of increase diminishes with age. He concludes that the concavity of the function is consistent with investment behavior implied by the optimal distribution of human capital investment over the life cycle. The quadratic parametric relationship between earnings and age has been challenged recently by Murphy and Welsch (1990). They have shown that the quadratic specification does not fit the data well, resulting in severely biased estimates of the earnings profile. They conclude that the quartic specification has a sufficiently small bias and could be used as the standard specification. Regarding the profile of the variability of earnings with age, using grouped data Mincer (1974) finds that it changes with the level of schooling.

Our main interest here is to explore the specifications of the mean and variance of earnings with age by nonparametric methods. For this purpose we considered two data sets: Canadian data (1971 Canadian Census Public Use Tapes) on 205 individuals and 1988 Chinese data on 2,449 urban males and 2,342 urban females. The individuals in both data sets were educated to grade 13, and thus schooling was assumed to be constant for simplicity (i.e., z_i does not appear in the relation). For the details on data and various other findings, see Ullah (1985), Singh et al. (1987), Chu and Marron (1991), and Basu and Ullah (1992). The conditional mean and variance of earnings (y) were calculated by using the formulae in Sections 3.2.2 and 3.2.6 with $q = 1$, a normal kernel, and $h = sn^{-1/5}$; $s^2 = \sum(x_i - \bar{x})^2/n$. The use of cross-validated h did not make any difference to the results.

We observe from Figure 3.4 that the quadratic parametric specification provides a smooth concave least squares estimate of the earnings profile. However, the nonparametric specification indicates a "dip" around the mean age of 40. This dip is also found if we use higher order or convolution kernels (Chu and Marron, 1991), and even if we consider the nonparametric regression of earnings on age and schooling. A possible explanation for this dip is the generation effect, because the cross section data represent the earnings of people at a point of time who essentially belong to different generations. Thus the plot of earnings represents the overlap of the earnings trajectories of different generations. Only if the sociopolitical environment of the economy has remained stable intergenerationally can we assume these trajectories to be the same. But this is not the case; one obvious counterexample being the Second World War. Therefore, the dip in the nonparametric regression might be attributed to the generation between 1935 and 1945. This is an important fact about the data

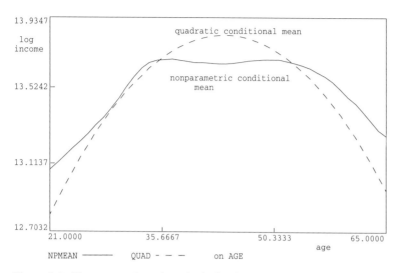

Figure 3.4. Nonparametric and quadratic fits, income/age relation (Canadian data).

observed from the nonparametric specification, but it is missed by a parametric specification. The dip also indicates the lack of global concavity and that the quartic relationship may be more appropriate than the quadratic specification; also see Murphy and Welch's (1990) parametric findings on this point. The question of whether the dip is significant or not can be answered by using the parametric and nonparametric specification testing procedures described in Section 3.13.

Looking at Figure 3.5 we find that, for Chinese data, male earnings increase at an increasing rate in the early part of their career. The peak is not found at the mean age, 37, but much later after retirement (65–66), and then it declines; the retirement age is 55. This is in contrast to the Canadian case where the decline begins around the mean age. Overall, the earnings profile appears to be quadratic. For females, however, the relationship is peculiar since between the ages 44 and 50 there is a decline in earnings and then an increase till around 60 after which it falls again. One explanation for the dip around ages 44–50 is again the cohort effect. This time it might be attributed to the cultural revolution in the 1950s. However, if true, the reason why the cultural revolution affected females ages 44–50, but not males, is unclear and needs further institutional details on the role of women in China. Finally, the observation that, for the same level of schooling, male earnings are uniformly higher than those for the female earnings indicates the possiblity of "wage discrimination." The test for the significant difference between male and female earning functions can be done by using the test due to Lavergne (1998).

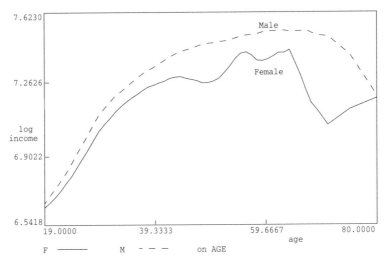

Figure 3.5. Nonparametric conditional mean, age/income relation (Chinese data, male and female).

Looking at Figure 3.6, we see that the Canadian data clearly exhibit variability in earnings that is a convex function of age; in particular, it appears to be inversely related to the mean earnings, that is, $\hat{V}(y|x) \propto (\hat{E}(y|x))^{-1}$ (this is also true of the Chinese data). The result is consistent with Mincer's (1974, p. 101) finding based on U.S. data. However, we should note that, although Mincer calculates a variance based on an arbitrary grouping of age, the nonparametric analysis does not need such a grouping. A useful implication of the above finding is that, in practice, one can circumvent the need for parametric specifications of $\hat{V}(y \mid x)$, the conditional heteroskedasticity – see Chapter 5 for more on this point.

Another observation from Figure 3.6 is that, for the early ages, the income is high and the variability (uncertainty) is low, but for the later ages the income is low and the variability is high. This implies that the income inequality may be influenced by life cycle effects. To analyze this hypothesis one can estimate several inequality measures conditional on age. Usually, this is done by calculating interage group inequality, which is then interpreted as a measure of inequality caused by life-cycle effects. The main criticism of this approach is that the results may be sensitive to the choice of the arbitrarily chosen age groups and their widths. Alternatively, one can calculate various inequality measures conditional on age. Some well-known inequality measures that satisfy the principle of transfers are Atkinson's (A) inequality measure, Theil's entropy (TE)

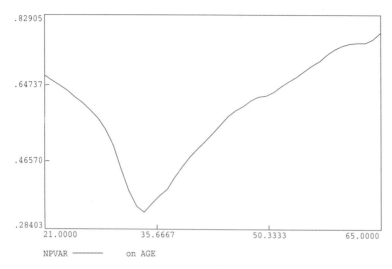

.82905

.64737

.46570

.28403
   21.0000   35.6667   50.3333   65.0000

NPVAR ——————— on AGE

Figure 3.6. Nonparametric conditional variance for income/age relation (Canadian data).

measure, and the coefficient of variation (C.V.); see Kakwani (1980) for an excellent description. The conditional versions of these measures can be written as

$$A(x) = 1 - [E(y^{1-\epsilon}|x)]^{1/(1-\epsilon)} (E(y|x))^{-1},$$
$$TE(x) = (E(y|x))^{-1} E[y \log y|x] - \log E(y|x),$$
$$C.V.(x) = \sqrt{V(y|x)}/E(y|x),$$

where the parameter $\epsilon \geq 0$ controls the degree of inequality aversion or perception. When $\epsilon = 0$ there is no perceived inequality and when $\epsilon = \infty$ there is concern for the poor only. In practice ϵ is usually considered to be between 0 and 2.

Though we do not perform such a calculation here, the inequality measures $A(x)$ and $TE(x)$ can easily be calculated by using the results of Section 3.2.6. For example, the $C.V.(x)$ follows directly from the calculation of $V(y|x)$ and $E(y|x)$. In fact, since in the above study, $\hat{V}(y|x) \propto (\hat{E}(y|x))^{-1}$, it will be the case that $\hat{C.V.}(x) \propto (\hat{E}(y|x))^{-3/2}$.

3.14.3   Review of Applied Work on Nonparametric Regression

There has been an increasing use of nonparametric methods in applied econometrics in recent years and an exhaustive treatment is impossible. Consequently, we limit ourselves to an interesting selection of the papers that have made applications of nonparametric regression to various areas of economics. The details can be found in the papers cited here.

Using Canadian longitudinal data Burbidge and Davies (1994) have examined age profiles of saving and wealth-holding. An important finding is that saving rates vary much more by income level than by age. Similar studies for the Netherlands, based on socio-economic panel data, have been done by Alessie et al. (1997). Essentially they examine income, savings, and wealth of the same household over time and over the life cycle. Zheng (1999) has done extensive work on the nonparametric earnings–age profile for U.S. males and females, and for various educational groups. Pudney (1993) and Basu and Ullah (1992) analyze the Chinese earnings–age profile, with the former concentrating upon nonparametric inequality measures.

In addition to the earnings–age profile studies mentioned in Section 3.14.2 there are studies on wealth–age profiles by Magee et al. (1991) and consumption–age profiles by Robb et al. (1992). These studies calculate nonparametric estimates of quantiles (median, 80%, 20%) of the conditional distribution of consumption (Y) given age $(X = x)$ instead of the conditional mean. The nonparametric estimator of the α quantile, $\hat{q}_\alpha(x)$, is the solution of $\hat{f}(\hat{q}_\alpha(x)|x) = \alpha$, where $\hat{f}(y|x)$ is the kernel estimator of $f(y|x)$. Robb et al. use the Canadian data (1978 to 1986) and analyze both a cross section of consumption–age profiles and the consumption pattern of cohorts for various educational groups. The main issue adressed is whether the consumption–age pattern observed in the cross section reasonably reflects what happens to actual cohorts. Based on the second, fifth, and eighth quantiles, their findings indicate that the cohort patterns are very similar to those in the cross section, thus they conclude that consumption–age profiles are generally representative of life-cycle behavior.

Microeconomic applications to production and demand relations are also common. For example Deaton and Ng (1998) look into the effect of price and tax reforms by nonparametric methods. Gallant (1981) and Vinod and Ullah (1988) look at production functions while McAllister and McManus (1993) analyze scale efficiencies of small and large banks. Demand curves have been estimated by Härdle et al. (1991) and McMillan et al. (1989). More specifically, nonparametric Engle curves have been extensively investigated in the work of Lewbel (1991), Gozalo (1997), Härdle et al. (1991), Bierens and Pott-Buter (1990), and Nicol (1993). In time series analysis, various authors have made forecasts by nonparametric regression. This includes the work of Diebold and Nason (1990) for exchange rates, Prescott and Stengos (1991) for gold prices, and Zhou (1993) for stock market returns. An interesting comparative study of the forecasting ability of nonparametric methods for exchange rates is by Mizrach (1992). Unlike most studies, which tend to use the kernel estimator, he compares a nearest neighbour and a locally linear regression smoother, finding that the latter produced far superior forecasts. In another area of macroeconomic time series, Wulwick and Mack (1990) explore the relationship between inflation and unemployment using Phillips's data and find that the parametric relationship often used does not hold globally, that is, for the entire range of data values.

Besides the above papers exploring the applications of nonparametric regression in micro- and macroeconomics, other work has started to appear in various other areas of economics and business. Finance is an attractive area, due to the large number of observations available. Early work with kernel- and series-based estimates, such as that of Pagan and Hong (1991) on the shape of the risk premium, has broadened out. There has been a noticeable recent use of local linear regression smoothers, for example, McCallister and McManus (1993) on the rate of return to banking, Gourieroux and Scaillet (1994) on estimating the term structure, and Bossaerts and Hillion (1997) on the relation between options prices and their determinants, such as strike price and volatility. Hutchison et al. (1994) also model the last function using neural network methods, whereas Kearns (1993) applied a flexible Fourier form. In development economics Deaton (1989) estimates the proportion of households producing and selling rice in various rural regions of Thailand. Essentially he estimates a nonparametric regression where the independent variable is consumption expenditure and the dependent variable is a dichotomous variable taking the value one if the household produces rice and zero if not. Subramanian and Deaton (1996) used Indian National Sample Survey data to explore the relationship between calories and per capita household expenditure for the state of Maharashtra. Budd (1993) has analyzed food prices and rural welfare for Ivory Coast. In resource economics Racine and Smith (1991) study the modeling of the growth process of fish populations. Rust (1988) describes a number of ways in which nonparametrics can be applied to the area of marketing research.

4 Nonparametric Estimation of Derivatives

4.1 Introduction

The econometric model considered in Chapter 3 was

$$Y = m(X) + U,$$

where Y is a dependent variable, X is a vector of regressors, U is the disturbance, and $m(x)$ is the regression function (conditional mean of Y given $X = x$). Often in econometric analysis it is the derivatives of $m(x)$ as well as $m(x)$ itself that are of interest. For example, the first derivative indicates the response coefficient (regression coefficient if m is linear) of Y with respect to X, and hence it describes the effect on the dependent variable due to changes in the regressors. The second derivative indicates the curvature of m and relates to questions concerning the concavity and convexity of m. Both of these derivatives appear in many quantities that need to be computed when assessing the utility of some economic action. A good example occurs in the modern theory of options pricing. It is known that the option price depends upon a number of underlying random variables; one is the asset price that the option is based on and another is the level of volatility in this price. As mentioned in the previous chapter, nonparametric methods have been used to estimate the response surface connecting the options price and these two quantities. The first and second derivatives of the expected value of the option price with respect to the asset price are generally referred to as delta and gamma risk, whereas the first derivative with respect to the volatility is vega risk. Under the guidelines for measuring market risk for the purpose of prudential supervision of banks set out by the Basle Committee on Banking Supervision, each of these risks must be quantified, so that estimates of the underlying derivatives of the response function need to be made.

In parametric econometrics the estimation of these derivatives and testing of associated hypotheses are carried out by assuming some functional form for the relationship (see, e.g., Diewert (1971) and the survey article by Lau (1986)), quite often a linear one (see a textbook of econometrics, e.g., Greene (1997)). In the options pricing case one might use the Black–Scholes formula, although it is known that its functional form is dependent on assumptions that are incorrect for financial assets. Any misspecification in the functional form of m leads to inconsistent estimates of the true derivatives and may affect the size and power of any test performed on them. Consequently, it is of some interest to investigate whether the nonparametric mode of analysis introduced in the preceding two chapters might be gainfully applied to the estimation of partial derivatives. This chapter therefore shows how partial derivatives may be estimated and tests of relevant economic hypotheses may be performed, by using the nonparametric regression estimators set out in Chapter 3.

Section 4.2 sets out the basic model and formulae to compute partial derivatives. Broadly, there are two ways of doing this: by numerical perturbation of the conditional mean or by directly differentiating the nonparametric estimator of the conditional mean. Section 4.3 considers how to devise estimators from these formulae, both for partial derivatives and for the average of these over the variable space. There are important uses for such "average dervatives" in later chapters, but they may also be of interest in their own right. Section 4.4 deals with hypothesis testing after derivatives have been estimated; Section 4.5 details the asymptotic theory of kernel and series estimators of the derivatives. Modifications needed to analyze average derivatives is the concern of Section 4.6 while Section 4.7 treats some of the issues arising in implementing the estimators. Finally, two illustrations of the techniques are provided in Section 4.8 along with a short review of applications in the literature. The first illustration involves a simple Monte Carlo study to estimate elasticities in a production relation; the second uses the Canadian and Chinese data sets of Chapter 3 to explore the shape of the function relating earnings to experience.

4.2 The Model and Partial Derivative Formulae

Suppose we have $q + 1 = p$ economic variables $Y, X_1, \ldots, X_q$, where Y is the dependent variable and the Xs are "regressors." The unknown joint density of these variables at the point (y, x) is $f(y, x)$. If $E|Y| < \infty$, the conditional mean of Y given $X = x$ exists and takes the form

$$E(Y|X = x) = m(x) = \frac{\int yf(y, x)\,dy}{f(x)} = \frac{g(x)}{f(x)}, \tag{4.1}$$

where $f(x)$ is the marginal density of X. The regression function $m(x)$ is a real-valued function of x and, replicating (4.1) for $i = 1, \ldots, n$,

$$y_i = m(x_i) + u_i = m(x_{i1}, \ldots, x_{iq}) + u_i, \tag{4.2}$$

where, by construction, the disturbance u_i is such that $E(u_i | X = x) = 0$ and $V(u_i | X = x) = \sigma^2$.[1] When $m(x) = x_1\beta_1 + \cdots + x_j\beta_j + \cdots + x_q\beta_q$ is linear, as often specified in parametric econometrics, then $\beta_j = \partial m(x)/\partial x_j$ is the jth regression coefficient, or first partial derivative, which gives the change in Y due to a unit change in x_j. The regression coefficient β_j is fixed for all x. However, when $m(x)$ is nonlinear, say $m(x) = x_1\beta_1 + \cdots + x_j^2\beta_j + \cdots + x_q\beta_q$, then the derivative of interest, $\partial m(x)/\partial x_j$, is not fixed but varies with x, that is, $\partial m(x)/\partial x_j = \beta_j(x) = 2x_j\beta_j$. A fixed value of the derivative can be calculated at, say, the mean value of data on x_j. Below we develop the derivatives of interest in economics when $m(x)$ is not specified a priori as a linear or nonlinear parametric function.

The response coefficient of Y with respect to a change in a regressor, say $x_j (j = 1, \ldots, q)$, is defined as the first-order partial derivative of $m(x)$ with respect to x_j and is

$$\beta_j(x) = \frac{\partial m(x)}{\partial x_j} = \lim_{h \to 0} (2h)^{-1}[m(x + e_jh) - m(x - e_jh)]. \quad (4.3)$$

In (4.3) e_j is a $q \times 1$ vector with unity in the jth position and zeros elsewhere, meaning that $m(x + e_jh) = m(x_1, \ldots, x_j + h, \ldots, x_q)$. When $q = 1, x = x_1$ and $\beta_1(x_1) = (m(x_1 + h) - m(x_1 - h))/2h$ as $h \to 0$. Note that (4.3) is a varying response coefficient since it is a function of x. A fixed response coefficient could be defined as $\beta(\bar{x})$, that is, $\beta(x)$ evaluated at some specific value of x, say the mean of x_i, $\bar{x} = (\bar{x}_1, \ldots, \bar{x}_q)$, or by calculating the average derivative $\bar{\beta}(x) = E\beta(x) = \int \beta(x) f(x) dx$. Note that when $m(x)$ is linear, the first partials of $m(x)$ are equivalent to regression coefficients.

An alternative formula for $\beta_j(x)$ can be obtained by taking the analytical derivative of $m(x)$. From (4.1), we have

$$m(x)f(x) = g(x), \quad (4.4)$$

and differentiating (4.4) with respect to x_j gives the first derivative of $m(x)$ as

$$\beta_j(x) = f(x)^{-1}\left[g_j^{(1)}(x) - f_j^{(1)}(x)m(x)\right], \quad (4.5)$$

with $g_j^{(1)}(x) = \partial g(x)/\partial x_j$ and $f_j^{(1)} = \partial f(x)/\partial x_j$.

Economic theory often imposes theoretical curvature conditions (concavity or convexity) on $m(x)$. For example, the Slutsky matrix is symmetric and

---

[1] x_{ij} is the ith observation upon the jth element in x. Some typographical problems arise in this chapter because we sometimes wish to differentiate with respect to an element of x. Normally the convention in this book is that the subscript on x represents an observation. As it is cumbersome to carry a double subscript it is convenient to adhere to a convention whereby a "j" subscript will be adopted when reference is being made to an element in x and an "i" subscript when designating an observation.

negative semidefinite whereas the price elasticity of demand may be an increasing function of price. Thus the behavior of the second-order partial derivative of $m(x)$ is also of interest. This is

$$\beta_j^{(2)}(x) = \frac{\partial^2}{\partial x_j^2} m(x)$$

$$= \lim_{h \to 0} (2h)^{-2} [m(x + 2e_j h) - 2m(x) - m(x - 2e_j h)]. \quad (4.6)$$

The analytical expression for $\beta_j^{(2)}(x)$, though complicated, can be written by taking the derivative of $\beta_j(x)$ in (4.5). In some other situations, for example in the estimation of demand and production functions, the cross elasticities (cross derivatives of $m(x)$) are also of some interest, for example, $\partial^2 m(x)/\partial x_1 \partial x_2$.[2] We observe that the derivatives described above are the pointwise derivative at any given value x. These derivatives describe the local behavior of the shape of the regression function. This will be useful if we want to analyze, for example, the earnings behavior of the cross section of individuals at different age levels including the mean age. However, sometimes one might be interested in analyzing the global behavior of the shape of the earnings function. In this case, a measure of interest would be the expected (average) value of the derivative over all x, that is,

$$\bar{\beta}_j = E\beta_j(X) = \int_x \beta_j(x) f(x) \, dx, \quad (4.7)$$

or the weighted average

$$\bar{\beta}_j^* = E\beta_j(X) w(X), \quad (4.8)$$

where $w(x)$ is a weight function. One choice of w could be the density function of X itself.

In the following section we consider the estimation of the partial derivatives of $m(x)$. Before presenting these results it should be noted that the partial derivatives of interest described above are easily extended to situations in which X are lagged values of Y or for systems of equations. For example, for a stationary, nonlinear, first-order autoregressive model, the regression function (4.1) becomes $E(Y|Y_{-1})$, where Y_{-1} is the lagged value of the stationary variable Y. Similarly, for the system model, Y will be a vector of (say) k endogenous variables and $E(Y|X)$ will be a vector regression function. Extension of the results to the simultaneous equations model is discussed in Chapter 6.

---

[2] In general, the sth-order ($s = 1, 2, \ldots$) partial or cross partial derivatives of $m(x)$ can be written as $\beta_j^{(s)} = \partial^s m(x)/\partial x_1^{s_1} \ldots \partial x_q^{s_q}$ where $s = s_1 + \cdots + s_q \geq 0, s_j \geq 0$. For $s = 1$ we write $\beta_j^{(1)} = \beta_j(x)$. Explicit expressions for $\beta_j^{(s)}$ are given in Ullah (1988a).

4.3 Estimation

4.3.1 *Estimation of Partial Derivatives by Kernel Methods*

From Section 2.8 of Chapter 2 the kernel estimator of the joint density $f(y, x)$ is

$$\hat{f}(y, x) = \frac{1}{nh^p} \sum_{i=1}^{n} K_1 \left(\frac{y_i - y}{h}, \frac{x_i - x}{h} \right), \tag{4.9}$$

whereas that of the marginal density $f(x)$ is

$$\hat{f}(x) = \frac{1}{nh^q} \sum_{i=1}^{n} K \left(\frac{x_i - x}{h} \right). \tag{4.10}$$

Using the definition of $m(x)$ given in (4.1), an estimator of the numerator is

$$\hat{g}(x) = \int y \hat{f}(y, x) \, dy = \frac{1}{nh^q} \sum_{i=1}^{n} y_i K \left(\frac{x_i - x}{h} \right), \tag{4.11}$$

exactly as derived in (3.13); see Section 3.2.3 for details. As described in that section the Nadarya–Watson kernel regression estimator of $m(x)$ is

$$\hat{m}(x) = \sum_{i=1}^{n} K \left(\frac{x_i - x}{h} \right) y_i \bigg/ \sum_{i=1}^{n} K \left(\frac{x_i - x}{h} \right) = \frac{\hat{g}(x)}{\hat{f}(x)}. \tag{4.12}$$

Now (4.3) suggests that we can estimate $\beta_j(x)$ by the formula there provided that h is small enough, or at least tends to zero as $n \to \infty$. Intuitively, a consistent estimator of $\beta_j(x)$ is simply

$$b_j(x) = \frac{1}{2h} [m(x + e_j h) - m(x - e_j h)],$$

where $h = h_n \to 0$ as $n \to \infty$. But this is not operational since $m(x \pm e_j h)$ is unknown, leading to the modified estimator

$$\tilde{\beta}_j(x) = \frac{1}{2h} [\hat{m}(x + e_j h) - \hat{m}(x - e_j h)]. \tag{4.13}$$

The estimator (4.13), described in Ullah (1988a) and Rilstone and Ullah (1989), merely involves the calculation of $\hat{m}(x)$ in (4.12) at the points $x \pm e_j h$ and represents the standard two-sided finite difference formula used in the numerical approximation of first derivatives.

Instead of computing a derivative by perturbation, Vinod and Ullah (1988) proposed the estimator of $\beta_j(x) = \partial m(x)/\partial x_j$ as the analytical derivative of $\hat{m}(x)$ in (4.12). By substituting (4.10) and (4.11), and their derivatives, into (4.5), this estimator can be written as

$$\hat{\beta}_j(x) = \hat{f}(x)^{-1} \big[\hat{g}_j^{(1)}(x) - \hat{f}_j^{(1)}(x) \hat{m}(x) \big], \tag{4.14}$$

where

$$\hat{g}_j^{(1)}(x) = -\frac{1}{nh^{q+1}} \sum_{i=1}^{n} y_i K_j^{(1)} \left(\frac{x_i - x}{h} \right),$$

$$\hat{f}_j^{(1)}(x) = -\frac{1}{nh^{q+1}} \sum_{i=1}^{n} K_j^{(1)} \left(\frac{x_i - x}{h} \right),$$

(4.15)

and $K_j^{(1)}(\psi_i) = \partial K(\psi_i)/\partial \psi_{ij}$, $\psi_i = (x_i - x)/h$, and ψ_{ij} is the jth component of ψ_i.

We observe that the estimator based on the numerical derivative $\tilde{\beta}_j(x)$ is approximately the same as the estimator based on the analytical derivative $\hat{\beta}_j(x)$, that is, $\tilde{\beta}_j(x) \simeq \hat{\beta}_j(x)$. Also, the asymptotic properties of $\tilde{\beta}_j(x)$ are the same as those of $\hat{\beta}_j(x)$. This can be seen by using a Taylor series expansion and writing, say for $q = 1$,

$$\hat{m}(x \pm h) = \hat{m}(x) \pm h\hat{m}^{(1)}(x) + O(h^2) = \hat{m}(x) \pm h\hat{\beta}_j(x) + O(h^2).$$

Substituting this into (4.13) then gives $\tilde{\beta}_j(x) - \hat{\beta}_j(x) = O(h)$, which tends to zero for large n. Details on the asymptotic properties of the derivative estimators are given in Section 4.5.

It is easily seen that the numerical derivative estimator can be extended for the second- and higher order derivatives. For example, the estimator for the second-order derivative of $m(x)$ from (4.6) is simply

$$\tilde{\beta}_j^{(2)}(x) = (\hat{m}(x + 2e_jh) - 2\hat{m}(x) - \hat{m}(x - 2e_jh))/(2h)^2.$$

Likewise, for $s > 2$, the expression for $\tilde{\beta}_j^{(s)}(x)$ can be written in a straightforward way; see Ullah (1988b). However the analytical formulae for $\hat{\beta}_j^{(s)}(x)$ for $s \geq 2$ quickly become quite unwieldy because of the ratio form of the kernel estimates. In view of this Mack and Muller (1989) have considered the following estimator. Suppose $Y^* = Y/f(X)$ is a scaled version of Y, making the joint density of the transformed variables Y^* and X at the points y^* and x, respectively, $f(y^*, x) = f(y, x)f(x)$. Consequently,

$$m(x) = \int yf(y|x)\, dy = \int y^* f(y^*|x)\, dy^*$$

(4.16)

and its estimator becomes

$$\hat{m}(x) = \frac{1}{nh^q} \sum_{i=1}^{n} K\left(\frac{x_i - x}{h} \right) y_i^*$$

$$= \frac{1}{nh^q} \sum_{i=1}^{n} K\left(\frac{x_i - x}{h} \right) \frac{y_i}{f(x_i)}.$$

(4.17)

The estimator of the derivative of $m(x)$ with respect to x_j is then

$$\tilde{\tilde{\beta}}_j(x) = -\frac{1}{nh^{q+1}} \sum_{i=1}^{n} K_j^{(1)} \left(\frac{x_i - x}{h} \right) \frac{y_i}{f(x_i)}. \tag{4.18}$$

In practice $f(x_i)$ in (4.18) is replaced by $\hat{f}(x_i)$ in (4.10) or any other density estimator from Chapter 2, making

$$\tilde{\beta}_j(x) = -\frac{1}{nh^{q+1}} \sum_{i=1}^{n} K_j^{(1)} \left(\frac{x_i - x}{h} \right) \frac{y_i}{\hat{f}(x_i)}. \tag{4.19}$$

This estimator has the advantage that only a derivative of the numerator is needed and thus it may be simpler to work with for the sth derivative $\tilde{\beta}_j^s(x)$ compared to $\hat{\beta}_j^{(s)}(x)$, although it may not have much advantage over $\tilde{\beta}_j^{(s)}(x)$. Its principal disadvantage is that $\hat{f}(x_i)$ has to be computed at every point in the sample and this will be computationally expensive if n is large.

The derivative estimators defined above are based on the kernel estimator of $m(x)$. Other estimators, based on different ways of estimating $m(x)$, are also possible. For this purpose, consider the general class of conditional mean estimators

$$\tilde{m}(x) = \sum_{i=1}^{n} w_{ni}(x) y_i, \tag{4.20}$$

where $w_{ni}(x)$ is a weight function depending on the distance of x_i from x. For the kernel regression case $w_{ni}(x) = K((x_i - x)/h)/\sum_{i=1}^{n} K((x_i - x)/h)$; weights for nearest neighbor and other regression estimators are described in Section 3.2.5. With the definition of the conditional moment as in (4.20) a general class of sth-order derivative estimators is

$$\beta_j^{*(s)}(x) = \sum_{i=1}^{n} w_{ni}^{(s)}(x) y_i, \tag{4.21}$$

where $w_{ni}^{(s)}(x) = \partial^s w_{ni}(x) / \partial x_j^s$ can be obtained either by finite differences or analytically. When X is a fixed design variable and $q = 1$, the estimator (4.21) has been considered in Georgiev (1984), Gasser and Müller (1984), Müller (1988), and Härdle and Gasser (1985). We also note that substituting (4.15) into (4.14) we can write $\hat{\beta}_j(x)$ as a weighted sum of ys, as in (4.21) with $s = 1$ and w_{ni} as the kernel weights (see (4.46)). The weights of y in $\hat{\beta}_j(x)$ sum to zero. These features are similar to the least squares estimator of the slope coefficients in a linear regression model that are weighted sums of ys with weights that sum to zero.

4.3.2 Estimation of Partial Derivatives by Series Methods

Section 3.8 discussed the estimation of $m(x)$ by series methods. These involve replacing $m(x)$ by a series approximation and then using the predictions from an OLS regression of y_i against the approximating terms as the estimator of $m(x)$. Estimators of the partial derivatives by series methods would just use (4.13) or the partial derivative of the approximating function. Thus, taking x to be scalar, if $m(x_i)$ was approximated by $\sum_{k=1}^{(M/2)}[\cos(kx_i)\gamma_k + \sin(kx_i)\delta_k]$, the estimator of $m(x)$ would be $\bar{m}(x) = \sum_{k=1}^{(M/2)}[\cos(kx_i)\hat{\gamma}_k + \sin(kx_i)\hat{\delta}_k]$, where $\hat{\gamma}_k$ and $\hat{\delta}_k$ are the OLS estimates from the regression of y_i against $\cos(kx_i)$ and $\sin(kx_i)$, $k = 1, \ldots, (M/2)$. Perturbation of x and reevaluation of $\bar{m}(x)$ would enable the construction of the derivative estimator in (4.13). Alternatively, one could just differentiate $\bar{m}(x)$ with respect to x_j.

4.3.3 Estimation of Average Derivatives

It was indicated in Section 4.2 that an alternative to the pointwise derivative is the average derivative. This provides information on the global behavior of the curvature of the regression function. Härdle and Stoker (1989) and Rilstone (1991b) have developed the estimation of such an average derivative over the sample space, that is, they estimate

$$\bar{\beta}_j = E\beta_j(x) = \int_x \beta_j(x)f(x)\,dx \tag{4.22}$$

$$= \int_x \left(\frac{\partial}{\partial x_j}m(x)\right)f(x)\,dx \tag{4.23}$$

$$= -\int_x \left(m(x)\frac{\partial f(x)}{\partial x_j}\right)dx \tag{4.24}$$

$$= E[m(x_i)s_j(x_i)], \tag{4.25}$$

where $s_j(x) = -f_j^{(1)}(x)/f(x)$ is the negative of the score function of the density with respect to the jth element in x.[3] Therefore

$$\bar{\beta}_j = E[y_i s_j(x_i)], \tag{4.26}$$

since $E[(y_i - m_i)|x_i] = 0$.

---

[3] The step from (4.23) to (4.24) involves integration by parts. When X is a single bounded random variable, $a \le X \le b$, with density zero at the boundary, we would get $m(b)f(b) - m(a)f(a) = \int_a^b [\partial m(x)/\partial x]f(x)dx + \int_a^b m(x)[\partial f(x)/\partial x]\,dx$ and the equality holds because $f(a) = f(b) = 0$. When X is a vector of unbounded random variables a more delicate argument is required; see Powell et al. (1989, Appendix 1).

Instead of the "raw" average derivatives Powell et al. (1989) considered the *weighted* average derivative, which can be written as

$$\bar{\beta}_j^* = E\left(\frac{\partial}{\partial x_j} m(x) f(x)\right) = \int \left(\frac{\partial}{\partial x_j} m(x)\right) f^2(x)\, dx \qquad (4.27)$$

$$= -2E\left(m(x) \frac{\partial f(x)}{\partial x_j}\right) \qquad (4.28)$$

$$= -2E\left[y_i f_j^{(1)}(x_i)\right]. \qquad (4.29)$$

Again the transition from (4.27) to (4.28) follows after integration by parts.

An estimator of $\bar{\beta}_j$ is

$$\tilde{\bar{\beta}}_j = \frac{1}{n} \sum_{i=1}^n y_i \hat{s}_j(x_i) = -\frac{1}{n} \sum_{i=1}^n y_i \frac{\hat{f}_j^{(1)}(x_i)}{\hat{f}(x_i)}, \qquad (4.30)$$

where $\hat{f}(x_i)$ is the kernel density estimator and $\hat{f}_j^{(1)}(x_i)$ is its derivative with respect to x_j. Since $\hat{f}(x_i)$ is in the denominator, the function $\hat{s}(x_i)$ may not be well behaved when $\hat{f}(x_i)$ is very small. To circumvent this problem, Härdle and Stoker (1989) recommended trimming, retaining only those observations for which $\hat{f}(x_i)$ is above a bound (b), and the trimmed estimator becomes

$$\bar{\beta}_{jT} = \frac{1}{n} \sum_{i=1}^n y_i \hat{s}_j(x_i) I[\hat{f}(x_i) > b], \qquad (4.31)$$

where b is a trimming parameter such that $b \to 0$ as $n \to \infty$. One disadvantage with this approach is that one has to drop some of the n observations in the calulation of $\tilde{\bar{\beta}}_j$, and this may have a deleterious effect on its small-sample properties. An alternative that is closer to a "pure" trimming approach is to replace $\hat{f}(x_i)$ in (4.30) by the maximum of $\hat{f}(x_i)$ and b, producing

$$\bar{\beta}_{jT} = -\frac{1}{n} \sum_{i=1}^n y_i \frac{\hat{f}_j^{(1)}(x_i)}{\hat{f}^*(x_i)}, \qquad (4.32)$$

where $\hat{f}^*(x_i) = \max\{\hat{f}(x_i), b\}$. This estimator will use all the n observations and its analytical properties may be easier to find than if (4.30) was selected.

The estimator $\tilde{\bar{\beta}}_j$ above requires a boundary assumption (see Footnote 3) on $f(x)$, and Stoker (1991) refers to $\tilde{\bar{\beta}}_j$ as an indirect estimator since it is based on the estimation of (4.26). For the calculation of $\tilde{\bar{\beta}}_j$ one needs the density estimate, and its derivative. Alternatively, a direct estimator of $\bar{\beta}_j$ can be obtained from (4.22) as

$$\hat{\bar{\beta}}_j = \frac{1}{n} \sum_{i=1}^{n} \hat{\beta}_j(x_i) = \int \hat{\beta}_j(x) \, d\hat{F}(x), \tag{4.33}$$

where $\hat{F}$ is the empirical distribution function and $\hat{\beta}_j(x_i)$ is the Vinod–Ullah pointwise estimator given in (4.14) with $\hat{f}$ replaced by $\hat{f}^*$ as in (4.32). Rilstone (1991b) has shown that $\hat{\bar{\beta}}_j$ is asymptotically equivalent to $\tilde{\tilde{\beta}}_j$.

An alternative form of the direct estimator (4.33) can be obtained by using the Mack and Muller pointwise derivative estimator in (4.19). This is

$$\bar{b}_j = \frac{1}{n} \sum_{k=1}^{n} \tilde{\tilde{\beta}}_j(x_k). \tag{4.34}$$

Using (4.19) it can easily be seen that

$$\bar{b}_j = -\frac{1}{n} \sum_{k=1}^{n} \frac{1}{nh^{q+1}} \sum_{i=1}^{n} K_j^{(1)} \left(\frac{x_i - x_k}{h} \right) \frac{y_i}{\hat{f}(x_i)} \tag{4.35}$$

$$= -\frac{1}{n} \sum_{i=1}^{n} y_i \frac{\hat{f}_j^{(1)}(x_i)}{\hat{f}(x_i)} = \tilde{\tilde{\beta}}_j. \tag{4.36}$$

This equality holds even when we consider trimming of types (4.31) and (4.32) in (4.19). Thus, interestingly the direct estimator of the average derivatives $\bar{b}_j$, based on the Mack–Muller pointwise derivative estimator, is identical with the Härdle and Stoker indirect estimator $\tilde{\tilde{\beta}}_j$. But note that $\hat{\bar{\beta}}_j$ in (4.33) is not identical to $\tilde{\tilde{\beta}}_j$. These results are not surprising because both $\bar{b}_j$ and $\tilde{\tilde{\beta}}_j$ avoid taking derivatives of the ratio, in contrast to $\hat{\bar{\beta}}_j$. Fan (1990b) has shown that the above results hold for the sth-order derivative estimator as well.

The weighted average derivative estimator can be formed as

$$\hat{\beta}_j^* = -2n^{-1} \sum y_i \hat{f}_j^{(1)}(x_i). \tag{4.37}$$

An alternative way of estimating $\bar{\beta}^*$ (the $q \times 1$ vector of derivatives $\bar{\beta}_j^*$, $j = 1, \ldots, q$) is to write $v_i = y_i - x_i' \bar{\beta}^{**}$, where $\bar{\beta}^{**} = \bar{\beta}^*/E(f(x_i))$ is a normalized weighted average derivative, and to recognize that $E(f_j^{(1)}(x_i)v_i) = 0$. This last equality is found from the following steps. Reversing the operations in (4.24) and (4.23) we have

$$E\left[f_j^{(1)}(x_i)v_i\right] = -E\left\{ f(x_i) \partial \left[m(x_i) - x_i' \bar{\beta}^{**} \right] / \partial x_{ij} \right\} \tag{4.38}$$

$$= -E\left[f(x_i)(\partial m(x_i)/\partial x_{ij}) - f(x_i)\bar{\beta}_j^* \right] \tag{4.39}$$

$$= -\int \left[f^2(x_i)(\partial m(x_i)/\partial x_{ij}) \, dx_i \right] + \bar{\beta}_j^*, \tag{4.40}$$

which equals zero by the definition of $\bar{\beta}_j^*$ in (4.27). Now the orthogonality conditions $E(f_j^{(1)}(x_i)v_i) = 0$ give a method of moments estimator of $\bar{\beta}^{**}$ that is just the instrumental variable estimator in which $\hat{f}_j^{(1)}(x_i)$ is used as an instrument for x_{ij}. Once $\bar{\beta}^{**}$ is found, $\bar{\beta}^*$ can be estimated by replacing $E(f(x_i))$ by $n^{-1} \sum \hat{f}(x_i)$. Powell et al.'s (1989) Monte Carlo study indicates that the instrumental variables estimator of $\bar{\beta}^*$ is superior in small samples to that in (4.37).

An instrumental variables estimator of the vector $\bar{\beta} = E[y_i s(x_i)]$, $s(x) = (s_1(x)\ldots, s_q(x))'$ as in (4.26), can also be obtained. Since $Es(x) = 0$, $\bar{\beta} = \text{cov}(s(x_i), y_i)$. Further, it can be shown that $\text{cov}(s(x_i), x_i) = E[s(x_i)x_i'] = E(\partial x_i'/\partial x_i) = I_q$ (again reversing the operations in (4.23) and (4.24)). Therefore $\bar{\beta} = [\text{cov}(s(x_i), x_i)]^{-1} \text{cov}(s(x_i), y_i)$, and $\hat{\bar{\beta}}_M = \left[\sum_{i=1}^n \hat{s}(x_i)x_i' \right]^{-1} \sum_{i=1}^n \hat{s}(x_i)y_i$ is a method of moments estimator of $\bar{\beta}$. This estimator can also be interpreted as an instrumental variable estimator of $\bar{\beta}$, $\hat{\bar{\beta}}_{IV}$, in the regression $y_i = x_i'\bar{\beta} + v_i$, where the instrument for x_i is $\hat{s}(x_i)$. Stoker (1991) has shown that $\hat{\bar{\beta}}_{IV}$ is asymptotically equivalent to $\hat{\bar{\beta}}_j$ in (4.30). However, these two estimators may have different small-sample efficiencies.

A point to be noted here is that all the average derivative estimators can be expressed as a weighted sum of y_i, that is, $\sum w_{ni}(x_i)y_i$. As observed before this was also the case with the pointwise derivatives; the difference is that $w_{ni}(x_i)$ is now evaluated at x_i and not at x. Furthermore, whereas the weights for the average derivative estimator $\bar{\beta}$ sum to zero in the limit, this is not the case with either the Härdle and Stoker or Powell et al. estimator.

4.3.4 *Local Linear Derivative Estimators*

As described in Chapter 3, the local linear regression estimator for $q = 1$ is obtained by performing a weighted regression of y_i against $z_i' = (1, (x_i - x))$ using weights $w_i^{1/2} = \left[K\left(\frac{x_i - x}{h}\right) \right]^{1/2}$. This gives the estimator of $m(x)$ as the weighted least squares estimator of the intercept that minimizes $\sum K\left(\frac{x_i - x}{h}\right)u_i^2$, where

$$u_i = y_i - m(x) - (x_i - x)\beta(x). \tag{4.41}$$

This is given by

$$\hat{m}(x) = e_1'\left(\sum z_i w_i z_i' \right)^{-1} \sum z_i w_i y_i, \tag{4.42}$$

where e_1 is a vector with unity in the first place and zero elsewhere. In the Nadaraya–Watson estimator considered above $z_i' = 1$ and e_1' is dropped because it is an estimator obtained by a weighted regression of y_i on unity. The estimator of the derivative $\beta(x) = \partial m(x)/\partial x$ can then be obtained as

$$b^*(x) = \frac{\partial}{\partial x}\hat{m}(x), \tag{4.43}$$

where $\hat{m}(x)$ is as in (4.42). The average derivative estimators in Section 4.3.3 can also be constructed by calculating $b^*(x_i)$ for $i = 1, \ldots, n$. The properties of the estimator, b^*, are not known, although they might be developed in the same way as was done for those in (4.13) and (4.14).

An alternative estimator of the derivative can be obtained by considering the weighted least squares estimator of the slope coefficient in (4.41). This is

$$b^{**}(x) = e_2' \left(\sum z_i w_i z_i' \right)^{-1} \sum z_i w_i y_i, \qquad (4.44)$$

where e_2 is a vector with unity in the second place. The logic of this estimator is apparent from (3.41), where it is clear that the slope coefficient is $\partial m(x^*)/\partial x$, where x^* lies between the points x_i and x. As $n \to \infty$, $h \to 0$ and only those x_i close to x are retained, ensuring that $x^* \to x$. The properties of the estimator b^{**} are discussed in Section 4.5.1. Its average derivative version $\bar{b}^{**} = n^{-1} \sum_{i=1}^n b^{**}(x_i)$ has been studied by Li et al. (1996).

Higher order derivatives can also be estimated by using the local polynomial approach, minimizing

$$\sum_{i=1}^n (y_i - m(x) - (x_i - x)\beta_1(x) - \cdots$$
$$- (x_i - x)^s \beta_s(x))^2 K\left(\frac{x_i - x}{h}\right),$$

where $\beta_s(x) = \partial^s m(x)/\partial x^s$.

One can also obtain the local estimators of the parameters α and β in the regression model $y_i = \alpha + x_i \beta + u_i$ by minimizing

$$\sum K\left(\frac{x_i - x}{h}\right) u_i^2 = \sum K\left(\frac{x_i - x}{h}\right) (y_i - \alpha - \beta x_i)^2.$$

This will give the estimators $\hat{\beta} = \hat{\beta}(x)$ and $\hat{\alpha}(x) = \hat{\alpha}$. The former is identical to that given in (4.44) whereas the relationship of $\hat{\alpha}$ to $m(x)$ was discussed in Chapter 3. Of course one does not need to use a linear function as the basis function. In some instances, as with production relations, one might want to use (say) a trans-log quadratic function. Gozalo and Linton (1995) perform derivative estimation by specifying some parametric form $g(x_i, \theta)$ and then finding the $\hat{\theta}$ that minimizes $\sum_{i=1}^n (y_i - g(x_i; \theta))^2 K\left(\frac{x_i-x}{h}\right)$, after which the requisite derivatives are computed by differentiating g with respect to x. Note that the key to the method is that $\hat{\theta}$ varies with the point x at which the derivative is being computed, so that $m(x)$ is only being assumed to behave like $g(x)$ locally around the point x and not globally.

4.3.5   Pointwise Versus Average Derivatives

Two types of derivatives have been discussed above, pointwise and average. Although the pointwise derivatives capture the varying response coefficients across the values of x, the average derivatives provide the constant (fixed) response coefficients. In this sense the pointwise derivative captures the local behavior of the shape of the regression function whereas the average derivative gives the global behavior. On the one hand, in the situation where a regression function is subject to severe local variability, an average derivative estimate may miss the local details of the regression function. On the other hand, the pointwise derivative may not capture the "typical" behavior of the regression function, as is possible with the average derivative. For example, as indicated by Rilstone (1991b, p. 210), in a quasi-concave production function with a single input ($q = 1$), the point estimate at the mean level of the input would tend to underestimate the "typical" slope of the production function.

A disadvantage with the average derivative is that it may not have any direct economic interpretation. There is one situation though in which it is a natural quantity to estimate; namely when the regression function has an "index" form, $m(x) = G(x'\delta)$. In such a model, there is a direct relationship between $\bar{\beta}_j$ and δ_j. In particular, $\bar{\beta}_j = E[dG(x'\delta)/d(x'\delta)\delta_j] = \delta_j\gamma$, where $\gamma = E[dG(x'\delta)/d(x'\delta)]$ is a scalar. Thus, when the mean response is a function of the single index $x'\delta$, the vector of average derivatives $\bar{\beta}$ is a constant multiple of the coefficient vector δ. For example, in the case where $m(x'\delta) = \delta_0 + x'\delta_1$, it is obvious that an estimator of δ_1 is available from the average derivative. An important example in econometrics when m is a function of a single index $x'\delta$ is the discrete choice regression model, where y_i is 1 or 0 and $m(x_i) = G(x_i'\delta)$. Chapter 7 has further discussion of this point.

It is easy to see that whenever $m(x)$ takes the form $G(x'\delta)$, it can be rewritten as $m(x) = G^*(x'\bar{\beta})$. This follows by noting that, if $m(x) = G(x'\delta)$, we can reparameterize $m(x)$ as $m(x) = G(x'\delta\gamma/\gamma) = G(x'\bar{\beta}/\gamma) = G^*(x'\bar{\beta})$. This observation shows that, for all single-index models having $m(x) = G(x'\delta)$, we can estimate $m(x)$ as $\hat{m}(x) = G^*(x'\hat{\bar{\beta}})$, where $\hat{\bar{\beta}}$ is the average derivative estimator described above. Average derivatives are also of interest in a number of other situations. For example, Stoker's (1986) stochastic aggregation method features average derivatives as the macroeconomic analogues of microeconomic relations, whereas averaging over part of the x space could correspond to an arc rather than a point elasticity.

An important statistical advantage of an average derivative estimator is its $\sqrt{n}$ consistency and asymptotic normality, which is the usual rate of convergence of parametric estimators. Moreover, the asymptotic rate of convergence is affected neither by the dimension, q, of x nor the window width h. In contrast, pointwise derivative estimators, which are based on the data in the neighborhood of a point, have less than $\sqrt{n}$ rate of convergence and this rate depends on h, becoming worse with an increasing size for q (see Section 4.5). The implication of all this is that, for efficient estimation and hypothesis testing, one may need much smaller samples with average derivative estimators compared to pointwise estimators. Despite this advantage, the pointwise estimates can not be ignored, as they do provide useful information, so that the two sets of statistical measures may be viewed as complements to each other.

4.4   Restricted Estimation and Hypothesis Testing

Economic theory often imposes derivative restrictions on $m(x)$, for example homogeneity and symmetry. In addition, there may be some simplifying restrictions of interest on $m(x)$, such as exclusion and linearity restrictions. Such restrictions can generally be expressed as a set of linear equality and inequality restrictions on the first- and second-order partial derivatives, that is, $\beta_j(x)$ and $\beta_j^{(2)}(x)$. For example, a zero or exclusion restriction on the jth variable x_j implies $\beta_j(x) = 0$, that is, x_j is not a relevant variable when explaining y. If $m(x)$ is a profit function and x is output, the restriction $\beta_j(x) = 0$ becomes a first-order condition for profit maximization, whereas if $m(x)$ is a consumption function with $q = 1$ and x as income, there is an inequality restriction $0 < \beta_j(x) < 1$, that is, the marginal propensity to consume lies between 0 and 1. A linearity restriction on $m(x)$, with $q = 2$ say, implies that all the second-order partial and cross partial derivatives are zero, that is, $\beta_j^{(2)} = 0$, for $j = 1, 2$. Similarly, if y and x are in logs, a homogeneity restriction implies $\sum_{j=1}^{q} \beta_j(x) = \lambda$, where $\lambda = 0$ represents homogeneity of degree zero, $\lambda = 1$ is constant returns to scale, $\lambda > 1$ is increasing returns, and $\lambda < 1$ is decreasing returns. Finally, if $m_l(y, x) = m_l(z)$ and $l = 1, \ldots, q$ is a system of q input demand equations derived from the cost function of a firm, then cost minimization implies the symmetry restrictions $\partial m_l(z)/\partial x_{l'} + \partial m_{l'}(z)/\partial x_l = 0$, where $l \neq l' = 1, \ldots, q$.

We observe that the linear equality restrictions described above can be written, at a point x, in a familiar notation, either as

$$R\beta(x) = r \tag{4.45}$$

or, more generally, as $R(x)\beta(x) = r(x)$, where $\beta(x) = [\beta_1(x), \ldots, \beta_q(x)]'$ is a $q \times 1$ vector of first-order derivatives, R is an $L \times q$ ($L \leq q$) matrix of constants, and r is an $L \times 1$ vector of known constants. Linear equality restrictions on both first- and second-order derivatives can be expressed as $R^*\beta^*(x) = r^*$, where $\beta^*(x) = [\beta'(x), \beta^{(2)'}(x)]'$ with $\beta^{(2)}(x)$ as the column vector of all the second-order partial and cross partial derivatives. Inequality restrictions can similarly be expressed as $R\beta(x) > r$ or $R\beta(x) < r$. We now turn to the estimation of $\beta(x)$ under equality restrictions and describe methods for testing the validity of these restrictions.

4.4.1   Imposing Linear Equality Restriction on Partial Derivatives

It can be seen from (4.14) and (4.15) that the unrestricted estimator of $\beta_j(x)$ can be rewritten as

$$\hat{\beta}_j(x) = \sum_{i=1}^{n} y_i w_{nij}^{(1)}(x),$$ (4.46)

where

$$w_{nij}^{(1)}(x) = h^{-1} \left(\sum K(\psi_i) \right)^{-2}$$

$$\times \left[K(\psi_i) \sum K_j^{(1)}(\psi_i) - K_j^{(1)}(\psi_i) \sum K(\psi_i) \right]$$

is such that $\sum w_{nij}^{(1)}(x) = 0$. Alternatively, defining $\xi_i(j) = w_{nij}^{(1)}(x) + n^{-1}$ we see that $\sum \xi_i(j) = 1$ and therefore it is possible to write $\hat{\beta}_j(x) = \sum(y_i - \bar{y})\xi_i(j)$, giving $\sum \xi_i(j)(y_i - \bar{y} - \hat{\beta}_j(x)) = 0$. In turn this may be regarded as the weighted least squares estimator found by minimizing $\sum(y_i - \bar{y} - \beta_j(x))^2 \xi_i(j)$.

To obtain the unrestricted least squares estimator of the vector $\beta(x) = [\beta_1(x) \ldots \beta_q(x)]'$, we can conceive of each estimator of $\beta_j(x)$ as coming from a weighted regression, with the equations generating them stacked like a seemingly unrelated regressions problem. Thereupon, if y is an $(n \times 1)$ vector of observations on y_i, $y^* = (y - \bar{y}) \otimes \iota_q$, ι_q is a $q \times 1$ unit vector, $Z = \iota_n \otimes I_q$, and D is an $(nq \times nq)$ diagonal matrix $\text{diag}\{\xi_1(1), \xi_2(2), \ldots, \xi_n(q)\}$, the kernel estimator of $\beta(x)$ minimizes

$$S = (y^* - Z\beta(x))'D(y^* - Z\beta(x)).$$ (4.47)

The solution for $\beta(x)$ is

$$\hat{\beta}(x) = (Z'DZ)^{-1}Z'Dy^*.$$ (4.48)

Now we turn to the estimation of $\beta(x)$ subject to exact linear restrictions $R\beta(x) = r$ as described in (4.45). An estimator of $\beta(x)$ subject to $R\beta(x) = r$ can be obtained by minimizing the Lagrangian

$$L = (y^* - Z\beta(x))'D(y^* - Z\beta(x)) + \lambda'(R\beta(x) - r)$$ (4.49)

with respect to $\beta(x)$ and λ, where λ is an $L \times 1$ vector of Lagrangian coefficients. This is the standard format for restricted least squares estimation problems, and it is easy to verify that the solution of $\partial L / \partial \beta(x) = 0$ provides

$$\hat{\beta}_R(x) = \hat{\beta}(x) - (Z'DZ)^{-1} R' \left(R(Z'DZ)^{-1} R' \right)^{-1} \left(R\hat{\beta}(x) - r \right)$$

$$= \hat{\beta}(x) - R' \left(RR' \right)^{-1} \left(R\hat{\beta}(x) - r \right),$$ (4.50)

as $Z'DZ = I_q$ because $\sum \xi_i(j) = 1$ for all $j = 1, \ldots, q$. Thus, if $\beta_1(x) = \beta_2(x)$ is the restriction, $R = (1, -1)$ and application of (4.50) gives the restricted estimators of the two derivatives as $.5(\hat{\beta}_1(x) + \hat{\beta}_2(x))$ and $.5(\hat{\beta}_1(x) - \hat{\beta}_2(x))$ respectively. Since Z can be regarded as fixed, the asymptotic properties of $\hat{\beta}_R(x)$ follow directly from the properties of $\hat{\beta}(x)$. The analysis for second-order derivatives follows in the same way as for the first-order case discussed above by noting that $\hat{\beta}^{(2)}(x) = \partial \hat{\beta}(x)/\partial x_j = \sum y_i w_{nij}^{(2)}(x)$, where $w_{ni}^{(2)}(x)$ is such that

$$\sum w_{nij}^{(2)}(x) = \sum \partial w_{nij}^{(1)}(x)/\partial x_j = \partial/\partial x_j \sum w_{nij}^{(1)}(x) = 0.$$

Restricted estimators of average derivatives can be developed in a similar fashion. For example, the unrestricted estimator $\bar{\beta}_j$ in (4.33) is the value of $\bar{\beta}$ that minimizes $(\hat{\beta}(x) - \bar{\beta})'(\hat{\beta}(x) - \bar{\beta})$. Thus the restricted estimator $\hat{\bar{\beta}}_R$ is the value of $\bar{\beta}$ that minimizes $(\hat{\beta}(x) - \bar{\beta})'(\hat{\beta}(x) - \bar{\beta}) + \lambda'(R\bar{\beta} - r)$. This gives

$$\hat{\bar{\beta}}_R = \hat{\bar{\beta}} - R'(RR')^{-1}(R\hat{\bar{\beta}} - r). \tag{4.51}$$

The restricted versions of instrumental variable and the Härdle and Stoker estimators can be given a similar treatment and is left as an exercise for the readers.

The restricted version of the local linear estimator in Section 4.3.4 can be obtained in a much more straightforward way. This is because, from Sections 3.3.2 and 4.3.2, the local linear estimator of the $q + 1$ vector $\delta(x) = [m(x), \beta'(x)]'$ is obtained by minimizing $(y - Z(x)\delta(x))'(y - Z(x)\delta(x))$ as

$$\hat{\delta}(x) = \left(\sum z_i w_i z_i' \right)^{-1} \sum z_i w_i y_i$$

$$= (Z'(x)W(x)Z(x))^{-1} Z'(x)W(x)y$$

where $Z(x)$ is an $n \times (q + 1)$ matrix generated by $z_i' = [1, (x_i - x)']$ and $W(x)$ is an $n \times n$ diagonal matrix of w_i. Now $R\beta(x) = r$ can be written as $R^*\delta(x) = r^*$ where $R^* = [0 \ R]$ with $L \times 1$ vector 0 and $r^* = [0 \ r']'$ with the scalar 0. Then the restricted estimator of $\delta(x)$ can be obtained by minimizing $(y - Z(x)\delta)'(y - Z(x)\delta)$ subject to $R^*\delta(x) = r^*$. This gives

$$\hat{\delta}_R(x) = \hat{\delta}(x) - (Z'(x)W(x)Z(x))^{-1} R^{*\prime}$$

$$\times (R^*(Z'(x)W(x)Z(x)R^*))^{-1} (R^*\hat{\delta}(x) - r^*).$$

4.4.2 Imposing Linear Inequality Restrictions

Now consider the case of inequality restrictions on, say, the jth response coefficient $\beta_j(x)$, in the form $\beta_j(x) \geq r$ where r is a known scalar. The inequality-restricted estimator that combines both the sample and inequality restriction in estimating $\beta_j(x)$ may be expressed as

$$b_j^{IR}(x) = I[-\infty < \hat{\beta}_j(x) < r]r + \hat{\beta}_j(x)I[r < \hat{\beta}_j(x) < \infty]. \quad (4.52)$$

In the general case of m linear inequality restrictions $R\beta(x) \geq r$, the inequality restricted estimator becomes

$$b^{IR}(x) = \hat{\beta}_R(x)I(-\infty < R\hat{\beta}(x) < r) + \hat{\beta}(x)I[r < R\hat{\beta}(x) < \infty], \quad (4.53)$$

where $\hat{\beta}_R(x)$ is as given in (4.50). The estimators (4.52) and (4.53) are similar to those given in parametric econometrics; see Judge and Yancey (1986) for details of that literature.

4.4.3   Hypothesis Testing

Suppose it is desired to test L linear restrictions,

$$H_0 : R\beta(x) = r \text{ against } H_1 : R\beta(x) \neq r, \quad (4.54)$$

at a point x, where R and r are as defined before. A test of (4.54) can be carried out by using the Wald-type statistic

$$W(x) = (R\hat{\beta}(x) - r)'[RV(\hat{\beta}(x))R']^{-1}(R\hat{\beta}(x) - r), \quad (4.55)$$

where $V(\hat{\beta}(x))$ is the asymptotic variance covariance matrix of $\hat{\beta}(x)$ given later in Section 4.5. It follows from the asymptotic normality result for $\hat{\beta}(x)$ in Section 4.5 that $R\hat{\beta}(x) - r$ is asymptotically normal, and hence W in (4.55) is asymptotically a central χ_L^2 under H_0. The test statistic for linear restrictions on both first- and second-order derivatives, $H_0 : R^*\beta^*(x) = r^*$ against $H_1 : R^*\beta^*(x) \neq r^*$, can be similarly written by substituting R, $\beta(x)$, and r by R^*, $\beta^*(x)$, and r^* (defined in Section 4.4), respectively, in (4.55). Testing for the significance of the jth variable, $H_0 : \beta_j(x) = 0$, is a special case of (4.54), and it can be done by either using (4.55) or $\hat{\beta}_j(x)/\sqrt{V(\hat{\beta}_j(x))} \sim \mathcal{N}(0, 1)$ as $n \to \infty$. An alternative is to use tests described in Section 3.13.

A general formulation for testing linear and nonlinear restrictions on $\beta^*(x)$ is

$$H_0 : \eta(\beta(x), \beta^{(2)}(x)) = \eta(\beta^*(x)) = 0,$$

$$H_1 : \eta(\beta(x), \beta^{(2)}(x)) = \eta(\beta^*(x)) \neq 0,$$

where $\eta()$ is a totally differentiable function of all first- and second-order derivatives. Examples of hypotheses of this form would be tests with respect to elasticities of scale or the degree of substitutability and questions regarding relative and absolute measures of risk aversion. A suitable test statistic for H_0 is

$$t_n(x) = (nh^{q+4})^{1/2} \frac{\eta(\hat{\beta}^*(x))}{\sigma_n(x)},$$

where $\sigma_n^2(x) = \eta^{(1)'} \Omega^*(x)\eta^{(1)}$, $\eta^{(1)} = \partial\eta/\partial\hat{\beta}^*(x)$, and $\Omega^*(x)$ is the variance co-variance matrix given later in Section 4.5. Under H_0, as $n \to \infty$, $t_n \sim \mathcal{N}(0, 1)$. For this and estimation of $\sigma_n(x)$, see Section 4.5.3.

There are two concerns about the pointwise tests described above. First, if H_0 is accepted at a point x it may be rejected at some other point x_0. Such conflicting outcomes at various points in the sample space of X make tests of H_0 indecisive. A possible solution to this dilemma is to develop simultaneous confidence bands, and that strategy requires future research. An alternative is to obtain the supremum of the test statistics or do the random search over x as advocated by Gozalo (1993) in the conditional mean case (see Section 3.13). Second, the pointwise estimates tend to have high standard errors for moderately sized samples. Put another way, they suffer from exhibiting less than $\sqrt{n}$ consistency.

In view of the above problems with the pointwise tests Racine (1997) proposes a procedure for testing the global significance of explanatory variables. The null and alternative hypothesis are $H_0 : R\beta(x) = r$ for all x in X against $H_1 : R\beta(x) \neq r$ for some x in X. It can be transformed into testing $H_0 : E[(R\beta(X) - r)'(R\beta(X) - r] = 0$ against $H_1 : E[(R\beta(X) - r)'(R\beta(X) - r)] > 0$. The test statistic used to test H_0 is given by

$$t = \frac{W}{\sqrt{V(W)}},$$

where $W = n^{-1} \sum_1^n W(x_i)$ with $W(x_i)$ as given in (4.55). Racine considers the case where $r = 0$ and R is a vector of unit elements, and obtains the sampling distribution of t, under H_0, by a nested bootstrap resampling scheme.

His results suggest that the test statistic is insensitive to the choice of window width, and that the empirical test size is very close to the nominal size of the test. The test was shown to have good power.

4.5 Asymptotic Properties of Partial Derivative Estimators

In this section a study is made of the large-sample properties of $\hat{\beta}_j(x)$. As in Chapter 3, for the sake of simplicity the results are derived for $q = 1$, and therefore in this section $\hat{\beta}_j(x) = \hat{\beta}(x) = \partial\hat{m}(x)/\partial x$.

Throughout this section we retain the assumptions used in previous chapters that follow.

(B0) $\{x_i, u_i\}$ is i.i.d for $i = 1, \ldots, n$ and x_i is independent of u_i, with $E(u_i) = 0$.

(B1) For asymptotic results K is taken to belong to the class of all Borel measurable real-valued functions $K(\psi)$ with bounded first-order partial derivative such that

(i) $\int K(\psi)\,d\psi = 1$,

(ii) $\int |K(\psi)|\,d\psi < \infty$,

    (iii) $|\psi| |K(\psi)| \to 0$ as $|\psi| \to \infty$,

    (iv) $\sup |K(\psi)| < \infty$.

(B2) $h \to 0$ and $nh^3 \to \infty$ as $n \to \infty$.

(B3) The partial derivatives of $f(x)$ at x exist up to the third order and are bounded.

(B4) The partial derivatives of $m(x)$ at x exist up to the third order and are bounded.

(B5) The partial derivatives of $v(x) = \int y^2 f(y, x) \, dy$ exist up to the third order and are bounded.

(B6) $E|u_i|^{2+\delta}$ exists for some $\delta > 0$ and $\int |K(\psi)|^{2+\delta} \, d\psi < \infty$ for some $\delta > 0$.

(B7) $\int \psi K(\psi) \, d\psi = 0$, and $\mu_2 = \int \psi^2 K(\psi) \, d\psi < \infty$.

It should be noted though that, instead of (B1), kernels K that are bounded densities with compact support might be assumed. However, (B1) is kept both for the sake of exposition and uniformity with the conditions on kernels in Chapters 2 and 3. The conditions (B3) and (B4) are smoothness conditions on f and m implying that f and m are continuous. They impose a high degree of regularity upon the functions, but they are sufficient conditions and can be relaxed. The boundedness assumption is useful for using dominated convergence results (Lemma 2.1), whereas a differentiability assumption is useful for Taylor series expansions. Assumption (B5) ensures that $V(Y|X = x) = V(U|Xx) = E(U^2|X = x)$ exists; in the case of homoskedasticity $E(U^2|X = x) = \sigma^2$, and this was the situation considered for simplicity in the derivation of the results in Chapter 3. Condition (B6) is needed in the proof of asymptotic normality, and (B7) for both approximate and asymptotic results. Both were used in Chapter 3 also.

4.5.1 *Asymptotic Properties of Kernel-Based Estimators*

Here we analyze consistency and normality of the pointwise kernel estimators.

        Theorem 4.1: When Assumptions (B0), (B1), and (B2) hold, $\hat{\beta}(x)$ is weakly consistent, that is,

$$p \lim_{n \to \infty} \hat{\beta}(x) = \beta(x). \tag{4.56}$$

    Proof: Notice that, from (4.14),

$$\hat{\beta}(x) = (\hat{f}(x))^{-1} \left[\hat{g}^{(1)}(x) - \hat{m}(x) \hat{f}^{(1)}(x) \right]. \tag{4.57}$$

Thus

$$p \lim \hat{\beta}(x) = (f(x))^{-1} \left[p \lim \hat{g}^{(1)}(x) - m(x) p \lim \hat{f}^{(1)}(x) \right],$$

where we use $p \lim \hat{f}(x) = f(x)$ and $p \lim \hat{m}(x) = m(x)$ from Theorem 2.6 in Chapter 2 and Theorem 3.4 in Chapter 3, respectively.

Now, because of i.i.d observations, and because K and f are bounded, we may interchange integration and differentiation to get

$$E \hat{f}^{(1)}(x) = E\left[\frac{\partial}{\partial x} \hat{f}(x)\right] = \frac{\partial}{\partial x}\left[E\hat{f}(x)\right] \to f^{(1)}(x) \tag{4.58}$$

by using Theorem 2.4, which shows that $E\hat{f}(x) \to f(x)$. Similarly

$$E\hat{g}^{(1)}(x) = \frac{\partial}{\partial x} E\hat{g}(x) \to g^{(1)}(x), \tag{4.59}$$

as $E\hat{g}(x) \to g(x)$ (Lemma 2.1 or Theorem 3.4). Furthermore, following steps similar to those in Theorems 2.5 and 3.5 we can show that

$$(nh^3)^{1/2} V\left(\hat{f}^{(1)}(x)\right) \to f(x) \int \left(K^{(1)}(\psi)\right)^2 d\psi \tag{4.60}$$

and

$$(nh^3)^{1/2} V\left(\hat{g}^{(1)}(x)\right) \to (m^2 + \sigma^2) f(x) \int \left(K^{(1)}(\psi)\right)^2 d\psi.$$

These results, along with Chebychev's inequality, mean that $p \lim \hat{f}^{(1)}(x) = f^{(1)}(x)$ and $p \lim \hat{g}^{(1)}(x) = g^{(1)}(x)$. Thus

$$p \lim \hat{\beta}(x) = (f(x))^{-1}\left[g^{(1)}(x) - m(x)f^{(1)}(x)\right] = \beta(x). \quad \text{Q.E.D.}$$

Having determined consistency of the estimator we move on to establish asymptotic normality of $(nh^3)^{1/2}(\hat{\beta} - \beta)$. Just as in Chapter 3 it is easiest to establish the limiting distribution by first centering $\hat{\beta}$ at its expectation conditional upon $x_1 \ldots x_n$, $E_X(\hat{\beta})$ and then finding conditions under which the estimators centered at β and $E_X(\hat{\beta})$ are asymptotically equivalent. Such a procedure is followed in Theorems 4.2 and 4.3.

Theorem 4.2: If Assumptions (B2)–(B6) hold, as $n \to \infty$,

$$(nh^3)^{1/2}(\hat{\beta} - E_X\hat{\beta}) \sim \mathcal{N}\left(0, \frac{\sigma^2}{f(x)} \int \left(K^{(1)}(\psi)\right)^2 d\psi\right). \tag{4.61}$$

Proof: From the definition of $\hat{\beta}$ in (4.14)

$$(nh^3)^{1/2}\hat{\beta} = (nh^3)^{1/2}\hat{f}^{-1}\left[\hat{g}^{(1)} - \hat{m}\hat{f}^{(1)}\right] \tag{4.62}$$

and

$$(nh^3)^{1/2}E_X\hat{\beta} = (nh^3)^{1/2}\hat{f}^{-1}\left[E_X\hat{g}^{(1)} - (E_X\hat{m})\hat{f}^{(1)}\right]. \tag{4.63}$$

Therefore,

$$(nh^3)^{1/2}(\hat{\beta} - E_X\hat{\beta}) = \hat{f}^{-1}\big[(nh^3)^{1/2}\big(\hat{g}^{(1)} - E_X\hat{g}^{(1)}\big)$$

$$- h(nh)^{1/2}(\hat{m} - E_X\hat{m})\,\hat{f}^{(1)}\big].$$

Now, from Theorem 3.5, $(nh)^{1/2}(\hat{m} - E_X\hat{m})$ tends to a random variable in distribution, and $\hat{f}^{(1)} \to f^{(1)}$. Thus, using Rao (1973, p. 385) and noting that $h \to 0$, we find that the asymptotic distribution of $(nh^3)^{1/2}(\hat{\beta} - E_X\hat{\beta})$ is the same as that of $\hat{f}^{-1}(nh^3)^{1/2}(\hat{g}^{(1)} - E_X\hat{g}^{(1)})$. But $\hat{f} \to f$, and

$$(nh^3)^{1/2}\big(\hat{g}^{(1)} - E\hat{g}^{(1)}\big) = (nh)^{-1/2}\sum_i K_i^{(1)}u_i,$$

which is similar to (3.69). Accordingly, following the arguments in the proof of Theorem 3.5, we see that $(nh)^{-1/2}\sum K_i^{(1)}u_i$ tends in distribution to $\mathcal{N}(0, \sigma^2 f(x)\int(K^{(1)}(\psi))^2\,d\psi)$, making the limit distribution of $(nh^3)^{1/2}(\hat{\beta} - E_X\hat{\beta})$ as given in (4.61).   Q.E.D.

Theorem 4.3: Suppose Assumptions (B1) to (B7) hold and

(B8) $(nh^3)^{1/2}h^2 \to 0$ as $n \to \infty$.

Then, as $n \to \infty$, $(nh^3)^{1/2}(\hat{\beta} - \beta)$ has the same distribution as $(nh^3)^{1/2}(\hat{\beta} - E_X\hat{\beta})$ in Theorem 4.2.

Proof: Writing

$$(nh^3)^{1/2}(\hat{\beta} - \beta) = (nh^3)^{1/2}[(\hat{\beta} - E_X\hat{\beta}) + (E_X\hat{\beta} - \beta)]$$

it is necessary to show that $(nh^3)^{1/2}(E_X\hat{\beta} - \beta) \to 0$ as $n \to \infty$. Now since $\hat{f} \to f$ and $\hat{f}^{(1)} \to f^{(1)}$ as $n \to \infty$, it follows that

$$(nh^3)^{1/2}(E_X\hat{\beta} - \beta) \to f^{-1}\big[(nh^3)^{1/2}\big(E_X\hat{g}^{(1)} - g^{(1)}\big)$$

$$- (nh^3)^{1/2}(E_X\hat{m} - m)\,f^{(1)}\big]. \qquad (4.64)$$

Further, following the arguments in the proof of Theorem 3.6, we can easily verify that, under (B8), both $(nh^3)^{1/2}(E_X\hat{g}^{(1)} - g^{(1)})$ and $h(nh)^{1/2}(E_X\hat{m} - m) \to 0$ as $n \to \infty$. Note that $h(nh)^{1/2}(E_X\hat{m} - m) \to 0$ when $(nh)^{1/2}h^3 \to 0$ or $nh^7 \to 0$, which is true if (B8) holds. Thus $(nh^3)^{1/2}(E_X\hat{\beta} - \beta) \to 0$, which gives the result in Theorem 4.3.   Q.E.D.

In practice h needs to satisfy both (B2) and (B8), that is, h should be such that $nh^3 \to \infty$ and $nh^7 \to 0$ as $n \to \infty$. In previous instances a similar conflict was removed by the use of higher order kernels. It is certainly true that the bias can be eliminated in this way (see the remarks following Theorem 3.6). Jacknifing of the estimator (see Section 2.4.3) would however eliminate the bias without the need for (B8), and its use may be an important component of derivative estimation if the optimal h is deemed desirable.

The results in the theorems above extend to the multivariate context, with q elements in x and $\beta(x) = \beta_j(x)$ defined as the derivative of $m(x)$ with respect to the jth variable x_j, simply by replacing nh^3 by nh^{2+q}.[4] If the window width h_j varies by regressor (i.e., is h_j for $j = 1, \ldots, q$ regressors) the results in Theorems 4.1 to 4.3 will remain the same except h^{q+2} and h^{q+4} are replaced by $(\prod^q h_j)h_j^2$ and $(\prod h_j)h_j^4$ respectively.[5]

From Theorems 4.2 and 4.3 a $100(1 - \alpha)\%$ confidence interval for $\hat{\beta}_j$ is given by

$$\hat{\beta}_j(x) \pm Z_{\alpha/2}(nh^{2+q})^{-1/2}(w^2(x))^{1/2}, \tag{4.65}$$

where $w^2(x) = \sigma^2(x)(f(x))^{-1} \int (K_j^{(1)}(\psi))^2 \, d\psi$ and $Z_{\alpha/2}$ is the critical value for the $(1 - \alpha)$ level of significance of an $\mathcal{N}(0, 1)$ random variable. In practice, $w^2(x)$ can be replaced by its consistent estimator $\hat{\sigma}^2(x)(\hat{f}(x))^{-1} \int (K_j^{(1)}(\psi))^2 \, d\psi$, with $\hat{f}(x)$ as given in (4.10) and

$$\hat{\sigma}^2(x) = \sum_{i=1}^{n}(y_i - \hat{m}(x_i))^2 K\left(\frac{x_i - x}{h}\right) \Big/ \sum_{i=1}^{n} K\left(\frac{x_i - x}{h}\right). \tag{4.66}$$

Theorems 4.2 and 4.3 give the asymptotic distribution of $\hat{\beta} = \hat{\beta}_j$, the estimator of the partial derivative of $m(x)$ with respect to the jth regressor. Arranging the partial derivatives in a $q \times 1$ vector $\beta = [\beta_1, \ldots, \beta_q]'$ with $\hat{\beta}$ as its estimator, the joint distribution may be found from Theorem 4.3 as normal with a zero mean vector and covariance matrix $\Omega(x)$, that is,

$$\left(nh^{q+2}\right)^{1/2}(\hat{\beta}(x) - \beta(x)) \sim \mathcal{N}(0, \Omega(x)),$$

where the (j, j')-th element of $\Omega(x)$ is

$$\omega_{jj'}(x) = \left(nh^{2+q}\right)\mathrm{cov}(\hat{\beta}_j, \hat{\beta}_{j'}) = \frac{\sigma_u^2(x)}{f(x)} \int K_j^{(1)}(\psi)K_{j'}^{(1)}(\psi) \, d\psi, \tag{4.67}$$

where $K_j^{(1)}(\psi)$ is the partial derivative of $K(\psi) = K(\psi_1, \ldots, \psi_q)$ with respect to ψ_j.

---

[4] $K^{(1)}$ is replaced by $K_j^{(1)}$, the first derivative of $K(\psi)$ with respect to the jth element in ψ.

[5] We also note that, as in Chapter 3, when $E(u_i^2|x_i) = \sigma^2(x_i)$ we need to replace σ^2 by $\sigma^2(x)$ in Theorems 4.2 and 4.3.

From the above results we observe that the distribution of $(nh^{q+2})^{1/2}R(\hat{\beta}(x) - \beta(x))$ is $\mathcal{N}(0, R\Omega(x)R')$ as $n \to \infty$. Furthermore, the distribution of the Wald statistic in Section 4.4.3, under H_0, is asymptotically χ^2 with L degrees of freedom. In practice $\Omega(x)$ can be replaced by $\hat{\Omega}(x)$ after $\sigma^2(x)$ and $f(x)$ are estimated by $\hat{\sigma}^2(x)$ and $\hat{f}(x)$.

4.5.2   Series-Based Estimators

Series-based nonparametric estimators of $m(X)$ approximate it by $z_i'\theta$ (see (3.88) in Section 3.9) and then use $z'(x)\hat{\theta}$ as the estimator, where $\hat{\theta}$ is found by the regression of y_i against z_i and $z(x)$ represents the value of the regressors z when $X = x$. Partial derivatives of $m(x)$ are easily found as $(\partial z'(x)/\partial x_j)\hat{\theta}$. Clearly, the partial derivative is linear in $\hat{\theta}$, and therefore the proof of asymptotic normality is very similar to that for $(nh)^{1/2}(\hat{m}(x) - m(x))$ in Theorems 3.8 and 3.9, the main difference coming from the fact that Q_2 in (3.91) is now the difference between the derivative at $X = x$ and the series approximation estimate. For Assumption (B7) of Section 3.9 to hold, the rate of expansion of the number of elements in the approximating series is now slower, just as it was for the kernel estimator. The variance of the estimator will be $(\partial z(x)/\partial x)'\text{var}(\hat{\theta})(\partial z(x)/\partial x)$ and so is easily computed from the results of the OLS regression yielding $\hat{\theta}$.

4.5.3   Higher Order Derivatives

The properties of higher order partial and cross partial derivative estimators $\hat{\beta}^{(s)}$, $s = s_1 + \cdots + s_q$, can be obtained in exactly the same way as was done for $q = 1$. The results will be the same as before, except for the need to replace $K^{(1)}$ by $K^{(s)}$, nh^3 by nh^{q+2s}, and the derivatives of order three with the derivative of order $s + 2$ in the theorems and assumptions. Thus, for example, Theorems 4.2 and 4.3 would become

$$\left(nh^{q+2s}\right)^{1/2}\left(\hat{\beta}_j^{(s)} - \beta_j^{(s)}\right) \sim \mathcal{N}\left(0, \frac{\sigma^2(x)}{f(x)}\int\left(K_j^{(s)}(\psi)\right)^2 d\psi\right).$$

(4.68)

Similarly the joint distribution of $\hat{\beta}^{(s)}(x) = [\hat{\beta}_1^{(s)}(x), \ldots, \hat{\beta}_q^{(s)}(x)]$ will be the same as (4.67) with nh^{q+2} replaced by nh^{q+2s} and $K_j^{(1)}$ replaced by $K_j^{(s)}$. For details of these results and other asymptotic properties of $\hat{\beta}^{(s)}$, see Ahmad and Ullah (1987) and Rilstone (1987, 1992a).

As described in Section 4.4.3, quite often one is interested in testing the joint restrictions on both the first- and second-order derivatives. In such situations one needs to know the joint distribution of the vector of first- and second-order derivatives. Let the latter be $\beta^*(x) = [\beta(x)'\ \beta^{(2)}(x)']'$. Then

$$\left(nh^{q+4}\right)^{1/2}(\hat{\beta}^*(x) - \beta^*(x)) \sim \mathcal{N}(0, \Omega^*(x)),$$

(4.69)

where

$$\Omega^*(x) = \begin{bmatrix} 0 & 0 \\ 0 & \Omega_1(x) \end{bmatrix}.$$

Here $\Omega_1(x)$ is the covariance matrix of $\hat{\beta}^{(2)}(x)$, and would just be $\Omega(x)$ with $K^{(1)}$ replaced by $K^{(2)}$. Note that the above result follows from the degeneracy of

$$\left(nh^{q+4}\right)^{1/2}(\hat{\beta} - \beta) = \left(nh^{q+2}\right)^{1/2}(\hat{\beta} - \beta)h.$$

From the joint distribution of $\hat{\beta}^*$ and the application of the Mann–Wald Theorem (Rao, 1973, p. 387 and the appendix) one can easily verify that

$$\left(nh^{q+4}\right)^{1/2}\frac{\eta(\hat{\beta}^*)}{\sigma_n(x)} \sim \mathcal{N}(0, 1), \tag{4.70}$$

where $\eta()$ and $\sigma_n(x)$ are as defined in Section 4.4.3. The estimate of $\Omega_1(x)$ is obtained in the same way as described for $\Omega(x)$ in (4.67). Details can be found in Rilstone (1992a).

4.5.4 Local Linear Estimators

Following the same procedure as in Chapter 3 the mean and variance, conditional on x_i, can be written from (4.44) as

$$E(b^{**}(x)|x_i) = e_2'\left(\sum z_i w_i z_i'\right)^{-1}\sum z_i w_i m(x_i)$$

and

$$V(b^{**}(x)|x_i) = \sigma^2 e_2'\left(\sum z_i w_i z_i'\right)^{-1}\left(\sum z_i w_i^2 z_i'\right)$$
$$\times \left(\sum z_i w_i z_i'\right)^{-1}e_2.$$

Then, for large n, we can obtain the asymptotic mean and variance as

$$E(b^{**}(x)|x_i) - \beta(x) = \frac{h^2}{2\mu_2}\left[\mu_4 m^{(3)} + \left(\mu_4 - \mu_2^2\right)\frac{m^{(2)}f^{(1)}}{f}\right]$$

and

$$V(b^{**}(x)|x_i) = \frac{1}{nh^3}\frac{\sigma^2}{f\mu_2^2}\int \psi^2 K^2(\psi)\,d\psi,$$

where $\mu_4 = \int \psi^4 K(\psi)\,d\psi$. Again, conditional and unconditional moments must be identical since the former are free of x_i – see Ruppert and Wand (1994) for details.

The asymptotic bias of the derivative estimator $\tilde{\beta}(x) = \partial \hat{m}(x)/\partial x$ in (4.13) or (4.14), where $\hat{m}$ is the Nadaraya–Watson estimator, can be obtained from

$$E\tilde{\beta}(x) = (2h)^{-1}[E\hat{m}(x+h) - E\hat{m}(x-h)],$$

which is $\partial E\hat{m}(x)/\partial x$ as $h \to 0$. Using the result (3.54) of Theorem 3.2 and differentiating it with respect to x produces

$$E(\tilde{\beta}(x)) - \beta(x)$$

$$= \frac{h^2}{2}\mu_2 \left[m^{(3)} + 2\left\{ \frac{f^{(2)}}{f}m^{(1)} + \frac{m^{(2)}f^{(1)}}{f} - \left(\frac{f^{(1)}}{f}\right)^2 m^{(1)} \right\} \right].$$

Similarly, the asymptotic bias of the b^* in (4.43), which is based on the local linear estimator $\hat{m}$, can be derived by using (3.65) in Theorem 3.3 to be

$$E(b^*(x)) - \beta(x) = \frac{h^2}{2}\mu_2 m^{(3)}(x).$$

We recall from Chapter 3 that the bias behavior of the local linear regression estimator was superior to that of the Nadaraya–Watson estimator. This superiority does not seem to extend to the usual local linear derivative estimator $b^{**}(x)$ (see Fan (1992, 1993) and Ruppert and Wand (1994)), at least in comparison to $\tilde{\beta}$ based on a Nadaraya–Watson estimator. Both $\tilde{\beta}$ and b^{**} depend on f, and both can behave poorly if either $f^{-1}f^{(1)}$ or $m^{(2)}$ are large. The estimator $\tilde{\beta}$ has other disadvantages as well, exhibiting poor performance when either $f^{-1}f^{(2)}$ or $m^{(1)}$ are large and being biased when $m(x)$ is linear. In this last instance b^{**} is unbiased. In contrast to these deficiencies the bias behavior of b^* is much better than that for either b^{**} or $\tilde{\beta}$. To support this conclusion we offer three pieces of evidence. First, b^* is unbiased when $m(x)$ is linear or quadratic. Second, because it does not depend upon f, it is "design adaptive," in the sense of Fan (1992). Finally, it is not affected by any of $f^{-1}f^{(1)}$, $f^{-1}f^{(2)}$, $m^{(1)}$, and $m^{(2)}$. Regarding the asymptotic variance, if a Gaussian kernel is used, the asymptotic variance of b^{**} is the same as that of $\hat{\beta}$ in (4.61). In general, however, they will be different. The asymptotic variance of b^* is not yet known. A comparative study of b^{**}, b^*, and $\tilde{\beta}$ will be a useful subject of future research.

4.6   Asymptotic Properties of Kernel-Based Average Derivative Estimators

Various average derivatives were set out in Section 4.3.3. Consider the weighted average derivative of Powell et al. (1989), $\hat{\bar{\beta}}^* = -2n^{-1}\sum_{i=1}^{n} y_i \hat{f}^{(1)}(x_i)$, where it is assumed that x_i is univariate so that the j subscript may be dropped. Powell et al. find it theoretically convenient to use the leave-one-out estimator

$$f^{(1)}(x_i) = -(n-1)^{-1} \sum_{\substack{k=1 \\ k \neq i}}^{n} h^{-2} K^{(1)}(h^{-1}(x_i - x_k))$$

(see (2.28) in Section 2.3) so that

$$\hat{\beta}^* = -2n^{-1}(n-1)^{-1} \sum_{i=1}^{n} \sum_{\substack{k=1 \\ k \neq i}}^{n} h^{-2} K^{(1)}(h^{-1}(x_k - x_i)) y_i. \qquad (4.71)$$

Equation (4.71) shows that the difficulty in devising an asymptotic theory for $\hat{\beta}^*$ resides in the double summation. If $K(\psi)$ is symmetric, $K^{(1)}(\psi)$ is anti-symmetric (i.e., $K^{(1)}(\psi) = -K^{(1)}(-\psi)$), allowing (4.71) to be written in the "U-statistic" form (see appendix)

$$\hat{\beta}^* = -\binom{n}{2}^{-1} \sum_{i=1}^{n} \sum_{k=i+1}^{n} h^{-2} K^{(1)}\left(h^{-1}(x_i - x_k)\right)(y_i - y_k) \qquad (4.72)$$

$$= -\binom{n}{2}^{-1} \sum_{i=1}^{n} \sum_{k=i+1}^{n} \xi_n(\zeta_i, \zeta_k), \qquad (4.73)$$

where

$$\xi_n(\zeta_i, \zeta_k) = h^{-2} K^{(1)}(h^{-1}(x_k - x_i))(y_i - y_k)$$

and $\zeta_i' = (x_i, y_i)$.

Denoting the right-hand side of (4.73) as U_n and defining $r_n(\zeta_i) = E(\xi_n (\zeta_i, \zeta_k)|\zeta_i)$ and the "projection" of the statistic U_n as

$$\hat{U}_n = E(r_n(\zeta_1)) + 2n^{-1} \sum_{i=1}^{n} [r_n(\zeta_i) - E(r_n(\zeta_i))],$$

we can decompose $\hat{\beta}^* - \bar{\beta}^*$ as

$$\hat{\beta}^* - \bar{\beta}^* = \{\hat{\beta}^* - E(\hat{\beta}^*)\} + [E(\hat{\beta}^*) - \bar{\beta}^*]$$

$$= \{[U_n - \hat{U}_n] + [\hat{U}_n - E(r_n(\zeta_1))]\} + [E(\hat{\beta}^*) - \bar{\beta}^*], \qquad (4.74)$$

using the fact that

$$E(\hat{\beta}^*) = E(U_n) = E(\hat{U}_n) = E(r_n(\zeta_1)) = E(r_n(\zeta_i)).$$

If the derivative $f^{(1)}(x_i)$ had been known, $\hat{\beta}^*$ would be the sample average of $-2y_i f^{(1)}(x_i)$, and it would therefore be expected that $n^{1/2}(\hat{\beta}^* - \bar{\beta}^*)$ would have a limiting distribution. For the same outcome when $f^{(1)}(x_i)$ is estimated, the first and third terms in (4.74) must be $o_p(1)$ when normalized by $n^{1/2}$, whereas the second must have a limiting distribution (after normalization). Theorem 4.4, which uses Lemmas 4.1 and 4.2, establishes the limiting distribution of $n^{1/2}(\hat{\hat{\beta}}^* - E(\hat{\hat{\beta}}^*))$, after which a discussion is provided of the circumstances under which the bias term $n^{1/2}(E(\hat{\hat{\beta}}^*) - \bar{\beta}^*)$ disappears. Rigorous proofs of the results are quite complex and we merely reproduce the essentials of Powell et al.'s argument. To do so requires some special assumptions.

(C1) $h \to 0$ and $nh^3 \to \infty$ as $n \to \infty$.
(C2) The support of f is a convex and possibly unbounded subset of R^q; the density f is zero on the boundary of its support; and both m and f are continuously differentiable.
(C3) With $m^{(1)}$, $f^{(1)}$, and $(mf)^{(1)}$ being the partial derivatives of m, f, and (mf) with respect to x respectively, $f^{(1)}$ and $(mf)^{(1)}$ satisfy the Lipschitz conditions,

$$\left\| f^{(1)}(x+v) - f^{(1)}(x) \right\| < c(x)\|v\|,$$

$$\left\| (mf)^{(1)}(x+v) - mf^{(1)}(x) \right\| < c(x)\|v\|$$

for some $c(x)$.
(C4) $m^{(1)}$, $f^{(1)}(y,x)$ have finite second moments and $E[(1+|y|+\|x\|)c(x)]^2 < \infty$ for the $c(x)$ in (C3).

Lemma 4.1: $n^{1/2}(U_n - \hat{U}_n)$ is $o_p(1)$ if $E\|\xi_n(\zeta_i, \zeta_k)\|^2$ is $o(n)$.

Proof: See Powell et al. (1989, Appendix 1). Q.E.D.

Lemma 4.1 is a standard result in U-statistic theory (e.g., Serfling, 1980, pp. 196–98). A special proof is needed, however, because of the dependence of ξ_n upon n through the window width h.

Lemma 4.2: Under Assumptions (B0), (B1), (B6), (C1), and (C2), $n^{1/2}(\hat{U}_n - U_n)$ is $o_p(1)$.

Proof: we have

$$E\|\xi_n(\zeta_i, \zeta_k)\|^2 = \int h^{-4} \left\| K^{(1)}(h^{-1}(x_k - x_i)) \right\|^2$$

$$\times E\{(y_i - y_k)^2 | x_i, x_k\} f(x_i) f(x_k)\, dx_i\, dx_k \quad (4.75)$$

$$= \int h^{-4} \left\| K^{(1)}\left(h^{-1}(x_k - x_i)\right) \right\|^2 [m^2(x_i) + m^2(x_k)$$

$$+ 2\sigma^2 - 2m(x_i)m(x_k)] f(x_i) f(x_k)\, dx_i\, dx_k \quad (4.76)$$

exploiting the independence of x_i and u_i. With the change of variable $\psi_i = (x_k - x_i)/h$, this becomes

$$E\|\xi_n(\zeta_i, \zeta_k)\|^2 = \int h^{-3} \left\| K^{(1)}(\psi) \right\|^2 [m^2(x_i) + m^2(x_i + h\psi_i)$$

$$+ 2\sigma^2 - 2m(x_i)m(x_i + h\psi)]$$

$$\times f(x_i) f(x_i + h\psi)\, dx_i\, d\psi_i \quad (4.77)$$

$$= O(h^{-3}) = O\left[n(nh^3)^{-1}\right] \quad (4.78)$$

using the continuity of $m(x)$ and $f(x)$. Since (4.78) gives the bound on $E\|\xi_n\|^2$ needed by Lemma 4.1 when (C1) holds, the theorem follows.   Q.E.D.

We turn now to the second term in (4.74), and Theorem 4.4 deals with its asymptotic normality.

Theorem 4.4: Under the same conditions as Lemma 4.2 augmented by (C3) and (C4) we have

$$n^{1/2}(\hat{\beta}^* - E(\hat{\beta}^*)) \quad \text{is} \quad \mathcal{N}(0, V_{\hat{\beta}^*}),$$

where $V_{\hat{\beta}^*} = 4\,\mathrm{var}[m^{(1)}(x_i) f(x_i) - (y_i - m(x_i)) f^{(1)}(x_i)] - 4[E(r_n(\zeta_1))]^2$.

Proof: Using Lemma 4.2 we obtain

$$n^{1/2}(\hat{\beta}^* - E(\hat{\beta}^*)) = n^{1/2}(\hat{U}_n - E(r_n(\zeta_1)) + o_p(1)$$

$$= 2n^{-1/2} \sum_{i=1}^{n} [r_n(\zeta_i) - E(r_n(\zeta_i))],$$

and, since $r_n(\zeta_i)$ are i.i.d., it follows from standard central limit theorems that $n^{1/2}(\hat{\beta}^* - E(\hat{\beta}^*))$ is asymptotically normal with variance $4\,\mathrm{var}(r_n(\zeta_1)) - 4(E(r_n(\zeta_1)))^2$. Now

$$r_n(\zeta_i) = -\int h^{-2} K^{(1)}(h^{-1}(x_k - x_i))(y_i - m(x_k)) f(x_k)\, dx \quad (4.79)$$

$$= \int h^{-1} K^{(1)}(\psi)(y_i - m(x_i + h\psi)) f(x_i + h\psi)\, d\psi \quad (4.80)$$

$$= \int (mf)^{(1)}(x_i + \psi h) K(\psi) \, d\psi$$

$$- y_i \int f^{(1)}(x_i + \psi h) K(\psi) \, d\psi \qquad (4.81)$$

using integration by parts and the fact that, on the boundary, $f(x) = 0$ (C2 and Footnote 3). Writing terms like $(mf)^{(1)}(x_i + h\psi)$ as $(mf^{(1)})(x_i) + \{(mf)^{(1)}(x_i + h\psi) - (mf)^{(1)}(x_i)\}$, and using

$$\int (mf)^{(1)} K(\psi) \, d\psi = \int [\partial (mf)/\partial x] K(\psi) \, d\psi$$

$$= \partial (mf)/\partial x \int K(\psi) \, d\psi = \partial (mf)/\partial x$$

(see B1(i)), followed by $\partial (mf)/\partial x = (\partial m/\partial x) f + (\partial f/\partial x) m$, we get

$$r_n = f(x_i) m^{(1)}(x_i) - (y_i - m(x_i)) f^{(1)}(x_i)$$

$$+ \int \left[(mf)^{(1)}(x_i + h\psi) - (mf)^{(1)}(x_i) \right] K(\psi) \, d\psi$$

$$- y_i \int \left[f^{(1)}(x_i + h\psi) - f^{(1)}(x_i) \right] K(\psi) \, d\psi. \qquad (4.82)$$

The last two terms in (4.82) have second moment bounded by

$$4h^2 E \left[\{(1 + |y|) c(x)\}^2 \int \|\psi\| \, |K(\psi)| \, d\psi \right]^2,$$

after applying (C3) with $\nu = h\psi$. Using (C4) this second moment is $O(h^2)$ and so the last two terms in (4.82) become $o_p(1)$. The distribution of $n^{1/2}(\hat{\beta}^* - E(\hat{\beta}^*))$ is therefore that of the first term, as asserted by the theorem.   Q.E.D.

It remains only to ensure that there is no asymptotic bias for $n^{1/2}(\hat{\beta}^* - \bar{\beta}^*)$, so that the estimator, centered on the true value, has a limiting normal distribution with the same covariance matrix as in Theorem 4.4 (i.e., that the last term in (4.74) disappears). Expanding $n^{1/2}[E(\hat{\beta}^*) - \bar{\beta}^*]$ as a Taylor series in h gives $b_1 n^{1/2} h + \frac{1}{2} b_2 n^{1/2} h^2 + \cdots$, where b_j are the derivatives of $E(\hat{\beta}^*)$ with respect to h, and the jth term in the expansion equals $-2(j!)^{-1} \int \psi^j K(\psi) m(x_1) f^{(j+1)} f(x_1) dx_1 d\psi$. From (B2), $nh^3 \to \infty$ circumscribes the choice of h, but this is consistent with $n^{1/2} h^2 \to 0$, meaning that the bias is $o(1)$ if $b_1 = 0$, that is, if $\int \psi K(\psi) \, d\psi = 0$, which it is by (B7). Problems arise when x is multivariate, as Lemma 4.2 would then require $nh^{q+2} \to \infty$, leaving the higher order terms involving $h^{(q+1)/2}$ (if $q > 1$ is odd) or $h^{(q+2)/2}$ (if q is even). To force these to be zero requires a laxer window width or higher order kernels that make the corresponding b_j zero.

The covariance matrix of the weighted average derivative estimator can be estimated by replacing unknowns such as $m(x_i)$, $f(x_i)$, etc. by consistent estimators, and then forming

$$4n^{-1} \sum \left[\hat{f}(x_i)\hat{m}^{(1)}(x_i) - (y_i - \hat{m}(x_i))\hat{f}^{(1)}(x_i)\right]^2 - 4(\hat{\bar{\beta}}^*)^2.$$

Alternatively, Powell et al. suggest forming the sample average of $\xi_n(\zeta_i, \zeta_k)$ over $k = 1, \ldots, n$, excluding the ith point, and then using the sample variance of this quantity to estimate the first part of $V_{\hat{\bar{\beta}}^*}$.

Li et al. (1996) have studied the asymptotic properties of the average derivative estimator $\bar{b}^{**} = n^{-1} \sum_{i=1}^{n} b^{**}(x_i)$, where $b^{**}(x_i)$ is the local linear estimator at the point $x = x_i$. Using the conditions $nh^4 \to 0$ and $nh^3 / \log n \longrightarrow \infty$ as $n \longrightarrow \infty$; they show that $n^{1/2}(\bar{b}^{**} - \bar{\beta})$ has the same asymptotic distribution as Härdle and Stoker's and Rilstone's estimators.

4.7 Implementing the Derivative Estimators

Implementation of derivative estimators raises issues regarding the selection of kernel K and window width h. Because we are effectively computing estimates of the density and the regression function, all the kernels described in Chapters 2 and 3 can be utilized again. Such material will not be repeated here, except that readers are reminded that the choice of kernel is not very important and that there are a number of ways to eliminate the asymptotic bias problem.

In choosing a window width for pointwise derivative estimation, it is necessary to minimize the mean square error. By definition

$$E(\hat{\beta}(x)) = E\left(\frac{\partial \hat{m}(x)}{\partial x}\right) = \frac{\partial E(\hat{m}(x))}{\partial x},$$

after interchanging integration and differentiation, and the bias in $\hat{\beta}(x)$ is therefore the same as that in $\hat{m}(x)$ (i.e., $O(h^2)$ under a symmetric kernel). Since the variance of $\hat{\beta}(x)$ is $O(\frac{1}{nh^3})$, minimizing the mean square error with respect to h produces

$$h_{opt} \propto n^{-1/7} \tag{4.83}$$

and a speed of convergence for the MSE of $n^{-4/7}$. With q regressors and estimation of an sth-order derivative, $h_{opt} \propto n^{-1/(q+4+2s)}$. For $s = 0$, $h \propto n^{-1/(q+4)}$, as obtained for the conditional mean case in Chapter 3. The implication is that the optimal window width used in the latter situation is not adequate when estimating derivatives. We also note from the analysis of Chapters 3 and 4, that for rth-order kernels, the h_{opt} becomes proportional to $n^{-1/(q+2r+2s)}$. For the case considered in this chapter, $r = 2$.

Another point is that, although h_{opt} above minimizes the MSE, it does not quite satisfy the condition (B8) that $nh^4 \to 0$ ($nh^{2r} \to 0$ with higher order kernels). The estimates based on h_{opt} may therefore be asymptotically biased. Thus one might consider a narrower window width and jacknifing procedures, though in practice these have been found to provide results similar to that based on h_{opt}.

We now turn to the optimal h for the average derivative estimator. As noted before, in this case the asymptotic variance does not depend on K, q, and h. Thus the effect of the choice of h on asymptotic efficiency cannot be analyzed. In view of this Härdle et al. (1992) and Powell and Stoker (1996) have considered the choice of h that minimizes the finite-sample approximation to the MSE of the average derivative estimators. From the result of Härdle et al. (1992) it follows that, for $q = 1$, the h that minimizes the MSE of $\hat{\beta}$ to $O(n^{-2}h^{-3}+h^4)$ is

$$h^*_{opt} = hn^{-2/7},\qquad(4.84)$$

where

$$h = \left(3\int \sigma^2(x)\,dx \int K^{(1)}(\psi)^2\,d\psi/a\right)^{1/7}$$

and

$$a = \mu_2^2\left(\int m(x)f^{-1}\left(f^{(1)}f^{(2)} - ff^{(3)}\right)dx\right)^2.$$

A plug-in estimator of h, with f, $f^{(1)}$, $m(x)$, and $\sigma^2(x)$ replaced by their estimates, can be used in practice. Powell and Stoker (1992) extend the result for the weighted average derivative estimator to handle q xs and rth-order kernels. Their results lead to $h^*_{opt} \propto n^{-2/(2r+q+2)}$. When $q = 1$ and $r = 2$, this reduces to (4.84). It is clear from these results that the optimal window width for the average derivative estimators is substantially smaller than the optimal h for the pointwise derivative estimator, as the latter must be of order $n^{-1/7}$.

4.8   Illustrative Examples

4.8.1   A Monte Carlo Experiment with a Production Function

An experiment was conducted to assess how the pointwise nonparametric estimators of partial derivatives perform when the true form of the regression function is known, and the data are generated from a known population. For this purpose the model considered was that constructed by White (1980a), which has also been used by Byron and Bera (1983). It constitutes a two-input constant returns to scale stochastic production function

$$y_i = -\frac{1}{5}\log\left(e^{-5x_{i1}} + 2e^{-5x_{i2}}\right) + u_i, \qquad i = 1, \ldots, 200, \qquad(4.85)$$

where y_i, x_{i1}, and x_{i2} are intended to represent the log values of variables such as output, capital, and labor. Data were generated in the experiment by drawing random numbers for u_i from a normal distribution with mean zero and variance .01, and observations on x_{i1} and x_{i2} are found from two independently distributed uniform random variables with mean .5 and variance $1/12$.

Our aim is to estimate the first and second partial derivatives of y in (4.85) with respect to $x_j (j = 1, 2)$. In the extensive literature on production economics parametric approximations are often used for this purpose, prominent representatives being

$$y_i = \beta_0 + \beta_1 x_{i1} + \beta_2 x_{i2} + u_i \quad \text{(Cobb–Douglas)},$$

$$y_i = \beta_0 + \beta_1 x_{i1} + \beta_2 x_{i2} + \beta_3 x_{i1}^2 + \beta_4 x_{i1} x_{i2}$$
$$+ \beta_5 x_{i2}^2 + u_i. \quad \text{(Trans-log)} \tag{4.86}$$

In general these approximations to (4.85) may not be good, making for bias in the estimates of derivatives. For example, the Cobb–Douglas specification implicitly constrains all higher order derivatives to zero, when this may not be true. In fact an important aim of White's paper was to show the difficulties inherent in using a specific functional form for inference when the actual form is unknown, thereby creating a rationale for considering the estimation of derivatives using nonparametric methods.

The nonparametric model can be written as

$$y_i = m(x_{i1}, x_{i2}) + u_i = E(y_i | x_{i1}, x_{i2}) + u_i, \tag{4.87}$$

which is a special case of (4.2) for $q = 2$. Note that the estimate of m and its partial derivatives with respect to x_1 and x_2 can be calculated by using (4.13). To compute the first derivative the kernel used was the product kernel

$$K(\psi_j) = \prod_{j=1}^{2} K(\psi_j), \qquad K(\psi_j) = (2\pi)^{-1/2} \exp\left(-\frac{1}{2}\psi_j^2\right),$$

but to avoid bias the kernel for the second-order derivative was the second-order kernel $K_3(\psi_j) = \frac{1}{2}(3 - \psi_j^2)K(\psi_j)$, as given in (2.122). Following the discussion in Section 4.5, the window widths h_j were varied with the derivatives estimated and each conditioning variable, being $s_j n^{-1/8}$ (for the first derivatives) and $s_j n^{-1/10}$ (for the second derivatives), where s_j is the estimated standard deviation of x_j. The cross-validation technique of determining window width was also used but it did not change the thrust of the results in Table 4.1 (for more details see Rilstone (1987)).

Table 4.1 gives the "true" values of the partial derivatives evaluated at the population means of x_1 and x_2, the latter being .33 and .66 respectively. Also given are estimates based on the Cobb–Douglas (CD) and Trans-Log (TL)

Table 4.1. *Response coefficients.*

$b(x)$	CD	TL	NP	ML	True value
$\hat{\beta}_1$	.3900	.3917	.3534	.3263	.3333
	$(.0364)^a$	(.0256)	(.1059)	(.039)	
$\hat{\beta}_2$	.6064	.6078	.6599	.6737	.6667
	(.0340)	(.0278)	(.1054)	(.0439)	
$\hat{\beta}_1^{(2)}$		−.6964	−.975	−1.1184	−1.111
		(.1921)	(1.14)	(1.072)	
$\hat{\beta}_2^{(2)}$		−.7594	−.8808	−1.118	−1.111
		(.2072)	(.2011)	(.1905)	
$\hat{\beta}_{1,2}^{(2)\,b}$		.8088	1.0599	1.118	1.111
		(.0893)	(.6881)	(.1905)	

Note: [a] Standard errors in parentheses.
[b] $\hat{\beta}_{1,2}^{(2)}$ denotes the cross partial derivative with respect to x_1 and x_2.

approximations, the nonparametric estimates (NP), and the maximum likelihood (ML) estimates using the true model. It is clear from the table that, in terms of bias, the nonparametric estimates of both first- and second-order derivatives are much superior to the parametric estimates, except for the MLE. In practice, however, the true model is unknown and hence the MLE is unavailable; however, it does illustrate the losses suffered by a failure to know functional form. The standard errors for the Cobb–Douglas and trans-log approximations were calculated by using White's robust asymptotic covariance matrix. These standard errors are somewhat smaller than the nonparametric standard errors and this must be because of the slow speed of convergnece for the nonparametric estimators.

4.8.2   Earnings–Age Relationship

In Chapter 3 we analyzed the mean and variance of the earnings–age profiles for China and Canada. Here, for the same data sets, we consider the estimation of pointwise and average response coefficients. Looking at Figures 4.1 and 4.2 one may conclude that Chinese male and female earnings are significantly affected by the early ages (including the mean age 40 for male and 32 for female) but, after that, especially in the later ages, the effect is insignificant. This sort of analysis is possible only if we compute pointwise derivatives. However, if we consider the average derivative estimator, $\hat{\bar{\beta}}$, we get values of 34.38 for males and 37.74 for females, with standard errors of 19.82 and 28.81 respectively. This suggests that, overall, age is a significant variable at the 10% level of significance.

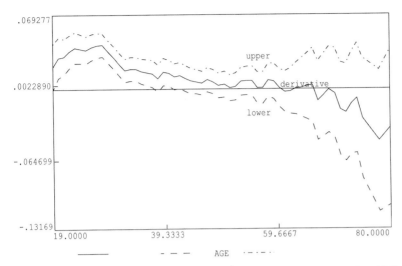

Figure 4.1. Nonparametric derivative of age w.r.t. income (Chinese males; 95% confidence intervals).

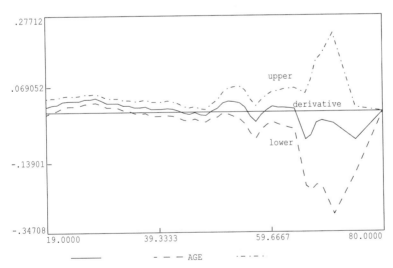

Figure 4.2. Nonparametric derivative of income w.r.t. age (Chinese females; 95% confidence intervals).

A similar finding was observed for the Canadian data. For these data the average derivative estimator was .0162 and its standard error .002. A parametric relationship $y = \alpha + \beta x_i + \gamma x_i^2$ was also estimated, producing $y = 10.041 + .173x - .002x^2$, with the standard errors of $\hat{\beta}$ and $\hat{\gamma}$ being .027 and .003, respectively. Based on this result, the estimate of the average partial derivative is $.173 - .002\bar{x} = .0184$, and its standard error is .003. These results are somewhat similar to those for average derivatives. The slight difference, however, may be due to the use of a quadratic functional form, given that the nonparametric estimates indicate a 'dip' in the relationship.

4.8.3   Review of Applied Work

In Section 4.8.1 we analyzed the estimation of a production function using generated data. Rilstone (1992a) has applied the techniques to describe the properties of a production function $y = m(x_1, x_2, x_3, x_4) + u_i$ fitted to the well-known data of Berndt and Khaled (1979), which consists of 25 annual observations on the log of output y, the log of capital x_1, the log of labor x_2, the log of energy x_3, and the log of other intermediate inputs x_4. The average elasticities and their standard errors (in parentheses) are .1987(.027), .3850(.068), .2215(.024), and .248(.0410). This gives a returns to scale parameter of 1.0533 in the industry. The Cobb–Douglas estimates were .0235(.012), .3360(.020), .047(.018), and .812(.016). The small size of sample here must make one somewhat guarded about the conclusions, but the large differences between the point estimates emphasize the need to examine how good the Cobb–Douglas specification is in this instance. Jung (1995) estimates the marginal product of slaves on plantations in the Ante-Bellum south for different plantation sizes and with a variety of nonparametric methods. Like Rilstone he has four conditioning variables, but now x_2 and x_3 are slave and free labor while x_4 is land. His work shows that the trans-log function used previously in such investigations seems misspecified.

In another study Rilstone (1991b) estimated the average uncompensated price elasticities in the model $y_{ji} = m(x_{1i}, x_{2i}, x_{3i}) + u_i$ with 44 annual observations on the logs of quantities y_{ji}, and normalized prices x_{ji}, $j = 1, \ldots, 3$ of U.S. durables, nondurables, and services respectively. The data are given in Gallant (1981). The nonparametric results showed similar effects to parametric results based on a Cobb–Douglas functional form, just as in the case of the production function analysis above. Tests of significance for each elasticity indicated a rejection of zero elasticities. In a related paper Lewbel (1993) provides nonparametric estimation of average compensated price elasticities; Lewbel (1995) nonparametrically tests demand theory constraints. In particular, he tests Slutsky symmetry in a system of demand equations. He compares this nonparametric test with the standard parametric version derived by assuming that the demand system has the quadratic, almost ideal, format. Generally, both tests agree on the rejection of symmetry for U.K. survey data. For the estimation of second-order derivatives of demand functions, see McMillan et al. (1989).

More applications of derivative estimation and hypothesis testing have begun to appear in econometrics. For example, Subramanian and Deaton (1996) and Ullah and Roy (1998) analyze the income elasticity of calorie intake for the Indian data and show the implications of their results for the policy issues related to poverty. Hausman and Newey (1995) and Breslaw (1995) explore the nonparametric estimation of consumer surplus. Hausman and Newey, for example, estimate the gasoline demand curve by a nonparametric method and then derive estimates of the average magnitude of the welfare loss from a tax on gasoline. In another paper Lewbel (1992) provides various applications of the derivative estimators.

5 Semiparametric Estimation of Single-Equation Models

5.1 Introduction

Chapters 3 and 4 have been concerned with the estimation of the conditional moments of Y given that X equals some value x and the derivatives of this measure. We have referred to the techniques for doing this as nonparametric, even though it was either necessary to prescribe "parameters" such as the window width for kernel estimators or the number of approximating terms for series estimators. Our use of the term "nonparametric" in that context was prompted by the fact that the "parameters" mentioned did not have any economic meaning. This chapter looks at a different scenario, distinguished by the feature that the models considered contain parameters with some economic meaning and which are the fundamental concern of an investigator, but which also have other aspects that may be difficult to describe convincingly in a parametric fashion. We will refer to these as the class of semiparametric (SP) models, and we will explore a number of members of this class in the following sections. An alternative description would have been seminonparametric (SNP), depending upon where one wishes to place the emphasis, and both terms have appeared in the literature.

Section 5.2 explores the situation when the relationship governing y_i can be written as a linear function of some variables x_{1i} and a nonlinear function of other variables x_{2i}, where the nonlinearity is unknown and it is the coefficients of x_{1i} that are of primary interest. By adapting the estimators of Chapter 3, Robinson (1988a) has shown that it is possible to construct an estimator of the parameters of the linear part that exhibits $\sqrt{n}$ consistency. A subsection of Section 5.2 exploits this outcome to derive diagnostic tests for model inadequacy after nonparametric regression and to compare parametric and semiparametric models.

Section 5.3 turns to a linear regression model with conditionally heteroskedastic disturbances of unknown form. It is well known that least squares is not efficient in that context, and the Generalized Least Squares (GLS) estimator was developed to produce a more efficient estimator. Unfortunately, the GLS estimator cannot normally be implemented, as it requires an estimate of the unknown conditional variance of the errors. Because these can be found with the techniques of Chapter 3, it is possible to follow Robinson (1987) and Carroll (1982) and define an SP estimator of the linear coefficients that is as efficient as if the true conditional variances were known. This section also reviews generalizations of this estimator to allow for models in which the conditional variance depends upon the parameters of the conditional mean, as occurs with Engle's (1982) autoregressive conditional heteroskedastic (ARCH) models.

Finally, if y_i and x_i are jointly normal it is well known that $E(y_i|x_i) = x_i'\beta$, or $y_i = x_i'\beta + u_i$, and the best estimator of β is the ordinary least squares (OLS) estimator $\hat{\beta} = (\Sigma x_i x_i')^{-1} \Sigma x_i y_i$. If u_i is not normal, the OLS estimator retains the property of being best, linear, and unbiased (BLUE) (conditional upon x_i). However, there is no obvious reason why linearity (in y_i) is an attractive property for an estimator once the normally distributed data paradigm is departed from. In fact, it might be anticipated that the best estimator would be a *nonlinear* function of y_i, and so OLS is unlikely to be the preferred choice. Interest has therefore grown in choosing a best estimator of β when $E(y_i|x_i) = x_i'\beta$ but u_i is not normal, particularly with the growth of cross-section data sets that seem to exhibit severe nonnormality. One way to proceed would be to endow the random variable u_i with some density and to then devise an optimal estimator under this specification by maximum likelihood methods. Unfortunately, if the density chosen for u_i is incorrect, more harm might be done by proceeding in this fashion than is incurred by invalidly acting as if the disturbances were normally distributed. Considerations of this sort have stimulated interest in estimating β as efficiently as possible by employing nonparametric estimates of the density of u_i. Section 5.4 sets out the types of models for which efficient estimation is possible, describing concepts such as the semiparametric efficiency bound and adaptive estimation, which aim to describe the minimum variance that can be attained, as well as situations when an estimator can be designed that adapts to the unknown density. Section 5.5 deals with methods for performing the latter task, which are described in Gallant and Nychka (1987); Stone (1975), Bickel (1982), and Manski (1984); and Chamberlain (1984) and Newey (1990a). The first of this trio of approaches approximates the unknown density as the product of a polynomial in u_i and the normal density; the second employs kernel methods to nonparametrically estimate the unknown density and its derivatives and subsequently employs these to devise an asymptotically efficient estimator; the last exploits an equivalence between a generalized method of moments approach and the MLE that would hold if the density of u_i was actually known.

Section 5.6 looks at the estimation of "variance parameters" in a linear model, and Section 5.7 uses the theory of Sections 5.4 and 5.5 to construct optimal diagnostic tests for misspecification. Section 5.8 briefly reviews work on efficient estimation when observations are dependent, as most of the theory to this point has been done under the presumption of independence, while Section 5.10

indicates a general method of constructing an estimator that attains the efficiency bound through the use of conditional moment restrictions. Section 5.11 closes with some applications.

Although the methods described in Section 5.5 will produce the most efficient estimator of β, the samples required to invoke the asymptotic properties may be very large, and there is a need for an estimator that is not fully efficient but which improves over OLS. For this purpose Huber (1964) proposed a class of M-estimators (for "like maximum likelihood"), and Section 5.9 outlines this class along with important members of it such as the quantile estimators of Koenker and Bassett (1978). Although these estimators have had limited use in the ordinary regression model, they assume far greater importance when the realm of censored regression models is entered, and an early discussion of this approach in a familiar context is advantageous for understanding later developments. Moreover, there are instances in which it is desirable to be able to characterize the quantiles of the conditional density of y given x rather than the conditional mean dealt with in Chapter 4.

5.2 Semiparametric Estimation of the Linear Part of a Regression Model

5.2.1 General Results

A number of models exist in the literature that have the distinguishing feature that part of the model is linear and part constitutes an unknown nonlinear format. Instead of the general nonlinear specification of (3.1) we would now have

$$y_i = x'_{1i}\beta + g_1(x_{2i}) + u_i, \tag{5.1}$$

which could be written in matrix form as

$$y = X_1\beta + g_1 + u. \tag{5.2}$$

In (5.1) $E(u_i|x_{1i}, x_{2i}) = 0$. Further x_{2i} cannot have unity as an element. This intercept restriction is an identification condition arising from the fact that $g_1(x_{2i})$ is unconstrained and therefore can have a constant term as part of its definition. Hence, it would always be possible to add any constant number to (5.1) and then absorb it into $g(x_{2i})$, showing that, without some further restriction upon the nature of $g_1(x_{2i})$, it is impossible to consistently estimate an intercept. This issue of identification of parameters, particularly in regards to the intercept, but sometimes a scale parameter as well, arises a good deal in the semiparametric literature and needs to be dealt with by imposing some restrictions. For example, if x_{2i} was replaced by $\delta_1 x_{2i} + \delta_2 x_{3i}$, then clearly we can only identify the ratio δ_1/δ_2 as $g_1(\cdot)$ can be redefined as a scalar multiple of the original function. Setting $\delta_2 = 1$ or $\delta_1^2 + \delta_2^2 = 1$ would be appropriate restrictions.

These considerations are especially important in later chapters dealing with discrete choice and selection models.

The parameter of interest is β so that the issue is how to estimate it in the presence of the unknown function g_1. Because Chapter 3 dealt with methods of estimating functions such as g_1, it is natural to employ the methods detailed there to account for g_1 and to thereby produce estimators of β. Throughout the remainder of this section the notation adopted is that connected with Theorems 3.1, 3.2, 3.5, and 3.6.

(i) A Semiparametric Estimator of β

Taking the conditional expectation of (5.1) leads to $E(y_i|x_{2i}) = E(x_{1i}|x_{2i})'\beta + g_1(x_{2i})$. Consequently

$$y_i - E(y_i|x_{2i}) = (x_{1i} - E(x_{1i}|x_{2i}))'\beta + u_i \qquad (5.3)$$

and

$$g_1(x_{2i}) = E(y_i|x_{2i}) - E(x_{1i}|x_{2i})'\beta. \qquad (5.4)$$

Since (5.3) has the properties of a linear regression model with dependent variable $y_i - E(y_i|x_{2i})$ and independent variables $(x_{1i} - E(x_{1i}|x_{2i}))$, an obvious estimator of β is

$$\hat{\beta} = \left[\sum_{i=1}^{n} (x_{1i} - \hat{m}_{12i})(x_{1i} - \hat{m}_{12i})' \right]^{-1}$$

$$\times \left[\sum_{i=1}^{n} (x_{1i} - \hat{m}_{12i})(y_i - \hat{m}_{2i}) \right], \qquad (5.5)$$

where $\hat{m}_{12i}$ and $\hat{m}_{2i}$ are the kernel-based estimators of $m_{12i} = E(x_{1i}|x_{2i})$ and $m_{2i} = E(y_i|x_{2i})$ respectively from (3.5). Once $\hat{\beta}$ is found, $g_1(x_{2i})$ can be estimated from (5.4) as $\hat{g}_1(x_{2i}) = \hat{m}_{2i} - \hat{m}'_{12i}\hat{\beta}$; for example, Stock (1989) works with this model but is particularly interested in estimating $g_1(x_{2i})$ rather than β. Alternatively, this estimator of $g_1(x_{2i})$ can be obtained by first substituting (5.5) into (5.1) so that $y_i^* = y_i - x'_{1i}\hat{\beta} = g_1(x_{2i}) + u_i$ and then writing the kernel estimator of $g_1(x_{2i})$ as the weighted sum of y_i^* given in (3.5). If $g_1(x_{2i})$ were linear in x_{2i}, $\hat{\beta}$ would just be the familiar estimator obtained by regressing the residuals from the (y_i, x_{2i}) regression against the residuals from the (x_{1i}, x_{2i}) regression. Notice also that if $E(x_{1i}|x_{2i}) = x'_{2i}\pi$ then $\hat{m}_{12i} = x'_{2i}\hat{\pi}_{OLS}$ and (5.5) could be given the matrix form $\hat{\beta} = (X'_1 M_2 X_1)^{-1} X'_1 M_2 \hat{v}$, where $M_2 = I - X_2(X'_2 X_2)^{-1} X'_2$, with X_1, X_2, and $\hat{v}$ the matrices containing, in the ith rows, x'_{1i}, x'_{2i}, and $\hat{v}_i = y_i - \hat{m}_{2i}$, respectively. But this means that $\hat{\beta}$ would be the OLS estimator of the coefficient of x_{1i} in the regression of $\hat{v}_i$ against x_{1i} and x_{2i}.

The kernel estimator for β in the context of (5.2) was analyzed by Robinson (1988a) and Speckman (1988), although both Stock (1989) and Denby (1986) work with the estimator. Two important questions are: 1. What is the asymptotic distribution of this estimator? and 2. How efficient is it relative to an estimator that used $g_1(x_{2i})$? These questions arise over many of the semiparametric (SP) estimators introduced in this chapter. At this juncture we concentrate upon the former issue. Looking at (5.3) the natural estimator of β is OLS on that equation, and the SP estimator $\hat{\beta}$ could be viewed as an analogous estimator in which the unknown quantities m_{12i} and m_{2i} were replaced by their nonparametric estimators $\hat{m}_{12i}$ and $\hat{m}_{2i}$. Accordingly, to prove asymptotic properties about $\hat{\beta}$ there will be a need for a law of large numbers and a central limit theorem that can be applied to sample means that are functions of nonparametric estimators of unknown variables, and it therefore helps to have a general result for this situation.

Suppose that $v_i = v(\bar{w}_i, \theta, \tau_i)$ is a function of some random variables $\bar{w}_i$, the unknown parameters of the model θ, and a quantity τ_i that is a function of random variables w_i that may be a subset of $\bar{w}_i$. Because τ_i is unknown it is replaced by a nonparametric estimator $\hat{\tau}_i$ of τ_i. The estimator will be assumed to be constructed from $\{w_i, \bar{w}_i\}$; for the applications discussed in this book such a requirement is not restrictive. Suppressing the dependence on $\bar{w}_i$, define the sample mean $\bar{v}(\theta, \tau) = n^{-1} \sum v(\theta, \tau_i)$, where τ is an $n \times 1$ vector containing τ_i. In most models it will be the case that sufficient restrictions can be placed upon $\bar{w}_i$, τ_0, and θ_0 (the zeros designating the true values) that $\bar{v}(\theta_0, \tau_0) \xrightarrow{p} \lim_{n \to \infty} E(\bar{v}(\theta_0, \tau_0))$ and $n^{1/2}[\bar{v}(\theta_0, \tau_0) - E(\bar{v}(\theta_0, \tau_0))]$ has a limiting normal distribution. For example, in (5.3) we would be interested in $v_i = (x_{1i} - \tau_i)u_i$, where $\tau_i = E(x_{1i}|x_{2i})$, and we could restrict the properties of x_{1i} and x_{2i} so that the sample mean $\bar{v}(\theta_0, \tau_0) = n^{-1} \sum(x_{1i} - E(x_{1i}|x_{2i}))u_i$ converged to zero and a central limit theorem applied to it.

What is needed are equivalent results when τ_i is replaced by a nonparametric estimator $\hat{\tau}_i$. The problem has many similarities to the sequential estimators studied in Newey (1984), Pagan (1984b), and Pagan (1986), in that a parameter, θ, is being estimated after another, τ, has been replaced by some estimate; in this case however the "parameter" τ is infinite dimensional (as $n \to \infty$) so that the results from that literature do not apply. Nevertheless, it should be obvious that all of the problems identified in those papers will still be present, since the move from τ being finite dimensional to infinite dimensional cannot be helpful. In fact, in many instances it is useful to first ask what would happen if τ was a finite-dimensional parameter, since this can alert us to whether there are likely problems in the infinite-dimensional case.

To illustrate the issues that will arise later, it is helpful to consider the *parametric* case in a simplified context. In particular it is assumed that τ is a scalar parameter and that all derivatives of $\bar{v}$ with respect to θ are zero after first order, as are all the cross derivatives between θ and τ. Defining $\hat{\tau}$ as a preliminary estimator of τ_0 and $\hat{\theta}$ as solving $\bar{v}(\hat{\theta}, \hat{\tau}) = 0$, we expand $\bar{v}(\hat{\theta}, \hat{\tau}) = 0$ around θ_0 to yield

$$\bar{v}(\hat{\theta}, \hat{\tau}) = 0 = \bar{v}(\theta_0, \hat{\tau}) + \bar{v}_\theta(\theta_0, \hat{\tau})(\hat{\theta} - \theta_0), \qquad (5.6)$$

where the subscript θ indicates the derivative with respect to θ. Now, if $\hat{\tau}$ is finite dimensional, we can generally expand $\bar{v}(\theta_0, \hat{\tau})$ around τ_0 to give (ignoring cross terms between $(\hat{\tau} - \tau_0)$ and $(\hat{\theta} - \theta_0)$)

$$\begin{aligned}\bar{v}(\hat{\theta}, \hat{\tau}) = 0 = &\ \bar{v}(\theta_0, \tau_0) + \bar{v}_\theta(\theta_0, \tau_0)(\hat{\theta} - \theta_0) \\ &+ \bar{v}_\tau(\theta_0, \tau_0)(\hat{\tau} - \tau_0) + \bar{v}_{\tau\tau}^*(\hat{\tau} - \tau_0)^2,\end{aligned} \qquad (5.7)$$

where the $*$ indicates evaluation between $\hat{\tau}$ and τ_0 and the number of subscripts indicates order of differentiation. Inverting (5.7) to get $\hat{\theta} - \theta_0$ we have

$$\begin{aligned}n^{1/2}(\hat{\theta} - \theta_0) = &\ -\bar{v}_\theta^{-1} n^{1/2} \bar{v}(\theta_0, \tau_0) - \bar{v}_\theta^{-1}\left(n^{1/2}\bar{v}_\tau(\hat{\tau} - \tau_0)\right) \\ &- \bar{v}_\theta^{-1}\bar{v}_{\tau\tau}^* n^{1/2}(\hat{\tau} - \tau_0)^2.\end{aligned} \qquad (5.8)$$

Now, it is clear from (5.8) that $n^{1/2}(\hat{\theta} - \theta_0)$ has the same distribution as $-\bar{v}_\theta^{-1} n^{1/2}\bar{v}(\theta_0, \tau_0)$ only if a number of conditions hold, unless one can ignore the fact that τ has to be estimated and act as if $\hat{\tau} = \tau_0$. First, the third term on the right-hand side must be $o_p(1)$. This could occur in a number of ways – either $\bar{v}_{\tau\tau}^*$ could converge to zero or $n^{1/2}(\hat{\tau} - \tau_0)^2 = \left[n^{1/4}(\hat{\tau} - \tau_0)\right]^2$ could be $o_p(1)$. For parametric models $n^{1/2}(\hat{\tau} - \tau_0)$ is typically $O_p(1)$, so that the latter condition eliminates the third term. Turning to the second term, the limiting distribution of $n^{1/2}(\hat{\theta} - \theta_0)$ will depend on that of $n^{1/2}(\hat{\tau} - \tau_0)$ unless $n^{1/2}\bar{v}_\tau(\hat{\tau} - \tau_o)$ is $o_p(1)$; in likelihood problems where $\bar{v}$ is the sample mean of the score for θ, this becomes the well-known requirement that the information matrix is block diagonal between θ and τ, since $\bar{v}_\tau$ is just the sample mean of the cross derivative of the log likelihood.

Now let us turn to the case where $\hat{\tau}$ is a nonparametric estimator. Expansions such as (5.7) are now more problematic since τ is an infinite-dimensional vector, and differentiation needs to be done more carefully. Nevertheless, Newey (1994a) indicates that such an expansion might be possible and this means that we might examine the last two terms in (5.8) to establish what the limiting distribution of $n^{1/2}(\hat{\theta} - \theta_0)$ would look like. With respect to the final term in (5.8), when $\hat{\tau}$ is a nonparametric estimator it is no longer true that $n^{1/2}(\hat{\tau} - \tau_0)$ is $O_p(1)$ (see Chapter 3). Consequently, either $n^{1/4}(\hat{\tau} - \tau_0)$ or $\bar{v}_{\tau\tau}^*$ would need to be $o_p(1)$. These would be necessary conditions to truncate the expansion and both will arise frequently later. Even when these conditions are satisfied, however, it is still possible that $\bar{v}_\tau n^{1/2}(\hat{\tau} - \tau_o)$ is not $o_p(1)$ so that the second term in (5.8) cannot be ignored, and this situation will need careful treatment. This heuristic analysis is a useful vehicle for illustrating the problems arising when $\hat{\tau}$ is infinite dimensional, but a more precise treatment is now provided.

Andrews (1994) has provided conditions under which a law of large numbers (LLN) and a central limit theorem (CLT) apply to $\bar{v}(\theta, \hat{\tau})$ when $\hat{\tau}_i$ is a non-parametric estimator of τ_i. Lemma 5.1 is adapted from his more general results, which will be discussed in Chapter 7 and which are summarized in the appendix.

Lemma 5.1:

(A) LLN: If   (i) $\hat{\tau}_i \xrightarrow{p} \tau_i$ with respect to some metric $\rho(.,.)$, for example

$$\rho(\hat{\tau}, \tau_0) = \lim_{n\to\infty} \left[n^{-1} \sum E \| v_i(\theta_0, \hat{\tau}_i) - v_i(\theta_0, \tau_i) \|^s \right]^{1/s},$$

$$1 \le s \le \infty,$$

(ii) $\lim_{n\to\infty} E(\bar{v}(\theta_0, \tau_0)) = c(\theta) < \infty$, and (iii) $\bar{v}(\theta, \tau_0)$ satisfies a uniform weak law of large numbers over Θ, where $\theta_0 \in \Theta$, then

$$\bar{v}(\theta, \hat{\tau}) \xrightarrow{p} c(\theta).$$

(B) CLT: If   (i) A(i) holds, (ii) $n^{1/2} E(\bar{v}(\theta_0, \hat{\tau})) \xrightarrow{p} 0$, (iii) $n^{1/2}[\bar{v}(\theta_0, \tau_0) - E(\bar{v}(\theta_0, \tau_0))] \xrightarrow{d} \mathcal{N}(0, V)$, and $\bar{v}(\theta, \tau_0)$ is stochastically equicontinuous, then

$$n^{1/2}[\bar{v}(\theta_0, \hat{\tau}) - E(\bar{v}(\theta_0, \tau_0))] \xrightarrow{d} \mathcal{N}(0, V).$$

Proof: The LLN is straightforward; the CLT follows from the discussion between equations A13 and A16 of the appendix to Andrews (1994).
Q.E.D.

To understand the origin of these conditions return to (5.6) and write $n^{1/2}\bar{v}(\theta_0, \hat{\tau})$ as

$$n^{1/2}\bar{v}(\theta_0, \hat{\tau}) = n^{1/2}\bar{v}(\theta_0, \tau_0) + n^{1/2}\{(E(\bar{v}(\theta_0, \tau_0)) - \bar{v}(\theta_0, \tau_0))$$
$$+ (\bar{v}(\theta_0, \hat{\tau}) - E(\bar{v}(\theta_0, \hat{\tau})))\} + n^{1/2}E(\bar{v}(\theta_0, \hat{\tau})),$$

where $E(\bar{v}(\theta_0, \tau_0)) = 0$ and now $\hat{\tau}$ is infinite dimensional. For the same reasons as when τ was finite dimensional the last two terms need to be $o_p(1)$ for $n^{1/2}(\hat{\theta} - \theta_0)$ to have a limiting distribution that does not depend upon $\hat{\tau}$. The last term is zero if condition B(ii) holds, while stochastic equicontinuity implies that the term in curly brackets is $o_p(1)$ (see Andrews (1994, eq. (2.9), p. 48)). As explained there, stochastic equicontinuity is a stochastic and asymptotic version of continuity in a function and effectively implies continuity of $\bar{v}(\theta_0, \tau)$ at τ_0 with probability close to one for large n. These conditions therefore replace those stated in terms of derivatives of $\bar{v}$ and the behavior of $\hat{\tau} - \tau_0$, which are well known from the finite-dimensional case. Because $E(\bar{v}(\theta_0, \hat{\tau}))$ involves $\hat{\tau}$, it will be the case that the convergence rate of $\hat{\tau} - \tau_0$ will still appear as an important item that needs to be considered. Thus condition B(ii), sometimes referred to as the "asymptotic independence" condition, effectively combines in a single format the requirement that $\bar{v}_\tau n^{1/2}(\hat{\tau} - \tau_0) + \bar{v}_{\tau\tau}^* n^{1/2}(\hat{\tau} - \tau_0)^2$ be $o_p(1)$ if the distribution of $n^{1/2}(\hat{\theta} - \theta_0)$ is to be independent from that of $\hat{\tau} - \tau_0$. For this reason, $n^{1/4}(\hat{\tau} - \tau_0)$ being $o_p(1)$ frequently arises in the discussion later; when it doesn't it is because $\bar{v}_{\tau\tau}^*$ is $o_p(1)$. Newey's (1994a) approach is to discuss the two terms separately, since he is interested in instances where $\bar{v}_\tau$ is not $o_p(1)$.

In Lemma 5.1 the notation $E(\bar{v}(\theta_0, \hat{\tau}))$ in B(ii) should be read as implying that the expectation is taken with respect to the density of $(w_i, \bar{w}_i)$, first with τ_i an arbitrary function of its conditioning elements, *after which* it is replaced by $\hat{\tau}_i$ in testing the condition. To illustrate this procedure, consider setting $v(\theta, \hat{\tau}_i) = x_{1i} - \hat{m}_{12i}$, with the notation drawn from the example beginning this section. In the first step to verifying B(ii), $\hat{m}_{12i}$ is replaced by τ_i, which is an arbitrary function of x_{2i} rather than the specific one used by the nonparametric estimator. That step yields $v(\theta_0, \tau_i) = x_{i1} - m_{12i} + m_{12i} - \tau_i$. Subsequently, taking the expectation of this quantity produces $E_{x_2}(m_{12i} - \tau_i)$ and, after substituting $\hat{m}_{12i}$ for τ_i, we see that $E_{x_2}(m_{12i} - \hat{m}_{12i})$ must tend in probability to zero if B(ii) is to be satisfied. Once B(ii) holds the asymptotic distribution of $n^{-1/2}\sum(x_{i1} - \hat{m}_{12i})$ would be just that of $n^{-1/2}\sum(x_{i1} - m_{12i})$. It might also be observed that in most instances the expectation over $\bar{w}_i$ and w_i reduces to one based upon w_i alone but, because $\hat{\tau}_i$ can be constructed from data consisting of not just w_i, $E(\bar{v}(\theta_0, \hat{\tau}))$ may be stochastic, accounting for the statement of B(ii) as involving convergence in probability rather than a limit.

One needs to ask how likely the other conditions are to be met. Consistency of $\hat{\tau}_i$ needs to be defined with respect to some norm, although L^2 is most common in what follows, whereas uniform laws of large numbers are fairly readily available for both independent and dependent random variables (e.g., Andrews, 1991d; Pötscher and Prucha, 1989). Because it was assumed that $\hat{\tau}_i$ was constructed from w_i and $\bar{w}_i$, $\rho(\hat{\tau}, \tau_0)$ is not random; Andrews actually allows for the more general case. Condition A(ii) is a model property that needs to be verified. Of the requirements under B, the CLT in (iii) holds fairly generally, provided dependence wears off sufficiently rapidly and there exist enough moments (for example, see White, 1984). Stochastic equicontinuity could be hard to verify and we will just assume in this book that $\bar{v}$ is stochastically equicontinuous. Andrews (1994) provides a variety of theorems to justify the assumption when the w_i are both independent and dependent and v_i takes a variety of forms. It is B(ii) which is most important, as it is a function of the model and the properties of the nonparametric estimator of τ_i. As will be seen it places restrictions upon the choice of window width and kernel that might be used for getting $\hat{\tau}_i$.

Theorem 5.1 describes the conditions under which the SP estimator of β (taken to be a scalar) in (5.5) is asymptotically normal and equivalent to the estimator of β one would get by substituting the true conditional expectations in (5.5). As might be expected, using the knowledge that $E(y_i|x_{1i}, x_{2i})$ is linear in x_{1i} is beneficial to estimation of β, allowing convergence to its true value at the same rate as if $g_1(\cdot)$ was parameterized.

Theorem 5.1: Let $\bar{w}'_i = (y_i, x_{1i}, x_{2i})$ be i.i.d. and $\eta_i = x_{1i} - E(x_{1i}|x_{2i})$, and assume that the moments of η_i and u_i up to fourth order are bounded, $E(\eta_i u_i) = 0$, and a CLT and LLN applies to $n^{-1/2}\sum \eta_i u_i$ and $n^{-1}\sum \eta_i \eta'_i$ respectively. If $\hat{\beta}$ is estimated from (5.5) and the nonparametric estimators of $m_{2i} = E(y_i|x_{2i})$ and $m_{12i} = E(x_{1i}|x_{2i})$ are such that $E_{\bar{w}}\left[n^{1/4}(\hat{m}_{12i} - m_{12i})^2\right]$ and $E_{\bar{w}}\left[n^{1/4}(\hat{m}_{2i} - m_{2i})^2\right]$ converge in probability to zero, $n^{1/2}(\hat{\beta} - \beta)$ is asymptotically $\mathcal{N}(0, \sigma^2 V_{\eta\eta}^{-1})$, where $V_{\eta\eta} = E(\eta_i\eta'_i)$ and $E_{\bar{w}}$ indicates that the expectation is taken with respect to the joint density of $\bar{w}_i$.

Proof (for scalar x_{1i} and x_{2i}): Substituting $y_i = m_{2i} + \eta_i\beta + u_i = m_{2i} + \hat{\eta}_i\beta + (\eta_i - \hat{\eta}_i)\beta + u_i$ into (5.5) gives

$$n^{1/2}(\hat{\beta} - \beta) = \left(n^{-1}\sum \hat{\eta}_i^2\right)^{-1}\left[n^{-1/2}\left(\sum \hat{\eta}_i((m_{2i} - \hat{m}_{2i})\right.\right.$$
$$\left.\left. + (\eta_i - \hat{\eta}_i)\beta + u_i)\right)\right]. \tag{5.9}$$

Consider the denominator, putting $v(\theta, \hat{\tau}_i) = \hat{\eta}_i^2 = (\eta_i + m_{12i} - \hat{m}_{12i})^2$. Now $E(\bar{v}(\theta_0, m_{12i})) = n^{-1}\sum E(\eta_i^2) = V_{\eta\eta}$ so that A(ii) of Lemma 5.1 is satisfied and the conditions given in the theorem also guarantee A(iii), leaving only A(i) to be checked. But this simply requires that $\hat{m}_{12i}$ tends to m_{12i} in some metric. Taking the metric as in A(i) with $s = 1$, we obtain

$$\rho(\hat{m}, m_0) = E(m_{12i} - \hat{m}_{12i})^2, \tag{5.10}$$

which tends to zero from the results of Chapter 3. Hence by the LLN the denominator converges to $V_{\eta\eta}$.

Turning to the numerator put $\theta = \beta$ and $\hat{v}_i = v_i(\theta, \hat{\tau}_i)$, which equals

$$\hat{\eta}_i\left[(m_{2i} - \hat{m}_{2i}) + (\hat{m}_{12i} - m_{12i})\beta + u_i\right].$$

Since m_{12i} and m_{2i} are the true values of the conditional means let $\tau'_i = (\tau_{2i}, \tau_{12i})$ be arbitrary functions of x_{2i}. Since $E(\bar{v}(\beta_0, \tau_0)) = 0$, Lemma 5.1 says that the numerator of (5.9), $n^{-1/2}\sum \hat{v}_i = n^{1/2}(n^{-1}\sum \hat{v}_i) = n^{1/2}\bar{v}(\beta_0, \hat{\tau})$, converges to the same limit distribution as $n^{1/2}\bar{v}(\beta_0, \tau_0) = n^{-1/2}\sum \eta_i u_i$ if conditions B(i) and B(ii) are satisfied. Condition B(ii) implies $E\left(n^{1/2}\bar{v}(\beta_0, \hat{\tau})\right) = 0$, where the expectation is taken with τ arbitrary and then τ_{2i} and τ_{12i} are set to $\hat{m}_{2i}$ and

$\hat{m}_{12i}$. Now

$$n^{-1/2} \sum_{i=1}^{n} E(v_i(\beta_0, \tau_{2i}, \tau_{12i}))$$

$$= n^{-1} \sum_{i=1}^{n} E[(\eta_i + (m_{12i} - \tau_{12i})][n^{1/2}(m_{2i} - \tau_{2i})$$

$$+ n^{1/2}(\tau_{12i} - m_{12i})\beta_0 + n^{1/2}u_i]$$

$$= E_{x_2} [n^{1/2}(m_{12i} - \tau_{12i})(m_{2i} - \tau_{2i}) - n^{1/2}(\tau_{12i} - m_{12i})^2 \beta_0],$$

$$(5.11)$$

where $E_{x_2}(\cdot)$ indicates that the expectation is taken with respect to x_2 only, as τ_{12i} and m_{21i} are functions solely of x_{2i}. Finally, $E(n^{1/2}\bar{v}(\beta_0, \hat{\tau}))$ is the right-hand side of (5.11) with τ_{21i} and τ_{2i} replaced by $\hat{m}_{21i}$ and $\hat{m}_{2i}$. Applying the Cauchy–Schwartz inequality to the first term in (5.11), the right-hand side becomes

$$\leq \left[E\left(n^{1/4}(\hat{m}_{12i} - m_{12i})\right)^2 \right]^{1/2} \left[E\left(n^{1/4}(\hat{m}_{2i} - m_{2i})\right)^2 \right]^{1/2}$$

$$+ E\left(n^{1/4}(\hat{m}_{12i} - m_{12i})\right)^2 |\beta_0|,$$

and it is clear that $n^{1/4}$ consistency is needed for the estimators of m_{12i} and m_{2i}.

Finally, condition B(i) of Lemma 5.1 needs to be checked with this different definition of v_i. Andrews (1994) finds that the condition holds if $E(\eta_i^4)$ and $E(u_i^4)$ are bounded and $E(\hat{m}_{12i} - m_{12i})^4$ and $E(m_{2i} - \hat{m}_{2i})^4$ tend to zero. Consequently, the asymptotic distribution of the numerator of (5.9) is that of $n^{-1/2} \sum \eta_i u_i$, which is $\mathcal{N}(0, \sigma^2 V_{\eta\eta})$, making the distribution of $n^{1/2}(\hat{\beta} - \beta_0)$, $\mathcal{N}(0, \sigma^2 V_{\eta\eta}^{-1})$. Q.E.D.

The application discussed in Theorem 5.1 illustrates nicely the way in which the need to estimate a nonparametric component impacts upon the properties of the semiparametric estimator. Not just any consistent estimator of the conditional means will work to give $n^{1/2}$ consistency for $(\hat{\beta} - \beta_0)$. If the conditional moments could be estimated parametrically then $n^{1/2}(\hat{m}_{2i} - m_{2i})$ would be $O_p(1)$ and $n^{1/4}$ consistency is straightforward, but from Chapter 3 the convergence rate of nonparametric estimators is slower than $n^{1/2}$ and depends upon the window width and the number of conditioning variables (q). To illustrate this, from Chapter 3 $(nh^q)^{1/2}(\hat{m}_{2i} - m_{2i})$ is stochastically bounded if data are independently distributed and the kernel is of the higher order variety with moments up to second order being zero. Hence, $n^{1/4}(\hat{m}_{2i} - m_{2i})$ converges to zero if $n^{-1/4}h^{-q/2}$ converges to zero (i.e., if nh^{2q} tends to infinity). Both Stock (1989) and Robinson (1988a) restrict the window width in this way. Notice

that, even though the kernel estimate of the conditional means converge to their
true values quite slowly, the fact that these are used in a regression indicates
that the values are effectively being "averaged," and it is this feature that makes
it possible for the estimator of β to exhibit the same convergence rate as in a
parametric model. In most cases it will be important to use higher order kernels
to eliminate the asymptotic bias problem, as this gives a wider range of potential
window widths and so makes $n^{1/4}$ consistency more likely.

A heuristic derivation of the results in Theorem 5.1 is available from the
requirements deduced from the parametric version discussed in the context of
(5.8). By inspection of (5.3), the moment condition defining the estimator $\hat{\beta}$ is
$E(\bar{v}) = 0$, where

$$\bar{v} = n^{-1} \sum [(y_i - m_{2i} - (x_{1i} - m_{12i})'\beta)(x_{1i} - m_{12i})]$$

and differentiating $\bar{v}$ gives $\bar{v}_{\tau_2} = -n^{-1} \sum (x_{1i} - m_{12i})$, $\bar{v}_{\tau_1} = -(y_i - m_{2i}) - 2n^{-1}$
$\sum (m_{12i} - x_{1i})\beta$, treating β as a scalar and identifying τ_j as m_{12i} and m_{2i} respectively. Differentiating again, we get $\bar{v}_{\tau_2 \tau_2} = 0$, $\bar{v}_{\tau_1 \tau_1} = -2\beta$, and $\bar{v}_{\tau_1 \tau_2} = 1$,
meaning that the third term in (5.8) disappears only if $n^{1/4}(\hat{\tau}_j - \tau_j)$ is $o_p(1)$ ($j =$
$1, 2$). Notice that the term $\bar{v}_{\tau_1 \tau_1}(\hat{\tau}_1 - \tau_1)$ is $o_p(1)$ if $\beta = 0$, but the cross term
remains and necessitates $n^{1/2}(\hat{\tau}_1 - \tau_1)(\hat{\tau}_2 - \tau_2)$ being $o_p(1)$. Thus, Andrews's
conclusions emerge out of the parametric analogy.

(ii)   A Series Estimator of β

A series estimator of β could be found by approximating m_{12i} and
m_{2i} in (5.5) by $w_i'\delta_1$ and $w_i'\delta_2$ respectively, where w_i are functions of x_{2i}. This
means that $\hat{m}_{12i}$ and $\hat{m}_{2i}$ would be the predictions from the regressions of x_{1i}
and y_i against w_i. In matrix notation the estimator of β would be $\hat{\beta} = \left(X_1'(I - P_W)^{-1} X_1 \right)^{-1} X_1'(I - P_W)y$, where $P_W = W(W'W)^{-1}W'$. But this would give
the same estimate of β as the regression of y against X_1 and W, indicating that
one is really approximating g_{1i} with a series $w_i'\delta$. What is of interest here are
the properties of $\hat{\beta}$. Theorem 5.2 deals with this.[1]

Theorem 5.2: Under the same assumptions as Theorem 5.1, and $\hat{\beta}$
estimated by regressing y_i against x_{1i} and w_i, $n^{1/2}(\hat{\beta} - \beta)$ is asymptotically

$$\mathcal{N}\left(0, \sigma^2 \left[p \lim_{n \to \infty} n^{-1} X_1'(I - P_W)X_1 \right]^{-1} \right).$$

---

[1] Donald and Newey (1994) derive the distribution of $\hat{\beta}$ under weak conditions, allowing x_{2i} to
be multidimensional and possibly discrete, with u_i being heteroskedastic. The assumptions of
Theorem 5.2 clearly place restrictions upon the nature of the basis functions and the rate at
which the number of terms in the series approximation can increase, but we leave these implicit.

Proof: Since the proposed estimator is a special case of (5.5) where the conditional means have been replaced by series rather than kernel estimators, Theorem 5.1 shows that $n^{1/2}(\hat{\beta} - \beta)$ is normally distributed provided the series estimators of m_{12i} and m_{2i} are $n^{1/4}$ consistent etc. Because $V_{\eta\eta} = \sigma^2 p$ $\lim n^{-1} X_1'(I - P_W)X_1$ the result follows. Q.E.D.

We note that both Theorems 5.1 and 5.2 assume $V(u_i|x_{1i}, x_{2i}) = \sigma^2$. Fan et al. (1995) extend the result of Theorem 5.1 to the case where u_i has a conditionally heteroskedastic variance, $V(u_i|x_{1i}, x_{2i}) = \sigma^2(x_{1i}, x_{2i})$, of unknown form. This extension required the boundedness of slightly more than the fourth moments of y and x. Further, although Theorems 5.1 and 5.2 made the assumption of i.i.d. data, Andrews (1994) shows that one can allow for dependence and heterogeneity. If one does that the conditions in the theorems need to be modified to reflect the fact that random variables need not have the same expectation at every point i – a feature exploited extensively above. In addition, verification of stochastic equicontinuity may be difficult; Andrews needs to restrict x_{2i} to be a bounded random variable to do so, although this does not seem a serious limitation.

There are two other problems with the asymptotic results in Theorems 5.1 and 5.2. First, the Monte Carlo evidence in Stock (1989) suggests that the first-order asymptotic distribution may provide poor approximations to the behavior of semiparametric estimators in small samples. Second, the asymptotic variance results do not depend on h and hence do not provide a way of choosing h in practice. Moreover, the dependence of $\hat{\beta}$ on the nonparametric estimators $\hat{\tau}$ disappears asymptotically. In view of these problems Linton (1995) has derived a second-order asymptotic expansion of the MSE of $\sqrt{n}(\hat{\beta} - \beta)$ to $o(n^{-2\lambda})$, where $0 < \lambda < 1/2$, thereafter obtaining the optimal h by minimizing the approximate MSE as was done in Chapters 2 to 4. Considering x_{2i} to be a vector of p variables and using second-order kernels (see Chapters 2 to 4) Linton shows that the asymptotic expansion has the form

$$\text{MSE}(\sqrt{n}(\hat{\beta} - \beta)) \approx V(\sqrt{n}(\hat{\beta} - \beta)) + [\text{bias}][\text{bias}]'$$
$$= V_0 + \frac{V_1}{nh^p} + nh^8 B,$$

where $V_0 = \sigma^2 V_{\eta\eta}^{-1}$, and the matrices V_1 and B are free of n and h. The optimal h that minimizes this MSE is $h(n) = o(n^{-2/(8+p)})$. Using such a value for h, the resulting correction to the asymptotic MSE, V_0, is of order $n^{-2\lambda}$, where $\lambda = \frac{8-p}{2(8+p)}$. For $p = 1$, $h(n) = o(n^{-2/9})$ and $\lambda = 7/18$. It is clear that the optimal order of magnitude of h for $\hat{\beta}$ is different than the order of magnitude of h in the first stage estimation of $\hat{\tau}$.

Linton (1996a) also provides a second-order Edgeworth approximation, to $o(n^{-1})$, of the distribution of the semiparametric estimator $\hat{\theta}$ that is a solution of $\bar{v}(\hat{\theta}, \hat{\tau}) = 0$. This includes, among others, $\hat{\beta}$ in (5.5) and the estimation of a regression parameter in the heteroskedastic model discussed later in Section 5.3. Linton's approximations are computationally intensive and they depend on unknown population parameters, so that it is currently unclear whether they will experience much use in improving the critical values of the standardized distribution of $\hat{\theta}$.

5.2.2   Diagnostic Tests after Nonparametric Regression

After estimating (3.1), $y_i = m(x_i) + u_i$, by the nonparametric regression methods of Chapter 3, information might be sought about the adequacy of the formulation, particularly about the common assumptions that the x_i are the only important variables to enter the conditional mean and that the conditional variance can be taken as constant. It is natural to proceed to do this in the same fashion as for the linear regression model, namely by substituting the nonparametric residuals $\hat{u}_i = y_i - \hat{m}_i$ into the standard diagnostic tests associated with most regression programs. Doing so inevitably raises the question of whether one can judge the significance of the test statistic values formed in this way as if one had a linear regression. It is not hard to establish that this cannot be so for finite samples as the nonparametric residuals are not linear functions of the errors u_i. To see this write $\hat{m}_i = \Sigma w_{ij} y_j$, where w_{ij} are the weights in kernel regression, doubly indexed because $x = x_i$, making $\hat{u}_i = y_i - \hat{m}_i = \{u_i - \Sigma w_{ij} u_j\} + \{m_i - \Sigma w_{ij} m_j\}$. The first part of this expression corresponds to the linear projection property of the OLS residuals, assuming that the x_i are fixed, but the second term only tends to zero asymptotically.

Nevertheless, this last feature suggests that the *asymptotic* distributions may be the same and the key to a demonstration of that fact is to pose diagnostic tests in the variable addition framework set out in Pagan (1984a). The basic idea of that paper was to augment the maintained model (3.1) with another set of variables z_i, giving

$$y_i = E(y_i|x_i) + z_i'\gamma + u_i, \tag{5.12}$$

and to then test if γ is zero. By varying the nature of z_i Pagan showed that it was possible to get most diagnostic tests as special cases. One point, made in that paper, needs to be emphasized. The role of z_i is to be a proxy for the specification error in the conditional mean of (3.1); it does not need to be the actual omitted variables. Hence a linear format could be assumed, at the risk of having a test with low power. A more extensive discussion of this point is given in that article and also in Pagan and Hall (1983).

Now consider what happens when $E(y_i|x_i)$ is estimated nonparametrically and (3.1) is the maintained model. If done by a series estimator the adequacy of the maintained model may be determined by adding z_i to the approximating regression and then testing if γ equals zero by the standard F-test; the justification is that (5.12) is a special case of (5.2) with $x_{1i} = z_i$ and $x_{2i} = x_i$, and Theorem 5.2 showed that $n^{1/2}(\hat{\gamma} - \gamma)$ had a limiting normal distribution.

A similar approach can be taken for kernel regression where the appropriate estimator of γ is provided in (5.5) and shown to be asymptotically normal in Theorem 5.1. In words, the estimate of γ is found by regressing the nonparametric residuals $\hat{u}_i$ against the residuals from the nonparametric regression of z_i against x_i. The standard F-test that γ is zero in such a regression will then provide a diagnostic test statistic. *Prima facie* this strategy is different to the way such tests are done in the linear model, where $\hat{u}_i$ would be regressed against z_i and x_i. One case in which they coincide, mentioned under (5.5), is when $E(z_i|x_i)$ was linear in the x_i. However, the regression of $\hat{u}_i$ against z_i and x_i will still yield a valid test statistic even if $E(z_i|x_i)$ is not linear in x_i. To show this consider replacing $E(x_{1i}|x_{2i})$ in (5.3) by $x_{2i}'\hat{\pi}$. Under *the null hypothesis* that $\beta = 0$ the limiting distribution of $n^{1/2}(\hat{\beta} - \beta)$ is not influenced by this substitution. Clearly, the *power* of the test will be affected and it would be best to use the SP estimator of γ rather than this linear version of it.

Following through the structure of Pagan (1984a), tests for the second moment assumption that σ^2 is a constant proceed by a series of substitutions from the relation

$$E\left(u_i^2\right) = \sigma_i^2 = \sigma^2 + z_i'\gamma \tag{5.13}$$

to

$$\hat{u}_i^2 = \sigma^2 + z_i'\gamma + \left(u_i^2 - E\left(u_i^2\right)\right) + \left(\hat{u}_i^2 - u_i^2\right), \tag{5.14}$$

and $H_0 : \gamma = 0$ is tested by regressing $\hat{u}_i^2$ against a constant and z_i. Defining

$$v_i = z_i \left[(y_i - m_i)^2 - \sigma^2 - z_i'\gamma\right],$$

$\hat{\gamma}$ solves $\bar{v}(\hat{\gamma}, \hat{\sigma}^2, \hat{m}_i) = 0$ and Lemma 5.1 can be applied to show that $n^{1/2}\sum \hat{v}_i$ has the same limiting normal distribution as $n^{1/2}\sum v_i$, where $\hat{v}_i = z_i(\hat{u}_i^2 - \sigma^2 - z_i'\gamma)$. Replacing $\hat{u}_i$ by $u_i + (m_i - \hat{m}_i)$, condition B(ii) requires that $n^{1/2}E(z_iu_i(m_i - \tau_i)) = 0$ and $n^{1/2}E(z_i|x_i)(\hat{m}_i - m_i)^2$ be $o_p(1)$. The two restrictions to ensure this outcome are that $\hat{m}_i$ is $n^{1/4}$ consistent and $E(m_iz_iu_i) = 0$. Of these the one most likely to be violated is the latter; if m_i or z_i were functions of endogenous variables or if they depended upon y_{i-1} when u_i was serially correlated, it would not be true. It is useful to think of what would happen to the test in a parametric setting. Following the argument in Pagan and Hall (1983) we see clearly that a failure of $E(m_iz_iu_i)$ to be zero means that the distribution of $n^{1/2}(\hat{\gamma} - \gamma)$ depends upon that for $\hat{m}$; in parametric models suitable adjustments can sometimes be made to allow for this effect and it may be possible to also do this for nonparametric models.

An alternative approach to diagnostic tests that effectively deals with some of these issues is the conditional moment approach of Newey (1985) and Tauchen (1985), wherein it is recognized that there are a number of moment restrictions implicit in the maintained models that might be tested. In terms of the discussion above about the extensiveness of the conditioning set for the mean of y_i, the implicit convention is that $E(z_i(y_i - E(y_i|x_i))) = c_0 = 0$. Newey and Tauchen proposed testing if $c_0 = 0$ by examining the sample moment, and this would be $\hat{c} = n^{-1}\Sigma z_i \hat{u}_i$.

Defining $v_i = z_i(y_i - E(y_i|x_i))$ it is apparent that $\hat{c} = n^{-1}\sum_{i=1}^{n} \hat{v}_i$, allowing the asymptotic distribution of $n^{1/2}(\hat{c} - c_0)$ to be established by an application of Lemma 5.1. Whang and Andrews (1993) use this approach. It is important to verify that the conditions of the lemma hold, in particular B(ii). Whang and Andrews also allow for the fact that θ is estimated. Condition B(ii) eliminates any dependence between $\hat{c}$ and $\hat{\tau}$ but does not ensure that the same is true of $\hat{c}$ and $\hat{\theta}$. To perform the extension assume that

$$n^{1/2}(\hat{\theta} - \theta_0) = n^{-1/2} \sum_{i=1}^{n} \zeta_i + o_p(1).^2$$

The ζ_i is termed the *influence function*, as it shows the influence of the ith data point upon $\hat{\theta}$, and, when random variables are i.i.d., $\text{var}(n^{1/2}(\hat{\theta} - \theta))$ will be $\text{var}(\zeta_1)$. If $\hat{\theta}$ is the MLE, $\zeta_i = \mathcal{I}_{\theta\theta}^{-1}d_{\theta,i}$, where $\mathcal{I}_{\theta\theta}$ is the information matrix for θ and $d_{\theta,i}$ is the ith observation on the score for θ. Substituting this into the expansion

$$n^{1/2}(\hat{c} - c_0) = n^{-1/2} \sum_{i=1}^{n} v(\theta_0, \tau_i) + \bar{v}_\theta n^{1/2}(\hat{\theta} - \theta_0) + o_p(1)$$

gives an influence function for $n^{1/2}(\hat{c} - c)$ of $v(\theta_0, \tau_i) + \bar{v}_\theta \zeta_i$ and hence

$$\text{var}(n^{1/2}(\hat{c} - c_0)) = \text{var}(v_i) + \text{cov}(v_i, \zeta_i')\bar{v}_\theta'$$
$$+ \bar{v}_\theta \text{cov}(\zeta_i, v_i') + \bar{v}_\theta \text{var}(\zeta_i)\bar{v}_\theta'.$$

This variance may then be used to form the test statistic $n(\hat{c} - c_0)'[\text{var}(n^{1/2}(\hat{c} - c_0))]^{-1}(\hat{c} - c_0)$, which will be asymptotically $\chi^2(\dim(c))$ under the null hypothesis that c_0 is zero.

5.2.3 *Semiparametric Estimation of Some Macro Models*

A number of models exist in macro economics in which there is interest in a variable that may be best estimated nonparametrically. Thus in (5.15)

$$y_i = x_i'\beta + z_i'\gamma + u_i, \tag{5.15}$$

z_i might be an anticipated value of a variable ξ_i given information w_i; the unanticipated value of such a variable; or its "volatility" as measured by the

---

[2] An estimator having this structure is referred to as asymptotically linear.

conditional variance $E\left[(\xi_i - E(\xi_i|w_i))^2|w_i\right]$. We desire to get an estimator of β and γ. Barro (1977) was interested in testing if $\gamma = 0$ when z_i was an expected value; many other studies are concerned with the impact of volatility, for example, Coulsen and Robins (1985) and Engle, Lillien, and Robins (1987). Most of this work determines a series for z_i by adopting a parametric model for the anticipated variable (or unanticipated variable) as a function of the information w_i, but there have been papers that advocated a nonparametric approach, for example Pagan and Ullah (1988) and Lee (1988).

Lemma 5.1 and the method of proof in Theorem 5.1 can be adapted to exploring the consequences of a switch from parametric to nonparametric methods. To illustrate, take z_i as $E(\xi_i|w_i)$ and suppose γ is estimated by regressing y_i against x_i and $\hat{z}_i$, the kernel estimator of the conditional mean z_i. When the z_i are replaced by $\hat{z}_i$ in (5.15) the error term becomes $u_i + (z_i - \hat{z}_i)'\gamma$ and the $\bar{v}(\theta_0, \hat{\tau})$ for use in Lemma 5.1 would be composed of $\hat{v}_i = x_i(u_i + (z_i - \hat{z}_i)'\gamma)$ and $\hat{v}_i = \hat{z}_i(u_i + (z_i - \hat{z}_i)'\gamma)$. To determine if the OLS estimator of γ described above is asymptotically normal we need to apply the tests in Lemma 5.1. Looking at B(ii) it is necessary to show that $E_w\left(\hat{z}_i n^{1/2}(z_i - \hat{z}_i)'\gamma\right)$ tends in probability to zero, and this would indicate that $\hat{z}_i$ has to be $n^{1/2}$ consistent. This is impossible; if $z_i = w_i'\alpha$ and $\hat{z}_i$ was estimated parametrically as $\hat{z}_i = w_i'\hat{\alpha}$, then $n^{1/2}(\hat{z}_i - z_i) = n^{1/2}w_i'(\hat{\alpha} - \alpha)$ and this is $O_p(1)$ rather than $o_p(1)$. In fact this conclusion is just the familiar one that "generated regressors" affect the sampling distributions of estimators that employ them.

In the parametric literature the problem just identified is circumvented by replacing $z_i = E(\xi_i|w_i)$ in (5.15) with ξ_i and then using $\hat{z}_i$ as an instrument for ξ_i. Then the v_i would be $\hat{z}_i(u_i + (z_i - \xi_i)'\gamma)$ and $x_i(u_i + (z_i - \xi_i)'\gamma)$, and it is easily seen that the expectation of these is zero for any $\hat{z}_i$ that are functions of w_i (it is assumed that x_i appears in agents' information sets and is therefore uncorrelated with the unanticipated quantities $(z_i - \xi_i)$). When the z_i is a conditional variance the analogous instrumental variable estimator involves replacing z_i with $(\xi_i - E(\xi_i|w_i))^2$, which is estimated by $(\xi_i - \hat{m}_i)^2$, and using $\hat{z}_i$, the estimated variance of ξ_i conditional upon w_i, as an instrument; see Pagan and Ullah (1988). Ignoring β in (5.15) and taking γ to be a scalar, we get

$$v_i = \hat{z}_i\left[u_i - \left((\xi_i - \hat{m}_i)^2 - z_i\right)\gamma\right]$$

$$= \hat{z}_i\left(u_i - (\xi_i - m_i)^2\gamma + z_i\gamma\right)$$

$$- 2(m_i - \hat{m}_i)(\xi_i - m_i)\gamma - (m_i - \hat{m}_i)^2\gamma\right).$$

Applying B(ii) for $\hat{m}_i$ and $\hat{\tau}_i = \hat{z}_i$ being functions of w_i shows that the expectation of the sum of the first four terms is zero and B(ii) becomes $E_w\left[(n^{1/4}(\hat{m}_i - m_i))^2\right]\gamma$ which must be $o_p(1)$. Once again $n^{1/4}$ consistency of the conditional moment is needed (unless $\gamma = 0$). Reference to the parametric analogue shows that the difference between instrumenting a conditional mean and a conditional variance is the fact that v_i goes from being a linear function of m_i to a quadratic, and this means that $v_{\tau\tau}$ in (5.8) is not $o_p(1)$ unless γ is zero, forcing the necessity of $n^{1/4}$ consistency of $\hat{m}_i$.

Some use has been made of the SP estimator in models featuring anticipations. In Lee's (1988) work y_i is consumption while z_i was a vector of anticipations on interest rates, government expenditure, and hours. To keep the number of conditioning variables low, he made the w_i principal components of variables in the agent's information set. When the x_i were properly specified he did not find that the results were much different from Bean's (1986) study, which made the anticipated values a linear function of information variables. Pagan and Hong (1991) reconsider Engle, Lillien, and Robins's (1987) model of the excess holding yield on U.S. Treasury Bills (y_i), which is assumed to be a function of z_i, the conditional variance of the excess holding yield of U.S. Treasury bills, as well as other variables such as the yield differential (x_i). They found that measuring z_i nonparametrically rather than with the parametric ARCH form used by Engle et al. led to a substantial increase in the explanatory power of the equation.

5.2.4 The Asymptotic Covariance Matrix of SP Estimators without Asymptotic Independence

As mentioned in the preceding subsection, there are models where Andrews's asymptotic independence condition is violated, which leads to the question of how some adjustment should be made to the asymptotic covariance matrix of the SP estimator to reflect the dependence. Newey (1994a) has a general discussion of this for SP estimators and also looks at some special cases. In particular, the case where the "nuisance variable" is a conditional moment. For many of the applications of this book, such a special case is of most interest.

Previously it was found that a study of estimation with a finite number of nuisance parameters could be very informative about the infinite-parameter or "nuisance variable" situation, and this will be true again. Using the same notation as in Section 5.2.1 suppose that v_i depends upon a conditional moment $m(w_i, \tau)$ and that this moment is the conditional mean of some variable ξ_i, that is, $\xi_i = m(w_i, \tau) + \eta_i$, where η_i is a random variable with $E(\eta_i|w_i) = 0$, and τ is an $(r \times 1)$ vector of parameters. A parametric approach to estimation would be to find the nonlinear least squares estimate $\hat{\tau}$ minimizing $\sum_{i=1}^{n}(\xi_i - m(w_i, \tau))^2$ and to then substitute $m(w_i, \hat{\tau})$ for m_i when solving for the parametric estimator $\hat{\theta}_P$. From (5.8), whether $n^{1/2}(\hat{\theta}_P - \theta_0)$ is asymptotically dependent upon $n^{1/2}(\hat{\tau} - \tau_0)$ is determined by $n^{1/2}\bar{v}_\tau(\hat{\tau} - \tau_0)$.

Now,

$$\bar{v}_\tau(\theta_0, \tau_0) = n^{-1} \sum (\partial v_i/\partial \tau) = n^{-1} \sum (\partial v_i/\partial m_i)(\partial m_i/\partial \tau)$$

$$= n^{-1} V_m' M_\tau,$$

where V_m and M_τ are $(n \times 1)$ and $(n \times r)$ matrices containing $\partial v_i/\partial m_i$ and $\partial m_i/\partial \tau$ respectively. From standard nonlinear least squares theory

$$n^{1/2}(\hat{\tau} - \tau_0) = -\left(n^{-1} M_\tau' M_\tau\right)^{-1} n^{-1/2} M_\tau'(\xi - m) + o_p(1),$$

meaning that

$$n^{1/2}\bar{v}_\tau(\theta_0, \tau_0)(\hat{\tau} - \tau_0) = -n^{-1/2}\left(V_m' M_\tau\right)\left(M_\tau' M_\tau\right)^{-1} M_\tau'(\xi - m)$$

$$= -n^{-1/2} \sum \hat{v}_{\tau,i}(\xi_i - m_i),$$

where $\hat{v}_{\tau,i}$ are the predictions from the regression of $\partial v_i/\partial m_i$ against $\partial m_i/\partial \tau$. Substituting this into (5.8), and assuming the third term on the right-hand side of (5.8) is $o_p(1)$, gives

$$n^{1/2}(\hat{\theta}_P - \theta_0) = -\bar{v}_\theta^{-1} n^{1/2} \bar{v}(\theta_0, \tau_0) + \bar{v}_\theta^{-1} n^{-1/2} \sum \hat{v}_{\tau,i}(\xi_i - m_i),$$
$$(5.16)$$

from which the variance of the limiting distribution of $n^{1/2}(\hat{\theta}_P - \theta_0)$ can be determined once the stochastic assumptions on v_i and $\eta_i = \xi_i - m_i$ are spelled out, since the influence function will be

$$\zeta_i = -\bar{v}_\theta^{-1} v_i + \bar{v}_\theta^{-1} \hat{v}_{\tau,i}(\xi_i - m_i).$$

To extend this treatment to the context where m_i is first estimated nonparametrically and then used to get $\hat{\theta}_{SP}$, it needs to be recognized that the essence of the nonparametric approach is to represent m_i as a linear sum of functions of w_i, that is, $m_i = \sum_{j=1}^{M} \psi_j(w_i)\tau_j$, where $M \to \infty$ as $n \to \infty$ and the terms $\psi_j(w_j)$ might be polynomials or trigonometric functions of the w_i. This was the series approach to the estimation of conditional moments in Section 3.8. Consequently, $\partial m_i/\partial \tau_j = \psi_j(w_i)$ and the regression of $\partial v_i/\partial m_i$ against $\partial m_i/\partial \tau$ is really one of $\partial v_i/\partial m_i$ against the functions $\psi_1(w_i), \psi_2(w_i), \ldots, \psi_M(w_i)$. From the results in Section 3.8, it would be expected that the predictions from this regression would converge, as $M \to \infty$, to $E(\partial v_i/\partial m_i | w_i)$, and (5.16) is therefore the nonparametric analogue of (5.16):

$$n^{1/2}(\hat{\theta}_{SP} - \theta_0) = -\bar{v}_\theta^{-1} n^{1/2} \bar{v}(\theta_0, \tau_0)$$

$$+ \bar{v}_\theta^{-1} n^{-1/2} \sum E\left[(\partial v_i/\partial m_i)| w_i\right](\xi_i - m_i).$$
$$(5.17)$$

Equation (5.17) is Newey's (1994a) formula for finding the covariance matrix of the SP estimator, $\hat{\theta}_{SP}$, when asymptotic independence does not hold and when a nonparametric estimator of the conditional mean is used that produces an influence function of

$$\zeta_i = -\bar{v}_\theta^{-1} v_i + \bar{v}_\theta^{-1} E\left[(\partial v_i / \partial m_i) | w_i\right] (\xi_i - m_i). \tag{5.18}$$

As an application of these ideas consider the model in (5.15) (with x_i omitted). In terms of (5.17) $\theta = \gamma$, $z_i = m_i$, and $v_i = z_i(y_i - z_i'\gamma)$. If $\eta_i = \xi_i - E(\xi_i | w_i) = \xi_i - m_i$ is taken to be i.i.d. $(0, \sigma_\eta^2)$, u_i is i.i.d. $(0, \sigma_u^2)$ and $E(u_i \eta_i) = 0$. Pagan (1984b) pointed out that the covariance matrix of an estimator of γ obtained by regressing y_i against z_i, when these were the predictions from an auxiliary regression of ξ_i against w_i, was $(\sigma_u^2 + \gamma^2 \sigma_\eta^2)(p \lim n^{-1} \sum z_i^2)^{-1}$. It is easily seen that this remains true if z_i is estimated nonparametrically, because $\partial v_i / \partial m_i = -z_i'\gamma$ and, from (5.18) the influence function will be $-(p \lim n^{-1} \sum z_i^2)^{-1} n^{-1/2} \sum z_i(u_i + \gamma \eta_i).$[3]

Another important special case is when the quantity being replaced (τ_i) is a density or its derivative and we wish to estimate $\mu = n^{-1} \sum_{i=1}^n v(\theta, \tau_i)$. Newey shows that the influence function of the SP estimator of μ is

$$\zeta_i = v_i - E(v_i) + \alpha_i - E(\alpha_i),$$

where $\alpha_i = (-1)^k D^{(k)}[E((\partial v_i / \partial \tau_i)|w_i) f(w_i)]$, k is the order of derivative of the density appearing in v_i, and $D^{(k)}$ is the kth-order derivative ($D^{(0)}[\cdot]$ equalling $f(w_i)$). More generally, if there is a vector of variables $\tau_{ij} (j = 1, ..., q)$ that appear in the $v_i(\theta, \tau)$, the influence function will become

$$\zeta_i = v_i - E(v_i) + \sum_{j=1}^q (\alpha_i - E(\alpha_i)),$$

and α_{ij} will be defined in the same way as α_i was for each variable.[4] As an illustration of this principle consider estimating $\mu = \int f(w)^2 dw = E(f(w))$, whereupon $\hat{\mu} = n^{-1} \sum \hat{f}(w_i)$ and $\hat{v}_i = \hat{f}(w_i)$. Then, with $\hat{\tau}_i = \hat{f}(w_i)$, $\partial v_i / \partial \tau_i = 1$, $\alpha_i = f(w_i) - E(f(w_i))$, and the influence function will be $\zeta_i = 2[f(w_i) - E(f(w_i))]$.

5.3 Efficient Estimation of Semiparametric Models in the Presence of Heteroskedasticity of Unknown Form

The standard linear model discussed in most econometrics texts is

$$y_i = x_i'\beta + u_i, \tag{5.19}$$

---

[3] For convenience we assume $x_i'\beta$ is not in the model and that γ is a scalar.
[4] Newey (1994b) also suggests a numerical way of computing ζ_i when it is difficult to find an analytic expression for it.

where u_i are i.i.d. $(0, \sigma^2)$ and x_i is a $(q \times 1)$ vector. It is well known that the OLS estimator of β is not efficient unless the variance of the u_i really is a constant. To allow for the possibility that this is not so, the Generalized Least Squares (GLS) estimator $\beta^* = \left(\Sigma x_i x_i' \sigma_i^{-2}\right)^{-1} \left(\Sigma x_i y_i \sigma_i^{-2}\right)$ is frequently proposed, where $\sigma_i^2 = E(u_i^2 | z_i)$. Here z_i includes x_i but might also involve certain transformations constructed from x_i and lagged values of y_i as discussed later. It may also be that certain variables are known to be excluded from the mean but are likely to appear in the variance, the most common being dummy variables describing shift terms, and the use of z_i allows for this possibility.

The central problem with GLS is that σ_i^2 is unknown and the estimator is therefore infeasible. Traditionally this complication has been resolved by parameterizing σ_i^2 as $g(z_i, \gamma)$, where $g(\cdot)$ is a known function. After consistent estimation of γ to get $\tilde{\gamma}$, σ_i^2 is replaced by $\tilde{\sigma}_i^2 = g(z_i, \tilde{\gamma})$ in the GLS formula, and a feasible GLS estimator $\tilde{\beta}^* = \left(\Sigma x_i x_i' \tilde{\sigma}_i^{-2}\right)^{-1} \left(\Sigma x_i y_i \tilde{\sigma}_i^{-2}\right)$ emerges. Under weak conditions $n^{1/2}(\tilde{\beta}^* - \beta)$ and $n^{1/2}(\beta^* - \beta)$ have the same limiting distribution.

When the function $g(\cdot)$ is unknown it is natural to emulate the process above by estimating σ_i^2 nonparametrically, as described in Chapter 3, to produce $\hat{\sigma}_i^2$ and thereby $\hat{\beta}^* = \left(\Sigma x_i x_i' \hat{\sigma}_i^{-2}\right)^{-1} \left(\Sigma x_i y_i \hat{\sigma}_i^{-2}\right)$. Rose (1978) was an early proponent of this estimator, setting $\hat{\sigma}_i^2 = \sum_{j=1}^n w_{ij} \tilde{u}_j^2$, where $\tilde{u}_j = y_j - x_j' \hat{\beta}_{OLS}$ and the weights w_{ij} are the kernel weights

$$K\left(h^{-1}(z_i - z_j)\right) \Big/ \sum_{s=1}^n K\left(h^{-1}(z_i - z_s)\right).$$

Carroll (1982) formally proved that $n^{1/2}(\hat{\beta}^* - \beta)$ and $n^{1/2}(\beta^* - \beta)$ were asymptotically equivalent when $\dim(z_i) = 1$, $z_i = x_i$, and the x_i were i.i.d. Since then the restriction to a single conditioning variable has been relaxed by Singh et al. (1987), and Robinson (1987) who employed nearest neighbour weights w_{ij} in his definition of the conditional variance, also see Carroll and Ruppert (1982, 1984, 1988). More general estimators of the conditional variance can be justified by Andrews's (1994) results, in particular Lemma 5.1 above may be used. Define

$$\bar{v}(\beta_0, \hat{\tau}) = n^{-1} \sum x_i \hat{\tau}_i^{-1} u_i = n^{-1} \sum x_i \hat{\sigma}_i^{-2} u_i$$

and observe that $E\left(x_i \tau_i^{-1} u_i\right) = 0$ thereby satisfying condition B(ii). Examination of B(i) establishes that it needs $\hat{\sigma}_i^2$ and σ_i^2 to be bounded away from zero and $E\left(\hat{\sigma}_i^2 - \sigma_i^2\right)^2$ to tend to zero as $n \to \infty$. Andrews's work also covers the case where x_i contains lagged values of y_i.

There has been some debate over the estimation of $\hat{\sigma}_i^2$. Rose's formula, exploiting the linearity of the conditional mean for y_i, would seem better than the pure nonparametric alternative used in Chapter 3, $\Sigma w_{ij}(y_j - \hat{m}_i)^2$, but Delgado

(1992) presents some simulation evidence that this may not be so (at least for small q). Hidalgo (1992) considers heteroskedasticity in the case of time series regression. Linton (1996b) develops a second-order asymptotic expansion of the MSE of $\hat{\beta}^*$ and shows that the optimal window width is $o(n^{-1/(4+q)})$ in which case the asymptotic MSE is $o(n^{-4/q+4})$. His work also indicates that there is no general ranking of the estimators mentioned above according to mean square error.

The principle for the design of an efficient estimator followed above involved expressing the most efficient estimator of β as a function of σ_i^2 and then substituting nonparametric estimates for any unknown quantities. Accordingly, it seems reasonable to employ the same strategy in contexts where the most efficient estimator of β can only be defined implicitly. Consider therefore the estimation of β when u_i is normal, not identically distributed (n.i.d.) $(0, \sigma_i^2)$ and $\sigma_i^2 = g[z_i(\beta)]$, where z_i is an $r \times 1$ vector of known functions of the data and β. Examples of z_i would arise in the "variance proportional to mean" model where $z_i = x_i'\beta$ and in generalized versions of Engle's (1982) ARCH model where $z_{ki}(\beta) = (y_{i-k} - x_{i-k}'\beta)$, $k = 1, \ldots, r$.

Following Schweppe (1965) the log likelihood of $y_1, y_2, \ldots, y_n$ is

$$L = -(n/2)\log(2\pi) - (1/2)\Sigma \log \sigma_i^2 - (1/2)\Sigma\sigma_i^{-2}(y_i - x_i'\beta)^2$$

(5.20)

and the scores with respect to β will be

$$\partial L/\partial\beta = (1/2)\Sigma\sigma_i^{-2}\left[\left((y_i - x_i'\beta)/\sigma_i\right)^2 - 1\right](\partial\sigma_i^2/\partial\beta)$$
$$+ (1/2)\Sigma\sigma_i^{-2}x_i(y_i - x_i'\beta).$$

(5.21)

If $(\partial\sigma_i^2/\partial\beta)$ and σ_i^2 were known (5.21) could be solved for β. Following our basic principle σ_i^2 can be replaced by its nonparametric estimate. By the chain rule $\partial\sigma_i^2/\partial\beta = \sum_{k=1}^{r}(\partial\sigma_i^2/\partial z_{ki})'(\partial z_{ki}/\partial\beta)$ and, as the second element is known, it only remains to estimate the derivatives of the first element by the methods discussed in Chapter 4. In applying the formulae of that chapter y_i becomes $\tilde{u}_i^2$ as $E(u_i^2) = \sigma_i^2$ and $\hat{\beta}_{OLS}$ is consistent. Accordingly, even though no explicit expression for the semiparametric MLE is available from (5.21), a solution may be found after all unknowns are replaced by their nonparametric estimates.

An alternative way of proceeding would be to construct an asymptotically efficient two-step estimator (Rothenberg and Leenders, 1964) as

$$\hat{\beta} = \hat{\beta}_{OLS} - \left[\Sigma(\partial\hat{L}_i/\partial\beta)(\partial\hat{L}_i/\partial\beta)'\right]^{-1}\Sigma(\partial\hat{L}_i/\partial\beta),$$

(5.22)

where $L = \sum_{i=1}^{n} L_i$, $(\partial L/\partial\beta) = \Sigma\partial L_i/\partial\beta$, the hats indicate that β is replaced by $\hat{\beta}_{OLS}$, and other unknowns are eliminated nonparametrically. This is one step of the scoring algorithm for maximizing L in (5.20), starting from an initial consistent estimator $(\hat{\beta}_{OLS})$ and replacing the information matrix by the outer product of the estimated scores. Robinson (1988b) describes this estimator when applied to the "variance proportional to mean" and ARCH models. The consistency and asymptotic normality of $\hat{\beta}$ may be established by following Andrews's (1994) approach, outlined in Chapter 7; also see Drost and Klassen (1997).

5.4   Conditions for Adaptive Estimation

In the following section we will be interested in the construction of an efficient estimator of the parameters of (5.19) when the form of the density of u_i is unknown. A question to settle prior to any discussion of estimation issues is under what conditions it is possible to construct an estimator that is fully efficient regardless of the density of u_i. One way to make this question more precise is to conceive of the unknown density as being characterized by an unknown vector of parameters η in addition to the parameters of interest θ. For example, suppose that the true density is normal. In (5.19) θ' would be (β', σ^2), while the density of the u_i might be regarded as Student's t, with η being the degrees of freedom. Alternatively, η might index the degree of heteroskedasticity when the density of u_i is normal. Within this family η_0 will indicate the true model. Given this *parametric submodel* the parameters θ may be estimated by a variety of techniques. Provided the class of estimators is suitably restricted, the minimum variance that can be attained for any specific value of η will be given by the Cramer–Rao bound. Now, recognize the fact that there is a potentially infinite number of densities or parametric submodels, every one of which has an associated Cramer–Rao bound (computed by taking the expectation with respect to the true density). Consequently, the variance of the best estimator of θ can be no smaller than the largest of these bounds. Such a supremum will be denoted by Ω.

The qualification "suitably restricted" is important, both to ensure the existence and relevance of the Cramer–Rao bound and to rule out deviant estimators like the "superefficient" ones discussed in Cox and Hinkley (1974); in the jargon of this literature the estimators need to be "locally regular." Newey (1990a) gives an intuitive discussion of the criteria that need to be satisfied if estimators are to be locally regular, and Bickel et al. (1993) have a more technical account. In what follows we borrow heavily from Newey's (1990a) excellent survey of this literature. It is assumed that the conditions needed for local regularity are satisfied in our models, allowing us to invoke the important property of such estimators summarized in Lemma 5.2.

Lemma 5.2 (Generalized Hajek Representation Theorem): If $\hat{\theta}$ is locally regular, the limiting distribution of $n^{1/2}(\hat{\theta} - \theta)$ is equal to $\mathcal{Z} + \mathcal{X}$, where $\mathcal{Z}$ is distributed as $\mathcal{N}(0, \Omega)$ and $\mathcal{X}$ is independent of $\mathcal{Z}$.

Proof: See Chamberlain (1987), Hajek (1970), or Begun et al. (1983).
Q.E.D.

Lemma 5.2 obviously leads us to conclude that a semiparametric estimator would be efficient if its variance is Ω, but it raises three questions that will recur in the following sections and chapters. Answers to them have been provided in many instances, but the body of pertinent knowledge is still fragmentary. First, is it possible to find an efficient estimator of θ that does not require knowledge of the parameter η in its construction (i.e., that is robust to the true form of the density)? If the answer is yes, it will be said that θ is *adaptively estimable*; the terminology "adaptive" obviously derives from the fact that the estimator adapts to the form of the density. Second, if adaptive estimation is not feasible, can we characterize the minimum variance of the best estimator, that is, determine the *semi-parametric efficiency bound* Ω? Finally, can an estimator be designed that attains this bound? Section 5.4 deals with the first two questions in the context of the linear regression model with unknown error density, while Section 5.5 takes up the problem of adaptive estimation. Section 5.10 discusses semiparametric efficiency bounds for estimators that are derived from a set of population moment relations.

To analyze the first query, return to the parametric submodel. Then it is apparent that η has an influence upon the efficiency of estimation. Defining the score for θ as d_θ and Fisher's asymptotic information matrix as $\mathcal{I}_{\theta\theta} = p \lim_{n\to\infty} n^{-1} E(d_\theta d_\theta')$, the Cramer–Rao bound when η is known will be $\mathcal{I}_{\theta\theta}^{-1}$, whereas, if η is not known and must be estimated, the bound becomes $\left(\mathcal{I}_{\theta\theta} - \mathcal{I}_{\theta\eta}\mathcal{I}_{\eta\eta}^{-1}\mathcal{I}_{\eta\theta}\right)^{-1}$ (see Durbin (1970)). The latter exceeds $\mathcal{I}_{\theta\theta}^{-1}$ unless $\mathcal{I}_{\theta\eta} = 0$, establishing the fact that knowledge of η is asymptotically irrelevant to estimation of θ if $\mathcal{I}_{\theta\eta} = 0$. Since this is true for any parametric submodel it must also hold over all densities compatible with the model, prompting Stein (1956) to give the following definition of an adaptive estimator.

Definition 5.1: An estimator $\hat\theta$ is adaptive if

$$n^{1/2}(\hat\theta - \theta) \overset{d}{\longrightarrow} \mathcal{N}\left(0, \mathcal{I}_{\theta\theta}^{-1}\right)$$

and a necessary condition for adaption is that $\mathcal{I}_{\theta\eta} = 0$.

Let us put this definition into perspective by writing down the log likelihood of (5.19), where x_i and u_i are independently distributed of one another, as

$$L = \sum_{i=1}^{n} \log f\left(y_i - x_i'\beta; \eta\right). \tag{5.23}$$

In (5.23) $f(\cdot)$ is the density of y_i while the ηs describe its parameters (over and above β). Independence of x_i and u_i is a strong assumption. Sometimes it is made in regression analysis to simplify proofs, but in the design of an efficient estimator it is not innocuous. The SP efficiency bound depends upon the type of assumptions imposed on the joint stochastic properties of x_i and u_i. Independence of x_i and u_i imply that any function of x_i and any odd function of u_i have zero covariance. By contrast the regression estimator is derived from the moment restrictions $E(x_i u_i) = 0$ or $E(u_i | x_i) = 0$ and these are only a subset of the restrictions provided by independence. Section 5.10 is concerned with the semiparametric bound if only the latter type of restrictions are imposed.

In (5.23) $\theta = \beta$ and a parametric submodel involves a specific choice for $f(\cdot)$ to get an efficient estimator of β regardless of the nature of f. Definition 5.1 indicates that $\mathcal{I}_{\beta\eta}$ computed for *any* $f(\cdot)$ must be zero. Obviously it is easy to verify that $\mathcal{I}_{\beta\eta} = 0$ for a given $f(\cdot)$, but much harder for general $f(\cdot)$. Some assistance is available from the fact that there may be conditions imposed upon the class of admissible densities from the assumptions made about (5.19). For example, if u_i has finite variance and is symmetrically distributed, this would eliminate from consideration densities such as Cauchy and Beta. Nevertheless, the range of densities is vast, and Bickel (1982) proposed a simpler way of checking for the possibility of adaption, which is stated as Lemma 5.3.

Lemma 5.3: A necessary condition for θ to be adaptively estimable is that

$$E\left(\partial \log f(\theta, \eta_0)/\partial\theta\right) = 0, \tag{5.24}$$

where $f(\theta, \eta)$ is the density of y_i conditional upon x_i, η_0 indexes the true density, and the expectation is taken over all possible densities that satisfy the constraints of the model.

Proof: Equation (5.24) can be written

$$\int \left[\partial \log f(\theta, \eta_0)/\partial\theta\right] f(y; \theta, \eta) \, dy = 0. \tag{5.25}$$

Differentiating (5.25) with respect to η gives

$$\int [\partial \log f(\theta, \eta_0)/\partial\theta][\partial f(\theta, \eta)/\partial\eta] \, dy$$

$$= \int [\partial \log f(\theta, \eta_0)/\partial\theta][\partial \log f(\theta, \eta)/\partial\eta] f(y; \theta, \eta) \, dy$$

$$= \mathcal{I}_{\theta\eta} = 0. \qquad \text{Q.E.D.}$$

In many instances Bickel's condition in Lemma 5.3 may be easier to apply than the diagonality of the information matrix in Definition 5.1. One extension to it needed in many applications is when adaption is only being entertained for a subset of θ. Lemma 5.4 covers that case.

Lemma 5.4: Necessary conditions for a subset θ_1 of $\theta' = (\theta_1', \theta_2')$ to be adaptively estimable are

(i) $E(\partial \log f(\theta, \eta_0)/\partial \theta_1) = 0$ and

(ii) $\mathcal{I}_{\theta_1 \theta_2} = E[(\partial \log f/\partial \theta_1)(\partial \log f/\partial \theta_2)'] = 0.$

Proof: For adaption to take place $\Omega = \mathcal{I}_{\theta_1 \theta_1}^{-1}$ and so the information matrix must be block diagonal between θ_1 and (θ_2, η). Condition (i) ensures that $\mathcal{I}_{\theta_1 \eta} = 0$ whereas (ii) completes the block diagonality.   Q.E.D.

Within the context of the linear model with log likelihood (5.23) it is possible to establish which parameters may be adaptively estimated by analyzing the scores for β

$$d_\beta = \partial L/\partial \beta = -\sum_{i=1}^{n} x_i f^{-1}(u_i) f^{(1)}(u_i) = -\Sigma x_i \psi_i, \qquad (5.26)$$

where $f^{(1)}(\cdot) = \partial f(u)/\partial u$ and $\psi_i = f^{-1}(u_i) f^{(1)}(u_i)$ is the negative of the *density score* of u_i.[5] Bickel's condition can now be applied to (5.26) to determine the adaptive estimability of β, and the outcomes are listed in Theorem 5.3.

Theorem 5.3: (i) If an intercept (β_2) appears in (5.19) the necessary condition for the slope parameters (β_1) to be adaptively estimable is satisfied. (ii) In the model (5.19), the necessary condition for the intercept to be adaptively estimable is met if the density of u_i is symmetric around zero. (iii) If the density of u_i has the form $f(u_i/\sigma)$ the scale parameter σ is not adaptively estimable.

Proof:

(i) If an intercept appears in (5.19) all regressors except that corresponding to the constant can be taken to have zero expectation without loss of generality. Hence the expected value of the scores for the slope parameters is $-E(x_i)a$, where a is the expectation of ψ_i and $E(x_i) = 0$. This satisfies

---

[5] We will generally refer to ψ_i as the score of the density in what follows, ignoring the sign.

(i) of Lemma 5.4. To verify (ii) of that lemma, $\mathcal{I}_{\beta_1 \beta_2} = E(x_i \psi_i^2)$, which is zero by the same argument.

(ii) When $f(u)$ is symmetric in u, $f^{-1}(u) f^{(1)}(u)$ is an odd function of u making the expectation of ψ_i, conditional upon x_i, zero. Hence, from (5.26), the score for the intercept, $-\Sigma \psi_i$, has zero expectation.

(iii) The score for σ^2 has expectation $-.5 E(\psi_i \sigma^{-3} u_i)$, where $\psi_i = f(u_i/\sigma)^{-1}$ $f^{(1)}(u_i/\sigma)$, and this need not be zero for arbitrary densities. Manski (1984, p. 167) gives the example where the true density is taken to be $\gamma^{-1} \exp(-.25 \delta^{-1} u^4)$, with γ and δ being such that the mean of u_i is zero and the variance (σ^2) is unity. In this case $E(\psi_i \sigma^{-3} u_i) \neq 0$.   Q.E.D.

Notice that symmetry is not required for adaptive estimation of the slope parameters, but the density of u_i must not depend upon x_i in order that the conditional expectation of ψ_i be invariant to x_i.

As seen in the example above there are parameters that cannot be adaptively estimated, and in those circumstances one would like to be able to compute Ω to ascertain the size of the efficiency loss. To get this bound it will be necessary to evaluate $\left(\mathcal{I}_{\theta\theta} - \mathcal{I}_{\theta\eta} \mathcal{I}_{\eta\eta}^{-1} \mathcal{I}_{\eta\theta} \right)^{-1}$ over all possible densities. There is no one way of doing such a computation and a variety of methods has evolved for application to specific models. Many of these demand long and involved derivations and we will merely record the conclusion. Others, particularly in the linear regression model, are relatively easy to understand. Bickel et al. (1993) give an extensive treatment and Newey (1990a) offers a simplified account of much of this literature. One general approach has been set out in Begun et al. (1983). An intuitive understanding of their method can be had by considering a parametric submodel and observing that $n^{-1/2} d_\theta$ and $n^{-1/2} d_\eta$ will be jointly asymptotically normally distributed with the asymptotic information matrix as covariance matrix. Defining $\tilde{d}_\theta = d_\theta - E(d_\theta | d_\eta)$, from the properties of the multivariate normal, we have

$$E\left(n^{-1} \tilde{d}_\theta \tilde{d}_\theta' \right) = \mathcal{I}_{\theta\theta} - \mathcal{I}_{\theta\eta} \mathcal{I}_{\eta\eta}^{-1} \mathcal{I}_{\eta\theta}. \tag{5.27}$$

Here $\tilde{d}_\theta$ are the *efficient* scores and (5.27) is their covariance matrix. The efficient scores have many interpretations. A useful one is that they are the scores for θ after the η have been concentrated out of the log likelihood (see Amemiya (1985) for this correspondence). When data is i.i.d., $\tilde{d}_\theta(i) = d_\theta(i) - E(d_\theta(i) | d_\eta(i))$, where the i indicates the ith component in the summation defining the relevant scores.

Extension of this idea to the class of all parametric submodels is hampered by the fact that, for a given sample size, there are an infinite number of forms for d_η. Begun et al. (1983) refer to the union of all vectors of the form $A d_\eta(i)$, where A has $q = \dim(\theta)$ rows, as the *tangent set*, and they define the efficient score as the residuals from the projection of $d_\theta(i)$ against this tangent set.[6] When the tangent set is linear and closed

$$\Omega = \left[\lim_{n \to \infty} n^{-1} E \left(\tilde{d}_\theta \tilde{d}'_\theta \right) \right]^{-1} = \left[E \tilde{d}_\theta(i) \tilde{d}_\theta(i)' \right]^{-1}.$$

Determination of the efficient scores is critical for the solution of Ω and plays an important role in checking on adaption – Lemma 5.3 could be rephrased as the equivalence $\tilde{d}_\theta = d_\theta$, that is, the scores for η have no predictive power for those of θ. Another important role is that they can also point to estimators that attain the SP bound. In particular, if $\hat{\theta}$ solves $\tilde{d}_\theta(\hat{\theta}) = 0$, standard expansions give

$$n^{1/2}(\hat{\theta} - \theta_0) = -\left[n^{-1} E \left(\sum \partial \tilde{d}_\theta(\theta_0)/\partial \theta \right) \right] n^{-1/2} \sum \tilde{d}_\theta(\theta_0) + o_p(1),$$

and

$$n^{1/2}(\hat{\theta} - \theta_0) \xrightarrow{d} \mathcal{N}(0, \ \Omega)$$

as $E \left(\partial \tilde{d}_\theta(i)/\partial \theta \right) = - E \left(\tilde{d}_\theta(i) \tilde{d}_\theta(i)' \right)$ by the standard information equality obtained by differentiating $E \left(\tilde{d}_\theta(i) \right) = 0$. Although finding $\hat{\theta}$ to solve the efficient scores gives a desirable estimator it may be computationally cumbersome, and so its role is frequently that of a benchmark.

The linear regression model (5.19) is a good vehicle for illustrating some of these points. Differentiating (5.23) with respect to η gives

$$d_\eta = \sum d_\eta(i) = \Sigma f(u_i)^{-1} \left(\partial f(u_i; \eta)/\partial \eta \right),$$

and there will be an infinite number of the d_η corresponding to different $f(\cdot)$. However, since both $f^{-1}(u)$ and $\partial f/\partial \eta$ are functions of u, we could write their product as $B(u)$. What restrictions upon this function $B(u)$ are then mandated by the model (5.19)? Theorem 5.3 showed that adaption was possible under the assumptions that the expected value of the u_i was zero and the variance finite (the latter to ensure that the variance of the adaptive estimator exists). Consequently, $B(u)$ is restricted only in this way and the tangent set will consist of all such functions. The projection of $d_\beta(i) = x_i \psi_i$ against $B(u_i)$ is $E(x_i \psi_i | B(u_i)) = E(x_i \psi_i | u_i) = E(x_i) \psi_i$, making the efficient score $\tilde{d}_\beta = \sum \tilde{d}_\beta(i) = \Sigma (x_i - E(x_i)) \psi_i$ and

$$\Omega = \left[E \left(\tilde{d}_\beta(i) \tilde{d}_\beta(i)' \right) \right]^{-1} = \left[\text{var}(x_i) E \left(\psi_i^2 \right) \right]^{-1}$$

$$= \left[E(d_\beta(i) d_\beta(i)') \right]^{-1},$$

---

[6] Technically, the tangent set is the mean square closure of all q-dimensional linear combinations of the scores $d_\eta(i)$.

agreeing with the earlier finding that β was adaptively estimable. What is particularly interesting about this expression is that it allows a simple statement about the efficiency loss sustained by the OLS estimator, as described in Theorem 5.4.

Theorem 5.4: The efficiency index φ of the OLS estimator of β in (5.19) is defined as the ratio of its asymptotic variance to the SP efficiency bound Ω and is $\varphi = \sigma^2 E(\psi_i^2)$. When the errors u_i are Gaussian $\varphi = 1$.

Proof: Since $\Omega = \left[\text{var}(x_i)E(\psi_i^2)\right]^{-1}$, while the asymptotic variance of $n^{1/2}(\hat{\beta}_{OLS} - \beta)$ is $\sigma^2(\text{var}(x_i))^{-1}$, and φ is as described. For u_i Gaussian,

$$f(u_i) = (2\pi\sigma^2)^{-1/2} \exp\left(-(1/2)\sigma^{-2}u_i^2\right)$$

and $f^{(1)}(u_i) = -f(u_i)\sigma^{-2}u_i$, so that $E(\psi_i^2) = \sigma^{-4}E(u_i^2) = \sigma^{-2}$ and $\varphi = 1$.

Q.E.D.

Theorem 5.4 indicates that the impact of nonnormal errors upon the OLS estimator could be assessed by computing the index φ. A consistent estimator of φ, $\hat{\varphi}$, is available from $\hat{\sigma}_{OLS}^2 \left[n^{-1}\Sigma \hat{f}^{-2}(\hat{u}_i)(\hat{f}^{(1)}(\hat{u}_i))^2\right]$, where $\hat{u}_i$ are the OLS residuals and the density and its derivative are estimated by one of the methods discussed in Chapter 2. Consistency of the estimator is easily established under a variety of conditions. Because a Gaussian density has $\psi(u) = -\sigma^{-2}u$, it might also be useful to plot the estimate of $\psi(u = u^*) = \hat{f}^{-1}(u^*)f^{(1)}(u^*)$ against u^*; a graphical indication of how nonnormal the errors are will then be available from the degree to which this function deviates from a straight line. Confidence intervals could be placed around the estimated function; using Newey's (1994b) method of finding the influence function it becomes

$$\zeta_i = -\sigma^2\psi_i^2 - 2(\partial\psi_i/\partial(\sigma^{-1}u_i)) - E(\varphi),$$

enabling a consistent estimator of the variance to be found from $n^{-1}\sum_{i=1}^{n}\hat{\zeta}_i^2$. Alternatively one can test for the linearity of $\psi(u)$ in a regression of $\psi(u)$ on u and higher powers of u. This is the approach considered in Bera and Ng (1992) who provide evidence on the performance of the test statistics showing that they seem to have superior finite sample properties compared to the standard tests of normality, see Bera and Jarque (1981).

An interesting question is whether it is possible to adaptively estimate other parameters that are sometimes introduced into the linear model, for example those associated with heteroskedasticity. To explore this issue define the scale parameter of the errors u_i in (5.19) as $\sigma_i = (z_i'\gamma)^{1/2}$, where z_i is a $(p \times 1)$ vector of variables that is i.i.d., distributed independently of $v_i = u_i/(z_i'\gamma)^{1/2}$, and does not contain β. The scale parameter is written in this way so that when u_i is normal its variance is $z_i'\gamma$, and this agrees with the treatment in Section 5.3.

Now replace the distributional assumption on u_i with one on v_i. Specifically, this random variable is taken to be i.i.d. with density $f(v)$.

Under these assumptions the log likelihood of $y_1, \ldots, y_n$ is

$$L = -(1/2)\Sigma \log \left(z_i'\gamma\right) + \Sigma \log \left\{ f\left[\left(y_i - x_i'\beta\right)/\left(z_i'\gamma\right)^{1/2}\right]\right\} \quad (5.28)$$

and the scores will be

$$\partial L/\partial \beta = -\Sigma x_i \left(z_i'\gamma\right)^{-1/2} f^{-1}(v_i) f^{(1)}(v_i), \quad (5.29)$$

$$\partial L/\partial \gamma = (1/2)\Sigma z_i \left(z_i'\gamma\right)^{-1} \left[-v_i f^{-1}(v_i) f^{(1)}(v_i) - 1\right]. \quad (5.30)$$

The presence of the random variables z_i in the denominator of (5.29) makes adaption much less likely than before, although there might be a number of ways that one could justify conditioning upon the z_i, for example if z_i is independent of x_i or the z_i are fixed. If one ignores the latter, Theorem 5.5 collects together the most likely outcomes.

Theorem 5.5: For the model (5.19) and the conditions described above, (i) the parameters β will be adaptively estimable if the density of v_i is symmetric around zero and (ii) the parameters $\gamma = [\gamma_1 \ldots \ldots \gamma_p]'$ will generally not be adaptively estimable, although they will be up to a scale parameter.

Proof:

(i) Since z_i and x_i are independently distributed of v_i, $E(\partial L/\partial \beta) = 0$ when $f^{-1}(v) f^{(1)}(v)$ is an odd function of v, which it is under symmetry. Similarly the information matrix between β and γ involves $E\left(f^{-2}(v_i)(f^{(1)}(v_i))^2 v_i\right)$, which is again an odd function. Application of Lemma 5.4 then produces the desired result.

(ii) The expected scores for γ will rarely equal zero and this is a necessary condition for adaption. Because $\partial L/\partial \gamma$ is the product of two independent random variables, $z_i(z_i'\gamma)^{-1}$ and $\left(-v_i f^{-1}(v_i) f^{(1)}(v_i)\right)$, it will have a zero expectation if either random variable has one. When v_i is $\mathcal{N}(0, 1)$, $E(-f^{-1} f^{(1)} v - 1) = E(v^2 - 1) = 0$, but this is likely to be the only density for which it is true. The other possibility is that $E(z_i/(z_i' \gamma)) = 0$. Because this is the ratio of random variables it will be hard to establish the expected value of $(z_i'\gamma)^{-1} z_i$, let alone a value for it. To derive the quoted result we restrict $p = 2$ for simplicity, and, without any loss of generality, follow Linton (1993) in reparameterizing σ_i^2 as $\sigma_i^2 = e^\delta(1 + \omega(z_{2i} - \alpha))$, where $\omega = e^{-\delta}\gamma_2$, $e^\delta = \gamma_1 + \gamma_2\alpha$, and α is a fixed number. Then we now need $E[\sigma_i^{-2}(z_{2i} - \alpha)] = 0$ for ω to be adaptively estimable and α can be chosen to make this hold. Finally, as Lemma 5.4 shows, it is also necessary that $\mathcal{I}_{\delta\omega} = 0$. But the score for δ is just

$\frac{1}{2}\left(-v_i f^{-1}(v_i)(f^{(1)}(v_i))^{-1}\right)$, and so the choice of α that sets $E(d_\omega)$ equal to zero also puts $\mathcal{I}_{\delta\omega}$ to zero.   Q.E.D.

Theorem 5.5 was established by Linton (1993) and Steigerwald (1993), albeit in the more complicated case of ARCH models where the z_i involve β. It is unclear whether it is very useful in the ARCH case as most applications require estimates of σ_i^2, and the inability to estimate γ_1 is therefore a critical limitation. Drost and Klassen (1997) also discuss adaptation in the GARCH model. One situation in which the subset of γ, $\{\gamma_2, \ldots, \gamma_p\}$, is adaptively estimable is when $\gamma_2 = \cdots = \gamma_p$ are zero, since then $z_i'\gamma = \gamma_1$ and $E(\gamma_1^{-1}z_{ki}) = 0 (k = 2, \ldots, p)$, owing to the fact that the intercept γ_1 enables us to assume that $E(z_{kt}) = 0$. In contrast, γ_1 will not have a score with zero expectation as it is just $-\frac{1}{2}\gamma_1^{-1}E(-f^{-1}f^{(1)}v - 1)$. This result is useful in constructing diagnostic tests of the null hypothesis that there is no heteroskedasticity and we will use this result when discussing diagnostic tests in Section 5.7.

Perhaps of greater significance, the parameter γ_1 is not identifiable, as can be inferred from an inspection of the scores for η in the density $f(v_i; \eta)$ and those for δ. The former were previously shown to be a function $\sum_{i=1}^n B(v_i)$ of v_i that is unrestricted unless some restrictions are placed upon the nature of $f(\cdot)$, whereas the latter is $\sum_{i=1}^n v_i f_i^{-1} f^{(1)}(v_i)$, and so it can be written as $\sum_{i=1}^n c(v_i)$, where $c(\cdot)$ will be an even function of v_i if $f(\cdot)$ is symmetric. Consequently, the score for η could be set to that for δ and this would make the information matrix singular, leading to a lack of identification along the lines of the arguments in Bowden (1973). Linton (1993) makes this point.

5.5 Efficient Estimation of Regression Parameters with Unknown Error Density

As mentioned in the introduction investigators may be happy to entertain a linear conditional mean but to feel ignorant about the density of u_i. If u_i is not normal the OLS estimator will not be the most efficient one possible, and it could be very inefficient indeed. This has led to interest in devising estimators that are more efficient than OLS when the regression errors are nonnormal but that do not lose too much efficiency if normality holds. A variety of solutions have been proposed, loosely grouped under the heading of "robust regression," but this book looks at a particular set of methods that emphasise nonparametric procedures.

5.5.1 Efficient Estimation by Likelihood Approximation

Because β in (5.19) was adaptively estimable it seems reasonable that maximizing (5.23) with respect to it will produce an efficient estimator. Three strategies have emerged in the literature for doing this, although other variants could be constructed by tying together the basic ideas with different approximation schemes. This subsection looks at direct approximation to the likelihood; in the next two the scores in (5.26) are the focus.

Gallant and Nychka (1987) worked within the framework of the classical approach to density approximation (Spanos, 1986, p. 204), whereby the unknown density $f(u)$ is approximated by

$$f^*(u) = P(u)\varphi(u) = \left(\sum_{j=0}^{M} H_j(u)\right)\varphi(u),$$

where the $H_j(u)$ are Hermite polynomials in u and $\varphi(u)$ is the normal density. Their suggestion was to maximize a likelihood based on this approximate density. Rather than work with Hermite polynomials, however, they chose to replace $\Sigma\, H_j(u)$ by a simple polynomial $P(u) = \left(1 + \gamma_1 u + \cdots + \gamma_M u^M\right)^2$ or, as in Gallant and Tauchen (1989), by a rational polynomial $P(u) = R(u)/Q(u)$.

To illustrate this technique let $P(u) = [\sum_{j=0}^{M} \gamma_j u^j]^2$, $\gamma_0 = 1$, the square ensuring that the approximate density is nonnegative. Then the approximate likelihood is $\Pi_i f^*(u_i)$ and the associated log likelihood will be (ignoring constants)

$$-2\sum_{i=1}^{n} \log\left(\sum_{j=0}^{M} \gamma_j \left(y_i - x_i'\beta\right)^j\right) - (n/2)\log\sigma^2$$

$$- (1/2\sigma^2)\sum_{i=1}^{n} \left(y_i - x_i'\beta\right)^2. \tag{5.31}$$

Expression (5.31) is maximized with respect to $\gamma_1, \ldots, \gamma_M$, β, and σ^2, appending the constraint that the approximate density be proper (i.e., $\int (\Sigma\gamma_j u^j)^2 \varphi(u)du = 1$). Because of the nature of $P(u)$ it is easy to impose this constraint, the elements in the summation being the moments of a normally distributed random variable taken around zero. To illustrate this point let $M = 2$, producing

$$\int f^*(u)\,du = \int \left(1 + \gamma_1 u + \gamma_2 u^2\right)^2 \varphi(u)\,du$$

$$= 1 + \left(\gamma_1^2 + 2\gamma_2\right)\sigma^2 + 3\gamma_2^2\sigma^4 = 1,$$

or $(\gamma_1^2 + 2\gamma_2) + 3\gamma_2^2\sigma^2 = 0$.

There have been an increasing number of applications of the idea to date. Gallant and Tauchen (1989) and Gallant, Hsieh, and Tauchen (1991) give time series–based applications to asset prices and exchange rates respectively. In these studies the optimization was done using the NPSOL routine for constrained maximization, and standard errors were found by inverting the Hessian of the approximate log likelihood. Also, the consistency of the estimator, as $M \to \infty$, has been established (Gallant and Nychka, 1987; Gallant, 1987), though only for the case when the y_i are not dependent. Bearing in mind the strict conditions upon the nature of the approximation needed to get asymptotic normality of the series estimator of the conditional mean in Chapter 3, it would seem very likely that, in this much more general context, similar restrictions will be needed.

5.5.2 *Efficient Estimation by Kernel-Based Score Approximation*

Rather than attempt to maximize the likelihood most efforts to get an adaptive estimator have done so by setting the first-order conditions in (5.26), or some approximation to it, to zero. Let $d_\beta = -\Sigma\, x_i \psi_i$ be the scores for β and define the asymptotic information matrix for β as

$$\mathcal{I}_{\beta\beta} = n^{-1} E \left(\sum x_i x_i' \psi_i^2 \right) = n^{-1} \Sigma E\left(x_i x_i'\right) E\left(\psi_i^2\right) = E\left(x_i x_i'\right) E\left(\psi_i^2\right),$$

using the fact that the x_i and u_i are i.i.d. and independent of each other. For convenience x_i is taken to have a zero mean so that d_β is also the efficient score $\tilde{d}_\beta = - \sum (x_i - E(x_i)) \psi_i$, and the estimator of β solving $\tilde{d}_\beta(\hat{\beta}_{MLE}) = 0$ will attain the SP efficiency bound. Now if we knew the true density it is a well-established fact that a two-step estimator that is asymptotically as efficient as the MLE can be found by setting

$$\hat{\beta} = \tilde{\beta} + n^{-1} \mathcal{I}_{\beta\beta}^{-1}(\tilde{u}) d_\beta(\tilde{u}). \tag{5.32}$$

In (5.32) $\tilde{\beta}$ is some $\sqrt{n}$ consistent estimator while the information matrix and scores, which have as arguments functions of $u_i = y_i - x_i'\beta$, are evaluated by setting β to $\tilde{\beta}$. This estimator is extensively discussed in econometrics by Rothenberg and Leenders (1964).

Stone (1975) and Bickel (1982) both adopted this two-step estimator strategy when devising an efficient nonparametric estimator of β. They replace ψ_i in the information matrix and scores by the kernel estimators of $f^{(1)}(u_i)$ and $f(u_i)$, that is, $\psi_i = \hat{f}^{-1}(\tilde{u}_i) \hat{f}^{(1)}(\tilde{u}_i)$, where $\hat{f}(\tilde{u}_i) = \sum_j K((\tilde{u}_i - \tilde{u}_j)/h)$ and $\hat{f}^{(1)}(u_i)$ is the derivative of this with respect to u_i. To recognize this dependence we will designate the corresponding estimators for ψ_i, $\mathcal{I}_{\beta\beta}$, and d_β as $\hat{\psi}_i$, $\widehat{\mathcal{I}}_{\beta\beta}^{-1}(\tilde{u}_i) = \left(n^{-1}\Sigma x_i x_i'\right)\left(n^{-1}\Sigma \hat{\psi}^2(\tilde{u}_i)\right)$, and $\hat{d}_\beta = -\Sigma x_i \hat{\psi}_i$, leading to the definition of the two-step nonparametric MLE of β as

$$\hat{\beta}_{2SNP} = \tilde{\beta} + n^{-1} \widehat{\mathcal{I}}_{\beta\beta}^{-1}(\tilde{u}) \hat{d}_\beta(\tilde{u}). \tag{5.33}$$

Given the lineage of the estimator in (5.33) it might be expected to be as efficient as the MLE when the density of u_i is unknown. However, it has not been easy to prove this contention although see the excellent work of Ai (1997) where he gives the proofs of the consistency and asymptotic normality of the estimator in (5.33) for a very general class of semiparametric models which include the models in the previous section and some of the models in Chapters 7 to 9. Here we will merely give an outline of what appear to be the essential conditions needed for the estimator to have the desired properties.

It is useful to think about the proof in a number of stages. Consider first the estimator in (5.32). Under fairly general conditions $d_\beta(\tilde{u})$ can be expanded around $d_\beta(\beta_0) = d_\beta(u)$ to give $d_\beta(u) - n\mathcal{I}_{\beta\beta}(u)(\tilde{\beta} - \beta_0) + o_p(1)$ and therefore (5.32) becomes

$$\hat{\beta} = \beta_0 + n^{-1}\widehat{\mathcal{I}}_{\beta\beta}^{-1}(u)d_\beta(u) + o_p(1). \tag{5.34}$$

A similar argument may be made for (5.33), although the proof is quite complex if it is done directly by mean value expansions. Instead, authors in the field, for example Bickel (1982) and Manski (1984), have relied heavily on the notion of contiguity of probability measures. In particular, it is shown that the densities of the residuals $\tilde{u}_i$ and the errors u_i are contiguous, following Hajek and Sidak (1967). The argument is too involved to repeat here but, given the relation between (5.32) and (5.34), it seems reasonable to replace (5.33) by

$$\hat{\beta}_{2SNP} = \beta_0 + n^{-1}\widehat{\mathcal{I}}_{\beta\beta}^{-1}(u)\,\hat{d}_\beta(u). \tag{5.35}$$

Subtracting (5.34) from (5.35) shows that $n^{1/2}(\hat{\beta}_{2SNP} - \hat{\beta})$ is $o_p(1)$ if $\widehat{\mathcal{I}}_{\beta\beta} \xrightarrow{p} \mathcal{I}_{\beta\beta}$ and $n^{-1/2}(\hat{d}_\beta(u) - d_\beta(u)) \xrightarrow{p} 0$. Theorem 5.6 therefore states a necessary condition for $n^{1/2}(\hat{\beta}_{2SNP} - \hat{\beta})$ to be $o_p(1)$.

Theorem 5.6: If the estimator of $\psi(u_i)$, $\hat{\psi}_i$, is i.i.d and independent of x_i a sufficient condition for $\hat{\beta}_{2SNP}$ to be asymptotically efficient relative to β is that $E(\psi_i - \hat{\psi}_i)^2 \to 0$ as $n \to \infty$.

Proof: It needs to be shown that $n^{1/2}(\hat{\beta}_{2SNP} - \hat{\beta})$ is $o_p(1)$. By definition

$$n^{-1/2}(\hat{d}_\beta(u) - d_\beta(u)) = -n^{-1/2}\Sigma\, x_i(\hat{\psi}_i - \psi_i).$$

When $\hat{\psi}_i$ is i.i.d., $\hat{\psi}_i - \psi_i$ is i.i.d. and therefore

$$\mathrm{cov}\left[n^{-1/2}(\hat{d}_\beta(u) - d_\beta(u))\right] = E\left(x_i x_i'\right)E(\hat{\psi}_i - \psi_i)^2$$

tends to zero under the conditions of the theorem, establishing that $n^{-1/2}(\hat{d}_\beta(u) - d_\beta(u)) \xrightarrow{p} 0$. A similar argument shows that $\widehat{\mathcal{I}}_{\beta\beta} \xrightarrow{p} \mathcal{I}_{\beta\beta}$.   Q.E.D.

The requirements of the theorem are exceedingly restrictive, since it will be very rare for the kernel estimator of the score of the density to be i.i.d.

Stone and Bickel ensured that it was i.i.d. by forming the kernel estimator from a different sample ($j = -n_1 + 1, \ldots, 0$) from that used for solving for $\beta(i = 1, \ldots, n)$. Under such a scenario the density estimator forming the basis of $\hat{\psi}_i$ becomes

$$\hat{f}(u_i) = (n_1 h)^{-1} \sum_{j=-n_1+1}^{0} K((u_j - u_i)/h).$$

Now, $\hat{\beta}$ can be estimated by conditioning upon the earlier observations, and that means the only random element in $\hat{f}_i$ is u_i, making $\hat{\psi}_i$ i.i.d. The assumption simplifies the proof enormously and highlights the fact that the crucial assumption for the ability of a two-step nonparametric estimator to have the same efficiency as the MLE maximizing (5.23) is that the approximation employed for ψ converges to the true value in mean square. Indeed, Andrews (1994) finds that this conclusion holds out of the i.i.d. setup here, even when the sample ($i = 1, \ldots, n$) is used to estimate ψ.[7] Condition B(ii) is satisfied when ψ_i is symmetric in u_i so that only consistency of $\hat{\psi}_i$ in some metric is needed. Hence any proofs of the construction of an adaptive estimator effectively must prescribe values of the window width parameter etc. that need to be satisfied to get mean square convergence of the estimator of the score for u.

In many of the papers dealing with the adaptive estimation of β there has been concern that the presence of the density in the denominator of ψ_i means that poor estimates would follow if a near-zero value occurs for $\hat{f}_i$, leading to a decision to replace $f(\tilde{u}_i)$ with a more suitable value. For this reason it is customary to trim the estimator in the following way:

$$\hat{\psi}_i = \hat{f}^{-1}(\tilde{u}_i)\hat{f}^{(1)}(\tilde{u}_i) \quad \text{if} \quad |\tilde{u}_i| \leq b_n, \quad \hat{f}(\tilde{u}_i) \geq c_n \quad \text{and,} \tag{5.36}$$

$$\left|\hat{f}^{(1)}(\tilde{u}_i)\right| \leq a_n \hat{f}(\tilde{u}_i) \quad \text{otherwise.} \tag{5.37}$$

With these definitions it is possible to state restrictions upon h, the window width, and the trimming parameters, b_n, c_n, and a_n, such that the desired mean square convergence of the density score estimator is achieved.

Theorem 5.7: If $b_n \to \infty$, $c_n \to 0$, $a_n \to \infty$, $h \to 0$, $n^{-1}b_n h^{-3} \to 0$, and $hb_n \to 0$ as $n \to \infty$ then $E(\hat{\psi}_i - \psi_i)^2 \to 0$ as $n \to \infty$.

Proof: See Bickel (1982, Section 6.1). Q.E.D.

---

[7] Since Theorem 5.6 aims to establish that $n^{-1/2}\hat{d}_\beta$ has the same limiting distribution as $n^{-1/2}d_\beta$, and the difference is that ψ_i is estimated nonparametrically in the former, Lemma 5.1 could be applied to demonstrate the equivalence.

One advantage of the two-step adaptive estimator of β is that it is very easy to implement. Perhaps the simplest way to do so is to obtain the correction term $\hat{\beta}_{2SNP} - \tilde{\beta}$ as the estimated coefficients in the regression of unity against $x_i \tilde{\psi}_i$. The only difficulties concern the construction of the initial consistent estimator $\tilde{\beta}$ and the estimated score $\tilde{\psi}_i$. As Andrews (1994) shows, and Manski (1984) found in Monte Carlo experiments, the Stone–Bickel sample splitting idea is not needed to get an efficient estimator of β, and therefore $\tilde{\beta}$ is most easily computed as the OLS estimator of β using all the available data. To estimate $\tilde{\psi}_i$ requires the selection of trimming parameters. As Robinson (1987) comments in a related context, the statement of how they must vary with n in Theorem 5.7 is almost useless to a practitioner. In his Monte Carlo experiments with $n = 25$ and $n = 100$ Manski set (h, b_n, c_n, a_n) to (.08, 4.0, .004, 30.0) and (.06, 5.0, .002, 36.0) respectively. At this stage the best strategy in applied work is likely to involve some experimentation to establish how sensitive the answers are to trimming.

5.5.3 Efficient Estimation by Moment-Based Score Approximation

A key factor enabling adaptive estimation in Section 5.5.2 was the ability to ensure mean square estimation of the score function ψ_i by kernel estimation of the density of u_i and its first derivative. That fact is emphasized by Theorems 5.6 and 5.7 and it leads us to wonder whether there are other ways that might be used to estimate ψ_i. A very simple procedure involving moment approximations has been advocated and studied by Beran (1976), Chamberlain (1984), and Newey (1988). To appreciate the basis of this estimator, assume initially that $f(u_i)$ is known to be symmetric and that all moments of u_i up to rth order are finite. Because ψ_i is a function of the scalar u_i one approximation is to express it as a polynomial in u_i. Since ψ_i is known to be an odd function of u_i, due to the symmetry assumption, only odd powers of u_i will be needed. An estimator of ψ_i may then be obtained as the predictions of ψ_i against $\zeta'_i = (u_i, u_i^3, \ldots, u_i^r)$, where r is taken to be odd here. Arranging the ζ_i in an $n \times s$ matrix ζ and $\psi' = (\psi_1 \ldots \psi_n)$, the estimator is $\bar{\psi}_i = \zeta'_i (\zeta' \zeta)^{-1} \zeta' \psi$. An efficient two-step MLE constructed like $\hat{\beta}_{2SNP}$ in (5.33) would be

$$\bar{\beta} = \tilde{\beta} + n^{-1} \bar{\mathcal{I}}_{\beta\beta}^{-1}(\tilde{u}) \bar{d}_\beta(\tilde{u}), \tag{5.38}$$

where $\bar{\mathcal{I}}_{\beta\beta}(u) = \left(n^{-1} \Sigma\, x_i x'_i \right) \left(n^{-1} \Sigma \bar{\psi}_i^2 \right)$ and $\bar{d}_\beta(u) = -\Sigma\, x_i \bar{\psi}_i$. That this estimator is likely to be asymptotically efficient follows from Theorem 5.6 and the fact that $E \left(\bar{\psi}_i - \psi_i \right)^2 \to 0$ as $r \to \infty$, a fact established by Newey (1988) and stated in Theorem 5.8.

Theorem 5.8: If the density of u_i is absolutely continuous and differentiable with $E \left(f(u_i)^{-2} f^{(1)}(u_i)^2 \right)$ finite, ζ_i are continuously differentiable functions of u with boundedness conditions on the powers and moments set out in Newey (1988, Lemma 2.2), and the density of u_i can be characterized by its moments,

$$\lim_{r \to \infty} E(\psi_i - \bar{\psi}_i)^2 = 0.$$

Proof: See Newey (1988). Q.E.D.

Theorem 5.8 indicates that the estimator $\bar{\beta}$ is likely to be adaptive. Of course it is infeasible because $\zeta'\psi$ is unknown and $\bar{\psi}_i$ cannot be formed. However, because $\bar{\psi}_i = \zeta_i(\zeta'\zeta)^{-1}E(\zeta'\psi) + o_p(1)$, and $E(\zeta'\psi)$ can be estimated, an operational version of (5.38) exists. It turns out that the resulting estimator is equivalent to an application of Hansen's (1982) generalized method of moments (GMM) estimator to the moment restrictions embodied in the conventions of the model, and for this reason we now concentrate upon deriving it in a form that enables an easy comparison with (5.38).

As the problem has been stated there are a number of moment restrictions that could be utilized to estimate β, stemming from the symmetry restrictions and the independence of x_i and u_i, namely $E(x_i\zeta_i') = 0$. In vectorized form these restrictions are $E(\rho(\beta)) = E((I_s \otimes X)'\text{vec}(\zeta)) = 0$. Hansen showed that it was best to estimate β by minimizing the expression $\rho(\beta)'V_{\rho\rho}^{-1}\rho(\beta)$ with respect to β (see also Section 5.10), where

$$V_{\rho\rho} = \text{cov}(\rho) = (I_s \otimes X')(V_{\zeta\zeta} \otimes I_N)(I_s \otimes X) = (V_{\zeta\zeta} \otimes X'X)$$

and $V_{\zeta\zeta}$ is the covariance matrix of ζ_i. If $s = 1$, $\rho(\beta) = X'(y - X\beta)$ and the OLS estimator of β would emerge. Hence, the GMM estimator attempts to get efficiency gains by utilizing information about higher order moments.

The GMM estimator solves the first-order conditions $\Phi(\hat{\beta}_{GMM})\hat{V}_{\rho\rho}^{-1}\rho$ $(\hat{\beta}_{GMM}) = 0$, where $\Phi = \partial\rho/\partial\beta$. Just as for the MLE it is possible to define an asymptotically equivalent two-step estimator by linearizing $\rho(\beta)$ around an initial $\sqrt{n}$ consistent estimator, $\tilde{\beta}$, and solving for β from these linearized first-order conditions, that is,

$$\tilde{\Phi}\tilde{V}_{\rho\rho}^{-1}\left(\tilde{\rho} + \tilde{\Phi}'(\hat{\beta}_{2SGMM} - \tilde{\beta})\right) = 0. \tag{5.39}$$

Equation (5.39) may be solved for $\hat{\beta}_{2SGMM}$ by estimating a system of "seemingly unrelated regressions," where the underlying set of s equations has the form

$$\tilde{\rho} = -\tilde{\Phi}(\beta - \tilde{\beta}) + \xi. \tag{5.40}$$

where ξ is an error vector. Alternatively, (5.40) can be written as

$$\tilde{\rho} = -E(\tilde{\Phi}|X)(\beta - \tilde{\beta}) - \{(\tilde{\Phi} - E(\tilde{\Phi}|X))(\beta - \tilde{\beta}) + \xi\}, \tag{5.41}$$

where the estimator of β from this modified system will have the same asymptotic distribution because $n^{-1/2}E(\Phi|X)'(\Phi - E(\Phi|X))(\beta - \tilde{\beta})$ is $o_p(1)$ when $n^{1/2}(\beta - \tilde{\beta})$ is $O_p(1)$. Thus the first-order conditions (5.39) become

$$E(\tilde{\Phi}|X)\tilde{V}_{\rho\rho}^{-1}[\tilde{\rho} + E(\tilde{\Phi}|X)]'(\hat{\beta}_{2SGMM} - \tilde{\beta}) = 0, \tag{5.42}$$

giving

$$\hat{\beta}_{2SGMM} = \tilde{\beta} - \left[E(\tilde{\Phi}|X)\tilde{V}_{\rho\rho}^{-1}E(\tilde{\Phi}|X)'\right]^{-1}\left[E(\tilde{\Phi}|X)\tilde{V}_{\rho\rho}^{-1}\tilde{\rho}\right]. \tag{5.43}$$

We now proceed to simplify (5.43) in order to derive $\hat{\beta}_{2SGMM}$ by using

$$E(\Phi|X) = E((\partial\text{vec}(\zeta))/\partial\beta|X)(I_s \otimes X).$$

$E((\partial\text{vec}(\zeta))/\partial\beta|X)$ has ith element $-x_i E(\partial\zeta_i/\partial u_i)$. This equals $-x_i w'$, where $w_i = E(\partial\zeta_i/\partial u_i)$ is a constant, as the u_i are i.i.d., making $E(\Phi|X) = -(w' \otimes X'X)$. Substituting for $E(\Phi|X)$, $V_{\rho\rho}$, and ρ into (5.43) yields

$$\hat{\beta}_{2SGMM} = \tilde{\beta} + \left[(\tilde{w}' \otimes X'X)(\tilde{V}_{\zeta\zeta}^{-1} \otimes (X'X)^{-1})(\tilde{w}' \otimes X'X)\right]^{-1}$$
$$\times (\tilde{w}' \otimes X'X)(\tilde{V}_{\zeta\zeta}^{-1} \otimes (X'X)^{-1})((I_s \otimes X')\text{vec}(\tilde{\zeta})). \tag{5.44}$$

Equation (5.44) bears a close resemblance to (5.38) in that the denominator is a linear combination of $x_i x_i'$ while the numerator is a linear combination of the x_i. The correspondence can be strengthened by the use of the generalized information equality (Rao, 1973, Exercises 5.8 and 5.9) stated in Lemma 5.5.

Lemma 5.5: $E(\partial\zeta_i/\partial u_i) = -E(\psi_i\zeta_i')$, where ψ_i is the score of the density with respect to u_i.

Proof: Since $E(\zeta_i) = 0$,

$$\int \zeta_i f(u)\,du = 0, \tag{5.45}$$

and differentiating (5.45) with respect to u we get

$$\int (\partial\zeta_i/\partial u)f(u)\,du + \int \zeta_i'(\partial f(u)/\partial u)\,du = 0. \tag{5.46}$$

Noting that $\psi = f^{-1}(u)(\partial f(u)/\partial u)$, we can write (5.46) as

$$\int (\partial\zeta_i/\partial u)f(u)\,du + \int \zeta_i'\psi_i f(u)\,du = 0, \tag{5.47}$$

from which the lemma follows.   Q.E.D.

The beauty of Lemma 5.5 is that it enables the replacement of $w' = E(\partial \zeta_i / \partial u_i)$ by $-E(\psi_i \zeta_i')$ and this latter term may be (hypothetically) consistently estimated by $-n^{-1}\Sigma \, \psi_i \zeta_i' = -n^{-1}\psi'\zeta$. Furthermore, $V_{\zeta\zeta}$ can be consistently estimated by $n^{-1}\zeta'\zeta$. Combining these two features, $w'V_{\zeta\zeta}^{-1}w$ and $w'V_{\zeta\zeta}^{-1}$ can be estimated by $n^{-1}\psi'\zeta(\zeta'\zeta)^{-1}\zeta'\psi = n^{-1}\Sigma \hat{\psi}_i^2$ and $-\psi'\zeta(\zeta'\zeta)^{-1} = \hat{\pi}$ respectively. Note that $\bar{\psi}_i = -\zeta_i'\hat{\pi}'$ and the two terms are just the explained sum of squares and the negative of the regression coefficients from the regression of ψ_i against ζ_i. Substituting both simplifications into (5.44) leaves

$$\hat{\beta}_{2SGMM} = \tilde{\beta} - \left[\sum x_i x_i' \left(n^{-1}\sum \bar{\psi}^2(\tilde{u}_i)\right)\right]^{-1}$$
$$\times \left[\sum x_i \bar{\psi}(\tilde{u}_i)\right] + o_p(1)$$
$$= \tilde{\beta} + n^{-1}\tilde{\mathcal{I}}_{\beta\beta}^{-1}(\tilde{u})\bar{d}_\beta(\tilde{u}) + o_p(1), \tag{5.48}$$

establishing the asymptotic equivalence of $\hat{\beta}_{2SGMM}$ and $\bar{\beta}$ in (5.38). Consequently, the two-step GMM estimator of β based on the moment conditions $E(x_i u_i^j) = 0, j = 1, 3, 5 \ldots$, is adaptive. However, although the argument given above is suggestive, it is not rigorous. In particular the act of estimating the density score from sample data via a series approximation means that some restriction must be placed upon the rate at which r can increase with the sample size, just as occurred in Section 3.9. Newey gives the following result:

Theorem 5.9: The estimator $\hat{\beta}_{2SGMM}$ is adaptive if $r \to \infty$ and $r^2 \log r / \log n \to 0$ as $n \to \infty$.

Proof: See Newey (1988, Theorem 2.3). Q.E.D.

The growth rate of r in Theorem 5.9 is very slow and cannot even be of the form n^α, which was the standard format in the Fourier approximation approach in Chapter 3, although it seems likely that future work will improve upon this rate.

It is now time to return to the assumptions of symmetry and independence of x_i and u_i made at the beginning of this subsection. The role of symmetry was to indicate that ζ_i need only be constituted from odd powers of u_i, whereas independence could be replaced in the proofs by requiring the moments of u_i, conditional upon x_i, to be constant. However, such modifications seem to be beside the point. As Newey forcefully argues, the GMM orientation is much more general than the adaptive maximum likelihood one, since it is capable of handling heteroskedasticity in the u_i etc., which kernel-based methods might have trouble with. Moreover, it may be that only a small number of moment restrictions is needed to give a good approximation to the score. Newey notes that, in the models employed by Manski in his simulations, the worst case was when the score function was a cubic in u_i, and so only three moment restrictions were required to get performance as good as the two-step adaptive MLE.

Implementing the two-step GMM estimator is a simple task as good programs exist for GMM estimation. Some modifications do need to be made if the density is not known to be symmetric. Then the conditional moment restrictions would become $E[x_i(u_i^j - E(u_i^j))]$, $j = 1, 2, 3 \ldots$, as all the orders of u_i will be needed for approximation purposes. In this instance Newey proposes estimating $E(u_i^j)$, $j = 2, 4, 6 \ldots$ along with the β. He also prefers to utilize the powers of $u_i/(1 + |u_i|)$ rather than u_i, since this has better characteristics if some moments of the distribution of u_i do not exist.

5.6   Estimation of Scale Parameters

Although Theorem 5.5 was not encouraging about the prospect for efficient estimation of scale parameters when the error density is of unknown form, it would seem sensible to obtain estimates of β and γ by either maximizing approximations to (5.28) or solving the scores (5.29) and (5.30). Gallant, Hsieh, and Tauchen (1991) do the former, where the z_i are taken to be functions of the x_i. Working with the scores (5.29) and (5.30) looks straightforward. Initial consistent estimators of β and γ can be found from OLS regression; for β it is the regression of y_i against x_i whereas for γ the corresponding variables would be $\left(y_i - x_i'\hat{\beta}_{OLS}\right)^2$ and z_i. With these in hand $\hat{v}_i$ can be formed and a nonparametric estimate of the score function $\psi(v) = f^{-1}(v) f^{(1)}(v)$ can be made. Two-step estimation would then proceed exactly as described in Section 5.5.2. It is much harder to provide a method of moments interpretation like that in Section 5.5.3 since the presence of the term v_i in the scores (5.30) prohibits the simplifications employed in (5.38) to (5.48). It may be that a study of the semiparametric efficiency bound for this model could indicate a suitable GMM estimator.

5.7   Optimal Diagnostic Tests in Linear Models

A broad range of diagnostic tests has evolved for the linear regression model. Many of these have been found using the Lagrange multiplier or score tests approach; see Breusch and Pagan (1980) or Engle (1984). For the linear model, traditionally analysis has begun with the assumption that the u_i in (5.19) are normal and that the score test statistic for the postulated deficiency in the model has been isolated; it is then shown that the limit distribution of the statistic is invariant to a wide variety of densities for the u_i. Although this is a useful robustness property, it ignores the fact that the power of the test is dependent upon the correspondence of the density assumed in the derivation of the test with the actual density. Koenker and Bassett (1982) for example argue that the test for heteroskedasticity derived by Godfrey (1978) and Breusch and Pagan (1979) could have poor power if the true density of the u_i was a mixture of normals instead of normal, as the Breusch/Godfrey/Pagan analysis presupposed.

An optimal testing strategy would be based upon the efficient score $\tilde{d}_\gamma$, where γ is the parameter associated with the misspecification indicator of the alternative model, and when this equals d_γ it is possible for us to construct fully efficient diagnostic tests. Thus a test for an omitted variable z_i merely involves the addition of z_i to the maintained model and its reestimation by the adaptive estimator. To appreciate how this test differs from the regular score test for omitted variables, observe that the standard method is to test for $E(z_i u_i) = 0$, whereas (5.26) implies that the optimal test involves checking if $E(z_i \psi_i) = 0$. If the errors are Gaussian $\psi_i = -\sigma^{-2} u_i$ and the two coincide. It is easily seen that the optimal test can be computed as n times the R^2 from the regression of unity against $(x_i \hat{\psi}_i, z_i \hat{\psi}_i)$ and not $(x_i \hat{u}_i, z_i \hat{u}_i)$.

A similar view can be taken of tests for heteroskedasticity that seek to determine if (5.30) has zero expectation. As pointed out in Theorem 5.5 the efficient score for $\gamma_2, \ldots, \gamma_p$ is equal to (5.30) when the null hypothesis of no heteroskedasticity is correct, that is, adaptive estimation of $\gamma_2, \ldots, \gamma_p$ was possible. Because of the block diagonality of the information matrix between β and γ, the optimal test for heteroskedasticity will be found as $n R^2$ in the regression of unity against $z_i \left(\hat{v}_i \, \hat{f}^{-1}(\hat{v}_i) \hat{f}^{(1)}(\hat{v}_i) - 1 \right)$. Again, when errors are normal the regressors, under the null hypothesis, would be $z_i (v_i^2 - 1)$, which is the Studentized form of the Breusch/Godfrey/Pagan test recommended by Koenker (1982). Thus the theory of adaptive estimation in the linear model provides a complete account of the steps needed to derive fully efficient diagnostic test statistics. Bickel (1978) has a comprehensive discussion of this point. Gonzalez-Rivera and Ullah (1998) systematically develop Rao score (RS) or Lagrange-multiplier test statistics based on the ML estimation of the parameters under the nonparametric kernel density instead of quasi ML estimation (QMLE) under the normality. They refer to this class of test statistics as the semiparametric RS (SPRS) test and show that its asymptotic distribution, under the null hypothesis, is the usual Chi-square distribution. They also provide some simulation evidence on the performance of the SPRS test statistics showing that they seem to have superior finite-sample properties compared to the standard parametric RS tests.

5.8 Adaptive Estimation with Dependent Observations

Until now it has been assumed that x_i and u_i in (5.19) are both i.i.d. If x_i has a time series structure, but remains independent of u_i, most of the conclusions of the preceding sections remain valid. Andrews (1991d) deals with the case where both x_i and u_i are stationary and dependent, with u_i following an sth-order Markov process. He considers the estimator of the slope coefficients, β, obtained by maximizing (5.23), where now the density is that of u_i conditional upon $u_{i-1}, u_{i-2}, \ldots, u_{i-s}$ and it is to be estimated nonparametrically. The estimator of β is shown to be adaptive; asymptotic normality is established if x_i and u_i are bounded random variables and the nonparametric estimators of the derivatives of the density converge in mean square to their true values.

When x_i contains lagged values of y_i, the situation is much less clear. Derivation of the semiparametric bound by conditioning upon the u_i is now no longer an option, and more direct solutions are needed. Nevertheless, Kreiss (1987) has investigated adaption when

$$x_i'\beta = \beta_1 y_{i-1} + \cdots + \beta_r y_{i-r} + \beta_{r+1} u_{i-1} + \cdots + \beta_{r+s} u_{i-s},$$

that is, y_i is an autoregressive moving average process of order r and s, that is ARMA(r, s). If the u_i are i.i.d. random variables that are symmetrically distributed around zero with finite fourth moment, and the ARMA process is stationary and invertible, he establishes that adaption for β is possible. Moreover, the two-step estimator in (5.35) is fully efficient provided that nh^9 is bounded and the conditions of Theorem 5.7 on the interaction of trimming and window-width parameters are satisfied, with the exception that $n^{-1}b_n h^{-3} \to 0$ becomes $n^{-1}b_n h^{-4} \to 0$. Given the sample sizes in economics, the requirement that nh^9 be bounded means that very rough estimates of the score function of the density will need to be used, as the window width will be wide. Despite this, Kreiss reports that the two-step estimator performed quite well in Monte Carlo experiments, even for an n as low as 50. For example, when the density of u_i was a mixture of normals, he found that 90% confidence intervals for the OLS estimator of an AR(1) parameter with true value .5 was $(-1.65, 1.18)$, whereas it shrank to $(-.65, .58)$ for the two-step estimator.

Extensions outside of the case when u_i are i.i.d. have been empirical rather than theoretical. Let $v_i = u_i/\sigma_i$, and assume that the density of v_i, conditional upon $\aleph_{i-1} = (y_1, \ldots, y_{i-1}, x_1, \ldots, x_i)$, is $f(v_i|\aleph_{i-1})$. By focusing upon the conditional densities, Schweppe (1965) found the log likelihood of $y_1, \ldots, y_n$ to be

$$L = \sum_{i=1}^n \log f(v_i|\aleph_{i-1}) + \log f(v_0), \tag{5.49}$$

where $f(v_0)$ is the unconditional density for v_0. Asymptotically, the last term is dominated by the first and can therefore be ignored, making it simply a matter of finding a suitable expression for $f(v_i|\aleph_{i-1})$ to allow estimation to proceed. One possibility is to presume that $\sigma_i = (z_i'\gamma)^{1/2}$ and that $f(v_i|\aleph_{i-1})$ is identical for all i. This occurs for example in Engle's (1982) ARCH model, where

$f(v_i|\aleph_{i-1})$ is $\mathcal{N}(0, 1)$ and z_i are u_{i-j}^2. With the v_i having identical conditional densities, the log likelihood would be

$$L = \sum_{i=1}^{n} \log\, f\left[(z_i'\gamma)^{-1/2}(y_i - x_i'\beta)\right] + \log\, f(v_0), \qquad (5.50)$$

and one could proceed to estimation either by maximizing (5.50) or by approximating the scores for β and γ. Engle and Gonzalez-Rivera (1991) do this by using the penalized likelihood method described in Chapter 2. Since the information matrix is block diagonal between β and γ, there would be no loss of efficiency in solving for β alone after replacing γ by any $\sqrt{n}$ consistent estimator. However, in many models involving time series the γ are of equal interest to the β. Since γ was not adaptively estimable in the independent observation case (Section 5.4) one must be sanguine over the prospects for this with dependent observations.

A straightforward application of the likelihood approximation idea of Section 5.5.1 would replace $f(v_i|\aleph_{i-1})$ by $(2\pi)^{-1/2}\exp(-.5v_i^2)P^2(v_i)$, but it might be felt that this formulation constrains the dependence in the conditional density too much. One way to "loosen up" the specification is to allow the coefficients in the polynomial $P(v_i)$ to depend upon $\aleph_{i-1}$. Thus, if $\aleph_{i-1} = y_{i-1}$ and $P(\cdot)$ is a first-order polynomial, $P(v_i) = \alpha_0(y_{i-1})+\alpha_1(y_{i-1})v_i$ and $\alpha_j(\cdot)$ are polynomial functions of the form $\alpha_j(y_{i-1}) = \sum_{k=0}^{s} \alpha_{jk}y_{i-1}^k$, where $\alpha_{00} = 1$. In Gallant and Tauchen (1989) σ_i was assumed constant and conditional heteroskedasticity in v_i was introduced by this device. Gallant, Hsieh, and Tauchen (1991) made σ_i a linear function of $\aleph_{i-1}$, but they introduced more flexibility through the variable coefficient modification, that is, because the polynomial coefficients also depend on $\aleph_{i-1}$ there is "extra" heteroskedasticity. Despite this, for the foreign exchange data they used it would seem that a constant-coefficient polynomial was adequate.

5.9 *M*-Estimators

5.9.1 *Estimation*

In Section 5.5 the optimal estimator of β in (5.19) was found either by maximizing (5.23) or by solving the first-order conditions in (5.26). A natural concern arising from the theory of that section must be that the quality of the approximations to the unknown functions will be severely circumscribed by the sample size. Such reservations lead to the following question: Can we replace (5.23) and (5.26) by other functions, application of which could deliver estimators that, although not fully efficient, are nevertheless superior to OLS in the event that the unknown density of u_i is nonnormal? Proposals in this vein can be conveniently discussed under the heading of *M*-estimators, a general class of

Table 5.1. *Criteria for the M-estimation of β.*

$\rho(\cdot)$	Estimator
$\lvert y_i - \beta \rvert$	Median
$\lvert y_i - x_i'\beta \rvert$	Least Absolute Deviations (LAD)
$\lvert \alpha - I(y_i - \beta < 0) \rvert (y_i - \beta)$	α-Quantile Estimator
$\lvert \alpha - I(y_i - x_i'\beta < 0) \rvert (y_i - x_i'\beta)$	α-Quantile Regression Estimator
$\lvert \alpha - I(y_i - x_i'\beta < 0) \rvert (y_i - x_i'\beta)^2$	Asymmetric Least Squares (ALS)

estimators set out in Huber (1964) with the "*M*" signifying "like maximum likelihood."

Equations (5.23) and (5.26) each have an outstanding characteristic that needs to be preserved by any substitute function. For (5.23) it is that the true value of β, β_0, maximizes the Kullback–Liebler information criterion $E\left(n^{-1}\Sigma\log(y_i - x_i'\beta)\right)$, and this fact is central to any "Wald-type" proof of the consistency of the MLE. Equation (5.26) required β_0 to solve the first-order conditions

$$E\left[n^{-1}\Sigma x_i f^{-1}\left(y_i - x_i'\beta\right) f^{(1)}\left(y_i - x_i'\beta\right)\right] = 0.$$

This constraint is essential to "Cramer-type" proofs of the consistency of the MLE. Our objective is to replace these functions with $n^{-1}\Sigma\rho(y_i, x_i, \theta)$ or $n^{-1}\Sigma\rho_\theta(y_i, x_i, \theta)$, where ρ_θ is the derivative of ρ with respect to θ, insisting that, when evaluated at the true value of θ, θ_0, the expectation of the first is minimized while the second is zero. It is possible to interpret the series estimator of Section 5.5.1 in this way by defining $\rho(\cdot)$ as the negative of (5.31) and letting $\theta = (\beta, \gamma)$. However, the theoretical work to be described subsequently envisages that θ is of finite dimension whereas that estimator had θ with dimension dependent on the sample size. Recently Duncan (1987) has made an attempt to broaden the theory to this context.

Many proposals have been made concerning $\rho(\cdot)$ and Table 5.1 gives a selection for the estimation of "location" parameters. The list is not meant to be exhaustive and omits some of the more popular ones from the robust estimation literature, as described for example in Koenker (1982) or Huber (1981). It is designed to cover those that have arisen in the "semiparametric" rather than "robust" estimation literature. Such a distinction is, admittedly, a little artificial, but it also serves to rule out from consideration other robust estimators that derive from R, L, and S principles. Amemiya (1985) has a short discussion of these. Few seem to have been applied in economics, and the computational problems can be severe.

The first and third criteria in Table 5.1 are meant for the estimation of a model that has only a location parameter. One can verify that $E(\rho(\theta_0)) = 0$ for each of the functions, thereby retaining the essential condition associated with adaptive estimation.[8] Such a treatment is permissible provided the data are identically distributed. For the first criterion, minimizing $n^{-1} \Sigma E |y_i - \beta|$ with respect to β gives $\Pr\{y_i \leq \beta_0\} = .5$, as can be seen from the following argument. First

$$E(\rho) = E|y_i - \beta| = \int_{y > \beta} (y - \beta) \, dF(y) - \int_{y < \beta} (y - \beta) \, dF(y).$$

Second, after differentiating with respect to β using a variant of Liebniz's rule that

$$\partial/\partial x \int_{-\infty}^{g(x)} \psi(x, y) \, dy = \int_{-\infty}^{g(x)} \partial \psi/\partial x + (\partial g/\partial x) \psi(x, g(x)),$$

we have

$$E(\rho_\beta) = \int_{y < \beta} dF(y) - \int_{y > \beta} dF(y) = F(y < \beta) - (1 - F(y < \beta))$$

$$= 2F(y < \beta) - 1,$$

and this equals zero when β equals β_0 as defined above. The M-estimator of β is therefore the median and it treats $\beta_0 = F^{-1}(.5)$ as the location parameter. Notice that, if the "model" was $y_i = \gamma + u_i$, where γ is the "intercept" in the relation, some meaning could be attached to it; rather than its just being a location parameter for the error u_i, the M-estimator above estimates $\gamma + F_u^{-1}(.5)$ rather than γ. For this reason the intercept is only identified with further assumptions, for example that $F_u^{-1}(.5) = 0$. In what follows it is assumed that the primary features of interest in the model are either a general measure of location or the slope parameters. There seem to be few instances where theory has predictions about the intercept that one would wish to test. Even when it does, for example in the testing of efficient markets, it is really the location parameter that is of interest.

The LAD estimator is a generalization of the median to the linear regression model and it has been extensively analyzed in Carroll and Ruppert (1988). It seems to have been little used in the linear model framework, but it assumes importance in the analysis of censored models in Chapter 9, as do the quantile estimators arrayed in Table 5.1. Its major disadvantage is that the function generating it is nondifferentiable in β and this necessitates the use of a simplex algorithm for minimization. However, many such algorithms are available and so the computation problem may not be severe.

The quantile estimators are generalizations of the median and LAD estimators, producing the latter when $\alpha = .5$. To see this write the expected value of

---

[8] Throughout the remainder of this section the dependence of ρ upon data at the ith point will be suppressed.

the function for the third criterion in Table 5.1 as $\alpha \int_{y>\beta}(y-\beta)\,dF(y) + (\alpha - 1)\int_{y<\beta}(y-\beta)\,dF(y)$ and follow the same set of steps as for the median to get $E(\rho_\beta) = \alpha - F(\beta)$, which is zero when $\beta_0 = F^{-1}(\alpha)$, the α quantile of y.

Quantile estimators seek to find the relationship between y_i and x_i at different quantiles of the conditional density of y_i given x_i. If y_i was income and x_i age, then the .25 quantile would focus upon how the income of those individuals in the 25% quantile for given ages varies with age. Hence we are holding constant the relative position of these individuals. Numerically, one can think about this relation graphically by sorting income according to ages $x_1, \ldots, x_G$, finding the value of income corresponding to the 25% quantile at each age, $y_1(\alpha), \ldots, y_G(\alpha)$, and then plotting $y_j(\alpha)$ against x_j. If the relation is linear one could perform a regression. This estimator contrasts with the conditional mean $E(y_i | x = x^*)$ in that $y_j(\alpha)$ would be replaced by $\bar{y}_j$ (the sample mean for age x_j). Hence, quantile estimation gives a clearer view of how the conditional density changes with x_i than that provided by the conditional mean. It is not complete in that the number of quantiles is likely to be quite small, given the finite amount of data available. Quantile estimation is particularly attractive if y_i is censored below (above) some point δ. Provided the α quantile chosen is above (below) δ the picture obtained of the conditional density will be correct, whereas the conditional mean will be adversely affected by this censoring. Of course the estimator described above relies upon x_i being a discrete random variable; when it is continuous β will be estimated by the fourth criterion in Table 5.1. Buchinsky (1994) provides a linear programming algorithm to do this and programs such as STATA provide quantile regression estimation as an option.

The last estimator in the table, ALS, was proposed by Aigner et al. (1976) and has been investigated by Newey and Powell (1987). In its construction α is a user-defined parameter that lies between zero and one. Its sobriquet comes from the fact that it gives weight of α or $(1 - \alpha)$ to the squared errors depending upon their sign. A value of $\alpha = .5$ reproduces OLS. Perhaps its most attractive feature is that it is differentiable in β, and Newey indicates that it can be computed by iterated weighted least squares, solving for $\hat{\beta}$ at the nth iteration with (5.51),

$$\hat{\beta}_{(n)} = \left[\Sigma\left(\left|\alpha - I\left(y_i < x_i'\hat{\beta}_{(n-1)}\right)\right|\right)x_i x_i'\right]^{-1}$$
$$\times \left[\Sigma\left(\left|\alpha - I\left(y_i < x_i'\hat{\beta}_{(n-1)}\right)\right|\right)x_i y_i\right]. \tag{5.51}$$

Quite general theorems for the distribution of M-estimators have emerged from the literature (Huber, 1981; Bierens, 1981; Pollard, 1985), covering various types of dependency in the data as well as differentiability of the $\rho(\cdot)$ function. It is this last feature which is of greatest interest since, with the

Table 5.2. *Covariance matrix of estimators of Table 5.1.*

Median	$(1/4)f(\beta_0)^{-2}$ when $F(\beta_0) = 1/2$
LAD	$(1/4)f(0)^{-2}\left[p\lim_{n\to\infty} n^{-1}\sum x_i x_i'\right]^{-1}$ when $F(0) = 1/2$
α Quantile	$\alpha(1-\alpha)\left(f(\beta_0)^{-2}\right)$ where $F(\beta_0) = \alpha$
α-Quantile Regression	$\alpha(1-\alpha)f(\beta_0)^{-2}\left[p\lim_{n\to\infty} n^{-1}\sum x_i x_i'\right]^{-1}$
ALS	$[E(\xi_i^2(\alpha)u_i^2)/E(\xi_i(\alpha))^2]\left[p\lim_{n\to\infty} n^{-1}\sum x_i x_i'\right]^{-1}$ where $\xi_i(\alpha) = \alpha - I(y_i - x_i'\beta < 0)$

exception of ALS, all the functions to be minimized in Table 5.1 are not differentiable. If ρ had been differentiable the limiting distribution of $n^{1/2}(\hat{\theta} - \theta_0)$ would be obtained as that of $\left[E\left(n^{-1}\Sigma\rho_{\theta\theta}(i)\right)\right]^{-1}\left[n^{-1/2}\Sigma\rho_\theta(i)\right]$, from which it is generally $\mathcal{N}\left(0, [E(\rho_{\theta\theta})]^{-1}[E(\rho_\theta\rho_\theta')][E(\rho_{\theta\theta})]^{-1}\right)$. Without differentiability some analogues of the two quantities above are needed, and these must exhibit the property that the difference between $n^{1/2}(\hat{\theta} - \theta_0)$ and any approximation be $o_p(1)$; in Pollard's terms a "stochastic differentiability condition" needs to be satisfied by the substitute functions. The denominator in the expression for $n^{1/2}(\hat{\theta} - \theta_0)$ above can be simply replaced by $\partial^2 E(\rho)/\partial\theta\partial\theta'$, that is, the order in which expectations and differentiation are done is reversed. It is much harder, however, to isolate a suitable candidate, Δ_θ, for ρ_θ. No general results seem to be available, but it sometimes helps to act as if the function was differentiable and to examine whether the resulting "derivatives" are satisfactory choices. For example, when $\rho(\theta) = |y_i - \beta|$, exploiting the fact that $\partial|z|/\partial z = \text{sgn}(z)$ if $z \neq 0$, suggests that $\Delta_\theta = \text{sgn}(y_i - \beta)$, and this is indeed adequate. For all the functions of Table 5.1 such a strategy works, and for this reason it is relatively easy to determine the covariance matrix of the estimators.[9] Taking the median as an example, we find $\partial^2 E\rho/\partial\theta\partial\theta' = 2f(\beta_0)$ and $E\text{sgn}(y_i - x_i'\beta)^2 = 1$, yielding the variance recorded in Table 5.2. It is assumed in this table that x_i is independent of u_i. Otherwise $\rho_{\theta\theta}$ would involve $f(u|x)$ and not the unconditional density of $f(u)$ and the formulae would be different. Most applications in which the density of u_i is assumed to depend on x_i evaluate the distribution of $\hat{\beta}$ by bootstrapping

---

[9] Phillips (1991) presents a simple way of doing the asymptotics for LAD estimators involving the expansion of the first-order conditions for $\hat{\beta}$, $n^{-1}\sum_{i=1}^{n}\text{sgn}(y_i - \hat{\beta}) = 0$, around β_0, and then noting that $d\text{sgn}(z)/dz = 2\delta(z)$, where $\delta(z)$ is the delta (generalized) function.

methods – see Buchinsky (1994) for example. For complete derivations of the remainder of this table see Koenker and Bassett (1978) and Newey and Powell (1987).[10]

It is instructive to note that the covariance matrix of all estimators has the standard form of a constant times $\left[p\lim_{n\to\infty} n^{-1}\sum x_i x_i'\right]^{-1}$. Because the semi-parametric bound was $E\left(f^{(1)}(u)/f(u)\right)^2$ times $\left[p\lim_{n\to\infty} n^{-1}\sum x_i x_i'\right]^{-1}$, it is therefore very easy to compute the efficiency of each estimator relative to others or to assess the efficiency loss compared to the optimal estimator. Many comparisons of this type exist in the literature, principally motivated by a desire to show that OLS can be very inefficient relative to the more robust estimators of Table 5.1 when errors are (say) a mixture of normals.

With both the quantile and ALS estimators a parameter α must be selected. For some purposes it is useful to determine a number of estimates by varying α. If $\hat\beta(\alpha_1)$ and $\hat\beta(\alpha_2)$ represent estimators of β given values of α_1 and α_2 for the tuning parameter α, the estimators are jointly normal with variances as given in Table 5.2, covariances the product of $\left[p\lim_{n\to\infty} n^{-1}\Sigma x_i x_i'\right]^{-1}$, and scaling terms $\alpha_1(1-\alpha_2)f\left(F^{-1}(\alpha_1)\right)f\left(F^{-1}(\alpha_2)\right)$ (quantile estimators) or $E\left(\xi_i(\alpha_1)\xi_i(\alpha_2)u_i^2\right)/[E(\xi_i(\alpha_1)\xi_i(\alpha_2))]^2$ (ALS). In practice, consistent estimators of all of these covariances are available by replacing all unknowns by consistent estimators, for example, $f(0)$, the density of the errors at the origin, can be estimated by applying any of the estimators of Chapter 2 to the residuals $y_i - x_i'\hat\beta$.

5.9.2 Diagnostic Tests with M-Estimators

After estimation of the regression model with an M-estimator it may be desirable to test assumptions regarding specification error etc. If $\rho(\cdot)$ is differentiable this is most easily done within the framework set out by Newey (1985) and Tauchen (1985). In those articles the characteristic of the model to be checked is formulated as an $r \times 1$ vector of conditional moment restrictions, $c_i(\theta)$, where $\tau_0 = E(c_i(\theta)) = 0$ under the null hypothesis. A suitable test statistic is then based upon $\hat\tau = n^{-1}\Sigma c_i(\hat\theta)$, where $\hat\theta$ is an M-estimator. In most instances $c(\theta)$ is differentiable and a Taylor series expansion around θ_0 yields

$$n^{1/2}(\hat\tau - \tau_0) = \left(n^{-1/2}\Sigma c_i\right) + \left(n^{-1}\Sigma \partial c_i/\partial\theta\right)'\left(n^{1/2}(\hat\theta - \theta_0)\right) + o_p(1).$$

[10] If n is relatively small it may be preferable to determine the distribution of the quantile estimators by bootstrapping. For fixed x_i Hahn (1995) shows that one can use the residuals $y_i - x_i'\hat\beta$ for this purpose and that the bootstrapped distribution converges on to the asymptotic distribution as $n \longrightarrow \infty$, at least when there is no intercept present in the regression. In an earlier paper Arcones and Giné (1992) dealt with the case that x_i was stochastic and showed that one could bootstrap the quantile estimator by reshuffling the observed y_i, x_i.

If

$$n^{1/2}(\hat{\theta} - \theta_0) = B^{-1}(n^{-1/2}\Sigma\Delta_i) + o_p(1),$$

and the joint covariance matrix of $n^{-1/2}\Sigma c_i$ and $n^{-1/2}\Sigma\Delta_i$ is V, $n^{1/2}(\hat{\tau} - \tau_0)$ will generally be $\mathcal{N}(0, \ AVA')$, where

$$A = \left[I_r, \left(p \lim_{n\to\infty} n^{-1}\Sigma\partial c_i/\partial\theta \right)' B^{-1} \right].$$

With this asymptotic result $n\hat{\tau}'(AVA')^{-1}\hat{\tau}$ will be asymptotically $\chi^2(r)$ when $\tau_0 = 0$.

In the preceding section it was mentioned that M-estimators could be written in the requisite way, B being the second derivative of the expected value of the $\rho(\cdot)$ function and Δ being chosen as an approximation to the first derivative. A simple way to estimate V when observations are independent is as the outer product form of the sample counterparts; for example, the covariance $E(c_i(\theta)\Delta_i(\theta)')$ is estimated by $n^{-1}\Sigma c_i(\hat{\theta})\Delta_i(\hat{\theta})'$. Extensions to cases where the data are dependent have been given by Domowitz and White (1982), Newey and West (1987), and Andrews (1991d). It might be noted that for the LAD estimator $\Delta_i = -x_i \text{sgn}(y_i - x_i'\beta)$ (put $x_i = 1$ for the median), whereas B is $2(p\lim_{n\to\infty} n^{-1}\Sigma x_i x_i') f(0)$.

5.9.3 Sequential M-Estimators

It sometimes happens that a suitable function defining an M-estimator of θ involves another set of parameters, γ, for which an $n^{1/2}$ consistent estimator, $\tilde{\gamma}$, is readily available, leading to the determination of $\tilde{\theta}$ by either maximizing $n^{-1}\sum\rho(\theta, \tilde{\gamma})$ or solving the first-order conditions $n^{-1}\sum\rho_\theta(\hat{\theta}, \tilde{\gamma}) = 0$. This situation is sometimes referred to as two-step or sequential estimation of θ, and it has been extensively treated by Newey (1984) and Duncan (1987). Both papers are concerned with the sampling properties of $\hat{\theta}$ satisfying the first-order conditions $n^{-1}\sum\rho_\theta(\hat{\theta}, \tilde{\gamma}) = 0$, with the restriction that the $\tilde{\gamma}$ are regarded as also coming from a set of first-order conditions $n^{-1}\sum\zeta_i(\tilde{\gamma}) = 0$. As conditions for consistency and asymptotic normality of M-estimators are well documented, they propose to exploit that literature for establishing the properties of $\hat{\theta}$, by defining an expanded M-estimation problem in which $\delta' = (\theta', \gamma')$ is estimated by

$$\left[n^{-1}\sum\rho_\theta(\hat{\theta}, \tilde{\gamma}), n^{-1}\sum\zeta_i(\tilde{\gamma}) \right] = 0.$$

Clearly, the $\hat{\delta}$ from this program is identical to $(\hat{\theta}', \tilde{\gamma}')$. Accordingly, the properties of $\hat{\theta}$ are just those of $\hat{\delta}$, and the covariance matrix of $n^{1/2}(\hat{\theta} - \theta_0)$ can be found by partitioned inversion of that for $n^{1/2}(\hat{\delta} - \delta_0)$. Explicit formulae for the latter can be found in both the papers by Newey and by Duncan.

There is one instance in which the effects of the other parameters, γ, is easily accounted for, namely when $\tilde{\gamma}$ is an MLE and the first-order conditions defining $\tilde{\gamma}$ involve the scores, d_γ, from some log likelihood. Then

$$n^{-1/2} \sum \rho_\theta(\hat{\theta}, \tilde{\gamma}) = 0$$
$$= n^{-1/2} \sum \rho_\theta(\theta_0, \gamma_0)$$
$$+ \left(p \lim_{n \to \infty} n^{-1} \sum \rho_{\theta\theta} \right) n^{1/2}(\hat{\theta} - \theta_0)$$
$$+ \left(p \lim_{n \to \infty} n^{-1} \sum \rho_{\theta\gamma} \right) n^{1/2}(\tilde{\gamma} - \gamma_0) + o_p(1).$$
$$(5.52)$$

But $p \lim_{n \to \infty} n^{-1} \sum \rho_{\theta\gamma} = E[\partial\rho_\theta/\partial\gamma]'$ and, from the generalized information equality of Lemma 5.5 after replacing u_i by γ and ζ_i by ρ_θ, this equals $-E[\rho_\theta d_\gamma']$. Consequently, (5.52) becomes

$$0 = n^{-1/2} \sum \rho_\theta + E(\rho_{\theta\theta})n^{1/2}(\hat{\theta} - \theta_0)$$
$$- E(\rho_\theta d_\gamma')n^{1/2}(\tilde{\gamma} - \gamma_0) + o_p(1), \qquad (5.53)$$

leading to

$$n^{1/2}(\hat{\theta} - \theta_0) = -[E(\rho_{\theta\theta})]^{-1}$$
$$\times \left[n^{-1/2} \sum \rho_\theta - E(\rho_\theta d_\gamma')n^{1/2}(\tilde{\gamma} - \gamma_0) \right], \quad (5.54)$$

from which the dependence of the distribution of $n^{1/2}(\hat{\theta} - \theta_0)$ upon that of $n^{1/2}(\tilde{\gamma} - \gamma_0)$ is apparent. If $E(\rho_\theta d_\gamma') = 0$, it is possible to proceed as if γ was known to be $\tilde{\gamma}$, but in all other cases some adjustment must be performed.

Now, let $P' = [\rho_\theta(1) \ldots \rho_\theta(n)]$ and $D' = [d_\gamma(1) \ldots d_\gamma(n)]$ so that $E(\rho_\theta d_\gamma') = n^{-1}P'D + o_p(1)$. Furthermore, if $\tilde{\gamma}$ is an MLE, $\tilde{\gamma} - \gamma_0 = [\sum d_\gamma(i)d_\gamma(i)']^{-1} \sum d_\gamma(i) + o_p(1)$, giving

$$n^{1/2}(\tilde{\gamma} - \gamma_0) = (n^{-1}D'D)^{-1}n^{-1/2}D'J, \qquad (5.55)$$

where J is an $(n \times 1)$ matrix of units. Substituting (5.55) into (5.54) produces

$$n^{1/2}(\hat{\theta} - \theta) = -[E(\rho_{\theta\theta})]^{-1} \left[n^{-1/2}P'J \right]$$
$$+ \left[(n^{-1}P'D)(n^{-1}D'D)^{-1}n^{-1/2}D'J \right] \qquad (5.56)$$
$$= -[E(\rho_{\theta\theta})]^{-1} n^{-1/2} \left[P'(I - D(D'D)^{-1}D') \right] J$$
$$(5.57)$$

and $P'(I - D(D'D)^{-1}D')J$ is the sum of residuals, τ_i, from the regression of $\rho_\theta(i)$ against $d_\gamma(i)$. This result has been exploited by Newey (1985) and Tauchen (1985) in the simplification of diagnostic tests based upon MLEs; its implication here is that $n^{1/2}(\hat{\theta} - \theta_0)$ has covariance matrix $\{[(E\rho_{\theta\theta})^{-1}]E(\tau_i\tau_i')[E (\rho_{\theta\theta})]^{-1}\}^{-1}$, and the term $E(\tau_i\tau_i')$ can be consistently estimated by $n^{-1}\sum \tau_i\tau_i'$. For many of the sequential estimators discussed in later chapters $\tilde{\gamma}$ is an MLE, making this formula appropriate.

5.10 The Semiparametric Efficiency Bound for Moment-Based Estimators

A particular subclass of M-estimators are those in which the set of first-order conditions stem from a set of unconditional or conditional moment restrictions. For example the OLS estimator of β in (5.19) might be obtained from $E(x_i(y_i - x_i'\beta)) = 0$. Denote the vector of moment restrictions by either $E(\zeta_i) = 0$ or $E(\zeta_i|z_i) = 0$, where $\zeta_i = y_i - x_i'\beta$ in the regression case and $z_i = x_i$. Note that the conditional moment restriction is a much weaker restriction than the unconditional one. For M-estimators exploiting unconditional moment restrictions, the SP efficiency bound was derived by Hansen (1982) as

$$V_{SP}^u = \left\{ E(\zeta_\theta) \left[E(\zeta\zeta') \right]^{-1} E(\zeta_\theta') \right\}^{-1}, \tag{5.58}$$

where $\zeta_\theta = \partial\zeta_i/\partial\theta$ and $E(\zeta\zeta') = E(\zeta_i\zeta_i')$. When working with the conditional moments the bound was determined by Chamberlain (1987) to be

$$V_{SP}^c = \left\{ E(\zeta_\theta |z) \left[E(\zeta\zeta' |z) \right]^{-1} E(\zeta_\theta |z)' \right\}^{-1}, \tag{5.59}$$

where the expectation is taken conditional upon the random variable z_i.

The results in (5.58) and (5.59) characterize the variance of an optimal estimator *given a set of assumed moment conditions*, and need not produce estimators of θ that are optimal under different criteria. For example, if u_i in (5.19) is $\mathcal{N}(0, \sigma^2)$, the OLS estimator of β attains the SP efficiency bound given the restriction $E(x_i(y_i - x_i'\beta)) = 0$. However, when the density is known only to be symmetric it is possible to improve on this estimator by using the moment restriction $E(x_i\psi_i) = 0$, where ψ_i is the score of the density for u_i (see Section 5.5). This means that the issue is really one of finding the "best" set of moment restrictions. It is here that the SP bound literature is informative; as outlined in Section 5.4 the best estimator of θ is that which solves $\sum \tilde{d}_\theta(\hat{\theta}) = 0$, where $\tilde{d}_\theta$ are the efficient scores. When the error density in (5.19) is known to be $\mathcal{N}(0, \sigma^2)$, $\tilde{d}_\theta$ is just $-\sigma^{-2}x_i(y_i - x_i'\beta)$, and so $\hat{\beta}_{OLS}$ is the optimal estimator, but, under other densities for u_i, the efficient score will be different. Exactly what relationship exists between $\tilde{d}_\theta$ and moment restrictions will be explored in the next subsection.

*5.10.1 Approximating the SP Efficiency Bound by a Conditional
Moment Estimator*

Section 5.5.3 revealed the possibility of constructing an estimator of β in (5.19)
that attained the SP efficiency bound $E(\psi_i^2)E(x_i^2)$ from a set of moment restrictions of the form $E(x_i u_i^k) = 0$, k odd. This connection raises the question
of whether such a correspondence has wider validity. Newey (1993b) addressed
this issue, showing that it is possible to devise an estimator attaining the SP efficiency bound defined by the efficient scores if a sufficient number and variety
of moment conditions are employed. Although in practice it is best to introduce
such estimators in a specific context, it is helpful to understand the essential
logic of this argument, and a brief account follows.

Assuming that there are p parameters, θ, to be estimated, let ζ be a ($p \times
M$) matrix of restrictions so that $\zeta = [\zeta_1 \ldots \zeta_M]$ and $E(\zeta) = 0$. Again the "i"
subscript is ignored in derivations. Thus quantities such as $\tilde{d}_\theta$ are really $\tilde{d}_\theta(i)$.
Newey's argument rests upon repeated applications of the following lemma.

Lemma 5.6: $E(\partial\zeta_j/\partial\theta)' = -E(\zeta_j\tilde{d}_\theta')$, where $\tilde{d}_\theta$ is the efficient score
for θ.

Proof: By definition

$$E(\zeta_j) = 0 = \int \zeta_j f(\omega; \theta, \eta) \, d\omega = 0, \tag{5.60}$$

where ω are the random variables entering ζ_j and whose density $f(\cdot)$ depends
upon the parameters of interest θ as well as the nuisance parameters η char-
acterizing the parametric subfamily discussed in Section 5.4. Differentiating
(5.60) with respect to η gives

$$\int \zeta_j (\partial f/\partial\eta)' \, d\omega = 0 = E(\zeta_j d_\eta') = 0, \tag{5.61}$$

where d_η is the score for η. By definition the efficient score for θ is $\tilde{d}_\theta = d_\theta - Ad_\eta$,
with Ad_η representing the tangent set. Invoking Lemma 5.5, we get

$$E(\partial\zeta_j/\partial\theta)' = -E(\zeta_j d_\theta')$$
$$= -E(\zeta_j(\tilde{d}_\theta + Ad_\eta)') = -E(\zeta_j\tilde{d}_\theta')$$

from (5.61). Q.E.D.

Now since there are more restrictions here than parameters to estimate, con-
sider forming a linear combination of them, making $\xi = \sum_{k=1}^{N} \zeta_k \gamma_k$, and forming an M-estimator of θ, $\hat{\theta}$, from the first-order conditions $E(\xi) = 0$. The

covariance matrix of $n^{1/2}(\hat{\theta} - \theta)$ will be

$$(E\xi_\theta)^{-1} E(\xi\xi')(E\xi_\theta)^{-1}$$

$$= \left[E \sum_{k=1}^{N} (\partial\zeta_k/\partial\theta) \gamma_k \right]^{-1} E(\xi\xi') \left[E \sum_{k=1}^{N} (\partial\zeta_k/\partial\theta)' \gamma_k \right]^{-1}$$

$$= \left[E \left(\sum_{k=1}^{N} \zeta_k \gamma_k \tilde{d}_\theta' \right) \right]^{-1} E \left[\left(\sum_{k=1}^{N} \zeta_k \gamma_k \right) \left(\sum_{k=1}^{N} \zeta_k \gamma_k \right)' \right]$$

$$\times \left[E \left(\sum_{k=1}^{N} \zeta_k \gamma_k \tilde{d}_\theta \right)' \right]^{-1},$$

whereas the SP efficiency bound is

$$\left[E \left(\tilde{d}_\theta \tilde{d}_\theta' \right) \right]^{-1} \left[E \tilde{d}_\theta \tilde{d}_\theta' \right] \left[E \left(\tilde{d}_\theta \tilde{d}_\theta' \right) \right]^{-1}.$$

A comparison of the two formulae shows that the M-estimator $\hat{\theta}$ will attain the SP efficiency bound if $\tilde{d}_\theta \tilde{d}_\theta' \simeq \left(\sum_{k=1}^{N} \zeta_k \gamma_k \right) \tilde{d}_\theta'$, that is, there exists a linear combination of the ζ_k that perfectly predicts the efficient score $\tilde{d}_\theta$ in mean square. To illustrate this point return to the regression case of Section 5.5.3. There the ζ_k were $x_i u_i^{2(k-1)+1}$ while $\tilde{d}_\theta = x_i \psi_i$ and the requirement becomes that ψ_i be accurately approximated by a polynomial in u_i (Theorem 5.8).

In the presentation above γ_k was taken to be fixed and so the M-estimator, $\hat{\theta}$, is not feasible. However, it is possible to provide a consistent estimator of γ. Because we are attempting to linearly approximate $\tilde{d}_\theta$ by regressors $(\zeta_1), \ldots, (\zeta_N)$, one possibility is to replace γ by its OLS estimate from the regression of $\tilde{d}_\theta$ against $\zeta_1, \ldots \zeta_N$. Suppose for simplicity that there is a single θ and that $p = 1$, so that ζ is a $1 \times N$ vector. Then

$$\hat{\gamma} = \left[E(\zeta'\zeta) \right]^{-1} \left[E(\zeta'\tilde{d}_\theta) \right] = - \left[E(\zeta\zeta') \right]^{-1} \left[E(\partial\zeta'/\partial\theta) \right]$$

from Lemma 5.6, and both terms making up $\hat{\gamma}$ can be subsequently estimated by sample moments. What is crucial here is the ability to replace the unknown $E(\zeta'\tilde{d}_\theta)$ by the estimable $E(\partial\zeta'/\partial\theta)$. It was this step in Lemma 5.5 that led to the GMM approximation to the adaptive estimator of β. When $p > 1$, there will be a system of equations connecting $\tilde{d}_\theta$ and ζ and, as the regressors are different in each one, a seemingly unrelated regressions (SUR) estimator rather than an OLS estimator of γ would be appropriate.

Newey describes the construction of efficient estimators. He indicates the restrictions that must be placed upon the moments to get them to span the efficient scores and the rate at which M can tend to infinity. It does seem, however, that it is better to deal with these on a case-by-case basis. Ideally, it is desirable to work with the efficient score, and moment approximations appear only for computational reasons or because working with a subset of moments may be close to optimal and, yet, may provide a simple estimator. For this reason, a detailed description of Newey's results is not provided.

5.11 Applications

5.11.1 Semiparametric Estimation of a Heteroskedastic Model

One of the uses of nonparametric methods was to obtain efficient estimators of parameters in the presence of heteroskedasticity in the errors of unknown form. Hence, it is interesting to look at an application of the kernel estimator discussed in Section 5.3 as a solution to this problem. The model selected for illustrative purposes is taken from Ramanathan (1989) and constitutes data on domestic travel expenditure (EXPTRAV), population (POP), and income (INCOME) for the fifty United States plus the District of Columbia in the year 1984. Ramanathan (1989, Table 11-1) contains the data, and an analysis is given in his Chapter 11 concerning the presence of heteroskedasticity. It is assumed that there is a linear relation between EXPTRAV and INCOME, and he presents estimates of the unknown coefficients when the error variance σ_i^2 is assumed to be of the form $\sigma_i^2 = \sigma^2 POP_i^2$ (p. 460).

Let $\hat{u}_i$ be the OLS residuals from the regression of $EXPTRAV_i$ against a constant and $INCOME_i$. Assuming that σ_i^2 is some function of POP_i, a nonparametric estimate is available from (3.42). A Gaussian kernel was selected with a window width set according to (3.61). Figure 5.1 presents a plot of the nonparametric variance estimate against all values of POP_i in the data. For comparison purposes the figure also shows the predictions from the regressions of $\hat{u}_i^2$ against POP_i^2 and $\hat{u}_i^2$ against unity, POP_i and POP_i^2. There seems little doubt that the relation $\sigma_i^2 = \sigma^2 POP_i^2$ is a misspecification and that some centered relation of the form $\sigma_i^2 = \sigma^2(POP_i - \mu)^2$ is needed; the last induces terms such as POP_i and POP_i^2 into the relation for σ_i^2. But even this expanded specification does not appear entirely adequate, failing to capture the sharp peak in the relation between σ_i^2 and POP_i. To emphasize this fact the R^2 between the three estimates of σ_i^2 and $\hat{u}_i^2$ were .33 (nonparametric), .12 (POP_i/POP_i^2), and .04 (POP_i^2 alone); the nonparametric estimate accounts for substantially more of the variability of the $\hat{u}_i^2$ than is done by the two parametric alternatives that are common in the literature.

Table 5.3 presents estimates of the coefficients in the travel expenditure/income relation along with estimated standard errors when the GLS estimator is used with σ_i^2 either estimated nonparametrically or as $\sigma_i^2 = \sigma^2 POP_i^2$. For the constant (CNST) term the standard errors are close, but for the slope coefficient on income the use of a more flexible specification of σ_i^2 has reduced the standard

Table 5.3. *Efficient semiparametric estimation of a travel expenditures model.*

Coefficient estimates	Parametric $\hat{\sigma}_i^{2^a}$	Nonparametric $\hat{\sigma}_i^{2^b}$
CNST	.5540	.2762
INCOME	.0644	.0655
Standard Error		
CNST	.2544	.2360
INCOME	.0158	.0039

Notes: [a]The results in the first column agree with Ramanathan (1989, p. 460).
[b]The second column is computed using the GLS formula for $\hat{\beta}$, $\left(\sum x_i x_i' \hat{\sigma}_i^{-2} \right)^{-1} \left(\sum x_i y_i \hat{\sigma}_i^{-2} \right)$, with $\hat{\sigma}_i^2$ estimated nonparametrically as described in the text and where $\left(\sum x_i x_i' \hat{\sigma}_i^{-2} \right)^{-1}$ are the estimated standard errors.
Source: Data are taken from Table 11-1 of Ramanathan (1989).

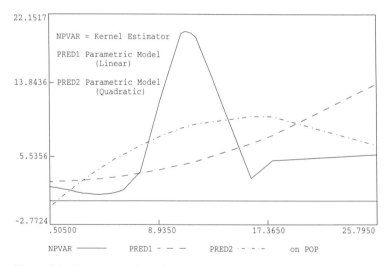

Figure 5.1. Nonparametric and parametric estimates of conditional variance of travel expenditures model.

error by some 400%. An attempt was made to compare the nonparametric-based estimate of β with one in which σ_i^2 is parameterized as a function of POP_i and POP_i^2. However, the first twelve predictions from the regression of $\hat{u}_i^2$ against unity, POP_i, and POP_i^2, are negative making the implied $\hat{\sigma}_i^2$ negative. If the

GLS regression is done only over the 13–51 sample, the standard errors on the income term are .0049 (parametric $\hat{\sigma}_i^2$) and .0038 (nonparametric $\hat{\sigma}_i^2$), showing an improvement in efficiency of around 50%. Thus, this estimator seems quite an attractive one if there is known to be heteroskedasticity in a model. Nevertheless, it is clear that the determinants of σ_i^2 will need to be limited in number. Many cross-section models have many regressors in x_i, and it would be impossible to get a good nonparametric estimate of σ_i^2 unless it is assumed to depend only upon a small number of the x_i (or other variables z_i).

5.11.2   Adaptive Estimation of a Model of House Prices

A comparison of the adaptive estimators discussed in Sections 5.5.2 and 5.5.3 seems useful. To this end we selected a data set on housing prices in San Diego (Ramanathan, 1989, Table 6.5, pp. 276–80). Ramanathan examines a number of models for these data. His model D (p. 309) is the basis for this investigation except that the variables FENCE and LNDRY are omitted as they were not significant in his Table 7.3.[11] These deletions leave a linear equation explaining house prices as a function of some twelve variables (including a constant). A test for normality of the errors (Bera and Jarque, 1981; Bowman and Shenton, 1975) gives a $\chi^2(2)$ of 83.7028. Table 5.4 provides OLS estimates of the coefficients along with their standard errors. Computing the efficiency index in Theorem 5.4 with a Gaussian kernel and window width set to that in (2.49), and differentiating $\hat{f}$ to obtain the derivative, gives a value of 1.76, indicating a substantial potential efficiency gain over OLS.

Table 5.4 presents estimates of the coefficients and their standard errors for the OLS, kernel-based adaptive estimator of Section 5.5.2, and the GMM estimator in Section 5.5.3. Standard errors are all heteroskedastic consistent.[12] The kernel-based adaptive estimator is calculated from (5.33), with the OLS estimator as $\tilde{\beta}$ and with $\hat{\psi}_i$ computed as mentioned above in the calculation of the efficiency ratio. To get robust estimates of the standard errors for $n^{1/2}(\hat{\beta}_{2SNP} - \beta)$ we use $\widehat{\mathcal{I}}_{\beta\beta}^{-1}\left(n^{-1}\sum x_i x_i' \hat{\psi}_i^2\right)\widehat{\mathcal{I}}_{\beta\beta}^{-1}$. GMM estimates of β are found by exploiting the orthogonality relations $E(x_i u_i) = 0$, $E(x_i u_i^3) = 0$; this yields twenty-four first-order conditions. Heteroskedastic-consistent standard errors are found as described in White (1982). Computations for the kernel-based estimator were done with a program written in GAUSS, whereas the GMM estimator was an adaption of a GAUSS program by David Runkle and Greg Leonard.

---

[11] The variables are described in Ramanathan. We will use his mnemonics as these are self-explanatory. One modification is that logs are taken to base ten rather than the natural log.

[12] There was evidence of heteroskedasticity in the residuals of the OLS regression. Since it is hard to discriminate between a lack of nonnormality and heteroskedasticity it seemed wise to make the computations robust to the latter.

Table 5.4. *Parameter estimates model of San Diego house prices.*

	OLS[a]	OLS/SE[b]	KER[c]	KER/SE	GMM[d]	GMM/SE[e]
SQFT	.243	.078	.246	.067	.559	.044
YARD	.008	.002	.007	.002	.005	.002
POOL	31.01	17.31	6.87	12.16	43.14	13.05
LAJOLLA	102.26	15.85	81.90	11.65	82.40	15.52
BATHS	25.89	22.20	−4.01	12.43	58.43	9.41
FIREPL	28.78	18.10	22.10	11.75	27.94	15.81
IRREG	45.31	20.22	35.07	8.88	69.30	13.62
SPRINK	48.62	14.87	41.88	12.55	96.40	13.61
VIEW	28.94	15.99	36.44	8.82	58.65	17.07
LSQFT	−964.00	394.27	−796.92	285.40	−2535.5	222.85
LYARD	95.49	47.92	−95.65	55.41	8.65	57.84
CNST	2997.3	1168.2	2548.4	800.66	7026.0	697.2

[a] OLS parameter estimates.
[b] Heteroskedastic consistent standard error for OLS.
[c] Kernel adaptive estimator.
[d] Optimal GMM estimator of coefficients using $E(x_i u_i) = 0$, $E\left(x_i u_i^3\right) = 0$.
[e] Heteroskedastic consistent standard errors for GMM.

Overall there does appear to be an efficiency gain over the OLS estimator, ranging from very small for the "YARD" coefficient to large for "IRREG." Only in one instance (LYARD) was the OLS variance estimate smaller than either of the adaptive estimators. Because of the heteroskedasticity adjustment, and the fact that there are only 59 observations, such a difference could easily arise due to sampling variation. With a program such as GAUSS it is simple to produce the estimates in Table 5.4, even when there are quite a large number of coefficients. Whether the efficiency gains were worth the effort is more problematical. Even though the test statistic for normality is quite high, the projected differences in standard errors (from the efficiency index) are only around 30% and, with only a few exceptions, that seems to have been typical of the actual differences. Accordingly, if this index proves to be a reliable indicator of efficiency gains, it would seem to be useful to compute it before going to the expense of doing adaptive estimation.

5.11.3 *Review of Other Applications*

Engle et al. (1986) analyzed the model (5.1) to estimate the effects of temperature (x_{2i}) on electricity demand (y); x_{1i} contained price and income among other regressors. Stock (1989) uses (5.1) to estimate the effect of the proximity of toxic waste on house prices. The effects of temperature and toxic waste in these two studies are highly nonlinear, though the effects of other variables (x_{1i}) are assumed to be linear. Given that there are a large number of variables in these two studies, nonparametric estimation would have a dimensionality problem, leading to the partially linear specification. In another study Anglin and Gencay (1996) investigate the effect of quality of a house on the price of a house in Windsor, Canada. They find the predictions from their semiparametric model to be better than those obtained from the linear parametric model and Box–Cox models. Other applications of (5.1) include: Roy's (1997) Indian panel data estimation where y is calorie intake, x_{2i} is income and x_{1i} includes variables such as education, age and sex; Ullah and Mundra's (1998) cross country analysis of the impact of immigration (x_{2i}) on U.S. exports or imports (y) with other variables x_{1i} consisting of population size, gross domestic product etc., Khanna et al.'s (1998) analysis of the cost efficiency (y) of public and private sector owned electricity firms in terms of input prices (x_{2i}) and factors (x_{1i}) such as age, ownership etc; and Kneisner and Li's (1996) analysis of labor supply models.

There are some applications on the semiparametric estimation of the models of type (5.15) where y_i depends on x_i and regressors z_i that need to be generated by a given information set. In Barro (1977) z_i represents an expectation variable; in Lee (1988) it is a "surprise" variable; and in Pagan and Ullah (1988) it is a conditional variance (volatility). In a recent study Appelbaum and Ullah (1998) look into the effects of higher (third and fourth) moments of an unknown output price distribution on the production decision of several U.S. manufacturing industries. The vector z_i in their case contains conditional second, third, and fourth moments that have been estimated nonparametrically (see Chapter 3).

Applications of the linear regression model (5.19) with unknown form of heteroskedasticity have also appeared in the literature; see, for example, Singh et al. (1987), Rilstone (1991c), Melenberg and Van Soest (1996), Altug and Miller (1998), and Whistler (1988). For the estimation of (5.17) under unknown density see Engle and Gonzalez-Rivera (1991), Gallant and Tauchen (1989), and Gallant et al. (1991). Finally, for an extensive application of robust M-estimators see Deaton (1997).

As mentioned earlier, quantile regression (i.e., an M-estimator minimizing $\sum_{i=1}^{n}(\alpha - I[(y_i - x_i'\beta) < 0])(y_i - x_i'\beta)$ at the α quantile) has become popular in recent years, particularly when it is felt that the conditional mean does not adequately portray the impact of values of x_i upon y_i. The conditional density would give a complete picture but this can be very demanding upon observations, so that a useful substitute is to model the quantiles of the conditional density, leading to the quantile regression estimator, where it is assumed that the conditional quantile is linear in the x_i. Buchinsky (1994) applies this estimator to study shifts in the conditional distribution of earnings as a function of various characteristics over time, whereas Conley and Galenson (1994) model the relationship between wealth and individual characteristics using a sample of residents of Chicago from the 1860 census. Quantile estimation was especially valuable here as it is known that the wealth data seem to be left censored and this distorts the relationship found by linear regression, whereas estimation at quantiles above this censoring point is robust to such an effect.

6 Semiparametric and Nonparametric Estimation of Simultaneous Equation Models

6.1 Introduction

In earlier chapters we have considered single-equation economic models where a dependent variable is a function of other variables. The basic assumption used in these models was that the right-hand side variables X are independent of the error term in the equation and therefore are not affected by the dependent variable Y. We did not allow for the possibility of a reverse causality, or feedback, where Y and X were jointly determined (endogenous) variables. There are a large number of economic models where some of the right-hand side variables are endogenous and these are referred to as a system of simultaneous equations models. Familiar examples are models of markets and the macro economy, as well as sets of factor demand equations. In all of these models, whether we are considering a single equation or a system as a whole, some of the right-hand side variables will be endogenous and hence correlated with the error term. For an overview of such system models, see Judge et al. (1985). In such systems direct application of the semiparametric and nonparametric regression estimators of Chapters 3 to 5 would lead to inconsistent estimators. Consequently, this chapter concentrates upon the modifications needed to those estimators when applied to random variables making up a system.

A primary division in the chapter is between those cases in which only a vector of parameters is unknown within the system and those when the system cannot be given a parametric form. In the first instance one wishes to devise an SP estimator of the parameters. Within this category a second division arises, distinguishing between estimators of the parameters of a single equation and those in the system as a whole. In each instance, a discussion is provided of popular parametric estimators followed by their semiparametric analogues. Thus, Section 6.2 considers single-equation SP estimation methods while Section 6.3 outlines those advocated for complete systems. Semiparametric instrumental variable estimators turn out to be what is needed and these are consistent; efficiency is attained by nonparametrically computing the unknown expectation

254

that defines the optimal instrument. As there are many ways of computing the latter a large range of proposals can be found in the literature. In some cases it is possible to define the SP efficiency bound and to provide a generalized method of moments (GMM) estimator that would attain this. Section 6.4 looks at Monte Carlo evidence on the performance of the estimators. Section 6.5 turns to the issues that arise when the system cannot be given a parametric form.

6.2 Single-Equation Estimators

Let us consider a general nonlinear structural equation

$$g_i(\beta) = g(z_i, \beta) = u_i, \qquad i = 1, \ldots, n, \tag{6.1}$$

where $g(\ )$ is a known function, $z_i = (y_i, x_{1i})$ contains y_i, a vector of endogenous variables that are correlated with the disturbances u_i, and x_{1i}, a vector of exogenous variables, while β is a $q_1 \times 1$ vector of unknown parameters. The error term u_i is i.i.d. such that

$$E(u_i|x_i) = 0, \qquad E\left(u_i^2|x_i\right) = \sigma^2, \tag{6.2}$$

where x_i is a vector of p "instrumental variables" that include x_{1i}. For convenience we have assumed homoskedastic disturbances, although it is not necessary for the asymptotic results.

The model (6.1) does not specify the distribution of y_i. In fact, Equation (6.1) may be one of many structural equations of an economic model that simultaneously define the distribution of y_i, but, except for Section 6.3, any parameters in other equations will not be regarded as of interest for estimation purposes. As a special case, the model in (6.1) might be

$$y_{1i} - g_1(y_{2i}, x_{1i}, \beta) = g(z_i, \beta) = u_i, \tag{6.3}$$

where y_i encompasses the endogenous variables y_{1i}, y_{2i}. Alternatively, (6.1) might be the first equation of the following model set out in Goldfeld and Quandt (1968), which has been a mainstay of research into the properties of estimators of nonlinear simultaneous equation systems:

$$y_{1i} = e^{y_{2i}} \beta_1 + \beta_2 x_{1i} + u_i, \tag{6.4}$$
$$y_{2i} = \alpha_1 + \alpha_2 \log y_{1i} + \alpha_3 x_{1i} + u_{2i}, \tag{6.5}$$

where y_{1i}, y_{2i}, and x_{1i} are scalar variables and α_j and β_j are parameters. This equation is nonlinear in variables only, and the problem of estimation arises because the reduced forms for y_1 and y_2 cannot be obtained explicitly.

6.2.1   Parametric Estimation

It is well known that nonlinear least squares (NLLS) on (6.1) generally lead
to inconsistent estimates of the parameter vector β, owing to the dependence
of y_i on u_i; see Kelejian (1971) and Zellner et al. (1965). In light of this difficulty, Amemiya (1974, 1977, 1983), Kelejian (1971), Jorgenson and Laffont
(1974), and Berndt et al. (1974), among others, developed nonlinear instrumental variable (NLIV) or nonlinear two-stage least squares (NL2SLS) methods for
estimating β. Such methods are motivated by the conditional moment restric-
tion of (6.2), $E(u_i|x_i) = E(g_i(\beta)|x_i) = 0$, and they can be obtained as Hansen's
(1982) GMM estimators, also see Ch. 5. Suppose that $w_i = [w_{1i}, \ldots, w_{ri}]'$ is
an $r \times 1$ ($r \geq q_1$) vector formed from x_i. In view of (6.2), the orthogonality
condition $E[w_i u_i] = E[w_i g_i(\beta)] = 0$ holds. If $r = q_1$, the GMM estimator of β,
$\hat{\beta}$, can therefore be obtained by imposing the sample analogue of this population
moment condition; that is, $\hat{\beta}$ is the solution to

$$\psi(\hat{\beta}) = \frac{1}{n} \sum_{i=1}^{n} w_i g_i(\hat{\beta}) = 0. \tag{6.6}$$

When there are more moment conditions than parameters to estimate, $\hat{\beta}$ is
obtained by minimizing the quadratic form

$$\left[n^{-1} \sum_{i=1}^{n} w_i g_i \right]' \left[\text{var} \left(n^{-1} \sum_{i=1}^{n} w_i g_i \right) \right]^{-1} \left[n^{-1} \sum_{i=1}^{n} w_i g_i \right].$$

With independence and homoskedasticity of u_i, $\text{var} \left(n^{-1} \sum_{i=1}^{n} w_i g_i \right)$ is proportional to $Q = n^{-1} \sum_{i=1}^{n} w_i w_i'$, leading one to minimize

$$S(\beta) = \psi'(\beta) Q^{-1} \psi(\beta). \tag{6.7}$$

This GMM estimator is the well-known NLIV estimator (e.g., Amemiya, 1977)
or the Generalized Instrumental Variables Estimator (GIVE) of Sargan (1958).

The asymptotic properties of the estimator $\hat{\beta}$, the minimizer of (6.7), have
been worked out by Amemiya (1974, 1977); Burguete, Gallant, and Souza
(1982); and Hansen (1982) among others. Such estimators attain the semiparametric efficiency bound given in (5.58), that is, $n^{1/2}(\hat{\beta} - \beta)$ will have asymptotic
variance

$$V(\hat{\beta}) = \sigma^2 \left[\left(E g_1^{(1)}(\beta) w_1' \right) \left(E w_1 w_1' \right)^{-1} \left(E w_1 g_1^{(1)}(\beta) \right) \right]^{-1}, \tag{6.8}$$

where $g_i^{(1)}(\beta) = g^{(1)}(z_i, \beta)$ is

$$g_i^{(1)}(\beta) = \partial g_i(\beta)/\partial \beta. \tag{6.9}$$

Although the optimal estimator of β is GMM when w_i are fixed, there will be different efficiencies for GMM estimators as the nature of w_i is varied. Various choices of w_i have been discussed in Amemiya (1975, 1983) and Bowden and Turkington (1981). For example, Kelejian (1971) suggests that they be constructed from the low order powers of the predetermined variables of the system; when estimating (6.4), and specifically β_1, Kelejian would construct w_i as the predictions of $e^{y_{2i}}$ in a regression of $e^{y_{2i}}$ on the powers of x_i. Bowden and Turkington suggested that better instruments can be obtained by first regressing the endogenous variables (for example y_{2i} in (6.4)) on a polynomial of the exogenous variables, taking the predictions $\hat{y}_{2i}$, and forming w_i as $e^{\hat{y}_{2i}}$. Amemiya (1975, 1983) referred to the "best" instrumental variable (BIV) estimator as that setting w_i to

$$w_i^* = m(x_i, \beta) = m_i(\beta) = E\big(g_i^{(1)}(\beta)|x_i\big). \tag{6.10}$$

Proofs of this fact are available in Amemiya (1974) and, under more general conditions, in Hansen (1982). Under this choice of w_i, the variance of the BIV estimator $\hat{\beta}^*$ follows from (6.8) as

$$V(\hat{\beta}^*) = \sigma^2 \big(E w_i^* w_i^{*\prime}\big)^{-1} = \sigma^2 \big[E m_1(\beta) m_1'(\beta)\big]^{-1} = V_{BIV}. \tag{6.11}$$

Tauchen (1986) points out that, for w_i^* in (6.10), $q_1 = r$; that is, the number of moment conditions has now been reduced to exactly the number of parameters. Hence the BIV estimator $\hat{\beta}^*$ can be directly defined as the solution of (6.6) with w_i^* as w_i. Viewing $\hat{\beta}^*$ in this framework helps us to develop the asymptotic distribution results in a simpler way. This is because the first-order conditions, $n^{-1}\sum w_i^* g_i(\hat{\beta}^*) = 0$, which produce $\hat{\beta}^*$, can be linearized as

$$0 = n^{-1} \sum w_i^* g_i(\hat{\beta}^*)$$
$$= n^{-1} \sum w_i^* g_i(\beta) + n^{-1}\left(\sum w_i^* g_i^{(1)\prime}(\beta)\right)(\hat{\beta}^* - \beta) + o_p(n^{-1/2}), \tag{6.12}$$

implying

$$n^{1/2}(\hat{\beta}^* - \beta) = -\left(n^{-1}\sum w_i^* g_i^{(1)\prime}(\beta)\right)^{-1}$$
$$\times n^{-1/2} \sum w_i^* g_i(\beta) + o_p(1). \tag{6.13}$$

The asymptotic distribution of $\hat{\beta}^*$ can then be shown to be normal with variance in (6.11) by applying standard central limit theorems to the right-hand side.

The problem with the BIV estimator is that the form of $m_i(\beta)$ is rarely, if ever, known. For example, for (6.4), $g_i^{(1)} = [e^{y_{2i}} \ x_{1i}]'$, $i = 1, \dots, n$, and $m_i(\beta) = [E(e^{y_{2i}}|x_{1i}) \ x_{1i}]'$ is not known. Some of the estimators previously discussed (e.g., those by Kelejian and Bowden and Turkington), may be viewed as approximating m_i by the use of finite-order polynomials in x_i. Other methods, such as the residual-based procedure of Brown and Mariano (1984), find the conditional expectation by computer simulation, using estimated residuals $\hat{u}_i$, constructed from some initial consistent estimator of β, as random numbers. In Section 5.10.1 it was pointed out that one might approximate the SP efficiency bound by expanding the number of moment conditions, and in the application of Section 5.5.3 that meant approximating the density score either by a kernel estimator or by a polynomial whose order expanded with sample size. It should be no surprise therefore that a similar outcome is observed here as exemplified in the semiparametric estimators of Newey (1990a) and Rilstone (1989, 1992b). Succeeding sections of this chapter are devoted to exploring these estimators.

6.2.2   Rilstone's Semiparametric Two-Stage Least Squares Estimator

As just mentioned, the objective is to nonparametrically estimate $m_i(\beta)$ for the purpose of estimating β semiparametrically. To this end let us form the regression

$$g_i^{(1)}(\beta) = E\left(g_i^{(1)}(\beta)|x_i\right) + \epsilon_i = m_i(\beta) + \epsilon_i, \tag{6.14}$$

where $E(\epsilon_i|x_i) = 0$, $i = 1, \ldots, n$. The regression in (6.14)) is similar to the nonparametric regression in (3.1) of Chapter 3.[1] Thus, from Sections 3.2.2 and 3.2.3, the kernel estimator is

$$\hat{m}_i(\beta) = \frac{\hat{\phi}_i(\beta)}{\hat{f}_i}, \tag{6.15}$$

where

$$\hat{\phi}_i(\beta) = (nh^p)^{-1} \sum_j K((x_j - x_i)/h) g_j^{(1)}(\beta),$$

$$\hat{f}_i = (nh^p)^{-1} \sum_j K((x_j - x_i)/h)),$$

and h is the window width. Of course, one could consider any member of the general class of nonparametric regression estimators described in Section 3.2.4. Newey (1990b), for example, considers nearest neighbor estimation and this is taken up in the following section. Here, we consider the kernel estimator for

---

[1] In contrast to (3.1), however, the dependent variable $g^{(1)}(\beta)$ in (6.14) is a function of random variables y_i, x_i and β unless g is linear. Moreover, we now need $E|g^{(1)}(\beta)| < \infty$, which may not be easy to verify (recall that $E|y| < \infty$ is needed for (3.1)).

its simplicity and implementability. A trimmed version of (6.15) can be written as

$$\hat{m}_i(\beta) = \frac{\hat{\phi}_i(\beta)}{\hat{f}_i^*},$$ (6.16)

where $f_i^* = \max\{\hat{f}_i, b\}$ and $b = b_n \to 0$ as $n \to \infty$; see Chapter 4.

Using $w_i = \hat{m}_i(\beta)$ in (6.6) the semiparametric BIV estimator, SPBIV, is the solution $\beta = \tilde{\beta}$ such that

$$\psi(\tilde{\beta}) = \frac{1}{n}\sum_{i=1}^{n} \hat{m}_i(\tilde{\beta})g_i(\tilde{\beta}) = 0.$$ (6.17)

The estimator $\tilde{\beta}$ is due to Rilstone (1989, 1992b) and it can also be regarded as the SP analogue of the two-stage least squares estimator (SP2SLS).

The consistency and asymptotic normality of the SPBIV estimator has been established in Rilstone (1989, 1992b) by imposing regularity conditions on the joint density functions of the i.i.d random variables $\{x_i, u_i\}$ and some functionals of these densities. Kernels considered were of higher (sth) order, as described in Section 2.7.2, and the window width was constrained to satisfy

$$nh^p \to \infty \quad \text{and} \quad nh^{2s} \to 0 \quad \text{as} \quad n \to \infty.$$ (6.18)

Under these conditions Rilstone has shown that, as $n \to \infty$,

$$\sqrt{n}(\tilde{\beta} - \beta) \sim \mathcal{N}(0, V_{BIV}),$$ (6.19)

where

$$V_{BIV} = \sigma^2\left[E\left(m_1(\beta)m_1'(\beta)\right)\right]^{-1}$$

can be consistently estimated by

$$\hat{V}_{BIV} = \hat{\sigma}^2\left(n^{-1}\sum \hat{m}_i(\tilde{\beta})\hat{m}_i(\tilde{\beta})'\right)^{-1},$$

and $\hat{\sigma}^2 = n^{-1}\sum g_i^2(\tilde{\beta})$.

Rilstone provides a detailed proof of (6.19) by a direct approach. Here we can heuristically establish it by appeal to the results in Chapter 5. Suppose $g_i(\beta)$ was linear in β. Then $\hat{m}_i(\beta)$ are being used as instruments for the variables associated with β. Such a scenario was discussed in Section 5.2.3, and it was observed there that the situation was one in which the asymptotic independence condition used by Andrews (1994) (condition B(ii) of Lemma 5.1) holds. To recap this result, it is sufficient that $E[(\tau_i - m_i)g_i^{(1)}(\beta)] = 0$, where τ_i is an arbitrary function of x_i. But this is true by assumption. Notice that linearity of $g_i(\beta)$ in β is not needed for asymptotic independence to pertain. In the nonlinear case the variable being instrumented is $g_i^{(1)}$, but the condition that must hold remains the same as for the linear case. Consequently, one can equate $\hat{m}_i$ with m_i when working out the asymptotic theory, explaining why the asymptotic variance is just that in (6.11).

6.3 Systems Estimation

Now we consider the estimation of a complete system of equations, for example, the estimation of (6.4) and (6.5) together. For this purpose we treat (6.1) as the representation of a general system of k nonlinear structural equations

$$g_i(\beta) = g(z_i, \beta) = u_i, \qquad i = 1, \ldots, n, \qquad (6.20)$$

which now has $g(z_i, \beta)$ as a $k \times 1$ vector of errors that depends on a data vector z and a $q \times 1$ vector of parameters β appearing in the k equations. It will be assumed throughout that $z_i = (y_i', x_i')'$, where y_i is a k-vector of endogenous variables and x_i is a vector of p exogenous variables (instrumental variables). Furthermore, the k-vector $u_i = [u_{1i} \ldots u_{ki}]'$ is an i.i.d. vector of random variables such that $E(u_i|x_i) = 0$ and $E(u_i u_i'|x_i) = \Omega$. The model (6.4)–(6.5) is a special case of (6.20) with $k = 2$, $p = 2$, and $q = 5$. Also, the number of endogenous variables is the same as the number of equations. In the econometrics literature such a model is known as a "full information" model. Limited information models are those where there are fewer equations in (6.20) than elements of y.

There are no straightforward methods of checking the identification of the nonlinear model in (6.20). Some work in this area can be found in Fisher (1966), Rothenberg (1971), Brown (1983), and more recently in Roehrig (1988). However, as Amemiya (1983) has indicated, "non-linearity generally helps rather than hampers identification, so that, for example, the number of excluded exogenous variables in a given equation need not be greater than or equal to the number of parameters of the same equation in a non-linear model."

6.3.1 A Parametric Estimator

Estimation of the system (6.20) can be done in the same way as for the single-equation case of Section 6.2, except for the need to allow for the presence of the cross-equation covariance matrix Ω. Thus, the GMM-based class of parametric instrumental variable estimators of β is now defined as minimizing

$$S(\beta) = \psi'(\beta) Q^{-1} \psi(\beta), \qquad (6.21)$$

where $\psi(\beta) = n^{-1} \sum W_i \hat{\Omega}^{-1} g_i(\beta)$ and $Q = n^{-1} \sum W_i \hat{\Omega}^{-1} W_i'$; W_i is an $r \times k$, $r \geq q$, matrix of instruments and $\hat{\Omega} = \hat{\Omega}(\tilde{\beta}) = n^{-1} \sum g_i(\tilde{\beta}) g_i(\tilde{\beta})'$, with $\tilde{\beta}$ as the SPBIV or SP2SLS of each equation. Subject to regularity conditions the resulting estimator is asymptotically normal with covariance matrix (see

Amemiya, 1977)

$$\left[E\left(G_1^{(1)}(\beta)\Omega^{-1}W_1'\right)\left(EW_1\Omega^{-1}W_1'\right)^{-1}E\left(W_1\Omega^{-1}G_1^{(1)}(\beta)'\right)\right]^{-1},$$

$$(6.22)$$

where $G_1^{(1)}(\beta)$ is a $k \times r$ matrix of the derivatives of $g_1(\beta)$ with respect to β'. Expression (6.22) is minimized, as in the single-equation case, by selecting

$$W_i^* = M(x_i, \beta) = M_i(\beta) = E\left[G_i^{(1)'}(\beta)\big|x_i\right]. \qquad (6.23)$$

With this optimal W_i^* the number of moment conditions becomes the same as the number of parameters to be estimated ($r = q$) and the covariance matrix in (6.22) reduces to

$$V = \left(EM_1(\beta)\Omega^{-1}M_1'(\beta)\right)^{-1}. \qquad (6.24)$$

Since $q = r$ the best three-stage least squares (3SLS) parametric estimator can be considered to be the solution of

$$\psi(\hat{\beta}) = \frac{1}{n}\sum_{i=1}^{n} M_i(\hat{\beta})\hat{\Omega}^{-1}g_i(\hat{\beta}) = 0. \qquad (6.25)$$

6.3.2 The SP3SLS Estimator

The SP3SLS estimator of β in (6.20) can be obtained in the same way as the SPBIV estimator in the single-equation case of Section 6.2. Essentially $\hat{M}(\beta)$ must be obtained by some nonparametric estimation method. If we substitute this into (6.25), the SP3SLS estimator β^* becomes the solution of

$$\hat{\psi}(\beta^*) = n^{-1}\sum \hat{M}_i(\beta^*)\hat{\Omega}^{-1}g_i(\beta^*) = 0.$$

Under some regularity conditions

$$\sqrt{n}(\beta^* - \beta) \to \mathcal{N}(0, V), \qquad (6.26)$$

where

$$\hat{V} = \hat{V}(\beta^*) = \left[n^{-1}\sum \hat{M}_i(\beta^*)\hat{\Omega}^{-1}\hat{M}_i'(\beta^*)\right]^{-1}$$

is a consistent estimator of V. The proof of (6.26) is similar to the proof of (6.19) in the single-equation case, after making an allowance for the fact that Ω must be replaced by a consistent estimator, $\hat{\Omega}$. For details, see Rilstone (1989, 1992b).

One important difference between SPBIV in the single-equation and system cases is that, although SPBIV for a single equation did not require any preliminary estimate of β, SPBIV for the system case does need a consistent preliminary estimator of $\tilde{\beta}$ in order to get $\hat{\Omega}$. An alternative generalization would be to obtain the estimate of β that solves $n^{-1} \sum \hat{M}_i(\beta)\hat{\Omega}^{-1}(\beta)g_i(\beta) = 0$, as this may give better finite-sample performance.

6.3.3 Newey's Estimator

Newey (1990b), independently of Rilstone (1989), considers a closely related SP3SLS estimator of β in (6.20). He uses a preliminary consistent estimator $\tilde{\beta}$ in both $\hat{M}_i(\tilde{\beta}) = \hat{M}(x_i)$ and $\hat{\Omega}$, takes the sample moment function as $\hat{\psi}(\beta) = n^{-1} \sum \hat{M}_i(\tilde{\beta})\hat{\Omega}^{-1}g_i(\beta)$, and defines an SPBIV estimator as that β for which $S(\beta) = \hat{\psi}(\beta)'\hat{\psi}(\beta)$ is minimized. Thus Newey's moment function is different from Rilstone's in two respects. First, Newey uses a preliminary estimator for both $\hat{\Omega}$ and $\hat{M}_i(\beta)$, whereas Rilstone uses one for $\hat{\Omega}$ only. For a single-equation case ($k = 1$), however, Ω becomes an irrelevant scaling factor, so that the only difference lies in the construction of $\hat{m}_i(\beta)$. Second, Newey adopts the nearest neighbor and series methods as his nonparametric techniques for estimating $M_i(\beta)$. However, since the limiting distribution of Newey's BIV is the same as that in (6.26), the above differences do not have any effect on the asymptotic efficiency of the two estimators. Such an equivalence might not extend to finite-sample efficiency however; see Section 6.4.

To prove asymptotic results Newey considers the linearized version of the instrumental variable estimator based on estimated optimal instruments. One Gauss–Newton step from $\tilde{\beta}$ toward the solution of $\sum \hat{M}_i(\tilde{\beta})\hat{\Omega}^{-1}g_i(\beta_N^*) = 0$ is

$$\beta_N^* = \tilde{\beta} - \left[\sum_{i=1}^n \hat{M}_i(\tilde{\beta})\hat{\Omega}^{-1}G_i^{(1)\prime}(\tilde{\beta}) \right]^{-1} \sum_{i=1}^n \hat{M}_i(\tilde{\beta})\hat{\Omega}^{-1}g(\tilde{\beta}), \quad (6.27)$$

where $\tilde{\beta}$ is the initial IV estimator and M_i and $G_i^{(1)}$ are as defined above; N in β_N^* refers to Newey's estimator. Then the details of the conditions under which consistency and asymptotic normality are obtained depend upon the nonparametric estimator chosen.

A nearest neighbor estimate of $M_i(\tilde{\beta})$ can be obtained in the following way. Let $m_i(\tilde{\beta})$ be a component of $M_i(\tilde{\beta})$ and $g_i^{(1)}(\tilde{\beta})$ be a component of $G_i^{(1)}(\tilde{\beta})$. Then a nearest neighbor estimator of $m_i(\tilde{\beta})$ is

$$\hat{m}_i(\tilde{\beta}) = \sum_{j=1}^n \omega_{ij} g_j^{(1)}(\tilde{\beta}), \quad (6.28)$$

where ω_{ij} is the k-nearest neighbor (k-NN) weights such as the uniform or triangular described in Chapter 3.[2] "Closeness" for values of x is here defined by a scaled version of the Euclidean norm, that is, the distance of x_i from x is given by $[(x_i - x)'D^{-1}(x_i - x)]^{1/2}$, where D is the matrix of variances of

---

[2] k appearing in k-NN should not be confused with k for the number of equations.

$x_l, l = 1, \ldots, p$. Although the k-NN estimator may be computationally more involved than kernel estimation it has the advantage of being free from the trimming problem encountered in the kernel case.

Various procedures, in practice, can be used for choosing k. One possibility is to choose a k that would minimize a bootstrap estimator of the standard deviation of β_N^*, as in Hsieh and Manski (1987). This will be computationally intensive. An alternative, suggested by Newey (1990a), is to use a cross-validated choice of k that would minimize

$$CV(k) = \sum_{i=1}^{n} \left(g_i^{(1)}(\tilde{\beta}) - \sum_{j=1}^{n} \omega_{ij} g_j^{(1)}(\tilde{\beta}) \right)^2. \tag{6.29}$$

The conditions required upon k are that $k/\sqrt{n} \to \infty$ and $k/n \to 0$ as $n \to \infty$.

Another method of estimating M, and hence constructing optimal instruments, is to perform nonparametric regression by series approximation. The series could be composed of polynomials or of trignometric terms, as discussed in Section 3.9. Consider, for simplicity, the case where x is a scalar and the problem is to estimate a component $m_i(\tilde{\beta})$ of $M_i(\tilde{\beta})$. Then the series estimator corresponding to (6.28) (see Section 3.9) is

$$\hat{m}(x_i, \tilde{\beta}) = \hat{m}_i(\tilde{\beta}) = P^L(x_i)'(P'P)^{-1}P'g^{(1)}(\tilde{\beta}), \tag{6.30}$$

where $P^L(x) = (p_1(x), \ldots, p_L(x))'$, $P = [P^L(x_1), \ldots, P^L(x_n)]'$, and $g^{(1)} = (g^{(1)}(z_1, \tilde{\beta}), \ldots, g^{(1)}(z_n, \tilde{\beta}))'$. When $p_\ell(x) = x^\ell$ we have Kelejian's (1971) estimator discussed above, except that the choice of L is no longer fixed but allowed to grow with n. The implementation of the series estimator crucially depends on the choice of the number of terms L. Newey suggests choosing L so as to minimize the sum of squared, cross-validated residuals

$$CV(L) = \sum_{i=1}^{n} (\hat{\mu}_i/\kappa_i)^2, \tag{6.31}$$

where $\hat{\mu}_i = g_i^{(1)}(\tilde{\beta}) - P^L(x_i)'(P'P)^{-1}P'\hat{g}^{(1)}$ is the ith residual from the regression of $\hat{g}_i^{(1)}$ on the series terms and $\kappa_i = 1 - P^L(x_i)'(P'P)^{-1}P^L(x_i)$. The resulting $\hat{L}$ will obviously be data dependent. Some conditions will need to be placed upon its asymptotic behavior. These turn out to be

(i) $\hat{L} \to \infty$ in probability and $\hat{L} = o_p(n^{(\nu-2)/2\nu})$ for some ν,
(ii) the error between $g_i^{(1)}$ and the series approximation tends to zero at rates similar to that in condition (B6) of Section 3.9,

with a more precise description being available in Newey's paper.

In general, Newey (1990b, p. 821) indicates that (i) will hold for any $\hat{L}$ if $g_i^{(1)}$ can be approximated by the series at a rate $L^{-\xi}$ for $\xi > 1$. He conjectures that this is the case with the cross-validated choice of $\hat{L}$. Furthermore, if the conditional variance of u_i given x_i is bounded, (i) can be weakened to $\hat{L} = o_p(n^{-1/2})$. Condition (ii) is more complex as it reflects a trade-off between flexibility in choosing L and the rate at which the series can approximate m. For example, if L is chosen from a finite number of possibilities, the approximation error should converge to zero in mean square as $L \to \infty$.

6.3.4 Newey's Efficient Distribution-Free Estimators

Parametric IV estimators of the parameter vector β due to Kelejian (1971) and Amemiya (1974, 1977), among others, were described in Section 6.2. These estimators are well known to be consistent under the assumption that $E(u|x) = 0$; knowledge of the functional form of the distribution is not required for this property.[3] Semiparametric IV estimators are also consistent under the same conditions. In this sense both parametric and SPIV estimators are distribution-free estimators. However, none of the methods discussed to date addresses the question of finding efficiency (although see Rilstone (1993)), and general results on this were discussed in Chapter 5. Under $E(u|x) = 0$, Chamberlain (1987) has shown that the IV estimator with optimal instrument given in (6.23) is efficient in the sense that it achieves the semiparametric efficiency bound – see also Section 5.10.

Newey (1989) has developed efficient SP estimators under two types of restrictions on the conditional distribution of u. The first is independence of u and x, that is,

$$f(u, x) = f(u)f(x), \tag{6.32}$$

whereas the second is a conditional symmetry restriction,

$$f(u|x) \text{ is symmetric around zero}, \tag{6.33}$$

which also implies $f(u, x) = f(-u, x)$. Conditional symmetry restricts the class of distributions to be symmetric but allows for heteroskedasticity, whereas independence allows for general classes of distributions but rules out heteroskedasticity.

The estimators developed by Newey, under either of the above two restrictions, are locally efficient, in the sense that they achieve the semiparametric efficiency bound for a specified parametric family of distributions of disturbances instead of all parametric distributions. That is, the asymptotic variance

---

[3] Because of the assumption that random variables are i.i.d. it is convenient in this section to drop the "i" subscript on u_i, x_i etc.

of the proposed estimators is the supremum of the Cramer–Rao bounds for regular parametric submodels. For more details on semiparametric efficiency and the construction of estimators attaining it see Sections 5.4 and 5.10.1. The basic idea is to derive estimators based on the efficient score (Section 5.4).

Consider a regular parametric submodel with parameters $\theta = (\beta', \eta')'$ and likelihood function $L(z|\theta)$ for a single observation z_1. The $q \times 1$ vector of parameters of interest is β, and η are the extra parameters in the parametric submodel $f(u, x; \eta)$ representing our lack of knowledge about the joint density of x and u. The likelihood function for z_1 is

$$L(z|\theta) = |\det(\partial g(z, \beta)/\partial y)| f(g(z, \beta), x; \eta). \tag{6.34}$$

Thus the respective score functions with respect to β and η, for a single observation, are

$$d_\beta = \frac{\partial \log L(z|\theta)}{\partial \beta} = J^{(1)}(z, \beta) + g^{(1)}(z, \beta)'\tau(u, x) \tag{6.35}$$

and

$$d_\eta = \frac{\partial \log L(z|\theta)}{\partial \eta} = \frac{\partial \log f(u, x; \eta)}{\partial \eta}, \tag{6.36}$$

where $J^{(1)}(z, \beta)$ is the derivative of $\log |\det(\partial g(z, \beta)/\partial y)|$ with respect to β, $\tau(u, x) = f^{-1}\partial f/\partial u$, and $f = f(u, x)$. Note that d_η and d_β depend on z and $\tau(u, x)$ depends on η.

When the restriction that u and x are independent is true, $d_\eta = d_\eta(u) + d_\eta(x)$, where $d_\eta(u)$ is the score of the marginal density of u and $d_\eta(x)$ is the score of the marginal density of x, both with respect to η. Following Begun et al. (1983) and Bickel et al. (1993), Newey (1989a) defines the efficient score as $\tilde{d}_\beta = d_\beta - \bar{d}_\beta$, where $\bar{d}_\beta = \text{proj}(d_\beta|\mathcal{T})$ is the projection of d_β on the tangent set $\mathcal{T}$; $\mathcal{T}$ is the mean square closure of all $q \times 1$ linear combinations of the scores d_η, and its elements, t, are such that $E(\tilde{d}_\beta' t) = 0$. With independence betweeen u and x, $d_\eta = d_\eta(u) + d_\eta(x)$, so that elements of the set $\mathcal{T}$, being linear combinations of these scores, must have the format

$$\{t = t(u) + t(x): Et(u) = Et(x) = 0\}.$$

Now suppose there exists a random variable ϕ and define

$$\bar{\phi} = E[\phi|u] - E[\phi] + E[\phi|x] - E[\phi].$$

Then, it is clear that $\bar{\phi}$ is a member of the tangent set. Moreover, $E[(\phi - \bar{\phi})' t] = 0$. As this othogonality property characterizes the efficient score, it follows that

$$\tilde{d}_\beta = d_\beta - E[d_\beta|u] - E[d_\beta|x] + 2E[d_\beta] \tag{6.37}$$

$$= d_\beta - E[d_\beta|u] = J^{(1)} - E(J^{(1)}|u) + \{g^{(1)} - E(g^{(1)}|u)\}'\tau(u), \tag{6.38}$$

where $J^{(1)} = J^{(1)}(z, \beta)$, $g^{(1)} = g^{(1)}(z, \beta)$, and $\tau(u, x) = (f(u))^{-1}\partial f(u)/\partial u = \tau(u)$ under independence. For the regularity conditions under which $\tilde{d}_\beta$ is an efficient score, see Newey (1989, Theorem 3.1).

Other restrictions upon the joint density $f(u, x)$ are possible. In the case of a conditional symmetry restriction, $f(u, x) = f(-u, x)$, and the density becomes an odd function of u, making the score $d_\eta = d_\eta(u, x) = d_\eta(-u, x)$. Thus, preserving this property, the tangent set must be restricted as

$$T = \{t : t(-u, x) = t(u, x), Et(u, x) = 0\}.$$

Letting the reduced form for y be $y = \pi(u, x, \beta)$, and choosing

$$\bar{\phi} = [\phi(\pi(u, x, \beta)) + \phi(\pi(-u, x, \beta), x)]/2 - E[\phi],$$

we find that this belongs to T and has the property that $E((\phi - \bar{\phi})'t) = 0$, due to symmetry. Therefore, the efficient score becomes

$$\tilde{d}_\beta = [d_\beta(\pi(u, x, \beta)) - d_\beta\{\pi(-u, x, \beta)\}]/2 \qquad (6.39)$$

$$= \{[J^{(1)}(\pi(u, x, \beta)) - J^{(1)}(\pi(-u, x, \beta))]$$

$$+ [g^{(1)}(\pi(u, x, \beta)) - g^{(1)}(\pi(-u, x, \beta))'\tau(u, x)]\}/2. \quad (6.40)$$

It is natural to use (6.38) and (6.40) as the estimating equations for β.[4] There are however some unknowns within them. Newey proposed that one replace $\tau(u, x)$ by what one would get from assuming some parametric joint density; for example, in the independence case we need $\tau(u)$ and this might be taken to be $-u/\sigma^2$, the quantity one would get from a normality assumption. Such substitutions do not affect the consistency of the estimator provided that densities are chosen that obey the conditions set out in the assumptions (e.g., densities that are conditionally symmetric in the conditional symmetry case), as the efficient score has a zero expected value by construction. The other terms that are unknown are items like $E[g^{(1)}(u_j, x_j)|u_i]$, which can be estimated by $n^{-1}\sum_{i=1}^n g^{(1)}(u_j, x_i)$, due to the independence of x_i and u_i. Finally, if one follows Newey's strategy of parameterizing $\tau(u, x)$, extra parameters such as σ^2 are introduced, as some auxiliary moment conditions will be needed to estimate these along with β. The augmented parameter vector will be designated θ, and $\hat{\theta}$ will be the GMM estimator that works with the vector of efficient scores and auxiliary moments. The asymptotic theory is then just that for a GMM estimator. This estimator is related to the M-estimators of McCurdy (1982), Taylor (1985), and Rupport and Aldershof (1989) and the instrumental variables estimators of

---

[4] For the case when there is both independence and symmetry Newey again provides an estimating equation based on the efficient score. The efficient score in that context can be obtained by combining the calculations of the separate cases given above.

Robinson (1991a), but they would be expected to be more efficient, to the extent that the selection of $\tau(u, x)$ closely approximates the efficient score.

6.4 Finite-Sample Properties

Goldfeld and Quandt (1968) and Bowden and Turkington (1981) have performed Monte Carlo studies to analyze the finite-sample behavior of parametric NL2SLS estimators. Both of these studies have used the model (6.4)–(6.5) in their Monte Carlo experimentation. Rilstone (1989) has also used the same model to analyze and compare the Monte Carlo properties of the NL2SLS and SP2SLS estimators.

Notice that the model (6.4)–(6.5) is nonlinear in variables only. Thus an explicit expression for the IV estimator of the parameters in (6.4) can be written as

$$\hat{\beta} = \left(\sum_{i=1}^{n} \hat{m}_i(\beta) g_i^{(1)}(\beta)' \right)^{-1} \sum_{i=1}^{n} \hat{m}_i(\beta) y_i, \tag{6.41}$$

where $g_i^{(1)}(\beta)' = (e^{y_{2i}}, x_{1i})'$, and $\hat{m}_i(\beta)$ is a 2×1 vector of instruments. Since an explicit solution for y_{2i} cannot be obtained, there are different ways in which the instrument for $e^{y_{2i}}$ can be generated. For example, whereas in the Kelejian–Amemiya method the predicted value of $e^{y_{2i}}$ is obtained by regressing $e^{y_{2i}}$ on polynomials of x_{1i}, in the Bowden–Turkington method the fitted values of y_{2i} are first obtained by a polynomial regression and are then used to form $e^{\hat{y}_{2i}}$. In the SP2SLS method $E(e^{y_{2i}}|x_i)$ is estimated by nonparametric methods.

The results of Rilstone's experiments favor the use of the semiparametric approach. Both in terms of bias and dispersion, the performance of kernel-based instruments was quite superior to their parametric counterparts. This remained so even where the sample was large, although the gains were not as striking. Only in the experiments where, say, the parameter value of β_1 was very small compared to β_2 did the parametric estimators tend to become more efficient compared to SP estimators. This makes sense because the expectation of y given x tends to a linear function for small values of β_1/β_2.

Rilstone's study finds that all estimators are biased downward with values of their biases in the range of -1.5 to $-.5$. Furthermore, the efficiency of each estimator was increased by including higher order polynomials in x, except when the sample size was very large, in which case they were equivalent. In general, however, the best results using a parametric technique, in terms of bias and dispersion, were no better than the worst results based on kernel regressions.

In both the parametric and semiparametric cases, estimators based on instruments generated by regressing the function $e^{y_{2i}}$ on polynomials in x performed better than the alternative of first regressing the endogenous variable y_{2i} on the polynomial in x_i and then forming $e^{\hat{y}_{2i}}$ as the instrument.

Thus, the Amemiya–Kelijian approach tends to perform better than the Bowden–Turkington approach, although, with large sample sizes, it was not clear which approach should be preferred.

Newey (1990b) has conducted a small sampling experiment focusing upon the performances of parametric and semiparametric IV estimators. His results indicate that the IV estimator of β based on a nearest neighbor estimate of the optimal instrument has less satisfactory performance than an estimator using an instrument based on series estimates. However, the efficiency of both procedures improves when data based choices of k in nearest neighbor and L in series estimation are adopted. With regard to nearest neighbor estimates it was found that, for nonstochastic choices of k, bias was usually substantial, and in most cases bias was more than two standard deviations away from zero. When a data-dependent choice of k was considered the reductions in both bias and variance were substantial. Also, the performance of a k-NN based estimator constructed with uniform weights was better than that which adopted triangular weights. For series estimators bias was very small and the variance substantially less than their k-NN counterparts. Performance was sensitive to the choice of L, but a data-dependent cross-validated choice performed well.[5]

Rilstone (1991a) also compares the performance of kernel, k-NN, and series estimators based on polynomials and finds little difference between them with respect to MSE. Bias for polynomial estimators was found to be smaller, which is consistent with Newey's results, but the ranking on efficiency was reversed. High order polynomials did not perform well in small samples. Other findings were (i) a substantial reduction in the MSE by using leave-one-out versions of all three estimators, (ii) good performance of cross-validated choice of smoothing parameters, (iii) invariance of the MSE due to changes in the weighting schemes of kernel and NN estimators, and (iv) a strong indication of an almost symmetric distribution for estimators, as evidenced by the mean being close to the median. We note that the similar performances of kernel and k-NN may be due to the fact that the model considered by Rilstone, (6.4)–(6.5), is linear in parameters. This causes both $m_i(\beta)$ and $g_i^{(1)}(\beta)$ to be free from β_1 and thus makes the optimization schemes of Newey and Rilstone similar. A better example for comparison will be a model that is nonlinear in the parameters.[6] It would

---

[5] Pagan and Jung (1993) point out that the performance of the SP2SLS estimator can become very poor as the quality of the instruments declines. In Newey's experiments the instruments are strongly correlated with the variables they instrument. When Pagan and Jung changed the parameters of Newey's experiments to produce poor instruments, the SP estimator performance declined quite dramatically. In particular, inferences were very unreliable.

[6] Jung (1995) observes that a problem with (6.4)–(6.5) as a sampling scheme is that (6.4) does not have an intercept, but an investigator would not know this in practice and would include one among the parameters to be estimated. Doing so considerably worsens the sampling performance of the SP2SLS estimator.

also be useful to incorporate the efficient score-based estimators described in Section 6.3.4.

6.5 Nonparametric Estimation

In earlier sections we considered the estimation of models represented by $g(z, \beta) = u$. Semiparametric estimation under the condition $E(u|x) = 0$ and robust estimation under independence and conditional symmetry assumptions were discussed. Here we consider a purely nonparametric model of the form

$$g(z, m) = u, \tag{6.42}$$

where m is a vector of unknown functions, u is the disturbance vector such that $E(u|x) = 0$, and, as before, x is the vector of instruments. The basic difference from the earlier model is that m can be infinite dimensional, that is, it may be a function rather than a vector of real numbers.

A special case of the model in (6.42) is a single equation of a structural system with one left-hand endogenous variable and a vector of endogenous variables y_1 on the right-hand side. Thus, $z = (y, y_1, x)$ such that

$$y = m(y_1) + u, \qquad E(u|x) = 0 \tag{6.43}$$

For this model $g(z, m) = y - m(y_1).$[7] The situation in (6.43) is like that in (6.4) but now the manner in which y_1 enters is not known to be e^{y_1}.

6.5.1 Identification

A general set of sufficient conditions for identification of the structural function (or functional parameter) m in model $g(z, m)$ is not yet known and may be difficult to obtain. However, a necessary identification condition is $E[g(z, m)|x] = 0$. When $g(z, m) = y - m(y_1)$, as in (6.43), the identification condition reduces to

$$\pi(x) = E(y|x) = E(m(y_1)|x) = \int m(y_1) f(y_1|x) \, dy_1, \tag{6.44}$$

where we can write

$$y = \pi(x) + v \quad \text{with} \quad E(v|x) = 0. \tag{6.45}$$

Equation (6.45) is a nonparametric version of the reduced form for y. Given the data, $f(y_1|x)$ and $\pi(x)$ can be estimated by the kernel methods of estimation in Chapters 2 and 3 respectively. The problem of identification of m is thus the problem of obtaining the unique solution of m from the integral equation (6.44). Newey and Powell (1990a) have indicated that the uniqueness of m is equivalent to the completeness of the conditional density of y_1 given x, a concept related to

---

[7] One could have $y = m(y_1, x_1) + u$, where x_1 belongs to x.

the Complete Sufficient Statistic (see Rao, 1973). An example of a conditional density that is complete is the family of exponential densities of the form

$$f(y_1|x) = a(y_1)b(x)\exp\{c(x)d(y_1)\},\tag{6.46}$$

where $a(y_1) > 0$, $d(y_1)$ is one to one, and the support of $c(x)$ contains an open set.

To see that the idea of completeness is also relevant for the well-known identification results in linear parametric models, consider $m(y_1) = y_1'\beta$, $E(y_1|x) = \Pi x$ and $E(y|x) = x\pi$. Note that the linearity of $E(y_1|x)$ implies that the conditional density of $y_1|x$ is a member of the exponential family. The unique solution of the integral equation (6.44) implies a unique solution for β in

$$x(\pi - \Pi'\beta) = 0,\tag{6.47}$$

or, if the distribution of x does not concentrate on a hyperplane, it implies that β can be solved from

$$\pi = \Pi'\beta,\tag{6.48}$$

which yields the well-known rank condition that Π' has full column rank.

An interesting necessary condition for identification of m in $y = g(z, m) + u$ is that the number of variables in x is the same as in y_1, that is, there are as many instruments as right-hand side variables. This is similar to the order condition for linear parametric models. Roehrig (1988) provides a rank condition for identification under a restriction that the instruments are continuously distributed and stochastically independent of the disturbances. Briefly, let (6.43) be an equation of a system of k equations $g(y, x, u) = 0$, with k endogenous variables y, p exogenous variables x, and $(y^{*\prime}, x^*)' = z^*$ excluded from (6.43) but appearing in the system. Then, if the Jacobian, $\partial g/\partial z^*$, has rank k, m is identified up to an additive constant. Development of a rigorous set of conditions for a more general set of models would be an interesting subject for future research.

6.5.2 *Nonparametric Two-Stage Least Squares (2SLS) Estimation*

Let us consider the model $y = m(y_1) + u$ and the problem of estimating m. Given the data on y, y_1, and instruments x we can first estimate $\pi(x) = E(y|x)$ by $\hat{\pi}(x)$ and $f(y_1|x)$ by $\hat{f}(y_1|x)$, where $\hat{\pi}$ and $\hat{f}$ are (say) kernel estimators. Then, at the second stage, an estimate of m can be obtained by solving the integral equation

$$\hat{\pi}(x) = \int m(y_1)\hat{f}(y_1|x)\,dy_1.\tag{6.49}$$

The solution of this integral equation is not straightforward. Newey and Powell (1990a) suggest that $m(y_1)$ might be approximated by a series expansion

$$m(y_1) = m(y_1, \gamma) = \sum_{j=1}^{J} \gamma_j p_j(y_1), \tag{6.50}$$

and this is then substituted for $m(y_1)$ in (6.49) to give

$$\hat{\pi}(x) = \sum_{j=1}^{J} \gamma_j \hat{E}(p_j | x), \tag{6.51}$$

with $\hat{E}(p_j | x) = \int p_j(y_1) \hat{f}(y_1 | x) \, dy_1$. An estimator of $m(y_1)$ is then available as $\hat{m}(y_1) = \sum_{j=1}^{J} \hat{\gamma}_j p_j(y_1)$, where $\hat{\gamma}_j$ is the value of γ_j that minimizes the Euclidean distance:

$$\sum_{i=1}^{n} \left\{ \hat{\pi}(x_i) - \sum_{j=1}^{J} \gamma_j \hat{E}(p_j(y_i) | x_i) \right\}^2. \tag{6.52}$$

The resulting estimator of m is a NP2SLS estimator in the sense that the first stage involves nonparametric estimation of $\pi(x)$ and $E(p_j | x)$ and the second stage involves a constrained least squares regression of $\hat{\pi}$ on $\hat{E}(p_j | x)$. To implement the estimator in practice it is necessary to specify the approximating series p_j, the number of included terms J, and the estimates $\hat{E}(p_j | x)$. Discussion of p_j and J was given in Section 6.3 whereas $\hat{E}(p_j | x)$ can be obtained by kernel, nearest neighbor, or series methods.

Newey and Powell (1990a) follow Gallant's (1981, 1987) methods in proving the consistency of the NP2SLS estimator obtained above. The consistency result depends crucially on the assumption of compactness of m in the norm $\|m\|$. Thus in practice one needs to check that the estimated function is smooth, and, if it is not, it should be rendered so by imposing constraints on the coefficients γ. Other assumptions for consistency relate to the finite-dimensional approximation of $m(y_1) = m(y_1, \gamma)$, a Lipschitz continuity condition on the residual u, and uniform convergence in probability of the objective function.

An alternative approach to estimation, in the spirit of "full information" estimation, is to consider the series approximations for both the structural equations and the distribution of unobservables and then apply maximum likelihood to estimate the parameters involved in series approximations. Note that the limited information approach in Newey and Powell avoids the specification of the joint distributions of the data. It will be interesting for future research to compare and analyze these alternative estimation strategies. The optimal data-dependent methods of choosing the smoothing parameters need to be investigated. Finally, it will be useful to develop computationally simpler estimators than those discussed here.

7 Semiparametric Estimation of Discrete Choice Models

7.1 Introduction

In many data sets occurring in the social sciences the object of interest is whether a decision has been made or an action carried out. Examples would be whether a durable good is purchased, a bond is issued, or, perhaps, whether a corporation removes its CEO. Generally, an investigator is interested in what it is that precipitates the decision or action, and a range of possible influences (x_i) is entertained. What makes this different from a regular regression problem is that the variable to be explained (y_i) is *qualitative* rather than quantitative; or, treating the decision outcome as a random variable taking the value zero or unity (reflecting negative and positive decisions or actions), y_i must be a *discrete* rather than a continuous random variable.

An enormous literature has built up on the types of models that can be employed to explain such data, a masterly exposition of which is Amemiya (1981). Economists imported many of these models from medical and biological statistics, and the traditional ways of estimating unknown parameters have revolved around formulating a suitable density function for the observed data. Section 7.2 reviews this literature, pointing to the fact that estimation has proceeded in either one of two ways. In the first, the discrete nature of the random variable enables one to formulate relationships as a heteroskedastic nonlinear regression. In the second, maximum likelihood methods are employed. Actually, the contrast turns out to be too sharp, as iteration of the former is known to lead to the latter, but the demarcation is useful when it comes to studying the nonparametric alternatives of Section 7.4. Section 7.2 also reviews problems with the parametric estimators if incorrect densities are adopted for the discrete random variable, and these constitute a case for nonparametric analysis.

Section 7.3 turns to the determination of the semiparametric efficiency bounds under a variety of assumptions. With this information in hand, Section 7.4 considers two classes of semiparametric estimators based on the "regression" and "maximum likelihood" principles distinguished in the parametric approach.

Ichimura (1993) is a representative of the first, Klein and Spady (1993), Gabler et al. (1993), and Gozalo and Linton (1994) constitute the second. It emerges that Klein and Spady's estimator attains the SP efficiency bound. Section 7.5 reviews some alternative estimators that appear in the literature. These are given only a short treatment since, with two exceptions, they either have a poorly developed asymptotic theory or they fail to be $\sqrt{n}$ consistent, so that they are dominated by the SP estimators of Section 7.4, at least from the viewpoint of asymptotic theory, although in finite samples such superiority may not be in evidence. Moreover, they are sometimes more robust to problems such as heteroskedasticity than the SP estimators of Section 7.4, and their potential application should be kept in mind if such problems are suspected in the data. Section 7.6 looks at the literature on polytomous choice models. Generally, these are straightforward extensions of the binary case. Section 7.7 considers work that has been done on specification tests for discrete choice models using the SP estimators. Finally, Section 7.8 reviews the literature on applications of the SP estimators discussed in the chapter.

7.2 Parametric Estimation of Binary Discrete Choice Models

Early work in medical statistics was concerned with the effects of drug dosage upon a unit. It was felt that the response could be thought of as a latent variable y_i^*, influenced by a number of factors x_i, to give a latent variable model:[1]

$$y_i^* = x_i'\beta + u_i^*. \tag{7.1}$$

If u_i^* is i.i.d.$(0, \sigma^2)$, Equation (7.1) would represent a standard regression model, except for the fact that y_i^* is not observed. Instead, all that is observed is whether the units respond in a certain qualitative way, in which case $y_i = 1$, or do not respond, whereupon $y_i = 0$. If there is an intercept in (7.1) we can say that $y_i = 1$ occurs if $y_i^* > 0$ and $y_i = 1$ if $y_i^* \le 0$, that is, $y_i = I(y_i^* > 0)$, and this means that

$$P\,[y_i = 1] = P\,[y_i^* > 0] = P\,[x_i'\beta + u_i^* > 0]$$
$$= P\,[u_i^* > -x_i'\beta] = F\,(x_i'\beta) = F_i,$$

where $F(u)$ is the cumulative distribution function (c.d.f.) of u_i and the random variable u_i is assumed to be symmetrically distributed around zero.[2]

---

[1] In what follows it will generally be convenient to drop the "0" subscript on β_0 that identifies the true parameter.

[2] If one does not wish to impose the symmetry assumption then $P\,(y_i = 1) = 1 - F(-x_i'\beta) = g(x_i'\beta)$. In the nonparametric case g is unknown and the sign information is irrelevant.

Given the probability that $y_i = 1$ is F_i, and the fact that y_i is a Bernouilli random variable, $E(y_i|x_i'\beta) = F(x_i'\beta)$. Consequently

$$y_i = F\left(x_i'\beta\right) + \epsilon_i, \tag{7.2}$$

where ϵ_i is easily seen to be i.d. $(0, F_i(1 - F_i))$. It is important to observe that $F(\cdot)$ is a function of a scalar $x_i'\beta$, leading to this being termed a *single-index* model. Because of this dependence the conditional expectation underlying (7.2) is based on the index $x_i'\beta$ not x_i. If β were known, and one wished to estimate the probability of a positive decision for an individual given characteristics x_i, nonparametric methods could be employed to estimate it by using y_i and $z_i = x_i'\beta$ as the data. The alternative of just computing $E(y_i|x_i)$ from (y_i, x_i), mentioned in Chapter 3, would fail to capture the single-index nature of the model.

Popular choices of $F(\lambda)$ are the cumulative distribution function (c.d.f.) of the standard normal density, yielding the probit model, or $F(\lambda) = e^\lambda (1+e^\lambda)^{-1}$, giving the logit model. The first-order conditions for the NLR estimator of β would be

$$\sum_{i=1}^{n} \frac{\partial F\left(x_i'\hat{\beta}\right)}{\partial \beta} \left[y_i - F\left(x_i'\hat{\beta}\right)\right] = 0, \tag{7.3}$$

and this estimator would be consistent and asymptotically normal under standard conditions. But it will not be efficient as the error term in (7.3) has variance $F_i(1 - F_i)$. Instead, weighted nonlinear regression needs to be performed, and this involves the first-order conditions

$$\sum_{i=1}^{n} \frac{\partial F\left(x_i'\tilde{\beta}\right)}{\partial \beta} F^{-1}\left(x_i'\tilde{\beta}\right)\left(1 - F\left(x_i'\tilde{\beta}\right)\right)^{-1} \left[y_i - F\left(x_i'\tilde{\beta}\right)\right] = 0. \tag{7.4}$$

Now the error term in (7.4) is not normally distributed and, based upon the results of Section 5.5, it might be conjectured that β can be more efficiently estimated by doing maximum likelihood rather than nonlinear regression. The log likelihood for y_i, conditional upon $\{x_i\}_{i=1}^{n}$, is easily shown to be

$$L = \sum_{i=1}^{n} \{(1 - y_i)\log(1 - F_i) + y_i \log F_i\}, \tag{7.5}$$

from which the scores for β are

$$\frac{\partial L}{\partial \beta} = \sum_{i=1}^{n} \left(\frac{\partial F_i}{\partial \beta}\right) F_i^{-1}(1 - F_i)^{-1}(y_i - F_i), \tag{7.6}$$

so that the $\tilde{\beta}$ setting $\partial L/\partial \beta = 0$ is exactly that from the first-order conditions for weighted NLR in (7.4). Accordingly, there are only two distinct estimators here – the unweighted NLR estimator with first-order conditions (7.3) and MLE with conditions (7.6).

If the assumed distribution function $F(\cdot)$ is correct the MLE $\tilde{\beta}$ is consistent and

$$
n^{1/2}(\tilde{\beta} - \beta) \xrightarrow{d} \mathcal{N}\left(0, \left[\lim_{n\to\infty} n^{-1} E \sum \left(\frac{\partial F_i}{\partial \beta}\right)\right.\right.
$$
$$
\left.\left. \times F_i^{-1}(1 - F_i)^{-1}\left(\frac{\partial F_i}{\partial \beta}\right)'\right]^{-1}\right).
$$

The covariance matrix can be consistently estimated by

$$
\left[n^{-1} \sum \left(\frac{\partial F_i}{\partial \beta}\right) F_i^{-1}(1 - F_i)^{-1}\left(\frac{\partial F_i}{\partial \beta}\right)'\right]^{-1},
$$

replacing β with $\tilde{\beta}$. Under specification error for the distribution function of y_i, the score in (7.6) is no longer guaranteed to have a zero expectation, and therefore $\tilde{\beta} \xrightarrow{p} \beta^*$, where β^* maximizes $E[n^{-1} \sum (1 - y_i) \log(1 - \bar{F}_i) + y_i \log \bar{F}_i]$, where the expectation is with respect to the true density for y_i and $\bar{F}_i$ is the *assumed* c.d.f. Some research has been done to characterize the subset of β^*, β_1^*, corresponding to the nonintercept coefficients in the model. Ruud (1983) showed that $\beta_1^* = \gamma \beta_{10}$ if $E(x_i|x_i'\beta_0)$ was linear in $x_i'\beta_0$; when the distribution of x_i is multivariate normal or spherically symmetric such a relation holds. Under such circumstances the slope coefficients can be consistently estimated up to a scale factor γ, whereas the intercept cannot be. The necessity for the latter qualifications, maintained throughout the remainder of this chapter, is readily apparent from (7.1) and the fact that $F(\cdot)$ is unknown. Dividing (7.1) by any constant leaves $P(y_i > 0)$ unchanged, while the addition of any constant term to $x_i'\beta$ can be absorbed into $F(\cdot)$. Thus the parameters β can only be identified up to a constant of proportionality, and the intercept cannot be identified unless further restrictions are placed upon $F(\cdot)$ (e.g., that the median of u_i^* is at zero). Identification issues are more complex if there is heteroskedasticity in the errors u_i^* as this may mean that $P(y_i = 1)$ may no longer be monotonic in $x_i'\beta_0$. Manski (1975, 1985) deals with identification when there is a lack of monotonicity. His result is that, if $P(y_i = 1)$ can be written as $v_1(x_1) + v_2(x_2, \theta)$, where x_1 and x_2 are vectors of continuous random variables, θ is identified if $\partial v_2(x_2, \theta_0)/\partial x_2 = \partial v_2(x_2, \theta_1)/\partial x_2$ implies that $\theta_0 = \theta_1$.

7.3 Semiparametric Efficiency Bounds for Binary Discrete Choice Models

At the end of the preceding section it was pointed out that an intercept cannot be estimated under a completely unknown specification for $F(\cdot)$, whereas slope parameters can only be determined up to a scale factor. Hence the number of estimable parameters is generally two smaller than $\dim(\beta)$, and they will be designated as θ, giving $P\{y_i = 1\} = F(v(x_i, \theta_0)) = F_i$, where $x_i'\beta = a + bv(x_i, \theta)$. As an illustration of this notation let

$$x_i'\beta = \beta_1 + x_{2i}\beta_2 + \cdots + x_{qi}\beta_q$$
$$= \beta_1 + \beta_2(x_{2i} + x_{3i}\theta_1 + \cdots + x_{qi}\theta_{q-2}),$$

producing

$$v(x_i, \theta) = x_{2i} + x_{3i}\theta_1 + \cdots + x_{qi}\theta_{q-2},$$
$$a = \beta_1, \quad b = \beta_2,$$
$$\theta_j = \beta_{j+2}/\beta_2, \quad j = 1, \ldots q - 2.$$

Such a transformation pre-supposes that a variable (x_{2i}) can be found whose associated coefficient (β_2) is nonzero so that θ_j exists. It must also be the case that at least one of the variables in x_i is a continuous random variable. A normalization such as the one above, in which x_{2i} is forced to have a coefficient of unity, means that, when x_{2i} is continuous, it cannot be rescaled without changing the value of its associated coefficient from unity and this fixes the value of the single index. However, if all the x_i were dummy variables, then the value of the single index should not be changed by transformations that preserve the ordering in the elements of x. Thus there would be a failure of identification. Although it is rare to see discrete choice models without at least one continuous random variable among the x_i, it may be that this regressor has only a weak influence on choices, and one might face a situation of near nonidentifiability. This complication must therefore be kept in mind when doing semiparametric estimation in discrete choice models that have many dummy variables as regressors.

To represent the class of potential distributions suppose also that $F(u) = \int_{-\infty}^{u} f(\lambda, \eta)\, d\lambda$, where η indexes the density in the same sense of a "parametric submodel" as discussed in Section 5.4. From that section the question of the possibility of efficient estimation can be handled by examining whether $E(d_\theta)$ is zero or not, and the semiparametric efficiency bound is $E\left(\tilde{d}_\theta(i)\tilde{d}_\theta(i)'\right)$, where $\tilde{d}_\theta(i)$ are the efficient scores. With i.i.d. data $\tilde{d}_\theta(i) = d_\theta(i) - E[d_\theta(i)|d_\eta(i)]$, under the presumption that the expectation can be taken over all the functions represented by $d_\eta(i)$. As mentioned earlier, verification of the legitimacy of this operation may be quite complex.

Having disposed of the above preliminaries, we have that the log likelihood will be

$$L = \sum_{i=1}^{n}(1 - y_i)\log(1 - F_i) + y_i \log F_i \qquad (7.7)$$

with scores

$$d_\theta(i) = (y_i - F_i) F_i^{-1} (1 - F_i)^{-1} \left(\frac{\partial F_i}{\partial v_i}\right) \left(\frac{\partial v_i}{\partial \theta}\right), \tag{7.8}$$

$$d_\eta(i) = (y_i - F_i) F_i^{-1} (1 - F_i)^{-1} \left(\frac{\partial F_i}{\partial \eta}\right). \tag{7.9}$$

Consider first the possibility of adaptive estimation. That would require $E(d_\theta(i)) = 0$ (Lemma 5.3) over arbitrary densities for u_i^*. Denoting the latter by $\bar{F}_i$, and using the law of iterated expectations, gives

$$E(d_\theta(i)) = E\left[(\bar{F}_i - F_i) F_i^{-1} (1 - F_i)^{-1} \left(\frac{\partial F_i}{\partial v_i}\right) E\left(\frac{\partial v_i}{\partial \theta}\bigg| v_i\right)\right]. \tag{7.10}$$

In general, it is unlikely that the right-hand side of (7.10) will equal zero, making adaption rare in the discrete choice model. One exception has been recounted by Cosslett (1987). If $E\left(\frac{\partial v_i}{\partial \theta}\big| v_i\right)$ was an odd function of v_i at the same time as symmetry in $f(\cdot)$ caused $\bar{F}_i$, F_i, and $\partial F_i/\partial v_i$ to be even functions, the term in square brackets in (7.10) will become an odd function. Ally these features with a further assumption of symmetry for the density of v_i and then $E(d_\theta(i)) = 0$. In fact, Cosslett shows that $E\left(\frac{\partial v_i}{\partial \theta}\big| v_i\right) - E\left(\frac{\partial v_i}{\partial \theta}\big| -v_i\right) = c v_i$ is necessary for adaption. Under this scenario the intercept is also estimable, although the scale parameter remains indeterminate. Although interesting from a theoretical viewpoint, the qualification would appear to have little practical relevance.

If adaption is not possible, knowledge of the semiparametric efficiency bound

$$\Omega = \left[E\left(\tilde{d}_\theta(i)\tilde{d}_\theta(i)'\right)\right]^{-1}$$

becomes important. Writing the right-hand side of (7.8) and (7.9) as $\zeta_i\left(\frac{\partial F_i}{\partial v_i}\right)$ $\left(\frac{\partial v_i}{\partial \theta}\right)$ and $\zeta_i\left(\frac{\partial F_i}{\partial \eta}\right)$ respectively, we see that ζ_i and the derivatives of F_i are both functions of v_i. Moreover, if there are no restrictions upon $F(\cdot)$, $\partial F_i/\partial \eta$ is essentially an arbitrary function of v_i, $B(v_i)$ (subject to the qualification of a finite variance). From these observations

$$E\left(d_\theta(i)|d_\eta(i)\right) = E\left[\zeta_i\left(\frac{\partial F_i}{\partial v_i}\right)\left(\frac{\partial v_i}{\partial \theta}\right)\bigg| \zeta_i B(v_i)\right]$$

$$= \zeta_i\left(\frac{\partial F_i}{\partial v_i}\right) E\left[\left(\frac{\partial v_i}{\partial \theta}\right)\bigg| v_i\right],$$

yielding the efficient score

$$\tilde{d}_\theta(i) = d_\theta(i) - E[d_\theta(i)|d_\eta(i)] = \zeta_i \frac{\partial F_i}{\partial v_i}\left[\frac{\partial v_i}{\partial \theta} - E\left(\frac{\partial v_i}{\partial \theta}\bigg| v_i\right)\right]. \tag{7.11}$$

It is important to note that $\tilde{d}_\theta(i)$ depends on assumptions made about $f(\cdot)$, as these constrain the class of functions $B(v_i)$. From (7.11), the SP bound is

$$\Omega^{-1} = E\left\{ \zeta_i^2 \left(\frac{\partial F_i}{\partial v_i}\right)^2 \left[\frac{\partial v_i}{\partial \theta} - E\left(\frac{\partial v_i}{\partial \theta}\bigg| v_i\right)\right]\right.$$
$$\left. \times \left[\frac{\partial v_i}{\partial \theta} - E\left(\frac{\partial v_i}{\partial \theta}\bigg| v_i\right)\right]'\right\}. \qquad (7.12)$$

Equation (7.12) is also the semiparametric bound when the class of alternatives is constrained to have a median of zero (i.e., $F(0) = .5$). One reason for imposing such a structure is that it enables an intercept to be estimated, in which case the intercept becomes an element of θ, say θ_1. However, because $\frac{\partial v_i}{\partial \theta_1} = 1$, $E\left(\frac{\partial v_i}{\partial \theta_1}\big| v_i\right) = 1$, $\tilde{d}_{\theta_1}(i) = 0$ and, based on Chamberlain's (1986) conclusion, the zero efficient score implies that no regular estimator of θ_1 exists in these circumstances. Essentially this eliminates the possibility of a $\sqrt{n}$ consistent estimator but not of an estimator that converges at a slower rate. Indeed it is known that there are consistent estimators of the intercept under a zero median restriction, in particular the maximum score estimators discussed in Section 7.5, but these do not exhibit $n^{1/2}$ convergence.

Cosslett (1987) also compares Ω to the Cramer–Rao bound in the case where $F(\cdot)$ is known to be F_0, and this exercise is very instructive. For simplicity, take θ to be a scalar, define $v_{1i} = \left(\frac{\partial v_i}{\partial \theta}\right)$ and $\xi_i = \zeta_i\left(\frac{\partial F_i}{\partial v_i}\right)$, and designate the information matrix ($\mathcal{I}$) and scores for the true density F_0 with a "0" superscript. In the parametric formulation there are two additional parameters, $\delta' = [a\ b]$, the unidentified location and scale parameters discussed at the beginning of this section. Thus the variance of $n^{1/2}(\hat{\theta} - \theta)$ would be $\left(\mathcal{I}_{\theta\theta}^0 - \mathcal{I}_{\theta\delta}^0(\mathcal{I}_{\delta\delta}^0)^{-1}\mathcal{I}_{\delta\theta}^0\right)^{-1}$, and we can therefore compare Ω^{-1} with $\mathcal{I}_{\theta\theta}^0 - \mathcal{I}_{\theta\delta}^0(\mathcal{I}_{\delta\delta}^0)^{-1}\mathcal{I}_{\delta0}^0$. Now, using (7.12),

$$\mathcal{I}_{\theta\theta}^0 = E\left(\xi_i^2 v_{1i}^2\right) = \Omega^{-1} + E\left(\xi_i^2\left(E\left(v_{1i}|v_i\right)\right)^2\right), \qquad (7.13)$$

from which it follows that the SP efficiency bound coincides with the Cramer–Rao bound if $E\left[\xi_i^2\left(E\left(v_{1i}|v_i\right)\right)^2\right]$ equals $\mathcal{I}_{\theta\delta}^0(\mathcal{I}_{\delta\delta}^0)^{-1}\mathcal{I}_{\delta\theta}^0$. But it is not hard to see that $\mathcal{I}_{\theta\delta}^0(\mathcal{I}_{\delta\delta}^0)^{-1}\mathcal{I}_{\delta\theta}^0$ can be regarded as the explained variance from the regression of $d_\theta^0(i) = \xi_i v_{1i}$ against $d_\delta^0(i)$, and the fact that $d_a^0(i) = \xi_i$ and $d_b^0(i) = \xi_i v_i$ makes the equivalent regression that of v_{1i} against unity and v_i. If $E\left(v_{1i}|v_i\right)$ had the form $c_0 + c_1 v_i$, the desired equality would be obtained. Consequently, the loss of efficiency of an SP estimator relative to that of a known parametric model stems from the combination of an inability to estimate all the unknown parameters and a failure of $E\left(v_{1i}|v_i\right)$ to be linear in v_i. If the latter feature was maintained, while a and b could be specified *a priori*, there would be no efficiency loss. What is interesting about this phenomenon is that it coincides exactly with Ruud's findings about the possibility of consistency of parametric estimators under distributional misspecification mentioned in Section 7.2. As he pointed out, it is remarkable that the result hinges solely upon the nature of x_i and does not depend upon $F(\cdot)$.

7.4 Semiparametric Estimation of Binary Discrete Choice Models

The problem is now how to estimate θ, a $p \times 1$ vector, when $P[y_i = 0] = F(v(x_i, \theta_0))$ of Section 7.3 is unknown.[3] Estimators are generally found from a set of first-order conditions $E(v_i(\theta_0, \tau_i)) = 0$, where τ_i is some function of data. In the GMM approach to estimation the sample mean $\bar{v}(\hat{\theta}, \tau) = n^{-1}\sum v_i(\hat{\theta}, \tau_i) = 0$ would define a suitable estimator if τ_i was known. What complicates this approach here is the fact that τ_i will be an unknown function of the data, but this difficulty was circumvented in Chapter 5 by replacing τ_i by its nonparametric estimate $\hat{\tau}_i$, and this strategy will be adopted again. Of course, formulating the estimator of θ as the solution to a set of first-order conditions $\bar{v}(\hat{\theta}, \hat{\tau}) = 0$ may be too restrictive, and Andrews (1994) has considered estimators that minimize some function $S(\bar{v}(\theta, \hat{\tau}))$. He terms these MINPIN (minimize a criterion function that depends on a preliminary infinite-dimensional nuisance parameter estimator) estimators. For this chapter $S = \bar{v}'\bar{v}$ is the only function needed, and the $\hat{\theta}$ minimizing S also solves $\bar{v}(\hat{\theta}, \hat{\tau}) = 0$; therefore it is not necessary to deal with the general case. Nevertheless, the formal proofs of the propositions set out below are all to be found in Andrews's work.

The two SP estimators studied in this section estimate θ either by solving the first-order conditions in (7.3) or (7.6) or by maximimizing (7.5), where $F(\cdot)$ and its derivatives are replaced by nonparametric estimates of the mean of y_i conditional upon $v(x_i, \theta)$. Ichimura (1993) used the equivalent of (7.3) as his method, whereas Klein and Spady adopt (7.6) (strictly both they and Gabler et al. maximize (7.5)). To gain some appreciation of the conditions under which these two estimators exhibit consistency and asymptotic normality, consider the properties of an estimator of θ solving $\bar{v}(\hat{\theta}, \hat{\tau}) = 0$. Following standard procedure, expand $\bar{v}(\hat{\theta}, \hat{\tau})$ around θ_0 to get

$$0 = \bar{v}(\theta_0, \hat{\tau}) + \bar{v}_\theta(\theta^*, \hat{\tau})(\hat{\theta} - \theta_0), \tag{7.14}$$

where $\bar{v}_\theta = \partial\bar{v}/\partial\theta$ and θ^* lies between $\hat{\theta}$ and θ_0. Inverting (7.14), we obtain $(\hat{\theta} - \theta_0) = -\bar{v}_\theta^{-1}\bar{v}(\theta_0, \hat{\tau})$, and the asymptotic properties of $n^{1/2}(\hat{\theta} - \theta_0)$ depend upon the behavior of $n^{1/2}\bar{v}_\theta$ and $n^{1/2}\bar{v}(\theta_0, \hat{\tau})$. Theorem 7.1 summarizes Andrews's (1994) results on this.

---

[3] It is assumed that $v(x_i, \theta_0)$ is linear. Matzkin (1992) considers SP estimation when this is incorrect.

Theorem 7.1: If $\hat{\theta}$ solves $\bar{v}(\hat{\theta}, \hat{\tau}) = 0$ and

1. the conditions of Lemma 1 of Chapter 5 are satisfied for v_i;
2. v_i is twice continuously differentiable in θ on Θ_0, $\forall \tau \in \Upsilon_0$;
3. v_i, $\partial v_i / \partial \theta$, and $b_t = \sup_{\theta \in \Theta_0, \tau \in \Upsilon_0} \|\partial^2 v_i / \partial \theta \partial \theta'\|$ satisfy a uniform weak law of large numbers over Θ_0 and Υ_0;
4. $\mu = \lim_{n \to \infty} E(\bar{v}(\theta_0, \tau_0))$, $D = \bar{v}_\theta(\theta, \tau) = \lim_{n \to \infty} E(\partial \bar{v}(\theta, \tau) / \partial \theta)$ exist uniformly over $\Theta_0 \times \Upsilon_0$ and are continuous at (θ_0, τ_0); and
5. $\lim_{n \to \infty} n^{-1} \sum E\, b_t < \infty$,

   then

$$\hat{\theta} \xrightarrow{p} \theta_0$$

and

$$n^{1/2}(\hat{\theta} - \theta_0) \xrightarrow{d} \mathcal{N}(0, D^{-1}VD^{-1}),$$

where $V = \mathrm{var}(n^{1/2}\bar{v}(\theta_0, \tau_0))$.

Assumptions (ii)–(v) in Theorem 7.1 guarantee that $\bar{v}_\theta(\theta^*, \hat{\tau}) - D$ is $o_p(1)$ so that $(\hat{\theta} - \theta_0) = -D^{-1}\bar{v}(\theta_0, \hat{\tau}) + o_p(1)$, whereas Lemma 5.1 shows that $\bar{v}_\theta(\theta_0, \hat{\tau}) \xrightarrow{p} 0$, $n^{1/2}\bar{v}(\theta_0, \hat{\tau}) \xrightarrow{d} \mathcal{N}(0, V)$. Consistency and asymptotic normality for $\hat{\theta}$ therefore follow directly. For most problems it is the conditions of Lemma 5.1 that are crucial rather than the extra ones given in Theorem 7.1, and they will occupy our attention in the following subsections.

7.4.1   Ichimura's Estimator

As noted above, Ichimura (1993) suggested that θ be estimated by $\tilde{\theta}$ defined by

$$\sum_{i=1}^{n} \left[\partial \hat{m}\left(v(x_i, \tilde{\theta})\right) / \partial \theta\right]\left(y_i - m\left(v(x_i, \tilde{\theta})\right)\right) = 0, \tag{7.15}$$

where

$$m\left(v(x_i, \theta_0)\right) = E\left(y_i | v(x_i, \theta_0)\right) = F\left(v(x_i, \theta_0)\right)$$

is the conditional mean of y_i and $\hat{m}$ is the nonparametric estimator of $E\left(y_i | v(x_i, \tilde{\theta})\right)$. Equation (7.15) differs from (7.3) because of the lack of identifiability of all elements of β, and $v(x_i, \theta)$ extracts from $x_i'\beta$ what is estimable (see Section 7.3). Because $m\left(v(x_i, \theta)\right)$ is the conditional expectation $E\left(y_i | v(x_i, \theta)\right)$, for any given value θ, say $\theta^{(1)}$, $z_i = v\left(x_i, \theta^{(1)}\right)$ and $m_i = \tau_{1i} = E\left(y_i | z_i\right)$ may be estimated by any of the nonparametric procedures described in Chapter 3, although only when $\theta = \theta_0$ will one obtain a consistent estimator.

Using the chain rule the derivatives of m_i with respect to θ can be written as $(\partial m_i/\partial v_i)\,(\partial v_i/\partial\theta)$; the latter term in the product follows from the definition of the model while the former can be estimated using the methods of Chapter 4. Designating $\partial m_i/\partial\theta$ by τ_{2i} and setting $v_i = \tau_{2i}(y_i - \tau_{1i})$, we find that $\tilde{\theta}$ solves $\bar{v}(\tilde{\theta}, \hat{\tau}) = 0$, where $\tau_i' = (\tau_{1i}, \tau_{2i})$.

To consider the asymptotic properties of the estimator $\tilde{\theta}$ it is important to investigate the nature of the first-order conditions that (7.15) is emulating. By definition $m(v(x_i, \theta_0)) = E(y_i|v(x_i, \theta_0))$, but the derivative in (7.15) is of $m(v(x_i, \theta))$ with respect to θ. Hence the implied first-order conditions are

$$E\left\{\sum_{i=1}^{n} [\partial m(v(x_i,\theta))/\partial\theta]_{\theta=\theta_0}\,[y_i - m(v(x_i,\theta_0))]\right\} = 0. \quad (7.16)$$

Lemma 7.1 then provides an alternative expression for $[\partial m(v(x_i,\theta))/\partial\theta]_{\theta=\theta_0}$, which is important for understanding the properties of the estimator.

Lemma 7.1:

$$\{\partial[m(v(x_i,\theta))]/\partial\theta\}_{\theta=\theta_0} = (\partial m(v(x_i,\theta_0))/\partial v_i)[\partial v(x_i,\theta)/\partial\theta$$
$$- E\{(\partial v(x_i,\theta))/\partial\theta|v_i\}]_{\theta=\theta_0}.$$

Proof:

$$m[v(x_i,\theta)] = E[y_i|v_i(x_i,\theta)] \quad (7.17)$$
$$= E\left[\{m(v_i(\theta_0)) - m(v_i(\theta)) + m(v_i(\theta))\}|v_i(\theta)\right] \quad (7.18)$$
$$= E\left[\{m_i(v(\theta_0)) - m(v_i(\alpha)) + m(v_i(\gamma))\}|v_i(\gamma)\right], \quad (7.19)$$

where $\alpha = \gamma = \theta$.
Differentiating (7.19) we obtain

$$\partial m(v(x_i,\theta_0))/\partial\theta = -\partial E[m(v(x_i,\alpha))|v(x_i,\gamma)]/\partial\alpha$$
$$+ \partial E[m(v(x_i,\gamma))|v(x_i,\gamma)]/\partial\gamma \quad (7.20)$$
$$= -E\left[\frac{\partial m_i}{\partial v_i}\frac{\partial v_i}{\partial\alpha}\bigg|v(x_i,\gamma)\right] + \left[\frac{\partial m_i}{\partial v_i}\frac{\partial v_i}{\partial\gamma}\right], \quad (7.21)$$

and evaluating the derivative at $\alpha = \gamma = \theta_0$ gives the desired result. Q.E.D.

Turning to the asymptotic properties of $\tilde{\theta}$, we can make recourse to Theorem 7.1 and, as mentioned earlier, it is really the conditions of Lemma 5.1 that need to be satisfied. Of these assumptions (B(ii)) (asymptotic independence) and

(B(iii)) (stochastic equicontinuity) are critical. Concentrating upon the former, we need $E\left(n^{1/2}v(\theta_0, \hat{\tau})\right) = 0$. If "0" designates true values, then

$$\hat{v}_i = \left(\tau_{2i}^0 + \left(\hat{\tau}_{2i} - \tau_{2i}^0\right)\right)\left(y_i - \tau_{1i}^0 - \hat{\tau}_{1i} + \tau_{1i}^0\right)$$

and

$$E(n^{1/2}\bar{v}(\theta_0, \tau)) = n^{1/2}E\left[\tau_{2i}^0\left(y_i - \tau_{1i}^0\right) - 2\tau_{2i}^0\left(\tau_{1i} + \tau_{1i}^0\right)\right.$$
$$+ \left(\tau_{2i} - \tau_{2i}^0\right)\left(\tau_{1i}^0 - \tau_{1i}\right)\bigg]$$
$$= n^{1/2}E\left[\left(\tau_{2i} - \tau_{2i}^0\right)\left(\tau_{1i}^0 - \tau_{1i}\right)\right]$$

as $E\left[\tau_{2i}^0 v(x_i, \theta)\right] = 0$, from Lemma 7.1, and $E\left((y_i - \tau_{1i}^0)\tau_{2i}^0\right) = 0$. Distributing $n^{1/2}$ as $n^{\delta_1 + \delta_2}$, where $\delta_1 + \delta_2 = 1/2$, we get that

$$E\left[n^{\delta_1}\left(\hat{\tau}_{2i} - \tau_{2i}^0\right)n^{\delta_2}\left(\hat{\tau}_{1i} - \tau_{1i}^0\right)\right] = 0$$

is needed. Immediately it follows that n^{δ_1} consistency must hold for $\hat{\tau}_{2i}$ and n^{δ_2} consistency for $\hat{\tau}_{1i}$. When $\delta_1 = \delta_2 = 1/4$, the $n^{1/4}$ consistency results prevalent in Chapter 5 would emerge, but that choice would seem inappropriate here as the convergence rate of a derivative estimator $(\hat{\tau}_{2i})$ is slower than that of a moment $(\hat{\tau}_{1i})$. Notice that $\hat{\tau}_{2i}$ is made up of the product of $\partial m_i/\partial v_i$ and $\partial v_i/\partial \theta$, meaning that a condition such as $E\|\partial v_i/\partial \theta\|^2 < \infty$ must also be imposed to get n^{δ_2} consistency for $\hat{\tau}_{2i}$. Now, if asymptotic bias has been removed from the kernel by some method, $(nh)^{1/2}\left(\hat{\tau}_{1i} - \tau_{1i}^0\right)$ and $(nh^3)^{1/2}\left(\hat{\tau}_{2i} - \tau_{2i}^0\right)$ are $O_p(1)$. Therefore $E\left[n^{1/2}\left(\hat{\tau}_{2i} - \tau_{2i}^0\right)\left(\hat{\tau}_{1i} - \tau_{1i}^0\right)\right]$ is $o_p(1)$ whenever $n^{1/2}\left[(nh)^{-1/2}(nh^3)^{-1/2}\right] = n^{-1/2}h^{-2} \to 0$ (i.e., $nh^4 \to \infty$), and this imposes a necessary condition upon the choice of window width. Ichimura states this restriction.[4]

Stochastic equicontinuity considerations also impose restrictions upon potential models and the nature of data. It is hard to be concise about these constraints as there are many possible combinations involving smoothness of the $F(\cdot)$ function and the existence of moments of the random variables y_i, x_i, etc. Andrews (1994) discusses various sets of sufficient conditions. Perhaps the simplest of these occurs when v_i is a bounded random variable. Unfortunately, this would create some complications in getting an asymptotically unbiased estimator of F_i and its derivatives by kernel methods if points close to the boundary were found in the data set. For this reason, it might be desirable to trim such points out of the formation of the first-order conditions; a suitable trimming function can

---

[4] To get $n^{1/2}\left(E(\bar{\theta}) - \theta_0\right)$ to be $o(1)$, a Taylor series expansion of $\bar{\theta}$ around θ_0 as a function of h shows that this occurs if either $n^{1/2}h^2$ or the term attached to h^2 is $o(1)$. Ichimura has a symmetric kernel thereby accounting for the term in h.

be found in Klein and Spady (1993) (see Section 7.4.2). One wonders whether this modification would be important in practice.

Ichimura's estimator is conceptually simple to implement. Once a nonparametric estimator of m_i is chosen, estimation of θ can be performed with a nonlinear regression program in which the quadratic function to be minimized is $\sum_{i=1}^{n}(y_i - \hat{m}_i)^2$. Standard errors of $\tilde{\theta}$ follow from Theorem 7.1. Because a consistent estimator of the derivative matrix D needs to be computed as part of the first-order conditions, only the covariance matrix of $n^{1/2}\bar{v}(\theta_0, \tau_0)$, V, demands enumeration. When the data are independent, a simple consistent estimator of this would be $n^{-1}\sum \hat{v}_i(\tilde{\theta}, \hat{\tau})\hat{v}_i(\tilde{\theta}, \hat{\tau})'$; dependent data could be handled with the autocorrelation and heteroskedastic consistent covariance matrix estimators of Newey and West (1987) or Andrews (1991b). Although conceptually simple, Ichimura's estimator is not cheap to compute owing to the need to solve for $\hat{m}_i$ and its derivatives for all $i = 1, \ldots, n$. Consequently, each time the function $\sum(y_i - \hat{m}_i)^2$ is evaluated n nonparametric regressions must be carried out. Obviously, it is important to keep the number of function evaluations low. If optimization can be performed by gradient methods some savings are available by observing that analytic derivatives can be expressed as a function of $\hat{m}_i$, $\partial\hat{m}_i/\partial v_i$, and the data alone, thereby avoiding the need to reevaluate the nonparametric estimators of m_i and $\partial m_i/\partial v_i$. In contrast, adoption of numerical derivatives would be very costly as these quantities would need to be recomputed nonparametrically after every parameter perturbation. Unfortunately, in many instances, gradient methods may not suffice as the optimand implicit in the estimator is badly behaved, with saddle points and local optima.

7.4.2 Klein and Spady's Estimator

Klein and Spady (1993) proposed that θ be estimated by maximizing

$$L = \sum(1 - y_i)\log(1 - \hat{m}(v(x_i, \theta))) + \sum y_i \log[\hat{m}(v(x_i, \theta))]$$

(7.22)

with respect to θ or by solving the first-order conditions

$$\sum_{i=1}^{n} \hat{m}(v(x_i, \hat{\theta}))^{-1}[1 - \hat{m}(v(x_i, \hat{\theta}))]^{-1}[\partial\hat{m}(v(x_i, \theta))/\partial\theta]$$

$$\times [y_i - \hat{m}(v(x_i, \hat{\theta}))] = 0.$$

(7.23)

Details of the construction of $\hat{m}(\cdot)$ are exactly as for Ichimura's estimator. In fact Klein and Spady have a slightly different way of estimating m_i. Because

y_i is either zero or unity,

$$\hat{m}_i = \sum_{j=1}^{n} y_j K((v_j - v_i)/h) \Bigg/ \sum_{j=1}^{n} K((v_j - v_i)/h)$$

$$= \sum_{j \in I_1} K((v_j - v_i)/h) \Bigg/ \sum_{j=1}^{n} K((v_j - v_i)/h),$$

where I_1 designates the set of j for which $y_j = 1$. Hence the numerator is an estimator of $f(v_i | y_i = 1)$ while the denominator estimates the unconditional density of $f(v_i)$. Viewed as a ratio of density estimates one will only get the $\hat{m}_i$ above if the same kernels and window widths are used for both calculations.

Application of Theorem 7.1 demonstrates the consistency and asymptotic normality of the estimator under the same conditions as for Ichimura with the addition of the requirement that the infimum of $\hat{m}(v(x_i, \hat{\theta}))(1 - \hat{m}(v(x_i, \hat{\theta})))$ over the range of $v(x_i, \theta_0)$ be nonzero. Difficulties can stem from this last restriction when $v(x_i, \theta_0)$ is a bounded random variable, since $F(\cdot)$ would be zero and unity at boundary points, leading Klein and Spady to recommend trimming of observations. Essentially their idea is to assign zero weight to those observations with v_i close to the lower and upper boundaries and unit weight to observations in the interior. As the sample size grows it is desirable to trim closer and closer to the boundaries and this suggests relating the trimming function ζ_i to the window width – see Klein and Spady (1993) for an exact statement. Certainly, for asymptotic proofs, trimming is indispensable, although it is less clear whether it is quite as important in practical application. Nevertheless, after making this modification they maximize the following function:

$$\sum \zeta_i [(1 - y_i) \log(1 - \hat{m}_i) + y_i \log(\hat{m}_i)].$$

Other computational details are exactly as for Ichimura's estimator, except that Klein and Spady recommend either the use of a higher order kernel or an adaptive estimator (Section 2.2.5) when estimating m_i and its derivatives. As mentioned earlier this removes bias. The covariance matrix of $n^{1/2}(\hat{\theta} - \theta_0)$ will be

$$V_{KS} = A^{-1} \left[\text{var} \left\{ n^{-1/2} \left(\sum_{i=1}^{n} m_i^{-1}(1 - m_i)^{-1} \right. \right. \right.$$
$$\left. \left. \left. \times (\partial m_i/\partial\theta)(y_i - m_i) \right) \right\} \right] A^{-1},$$

where

$$A = p \lim_{n\to\infty} n^{-1} \sum m_i^{-1}(1 - m_i)^{-1} (\partial m_i/\partial\theta)(\partial m_i/\partial\theta)'.$$

This is the equivalent of the variance of a parametric estimator where m_i replaces F_i. All the elements in V_{KS} can be consistently estimated; m_i etc. by $\hat{m}_i$ and the middle term either directly or with some robust estimator to take account of heterogeneity or dependence.

Klein and Spady's estimator attains the SP efficiency bound. To see this it is sufficient to show that (7.23) amounts to solving the first-order conditions $\sum \tilde{d}_\theta(i) = 0$. Equation (7.11) gives the efficient score

$$\tilde{d}_\theta(i) = (y_i - m_i) m_i^{-1} (1 - m_i)^{-1} (\partial m_i / \partial v_i)$$

$$\times [(\partial v_i / \partial \theta) - E((\partial v_i / \partial \theta) | v_i)],$$

and Lemma 7.1 shows that the product of the last two elements of this expression is just $\partial m_i / \partial \theta$, so that (7.23) is the sample efficient score. Note that from (7.21) the derivative of $\hat{m}((x_i, \theta))$ with respect to θ brings in the two elements in the last term.

Klein and Spady provide some simulation evidence on the properties of their estimator. Data are generated from a two-regressor linear model, implying a single unknown parameter after the normalization discussed in Section 7.3, with an error term that is normally distributed but which has conditional heteroskedasticity, thereby making for fatter tails than the normal in the density of u_i. Sample size was set to 100. They find little difference between the performance of the trimmed and untrimmed estimators, suggesting that one might dispense with this modification in practice, even though it was important to their proof of asymptotic normality. The efficiency loss, compared to Probit, is only 22% in the case that u_i is normal with no heteroskedasticity. When the density of u_i was not normal their estimator showed much lower bias and mean square error than the probit estimator. Particularly striking was the vastly better performance of the SP estimator in predicting $P(y_i = 1 | x_i' \beta)$. It would appear that this estimator has a promising future in the estimation of discrete choice models.

7.4.3 The SNP Maximum Likelihood Estimator

Following the suggestion of Gallant and Nychka (1987), Gabler et al. (1993) approximate the density of the underlying latent error u_i^* with the SNP procedure of earlier chapters. Designating this by $f^*(u_i)$ one can then find an approximation to F_i by integration. Once that quantity is computed, estimation is essentially the same as for Klein and Spady, with the likelihood being maximized with respect to θ and any tuning parameters used in the SNP approximation. Consequently, it is simply a matter of using a different estimator of $E(y_i | v(x_i, \theta))$ than that adopted in the kernel-based approach of Klein and Spady.

7.4.4   Local Maximum Likelihood Estimation

Gozalo and Linton observe that, since $\hat{m}(\nu(x_i, \theta))$ in (7.22) is a conditional mean one might replace it with the conditional mean of a parametric model $F(x_i'\beta)$ and then perform local likelihood analysis; for example, they maximize

$$\sum_{i=1}^{n} K\left(\frac{x_i - x}{h}\right) \left[(1 - y_i) \log\left(1 - F\left(x_i'\beta\right)\right) + y_i \log\left(F\left(x_i'\beta\right)\right)\right]$$

with respect to β. Such a procedure produces an estimate of the $P(y_i = 1)$ at the values $x_i = x$ and is the analogue of the local linear regression method discussed in Chapter 3.

7.5   Alternative Consistent SP Estimators

A number of other SP estimators for discrete choice models appear in the literature. Five of these, the maximum score estimator (Manski, 1975), the smoothed maximum score estimator of Horowitz (1992), the maximum rank correlation estimator (Han, 1987), Cosslett's (1983) approximation to the MLE, and the average derivative estimator of Powell et al. (1989) are discussed below. In every case consistency of the estimator has been shown, although, with the exception of the average derivative and rank correlation estimators, not $n^{1/2}$ consistency. Fundamentally, one wishes to estimate $P\{y_i = 1|x_i\}$, and this task is given more structure by assuming that $P\{y_i = 1\} = F(x_i'\beta)$, where $F(\cdot)$ is unknown; that is, the probability to be estimated has a single index form, reducing the problem to one of estimating β. As pointed out in Section 7.3, β is not identified. To solve the lack of invariance to scaling, a normalization was employed in Section 7.3, but an alternative is to require that $\beta'\beta = 1$. To solve the lack of invariance to translations, β could either be defined as exclusive of the intercept or some identifying constraint such as $F(0) = .5$ could be placed upon $F(\cdot)$; the latter identifies the intercept. In Subsections 7.5.1, 7.5.3, and 7.5.4 $\beta'\beta = 1$ is a constraint that needs to be adjoined to any optimization being performed, while the intercept is either deleted from β or $F(0) = .5$ is assumed. The estimators of Sections 7.5.2 and 7.5.5, due to Horowitz (1992) and Powell, Stock, and Stoker (1989), work with the reparameterization of Section 7.3.

7.5.1   Manski's Maximum Score Estimator

One way to motivate Ichimura's and Klein and Spady's estimators is to recognize that they optimize functions with respect to β whose expectation is optimized at β_0. Accordingly, in the same way as was true of the M-estimators of Chapter 5, other functions might be substituted to get a consistent estimator. In this vein

Manski (1975) proposed

$$Q_M(\beta) = \sum_{i=1}^{n} y_i I\left(x_i'\beta \geq 0\right) + (1 - y_i) I\left(x_i'\beta < 0\right), \qquad (7.24)$$

where $Q_M(\beta)$ gives the number of correct predictions (the "score") if y_i was predicted to be unity whenever $x_i'\beta \geq 0$. As Amemiya (1985, p. 343) shows $E\left(Q_M(\beta)\right)$ is minimized at $\beta = \beta_0$ when $F(0) = .5$. Strong consistency of the estimator has been established but $n^{1/3}(\hat{\beta} - \beta_0)$ has a nonnormal limiting distribution (Kim and Pollard, 1990). Because of this slow rate of convergence the estimator might be regarded as unattractive relative to the estimators of Section 7.4. However, this disadvantage is possibly offset by its being a little more robust to specification errors. Specifically, $E\left(Q_m(\beta)\right)$ is maximized at $\beta = \beta_0$ even if there is heteroskedasticity in the latent errors u_i^* in (7.1) (assuming that $F(0) = .5$). Given that feature, a comparison of the maximum score and other estimators may be advisable. Unfortunately, the different rates of convergence mean that specification tests of the Hausman (1978) variety cannot be done.

Computation of the maximum score estimator is not trivial as Q_M is not continuous in β. Manski describes algorithms for finding the optimum and Manski and Thompson (1988) show how to perform hypothesis tests with the bootstrap.

7.5.2 Horowitz's Smoothed Maximum Score Estimator

Because many of the difficulties with the maximum score estimator arise from the lack of continuity in the indicator function $I(v_i)$, Horowitz (1992) replaces it with a smooth function of v_i. A central property of the indicator function is that it takes the value unity when $v_i > 0$ and zero when $v_i \leq 0$, and this feature must be preserved by any smooth function used as a replacement. Let the smooth function be $\kappa(h^{-1}v_i)$, where h is a window width that depends on sample size and for which $\lim_{n \to \infty} h = 0$. Then, if $v_i < 0$, $\psi_i = h^{-1}v_i \to -\infty$ as $n \to \infty$, whereas, if $v_i > 0$, it will tend to infinity. Consequently, with $\kappa(\cdot)$ being chosen so that $\lim_{\psi \to \infty} \kappa(\psi) = 0$, $\lim_{\psi \to -\infty} \kappa(\psi) = 1$, the function acts like an indicator function when n is large. The obvious class of functions satisfying this restriction are c.d.f.s.[5]

---

[5] Notice that in Chapters 2 and 3 we sought a smooth function assigning a large weight when ψ was in a prespecified region around zero and giving zero if ψ lay outside that region. Hence the function needed to have the properties $K(-\infty) = 0$, $K(\infty) = 0$, as large positive or negative values of ψ would lie outside the designated region. In the current context only nonpositive values of ψ are to be penalized, necessitating the selection of a function with different characteristics.

Before replacing the indicator function by a smooth function it is useful to express the sample mean of (7.24) in the format adopted by Horowitz:

$$S' = n^{-1} \sum_{i=1}^{n} \{y_i I(v_i \geq 0) + (1 - y_i)I(v_i < 0)\} \tag{7.25}$$

$$= n^{-1} \sum_{i=1}^{n} \{y_i I(v_i \geq 0) + (1 - y_i)(1 - I(v_i \geq 0))\} \tag{7.26}$$

$$= n^{-1} \sum_{i=1}^{n} (2y_i - 1)I(v_i \geq 0) + 1 - n^{-1} \sum_{k=1}^{n} y_k \tag{7.27}$$

$$= n^{-1} \sum_{i=1}^{n} [2I(y_i = 1) - 1]I(v_i \geq 0) + \left(1 - n^{-1} \sum_{k=1}^{n} y_k\right). \tag{7.28}$$

Subsequently $I(v_i \geq 0)$ is replaced by the smooth function to yield

$$S = n^{-1} \sum_{i=1}^{n} [2I(y_i = 1) - 1]\kappa(h^{-1}v_i) + 1 - n^{-1} \sum_{i=1}^{n} y_i. \tag{7.29}$$

Because the last two terms in (7.29) do not depend upon θ, Horowitz maximizes the first one only, to produce $\hat{\theta}_H$. Differentiating S with respect to θ yields

$$\frac{\partial S}{\partial \theta} = (nh)^{-1} \sum_{i=1}^{n} [2I(y_i = 1) - 1] K\left(h^{-1}v_i\right) \frac{\partial v_i}{\partial \theta}, \tag{7.30}$$

where $K(\cdot)$, the derivative of $\kappa(\psi)$ with respect to ψ, is a density function. Because the kernel $K(\cdot)$ appearing in Chapters 2 and 3 had $K(-\infty) = K(\infty) = 0$, and integrated to unity, that nomenclature is retained.

Now (7.30) is similar to the expressions for the density and the numerator of the conditional mean estimators (see Equation (2.7) in Section 2.2.3 and Equation (3.5) in Section 3.2.2). As both of these quantities had a limiting distribution when normalized by $(nh)^{1/2}$ (see Theorems 2.9 and 3.5) by analogy it might be expected that $(nh)^{1/2}\partial S/\partial \theta$ would also have a limiting distribution, although, in line with the result in Theorem 2.10, it will be centered at $E\left[(nh)^{1/2}\partial S/\partial \theta\right]$ rather than at zero. Writing

$$(nh)^{1/2}\frac{\partial S}{\partial \theta} = (nh)^{1/2}\left[\frac{\partial S}{\partial \theta} - E\left(\frac{\partial S}{\partial \theta}\right)\right] + (nh)^{1/2}E\left(\frac{\partial S}{\partial \theta}\right),$$

the first term can be shown to be $\mathcal{N}(0, D)$, where $D = \int K^2(\psi)\tilde{x}_i\tilde{x}_i' f(0|\tilde{x}_i)$

$f_{\tilde{x}}(\tilde{x}_i)\,d\psi\,d\tilde{x}_i$, with $\tilde{x}_i = \partial v_i/\partial\theta$.[6] The second term is

$$(nh)^{1/2}E\left(\frac{\partial S}{\partial\theta}\right)$$

$$= (nh)^{1/2}E\left[n^{-1}\sum_{i=1}^{n}(2I(y_i=1)-1)K\left(h^{-1}v_i|\tilde{x}_i\right)\tilde{x}_i h^{-1}\right].$$

By using the law of iterated expectations

$$E\left(\frac{\partial S}{\partial\theta}\right) = \int[1-2F(-v_i|v_i,\tilde{x}_i)h^{-1}\tilde{x}_i K(h^{-1}v_i)$$

$$\times f(v_i|\tilde{x}_i)f_{\tilde{x}}(\tilde{x}_i)]\,dv_i\,d\tilde{x}_i$$

$$= \int[1-2F(-h\psi_i|h\psi_i,\tilde{x}_i)\tilde{x}_i K(\psi_i)$$

$$\times f(h\psi_i|\tilde{x}_i)f_{\tilde{x}}(\tilde{x}_i)]\,d\psi_i\,d\tilde{x}_i,$$

after the change of variable to $\psi_i = v_i/h$. One can also show that

$$-n^{-1}\frac{\partial^2 S}{\partial\theta\partial\theta'} \xrightarrow{p} Q = 2\int \tilde{x}_i\tilde{x}_i' F^{(1)}(0\mid 0,\tilde{x}_i)\, f(0|\tilde{x}_i)\, f_{\tilde{x}}(\tilde{x}_i)\,d\tilde{x}_i.$$

(7.31)

By design $\hat{\theta}_H$ satisfies $\partial S/\partial\theta(\hat{\theta}_H) = 0$. Linearizing these first-order conditions around θ_0, and using (7.31), gives

$$(nh)^{1/2}(\hat{\theta}_H-\theta_0) = -\left(\frac{\partial^2 S}{\partial\theta\partial\theta'}\right)^{-1}(nh)^{1/2}\frac{\partial S}{\partial\theta}$$

$$= Q^{-1}(nh)^{1/2}\frac{\partial S}{\partial\theta} + o_p(1).$$

From earlier arguments we have

$$(nh)^{1/2}\frac{\partial S}{\partial\theta} \xrightarrow{p} \mathcal{N}\left[\lim_{n\to\infty}(nh)^{1/2}E\left(\frac{\partial S}{\partial\theta}\right), D\right],$$

meaning that

$$(nh)^{1/2}(\hat{\theta}_H-\theta_0) \xrightarrow{d} \mathcal{N}\left(\lim_{n\to\infty}(nh)^{1/2}Q^{-1}E\left(\frac{\partial S}{\partial\theta}\right), Q^{-1}DQ^{-1}\right),$$

and the limiting distribution will not be centered on θ_0 unless $\lim_{n\to\infty}(nh)^{1/2}E(\partial S/\partial\theta)=0$. Following the strategy of Theorem 2.2, we expand $F(-h\psi_i|$

[6] From Section 7.3, v_i is linear in x_i so that $\partial v_i/\partial\theta$ is a subset of the vector x_i, and it is convenient to write this as $\tilde{x}_i$, rather than retain the $\partial v_i/\partial\theta$ representation. If (7.1) had been nonlinear in x_i, $\tilde{x}_i$ should be thought of as $\partial v_i/\partial\theta$ in what follows.

$h\psi_i, \tilde{x}_i)$ and $f\,(h\psi_i|\tilde{x}_i)$ around $h\psi_i = 0$, thereby expressing $E\,(\partial S/\partial\theta)$ as a polynomial in $h\psi_i$, making it clear that there will be a bias in the estimator. A similar situation occurred with density and moment estimators, and a number of methods to alleviate the problem were canvassed in Section 2.4.3. A popular solution is to construct an rth-order kernel for which $\int \psi^i K(\psi)\,d\psi = 0$, $i = 1, \ldots, r - 1$, as that will mean that only terms in h^r and above in the polynomial approximation to $E\,(\partial S/\partial\theta)$ are nonzero. Thereafter, if the window width is set so that $(nh)^{1/2}h^r \to 0$, the asymptotic distribution of $(nh)^{1/2}(\hat{\theta}_H - \theta_0)$ would be centered at zero. This is the condition termed (A15) in Section 2.5.3 and (A10) in Section 3.4.1, although in both cases $r = 2$, as it was only assumed that the underlying functions had derivatives existing up to second order. Unfortunately, this particular choice for h slows convergence. The optimum window width for an rth-order kernel was explored in (2.65), and it was found to be proportional to $n^{-1/(2r+1)}$.[7] With that value $(nh)^{1/2}h^r \to \lambda(\neq 0)$. For this reason Horowitz follows Bierens (1987a) and estimates the bias term.

Horowitz reports a simulation study of the estimator. Only an intercept is to be estimated and that is done under three alternative densities for u_i – logistic, uniform, and Student's t with three degrees of freedom. In all cases the median of u_i is zero so as to identify the intercept. Both second- and fourth-order kernels are used. For $r = 2$, he makes K the Gaussian kernel and κ will therefore be the cumulative normal. When $r = 4$ he selects an Epanechnikov-type kernel. δ is set to .10 and n ranges from 250 to 1000. Generally, results were the same for all densities, the principal determinant of performance was the variance of u_i rather than the shape of the density. Using the true optimal window width the estimator dominates Manski's unsmoothed estimator when $n = 1{,}000$ but is inferior to it if $n = 250$. Bias is around 5% of the true value, whereas the variance exceeds its asymptotic value by factors between 70 and 100% when $n = 250$ and $r = 2$. Opting for a fourth-order kernel proves to be very important; the ratio of the MSE of $\hat{\theta}_H$ to its asymptotic value is 1.68 for $r = 2$ but 1.28 for $r = 4$ ($n = 250$), when the density of u_i is logistic. The bias and variance interact to produce nominal test sizes roughly twice that predicted by asymptotic theory. One reason for the poor performance when $n = 250$ seems to be that, as the variance of u_i increases, S is nearly flat in the vicinity of its maximum, causing the matrix Q to be nearly zero and the estimate of the bias term to be very large. Horowitz (1993b) indicates that the size of the test statistics formed from the smoothed maximum score estimator can be determined more accurately by using a bootstrap method and he sets out the steps to implement this. He also

---

[7] The factor of proportionality will be different to that in (2.65) as the objective will be to minimize the MSE using the mean and variance of the asymptotic distribution of $\hat{\theta}_H$.

notes that S can have many local extrema and a global optimization is needed to get $\hat{\theta}_H$. The simulated annealing algorithm of Szu and Hartley (1987) seems to work well.

In practice the optimal window width could not be computed, and Horowitz examines how good an estimate of it can be made by plugging in sample estimates of its determinants. This strategy is similar to "plug-in" methods mentioned in Chapter 2. However, a new element enters owing to the dependence of the estimator of the bias upon $\hat{\theta}_H$. Because $\hat{\theta}_H$ has small sample bias, so to will the "bias" estimator, leading to the need for a further correction to properly estimate the bias. Even with this correction the estimated window width is much larger than the optimal one, although it would appear that the correspondence is close enough to produce an $\hat{\theta}_H$ that dominates Manski's estimator when $n = 1,000$. From all of this it is clear that selection of window width is crucial to estimator performance, and a good deal more work needs to be done on this topic. Nevertheless, the fact that $\hat{\theta}_H$ does have an asymptotic normal distribution, and that its convergence rate can be made close to $n^{-1/2}$, if r is large, makes it an attractive estimator worthy of further investigation.

7.5.3 Han's Maximum Rank Correlation Estimator

Another function that could be maximized is the rank correlation between y_i and $x_i'\beta$,

$$Q_H(\beta) = \frac{1}{n(n-1)} \sum_{j=1}^{n} \sum_{i \neq j} I(y_i > y_j) I\left(x_i'\beta > x_j'\beta\right)$$

$$+ I(y_i < y_j) I\left(x_i'\beta < x_j'\beta\right), \tag{7.32}$$

where the summation is taken over all $\binom{n}{2}$ combinations of two distinct elements (i, j) from $i = 1, \ldots, n; j = 1, \ldots, n$. The idea behind the estimator is simple. Because F is monotonically increasing in $x_i'\beta$, $P(y_i \geq y_j | x_i, x_j) \geq P(y_i \leq y_j | x_i, x_j)$ if $x_i'\beta_0 \geq x_j'\beta_0$, making it likely that $y_i \geq y_j$ whenever $x_i'\beta_0 \geq x_j'\beta_0$, so that a high correlation between the rank of y_i and the rank of $x_i'\beta$ should be observed when $\beta = \beta_0$, whereas a lower value would be exhibited when β departs from β_0. Formally, $E(Q_H(\beta))$ is maximized at $\beta = \beta_0$ (Han, 1987, p. 310–11), and that fact is the basis of a consistency proof for the estimator. Sherman (1993) reformulates $E(Q_H(\beta))$ as $2[E(\tau(z, \beta))]$, where

$$\tau(z, \beta) = P(Y < y) I(X'\beta < x'\beta) + P(Y > y) I(X'\beta > x'\beta),$$

where small letters indicate realizations of the random variables in large letters and $Z = [Y, X']'$. Thereafter the estimator of $\beta = \beta(\theta)$, the identifiable parameters, can be regarded as an M-estimator and will be asymptotically normal.

Computation of Han's estimator is complex owing to the lack of continuity in the function, and replacing the indicator function with a smooth function would probably be wise.[8]

7.5.4   Cosslett's Approximate MLE

In the same manner as that of Klein and Spady, Cosslett (1983) attempted to choose β by maximizing the log likelihood in (7.5) where F_i is replaced by a nonparametric estimator constructed as follows: For a given β it is possible to order the observations by increasing values of $z_i = x_i'\beta$. Selecting a value of z_i, say z^*, and constructing an interval around that value, the expected fraction of y_is equaling unity in this interval would be $F(z^*)$. Consequently $F(z^*)$ might be estimated by the ratio of the number of observed y_is in the interval equaling unity to the total number. It only remains to choose the intervals. Because $F(-\infty) = 0$ and $F(\infty) = 1$, the lowest interval will terminate at the first $y_i = 1$ to ensure that the estimate of $F(-\infty)$ is really zero. Similarly, the top interval will consist entirely of the last set of values of y_i that equal unity. In between these bounds Cosslett suggests that, starting from the bottom, an interval terminates whenever a $y_i = 0$ is encountered. After doing such a sorting, intervals can then be combined into larger intervals to ensure that $\hat{F}(\cdot)$ never decreases. For example, suppose that, after ordering of data by z_i, the y_i are

$$0\,0\,\vdots\,1\,1\,0\,\vdots\,0\,1\,1\,1\,0\,0\,\vdots\,1\,1.$$

Dotted lines now indicate the divisions established by application of the rules above, leading to $F(\cdot)$ being represented as $\left[0, \frac{2}{3}, \frac{1}{2}, 1\right]$. But this would not be satisfactory for a distribution function, leading to the combination of the second and third intervals to give

$$0\,0\,\vdots\,1\,1\,0\,0\,1\,1\,1\,0\,0\,\vdots\,1\,1,$$

making $\hat{F}(\cdot) = 0$ for $i = 1, 2$; $\hat{F}(\cdot) = \frac{5}{9}$ for $i = 3\text{--}11$; and $\hat{F} = 1$ for $i = 12, 13$. Clearly, the number of spikes used in approximating $F(\cdot)$, L, is much smaller than n, but L would be expected to grow with n. Cosslett shows that this strategy for estimating $F(\cdot)$ does yield a consistent estimator. However, as observed in Section 7.4, $n^{1/4}$ consistency of $\hat{F}$ may actually be needed for $n^{1/2}$ consistency

---

[8] In some correspondence with us Scott Thompson has observed that the rank correlation estimator is no more difficult to compute than the maximum score estimator since it can be viewed as the latter applied to the differences between each pair of observations in the original data set.

of the SP estimator of β. Wang and Zhou (1995, Appendix) suggest that results in Leurgans (1982) can be used to show that $\hat{F}$ is $n^{1/3}$ consistent. In the same way as Horowitz's estimator generalizes Manski's, Ming (1993) has suggested that a smoothed estimator of $F(\cdot)$ be used rather than a step function, and he shows consistency of such an estimator.

7.5.5 An Iterative Least Squares Estimator

Wang and Zhou (1995) consider the $E(y_i^* | x_i'\beta, y_i)$ and find $\hat{\beta}$ that solves the moment condition

$$\sum_{i=1}^{n} x_i \left[I(y_i > 0)\hat{E}\left(y_i^* | x_i'\hat{\beta}, y_i = 1\right) \right.$$
$$\left. + (1 - I(y_i > 0))\, \hat{E}\left(y_i^* | x_i'\hat{\beta}, y_i = 0\right) \right] = 0, \tag{7.33}$$

where

$$E\left(y_i^* | x_i'\beta, y_i = 1\right) = x_i'\beta + F^{-1}\left(x_i'\beta\right) \int_{-\infty}^{x_i'\beta} u^* dF(u^*),$$

$$E\left(y_i^* | x_i'\beta, y_i = 0\right) = x_i'\beta + \left(1 - F\left(x_i'\beta\right)\right)^{-1} \int_{x_i'\beta}^{\infty} u^* dF(u^*).$$

To estimate these expectations they replace β by some preliminary estimator and substitute Coslett's estimator of $F(\cdot)$ for F. It is easy to see that (7.33) is based on the moment condition

$$E\left[x_i \left[\begin{array}{c} I(y_i > 0)\left(E\left(y_i^* | x_i'\beta, y_i = 1\right) - x_i'\beta\right) \\ + (1 - I(y_i > 0))\left(E\left(y_i^* | x_i'\beta, y_i = 0\right) - x_i'\beta\right) \end{array} \right] \right] = 0,$$
$$\tag{7.34}$$

and this can be shown to be valid by using the law of iterated expectations and writing $E(\cdot)$ as $E\left[E\left(\cdot | y_i = 1 \text{ or } 0\right)\right]$. Thus, (7.34) becomes

$$E\left[x_i \left(F_i F_i^{-1} \int_{-\infty}^{x_i'\beta} u^* dF(u^*) \right) + (1 - F_i)(1 - F_i)^{-1} \int_{x_i'\beta}^{\infty} u^* dF(u^*) \right]$$

$$= E\left[x_i \int_{-\infty}^{\infty} u^* dF(u^*) \right],$$

which is zero.

Wang and Zhou iterate the estimator. They claim $n^{1/2}$ consistency of the estimator, but the method of proof assumes that $\hat{F}$ is $n^{1/2}$ consistent, and this cannot be correct for Coslett's estimator. However, in simulation experiments they show that the estimator has good finite-sample performance and its empirical density function is reasonably close to normal. It is obviously the case that regardless of whether $\hat{F}$ is $n^{1/2}$ or $n^{1/3}$ consistent the distribution of $\hat{\beta}$ will depend upon that for $\hat{F}$, and Wang and Zhou recommend that this dependence be allowed for by bootstrapping.

7.5.6 *Derivative-Based Estimators*

As mentioned in Section 4.3.3, it is possible to form a consistent estimator of θ from average derivatives of the conditional expectation of y_i with respect to x_i. Using the normalization of Section 7.3, let $v_i = x_{2i} + x_{3i}\theta_1 + \cdots + x_{qi}\theta_{q-2}$, from which the average derivatives are

$$\delta_k = E\left(\partial m_i/\partial x_{ki}\right)$$
$$= E\left[\left(\partial m_i/\partial v_i\right)\left(\partial v_i/\partial x_{ki}\right)\right] \quad (k = 2, \ldots, q)$$
$$= E\left(\partial m_i/\partial v_i\right)$$

for $k = 2$ and $E\left(\partial m_i/\partial v_i\right)\theta_{k-2}$ for $k > 2$. Accordingly, $\hat{\theta}_{k-2} = \hat{\delta}_k/\hat{\delta}_2$ and the average derivatives can be estimated from (4.31), (4.32), or (4.36). Alternatively, one could replace the $\hat{\delta} = \left(\hat{\delta}_3, \ldots, \hat{\delta}_q\right)$ with the weighted average derivatives in (4.37). In both instances $n^{1/2}\left(\hat{\theta} - \theta\right) = \hat{\delta}_2^{-1} n^{1/2}\left(\hat{\delta} - \delta\right) + o_p(1)$. Defining $(\delta^+)' = (\delta_2 \ \delta')$, if $n^{1/2}\left(\hat{\delta}^+ - \delta_0^+\right) \xrightarrow{d} \mathcal{N}(0, V_\delta)$, we find

$$n^{1/2}\left(\hat{\theta}_{k-2} - \theta_{k-2}\right) \xrightarrow{d} \mathcal{N}\left(0, \delta_2^{-2} e'_{k-2} V_\delta e_{k-2}\right),$$

where e_{k-2} is a $(q-2) \times 1$ vector with zero in the $(k-2)$th place and unity elsewhere. The conditions under which $n^{1/2}\left(\hat{\delta}^+ - \delta_0^+\right)$ was asymptotically normal and centered on zero were that $nh^{q+1} \to \infty$ and that bias had been removed from the kernel estimator up to and including $O\left(h^{(q+1)/2}\right)$.[9] Unfortunately, a large value of q is the norm rather than the exception in discrete choice models and that makes for a complex adjustment (although it may be that many of the x_i are discrete and that situation is discussed in the next subsection). In this regard the recursive formulae provided for higher order kernels in Section 2.7.2 may be very helpful. One point to notice is that the window-width condition for this estimator is far more stringent than for Klein and Spady's or Ichimura's estimator. Essentially, this stems from the fact that the single-index restriction is being lost; in the latter estimators the only nonparametric

---

[9] These conditions differ from those in Section 4.3.2 because the number of derivatives being estimated here is $(q-1)$ due to the decision to treat x_{1i} as unity in the discussion in Section 7.3 and the fact that the intercept is not estimable without extra prior information on the density.

derivative estimators being exploited are with respect to the *scalar* v_i, and this produces the window-width restriction for a single derivative, namely $nh^3 \to \infty$.

7.5.7   *Models with Discrete Explanatory Variables*

Suppose that the single index includes both continuous random variables (designated with C) as well as dummy variables (distinguished by a D). This makes the single index $v_i = v_i^C + v_i^D$. A further simplification is to replace the dummy variable contribution by a linear form to give $v_i = v_i^C + z_i'\alpha$, where z_i are the dummy variables. One might want to estimate the effects of the dummy variable on the probability of taking some action. Due to the discrete nature of these variables one cannot form the derivatives used by many of the methods just discussed. An elegant solution advanced by Horowitz and Härdle (1996) is as follows. In this discussion the i subscript is suppressed.

Initially $F(.)$ is taken to be known and it is assumed that, for any value of z, values for v^C exist, v_- and v_+, such that $F(v^C + z'\alpha) < \gamma_0$ for $v^C < v_-$ and $F(v^C + z'\alpha) > \gamma_1$ for $v^C > v_+$. Taking any value of z define

$$J(z) = \int_{v_-}^{v_+} \{\gamma_0 I[F(v^C + z'\alpha) < \gamma_0] + \gamma_1 I[F(v^C + z'\alpha) > \gamma_1]$$

$$+ F(v^C + z'\alpha)I[\gamma_0 \leq F(v^C + z'\alpha) \leq \gamma_1]\} dv^C. \tag{7.35}$$

Now, after a change of variable to $u = v^C + z'\alpha$, and a use of the definitions of $v_a = \max_z\{v_+ + z'\alpha\}$ and $v_b = \min_z\{v_- + z'\alpha\}$, (7.35) can be rewritten as

$$J(z) = \gamma_0 \int_{v_- + z'\alpha}^{v_a} I[F(u) < \gamma_0]du + \gamma_0 \int_{v_a}^{v_b} I[F(u) < \gamma_0]du$$

$$+ \int_{v_a}^{v_b} F(u)I[\gamma_0 < F(u) < \gamma_1]du + \gamma_1 \int_{v_a}^{v_b} I[F(u) > \gamma_1]du$$

$$+ \gamma_1 \int_{v_b}^{v_+ + z'\alpha} I[F(u) > \gamma_1]$$

$$= \gamma_0(v_a - v_- - z'\alpha) + \gamma_1(v_+ + z'\alpha - v_b)$$

$$+ \gamma_0 \int_{v_a}^{v_b} I[F(u) < \gamma_0]du$$

$$+ \int_{v_a}^{v_b} F(u)I[\gamma_0 < F(u) < \gamma_1]du + \gamma_1 \int_{v_a}^{v_b} I[F(u) > \gamma_1]du.$$

Consider any set of two values for the dummy variables $z^{(1)}$ and $z^{(0)}$. Then

$$J\left(z^{(1)}\right) - J\left(z^{(0)}\right) = \gamma_0\left(v_a - v_- - z^{(1)\prime}\alpha\right) + \gamma_1\left(v_+ + z^{(1)\prime}\alpha - v_b\right)$$
$$- \gamma_0\left(v_a - v_- - z^{(0)\prime}\alpha\right) - \gamma_1\left(v_+ + z^{(0)\prime}\alpha - v_b\right)$$
$$= (\gamma_1 - \gamma_0)\left(z^{(1)} - z^{(0)}\right)'\alpha.$$

Clearly, if γ_1, γ_2, and $J(z^{(1)}) - J(z^{(0)})$ can be measured one could estimate α by a simple regression. If one knew v_i^C then it would be possible to compute an estimate of $F(v^C + z'\alpha)$ using a kernel estimator of the conditional expectation of Y given that the continuous and discrete contributions to this index take specified values v^C and z. This information can then be used to find γ_0 and γ_1 from the extreme values of this quantity in the data. To find v_i^C we recognize that it will generally be linear in some parameters δ, and these may be estimated by using the average derivative estimator of the previous section so that a value for v_i^C can always be found. Horowitz and Hardle also provide expressions for the covariance matrix of their estimator as well as other details, such as the need to select a higher order kernel when estimating F.

7.6   Multinomial Discrete Choice Models

Consider now the situation when there is a set C of J alternative actions, and the probability that the ith individual will choose alternative j from this set is F_{ij}, which becomes the equivalent of F_i in the univariate case. The data consist of observations on which alternative is chosen by the ith individual. Define J variables $y_{ij}(j = 1, \ldots, J)$ that take the value unity if alternative j is selected by the ith individual and zero otherwise. Then, exactly as for the binary alternative situation, $E(y_{ij}) = F_{ij}$ and the random variable y_{ij} has variance $F_{ij}(1 - F_{ij})$. Consequently, the equivalent of (7.2) when there are multiple choices is

$$y_{ij} = F_{ij} + \epsilon_{ij}, \tag{7.36}$$

whereas the log likelihood is

$$\sum_{i=1}^{n}\sum_{j=1}^{J} y_{ij} \log F_{ij}. \tag{7.37}$$

Parametric models specify a form for F_{ij}; for example, the multinomial logit model sets $F_{ij} = \exp\left(x_{ij}'\beta\right) / \sum_{j=1}^{J} \exp\left(x_{ij}'\beta\right)$. Semiparametric estimation of β would proceed exactly as in the binary case by estimating F_{ij} nonparametrically. A complication now is that F_{ij} is a function of $v_{ij} = x_{ij}'\beta$, and so this is a multi-index model. Nevertheless $F_{ij} = E(y_{ij}|v_{ik}, k = 1, \ldots, J)$ and, conceptually, there is nothing new here. Ichimura and Lee (1991) have set out a formal asymptotic theory for an extension of Ichimura's estimator, (i.e., β is found by minimizing the sum of squares from (7.36)); Lee (1995) extends Klein and Spady's binary choice estimator by maximizing (7.37).[10] The main complication comes from the multiple indices, as higher order kernels now need to be used to estimate F_{ij} owing to the expansion in the number of conditioning variables. Because higher order kernels can be negative $\hat{F}_{ij}$ might become negative and trimming needs to be done to safeguard against this possibility. A Monte Carlo experiment to evaluate the finite-sample performance indicated that the estimator is quite sensitive to the choice of window width, the proper selection of which remains an open question.

Lee derives an SP efficiency bound as a straightforward extension of that in the binary case. Provided trimming was not operative his estimator would attain the bound. However, as mentioned in connection with various applications in Chapter 5, the SP bound depends upon whatever restrictions need to be imposed as a result of the underlying distributional assumptions. Thompson (1993) points out that Lee's SP bound is appropriate if one is only imposing the multiple index assumption (i.e., that the F_{ij} depend only upon indices). However, in general there will be other restrictions caused by the fact that the probabilities F_{ij} all depend upon the same underlying distribution. For example, one restriction that would need to be imposed is that the F_{ij} sum to unity. In the binary choice case this will be trivially true. Thompson points out a realistic case in which the SP bound is not that in Lee's paper: if one describes the underlying multinomial model by writing the utilities from each choice as a function of the x_{ij} and error terms with the error terms being distributed independently of the x_{ij}.

7.7 Some Specification Tests for Discrete Choice Models

Suppose a parametric model such as logit or probit has been applied to the data. Then the expected value of y_i conditional upon the single index $x_i'\hat{\beta}$ would be $\hat{m}_i^P$, where $\hat{m}_i^P = F(x_i'\hat{\beta})$ depends on the parametric form chosen and $\hat{\beta}$ is the parametric estimator. Horowitz and Härdle (1994) and Klein (1993) suggest a test of this specification by considering the deviation of $\hat{m}_i^P$ from a nonparametric estimator of the mean of y_i conditional upon the estimated single index $x_i'\hat{\beta}$; that is, $\hat{m}_i^{NP} = E(y_i|x_i'\hat{\beta})$ is estimated nonparametrically.[11]

---

[10] Ichimura and Lee's paper deals with the estimation of multiple index models and not specifically with polychotomous choice. A multiple index model can arise in a number of other ways, e.g, if there was heteroskedasticity in the latent error underlying a discrete choice model.

[11] Klein (1993) also looks at the comparison over a specified region of the space for $x_i'\hat{\beta}$ rather than all of it. Obviously one is comparing parametric and SP estimates of the probability that y_i is unity. Other specification tests have focused upon the difference between $\hat{\beta}$ estimated parametrically and semiparametrically, e.g., Pagan and Vella (1989).

Their test statistic is

$$HH = h^{1/2} \sum_{i=1}^{n} \omega(x_i'\hat{\beta})(y_i - \hat{m}_i^P)(\hat{m}_i^{NP} - \hat{m}_i^P),$$

where $\omega(\cdot)$ is a weighting function used to improve the power of the test. They show that this is asymptotically $\mathcal{N}(0, v_{HH})$, where v_{HH} is

$$v_{HH} = 2\left(\int_{-\infty}^{\infty} K(\psi)^2 d\psi\right)\int_{-\infty}^{\infty} \omega^2(z)\sigma^4(z)\,dz,$$

and where $K(\cdot)$ is the kernel used in forming $\hat{m}^{NP}$ and $\sigma^2(z)$ is var$[y_i|v_i = z]$. The normalizing factor of $h^{1/2}$ can be explained intuitively as follows, assuming that m_i and β are known, that is HH becomes

$$HH = n^{-1/2} \sum \omega(x_i)(y_i - m_i)(nh)^{1/2}(\hat{m}^{NP} - m_i).$$

Since $(nh)^{1/2}(\hat{m}_i^{NP} - m_i)$ will be asymptotically a random variable ζ_i we might expect that $n^{-1/2} \sum \omega(x_i)(y_i - m_i)\zeta_i$ would be asymptotically normal from the Central Limit Theorem. Thus the factor $h^{1/2}$ compensates for the nonparametric estimation of m_i. Notice that $(nh)^{1/2}(\hat{m}_i^{NP} - m_i)$ will only be centered on zero if bias of the kernel has been removed, and this explains why they use higher order kernels and jackknifing when forming $\hat{m}_i^{NP}$. To estimate v_{HH} write it as

$$\int_{-\infty}^{\infty} \omega(z)\sigma^4(z)\,dz = \int_{-\infty}^{\infty} \left[\frac{\omega(z)\sigma^4(z)}{f_v(z)}\right] f_v(z),$$

which is $E(\omega(v_1)\sigma^4(v_1)f^{-1}(v_1))$, leading to the consistent estimator n^{-1} $\sum_{i=1}^{n} \omega(v_i)\sigma^4(v_i)f^{-1}(v_i)$. This still leaves $\sigma^4(v_i)$ to be estimated, and that could either be done nonparametrically or, what may be better, from the parametric model constituting the null hypothesis.

The technique has the advantage that, if the single-index restriction is correct, and only the nature of $F(\cdot)$ is of issue, the curse of dimensionality is avoided, since conditioning is only done upon a single variable. Simulations in Horowitz and Härdle using a linear/nonlinear model comparison found the test to have good size and power. Proença (1993), however, found there were difficulties with the size of the test, when applying it to tests of a logit model with simulated data, due to the conditional variance of y_i not being a constant. She also found that the test was sensitive to the choice of weighting factor $\omega(\cdot)$.[12] Generally, this is taken to be unity for the range of $x_i'\hat{\beta}$ from the α to $(1 - \alpha)$th quantiles and zero elsewhere, with α being either .05 or .01. It is possible that the difficulties she noted in estimating the asymptotic variance come from the computation of the

---

[12] Fan and Liu (1997) suggest that one use $f(x_i'\hat{\beta})$ as the weighting function and they replace $\hat{m}_i^p$ by its convolution with a kernel.

conditional variance as $\hat{m}_i^{NP}\left(1 - m_i^{NP}\right)$. Since the test is to be evaluated under the null hypothesis of a parametric model $\hat{m}_i^{P}\left(1 - m_i^{P}\right)$ could be a more stable choice. Proença also determined that critical values found with the bootstrap procedure greatly improved the finite-sample behavior of the test.

A second issue with discrete choice models is whether the single-index assumption is correct. Stoker (1992) and Rodriguez and Stoker (1993) developed a test of this. Essentially, the question is whether the conditional mean can be written as a function of the scalar $x_i'\beta$ or whether it has the more general form $m(x_i)$. If the null hypothesis was that the model was a parametric one then one could just test this using the approaches described in Section 3.13 (e.g., basing it on $\sum \left(y_i - \hat{m}_i^{P}\right)\left(\hat{m}_i^{NP} - \hat{m}_i^{P}\right)$, where $\hat{m}_i^{NP} = E\left(y_i|x_i\right)$). Rodriguez and Stoker's variant is to take the maintained model as the semiparametric one, that is, instead of $\hat{m}_i^{P}$ they have $E\left(y_i|v\left(x_i, \hat{\theta}\right)\right)$, where $\hat{\theta}$ is an SP estimate of θ, in their case the average derivative estimator. In practice they also adopt a weighting function that trims out data according to the value of $\hat{f}(x_i)$. If $\hat{f}(x_i) > b$ the weighting function is given a value of unity but zero otherwise, where b is a small number. Although different in application, the use of an SP estimator rather than a parametric one should not matter, as both are $\sqrt{n}$ consistent, so that this test falls into the same class as those discussed in Section 3.13. Rodriguez and Stoker applied their test to study the structure of the Boston housing data model described in Stoker (1992). This features 500 observations on housing prices and nine regressors x_i. They find that both a log linear model and the single-index model were rejected against a nonparametric model.

7.8 Applications

Semiparametric estimation of discrete choice models has proven to be quite popular. Das (1991) used the maximum score estimator to determine the factors entering into a decision by cement firms to shut down their kilns; Horowitz (1993a) applies the maximum score and smoothed maximum score estimators to the choice of travel mode to work. As might be expected, labor force participation decisions are also popular vehicles for the techniques. Newey et al. (1990) adopted Ichimura's and Klein and Spady's estimators; Gabler et al. (1993) used the SNP estimator; and Gerfin (1996) applies the smoothed maximum score, Klein–Spady, and SNP estimators to data on women's participation rates from a variety of countries. The comparisons performed in the latter paper are very interesting. In line with theory, the SNP and Klein–Spady estimates of θ tend to be quite close. More surprising is the fact that the smoothed maximum score estimates are within a standard deviation of Klein–Spady. However, the predicted participation probabilities of the different estimators were markedly different for his German data set. He performed a number of tests on the estimators and found that Vuong's (1989) likelihood ratio test favored the Klein–Spady estimator.

8 Semiparametric Estimation of Selectivity Models

8.1 Introduction

When individual data are used to estimate the parameters of a model, a persistent question that has to be addressed is whether the sample of individuals has been randomly selected. If their presence in the sample is a consequence of some choice made, and selection has been a function of some economic variables, then it is possible that a failure to recognize the endogeneity of inclusion in the sample can lead to inconsistent parameter estimators. The presence of such endogenous sample-selection bias has been recognized for many years, for example Roy (1951), but its implication for estimation theory was left until the papers by Gronau (1974) and Heckman (1974). Since that time it has been recognized that the problems caused by sample selection are pervasive in the analysis of microeconomic data and some adjustment for its effects needs to be made.

Conceptually, the effects of sample selection are simple; selection transforms a linear model with errors having a zero conditional mean and being homoskedastic into one where the errors have a nonzero conditional mean and are heteroskedastic. Somehow an adjustment needs to be performed to compensate for these changes to the error term. Parametric approaches, in particular that of Heckman (1976), have proceeded by finding expressions for the conditional means and variances of the error term under self-selection, and then making corrections to compensate for these effects. Section 8.2 outlines this estimator. It involves a two-step procedure that is simple to use and is available in many computer packages. An alternative, also discussed in this section, is to do maximum likelihood estimation, and this is also a standard option in programs such as LIMDEP.

There is some dissatisfaction over the performance of the two-step estimator. Two reasons might be advanced as an explanation. One is that the estimator is very inefficient relative to the maximum likelihood estimator. A second problem is that the adjustments performed require precise distributional assumptions about the equation under study as well as the equation describing how selection occurs, in order that the probability of self-selection can be determined. In the standard solution the joint distribution of the errors from these equations is taken to be bivariate normal, but this assumption could be too strong. It is here that nonparametric methods have some potential. Section 8.3 outlines various semiparametric analogues of the parametric two-step method. These are due to Cosslett (1991), Powell (1987), Newey (1991a), and Ming and Vella (1994, 1995). Section 8.4 looks at the semiparametric efficiency bound for this model and describes a proposal by Newey (1991a) that attempts to find an estimator whose efficiency is close to the bound. To do this he utilizes the GMM principle and approximates the efficient scores with a sufficient variety of moment restrictions. Hence, the approach is reminiscent of his method for adaptively estimating parameters in the regression model discussed in Section 5.5.3 and is an application of the general principle of representing the efficient score as a linear combination of moment restrictions mentioned in Section 5.10. Section 8.5 briefly looks at an issue that arises from the fact that SP estimators are unable to directly estimate the intercept in the equation of interest, and a solution to the problem is described. Section 8.6 concludes with mention of some applications.

8.2   Some Parametric Estimators

The bivariate sample selection model has two equations – a structural one (8.2) describing a variable y_{2i} and another, (8.1), which determines if an individual appears in the sample of observations used to estimate the parameters of (8.2). One way to conceive of the latter is as a discrete choice model, that is, there is a latent variable y_{1i}^* with associated binary indicator variable y_{1i}; when $y_{1i} = 1$ the individual appears in the sample because y_{1i}^* exceeds the threshold value of zero. All variables $\{y_{1i}, y_{2i}\}$, $x_i = \{x_{1i}, x_{2i}\}$ are taken to be i.i.d., with $\{x_{1i}, x_{2i}\}$ being independent of the error terms $\{e_{1i}, e_{2i}\}$. Weaker conditions can generally be imposed.

$$y_{1i}^* = x_{1i}'\beta_1 + e_{1i} \tag{8.1}$$

$$y_{2i} = x_{2i}'\beta_2 + e_{2i} \tag{8.2}$$

$$y_{1i} = I\left(y_{1i}^* > 0\right). \tag{8.3}$$

The essence of the selectivity problem is that there are "missing observations" upon the random variable y_{2i} caused by the fact that data on $\{y_{2i}, x_{2i}\}$ are only observed if the individual participates in the sample, that is, $y_{1i} = 1$. To make this clear let there be n observations on $\{y_{2i}, x_{2i}\}$ but n^* on $\{y_{1i}, x_{1i}\}$. It is convenient to assume that the extra observations are $n + 1, \ldots, n^*$ so that

$y_{1i} = 1$ for $i = 1, \ldots, n$ (the individual selects himself into the sample) and $y_{1i} = 0$ for $i = n+1, \ldots, n^*$ (the individual does not enter into the (8.2) sample). The classic prototype for (8.1) and (8.2) is the female labor supply decision, with y_{1i} indicating the decision to participate in the work force or not, y_{2i} the actual wage earned if the woman enters the work force, and y_{1i}^* the gap between the offered and reservation wage. Participation is induced only if $y_{1i}^* > 0$ and (8.1)–(8.3) give a full description of how the data are generated.

The objective is to estimate β_2 from $\{y_{2i}, x_{2i}\}_{i=1}^n$, taking account of the fact that observations on the random variable y_{2i} are available only if $y_{1i} > 0$. One way to conceive of a regression model is as an attempt to find the expectation of y_{2i} conditional upon its determinants x_{2i}; in this instance it needs to be recognized that the expectation must also be conditional upon $y_{1i} = 1$. From (8.1) this latter expectation is

$$E(y_{2i}|x_i, y_{1i} = 1) = x'_{2i}\beta_2 + E\left(e_{2i}|x_i, y_{1i}^* > 0\right), \qquad (8.4)$$

so that

$$y_{2i} = x'_{2i}\beta_2 + E\left(e_{2i}|x_i, y_{1i}^* > 0\right) + u_{2i}, \qquad (8.5)$$

where $u_{2i} = y_{2i} - E(y_{2i}|x_i, y_{1i}^* > 0)$. In (8.5) the error term has a zero mean by construction, but $\zeta_i = E(e_{2i}|x_i, y_{1i}^* > 0) + u_{2i}$ will not unless $E(e_{2i}|x_i, y_{1i}^* > 0) = 0$. Furthermore, $E(e_{2i}|x_i, y_{1i}^* > 0)$ will generally not be constant but will depend upon x_{1i}. These facts mean that an attempt to estimate β_2 by regressing y_{2i} against x_{2i} will fail. The precise effects depend upon the nature of $E(e_{2i}|x_i, y_{1i}^* > 0)$. If $E(e_{2i}|x_i, y_{1i}^* > 0)$ is nonzero, but a *constant*, it is only the intercept of (8.2) that would be inconsistently estimated, whereas if the conditional expectation varies with regressors correlated with x_{2i}, coefficients attached to these will also be inconsistently estimated.

Viewed as a regression problem the estimation issue is simple: Find a measure of

$$E\left(e_{2i}|x_i, y_{1i}^* > 0\right),$$

"purge" y_{2i} by forming $\tilde{y}_{2i} = y_{2i} - E(e_{2i}|x_i, y_{1i}^* > 0)$, and estimate β_2 by regressing $\tilde{y}_{2i}$ against x_{2i}. Both parametric and semiparametric estimation methods work in exactly this way. Beginning with the best-known parametric method, assume that e_{1i} and e_{2i} are multivariate normal, $\mathcal{N}(0, \Sigma)$, where

$$\Sigma = \begin{pmatrix} \sigma_{11} & \sigma_{12} \\ \sigma_{21} & \sigma_{22} \end{pmatrix}.$$

By the properties of the bivariate normal $E(e_{2i}|e_{1i}) = \sigma_{11}^{-1}\sigma_{12}e_{1i}$, and $e_{2i} = E(e_{2i}|e_{1i}) + \eta_i$, where η_i is independent of e_{1i} and x_i (i.e., of y_{1i}^* and x_i).

Consequently,

$$E\left(e_{2i}|x_i, y_{1i}^* > 0\right) = \sigma_{11}^{-1}\sigma_{12}E\left(e_{1i}|x_i, y_{1i}^* > 0\right).$$

Furthermore,

$$E\left(e_{1i}|y_{1i}^* > 0, \ x_{1i}\right) = \sigma_{11}^{-1/2}\phi\left(x_{1i}'\beta_1/\sigma_{11}^{1/2}\right)\Phi^{-1}\left(x_{1i}'\beta_1/\sigma_{11}^{1/2}\right),$$

where $\phi(z) = (2\pi)^{-1/2}\exp(-\frac{1}{2}z^2)$ and $\Phi(z) = \int_{-\infty}^z \phi(\lambda)\,d\lambda$ (Amemiya, 1985, p. 367). Making this substitution (8.5) becomes

$$y_{2i} = x_{2i}'\beta_2 + \sigma_{11}^{-1/2}\sigma_{12}\phi\left(x_{1i}'\alpha\right)\Phi^{-1}\left(x_{1i}'\alpha\right) + u_{2i}, \tag{8.6}$$

where $\alpha = \beta_1\sigma_{11}^{-1/2}$. It is apparent from (8.6) that β_2 could be estimated if $\lambda_i = \phi(x_{1i}'\alpha)\Phi^{-1}(x_{1i}'\alpha)$ was known. Since it depends upon the data (x_{1i}) and an unknown parameter α, the problem is how to estimate α. Because (8.1) could be reparameterized as $\sigma_{11}^{-1/2}y_{1i}^* = x_{1i}'(\sigma_{11}^{-1/2}\beta_1) + \bar{e}_{1i}$, where $\bar{e}_{1i}$ is n.i.d. (0, 1), this is a Probit model with unknown coefficients $\alpha = \sigma_{11}^{-1/2}\beta_1$, and α can therefore be estimated by maximum likelihood.

Perhaps the main issue with this estimator is to attach the correct covariance matrix to $\hat{\beta}_2$. The OLS estimator is inappropriate owing to the heteroskedasticity in u_{1i} and because of the fact that α is estimated. Amemiya (1985, p. 371, eq. (10.4.22)) gives the formula. In fact it is probably easiest to compute the covariance matrix from the general formula for a sequential M-estimator given in Chapter 5, since OLS upon (8.6) involves orthogonality conditions

$$\left(\sum x_{2i}'\left(y_{2i} - x_{2i}'\beta_2 - \hat{\delta}\hat{\lambda}_i\right)\sum\hat{\lambda}_i\left(y_{2i} - x_{2i}'\hat{\beta}_2 - \hat{\delta}\hat{\lambda}_i\right)\right) = (0 \quad 0),$$

and $\hat{\alpha}$ solves the scores for the probit likelihood.

It is instructive to consider maximum likelihood estimation of β_2 based upon all available observations. After defining $v_i = x_{1i}'\alpha$ and the joint density of e_{1i} and e_{2i}, conditional upon x_i, as $f(e_{1i}, e_{2i})$, we obtain

$$F(v_i) = \int_{-v_i}^{\infty}\int_{-\infty}^{\infty} f(e_1, e_2)\,de_1\,de_2 = P((e_{1i} \geq -v_i)|x_i)$$

and

$$f(e_{2i}|y_{1i} = 1) = f(y_{2i}|y_{1i}^* > 0, \ x_i) = F^{-1}(v_i)\int_{-v_i}^{\infty} f(t, e_{2i})\,dt.$$

Then the joint density of the data is

$$\Pi_{i=1}^n f(y_{2i}|y_{1i}^* > 0, \ x_i)P(y_{1i}^* > 0)\left\{\Pi_{i=n+1}^{n^*}P(y_{1i}^* \leq 0)\right\},$$

giving the log likelihood

$$L = \sum_{i=n+1}^{n^*} (1 - y_{1i}) \log (1 - F(v_i)) + \sum_{i=1}^{n} y_{1i} \log F(v_i)$$

$$+ \sum_{i=1}^{n} y_{1i} \log f(e_{2i}|y_{1i} = 1) \tag{8.7}$$

$$= L^p + \sum_{i=1}^{n} y_{1i} \log f(e_{2i}|y_{1i} = 1). \tag{8.8}$$

We differentiate (8.8) to get the scores,

$$\partial L/\partial \alpha = \partial L^p/\partial \alpha + \sum_{i=1}^{n} (\partial \log f(e_{2i}|y_{1i} = 1)/\partial v_i) (\partial v_i/\partial \alpha),$$
$$\tag{8.9}$$

$$\partial L/\partial \beta_2 = -\sum_{i=1}^{n} x_{2i} \partial \log f(e_{2i}|y_{1i})/\partial e_{2i}. \tag{8.10}$$

The specification of the density $f(e_{1i}, e_{2i})$ then determines the nature of (8.9) and (8.10). If the density is bivariate normal L^p is the log likelihood for a probit model and the density scores are

$$\partial \log f(e_{2i}|y_{1i})/\partial v_i = \lambda(v_i) - \psi_2^{-1}\lambda([v_i + \psi_1 e_{2i}]\psi_2), \tag{8.11}$$

$$\partial \log f(e_{2i}|y_{1i})/\partial e_{2i} = (e_{2i} - \sigma_{12}\psi_1\lambda([v_i + \psi_1 e_{2i}]\psi_2))\sigma_{22}^{-2},$$
$$\tag{8.12}$$

where $\psi_1 = \sigma_{22}^{-1}\sigma_{12}$ and $\psi_2 = (1 - \sigma_{22}^{-1}\sigma_{12}^2)^{1/2}$. Substituting (8.12) into (8.10) gives

$$\partial L/\partial \beta_2 = -\sum_{i=1}^{n} x_{2i} (e_{2i} - \sigma_{12}\psi_1\lambda([v_i + \psi_1 e_{2i}]\psi_2))\sigma_{22}^{-2}, \tag{8.13}$$

which could also be obtained by differentiating the log likelihood given in Amemiya (1985, eq. (10.7b)). It is noticeable that the first-order conditions for β_2 differ from those of the two-step estimator by the variable entering into the inverse Mill's ratio λ. The sequential estimator described earlier solved for α from $\partial L^p/\partial \alpha = 0$ and for β from $\sum_{i=1}^{n} x_{2i}(e_{2i} - \rho\sigma_{22}\lambda(v_i)) = 0$, and so it is apparent that the MLE exploits extra information.

8.3 Some Sequential Semiparametric Estimators

In Chapter 7 SP estimators were constructed to mimic parametric methods by replacing conditional moments by their nonparametric estimates. A similar strategy can be applied to the selectivity model. Consider Equation (8.4). It is always possible to write $E(e_{2i}|e_{1i}) = m(e_{1i})$ and

$$E(e_{2i}|x_i, y_{1i}^* > 0) = E[(m(e_{1i}) + \eta_i)|x_i, y_{1i}^* > 0]$$
$$= E[m(e_{1i})|x_i, y_{1i} = 1]$$
$$= g(x_{1i}'\beta_1), \qquad (8.14)$$

since the expectation will involve the integral of the density of e_{1i} conditional upon x_i and $y_{1i} = 1$ over the range $(-\infty, -x_{1i}'\beta_1)$. Making this substitution into (8.5) leaves

$$y_{2i} = x_{2i}'\beta_2 + g(x_{1i}'\beta_1) + u_{2i}. \qquad (8.15)$$

Now (8.15) has the form of the SP regression model discussed in Chapter 5, provided β_1 is known, and one might consider estimating β_2 by one of the methods discussed there. There is however a potential identification problem; in Chapter 5 $z_i = x_{1i}'\beta_1$ was assumed to be disjoint with x_{2i}, but that is less plausible for the selectivity model since there is no reason to believe that the set of variables affecting decisions regarding y_{2i} should not also determine the individual's presence or absence in the sample. If $x_{2i} = x_{1i}$, the fact that $g(\cdot)$ is unknown, and therefore might be linear in x_{1i}, means that β_2 could not be identified. For SP estimators, x_{1i} must therefore have some different members to x_{2i}. In theory, this restriction does not apply to parametric methods, as $g(\cdot)$ is a known nonlinear function of $z_i = x_{1i}'\beta_1$. In practice, the requisite nonlinearity might not be achieved in any given data set; as Amemiya (1985, p. 472) observes, when the errors are bivariate normal, $g(z)$ is linear over the range $-1 < z < 5$. Thus the relative natures of x_{1i} and x_{2i} are critical to the success of both SP and parametric estimators. Even when x_{1i} is a superset of x_{2i}, the precision of estimation of β_2 will hinge upon the effects of the extra elements. If these are few in number or exhibit little volatility, the prospects for SP estimation are poor.

A further problem arises in the SP context from the fact that β_1 is not known and may need to be estimated semiparametrically due to lack of knowledge about the joint density of the errors. As discussed in Chapter 7, it is not possible to estimate all members of β_1. In particular, the intercept and factor of proportionality in $x_{1i}'\beta_1$ cannot be estimated, leading us to write $x_{1i}'\beta_1 = v_i(\theta)$ earlier, where θ were the estimable parameters. Because $g(\cdot)$ is unknown, the intercept and proportionality factor can be absorbed into it so that $g(x_{1i}'\beta_1) = g(v_i(\theta))$, and the SP estimator of θ will be used to construct $z_i = v_i(\hat{\theta})$ for use in estimating β_2. Because $g(\cdot)$ is arbitrary we will henceforth write the unknown function as $g(v_i(\theta))$. Suppose then that we had an estimator of θ from some source. A sequential estimator of β_2 might then be obtained by semiparametrically estimating β_2, where $g(\cdot)$ is replaced by a nonparametric approximation. A number of variants of this idea appear in the literature and we turn to a description of these.

8.3.1   Cosslett's Dummy Variable Method

Cosslett (1991) notes that $v_i(\hat{\theta})$ is a scalar and its range could be divided into M sections $(-\infty, a_1), (a_1, a_2), \ldots, (a_{M-1}, \infty)$. Defining M dummy variables D_{ij} as taking the value unity if the ith observation has a value of $v_i(\hat{\theta})$ falling in the jth section and zero otherwise, he writes $g(v_i(\theta)) = \sum_{j=1}^{M} b_j D_{ij}$, and he finds β_2 by an OLS regression of y_{2i} against x_{2i} and the M dummy variables. To establish consistency of the estimator of β_2, M would need to grow with n, but Cosslett selects the Sections $(-\infty, a_1)$ etc. from the estimated distribution function for e_{1i} found by applying his SP estimator for discrete choice models (Section 7.5.4). A by-product of this latter estimator is a step-function estimate of the distribution function, and these steps are taken to define $a_1, a_2, \ldots, a_M$. Cosslett demonstrates consistency for his estimator of β_2 but not asymptotic normality. The latter property seems unlikely as $n^{1/4}$ consistency of the estimator of $g(\cdot)$ is needed (Section 5.2.1) and that does not seem plausible for the ramp function employed here. However, the estimator is very simple to apply, with most of the cost being the computation of $\hat{\theta}$, and therefore it is a useful device for getting a preliminary estimate of β_2.

8.3.2   Powell's Kernel Estimator

Powell (1987) set out an estimator of (8.15) that has a close connection with Robinson's SP estimator discussed in Section 5.2.1. To recapitulate that material, take the expectation of both sides of (8.15) conditional upon v_i and subtract this from (8.15) to leave

$$y_{2i} - E(y_{2i}|v_i) = [x_{2i} - E(x_{2i}|v_i)]' \beta_2 + u_{2i}. \tag{8.16}$$

Now it is possible to estimate β_2 in a number of ways. A straightforward extension of Robinson's estimator would be to estimate both $E(y_{2i}|v_i)$ and $E(x_{2i}|v_i)$ nonparametrically (with $v_i = v_i(\hat{\theta})$) and to then regress the nonparametric residuals $y_{2i} - \hat{E}(y_{2i}|v_i(\hat{\theta}))$ against $(x_{2i} - \hat{E}(x_{2i}|v_i(\hat{\theta})))$. Details of this estimator are the same as in Section 5.2.1 except that the errors in (8.15) are heteroskedastic and there is sampling variability induced by the need to use $\hat{\theta}$ rather than the true value. Note that one cannot have any element of x_{2i} equaling a constant since then $x_{2i} - E(x_{2i}|v_i)$ equals zero (i.e., the intercept in the equation describing y_{2i} cannot be estimated). Fundamentally, this lack of identification arises due to the fact that $g(x'_{1i}\beta_1)$ may involve a constant, because $g(\cdot)$ is an unknown function (see Heckman, 1990). The problem is studied in more detail in Section 8.5. Throughout this section the parameters to be estimated (β_2) are taken to be the slope coefficients in (8.2).

This estimator is related to Powell's but is not identical to it. The aim of both procedures is to eliminate the unobservable $g(v_i)$. Powell does this by "differencing", that is, by considering

$$y_{2i} - y_{2j} = (x_{2i} - x_{2j})'\beta_2 + g(v_i) - g(v_j) \tag{8.17}$$

and then applying weights ω_{ij} that would be close to zero whenever v_i was not close to v_j. That is, the weighted model

$$\omega_{ij}(y_{2i} - y_{2j}) = \omega_{ij}(x_{2i} - x_{2j})'\beta_2 \tag{8.18}$$

effectively eliminates the term $g(v_i) - g(v_j)$ as the observations for which $g(v_i)$ departs from $g(v_j)$ are given "zero" weights. To see the connection with (8.17), estimate $E(x_{2i}|v_i)$ with a kernel estimator using a uniform density as the kernel. Then $\hat{E}(x_{2i}|v_i) = n_h^{-1}\sum_{j\in I_h} x_{2j}$, where I_h are those values of $j = 1, \ldots, n$ that have x_j within $\pm h/2$ of x_i and n_h is their number. Clearly,

$$x_{2i} - \hat{E}(x_{2i}|v_i) = n_h^{-1}\sum_{j\in I^*}(x_{2i} - x_{2j}),$$

which might be written as $\sum_{j=1}^{n} \omega_{ij}^*(x_{2i} - x_{2j})$, where $w_{ij}^* = 0$ if $j \notin I_h$ and equals n_h^{-1} if $j \in I_h$. Performing a similar transformation upon $y_{2i} - y_{2j}$ leads us to replace (8.17) by

$$\sum_{j=1}^{n} w_{ij}^*(y_{2i} - y_{2j}) = \sum_{j=1}^{n} w_{ij}^*(x_{2i} - x_{2j})'\beta_2. \tag{8.19}$$

Comparing (8.18) and (8.19) we see that the latter simply sums over all observations rather than treating them as separate elements within a very large ($n(n+1)/2$ elements) regression as Powell has done. We will therefore refer to the estimator of β deriving from (8.16) as Powell's estimator, even though this is not strictly correct – Ming and Vella (1994) correctly point out that (8.19) is like a "within groups" estimator to remove fixed effects and they have extended the idea to handle the presence of endogenous regressors in (8.2).

Ming and Vella (1995) note that $\zeta_i = x_{2i} - E(x_{2i}|v_i)$ could instead be used as an instrument for x_{2i} in (8.2) as $E(e_{2i}|\zeta_i) = 0$ by the law of iterated expectations, and they investigate this estimator. It would however be inefficient relative to Powell's.[1] To see this, observe that the asymptotic variance of the estimator of β_2 from (8.16) is $\sigma_{u_2}^2\left(p\lim_{n\to\infty} n^{-1}\sum_{i=1}^{n}\zeta_i\zeta_i'\right)^{-1}$, whereas the Ming–Vella

---

[1] In the result that follows we assume that $E(x_{2i}|v_i)$ is known and so abstract from the complications arising from the need to estimate it.

instrumental variable estimator would have variance

$$
\left(p \lim_{n \to \infty} n^{-1} \sum_{i=1}^{n} \zeta_i x_{2i}' \right)^{-1} \left(\sigma_{e_2}^2 p \lim_{n \to \infty} n^{-1} \sum_{i=1}^{n} \zeta_i \zeta_i' \right)
$$

$$
\times \left(p \lim_{n \to \infty} n^{-1} \sum x_{2i} \zeta_i' \right)^{-1}.
$$

Now

$$
p \lim_{n \to \infty} n^{-1} \sum_{i=1}^{n} \zeta_i x_{2i}' = p \lim_{n \to \infty} n^{-1} \sum_{i=1}^{n} \zeta_i \zeta_i',
$$

so that this variance becomes $\sigma_{e_2}^2 \left(p \lim_{n \to \infty} \sum_{i=1}^{n} \zeta_i \zeta_i' \right)^{-1}$, and the Ming–Vella estimator will be inefficient relative to Powell's if $\sigma_{e_2}^2 > \sigma_{u_2}^2$. But this must be the case because $e_{2i} = u_{2i} + g(v_i)$ and $g(v_i)$ is uncorrelated with u_{2i} by assumption.

Ahn and Powell (1993) and Choi (1990) replace $E(x_{2i}|v_i)$ with $E(x_{2i}|x_{1i})$ to safeguard against the possibility that the *propensity score* (i.e., $P(y_i = 1)$) is not a function of a single index. Newey and Powell (1990b) investigate the SP efficiency bound when the selection rule is not a function of a single index linear in x_{1i}.

8.3.3 Newey's Series Estimator

Newey (1991b) observes that there have been many other ways to approximate $g(v_i(\theta))$ mentioned in the literature. Lee (1982) replaced the density of the errors by an Edgeworth approximation, the lead term of which is the bivariate normal, allowing $g(v_i)$ to be written as a power series $g(v_i) = \sum_{j=0}^{\infty} b_j \lambda_i v_i^j$, where λ_i is the inverse Mill's ratio evaluated at $v_i(\hat\theta)$. The first term in this series corresponds to the traditional parametric estimator. Heckman and Robb (1985) worked with a flexible Fourier form approximation. Newey allows for a general class of series approximations, although in his proofs he requires differentiability of the function with bounded first and second derivatives, and he also restricts the range of v_i.[2]

Newey's preference is for a series approximation of the form $\tau_j(v_i) = \psi(v_i)^j$, where $\psi(\cdot)$ is some monotonic function of v_i that is bounded between -1 and 1, for example $\psi(v) = 2\,\Phi(v) - 1$. Because the estimator is basically an application of the series approach described in Section 3.8–3.9, whatever approximation is chosen will have to satisfy conditions like (B1)–(B7) in Section 3.9. Of these (B5) and (B7) can be critical. Newey indicates that difficulties can arise if

---

[2] He estimates the boundaries of $v_i\, n^{1/2}$ consistently by using the order statistics $\min_{i \le n} v_i$ and $\max_{i \le n} v_i$.

mixtures of series, for instance polynomial and trigonometric terms, are used.[3] However, the rationale for the polynomials in this expansion is to improve small-sample properties, and it is not envisaged that the number of polynomial terms grows with the sample size. Hence, the series approximation is really of a single type. Whatever approximation is chosen the asymptotic theory is covered by Theorem 5.2 except that allowance must be made for heteroskedasticity in the disturbances u_{2i} and the fact that θ has been replaced by $\hat{\theta}$. Denoting the approximating terms as $\tau_1\left(v_i(\hat{\theta})\right), \ldots, \tau_M\left(v_i(\hat{\theta})\right)$, $\hat{\delta}' = \left(\hat{\beta}'_2, \hat{b}_1 \ldots \hat{b}_M\right)$ as the parameter estimates from the regression of y_{2i} against

$$z'_i = \left[x'_{2i}\tau_1\left(v_i(\hat{\theta})\right) \ldots \tau_M\left(v_i(\hat{\theta})\right)\right],$$

$$\hat{g}(\hat{\theta}) = \sum_{j=1}^{M} \tau_j\left(v_i(\hat{\theta})\right)\hat{b}_j,$$

$$G = n^{-1}\sum_{i=1}^{n} x_{2i}\left[\frac{\partial \hat{g}}{\partial v_i}\right]\left[\frac{\partial v_i}{\partial \theta}\right],$$

and $V_{\hat{\theta}}$ as the asymptotic covariance matrix of $n^{1/2}(\hat{\theta} - \theta_0)$, Newey gives a consistent estimator of the covariance matrix of $n^{1/2}(\hat{\beta}_2 - \beta_{20})$ as

$$\begin{bmatrix} I & 0 \end{bmatrix}\left(n^{-1}X'_2X_2\right)^{-1}\left\{n^{-1}\sum_{i=1}^{n} x_{2i}x'_{2i}\left(y_{2i} - z'_i\hat{\delta}\right)^2 + GV_{\hat{\theta}}G'\right\}$$

$$\times \left(n^{-1}X'_2X_2\right)^{-1}\begin{bmatrix} I & 0 \end{bmatrix}'. \tag{8.20}$$

The first term in the curly brackets of (8.20) accounts for the heteroskedasticity in the error term, and the second for the fact that θ is estimated.

Because only a scalar v_i is involved the series approximation method has greater appeal than the kernel-based procedure. Once approximating functions are selected estimation is just by least squares, and one can regard it as a simple extension of Heckman's two-step estimator. This connection can be formalized if $\tau_j = [\phi(v)/\Phi(v)]v^{j-1}$, as this will mean that the addition of τ_1 alone would just give Heckman's estimator.[4] However, such an approximation would not necessarily be accurate enough. Returning to (8.14), think of expanding $m(e_{1i})$ in a series involving e_{1i}^j. Then $E[m(e_{1i})|x_i, y_{1i} = 1]$ should be better represented as functions of $E[e_{1i}^j|x_i, y_{1i} = 1]$ than $\{E[e_{1i}|x_i, y_{1i} = 1]\}^j$, which these τ_j represent.

---

[3] Thus the flexible Fourier form of Gallant (1981) would be troublesome.
[4] Newey argues against this choice since the terms could be unbounded if v_i is unbounded, and that would induce sensitivity into the estimates. For this reason he favors approximation involving terms such as $[2\Phi(v) - 1]^k$.

8.3.4 Newey's GMM Estimator

One way to conceive of the previous estimator is as a GMM estimator working off the orthogonality condition $E(z_i(y_{2i} - x'_{2i}\beta_2 - g(v_i))) = 0$, where $g(v_i)$ has been replaced by a series approximation $\sum_{j=1}^{M} \tau_j(\hat{v}_i)\gamma_j$ and $z'_i = (x'_{2i}\,\tau_1(\hat{v}_i)$ $\ldots\tau_M(\hat{v}_i))$. But there are many more orthogonality conditions available by exploiting the independence of x_i and u_{2i}. As Newey (1991a) observes, independence implies that the conditional distribution of u_{i2}, given selection and x_i, depends only on v_i, meaning that the conditional expectation of *any* function of u_{i2} depends solely on v_i. This fact leads him to propose a GMM estimator for β_2. To do this define $\zeta_j(e_{2i})$ $(j = 1, \ldots, J)$ as some function of e_{2i}, and define $\psi_j(v_i) = E(\zeta_j(e_{2i})|x_i, v_i)$. By the independence of x_i and u_{2i}, $E(z_i(\zeta_j(e_{2i}) - \psi_j(v_i))) = 0$, when z_i is a function of x_{2i} and v_i. The GMM estimator derived from these orthogonality relations provides a potential efficiency gain over the simple sequential estimator discussed previously. Efficiency is dependent upon the preliminary estimator for θ and the nature of the functions $\zeta_j(v_i)$ and z_i. An interesting question, pursued later, is: What is an optimal choice of these functions?

8.4 Maximum Likelihood–Type Estimators

In Section 8.2 a maximum likelihood parametric estimator was set out as an alternative to the popular two-step method. Two SP analogues of this estimator have been developed, basically differing in whether it is the log likelihood or the scores that get approximated. Gallant and Nychka (1987) follow the first line of attack and Newey (1991a) the second.

8.4.1 Gallant and Nychka's Estimator

The log likelihood for the selectivity model was presented in (8.8), and it depended upon the conditional density $f(e_{2i}|v_i)$ and its cumulative form $F(v_i)$. Both of these are derivative from the joint density $f(e_{1i}, e_{2i})$, so that the log likelihood of the data is completely described once $f(e_{1i}, e_{2i})$ is specified. This feature leads to the idea of approximating $f(e_{1i}, e_{2i})$. A similar strategy was followed in the context of the regression model in Section 5.5.1. There the density was written as the product of a normal with a polynomial, but that would complicate estimation here. Instead, Gallant and Nychka proposed that $f(e_{1i}, e_{2i})$ be replaced by

$$\tilde{f}(e_{1i}, e_{2i})) = \left[\sum_{j=0}^{M}\sum_{k=0}^{M}\gamma_{jk}e_{1i}^j e_{2i}^k\right]^2 \exp\left\{-(e_{1i}/\delta_1)^2 - (e_{2i}/\delta_2)^2\right\}.$$

Integration with respect to this form of density is computationally very simple and, indeed,

$$\int_{a_1}^{b_1} \int_{a_2}^{b_2} \tilde{f}(e_{1i}, e_{2i}) = \sum_{j,k,p,q=1}^{M} \gamma_{jk} \gamma_{pq} \int_{a_1}^{b_1} e_{1i}^{j+p} \exp\left(-e_{1i}^2/\delta_1^2\right)$$

$$\times \int_{a_2}^{b_2} e_{2i}^{k+q} \exp\left(-e_{2i}^2/\delta_2^2\right). \qquad (8.21)$$

By using this formula to solve for $F(v_i)$ and $f(e_{2i}|v_i)$ it is a simple matter to approximate the log likelihood in (8.8). The SP estimator of β_2 and θ maximizes the approximate likelihood subject to the constraints that $\int \tilde{f}(e)\,de = 1$ and $\int e\tilde{f}(e) = 0$, where e is the (2×1) vector (e_{1i}, e_{2i}). Gallant and Nychka demonstrated consistency of the estimator as $M \to \infty$, but they did not provide a distribution theory.

8.4.2 Newey's Estimator

Rather than attempt to approximate the log likelihood, it makes sense to focus upon the efficient scores, since an estimator of β_2 from them should attain the SP efficiency bound (see Section 5.4). Letting $\psi' = [\theta' \ \beta_2']$, to derive the efficient scores $\tilde{d}_\psi$, we regard the density function $f(e_{1i}, e_{2i})$ as being indexed by a parameter η, and this nuisance parameter needs to be concentrated out of the log likelihood, leaving, for the ith observation $\tilde{d}_\psi(i) = d_\psi(i) - E(d_\psi(i)|d_\eta(i))$. Now $d_\eta(i)$ is an unrestricted function of $\xi_i = (y_{1i} - F_i)v_i$, since both $F(v_i)$ and $f(e_{2i}|v_i)$ making up the log likelihood in (8.7) are dependent on η. Consequently, $E[d_\psi(i)|d_\eta(i)] = E[d_\psi(i)|\xi_i]$ and

$$\tilde{d}_\theta = \sum_{i=1}^{n} [\partial v_i/\partial\theta - E((\partial v_i/\partial\theta)|v_i)] (\partial F_i/\partial v_i)$$

$$\times F_i^{-1}(1 - F_i)^{-1}(y_{1i} - F_i) + \sum_{i=1}^{n} [\partial v_i/\partial\theta - E((\partial v_i/\partial\theta)|v_i)]$$

$$\times [\partial \log f(e_{2i}|v_i)/\partial v_i] \qquad (8.22)$$

$$\tilde{d}_{\beta_2} = \sum_{i=1}^{n} [x_{2i} - E(x_{2i}|v_i)][\partial \log f(e_{2i}|v_i)/\partial e_{2i}]. \qquad (8.23)$$

One possibility would be to find an estimator of ψ, $\hat{\psi}$, that set $\tilde{d}_\psi(\hat{\psi}) = 0$, but this makes for a complex optimization problem. Moreover, there is structure to this problem that can be exploited to ease the computational load. Rather than work specifically with the selectivity model, the simplications are best seen in the context of a more general estimation environment that has the

Nonparametric Econometrics

selectivity model as a special case. To this end consider a bivariate problem in which the log likelihood for (y_{1i}, y_{2i}) is written as the sum of a conditional log likelihood $L^c(y_{2i}|y_{1i})$ and a marginal log likelihood $L^m(y_{1i})$. There are two sets of parameters – those of interest, β, and those that are a nuisance, α – and it happens that α appears only in the marginal likelihood. Consequently, the log likelihood is

$$L = L^c(\beta, \alpha) + L^m(\alpha). \tag{8.24}$$

Define the information matrix as $\mathcal{I}_{\beta\beta} = \lim_{n\to\infty} n^{-1} E\left(d_\beta d'_\beta\right)$ etc. and let a superscript of "c" or "m" designate whether the operation is being performed on the conditional or marginal log likelihood, that is, $d^c_\beta = \partial L^c/\partial\beta$, $\mathcal{I}^c_{\beta\beta} = \lim_{n\to\infty} n^{-1} E\left[d^c_\beta (d^c_\beta)'\right]$. If there is no superscript, quantities are relative to the complete likelihood. From the structure of (8.24) it is clear that $d_\beta = d^c_\beta$, $\mathcal{I}_{\beta\beta} = \mathcal{I}^c_{\beta\beta}$, and $\mathcal{I}_{\beta\alpha} = \mathcal{I}^c_{\beta\alpha}$. Since it is β that we are interested in, α can be concentrated out of (8.24), meaning that the MLE of β solves $\bar{d}(\hat\beta) = 0$, where

$$\bar{d}_\beta = d_\beta - \mathcal{I}_{\beta\alpha}\mathcal{I}^{-1}_{\alpha\alpha}d_a \tag{8.25}$$

$$= d^c_\beta - \mathcal{I}_{\beta\alpha}\mathcal{I}^{-1}_{\alpha\alpha}\left(d^c_\alpha + d^m_\alpha\right) \tag{8.26}$$

$$= \left(d^c_\beta - \mathcal{I}_{\beta\alpha}\mathcal{I}^{-1}_{\alpha\alpha}d^c_\alpha\right) - \mathcal{I}_{\beta\alpha}\mathcal{I}^{-1}_{\alpha\alpha}d^m_\alpha \tag{8.27}$$

$$= d^*_\beta - \mathcal{I}_{\beta\alpha}\mathcal{I}^{-1}_{\alpha\alpha}d^m_\alpha. \tag{8.28}$$

The following properties hold for d^*_β and $\tilde{d}_\beta$.

Lemma 8.1: $\lim_{n\to\infty} E\left[n^{-1}d^*_\beta(d^c_\alpha)'\right] = \mathcal{I}_{\beta\alpha}\mathcal{I}^{-1}_{\alpha\alpha}\mathcal{I}^m_{\alpha\alpha}$.

Proof: We have

$$\lim_{n\to\infty} E\left[n^{-1}d^*_\beta\left(d^c_\alpha\right)'\right]$$

$$= \lim_{n\to\infty} E\left[n^{-1}\left(d^c_\beta - \mathcal{I}_{\beta\alpha}\mathcal{I}^{-1}_{\alpha\alpha}d^c_\alpha\right)\left(d^c_\alpha\right)'\right] \tag{8.29}$$

$$= \mathcal{I}_{\beta\alpha} - \mathcal{I}_{\beta\alpha}\mathcal{I}^{-1}_{\alpha\alpha}\mathcal{I}^c_{\alpha\alpha}. \tag{8.30}$$

Because $\mathcal{I}_{\alpha\alpha} = \mathcal{I}^c_{\alpha\alpha} + \mathcal{I}^m_{\alpha\alpha}$, substitution for $\mathcal{I}_{\alpha\alpha}$ gives

$$\lim_{n\to\infty} E\left[n^{-1}d^*_\beta\left(d^c_\alpha\right)'\right] = \mathcal{I}_{\beta\alpha} - \mathcal{I}_{\beta\alpha}\left(\mathcal{I}^c_{\alpha\alpha} + \mathcal{I}^m_{\alpha\alpha}\right)^{-1}\mathcal{I}^c_{\alpha\alpha} \tag{8.31}$$

$$= \mathcal{I}_{\beta\alpha}\left[I - \left(\mathcal{I}^c_{\alpha\alpha} + \mathcal{I}^m_{\alpha\alpha}\right)^{-1}\mathcal{I}^c_{\alpha\alpha}\right] \tag{8.32}$$

$$= \mathcal{I}_{\beta\alpha} I_{\alpha\alpha}^{-1} \left[\left(\mathcal{I}_{\alpha\alpha}^c + \mathcal{I}_{\alpha\alpha}^m - \mathcal{I}_{\alpha\alpha}^c \right) \right] \tag{8.33}$$

$$= \mathcal{I}_{\beta\alpha} \mathcal{I}_{\alpha a}^{-1} \mathcal{I}_{\alpha\alpha}^m. \tag{8.34}$$

Lemma 8.2:

(i) $E\left[n^{-1}\partial d_\beta^*/\partial\beta\right] = -\lim\limits_{n\to\infty} E\left[n^{-1}\bar{d}_\beta \bar{d}_\beta'\right] = -\bar{V}.$

(ii) $E\left[n^{-1}\partial d_\beta^*/\partial\alpha\right] = -\lim\limits_{n\to\infty} E\left[n^{-1}d_\beta^*\left(d_\alpha^c\right)'\right] = -\mathcal{I}_{\beta\alpha}\mathcal{I}_{\alpha\alpha}^{-1}\mathcal{I}_{\alpha\alpha}^m.$

Proof: Part (i) follows from the generalized information equality (Rao, 1973), associated with $E\left(d_\beta^*\right) = 0$ and discussed in Lemma 5.5 and Lemma 7.1, that

$$\lim\limits_{n\to\infty} E\left[n^{-1}\partial d_\beta^*/\partial\beta\right] = -\lim\limits_{n\to\infty} E\left[n^{-1}d_\beta^*\left(d_\beta^c\right)'\right] \tag{8.35}$$

$$= -\lim\limits_{n\to\infty} E\left[n^{-1}\left(d_\beta^c - \mathcal{I}_{\beta\alpha}\mathcal{I}_{\alpha\alpha}^{-1}d_\alpha^c\right)\left(d_\beta^c\right)'\right] \tag{8.36}$$

$$= -\left[\mathcal{I}_{\beta\beta} - \mathcal{I}_{\beta\alpha}\mathcal{I}_{\alpha\alpha}^{-1}\mathcal{I}_{\alpha\beta}\right], \tag{8.37}$$

which is easily seen to be the negative of the asymptotic covariance matrix of $n^{-1/2}\bar{d}_\beta$.

For (ii) we have

$$E\left[n^{-1}\partial d_\beta^*/\partial\alpha\right] = \lim\limits_{n\to\infty} E\left[d_\beta^*\left(d_\alpha^c\right)'\right]$$

$$= E\left\{\left[d_\beta^c - \mathcal{I}_{\beta\alpha}\mathcal{I}_{\alpha\alpha}^{-1}d_\alpha^c\right]d_\alpha^{c\prime}\right\}$$

$$= \mathcal{I}_{\beta a} - \mathcal{I}_{\beta\alpha}\mathcal{I}_{\alpha a}^{-1}\mathcal{I}_{\alpha a}^c$$

$$= \mathcal{I}_{\beta a}\mathcal{I}_{\alpha\alpha}^{-1}\mathcal{I}_{\alpha a}^m,$$

using $\mathcal{I}_{\alpha\alpha} = \mathcal{I}_{\alpha\alpha}^m + \mathcal{I}_{\alpha\alpha}^c.$ Q.E.D.

By definition the MLE estimators of β and α solve $d_\beta(\hat\beta,\ \hat\alpha) = 0$, $d_\alpha(\hat\beta,\ \hat\alpha) = 0$ and the asymptotic covariance matrix of $n^{1/2}(\hat\beta - \beta_0)$ is $\bar{V}^{-1}$. A simpler estimator is to find $\tilde\alpha$ by maximizing $L^m(\alpha)$ (i.e., $d_\alpha^m(\tilde\alpha) = 0$) and then to find $\tilde\beta$ such that $d_\beta^*(\tilde\beta,\ \tilde\alpha) = 0$. In Theorem 8.1 it is shown that $n^{1/2}(\tilde\beta - \beta_0)$ and $n^{1/2}(\hat\beta - \beta)$ have the same limiting distribution.

Theorem 8.1: With $\tilde\alpha$ as the estimator of α maximizing L^m in (8.24), the estimator of β, $\tilde\beta$, solving $d_\beta^*(\tilde\beta,\ \tilde\alpha) = 0$ has limiting covariance matrix $\bar{V}^{-1} = \left(\mathcal{I}_{\beta\beta} - \mathcal{I}_{\beta\alpha}\mathcal{I}_{\alpha\alpha}^{-1}\mathcal{I}_{\alpha\beta}\right)^{-1}$ and is therefore efficient relative to the MLE of β that solves $d_\beta(\hat\beta,\ \hat\alpha) = d_\alpha(\hat\beta,\ \hat\alpha) = 0$.

Proof: Expanding $d_\beta^*(\tilde\beta,\ \tilde\alpha) = 0$ around β_0, α_0 we get

$$0 = n^{-1/2}d_\beta^* (\beta_0, \alpha_0) + \left(n^{-1}\partial d_\beta^*/\partial\beta\right) n^{1/2} \left(\tilde\beta - \beta_0\right)$$
$$+ \left(n^{-1}\partial d_\beta^*/\partial\alpha\right) n^{1/2} \left(\tilde\alpha - \alpha_0\right) + o_p(1) \tag{8.38}$$
$$= n^{-1/2}d_\beta^* (\beta_0,\ \alpha_0) - \bar V n^{1/2} \left(\tilde\beta - \beta_0\right)$$
$$- \mathcal{I}_{\beta\alpha}\mathcal{I}_{\alpha\alpha}^{-1}\mathcal{I}_{\alpha\alpha}^m n^{1/2} \left(\tilde\alpha - \alpha_0\right) \tag{8.39}$$

from Lemma 8.2. Now

$$0 = n^{-1/2}d_\beta^* (\beta_0,\ \alpha_0) - \bar V n^{1/2} \left(\tilde\beta - \beta_0\right)$$
$$- I_{\beta\alpha}I_{\alpha\alpha}^{-1}I_{\alpha\alpha}^m \left(\mathcal{I}_{\alpha\alpha}^m\right)^{-1} n^{-1/2}d_\alpha^m + o_p(1) \tag{8.40}$$

from the fact that $\tilde\alpha$ solves $d_\alpha^m(\tilde\alpha) = 0$ and so $n^{1/2}(\tilde\alpha - \alpha_0) = (\mathcal{I}_{\alpha\alpha}^m)^{-1}$ $n^{-1/2}d_\alpha^m + o_p(1)$. Thus

$$0 = n^{-1/2}\left[d_\beta^* (\beta_0,\ \alpha_0) - \mathcal{I}_{\beta\alpha}\mathcal{I}_{\alpha\alpha}^{-1}d_\alpha^m\right] - \bar V n^{1/2} \left(\tilde\beta - \beta_0\right) \tag{8.41}$$
$$= n^{-1/2}\tilde d_\beta - \bar V n^{1/2} \left(\tilde\beta - \beta_0\right) \tag{8.42}$$

from (8.28). Therefore

$$n^{1/2} \left(\tilde\beta - \beta_0\right) = \bar V^{-1}n^{-1/2}\tilde d_\beta$$

and, under standard conditions,

$$n^{1/2} \left(\tilde\beta - \beta_0\right) \xrightarrow{d} \mathcal{N}\left(0,\ \bar V^{-1}\right). \quad \text{Q.E.D.}$$

The selectivity model has exactly the structure described above, as the log likelihood segments into two parts (see (8.8)) with the first coming from the marginal density of y_{1i}, whereas the second represents the density of y_{2i} conditional upon y_{1i}. Furthermore, $\beta_2(= \beta)$ appears only in the conditional density whereas $\theta(= \alpha)$ is in the marginal density as well. Newey's idea is to solve for θ by maximizing L^m, which means that $\tilde\theta$ will be Klein and Spady's SP estimator of Section 7.4.2, and then to find $\tilde\beta_2$ from $d_{\beta_2}^*(\tilde\beta_2, \tilde\theta) = 0$, where $d_{\beta_2}^* = \tilde d_{\beta_2} - \mathcal{I}_{\beta_2\theta}\mathcal{I}_{\theta\theta}^{-1}\tilde d_\theta$ and $\tilde d_{\beta_2}$, $\tilde d_\theta$ were defined in (8.22) and (8.23). One way to do this would be to replace unknowns in (8.11) and (8.12) by nonparametric estimators. Because $\partial \log f(e_{2i}|v_i)/\partial v_i$ and $\partial \log f(e_{2i}|v_i)/\partial e_{2i}$ are functions solely of e_{2i} and v_i, these could be replaced by a single series expansion in e_{2i} and v_i. Newey shows that the resulting estimator is just the GMM estimator described in the previous section. Such a connection should not be surprising given the conclusion in Section 5.10 that any SP estimator can be approximated by a GMM estimator with a sufficient variety and number of moment restrictions, as well as the analysis in Section 5.5.3 of the linear model.

8.5 Estimation of the Intercept in Selection Models

As mentioned earlier there are problems in estimating the intercept in (8.2) owing to the fact that $g(\cdot)$ in (8.15) might be related to v_i with a nonzero intercept. It is of interest therefore to enquire into how an intercept in (8.2) might be estimated. We will assume that the first element of x_{2i} is unity and partition x'_{2i} as $[1 \; \bar{x}'_{2i}]$ with β'_2 being $[\gamma \; \delta']$.[5]

It is not always the case that one needs to estimate the intercept. If only the impact of *variations* in $\bar{x}_{2i}$ need to be studied it becomes irrelevant. However, there are enough instances where the "level" of y_{2i} needs to be estimated as to require some attention to be paid to the issue. Heckman (1990) suggested that an estimator of γ could be found by averaging those observations for which $E(e_{2i}|y^*_{1i} > 0) = g(v_i)$ is zero, that is, if $P(e_{2i}|y_{1i} = 1) = 1$. This leads to an estimator of the form

$$\hat{\gamma} = \frac{\sum_{i=1}^{n} \left(y_{2i} - \bar{x}'_{2i}\delta\right) y_{1i} I\left(\hat{v}_i > h_1\right)}{\sum_{i=1}^{n} y_{1i} I\left(\hat{v} > h_1\right)},$$

where h_1 is a window-width or smoothing parameter such that $h_1 \rightarrow 0$ as $n \rightarrow \infty$. Andrews and Schafgens (1998) modify $\hat{\gamma}$ by replacing the indicator function with a nondecreasing $[0, 1]$-valued smooth function $\kappa(z)$ with the properties that $\kappa(z) = 0$, for $\kappa(z) \leq 0$, and $\kappa(z) = 1$, for $z \geq b$; it posesses three bounded derivatives, that is, the function is like that used by Horowitz with his smoothed maximum score estimator. They establish the consistency and asymptotic normality of this estimator.

8.6 Applications of the Estimators

Newey et al. (1990) applied his series estimator to an equation explaining the wages earned by married women. In this case the probability of labor force participation was estimated either by a probit model or an SP estimator like Ichumura's or Klein and Spady's. Specification tests tended to favor the probit model so that $\hat{\beta}_1$ was estimated that way. The series expansion then involved $\frac{\phi(x'_{1i}\hat{\beta}_1)}{\Phi(x'_{1i}\hat{\beta}_1)}(x'_{1i}\hat{\beta})^j$ $(j = 1, \ldots, M)$, with M being chosen by cross validation. Ultimately $M = 2$ and the resulting $\hat{\beta}_2$ was found to be very close to the traditional two-step estimator; that is, the presence of the term $\frac{\phi(x'_{1i}\hat{\beta}_1)}{\Phi(x'_{1i}\hat{\beta}_1)}(x'_{1i}\hat{\beta})^2$ had little impact upon the estimation of β_2.

---

[5] Gallant and Nychka's series-expansion method avoids the difficulties we mention simply because it effectively uses a parametric density, and all elements of β_2 should be then identifiable. What is not clear however is what happens as $M \rightarrow \infty$ in their case; if the estimator of the density becomes "nonparametric" then it is hard to see how γ can be identified asymptotically, even though it is for any finite M.

Melenberg and Van Soest (1993) also model the wages of Dutch married females. They expand the range of estimators from series ones to those by Gallant and Nychka, Newey (GMM estimator), and Ahn and Powell. Gallant and Nychka's estimator performed very well for the data set under consideration, although numerical optimization of the likelihood requires substantial computational effort, and there is no guarantee that a global maximum will be attained. Powell's estimators work quite well, although computation of standard errors could be difficult. Their preference was for Newey's series or GMM estimators, with the latter being particularly attractive, owing to its ability to attain the SP efficiency bound.

Lee (1990) considered the asymptotic performance of some of the estimators for particular numerical models. This amounted to comparing the variance of Newey's and Powell's two-step estimators with the SP efficiency bound (SEB). Generally, these estimators proved to be very inefficient, having variances that could be some ten times the SEB. Unless there exists substantial variation in x_{2i} not associated with x_{1i} it is unlikely that two-step estimators will be very effective, and this suggests that it may pay to focus upon the GMM estimator in future SP applications to the selection problem.

8.7   Conclusions

This chapter has considered the semiparametric estimation of parameters in the traditional form of the selection problem wherein the observations are only available for those individuals who have made a positive choice. In line with the parametric literature, SP approaches either concentrate upon two-step estimation or attempt to replicate full maximum likelihood. This class of models is sometimes referred to as Type-2 Tobit since the observations consist of $y_{1i} = I(y_{1i}^* > 0)$, y_{2i}, and the exogenous regressors. Type-3 Tobit models also feature issues of selection but now there is partial observability of y_{1i}^*. In the simplest case one observes $y_{1i} = I(y_{1i}^* > 0)y_{1i}^*$, meaning that the auxiliary equation describing the selection rule is best thought of as involving censoring rather than discrete choice. Consequently, SP estimators will generally involve some of the methods discussed in the next chapter, although the underlying principles are similar to those of this chapter. Lee (1994) and Honore et al. (1997) are good references.

9　Semiparametric Estimation of Censored Regression Models

9.1　Introduction

Censoring of a variable whose behavior is to be explained is not uncommon with economic data. Tobin (1958) noted the fact that certain households purchased zero amounts of particular consumer durables in any given period (i.e., the expenditure variable was left censored at zero). Spells of unemployment are generally right censored owing to the fact that some individuals in the sample will not yet have terminated their spell of unemployment when sampled. Exchange rates can be censored at both ends if governments intervene at "support points." In such instances it is not appropriate to treat the variable to be explained as a continuous random variable, owing to the occurrence of multiple observations at the censoring point. Rather, the observations need to be treated as a mixture of a discrete and a continuous random variable, and estimation methods such as least squares regression cease to be appropriate.

Models of this form are generally given the designation of "Tobit," although, as Amemiya's (1985, Chapter 10) classification makes clear, there is considerable heterogeneity behind such nomenclature, owing to a plethora of possible censoring mechanisms. For example, the selectivity model analyzed in Chapter 8 is a Tobit model, but one in which the censoring point is determined by agents' actions. In this chapter we will concentrate upon the latent variable model

$$y_i^* = x_i'\beta + u_i \tag{9.1}$$

with the simplest left-censoring mechanism $y_i = \max(x_i'\beta + u_i, \ 0)$. If the model exhibited left censoring at some value δ, where δ is a known censoring point, it could be transformed to the format of (9.1) by defining $x_i'\beta - \delta = \tilde{x}_i'\tilde{\beta}$, where $\tilde{x}_i' = (x_i' \ 1)$ and $\tilde{\beta}' = (\beta' \ \delta)$, in which case only a subset of the parameters is unknown. This more general format also encompasses the case of right censoring, that is, $y_i = \min(x_i'\beta + u_i, \ \delta)$, by recognizing its equivalence to $-y_i = \max(-x_i'\beta - u_i, \ -\delta)$. Therefore, to allow for censoring points different than zero, it suffices to redefine $x_i'\beta$ as $\tilde{x}_i'\tilde{\beta}$, and the reader should replace x_i with $\tilde{x}_i$ in what follows (wherever x_i appears as a conditioning element or in an indicator function).

Traditionally β has been estimated by parametric methods that prescribe the density function for u_i, almost invariably as normal. Section 9.2 outlines the major suggestions. If the density of u_i is unknown though, semiparametric estimation of β becomes of interest. As is usual in this literature, the objective is to find the best estimator of β, in the sense of achieving the SP efficiency bound. But, as noted on previous occasions, this bound is a function of what is assumed about the density of u_i and the relation of x_i to u_i. In particular, there will be different bounds if (i) x_i and u_i are independently distributed, (ii) conditional upon x_i the median of u_i is zero, and (iii) conditional upon x_i, u_i is symmetrically distributed. Section 9.3 therefore sets out the efficient score and SP efficiency bounds corresponding to each case.

A basic theme in the estimation of censored regression models is the need to identify the cumulative distribution function (c.d.f.) for u_i, $F(u)$. In parametric models this is by prescription, but if β is to be estimated semiparametrically some estimator of $F(u)$ must be made. Because of the censoring, however, this is not as straightforward as when y_i is a continuous random variable. Nevertheless, Kaplan and Meier (1958) provided an estimator of $F(u)$, the product-limit estimator, that was consistent and asymptotically normal, and Section 9.4 provides an account of its construction.

Sections 9.5 and 9.6 turn to the SP estimation of β. The first of these sections describes a range of estimators, all of which seek to emulate parametric approaches. Essentially these utilize estimator-generating equations from parametric models, replacing the unknown distribution function $F(u)$ by the Kaplan–Meier or other estimator of it. Included in this class are the estimators of Buckley and James (1979), Horowitz (1986), Ichimura (1993), and Moon (1989). These estimators do not attain the SP bound under any of the conditions mentioned earlier. This leads to the suggestion of finding M-estimators of β that do solve the efficient scores. For the type (ii) constraint identified above, Newey and Powell (1990b) have shown that a variant of Powell's (1984) censored least absolute deviations estimator does so. Similarly, Newey (1991c) finds an estimator, loosely based on Powell's (1986b) symmetrically trimmed least squares estimator, that attains the bound, but now under (iii). Each of these estimators, along with others related to them, is discussed in Section 9.6.

Section 9.7 looks at some evidence on the relative performance of the various estimators. Horowitz (1988b) compared the asymptotic variances of various estimators to Cosslett's (1987) SP bound for type (i) constraints, whereas Paarsch (1984) and Moon (1989) present small Monte Carlo studies of a set of the estimators mentioned above.

9.2   Some Parametric Estimators

A basic idea in handling censored regression models is to retain the format of a regression but to "correct" the observations for the effects of censoring. Perhaps the simplest solution is to observe that the least squares principle in uncensored models finds that value of β minimizing $\sum_{i=1}^{n} (y_i - E(y_i|x_i))^2$, after $E(y_i|x_i)$ is replaced by $x_i'\beta$. When observations are censored application of this same principle would require the evaluation of $E(y_i|x_i)$. For a random variable Y that is nonnegative, it is a standard result that $E(Y) = \int_0^\infty (1 - F_Y(y)) \, dy$, where $F_Y(y)$ is the c.d.f. of Y. To prove this, integrate by parts, giving

$$[y(1 - F_Y(y))]_0^\infty + \int_0^\infty y \, f_Y(y) \, dy = E(Y),$$

where $f_Y(y)$ is the density of Y. After a change of variable,[1] we get

$$E(y_i|x_i) = \int_{-x_i'\beta}^{\infty} (1 - F(u)) \, du \tag{9.2}$$

$$= [u(1 - F(u))]_{-x_i'\beta}^{\infty} + \int_{-x_i'\beta}^{\infty} u f(u) \, du, \tag{9.3}$$

and integrating by parts yields

$$E(y_i|x_i) = x_i'\beta \left(1 - F(-x_i'\beta)\right) + \int_{-x_i'\beta}^{\infty} u f(u) \, du. \tag{9.4}$$

If the density $f(u)$ is symmetric around zero, (9.4) becomes

$$E(y_i|x_i) = x_i'\beta \, F(x_i'\beta) + \int_{-x_i'\beta}^{\infty} u f(u) \, du. \tag{9.5}$$

Further simplication to (9.5) depends upon the type of density assumed for u_i. If $f(u)$ is $\mathcal{N}(0, \sigma^2)$, the integral in (9.5) is $\sigma^2 f(x_i'\beta)$ (Amemiya, 1973, pp. 997–1016) and (9.5) becomes

$$E(y_i|x_i) = x_i'\beta \, F(x_i'\beta) + \sigma^2 f(x_i'\beta) \tag{9.6}$$

$$= x_i'\beta \, \Phi(x_i'\beta) + \sigma \, \phi(x_i'\beta), \tag{9.7}$$

---

[1] Strictly β should be replaced by β_0, the true value, but unless we wish to emphasize this fact, we will generally drop the subscript in this chapter.

where $\phi(\cdot)$ and $\Phi(\cdot)$ are the standard normal density and its c.d.f. respectively. Thus, under the normality assumption, one might minimize

$$\sum_{i=1}^{n} \left[y_i - x_i'\beta \, \Phi\left(x_i'\beta\right) - \sigma\phi\left(x_i'\beta\right) \right]^2$$

with respect to β, a strategy advocated in Wales and Woodland (1980).

Improvements can be made to the nonlinear regression estimator described above, by taking account of the heteroskedasticity in the errors $[y_i - E(y_i|x_i)]$. Their variance, conditional upon x_i, is

$$\sigma_i^2 = 2 \int_{-x_i'\beta}^{\infty} (1 - F(u)) \, u \, du + 2x_i'\beta \int_{-x_i'\beta}^{\infty} (1 - F(u)) \, du$$

$$- \left\{ \int_{-x_i'\beta}^{\infty} [1 - F(u)] \, du \right\}^2, \tag{9.8}$$

and this suggests that the GLS type of estimator minimizing $\sum_{i=1}^{n} \sigma_i^{-2}(y_i - E(y_i|x_i))^2$ would be more efficient than the OLS variant.

An alternative approach, which also utilizes all available observations, is to replace the "missing observations" on y_i^* by $E(y_i^*|y_i \leq 0)$ and to then perform a nonlinear regression of $I(y_i > 0) \, y_i^* + (1 - I(y_i > 0)) \, E(y_i^*|y_i \leq 0)$ against x_i to estimate β. The $\hat{\beta}$ that results solves the first-order conditions

$$\sum_{i=1}^{n} x_i \left\{ I(y_i > 0) \left(y_i - x_i'\hat{\beta} \right) \right.$$

$$\left. + (1 - I(y_i > 0)) \left(E\left(y_i^*|y_i \leq 0\right) - x_i'\hat{\beta} \right) \right\} = 0. \tag{9.9}$$

Use of (9.9) as an estimating equation is justified since the population quantity underlying (9.9) is

$$n^{-1} \sum_{i=1}^{n} x_i E\left[I(y_i > 0) \left(y_i - x_i'\beta \right) \right.$$

$$\left. + (1 - I(y_i > 0)) E(u_i|y_i \leq 0) \right] = 0.$$

To show that this is valid write the first term in the brackets as

$$E\left\{ E\left[I(y_i > 0) \left(y_i - x_i'\beta \right) \middle| y_i > 0 \right] \right\}$$

$$= E\left[I(y_i > 0) \int_{-x_i'\beta}^{\infty} uf(u) \left(1 - F\left(-x_i'\beta\right) \right)^{-1} du \right];$$

conditioning on the event of $y_i \leq 0$ makes the second term

$$E\left[(1 - I(y_i > 0)) \int_{-\infty}^{-x_i'\beta} uf(u) F^{-1}\left(-x_i'\beta\right) du \right].$$

Then $E\left(I\left(y_i > 0\right)\right) = 1 - F(-x_i'\beta)$, and the two terms sum to $\int_{-\infty}^{\infty} u f(u)\, du = 0$ from the fact that $E\left(u_i\right) = 0$.

A general expression for $E(y_i^* | y_i \leq 0)$ is

$$E(y_i^* | y_i \leq 0) = x_i'\beta + \int_{-\infty}^{-x_i'\beta} u\, f(u)\, du / F\left(-x_i'\beta\right). \tag{9.10}$$

Rather than utilize all the observations, some proposals concentrate upon the positive values only. Heckman (1976), for example, suggests estimating β from the positive values of y_i alone, minimizing $\sum [y_i - E\left(y_i | x_i, \ y_i > 0\right)]^2$ with respect to β. To implement this idea we need to find the conditional expectation

$$E\left(y_i | x_i, \ y_i > 0\right) = x_i'\beta + \left[1 - F\left(-x_i'\beta\right)\right]^{-1} \int_{-x_i'\beta}^{\infty} (1 - F(u))\, du. \tag{9.11}$$

When the error density for u_i is $\mathcal{N}(0, \sigma^2)$ it follows from the argument leading from (9.2) to (9.5) that

$$E\left(y_i | x_i, \ y_i > 0\right) = x_i'\beta + \sigma\phi\left(x_i'\beta/\sigma\right)/\Phi\left(x_i'\beta/\sigma\right),$$

which is the basis of Heckman's famous two-step estimator for sample-selection models.

Dispensing with the need to retain a regression structure for the estimator, maximum likelihood becomes the obvious alternative approach, given distributional knowledge. For data generated by i.i.d. random variables the log likelihood for $\{y_i\}_{i=1}^{n}$, conditional upon $\{x_i\}_{i=1}^{n}$, would be

$$\sum_{i=1}^{n} (1 - y_i) \log F\left(-x_i'\beta\right) + \sum_{i=1}^{n} y_i \log f\left(y_i - x_i'\beta\right), \tag{9.12}$$

and maximization of (9.12) with respect to β (and also any other parameters that characterize the density) would give the MLE of β. When $f(\cdot)$ is the $\mathcal{N}(0, \sigma^2)$ density, σ^2 would be an extra parameter to estimate along with β. Standard programs such as GAUSS, LIMDEP, RATS, and MICROFIT all provide routines to get the MLE of β when $f(\cdot)$ is normally distributed. The covariance matrix may be found from the information matrix or various sample approximations to it – see Greene (1997) for a good discussion.

It is clear from the analysis above that the estimators of β are heavily dependent upon distributional information. In (9.7) and (9.11), the conditional expectation of y_i, given x_i and any auxiliary information, is a specific nonlinear function of $x_i'\beta$ that is determined by $F(u)$. However, if the true density is different from the assumed one, the conditional mean will be misspecified and the estimator of β found by minimizing the squared deviations of y_i from this conditional expectation will be inconsistent. Hence, it is of interest to derive estimators of β that are consistent in the face of unknown shape for $F(u)$.

9.3   Semiparametric Efficiency Bounds for the Censored Regression Model

Semiparametric efficiency bounds for the censored regression model have been found under a variety of circumstances – a variety partly stimulated by there being no known estimator that will attain the bound when x_i and u_i are independent. Estimators can be found however that will reach the bound if independence is replaced by restrictions involving conditional symmetry of the density of u_i or on its conditional median.

As in Chapter 7, if the density for u_i is unrestricted, it will not be possible to estimate an intercept in $x_i'\beta$, leading to the reparameterization of $x_i'\beta$ as $v_i = v(x_i, \theta)$ (see Section 7.3), with θ being the estimable parameters.[2] If x_i and u_i are independently distributed, the log likelihood of $y_1 \ldots y_n$ (conditional upon x_i) will be

$$\sum_{i=1}^{n}\{\log\ F\ (-v_i;\eta)\ I\ (y_i < 0) + \log\ f\ (y_i - v_i;\eta)\ I\ (y_i > 0)\},$$

$$(9.13)$$

where $f(\cdot)$ is the density function for u_i and $F(\cdot)$ is its c.d.f. Following Section 5.4, η will index a parametric subfamily of densities, and $F\ (-v_i;\eta) = \int_{-\infty}^{-v_i} f(u;\eta)\,du$ will describe the corresponding family of c.d.f.s. As outlined in that section, the SP efficiency bound is found by deriving the efficient score for θ, whose inputs would be

$$d_\theta = -\sum_{i=1}^{n}\left[F^{-1}(-v_i)f(v_i;\eta)I\ (y_i < 0)\right.$$

$$\left. + f^{-1}(u_i;\eta)f^{(1)}(u_i;\eta)I\ (y_i > 0)\right]\frac{\partial v_i}{\partial\theta}, \qquad (9.14)$$

$$d_\eta = \sum_{i=1}^{n}\left[F^{-1}(-v_i)\left(\int_{-\infty}^{-v_i}\frac{\partial f_i}{\partial\eta}\,du\right)I\ (y_i < 0)\right.$$

$$\left. + f^{-1}(u_i;\eta)\frac{\partial f_i}{\partial\eta}I\ (y_i > 0)\right]. \qquad (9.15)$$

Clearly (9.14) and (9.15) are much more complex expressions than the corresponding duo for the discrete choice model (see Section 7.3), a complexity that partly stems from the dependence of the scores upon $F(\cdot)$ only in the discrete choice case and upon both $f(\cdot)$ and $F(\cdot)$ in censored regression. Such a singular dependence in the former instance allowed for $F(\cdot)$ to be directly

---

[2] Unlike in Section 7.3 it will normally be possible to identify the slope parameters themselves rather than just their ratio.

indexed with η, whereas now it is a complex indirect function of it. Finding the efficient score $\tilde{d}_\theta(i) = d_\theta(i) - E(d_\theta(i)|d_\eta(i))$ is also a much more complex operation than for the discrete choice model as $d_\eta(i)$ depends on v_i and u_i and no longer just on v_i. If η was parametric, $E(d_\theta(i)|d_\eta(i)) = \mathcal{I}_{\eta\eta}^{-1}\mathcal{I}_{\eta\theta}d_\eta(i)$, where $\mathcal{I}$ is the information matrix, and Cosslett (1987) uses this fact to suggest a solution for the efficiency bound, thereafter proceeding to verify the conjecture.[3] Maintaining independence between x_i and u_i, and making a number of other assumptions pertaining to boundness and continuity of functions such as $f(\cdot)$, f^2/F, etc., he derives the SP efficiency bound as (see his Appendix B)

$$V_I = \int_{-\infty}^\infty f(u)^{-1} F^2(u) \left[\frac{d}{du} \left(\frac{f(u)}{F(u)} \right) \right]^2$$

$$\times H(u)\mathrm{var} \left[\left. \frac{\partial v}{\partial \theta} \right| - v(x,\theta) < u \right], \tag{9.16}$$

where $H(u) = P(u > -v(x,\theta))$ and the "I" denotes that this bound applies under the independence assumption. Cosslett also investigated the bound when independence was *augmented* by the assumption that the density of u_i had zero median. Changing the condition allows the intercept to be estimated, but it does not change the bound for the slope coefficients, as the location parameter is actually being estimated in both situations. Under pure independence it is subsumed into the unknown density for u_i, and it is that which needs to be estimated, whereas in the extended case it is separated out.

Newey and Powell (1990b) dropped the assumption of independence of x_i and u_i, replacing it by the requirement that the density of u_i, conditional upon x_i, has zero median. To constrain the parametric subfamily of densities in this way leads them to set

$$f(u|x,\eta) = f(u|x)\{1 + [v(x)'\eta]\xi(u,x)\},$$

where η and $v(x)$ are $p \times 1$ vectors with $v(x)$ and $\xi(u,x)$ being bounded and continuously differentiable in u, while the derivative $\partial\xi/\partial u$ is bounded with

$$\int \xi(u,x)f(u|x)\,du = \int \mathrm{sgn}(u)\xi(u,x)f(u,x)\,du = 0.$$

The integral restriction forces members of this parametric subfamily to integrate to unity and to have zero median. Under the zero conditional median restriction the intercept can be estimated, and they demonstrate that the SP bound is

$$V_M = \left\{ E \left[4I \left(x_i'\beta > 0 \right) f^2 \left(0|x_i \right) x_i x_i' \right] \right\}^{-1}, \tag{9.17}$$

---

[3] Actually, he works with the derivative of the square root of the density of y_i^* with respect to θ, rather than with the scores. However, both ultimately give the information matrix.

with efficient score

$$\tilde{d}_\beta^M(i) = 2f\left(0|x_i\right) I\left(x_i'\beta > 0\right) \operatorname{sgn}\left(y_i - x_i'\beta\right) x_i. \tag{9.18}$$

The value of the efficient score depends upon whether $x_i'\beta$ is greater than zero or not. Their intuitive explanation for this feature is as follows: When censoring occurs the efficient score equals zero, because knowledge of the median is irrelevant (if the censoring point is to the left of the median), whereas, when observations are uncensored, it takes the value $2f\left(0|x_i\right)\operatorname{sgn}(y_i - x_i'\beta)x_i$, coinciding with what it would be in the regression model if a zero conditional median restriction was imposed. Of course $V_M \geq V_I$ and Cosslett (p. 576) formally demonstrates this. His argument exploits the fact that $H(u)$ var $\left[\frac{\partial v}{\partial \theta}\middle| v(x,\theta) < u\right]$ is an increasing function of u, possessing a lower bound when $u = 0$. Mapping this to an "upper bound" for V_I shows that it is no less than V_M, coinciding when $f(\cdot)$ is exponential. Based on this relation it seems likely that V_M exceeds V_I by a considerable margin, showing the efficiency loss sustained by the use of a weaker set of restrictions on the class of allowable densities.

Finally, when f is taken to be symmetric, Newey (1990a) finds the efficient score to be

$$\tilde{d}_\beta^{(S)}(i) = \sum_{i=1}^n I\left(x_i'\beta > 0\right) x_i \left\{\left[I\left(y_i \geq 2x_i'\beta\right) - I\left(y_i = 0\right)\right] J_i\right.$$
$$\left. - I\left(0 < y_i < 2x_i'\beta\right) f_i^{-1} f_i^{(1)}\right\}, \tag{9.19}$$

where the f_i is now the density of u_i conditional upon x_i, $f_i^{(1)}$ is the first derivative of f_i with respect to its argument u_i, and $J_i = E\left[f_i^{-1} f_i^{(1)}\middle| u_i \leq x_i'\beta\right]$. Inspection of this formula shows that the efficient score is zero for all observations for which $x_i'\beta < 0$. The logic of this is clearest when $x_i = 1$ so that only an intercept (location parameter) is to be estimated. When the true value of β is negative, censoring occurs above the location parameter so that the requirement of conditional symmetry provides no useful information for the estimation of β.

9.4   The Kaplan–Meier Estimator of the Distribution Function of a Censored Random Variable

As evidenced in earlier chapters semiparametric estimation largely involves replacing unknown densities, or functions of them, with their nonparametric estimates. As the parametric estimators of Section 9.2 all feature the cumulative distribution function (c.d.f.) of the errors u_i, $F(\cdot)$, it is obvious that it will need to be estimated. But, because the random variable u_i is censored, it is not immediately apparent how this should be done.

Kaplan and Meier (1958) formulated a solution to this problem, which has become known as the "product-limit" estimator. To appreciate its logic consider a random variable Y, with y_i, $i = 1, \ldots, n$, being observations. Kaplan and Meier actually prefer to estimate the survival curve $P\{Y > c\}$, but, as the c.d.f. of Y is $1 - P\{Y \geq c\}$, it is a simple matter to effect a conversion. Suppose initially that Y is uncensored. A standard estimator of $P\{Y > c\}$ would be $(\#y_i > c)/n$. An alternative way of building up this estimate would be as follows: First define ascending points $c_1, \ldots, c_s$ at which the c.d.f. is to be evaluated, and let $I_j = I(Y > c_j)$; that is, if Y survives past c_j the variable I_j has the value unity. Because I_j is a random variable

$$P(I_j = 1) = P(I_j = 1 | I_{j-1} = 1) \cdot P(I_{j-1} = 1). \tag{9.20}$$

By choosing c_1 small enough, say below the smallest point in the data, we can always ensure that the recursion in (9.20) starts with $P(I_1) = 1$, that is, all items survive initially. Now, estimating the two terms on the right-hand side of (9.20) by $[(\#y_i > c_j)/\#y_i > c_{j-1}]$ and $[(\#y_i > c_{j-1})/n]$ respectively, it is seen that (9.20) delivers the standard estimator, and repeated application of it would produce the empirical distribution function.

Kaplan and Meier proposed that (9.20) also be used for censored data but with

$$P(I_j = 1 | I_{j-1} = 1) = (\#y_i \geq c_{j-1})$$
$$- (\# \text{ uncensored } y_i \text{ in the range } c_{j-1} < y_i \leq c_j)/(\#y_i \geq c_{j-1})),$$

for $j = 1, \ldots, s$ and $P(I_j = 1 | I_{j-1} = 1) = 0$ after values of c_j exceed the censoring threshold. Notice that the numerator here differs from that for an uncensored random variable to the extent that there are censored observations in the range c_{j-1} to c_j. If all the observations in this range are censored $P(I_j = 1 | I_{j-1} = 1)$ is unity and the survival function estimate does not change. After c_j exceeds the censoring threshold the survival function is set to zero. Such a decision is arbitrary as there is no knowledge about survival past this point, but it matters little as the only part of the survival curve used in SP estimation is that up to the threshold. Meier (1975, p. 73) discusses an "extended product limit" estimator that treats the end-point differently in order to get an unbiased estimator at all points.

As an illustration of the methodology, twenty $(= n)$ random numbers from an $\mathcal{N}(0, 1)$ random variable, censored at unity, were generated and recorded in Table 9.1. Setting $s = n$, $c_i = y_i (i = 1, \ldots, n)$, this table also gives the conditional probabilities making up (9.20), the survival curve, and the c.d.f. Notice that, because of censoring, $F(\cdot)$ would be set to unity for any $c_i > 1$. In the applications of the Kaplan–Meier estimator reported later it is the density function of $u_i = y_i^* - x_i'\beta$ that is needed, and the censoring point is $-x_i'\beta$ and therefore variable. This does not change the estimator of the c.d.f. of u however, except that $c_i = -x_i'\beta$, and u_i will be the censored random variable. Of course in practice β is not observable and needs to be replaced with some estimate.

Table 9.1. *Illustration of the Kaplan–Meier estimator.*[a]

	Data $(= c_j)$	$P(I_j/I_{j-1})$	Survivor function $(P(y > c_j))$	c.d.f. $P(y \le c)$
1	−1.305	19/20	.95	.05
2	−1.242	18/19	.90	.10
3	−1.181	17/18	.85	.15
4	−.934	16/17	.80	.20
5	−.899	15/16	.75	.25
6	−.818	14/15	.70	.30
7	−.743	13/14	.65	.35
8	−.740	12/13	.60	.40
9	−.694	11/12	.55	.45
10	−.600	10/11	.50	.50
11	−.442	09/10	.45	.55
12	−.200	08/09	.40	.60
13	−.012	07/08	.35	.65
14	.257	06/07	.30	.70
15	.348	05/06	.25	.75
16	.450	04/05	.20	.80
17	.610	03/04	.15	.85
18	.918	02/03	.10	.90
19	1.00	1	.10	.90
20	1.00	1	.10	.90

Note: [a] Data have been stored in ascending order. As mentioned in the text the survivor function can be set to zero for values of y in excess of the censoring value of unity.

Various asymptotic properties of the product-limit estimator have been established, under both fixed and variable censoring, Strong uniform consistency was shown by Földes (1981) under variable censoring, whereas Shorack and Wellner (1986, p. 327) establish strong consistency for general censoring. Hall and Wellner (1980) find asymptotic confidence intervals for the estimator under variable censoring. Applications of the estimator to testing for specification errors in censored regression models are reported in Horowitz and Neumann (1989a).

9.5   Semiparametric Density-Based Estimators

Section 9.2 laid out various parametric estimators of β, all of which needed a complete specification of the c.d.f. of the errors u_i. It is natural therefore that semiparametric versions of these would arise wherein the c.d.f. of u_i is estimated jointly with β. As there were effectively three different types of parametric estimators, we will categorize the discussion in the same way for the SP analogues.

9.5.1 The Semiparametric Generalized Least Squares Estimator (SGLS)

Horowitz (1986, 1988a) and Ichimura (1993) recommended that an estimator of β be found by following the Generalized Least Squares principle. Suppose a consistent estimator of

$$\sigma_i^2 = \text{var}\left(y_i - E\left(y_i \mid x_i'\beta\right)\right)$$

is available. Then Horowitz suggested minimizing

$$\sum_{i=1}^{n} \tilde{\sigma}_i^{-2} \left[y_i - \int_{-x_i'b}^{\infty} (1 - F(u))\, du\right]^2$$

with respect to b to produce $\hat{\beta}_{\text{SGLS}}$.[4] It is possible to produce a consistent estimator of σ_i^2 by replacing β and $F(u)$ in (9.8) by consistent estimators of these quantities. Rather than work with integrals involving $F(u)$, both σ_i^2 and $E(y_i|x_i'\beta)$ are evaluated by integration by parts; the latter is given in (9.4), whereas σ_i^2 reduces to

$$\left(x_i'\beta\right)^2 \left(1 - F\left(-x_i'\beta\right)\right) + \int_{-x_i'\beta}^{\infty} u^2\, dF(u) + 2x_i'\beta \int_{-x_i'\beta}^{\infty} u\, dF(u)$$

$$- \left[\left(1 - F\left(-x_i'\beta\right)\right) x_i'\beta + \int_{-x_i'\beta}^{\infty} u\, dF(u)\right]^2.$$

Horowitz replaces $F(u)$ in the expressions for the conditional moments by the Kaplan–Meier estimator (KME), $\hat{F}(u)$, and estimates $dF(u)$ by $\hat{F}(u_j) - \hat{F}(u_{j-1})$, where u_j are the points at which $\hat{F}(u)$ is determined. In Horowitz (1986) $\hat{\beta}_{\text{SGLS}}$ is shown to be consistent. Initial estimates of β for forming $\tilde{\sigma}_i^2$ could be found by minimizing the same criterion but with $\tilde{\sigma}_i^2$ set to unity.

Because the problem is similar to nonlinear least squares, one way to proceed would be to find $\hat{\beta}_{\text{SGLS}}$ as the solution to the first-order conditions

$$\sum_{i=1}^{n} \tilde{\sigma}_i^{-2} \frac{\partial \hat{m}_i}{\partial \beta} (y_i - \hat{m}_i) = 0,$$

---

[4] As the intercept cannot be identified β will only contain slope coefficients. Since all of the estimators of this section are only of slope coefficients there should be no confusion with such a definition.

where $\hat{m}_i = E\left(y_i \,\middle|\, x_i'\hat{\beta}_{SGLS}\right)$ is evaluated with (9.4), where F is replaced by the KME. A difficulty in doing this is that $\hat{F}(u)$ is discontinuous in u, and hence in $\hat{\beta}_{SGLS}$, and there is therefore no guarantee of a solution. Further, the lack of continuity makes it hard to find distributional properties for $\hat{\beta}_{SGLS}$. These features led Horowitz to use a smoothed version of the KME rather than the original itself (see Horowitz, 1988a, p. 51). Even then, the proof of asymptotic normality of $n^{1/2}\left(\hat{\beta}_{SGLS} - \beta_0\right)$ is very complex, mainly because the derivative $\partial\hat{m}_i/\partial\beta$ is estimated as a finite difference of the original KME rather than the smoothed version of it, and conditions need to be imposed to ensure that the finite difference does converge to the requisite derivative. There are also many practical problems in implementing the estimator. Although $\hat{\beta}_{SGLS}$ is an M-estimator the expression for its asymptotic covariance matrix is lengthy (see Horowitz, 1988a, pp. 128–9), and initial computations of it (in FORTRAN) took many hours on a PC (see Horowitz and Neuman, 1987). In later work, Horowitz and Neuman (1989b) indicate that performing the computations in GAUSS results in significant savings. With the vastly faster microcomputers of today such computational constraints should no longer be an issue.

Because the difficulties in implementing Horowitz's SGLS estimator seem to stem from the use of the KME in estimating the conditional expectation of $m_i = E(y_i|x_i'\beta)$, it would seem sensible to estimate this expectation by kernel methods, as this will make $\hat{m}_i$ both continuous and differentiable, provided the kernel has these properties. Because $x_i'\beta$ is a scalar, it is relatively easy to use kernel methods for this purpose. Ichimura (1993) made this suggestion, finding the value $\hat{\beta}$ such that

$$\sum_{i=1}^{n} \frac{\partial\hat{m}_i}{\partial\beta}\left(y_i - E\left(y_i \,\middle|\, x_i'\hat{\beta}\right)\right) = 0.$$

An iterative procedure will need to be followed to determine $\hat{\beta}$. At each trial value for β, b, the single index $x_i'b$ is formed, kernel estimation gives $E(y_i|x_i'b)$, and then differentiation with respect to b of this formula provides $\partial\hat{m}_i/\partial\beta$. Such an estimator for the discrete choice model has already been detailed in Section 7.4.1. Alternatively, one could perform a weighted regression with weights $\tilde{\sigma}_i^{-2}$; $\tilde{\sigma}_i^2$ will be the estimated variance of y_i, given $x_i'\tilde{\beta}$, where $\tilde{\beta}$ is some initial consistent estimator of β. Because this estimator of β aims to solve the same problem as Horowitz's it is convenient to refer to it as the SGLS estimator as well. Consistency and asymptotic normality follow exactly as for the application of this estimator to the discrete choice model of Section 7.4.1.

9.5.2 *Estimators Replacing Part of the Sample*

The parametric estimator described in (9.9) replaced the censored observations on y_i^* by $E(y_i^*|y_i^* < 0)$; Equation (9.11) did the same for the uncensored observations. For the first of these procedures the sum of squares is defined over all observations, whereas in the latter only uncensored observations are used. Semiparametric analogues of these two estimators are given by Buckley and James (1979) and Moon (1989). Each estimator is implemented by replacing $F(u)$ in (9.9) and (9.11) by the KME. Consistency proofs are available for the β solving the associated first-order conditions, but nothing is known about the distributional properties, because of the discontinuity of the KM estimator. There would not seem to be any advantages to these estimators over $\hat{\beta}_{\text{SGLS}}$, and so no detailed analysis will be provided.

9.5.3 Maximum Likelihood–Type Estimators

Rather than work with least squares–type estimators there have been attempts to emulate maximum likelihood. In the parametric case, (9.12) is maximized with respect to β, and SP variants would replace the c.d.f. and density function of u_i with some smooth approximation that converges to the true quantities asymptotically. Duncan (1986) approximated $f(u)$ with a spline function, and other alternatives in this vein were mentioned in his paper. By contrast, Fernandez (1986) used a smoothed version of the KME, which is effectively the orthogonal series method discussed in Section 2.2.6 applied to $d\hat{F}(u)$ (for the "density" estimator) and to $\hat{F}(u)$ (for the c.d.f.). Consistency of the nonparametric MLE $\left(\hat{\beta}_{\text{NPMLE}}\right)$ is shown, but again a distributional proof is lacking.

9.6 Semiparametric Nondensity-Based Estimators

Parametric estimators all exploited knowledge of the density of u_i in their construction. Semiparametric estimators can be separated according to whether or not they estimate the unknown density for u_i as a prelude to estimating θ (or β). The situation is reminiscent of that in Section 5.9. Although the optimal estimator of regression parameters (β) depended upon the unknown error density, the M-estimators of Section 5.9 would produce consistent and asymptotically normal estimators of β by solving criterion functions whose expectation is minimized when β was set to its true value. These estimators would generally be inefficient, but they might be more robust than estimators of β that made assumptions about the error term. Although the latter should not be a problem for the estimators of Section 9.5, there may be computational advantages to working with M-estimators rather than attempting to mimic what would be optimal if the density of u_i was known. Moreover, it may be that these estimators may have better sampling performance in realistic sample sizes, even if they are not efficient in very large samples. It will also emerge that, in certain circumstances, they may attain the semiparametric efficiency bound.

9.6.1   Powell's Censored Least Absolute Deviation (CLAD) Estimator

Powell (1984) suggested applying the LAD estimator to the censored regression model, giving

$$\hat{\beta}_{CLAD} = \underset{\beta}{\text{argmin}} \sum_{i=1}^{n} \left| y_i - \max\left\{ x_i'\beta, 0 \right\} \right| \tag{9.21}$$

$$= \underset{\beta}{\text{argmin}} \sum_{i=1}^{n} I\left(x_i'\beta > 0 \right) \left| y_i - x_i'\beta \right|, \tag{9.22}$$

because, for observations $x_i'\beta \leq 0$, $\max[x_i'\beta, 0] = 0$ and $|y_i - \max\{x_i'\beta, 0\}| = |y_i|$ is not a function of β. Hence $\sum |y_i - x_i'\beta|$ is minimized using only those observations for which $x_i'\beta > 0$.[5] To see why suppose $x_i = 1$ (i.e., only a location parameter is to be estimated). If $\beta < 0$ the location parameter lies below the censoring point for y_i (zero), and so the data have no information about it. Only if β exceeds the censoring point are the data informative.

It is also instructive to analyze (9.21) as a special case of a result given in Section 5.9. There it was noted that minimizing $E\{[\alpha - I(y - \xi)](y - \xi)\}$ with respect to ξ gave the α quantile of y as the solution for ξ. When $\alpha = 1/2$, this criterion is $\frac{1}{2}E|y - \xi|$. Now, since the median of y_i (conditional on x_i) is $\max\{x_i'\beta + \mu_{1/2}, 0\}$, where $\mu_{1/2}$ is the *median* of u_i, minimizing $E|y_i - \max\{x_i'b, 0\}|$ with respect to b will mean that $x_i'b = x_i'\beta + \mu_{1/2}$. Thus, if the median of u_i is zero (i.e., $\mu_{1/2} = 0$), $b = \beta_0$ minimizes $E[y_i - \max\{x_i'b, 0\}]$, and this outcome was the basis of M-estimators. If the median of u_i is not zero the criterion is minimized by setting the slope parameter to its true value, but the intercept would be the true value plus $\mu_{1/2}$.

The first-order conditions implicit in (9.22) are

$$\sum_{i=1}^{n} I\left(x_i'\hat{\beta}_{CLAD} > 0 \right) x_i \, \text{sgn}\left(y_i - x_i'\hat{\beta}_{CLAD} \right) = 0, \tag{9.23}$$

and, when u_i and x_i are independent, the covariance matrix for $n^{1/2}\left(\hat{\beta}_{CLAD} - \beta_0 \right)$ is

$$V_{CLAD} = \left[E\left\{ 4f^2(0) \lim_{n \to \infty} n^{-1} \sum_{i=1}^{n} I\left(x_i'\beta_0 > 0 \right) x_i x_i' \right\} \right]^{-1}, \tag{9.24}$$

where $f(0)$ is the density of u_i at the origin (assuming that the median of u_i is zero). Notice that this covariance matrix is identical to that for the LAD estimator of parameters in an uncensored regression, after making an allowance for the

---

[5] Note that for left censoring at δ_i rather than zero we would have $x_i'\beta > \delta_i$.

fact that the criterion minimized in each case differs solely by the presence of the multiplicative term $I(x_i'\beta > 0)$.

Minimization of (9.21) is somewhat more complicated than for the conventional LAD estimator of Chapter 5, owing to the presence of the indicator function weights. In particular, linear programming algorithms can no longer be applied and there is some evidence that the CLAD optimand exhibits local optima. Moreover, just as for LAD, it is necesssary to compute $f(0)$ in the covariance matrix (9.24), but now in the presence of censored data. One possibility would be to utilize the Kaplan–Meier estimator of the c.d.f. and to then find an approximation to $f(0)$ by $[F(z^+) - F(z^-)]/(z^+ - z^-)$, where z^+ and z^- are the two values closest to zero at which the c.d.f. is estimated (z^+ exceeding zero and z^- being less than it). Alternatively, one might estimate the density by the empirical density function in a region around zero. For uncensored data $f(0)$ could be consistently estimated by $\#[-h/2 < \hat{u}_i < h/2]/nh$, as discussed in Chapter 2, that is, $(nh)^{-1}\sum_{i=1}^n I[-h/2 < \hat{u}_i < h/2]$ (where $\hat{u}_i = y_i - x_i'\hat{\beta}_{\text{CLAD}}$). Censoring creates some complications since it is possible that some of the censored y_i correspond to u_i close to zero. Powell (1984) uses the definition

$$f(0) = \lim_{h \to 0} h^{-1}[P(0 \le u_i < h)]$$
$$= \lim_{h \to 0} h^{-1}\left[P(0 \le u_i < h \,|\, x_i'\beta > 0)\right],$$

because of the independence of u_i and x_i. Then, just as in Section 2.2.1, the conditional probability can be estimated, yielding

$$\hat{f}(0) = \sum_{i=1}^n I\left(x_i'\hat{\beta}_{\text{CLAD}} > 0\right) I\left(0 \le \hat{u}_i < h\right) \Big/ \left\{ h \sum_{i=1}^n I\left(x_i'\hat{\beta}_{\text{CLAD}} > 0\right)\right\}.$$

The restriction that $x_i'\hat{\beta}_{\text{CLAD}}$ be positive, in conjunction with the fact that $0 \le \hat{u}_i \le h$, ensures, via $y_i^* = x_i'\beta + u_i$, that only uncensored data points are used in the density construction. Horowitz and Newman (1987) use a variant of this estimator:

$$\hat{f}(0) = \sum_{i=1}^n \left(-\frac{h}{2} \le \hat{u}_i < \frac{h}{2}\right) I(y_i > 0) \Big/ h \left\{ \sum_{i=1}^n I\left(x_i'\hat{\beta}_{\text{CLAD}} > \frac{h}{2}\right) \right.$$
$$\left. + \frac{1}{2}\left(1 + \frac{x_i'\hat{\beta}_{\text{CLAD}}}{(h/2)}\right) I\left(-\frac{h}{2} < x_i'\hat{\beta}_{\text{CLAD}} \le \frac{h}{2}\right)\right\}. \quad (9.25)$$

If the window width h declines to zero as $n \to \infty$, then it is clear that this estimator converges to Powell's.

Hall and Horowitz (1990) replace the indicator function in (9.25) by a kernel, as in the movement from Section 2.2.1 to 2.2.3. They also show that the optimal window width remains the same as in Chapter 2 for uncensored data. Although β is unknown and is replaced by $\hat{\beta}_{\text{CLAD}}$, the fact that it converges faster, at $O(n^{-1/2})$, than the nonparametric density estimator, means that it can be taken as known. They determine an exact expression for the optimal h, involving unknown quantities such as the derivatives of the function

$$g(u) = P\left[x_i'\hat{\beta}_{\text{CLAD}} > -u\right][f(u) - f(0)],$$

and indicate how it might be consistently estimated. Given the mixed performance of "plug-in" methods, when nonparametrically estimating a density, recounted in Chapter 2, one should be cautious in persuing this idea here. Nevertheless, as documented in Horowitz and Neumann (1987), the covariance matrix computations are sensitive to window-width choice, and further work is needed on automatic selection of h.

Newey and Powell (1990b) generalize the function to be minimized from (9.21) to

$$\sum w_i \left|y_i - \max\left\{x_i'\beta, 0\right\}\right|,$$

where w_i is allowed to be some nonnegative function of the censoring point and the regressors. This modification also makes (9.21) a weighted sum with weights w_i. The asymptotic covariance matrix of the resulting weighted censored least absolute deviation (WCLAD) estimator is

$$V_{\text{WCLAD}} = \lim_{n \to \infty} nA^{-1}E\left[\sum_{i=1}^{n} I\left(x_i'\beta > 0\right)w_i^2 x_i x_i'\right](A')^{-1}, \qquad (9.26)$$

where

$$A = 2E\sum_{i=1}^{n} f\left(0|x_i\right) I\left(x_i'\beta > 0\right) w_i x_i x_i',$$

which is minimized when $w_i = 2f\left(0|x_i\right)$. The optimal estimator therefore solves

$$\hat{\beta}_{\text{WCLAD}} = \overset{\text{argmin}}{b} \sum_{i=1}^{n} 2f\left(0|x_i\right) \left|y_i - \max\left\{x_i'b, 0\right\}\right| \qquad (9.27)$$

and has covariance matrix $\left\{E\left[4\sum_{i=1}^{n} I(x_i'\beta > 0)f^2\left(0|x_i\right)x_i x_i'\right]\right\}^{-1}$, and this was the SP bound for the censored regression model under a zero conditional median restriction (see (9.17)). If y_i and x_i are independent, $f\left(0|x_i\right)$ would be a constant and so $\hat{\beta}_{\text{WCLAD}}$ would just be Powell's CLAD.

Estimation of $\hat{\beta}_{\text{WCLAD}}$ proceeds exactly as for $\hat{\beta}_{\text{CLAD}}$, but the variance involves the conditional rather than the unconditional density. Consider estimating $f(0|x^*)$. Previously the sample used to form the estimator of $f(0)$ used all observations x_j such that $x_j'\beta > 0$, but now only those close to x^* should be used. Hence a suitable estimator of $f(0|x_i)$ would be

$$\sum_{j=1}^{n} I\left(x_i - \frac{h}{2} \leq x_j \leq x_i + \frac{h}{2}\right) I\left(0 \leq \hat{u}_j < h\right)$$

$$\times I\left(x_j'\hat{\beta}_{\text{WCLAD}} > 0\right) \Bigg/ \sum_{j=1}^{n} \left(x_j'\hat{\beta}_{\text{WCLAD}} > 0\right).$$

Since this needs to be evaluated at every point in the sample, allowing for dependence between u_i and x_i will be computationally expensive.

9.6.2 Powell's (1986a) Censored Quantile Estimators

Just as for the M-estimators in Section 5.9 the LAD estimator could be extended to quantiles other than the median, by minimizing $\sum_{i=1}^{n} \rho[y_i - \max\{0, x_i'\beta\}]$, where $\rho(z) = [\alpha - I(z < 0)]$, z is the function used in Section 5.9, and $0 < \alpha < 1$ defines which quantile is to be used. The argument for this estimator is the same as in Section 5.9. If μ_α denotes the α quantile of the distribution of u_i, then $\max\left(0, \mu_\alpha + x_i'\beta\right)$ is the α quantile of y_i conditional upon x_i. Since (see Section 5.9), for any random variable z, $E\left[\rho(z - \xi)\right]$ minimized with respect to ξ gives the α quantile of the z-distribution, the expected value of the criterion will be minimized at the true value of β, with the exception of the intercept, which will equal the true value plus μ_α, the α quantile of u_i. To identify the intercept, μ_α needs to be set to zero, that is, assume the α conditional quantile is zero. The covariance matrix of the censored quantile estimator is the same as (9.24) with the factor 4 replaced by $[\alpha(1 - \alpha)]^{-1}$ and $f(0)$ by $f(\mu_\alpha)$.

9.6.3 Powell's Symmetrically Censored Least Squares Estimators

If y_i^* in (9.1) was observed the OLS estimator of β in the latent variable model would be a consistent estimator of β_0, since it is the value of b minimizing

$$E\left[\sum_{i=1}^{n} \left(y_i^* - x_i'b\right)^2\right] = \int_{-\infty}^{\infty} \sum_{i=1}^{n} \left(y_i^* - x_i'b\right)^2 f(u_i)\, du.$$

However, this fails to be true if y_i^* is replaced by y_i. There are other criterion functions though for which the minimum is achieved at β_0. For example, for any nonrandom variable η_i, it must be the case that b minimizes

$$\int_{-\eta_i}^{\eta_i} \sum_{i=1}^{n} \left(y_i^* - x_i'b\right)^2 f(u_i) \, du_i$$

$$= E\left[\sum_{i=1}^{n} I\left(|u_i| < \eta_i\right) I\left(\eta_i > 0\right) \left(y_i^* - x_i'b\right)^2\right]$$

at the value β_0, provided that the density for u_i is symmetric around zero. An extension of this result is to allow $f(u_i)$ to be conditional upon x_i, in which case η_i can be made a function of x_i. In particular, setting $\eta_i = x_i'\beta_0$, b minimizes

$$S_1 = E\left[\sum_{i=1}^{n} I\left(|u_i| < x_i'\beta_0\right) I\left(x_i'\beta_0 > 0\right) \left(y_i - x_i'b\right)^2\right] \qquad (9.28)$$

at β_0; the substitution of y_i for y_i^* stems from the fact that y_i^* is observable and equal to y_i over the range $|u_i| < x_i'\beta_0$. This result points to the fact that minimizing

$$S_2 = n^{-1} \sum_{i=1}^{n} I\left(0 < y_i < 2x_i'b\right) I\left(x_i'b > 0\right) \left(y_i - x_i'b\right)^2 \qquad (9.29)$$

with respect to b would produce a consistent estimator of β_0.

A disadvantage of this estimator is that it effectively ignores all censored data points, as well as those with values of y_i exceeding $2x_i'\beta_0$, due to the effect of the indicator function $I\left(0 < y_i < 2x_i'\beta_0\right)$. Such a strategy would be appropriate to a truncated regression model but not to a censored one. To include the extra observations, and yet retain the minimum at β_0, it suffices to add to (9.28) functions of these observations that are equal and opposite at $b = \beta_0$. In particular we aim to augment (9.28) with the term

$$E\left[\sum_{i=1}^{n} I\left(x_i'\beta_0 > 0\right) I\left(u_i \leq -x_i'\beta_0\right) \left(x_i'b\right)^2\right.$$
$$\left. - \sum_{i=1}^{n} \left\{I\left(x_i'\beta_0 > 0\right) I\left(u_i \geq x_i'\beta_0\right) \left(x_i'b\right)^2\right\}\right],$$

as this is zero when u_i is symmetrically distributed around zero and $b = \beta_0$. Consequently, the augmented sample criterion is (omitting the sample-size divisor)

$$S = \left[\sum_{i=1}^{n} I\left(x_i'b > 0\right) \left\{I\left(u_i \leq -x_i'b\right) \left(x_i'b\right)^2 + I\left(0 < y_i < 2x_i'b\right)\right.\right.$$
$$\left.\left. \times \left(y_i - x_i'b\right)^2 - I\left(u_i \geq x_i'b\right) \left(x_i'b^2\right)\right\}\right], \qquad (9.30)$$

Table 9.2. *Contributions to criterion functions of data.*

Observations for which	Contribution to S	Contribution to S_p
$x_i'b < 0$	0	$\frac{1}{2}y_i^2$
$x_i'b > 0, y_i = 0$	$(x_i'b)^2$	$(x_i'b)^2$
$x_i'b > 0, 0 < y_i < 2x_i'b$	$(y_i - x_i'b)^2$	$(y_i - x_i'b)^2$
$y_i \geq 2x_i'b$	$-(x_i'b)^2$	$y_i^2 - (x_i'b)^2$

and it has the values collected in column two of Table 9.2, for various values of y_i.

Powell (1986b) investigates a symmetrically censored least squares estimator, $\hat{\beta}_{\text{SCLS}}$, that minimizes

$$S_p = \sum_{i=1}^{n} \left[y_i - \max \left\{ \frac{1}{2}y_i, \, x_i'b \right\}^2 \right]^2$$

$$+ \sum_{i=1}^{n} I\left(y_i > 2x_i'b \right) \left[\left(\frac{1}{2}y_i^2 \right) - \left(\max \left\{ 0, x_i'b \right\} \right)^2 \right]. \quad (9.31)$$

Inspection of S_p for various values of y_i gives the results in the third column of Table 9.2, from which it is obvious that S_p and S are both minimized at the same values for b, since the value y_i^2 is unchanged as b varies.

The quadratic terms in S and S_p are suggestive of least squares, but the analogy can be made tighter by noting that the value of b minimizing S_p is the solution to the first-order conditions

$$E\left[\sum_{i=1}^{n} I\left(x_i'\beta_0 > 0 \right) x_i \left(\min\left\{ y_i, 2x_i'\beta_0 \right\} - x_i'\beta_0 \right) \right] = 0, \quad (9.32)$$

and this would involve a least squares regression of z_i against x_i, where $z_i = y_i$ except when $y_i \geq 2x_i'\beta_0$, whereupon it is made equal to $2x_i'\beta_0$. This strategy of "artificially" censoring at $2x_i'\beta_0$, as a counterpart to the "natural" censoring at zero, "balances" the sample, since the probability of getting values of $y_i \geq 2x_i'\beta_0$ equals that for $y_i = 0$ under a symmetric density for u_i. Since all values of $y_i^* \leq 0$ are "collapsed" onto zero, symmetry points to the possibility of mapping all y_i^* values greater than or equal to $2x_i'\beta_0$ into $2x_i'\beta_0$. Unfortunately, replacing (9.32) with a sample moment and then solving for the value of b setting it to zero need not give $\hat{\beta}_{\text{SCLS}}$, because of the discontinuities induced by the indicator function. Multiple solutions may exist, $b = 0$ being one of them. Powell observes that, although the sample version of (9.32) is not zero for b close to $\hat{\beta}_{\text{SCLS}}$, this is just a local restriction, and large departures from $\hat{\beta}_{\text{SCLS}}$ may indeed satisfy the first-order conditions.

Powell shows that $\hat{\beta}_{\text{SCLS}}$ is consistent and $n^{1/2} \left(\hat{\beta}_{\text{SCLS}} - \beta_0 \right)$ is asymptotically normally distributed with covariance matrix

$$V_{\text{SCLS}} = C^{-1} \left(\lim_{n \to \infty} n^{-1} \sum_{i=1}^{n} E \left[I \left(x_i' \beta_0 > 0 \right) \right.\right.$$

$$\left.\left. \times \min \left\{ u_i^2, \left(x_i' \beta_0 \right)^2 \right\} x_i x_i' \right] \right) C^{-1}, \qquad (9.33)$$

where

$$C = \lim_{n \to \infty} n^{-1} \sum_{i=1}^{n} E \left[I \left(-x_i' \beta_0 < u_i < x_i' \beta_0 \right) x_i x_i' \right].$$

Replacing β_0 by $\hat{\beta}_{\text{SCLS}}$, u_i by $\hat{u}_i = y_i - x_i' \hat{\beta}_{\text{SCLS}}$, and the expectation by a sample moment produces a consistent estimator of V_{SCLS} that can be used for hypothesis testing.

There are some obvious limitations to the SCLS estimator. As with other estimators in this section, observations for which $x_i' \beta_0 \leq 0$ are lost. Additionally, however, information available from points with $y_i^* \geq 2 x_i' \beta_0$ is being discarded, so that the effective sample size may be much smaller than the actual one. From the nature of the covariance matrix it is also apparent that there must be sufficient variation in the regressors, as the "cross-product" matrix $\lim_{n \to \infty} n^{-1} \sum_{i=1}^{n} E[I(x_i' \beta_0 > 0) x_i x_i']$ must be nonsingular asymptotically. A lack of unimodality in the density of u_i can also be troublesome, since the presence of multiple modes implies the possibility of choosing a number of artificial censoring points that would retain symmetry, and this results in multiple minima for S_p (see Powell, 1986b, p. 1441).

9.6.4 *Newey's Efficient Estimator under Conditional Symmetry*

Since the efficient score for a censored regression model under conditional symmetry is known to be (9.19) it would be desirable to find the estimator $\hat{\beta}_{\text{ECS}}$ (efficient under conditional symmetry) that solves $\sum_{i=1}^{n} \tilde{d}_\beta^{(S)} \left(\hat{\beta}_{\text{ECS}} \right) (i) = 0$. One might attempt to estimate the unknown elements in (9.19) with nonparametric methods, but this is likely to be rather difficult. Instead Newey (1991c) applies his idea, described in Section 5.10, of forming a GMM estimator of β that would be asymptotically equivalent to $\hat{\beta}_{\text{ECS}}$. To do this it is necessary to specify a set of moment conditions that would reproduce the efficient score in large samples.

Newey selects as moment conditions

$$E\left[\sum_{i=1}^{n} I\left(x_i'\beta_0 > 0\right) g_j(u_i)\right] = 0, \tag{9.34}$$

$$E\left[\sum_{i=1}^{n} I\left(x_i'\beta_0 > 0\right) \psi_j(x_i)\left\{I\left(y_i \geq 2x_i'\beta_0\right) - I\left(y_i = 0\right)\right\}\right] = 0, \tag{9.35}$$

$j = 1, \ldots, M$, where $g_j(u_i)$ are odd functions of u_i and $\psi_j(\cdot)$ are prespecified functions of x_i. Equation (9.34) holds because $g_j(u_i)$ is odd whereas (9.35) is valid from the fact that

$$E\left\{x_i\left[I\left(y_i \geq 2x_i'\beta_0\right) - I\left(y_i = 0\right)\right]\right\} = 0,$$

again from conditional symmetry of the errors. Equation (9.34) is chosen to approximate the second part of the score in (9.19), as it is an odd function of u_i, whereas (9.35) performs the same task for the first part (J_i is a function of x_i). Following the same strategy as in Section 5.5.3, Newey recommends polynomials in $u_i/(1 + |u_i|)$ and $x_{ik}/(1 + |x_{ik}|)$ as the approximating functions, although for discrete x_{ik} the approximation involves enumerating all the possible outcomes of their products. The covariance matrix of the estimator will be that of the GMM estimator.

Under some technical conditions Newey finds that the number of approximating functions ($2M$) must tend to infinity such that $M \ln M/\ln(n) \to 0$, which demands a very slow rate of increase. He argues that it is difficult to allow for faster growth rates without imposing strong restrictions upon the nature of the densities of u_i and x_i; the limiting factor is the need for a lower bound on the eigenvalue of the variance matrix of the moment function – a constraint that also occurs in the series approximation techniques of Section 3.8. Ideally, it would be desirable to utilize the data to select the number of approximating terms as in Section 3.8. Newey suggests that bootstrapping might be used to choose M by minimizing the standard errors of $\hat{\beta}_{ECS}$, as was done by Hsieh and Manski (1987) for the linear regression model, but little is available on the theoretical and computational problems of this proposal.

9.7   Comparative Studies of the Estimators

A number of papers have considered the behavior of the estimators in small and large samples. Horowitz (1988b) studied the asymptotic behavior of the quantile and SGLS estimators. He compared the asymptotic covariance matrices for these estimators in a single-regressor model, when the regressor is from a beta distribution over a finite support and the error term is a mixture of symmetrically truncated normal densities. Some findings were expected; the asymptotic variance of all estimators rises with the degree of censoring and the variance of u_i. Generally the SGLS estimator was more efficient than any quantile estimator unless the degree of censoring was high or the density of u_i had large kurtosis. The latter effect is explicable by the fact that quantile estimators are "robust" estimators and are designed to be insensitive to outliers. All of the estimators had variance well above the efficiency bound (9.16), pointing to the importance of finding estimators that would attain this. An interesting feature of the experiments was that the best quantile estimator was for $\alpha > 1/2$ (i.e., above the median), probably because left censoring means that more data are available for estimation at high quantiles.

Small-sample behavior of a single estimator or a set of estimators is featured in a number of articles. Powell considered his SCLS estimator when $n = 200$. He found that the performance of the estimator was governed by the number of observations for which $x_i'\beta_0 > 0$. His basic experimental design meant that the R^2 for (9.1) when all data on y_i^* were observed would be .5. However, restricting attention to only those observations for which $x_i'\beta_0 > 0$, it drops to .2. Such sample reduction had a leading role in other effects as well. An asymmetry in the distribution of $\hat{\beta}_{SCLS}$ arose because trial values of b that are low result in many $x_i'b < 0$, and thus fewer observations are used in forming the criterion at these values than for high values of b. Another example occurred when he induced heteroskedasticity in the errors (linearly related to the single regressor squared). One of the attractive features of the SCLS estimator is that it should be consistent in the presence of heteroskedasticity. However, if the error variance rises with $x_i'\beta_0$, then there is a tendency to retain only those observations with high error variance, and that makes the SCLS estimator itself have a high variance. Of course such an effect disappears as $n \to \infty$, but the fact that it is present when $n = 200$ is significant. Since many of the other estimators discussed in Section 9.6 also eliminated observations for which $x_i'\beta_0 < 0$, presumably the same difficulties would occur for them.

Moon (1989) compared the LAD, Buckley–James, SGLS, and the "conditional least squares" estimator of Section 9.5.2. The latter estimator was generally inferior to the others, and he found that Buckley–James worked quite well, even when the true errors were normally distributed. Exactly how he implemented SGLS is unclear, although he did utilize Horowitz's approach of replacing $F(\cdot)$ with the KME. It would be interesting to see if Ichimura's variant was better, since the smoothing done in it seems more natural.

10 Retrospect and Prospect

Nonparametric (NP) and semiparametric (SP) methods potentially offer a very high return to applied researchers, owing to their ability to adapt to many unknown features of the data. Moreover, it can now be said with some confidence that there exists an NP or SP technique capable of handling any situation an applied researcher would encounter. Such breadth may not be fully evident from this book in that its table of contents reflects the typical set of topics covered in a first-year graduate course in econometrics. But, just as such courses aim to establish principles in parametric econometrics that can be applied in a more general context, so too does this book attempt to perform the same function for the NP and SP approaches. Topics dealt with, such as kernel and series estimation, choice of window widths, bias adjustments, and efficiency bounds, recur in many areas that we have left untouched; examples include the literatures on broad areas such as panel data and hazard function estimation as well as some more restricted topics, such as frontier production functions and dynamic optimal decisions. A knowledge of the basic principles of NP and SP estimation sets a vital foundation for understanding this latter literature.

As should be apparent from the book there is a well-defined asymptotic theory for most estimators, and one can generally find one that is consistent and asymptotically normal, at least under particular assumptions. How useful this feature really is remains to be decided. Although there have been simulation studies of estimators, these tend to be in the original papers justifying them, and little comparative work has appeared. As the "value at risk" literature emphasizes, "stress testing" is a mandatory activity when deciding on actions, and it would be preferable if one could point to independent studies of the performance of NP and SP estimators, particularly under conditions that substantially depart from the context for which they were developed. In many ways the small volume of such work is an inefficiency in econometrics itself; information about the relative effectiveness of new estimators is rarely codified in any way and a great deal of reliance is placed upon oral tradition as a way of disseminating the knowledge. What information we do have suggests that quite large samples are required to match the asymptotic theory; otherwise one faces a trade-off between a small-sample bias associated with the use of NP and SP techniques versus a possible large-sample bias for a parametric estimator in the event of specification error. Samples of information on financial transactions and survey data are generally of sufficient magnitude to tip the balance in favor of an NP or SP approach in those areas, at least provided the models being estimated are not too complex, whereas the small amount of information available on macroeconomic series makes it doubtful that parametric models will ever be replaced as the main tool for their analysis.

In practice the spread of NP and SP methods has not been as rapid as one might have expected, and certainly it has failed to keep pace with the burgeoning theory. Initially this could be explained by the fact that the methods were computationally intensive and easily overwhelmed early generations of PCs. However, this is no longer true and most methods can now be performed with moderate amounts of computer time on Pentium-equipped PCs. This is not to say that the computational issues have been fully resolved. One difficulty has been that many SP estimators optimize criteria featuring local optima and only the global optimum possesses the requisite properties. Thus there is a need for reliable algorithms to locate the global optimum. In this connection it is salutary to remember that three decades ago a similar situation existed in parametric econometrics. Maximum likelihood was not a widely used tool owing to the lack of good algorithms for locating local maxima. Today, however, researchers comfortably utilize the options available in packages such as LIMDEP and SHAZAM for describing and maximizing likelihoods. At a more prosaic level there is still no clear way of setting window widths, even though they are central to all of the techniques. As seen in Chapter 2, in the simple context of estimating a density, an enormous literature evolved on how to do this. Even in that case, despite a winnowing of the many methods proposed, no single procedure has come to dominate. Such unresolved questions probably make those who write computer packages rather hesitant about adding the techniques to their existing parametric ones. Although kernel density estimation now appears in many packages, few other NP and SP techniques have been made available. Mostly those who have used the methods have written their routines in something like GAUSS. Until widely used packages include the methods it seems likely that their adoption rate by applied researchers will be slow.

Although a natural response, it is unwise to treat NP and SP methods as strictly competitive with parametric alternatives. The former can be extremely useful as a complement to the latter, especially when trying to judge adequacy. Provided the number of conditioning variables is relatively small, or that one can restrict any nonlinearity to a subset of those variables, any researcher should find it of interest to estimate models using both parametric and NP/SP methods. Informal comparisons of the two sets of results provide a useful check on the robustness of any conclusions drawn from the analysis. Formal comparison, such as the Horowitz–Härdle (1994) specification test for the distributional assumptions in discrete choice models, can be a very insightful way of performing diagnostic tests on the fitted parametric model. Consequently, it is hard to believe that one will not see applied workers come to realize the utility of NP and SP methods, even for such restricted uses.

Nonparametric and semiparametric statistics is a dynamic area and there are ongoing advances, not mentioned in this book, that may still have a substantial impact upon econometrics. Wavelets (Daubechies, 1992; Meyer, 1993; and Hall et al., 1994) are perhaps the foremost example. Moreover, with the rapid development of computer hardware will likely come computer packages offering some variants of these methods. It is quite possible that a decade from now SP and NP techniques will be as common a component of the tool kit of applied econometricians as parametric methods such as maximum likelihood are today.

Appendix A: Statistical Methods

The asymptotic theories of semiparametric and nonparametric econometrics heavily depend on several statistical concepts. These include probability theory, convergence, and conditioning. Accordingly, the objective of this appendix is to present results and definitions related to these concepts that are useful for the asymptotic theory covered in this book. To do so it is assumed that the reader has a basic knowledge of probability and statistics.

A.1 Probability Concepts

The axiomatic approach to probability theory is based on the concept of a *probability space* and an associated probability triple (Ω, F, P) defined below:

> (i) *The Sample Space,* Ω
>
> The set Ω is called the sample space. This contains the set of all possible outcomes (elementary events) of a random experiment E. For example, consider the experiment of tossing a fair coin twice. Then the sample space is

$$\Omega = \{HT, TH, HH, TT\}$$
$$= \{\omega_1, \omega_2, \omega_3, \omega_4\}, \tag{A.1}$$

where $\omega_1 = HT$ etc. Note that ω_i, $i = 1, \dots, 4$, are the outcomes or elementary events.

> (ii) *The Class of Subsets of the Sample Space,* F
>
> Consider a nonempty collection of subsets (events) of Ω, F, satisfying the following two properties:

(a) If a subset $F_1 \in F$ then $F_1^* \in F$, where F_1^* is the complement of the subset F_1 with respect to Ω and $\in$ represents "belong to."

By definition the subset or event F_1 is the collection of elementary events in an experiment. For example, let F_1 denote the event of obtaining one head in the example (A.1). F_1 therefore consists of elementary events $\omega_1, \omega_2, \omega_3$, i.e., $F_1 = \{\omega_1, \omega_2, \omega_3\}$.

(b) If $F_i \in F$ for $i = 1, 2, \ldots$, then $\bigcup_i F_i \in F$, where $\bigcup$ represents union $\bigcup_i F_i = F_1 \bigcup F_2$, which is the set of all elementary events of either F_1 or F_2.

(c) $\phi, \Omega \in F$, where ϕ denotes a null (empty) set, which is the complement of Ω.

The class of subsets denoted by F is, by definition, a σ-*field* of subsets of Ω. Alternatively, a σ-field F is a nonempty class (from Ω) that is closed under complementation and under the formation of countable unions.

Consider the example of tossing two coins as in (i). It can be verified that the set of *all* subsets of Ω,

$$
\begin{aligned}
F = \{ &\Omega, \phi, \{\omega_1\}, \{\omega_2\}, \{\omega_3\}, \{\omega_4\}, \{\omega_1, \omega_2\}, \\
&\{\omega_1, \omega_3\}, \{\omega_1, \omega_4\}, \{\omega_2, \omega_3\}, \{\omega_2, \omega_4\}, \\
&\{\omega_3, \omega_4\}, \{\omega_1, \omega_2, \omega_3\}, \{\omega_1, \omega_2, \omega_4\}, \\
&\{\omega_2, \omega_3, \omega_4\}, \{\omega_3, \omega_4, \omega_1\}\}
\end{aligned}
\tag{A.2}
$$

is a σ-field and F might be written as $F = \{F_1, F_2, F_3, \ldots, F_{16}\}$, where, for example, $F_1 = \Omega$, $F_3 = \{\omega_1\}$, and $F_{16} = \{\omega_3, \omega_4, \omega_1\}$.

A σ-field of interest may be $F = \{\{\omega_1\}, \{\omega_3, \omega_2, \omega_4\}, \phi, \Omega\}$. It would not be the case however that the set $C = \{\{\omega_1, \omega_2\}\}$ is a σ-field because ϕ, Ω and $\{\omega_1, \omega_2\}^*$ do not belong to F. Nevertheless, in this case it is possible to start from C and construct the σ-field generated by its elements, simply by extending it to include C^* and taking countable unions of the elements of C. Eventually, this gives the *Borel* or σ-field, generated by C, namely, $F_c = \{\Omega, \phi, \{(HT), (TH)\}, \{(HH), (TT)\}\}$. Such a *Borel* or σ-*field* is called a minimal σ-field on Ω. This concept is useful in constructing Borel fields where Ω is either infinite or uncountable. For example, when Ω is the real line, defining F as the {countable union of intervals like $(a, b]$} makes it a Borel field, and the elements of F are called *Borel sets*. Essentially, the class of Borel sets is the smallest additive class of sets in the real line that includes all intervals (see, e.g., Cramér (1974)).

(iii) Probability as a Set Function P

For each $F_1 \in F$ we assign a value $P(F_1)$, which is the probability of F_1. This is a real-valued set function P on F satisfying axioms (well-known assumptions accepted without questioning):

(a) $P(F_1) \geq 0$, for all $F_1 \in F$,

(b) $P(\Omega) = 1$,

(c) $P\left(\bigcup_{i=1}^{\infty} F_i\right) = \sum_{i=1}^{\infty} P(F_i)$, where $\{F_i\}_{i=1}^{\infty}$ is a sequence of mutually exclusive events in F (that is, $F_i \cap F_j = \phi$ for $i \neq j$ where $\cap$ represents intersection and $F_i \cap F_j$ implies a set of elementary events in F_i and F_j).

Such a set function P defined for all sets in F is called a *probability measure*. For example, the probability measure over F, in the coin tossing example above, is $P(\Omega) = 1$, $P(\phi) = 0$, $P(\{\omega_1\}) = 1/4 = P(\{\omega_2\}) = P(\{\omega_3\}) = P(\{\omega_4\})$, $P(\{\omega_1, \omega_2\}) = 2/4, \cdots, P(\{\omega_3, \omega_4, \omega_1\}) = 3/4$. Note that if P is a real-valued function of F satisfying (a) and (c) and $P(\phi) = 0$, then P is simply defined as *measure*, (Ω, F) is called a measurable space, and (Ω, F, P) a *measure space*.

Given the above definition of probability, we can easily verify the following properties of $P(\cdot)$:

(i) $P(\phi) = 0$.

(ii) $P(F^*) = 1 - P(F)$.

(iii) $F_1 \subset F_2 \Rightarrow P(F_2 - F_1) = P(F_2) - P(F_1) \Rightarrow P(F_1) \leq P(F_2)$, where $\subset$ means "contained in."

(iv) $P(F_1 \cup F_2) = P(F_1) + P(F_2) - P(F_1 \cap F_2)$ giving the inequality $P(F_1 \cup F_2) \leq P(F_1) + P(F_2)$. Further, for $i = 1, \ldots, n$, we have from Poincare's result,

$$P(\cup F_i) = \sum P(F_i) - \sum_{i<j} P(F_i \cap F_j)$$
$$+ \sum_{i<j<k} P(F_i \cap F_j \cap F_k) + \cdots (-1)^{n-1} P(\cap F_i).$$

This gives $P(\cup F_i) \leq \sum P(F_i)$, $i = 1, \ldots, n$, which is Boole's inequality. Note that $P(\cup F_i) = \sum P(F_i)$ if the F_is are disjoint sets.

(v) Let $\{F_i\}$ be a nonincreasing sequence of sets in F such that $\lim_{i \to \infty} F_i = \cap F_i \in F$. Then $\lim P(F_i) = P(\lim F_i)$ as $i \to \infty$. If F_i is a nondecreasing sequence such that $\lim F_i = \cup F_i$ then $\lim P(F_i) = P(\cup F_i) = P(\lim F_i)$ as $i \to \infty$.

(vi) (Bonferroni's inequality): For $F_i \in F$, $i = 1, \ldots, n$

$$P(\cap F_i) \geq 1 - \sum P(F_i^*),$$
$$P(\cap F_i) \geq \sum P(F_i) - (n - 1).$$

Boole's inequality in (iv) gives an upper bound to the probability of *at least* one event whereas Poincare's result provides the exact probability. Bonferroni's inequality in (vi) is quite useful in econometrics in the hypothesis testing context. For example, suppose a sequence of n independent tests is performed with significance levels $\alpha_1, \ldots, \alpha_n$. Then Bonferroni's inequality says that the resulting overall significance level would be at most $\sum \alpha_i$. This is because

$$P(\cap F_i)^* = 1 - P(\cap F_i) \leq 1 - \left(1 - \sum P(F_i^*)\right) = \sum \alpha_i$$

where $\alpha_i = P(\text{reject } H_0 | H_0 \text{ is true at } i\text{th test})$ and F_is are the acceptance regions.

A.1.1 Random Variable and Distribution Function

Let us define R as the real line $x = (-\infty, \infty)$ and R^q by the q-dimensional real Euclidean space. Further let B be the nonempty collection of the subsets (Borel sets) of R such that

(i) all intervals $\{x : -\infty < x \leq x^*\} \in B$, $x^* \in R$;
(ii) if the subset $B_1 \in B$ then $B_1^* \in B$;
(iii) if the sequence $B_i \in B$ then $\bigcup_i B_i \in B$.

Such a set B is the Borel field on R. Note that the Borel sets would also be generated by all the open half-lines of R, all the open intervals of R, or all the closed intervals of R. These Borel sets have the property that, if P is a probability measure, and $B_1 \in B$, then $P(B_1)$ is well defined.

By construction R and B are the transformations of Ω and F in the event space. A random variable X is a real-valued function from Ω to R, $X = x(\omega)$, with value $x(\omega)$ at $\omega \in \Omega$, such that for every real number x the set $\{\omega : x(\omega) \leq x\} \in F$. More generally, for each Borel set $B_1 \in B$ on R, the set $\{\omega \in \Omega : x(\omega) \in B_1) \in F$. Thereupon, the probability of the set $x(\omega) \leq x$ is defined as the distribution function of X at $x \in R$, $F(x)$. That is, $F(x) = P(\{\omega : x(\omega) \leq x\})$, or, in brief, $F(x) = P(X \leq x)$.

The distribution function $F(x)$ satisfies the following properties:

(a) $F(x)$ is nondecreasing.
(b) $F(-\infty) = \lim_{x \to \infty} F(x) = 0$; $F(\infty) = \lim_{x \to \infty} F(x) = 1$.
(c) $F(x)$ is continuous from the right, that is,

$$F(x) = \lim_{h \to 0} F(x + h).$$

At every continuity point x, the density function $f(x)$ is given as

$$f(x) = \frac{d}{dx}F(x) = \lim_{h \to 0} \frac{F(x + h/2) - F(x - h/2)}{h}$$

$$= \frac{1}{h}\lim_{h \to 0} P(x - h/2 < X \leq x + h/2). \tag{A.3}$$

Thus

$$f(x)\,dx = f(x)h \simeq P(x - h/2 < X \leq x + h/2) \tag{A.4}$$

provides the probability of a continuous random variable in the interval $(x - \frac{h}{2}, x + \frac{h}{2})$. Note that $P(X = x) = 0$ for the continuous case; substitute $h = 0$. However, for discrete X the $P(X = x)$ is given by $f(x)$. The density function $f(x)$ is any function such that $f(x) \geq 0$ for all $x \in R$, $\int_R f(x)\,dx = 1$, and $P(a < X < b) = \int_a^b f(x)\,dx$. An important point to observe is that, although the distribution function gives the cumulative probabilities, the integral of a density function gives the probability in a given interval.

Let us consider the coin-tossing experiment again, defining the random variable X as the number of "tails." For this experiment, the functions $x(\omega_1) = x(\omega_2) = 1$, $x(\omega_3) = 0$, $x(\omega_4) = 2$ determine the random variable X, mapping all the elements of Ω onto the set $R = \{0, 1, 2\}$. The corresponding distribution function is

$$F(x) = \begin{cases} 1 & \text{if } x \geq 2, \\ 3/4 & \text{if } 0 \leq x < 2, \\ 1/4 & \text{if } 0 \leq x < 1, \\ 0 & \text{if } x < 0. \end{cases} \tag{A.5}$$

For specific classes of discrete and continuous distributions, see Johnson and Kotz (1969, 1970).

By introducing the concept of a random variable X on (Ω, F, P) we have in effect developed an alternative but equivalent probability space (R, B, P), where P is the set function on arbitrary sets. In general, by choosing the semi-closed intervals $(-\infty, 0]$, $(-\infty, 1]$, $(-\infty, 2]$ a Borel field on R can be generated that forms the domain of P. Because of its mathematical structure the probability space (R, B, P) is easier to work with for the probability models in this book, since data in economics are in R and hence are more easily identified with X, although fundamentally all statements can be traced back to the probability space (Ω, F, P).

The above definitions extend to the case of $X \in R^q$ defined on a probability space (Ω, F, P). Let the q-dimensional Borel field B^q be the class of Borel sets. Then X is a q-dimensional random vector on (Ω, F, P) if it is the case that $\{\omega \in \Omega : x(\omega) \in B_1^q\} \in F$ for every Borel subset $B_1^q \in B^q$. Note that $P(X \in B_1^q) = P(\omega \in \Omega : x(\omega) \in B_1^q)$ is the probability measure induced by X.

If B_1^q is the product sets $X_{j=1}^q(-\infty, x_j]$, where x_js are the components of a vector $x \in R^q$, then

$$F(x) = P(X \leq x) = P\left(\{\omega \in \Omega : x(\omega) \in X_{j=1}^q(-\infty, x_j]\}\right) \tag{A.6}$$

is the joint distribution function F. The density function is

$$f(x) = f(x_1, \ldots, x_q) = \frac{\partial^q F(x)}{\partial x} = \partial^q F / \partial x_1, \ldots, \partial x_q.$$

Here f is uniquely determined by the probability measure $P\left(X_{j=1}^q(-\infty, x_j]\right)$. The reverse is also true; that is, given a distribution function F on R^q, there exists a unique probability measure P on (R^q, B^q) defining F.

A.1.2 Conditional Distribution and Independence

Consider the random vector $X = (X_1, \ldots, X_q) = (X_{(1)}, X_{(2)})$, where $X_{(1)} \in R^{q_1}$ and $X_{(2)} \in R^{q_2}$, where $q_1 + q_2 = q$. Let $F(x) = F(x_{(1)}, x_{(2)})$ be the distribution function at x; $f(x) = f(x_{(1)}, x_{(2)})$ the joint density of $x_{(1)}$ and $x_{(2)}$; and $f_1(x_{(1)}) = \int f(x_{(1)}, x_{(2)}) \, dx_{(2)}$ the density of $X_{(1)}$ alone, termed the marginal density.

The conditional distribution of $X_{(2)}$ given $X_{(1)} \in B_1^{q_1}$ (B_1 belongs to B) is defined as

$$
\begin{aligned}
F\left(x_{(2)} \mid x_{(1)}\right) &= F\left(x_{(2)} \mid x_{(1)} \in B_1^{q_1}\right) \\
&= \frac{P\left[x_{(1)}(\omega) \in B_1^{q_1}, x_{(2)}(\omega) < x_{(2)}\right]}{P\left[x_1(\omega) \in B_1^{q_1}\right]} \\
&= \int_{B_1^{q_1}} \int_{-\infty}^{x_{(2)}} f\left(x_{(1)}, x_{(2)}\right) dx_{(1)} \, dx_{(2)} \\
&= \int_{B_1^{q_1}} f_1\left(x_{(1)}\right) dx_{(1)} \int_{-\infty}^{x_{(2)}} \frac{f\left(x_{(1)}, x_{(2)}\right)}{f_1\left(x_{(1)}\right)} dx_{(2)} \\
&= \int_{-\infty}^{x_{(2)}} \frac{f\left(x_{(1)}, x_{(2)}\right) dx_{(2)}}{f_1\left(x_{(1)}\right)},
\end{aligned}
\tag{A.7}
$$

where

$$\int f_1\left(x_{(1)}\right) dx_{(1)} = P\left[x_{(1)}(\omega) \in B_1^{q_1}\right] = 1.$$

The conditional density of $X_{(2)} \in R^{q_2}$ at $X_{(1)} = x_{(1)}$ is (writing $f_1(x_{(1)}) = f(x_{(1)})$)

$$f\left(x_{(2)} \mid x_{(1)}\right) = \frac{f\left(x_{(2)}, x_{(1)}\right)}{f\left(x_{(1)}\right)}. \tag{A.8}$$

Similarly, $f(x_{(1)}|x_{(2)}) = f(x_{(1)}, x_{(2)})/f(x_{(2)})$ is the conditional density of $X_{(1)} \in R^{q_1}$ given $X_{(2)} = x_{(2)}$.

Two random vectors $X_{(1)}$ and $X_{(2)}$ are said to be independent if

$$F\left(x_{(1)}, x_{(2)}\right) = F_1\left(x_{(1)}\right) F_2\left(x_{(2)}\right) \tag{A.9}$$

or

$$f\left(x_{(1)}, x_{(2)}\right) = f_1\left(x_{(1)}\right) f_2\left(x_{(2)}\right). \tag{A.10}$$

For q random variables $X = (X_1, \ldots, X_q)$ to be independent we have

$$f(x) = f(x_1, x_2, \ldots, x_q) = \prod_{j=1}^{q} f(x_j). \tag{A.11}$$

A.1.3   Borel Measurable Functions

Let X be a random vector on (Ω, F, P) transformed into (R^q, B^q, P), and let $f(x)$ be a real-valued function for $x \in R^q$. Then $f(x)$ on R^q is called a Borel measurable function if for every $a \in R$ the set $\{x \in R^q : f(x) \leq a\}$ is a Borel set in R^q. The usefulness of this definition is that, if $f(x)$ satisfies Borel measurability, the function of the random vector X, $f(X)$, is also a random variable.

A useful property of the Borel measurable function is that, if $\{f_i\}$, $i = 1$, $2, \ldots, n$ is a sequence of Borel measurable functions on R^q, the functions $\max\{f_i\}$, $\min\{f_i\}$, $\sup f_n$, $\inf f_n$, $\limsup f_n$, and $\liminf f_n$ are also Borel measurable. The proof of this result can be found in Chung (1974) and Royden (1968), among others. It can also be shown that continuous real functions on R^q are also Borel measurable. Another example of a Borel measurable function is a weighted sum of indicator functions,

$$f_n(x) = \sum_{i=1}^{n} a_i I\left(x \in B_i^q\right), \tag{A.12}$$

where $I(\cdot) = 1$ if the event in brackets is true and 0 otherwise; B_i^q are Borel sets whose pairwise intersections are null sets, and a_is are real numbers. Borel measurability of $f_n(x)$ follows from the fact that the set $\{x \in R^q : f(x) \leq a\}$ for this f is always a finite union of Borel sets.

There are conditions under which a function can be verified to be Borel measurable. An important result in this regard is that a nonnegative real function f is Borel measurable if and only if there is a nondecreasing sequence of weighted functions f_n of the type (A.12) such that $0 \leq f_n(x) \leq f(x)$ and $\lim f_n = f$. A real function, however, is measurable if and only if it is a limit of a sequence of simple functions.

Let $X \in R^q$ be a random vector on a probability space (Ω, F, P). Then the mathematical expectation of X, the mean value, is defined as

$$EX = \int x \, dF(x), \tag{A.13}$$

where $F(x)$ is the distribution function of X and the integral is Lebesgue–Stieltjes (see Rao (1973, p. 92)). When the density function $f(x)$ of X exists we have

$$EX = \int x \, dF(x) = \int x f(x) \, dx, \tag{A.14}$$

where the integral is now a Riemann integral.

If $g(X) = g(X_1, \ldots, X_q)$ is a Borel measurable function of $X \in R^q$ with density $f(x)$, then

$$Eg(X) = \int g(x) \, dF(x) = \int g(x) f(x) \, dx. \tag{A.15}$$

Note that Borel measurability ensures that $g(X)$ is a random variable with respect to the probability measure induced by X.

The following results are well known and can be easily verified.

(i) If the X_js are independent, $E(\prod_{j=1}^{q} X_j) = \prod_{j=1}^{q} EX_j$.

(ii) $E(\sum_{j=1}^{q} C_j X_j) = \sum_{j=1}^{n} C_j EX_j$, where the C_js are constants.

(iii) If X_1 and X_2 are independent and $g_1(X_1)$ and $g_2(X_2)$ are Borel measurable functions then $g_1(X_1)$ and $g_2(X_2)$ are also independent.

(iv) Let $X \in R^2$. Then the Law of Iterated Expectations provides

$$Eg(X_1, X_2) = E_{X_1}[E_{X_2}\{g(X_1, X_2) \mid X_1\}],$$

where $E_{X_2}\{g(X_1, X_2) \mid X_1\}$ is the expectation with respect to X_2 conditional on X_1.

Let $q = 1$ so that $X \in R$. The rth moment of X about a constant μ is

$$\mu'_r = E(X - \mu)^r = \int (x - \mu)^r \, dF$$

$$= \int (x - \mu)^r f(x) \, dx. \tag{A.16}$$

If X is discrete

$$\mu'_r = \sum_s (x_s - \mu)^r p_s, \tag{A.17}$$

where p_s is the probability of $X = x_s$. When $\mu = EX$ then the moments are said to be central and are represented by μ_r. Note that $\mu_0 = 1$, $\mu_2 = \mu'_2 - \mu'^2_1$ is the variance, $V(X)$, and so on.

A useful result to note is that for $g = g(X_1, X_2)$

$$V[g(X_1, X_2)] = E_{X_1}[V_{X_2}(g|X_1)] + V_{X_1}[E_{X_2}(g|X_1)]. \qquad (A.18)$$

A.1.4 Inequalities Involving Expectations

Many proofs in nonparametric statistics involve the application of inequalities, and we collect here some of the more important ones.

1. *Chebychev's inequality*: Let $g(x)$ be a positive Borel measurable function on R, monotonically increasing on $(0, \infty)$ and $g(x) = g(-x)$. Then for every random variable X on R and $\epsilon > 0$ we have

$$P[|X| > \epsilon] \leq Eg(X)/g(\epsilon).$$

   In the special case when $g(X) = X^2$, $P[|X| > \epsilon] \leq \frac{EX^2}{\epsilon^2}$, which is the best known form of Chebychev's inequality.

2. *Markov's inequality*: Let X be a positive random variable with $EX = \mu$. Then $P(X \geq t\mu) \leq \frac{1}{t}$, $t > 0$.

3. C_r *inequality*: Let X_1 and X_2 be two random variables. Then

$$E|X_1 + X_2|^r \leq c_r[E|X_1|^r + E|X_2|^r],$$

   where $c_r = 1$ if $r \leq 1$ and $c_r = 2^{r-1}$ if $r > 1$.

4. *Holder's inequality*: Let X_1 and X_2 be random variables. Then for $p > 1$ and $1/p + 1/q = 1$

$$|EX_1 X_2| \leq E|X_1 X_2| \leq \{E|X_1|^p\}^{1/p}\{E|X_2|^q\}^{1/q}.$$

   For $p = q = 2$ we obtain the well-known Cauchy–Schwarz inequality.

5. *Minkowski's inequality*: Let X_1 and X_2 be random variables. Then for $p \geq 1$

$$(E|X_1 + X_2|^p)^{1/2} \leq (E|X_1|^p)^{1/p} + (E|X_2|^p)^{1/p}.$$

   Note that for the inequalities in (3) to (5) we need the existence of $E|X|^r$ for some r.

6. *Liapounov's inequality*: Let X be a random variable. Then for $1 \leq p \leq q \leq \infty$

$$(E|X|^p)^{1/p} \leq (E|X|^q)^{1/q}.$$

   This is a special case of Holder's inequality with $X_2 = 1$, $X_1 = |X|^p$, and $p = q/p$.

7. *Jensen's inequality*: If $g(\ )$ is a convex Borel measurable real function on R, and X is the random variable such that $E|X| < \infty$ and $E|g(X)| < \infty$, then

$$Eg(X) \geq g(EX).$$

The inequalities given above can also be written with respect to summations in place of expectations. For example, Holder's inequality also implies

$$\left| \frac{1}{n} \sum_{i=1}^{n} x_{i1} x_{i2} \right| \leq \sum_{i=1}^{n} \left| \frac{1}{n} x_{i1} x_{i2} \right|$$

$$\leq \left(\frac{1}{n} \sum_{i=1}^{n} |x_{i1}|^p \right)^{1/p} \left(\frac{1}{n} \sum_{i=1}^{n} |x_{i2}|^q \right)^{1/q}, \qquad (A.19)$$

where x_{i1} and x_{i2} are real numbers. Taking $x_{i2} = 1$ yields

$$\left| \frac{1}{n} \sum_{i=1}^{n} x_{i1} \right| \leq n^{-1/p} \left(\sum_{i=1}^{n} |x_{i1}|^p \right)^{1/p} \qquad (A.20)$$

or

$$\left| \sum_{i=1}^{n} x_{i1} \right|^p \leq n^{p-1} \sum_{i=1}^{n} |x_{i1}|^p. \qquad (A.21)$$

This is sharper than the well-known inequality $\left| \sum x_{i1} \right|^p \leq n \max |x_{i1}|^p \leq n^p \sum |x_{i1}|^p$, $p > 0$.

A.1.5 Characteristic Function (c.f.)

Let X be a random vector on R^q with distribution function F. The characteristic function (c.f.) of this distribution is the complex-valued function

$$\phi(t) = E(e^{it'X}) = \int e^{it'x} dF(x)$$

$$= \int \cos(t'x) dF(x) + i \int \sin(t'x) dF(x), \qquad (A.22)$$

where $i = \sqrt{-1}$ and $t \in R^q$ is a real-valued vector. The integral above always exists since $|e^{it'x}| = |\cos t'x + i \sin t'x| = 1$ is bounded for all x.

An important feature of the c.f. is the fact that any continuous distribution function of X is uniquely determined by its c.f. This follows from the well-known Inversion formula: If $\int |\phi(t)| dt < \infty$, that is $\phi(t)$ is absolutely integrable, then the density function is given by

$$f(x) = \left(\frac{1}{2\pi}\right)^q \int e^{-it'x}\phi(t)\,dt.$$ (A.23)

A.2 Results on Convergence

In this section we deal with the concepts of weak and strong convergence of random variables, laws of large numbers, convergence in distribution, and central limit theorems. Definitions of uniform convergence of random functions will also be presented.

A.2.1 Weak and Strong Convergence of Random Variables

We assume throughout that the random variables involved are defined on a common probability space (Ω, F, P)

Definition 1: A sequence of random variables (r.v.s)$\{X_n\}$ converges in probability to a r.v. (or constant) X, if for every $\epsilon > 0$, $\lim_{n\to\infty} P(|X_n - X| \le \epsilon) = 1$.

We usually write this as $X_n \xrightarrow{p} X$ or $p\lim X_n = X$. This is known as weak convergence of $\{X_n\}$.

A stronger concept of convergence is almost sure convergence or strong convergence.

Definition 2: A sequence of r.v.s. $\{X_n\}$ converges to a r.v. (or constant) X almost surely (or with probability one) if

$$P\left(\lim_{n\to\infty} X_n = X\right) = 1.$$ (A.24)

This is also denoted by $X_n \xrightarrow{a.s.} X$. An equivalent definition is

$$\lim_{n\to\infty} P\left(\sup_{n_0 \ge n} |X_{n_0} - X| > \epsilon\right) = 0$$ (A.25)

for every ϵ.

The following important lemma provides a useful way for proving strong convergence.

Borel–Cantelli Lemma: The sequence of random variables $\{X_n\}$ converges to X almost surely (*a.s.*) if for every $\varepsilon > 0$

$$\sum_{n=1}^{\infty} P(|X_n - X| > \epsilon) < \infty. \tag{A.26}$$

Proof: See Rao (1973, p. 137). Q.E.D.

Definition 3: The sequence of r.v.s converge in rth mean to a r.v. (or constant) X if for some $r > 0$

$$\lim_{n\to\infty} E |X_n - X|^r = 0. \tag{A.27}$$

This mode of convergence is referred to as convergence in rth moment. For $r = 2$ one gets convergence in the mean square error (MSE).

The three modes of convergence described above are related as follows:

(i) Convergence in MSE implies convergence in probability. This follows by using Chebychev's inequality

$$P(|X_n - c| > \epsilon) \le \frac{1}{\epsilon^2} E(X_n - c)^2 \tag{A.28}$$

from Section A.1.4, and taking limits on both sides. Similarly we can show that convergence in rth moment implies convergence in probability.

Note, however, that the conditions under which we obtain convergence in MSE may not be the same as the conditions for convergence in probability. Also, convergence in probability may not necessarily imply convergence in MSE since, for example, the MSE may not even exist for some sequences. However, the following theorem gives a condition under which weak convergence will imply convergence in MSE or in rth mean.

Dominated Convergence Theorem: If $X_n \xrightarrow{p} X$ and if $|X_n| \le y$ a.s., where $Ey < \infty$, then $E|X_n - X| \to 0$ or $EX_n \to EX$.

Proof: See Rao (1973). Q.E.D.

If, in the above theorem, we replace $Ey < \infty$ by $Ey^r < \infty$ for some $r > 0$ then we have $E|X_n - X|^r \to 0$. This result can be used to prove the following well-known theorem. See, for example, Rao (1973).

Monotone Convergence Theorem: Let $\{X_n\}$ be a nonnegative and nondecreasing sequence of r.v.s. Then $E \lim X_n = \lim E X_n \leq \infty$.

(ii) Convergence in MSE implies strong convergence only if $\sum_1^\infty E(X_n - X)^2 < \infty$.

(iii) Strong convergence implies convergence in probability.

Let us consider an example of the sequence $\{X_n\}$ that illustrates the above concepts. This is

X_n	P
$-n$	$1/2n$
0	$1 - 1/n$
n	$1/2n$

(A.29)

The sequence in (A.29) converges a.s. to zero since $P(\lim X_n = 0) = 1$. Note that a.s. convergence implies weak convergence. To see this result we merely note that

$$\lim_{n \to \infty} P(|X_n| < \epsilon) = 1 - \lim_{n \to \infty} P(|X_n| > \epsilon) = 1$$

because $P(|X_n| > \epsilon) = 1/n$. Next $E X_n^2 = n$. Thus X_n does not converge in the MSE sense. The example in (A.29) thus illustrates that weak convergence does not imply MSE convergence. An example can, however, be constructed where weak convergence would imply MSE convergence. For an illustration, take $X_n = 1$ with probability $1 - 1/n$ and $X_n = 0$ with probability $1/n$. Then $P[|X_n - 1| < \epsilon] = 1 - 1/n \to 1$ as $n \to \infty$, and $E(X_n - 1)^2 = 1/n \to 0$ as $n \to \infty$. That is, weak convergence implies MSE convergence.

A.2.2   Laws of Large Numbers

The concepts of convergence discussed in Section A.2.1 are useful in analyzing the convergence of statistics that are based on repeated samples. These statistics may be the sample mean, sample variance, and econometric estimators and test statistics, among others. Here we present weak and strong laws of large numbers (W.L.L.N. and S.L.L.N.) for such statistics. The weak law represents convergence in probability and the strong law represents convergence a.s. (or with probability one). The proofs are omitted here but they can be found in textbooks such as those by Rao (1973) and Chung (1974).

(i) **Chebychev's Theorem:** Let the r.v.s X_i be such that $EX_i = \mu_i$, $V(X_i) = \sigma_i^2 < \infty$, and $\text{cov}(X_i, X_j) = 0$, $i \neq j$. Then

$$\bar{X}_n - \bar{\mu}_n \xrightarrow{p} 0$$

if $\bar{\sigma}^2 \to 0$ as $n \to \infty$, where $\bar{X}_n = n^{-1} \sum X_i$, $\bar{\mu}_n = n^{-1} \sum \mu_i$, and $\bar{\sigma}^2 = n^{-1} \sum \sigma_i^2$.

If $\mu_i = \mu$ and $\sigma_i^2 = \sigma^2$ the conditions of the theorem are satisfied and we have $\bar{X}_n \xrightarrow{p} \mu$.

(ii) **Khinchin's Theorem:** Let $\{X_i\}$ $i = 1, 2, \ldots$ be independent and identically distributed (i.i.d.) and $E(X_i) = \mu < \infty$. Then

$$\bar{X}_n \xrightarrow{p} \mu.$$

If we replace independence by uncorrelatedness a stronger condition $\sum_1^\infty (\sigma_i^2 (\log i)^2 / i^2) < \infty$ is needed for $\bar{X}_n - \bar{\mu}_n \xrightarrow{a.s.} 0$; see Doob (1953). An alternative moment condition for a.s. convergence is

$$\sup \frac{1}{n} \sum_{i=1}^n E|X_i - \mu_i|^{2+\delta} < \infty \quad \text{for some } \delta > 0. \tag{A.30}$$

If X_is are i.i.d. random variables then the condition on the second moment is not needed. In this case we can achieve a necessary and sufficient condition given in (iv) below.

(iii) **Kolmogorov's Theorem (I):** Let $\{X_i\}$ be independent r.v.s such that $EX_i = \mu_i$ and $V(X_i) = \sigma_i^2$. Then

$$\bar{X}_n - \bar{\mu}_n \xrightarrow{a.s.} 0$$

if $\sum_{i=1}^\infty (\sigma_i^2 / i^2) < \infty$.

(iv) **Kolmogorov's Theorem (II):** Let $\{X_i\}$ be i.i.d. random variables. Then a necessary and sufficient condition for $\bar{X}_n \xrightarrow{a.s.} \mu$ is that $EX_1 = \mu$ exists.

A.2.3 Convergence of Distribution Functions

Let us represent by $\{F_n(x) = P(X_n \leq x)\}$ or simply by $\{F_n\}$ the sequence of distribution functions of the random variables $\{X_n\}$.

Definition 4: The sequence of random variables $\{X_n\}$ is said to converge in distribution to a r.v. X with distribution function $F(x)$ or F if $F_n \to F$ as $n \to \infty$ at all continuity points of F. This can be written as $X_n \xrightarrow{d} X$ where d implies "in distribution."

The approximating distribution function F is called a limiting or asymptotic distribution. We can now note the following useful results. The proofs can be found in Feller (1968), Rao (1973), Chung (1974), and Serfling (1980).

(i) **Helly–Bray Theorem:** $F_n \to F$ implies $\int g\,dF_n \to \int g\,dF$, where g is any bounded and continuous function.

As a consequence of this theorem we have the following result:

$$X_n \xrightarrow{p} X \text{ implies } X_n \xrightarrow{d} X,$$
$$X_n \xrightarrow{d} c \text{ implies } X_n \xrightarrow{p} c,$$

(A.31)

where c is a constant and X is a r.v.

Suppose $\{Y_n\}$ is another sequence of r.v.s and $g(\ )$ is a continuous real function in x and y. Then if $X_n \xrightarrow{d} X$, $Y_n \xrightarrow{p} c$, then $g(X_n, Y_n) \xrightarrow{d} g(X, c)$, where c is a constant. For example, $X_n + Y_n \xrightarrow{d} X + c$. Note that the condition $Y_n \xrightarrow{p} c$ is important. For example, if $Y_n \xrightarrow{d} Y$, where Y is a random variable, then $X_n + Y_n \xrightarrow{d} X + Y$ may not be true. The results in (i) above also hold if X_n and Y_n are random vectors.

(ii) **Cramer–Wold Theorem:** The sequence of random vectors $\{X_n\}$, $X_n = (X_{1n}, \ldots, X_{qn})' \in R^q$, converges in distribution to the random vector X with distribution function F if for any real constant vector $\lambda = (\lambda_1, \ldots, \lambda_q)'$

$$\lambda' X_n \xrightarrow{d} \lambda' X.$$

(iii) **Continuity Theorem:** Let $\phi_n(t)$ be the sequence of c.f.s corresponding to F_n of random vectors X_n on R^q. If $X_n \xrightarrow{d} X$ and $\phi_n(t) \to \phi(t)$ then $\phi(t)$ is the c.f. of X.

This result establishes the link between the convergence in distribution and convergence of c.f.s. This is often used in proving central limit theorems. Allied with the Cramer–Wold device it gives the following result on asymptotic normality of a vector of random variables.

Theorem: If, for all vectors $\lambda \in R^q$, $\lambda' X_n \xrightarrow{d} \lambda' X \sim \mathcal{N}(\lambda'\mu, \lambda'\Omega\lambda)$, where Ω is a positive (semi) definite matrix, then $X_n \xrightarrow{d} X \sim \mathcal{N}(\mu, \Omega)$.

Proof: Let $X \in R^q$ be a random vector with $EX = \mu$ and $V(X) = E(X - \mu)(X - \mu)' = \Omega$. Suppose that for every λ vector, $\lambda'X \sim \mathcal{N}(\lambda'\mu, \lambda'\Omega\lambda)$. Then the c.f. of $\lambda'X$ (see, e.g., Rao (1973)), for every $t \in R$, is

$$\phi(t) = Ee^{it(\lambda'X)} = e^{[it\lambda'\mu - (1/2)t^2\lambda'\Omega\lambda]}.$$

(A.32)

Substituting $t = 1$ gives the c.f. of X,

$$e^{i\lambda'\mu - \frac{1}{2}\lambda'\Omega\lambda},$$ (A.33)

which corresponds to that of the q-variate normal distribution $\mathcal{N}(\mu, \Omega)$; see Rao (1973). Q.E.D.

A.2.4 Central Limit Theorems

Here we present some well-known results on the convergence of sequences to normality. For proofs see Feller (1968), Rao (1973), or Chung (1974).

Theorem (Lindberg–Levy): Let $\{X_i\}$ be a sequence of i.i.d. random variables such that $EX_i = \mu$, $V(X_i) = \sigma^2 < \infty$. Then

$$\sqrt{n}\frac{(\bar{X}_n - \mu)}{\sigma} \xrightarrow{d} \mathcal{N}(0, 1).$$

Proof: See Rao (1973, p. 127). Q.E.D.

Theorem Lindberg–Feller: Let $\{X_i\}$ be a sequence of independent r.v.s such that $EX_i = \mu_i$ and $V(X_i) = \sigma_i^2 < \infty$. Define

$$\sigma_n = \left(\sum_1^n \sigma_i^2\right)^{1/2}.$$

Then $\lim_{n\to\infty}\left[\max_{1\le i\le n}\frac{\sigma_i}{\sigma_n}\right] = 0$ and

$$\frac{\sum_1^n (X_i - \mu_i)}{\sigma_n} \xrightarrow{d} \mathcal{N}(0, 1)$$ (A.34)

hold if and only if, for every $\epsilon > 0$,

$$\lim_{n\to\infty}\frac{1}{\sigma_n^2}\sum_{i=1}^n \int_{|x-\mu_i|>\epsilon\sigma_n} (x - \mu_i)^2 dF_i(x) = 0.$$ (A.35)

The condition (A.35) is known as the *Lindberg condition*. As the condition is often difficult to verify, it is useful to have a simpler condition that implies it. This is contained in the next theorem, due to Liapounov. We state this theorem for the sequence of double arrays $\{X_{n,i}\}$, $i = 1, \ldots, n$ of independent random variables such that $EX_{n,i} = \mu_{n,i}$ and $V(X_{n,i}) = \sigma_{n,i}^2$. This is the kind of sequence we will be dealing with in this book since the random variable will depend directly upon the sample size n. Let $S_n = \sum_{i=1}^{n} X_{n,i}$. Then

$$E S_n = \mu_n = \sum_{i=1}^{n} \mu_{n,i}, \qquad V(S_n) = \sum_{i=1}^{n} \sigma_{n,i}^2 = \sigma_n^2 < \infty. \qquad (A.36)$$

Theorem (Liapounov): Let $\{X_{n,i}\}$ be the sequence of independent r.v.s as given above and let $E|X_{n,i}|^{2+\delta} < \infty$ for some $\delta > 0$. Denote $L_{n,i} = (X_{n,i} - \mu_{n,i})/\sigma_n$. Then

$$\frac{S_n - E S_n}{\sigma_n} = \sum_{i=1}^{n} L_{n,i} \xrightarrow{d} \mathcal{N}(0, 1) \qquad (A.37)$$

if, for some $\delta > 0$,

$$\lim \sum_{i=1}^{n} E \mid L_{n,i} \mid^{2+\delta} = 0. \qquad (A.38)$$

Proof: See Chung (1974, p. 209). Q.E.D.

A special case of the above theorem is where $\mu_{n,i} = 0$ and $\sigma_{n,i}^2$ is such that

$$\lim \frac{1}{n} \sigma_n^2 \to \sigma^2. \qquad (A.39)$$

Then

$$\frac{S_n}{\sqrt{n}\sigma} \xrightarrow{d} \mathcal{N}(0, 1), \qquad (A.40)$$

if, for some $\delta > 0$,

$$\lim \left[\sum_{i=1}^{n} E|X_{n,i}/\sqrt{n}|^{2+\delta} \right] = 0. \qquad (A.41)$$

This condition holds if

$$\sup_n \left[\frac{1}{n} \sum_{i=1}^{n} |X_{n,i}|^{2+\delta} \right] < \infty. \qquad (A.42)$$

We need to be reminded that Liapounov's theorem is usually stated in textbooks for $\{X_{n,i}\} = \{X_i\}$, that is, not for arrays, as in the case of the Lindberg–Levy and Lindberg–Feller theorems above.

Many situations involving semiparametric and nonparametric estimation end up with a double summation to describe the estimator or statistic. The central limit theorems for these situations are given by the following results on U-statistics.

Consider a general second-order U-statistic of the form

$$U_n = \binom{n}{2}^{-1} \sum_{1 \leq i < j \leq n} H_n(X_i, X_j),$$

where $X_i, i = 1, \ldots, n$ is an i.i.d. random vector and H_n is a symmetric function, that is, $H_n(X_i, X_j) = H_n(X_j, X_i)$. Now define $r_n(X_i) = E[H_n(X_i, X_j)|X_i]$ and

$$\hat{U}_n = Er_n(X_i) + 2n^{-1} \sum_{i=1}^{n} [r_n(X_i) - Er_n(X_i)].$$

The latter is called the "projection" of the statistic U_n (Hoeffding (1948)). Then $\sqrt{n}(U_n - \hat{U}_n) = o_p(1)$ if $E[\| H_n(X_i, X_j) \|^2] = o(n)$ (see Powell et al. (1989)), making the asymptotic distribution of $\hat{U}_n$ the same as that of U_n. But the asymptotic distribution of $\hat{U}$, which is an average of independent random variables $r_n(X_i) - Er_n(X_i)$ is normal by using the regularity conditions of the central limit theorems above. Thus the asymptotic distribution of U_n will be normal. For details see Hoeffding (1948), Serfling (1980), and Powell et al. (1989).

Some of the U-statistics are degenerate, that is $r_n(X_i) = 0$ almost surely for all X_i. In this case the following theorems are useful.

Theorem (Second-Order Degenerate U-Statistics): Consider U_n^* $= \binom{n}{2}^{-1} \sum_{1 \leq i < j \leq n} H_n(X_i, X_j)$, where $X_i, i = 1, \ldots, n$ is an i.i.d. random vector, H_n is symmetric, centred ($EH_n(X_1, X_2) = 0$), degenerate $E[H_n(X_1, X_2)| X_1] = 0$ a.s.), and $E[H_n^2(X_1, X_2)] < \infty$ for each n. Define $G_n(X_1, X_2) = E_{X_i}[H_n(X_1, X_i)H_n(X_2, X_i)]$. Then if

$$\left\{ E\left[G_n^2(X_1, X_2)\right] + n^{-1}E\left[H_n^4(X_1, X_2)\right] \right\} / \left\{ E\left[H_n^2(X_1, X_2)\right] \right\}^2 \to 0$$

as $n \to \infty$, U_n^* is asymptotically normal with mean zero and variance $2E[H_n^2 (X_1, X_2)]$. This result is due to Hall (1984).

Theorem (kth-Order Degenerate U-Statistics): Let

$$U_n^* = \binom{n}{k}^{-1} \sum_{(n,k)} H_n\left(X_{i_1}, \ldots, X_{i_k}\right)$$

be a kth-order U statistic, where H_n is a symmetric function (exchangeable) that depends on n, X_i is an i.i.d. random vector, and the summation $\sum_{(n,k)}$ extends over all combinations $1 \leq i_1 < \ldots < i_k \leq n$ of $\{1, \ldots, n\}$. Assume that $H_n(X_1, \ldots, X_k)$ is centred, degenerate $(E\{H_n(X_1, \ldots, X_k)|X_1\} = 0 \text{ a.s.})$, and define, for $c = 1, \ldots, k$,

$$H_{nc}(x_1, \ldots, x_c) = E\{H_n(X_1, \ldots, X_k)|X_1 = x_1, \ldots, X_c = x_c\}$$

with their variances being $\sigma_{nc}^2 = V\{H_{nc}(X_1, \ldots, X_c)\}$. Further define

$$G_n(X_1, X_2) = E_{X_3}[H_{n2}(X_1, X_3)H_{n2}(X_2, X_3)|X_1, X_2].$$

If $E[H_n^2(X_1, \ldots, X_k)] < \infty$ for each n, $\sigma_{nc}^2/\sigma_{n2}^2 = o(n^{(c-2)})$ for $c = 3, \ldots, k$ (when $k \geq 3$), and, as $n \to \infty$,

$$\frac{E[G_n^2(X_1, X_2)] + n^{-1}E[H_{n2}^4(X_1, X_2)]}{\{E[H_{n2}^2(X_1, X_2)]\}^2} \to 0,$$

then nU_n^* is asymptotically normal with mean zero and variance $\{k^2(k-1)^2 \sigma_{n2}^2/2\}$.

This result is due to Fan and Li (1996) and it reduces to the previous theorem due to Hall when $k = 2$. For the case of dependent observations, see Fan and Li (1996c).

A.2.5 *Further Results on the Law of Large Numbers and Convergence in Moments and Distributions*

In Section A.2.2 the law of large numbers for the sequence of r.v.s $\{X_n\}$ was investigated. Now we present below the law of large numbers for functions of X_n. These also hold for $\{X_n\} \in R^q$.

Theorem: Let $\{X_n\}$ be a sequence of independent r.v.s with the distribution functions $\{F_n\}$. Further consider $g(x)$ to be a continuous function. If

$$\frac{1}{n} \sum_{i=1}^n F_i \to F(x) \text{ pointwise}$$

and

$$\sup_n \frac{1}{n} \sum_{i=1}^n E |g(x_i)|^{1+\delta} < \infty \quad \text{for some } \delta > 0,$$

then

$$\frac{1}{n} \sum_{i=1}^n g(X_i) \xrightarrow{P} \int g(x) \, dF(x) = Eg(X).$$

Further using the additional restrictions $\sup n^{-1} \Sigma E |g(x_i)|^{2+\delta} < \infty$ for some $\delta > 0$, $n^{-1}\Sigma g(X_i) \xrightarrow{a.s} \int g(x) \, dF(x) = Eg(X)$.

Proof: See Bierens (1987b). Q.E.D.

Note that the above theorem goes through for the Borel measurable function g if we assume the convergence of $n^{-1}\Sigma F_i \to F$ setwise, where F is the distribution function induced by a probability measure. The convergence of, say, $\{F_n\}$ to F setwise means that for each Borel set B_0 in B the sequence of probability measures over B_0 converges to a probability measure over B_0.

Many semiparametric models feature estimators that are functions of the random vector $X \in R$ as well as a parameter vector $\theta \in \Theta$, where Θ is a compact Borel set in R. Let us denote this random function g as $g(X, \theta)$. If $g(x, \theta)$ is a continuous real function on $R \times \Theta$ then under the conditions of the above theorem (with $g(X)$ replaced by $g(X, \theta)$),

$$\frac{1}{n}\sum_{i=1}^{n} g(X_i, \theta) \to \int g(x, \theta)\,dF(x) = Eg(x, \theta),\qquad (A.43)$$

a.s. or in probability and uniformly on θ. This result will also be true when $g(x, \theta)$ is a Borel measurable function if the pointwise convergence of $n^{-1}\sum F_i$ is changed to setwise convergence. These results follow from Theorems 1 and 2 of Jennrich (1969).

A.2.6 Convergence in Moments

Section A.2.2 (Definition 3) considered the convergence of X_n in rth moment. Here we look into the conditions under which the limit of the rth moment is equal to the rth asymptotic moment (the rth moment of the asymptotic distribution). This is useful since, for some sequences, the rth moment of its asymptotic distribution is finite, but the limit of the exact rth moment of the sequence may be infinite. To relate the two moments, the important condition is that the sequence $\{X_n\}$ be uniformly integrable, that is,

$$\lim_{c\to\infty}\sup_n \int_{|x_n^r|>c} |x_n^r|\,dP = 0.\qquad (A.44)$$

With this concept we can state the desired result as:
If (i) $X_n \to X$ in probability or distribution, (ii) $E|X_n|^r < \infty$, and (iii) $\{X_n^r\}$ is uniformly integrable, then

$$\lim_{n\to\infty} EX_n^r = EX^r.$$

Proof: See Serfling (1980). Q.E.D.

Many results in this book hinge on the asymptotic behavior of a function of X_n that itself depends on n, in particular where $X_n = X/h, h = h_n$. Convergence of such quantities is an important result and is used extensively in proving asymptotic results in this book. Because of its usefulness we also provide a proof, which can be found in Parzen (1962), among others. We present the proof for $X \in R^q$.

Lemma 1: Suppose $g(x)$ is a Borel measurable function on R^q such that

  (i) $\int |g(x)|\, dx < \infty$,
  (ii) $\|x\|^q\, |g(x)| \to 0$ as $\|x\| \to \infty$,
  (iii) $\sup |g(x)| < \infty$,

where $\|x\|$ is the usual Euclidean norm of x. Let $f(x)$ be another function on R^q such that

  (iv) $\int |f(x)|\, dx < \infty$.

Then, at every point x_0 of continuity of f,

$$f_n(x_0) = \frac{1}{h^q} \int g\left(\frac{x}{h}\right) f(x_0 - x)\, dx \to f(x_0) \int g(x)\, dx, \quad \text{(A.45)}$$

as $n \to \infty$, where $h = h_n$ is a sequence of positive constants such that $h \to 0$ as $n \to \infty$. Furthermore, if f is uniformly continuous, then the convergence in (A.45) is uniform.

Proof: First, by change of variable and subsequent substitution of (A.45), write

$$f_n(x_0) - f(x_0) \int g(x)\, dx = f_n(x_0) - f(x_0) \frac{1}{h^q} \int g\left(\frac{x}{h}\right) dx$$

$$= \int [f(x_0 - x) - f(x_0)] \frac{1}{h^q} g\left(\frac{x}{h}\right) dx.$$

Setting $\delta > 0$ and splitting the region of integration into two regions, $\|x\| \le \delta$ and $\|x\| > \delta$, we have

$$\left| f_n(x_0) - f(x_0) \int g(x)\, dx \right|$$

$$\le \max_{\|x\| \le \delta} |f(x_0 - x) - f(x_0)| \int_{\|z\| \le \delta/h} |g(z)|\, dz$$

$$+ \int_{\|x\| > \delta} \left| \frac{f(x_0 - x)}{\|x\|^q} \right| \frac{\|x\|^q}{h^q} \left| g\left(\frac{x}{h}\right) \right| dx$$

$$+ |f(x_0)| \int_{\|x\| > \delta} \frac{1}{h^q} \left| g\left(\frac{x}{h}\right) \right| dx, \quad \text{(A.46)}$$

where we note

$$\int_{\|z\|\leq\delta/h} |g(z)|\,dz = \frac{1}{h^q} \int_{\|x\|\leq\delta} \left| g\left(\frac{x}{h}\right) \right| dx, \quad z = x/h.$$

Next observe that

$$\int_{\|x\|>\delta} \left| \frac{f(x_0 - x)}{\|x\|^q} \right| \frac{\|x\|^q}{h^q} \left| g\left(\frac{x}{h}\right) \right| dx$$

$$\leq \frac{1}{\delta^q} \sup_{\|z\|\geq\delta/h} \|z\|^q\,|(g(z)| \int |f(x)|\,dx \qquad (A.47)$$

because

$$\int |f(x_0 - x)|\,dx = \int |f(u)|\,du = \int |f(x)|\,dx.$$

Thus

$$\left| f_n(x_0) - f(x_0)\int g(x)\,dx \right| \leq \max_{\|x\|\leq\delta} |f(x_0 - x) - f(x_0)| \int |g(z)|\,dz$$

$$+ \frac{1}{\delta^q} \sup_{\|z\|\geq\delta/h} \|z\|^q\,|g(z)| \int |f(x)|\,dx$$

$$+ |f(x_0)| \int_{\|z\|\geq\delta/h} |g(z)|\,dz, \qquad (A.48)$$

which tends to zero if we let first $n \to \infty$ ($h \to 0$) and then $\delta \to 0$. This is because the first term is zero if $\delta \to 0$ and under (i). The second term is zero if $h \to 0$ under (ii) and (iv). And the third term is zero if $h \to 0$, for any $\delta > 0$.

It is easy to show that, if f is uniformly continuous, then the convergence in (A.45) is uniform. This feature stems from the fact that uniform continuity implies that the first and second terms in (A.48) are zero as $n \to \infty$, while the third term is zero because $|f(x)|$ is bounded. Thus

$$\lim_{n\to\infty} \sup_{x\in R^q} \left| f_n(x_0) - f(x_0) \int g(x)\,dx \right| = 0. \qquad (A.49)$$

$$\text{Q.E.D.}$$

An intuitive proof of the result (A.45) in Lemma 1 follows by noting that

$$f_n(x_0) = \frac{1}{h^q} \int g\left(\frac{x}{h}\right) f(x_0 - x)\,dx$$

$$= \int g(z) f(x_0 - hz)\,dz$$

$$\to f(x_0) \int g(z)\,dz, \qquad (A.50)$$

as $n \to \infty$. The last outcome is obtained by applying the Mean-Value Theorem to $f(x_0 - hz)$, which yields $f(x_0) - hzf'(x_0^*)$, where x_0^* lies in $[x_0 - hz, \ x]$, and therefore

$$\int g(z) f(x_0 - hz) \, dz = \int g(z)[f(x_0) - hzf'(x_0^*)] \, dz, \qquad (A.51)$$

after which the limit as $h \to 0$ produces the desired result. However, this requires differentiability of f and the existence of the moment of $g(z)$, thereby excluding densities such as the uniform. These conditions are avoided in the rigorous proof given above.

The result in Lemma 1 is known as the Dominated (Bounded) Convergence Theorem, which is another version of the Dominated Convergence Theorem in A.2.2.

An extension of the result in Lemma 1 is as follows:

Corollary 1: Let $f(x)$ and $g(x)$ be as in Lemma 1. Then for any $r \ge 0$, and every continuity point x of f, as $n \to \infty$,

$$\frac{1}{h^q} \int g^r \left(\frac{x_0 - x}{h} \right) f(x) \, dx \to f(x_0) \int g^r(x) \, dx, \qquad (A.52)$$

or

$$\int g^r(\psi) f(x_0 - h\psi) \, d\psi \to f(x_0) \int g^r(x) \, dx, \qquad (A.53)$$

where $\psi = (x_0 - x)/h$.

Proof: The proof follows by noting that, under (i) and (iii) of Lemma 1, $g^r(x)$ is bounded and absolutely integrable. Thus, for $y = x_0 - x$,

$$\frac{1}{h^q} \int g^r \left(\frac{x_0 - x}{h} \right) f(x) \, dx = \frac{1}{h^q} \int g^r \left(\frac{y}{h} \right) f(x_0 - y) \, dy.$$

$$(A.54)$$

Now using Lemma 1 on the right-hand side, we get $h^{-q} \int g^r \left(\frac{y}{h} \right) f(x_0 - y) \, dy \to f(x_0) \int g^r(y) \, dy$ or $f(x_0) \int g^r(x) \, dx$, as $n \to \infty$. The result in (A.53) follows by the substitution $\psi = (x_0 - x)/h$. Q.E.D.

Corollary 2: Let $f(x)$ and $g(x)$ be as in Lemma 1. In addition consider $f(x)$ to be a density function of the r.v. X. Then

$$\frac{1}{h^q} E g^r \left(\frac{x_0 - X}{h} \right) \to f(x_0) \int g^r(x) \, dx, \qquad (A.55)$$

or $h^{-q} E g^r(\psi) \to f(x_0) \int g^r(x) \, dx$, where $\psi = (x_0 - X)/h$.

Proof: This result is an alternative representation of the result in Lemma 1, since

$$\frac{1}{h^q} E g^r \left(\frac{x_0 - X}{h} \right) = \frac{1}{h^q} \int g^r \left(\frac{x_0 - x}{h} \right) f(x) \, dx. \tag{A.56}$$

Q.E.D.

A.3 Some Probability Inequalities

In Section A.1.1 we provided inequalities involving expectations. Here we present some inequalities of probabilities that can be useful in many applications. For the inequalities in (I) to (IV) below see Rao (1973).

(**I**) If X is a r.v. such that $E e^{aX} < \infty$ for $a > 0$, then

$$P(X \geq \epsilon) \leq E(e^{aX})/e^{a\epsilon}.$$

(**II**) If X_1, X_2 are i.i.d., then for $\epsilon > 0$

$$P[|X_1 - X_2| > \epsilon] \leq P[|X_1| > \epsilon/2] + P[|X_2| > \epsilon/2]$$
$$= 2P[|X_1| > \epsilon/2].$$

If X_is are i.i.d., $i = 1, \ldots, n$, then

$$2P[|X_1 + \cdots + X_n| \geq \epsilon] \geq 1 - e^{-n[1 - F(\epsilon) + F(-\epsilon)]}.$$

(**III**) *Kolmogorov's inequality:* Let $X_i, i = 1, \ldots, n$ be n independent random variables such that $E X_i = 0$, $V(X_i) = \sigma_i^2 < \infty$. Then

$$P \left(\max_{1 \leq k \leq n} \left| \sum_1^k X_i \right| > \epsilon \right) < \frac{1}{\epsilon^2} \sum_{i=1}^n \sigma_i^2.$$

(**IV**) *Berge inequality:* Let X_1, X_2 be r.v.s such that $E X_i = \mu_i$, $V(X_i) = \sigma_i^2$ and $\text{cov}(X_1, X_2) = \rho \sigma_1 \sigma_2$. Then

$$P \left\{ \max \left(\frac{|X_1 - \mu_1|}{\sigma_1}, \frac{|X_2 - \mu_2|}{\sigma_2} \right) \geq \lambda \right\} \leq \frac{1 + \sqrt{1 - \rho^2}}{\lambda^2}.$$

(**V**) *Chebychev's inequality for $\bar{X}_n$:* Let $\{X_i\}, i = 1, \ldots, n$ be n independent r.v.s with $E X_i = \mu_i$ and $V(X_i) = \sigma^2$. Then, from Chebychev's inequality in Section A.1.4, for $\epsilon > 0$

$$P[|\bar{X}_n - \bar{\mu}_n| \geq \epsilon] \leq \frac{\sigma^2}{n\epsilon^2},$$

where $\bar{X}_n = \sum_1^n X_i/n$ and $\bar{\mu}_n = \sum_1^n \mu_i/n$. In general

$$P\left[\left|\bar{X}_n - \bar{\mu}_n\right| \geq \epsilon\right] \leq \frac{\mu_r}{\epsilon^r},$$

where $\mu_r = E\left|\bar{X}_n - \bar{\mu}_n\right|^r$ is the rth central moment of $\bar{X}_n$.

(VI) *Cantelli inequality:* Under the assumptions of Chebychev's inequality, and for $\epsilon > 0$,

$$P\left(\bar{X}_n - \bar{\mu}_n \leq \epsilon\right) \geq \frac{\sigma^2}{\sigma^2 + n\epsilon^2}.$$

(VII) *Hoeffding (1963) inequality:* If $\{X_i\}$ are independent and $a_i \leq X_i - \mu_i \leq b_i$ a.s. for $i = 1, \ldots, n$, then for $\epsilon > 0$,

$$P\left[\left(\bar{X}_n - \bar{\mu}_n\right) \geq \epsilon\right] \leq e^{-2n^2\epsilon^2/\Sigma_1^n(b_i-a_i)^2}.$$

In a special case where $a \leq X_i - \mu_i \leq b$ for all $i = 1, \ldots, n$

$$P\left[\left(\bar{X}_n - \bar{\mu}_n\right) \geq \epsilon\right] \leq e^{-2n\epsilon^2/(b-a)^2}.$$

It is easy to verify that, assuming $a \leq |X_i - \mu_i| \leq b$,

$$P\left[\left|\bar{X}_n - \bar{\mu}_n\right| \geq \epsilon\right] = P\left[\left(\bar{X}_n - \bar{\mu}_n\right) \geq \epsilon\right]$$
$$+ P\left[-\left(\bar{X}_n - \bar{\mu}_n\right) \geq \epsilon\right] \leq 2e^{-2n\epsilon^2/(b-a)^2}.$$

For a proof see Hoeffding (1963).

(VIII) *Bennett's (1962) inequality:* If $\{X_i\}$ are independent, and $|X_i - \mu_i| < b$ for all i, then for $\epsilon > 0$

$$P[|\bar{X}_n - \bar{\mu}_n| > \epsilon] \leq 2e^{-n\epsilon^2/2(\sigma^2+b\epsilon)}.$$

If b above is replaced by $b/3$ we get Berstein's inequality as given in (2.13) of Hoeffding (1963).

Note that the probability inequalities stated above in (V) to (VII) are obtained by using the result in (I). That is, taking $\bar{\mu}_n = \mu$,

$$P\left[\bar{X}_n - \mu \geq \epsilon\right] = P\left[n\left(\bar{X}_n - \mu\right) \geq n\epsilon\right]$$
$$\leq e^{-an\epsilon} E e^{an(\bar{X}_n - \mu)}$$
$$= e^{-an\epsilon} \prod_{i=1}^n E e^{a(X_i - \mu)}.$$

For further details see Hoeffding (1963) and Bennett (1962).

We also note that Hoeffding's bound is tighter than Chebychev's except for small n or ϵ. However, whereas Chebychev's inequality applies very broadly, the inequalities of Hoeffding and Bennett are applicable only to bounded X_i.

Observe also that although Chebychev's and Bennett's inequalities both depend on σ^2, Hoeffding's inequality does not.

(IX) *Georgiev and Greblicki (1986) inequality:* Let $\{X_i\}$ be independent r.v.s such that $EX_i = 0$, $\sup_i |X_i| = b < \infty$ a.s. Then for c_{ni} as constants depending on n,

$$P\left[\left|\sum_{i=1}^{n} c_{ni} X_i\right| \geq \epsilon\right] < 2e^{-b/M},$$

where $M = \sup_i |c_{ni}| > 0$.

(X) *Owen's (1987) inequality:* If X_1 and X_2 are r.v.s then

$$P\left[|X_1| > \epsilon\right] \leq \epsilon + P\left[E\left(|X_1||X_2|\right) > \epsilon^2\right]$$

or

$$P\left[|X_1| > \epsilon\right] \leq \epsilon + P\left[(|X_1| > \epsilon |X_2) > \epsilon\right].$$

(XI) *Berry (1941) and Esseen (1945) theorem:* The central limit theorems described in A.2.4 tell us that under certain conditions the distribution of the standardized sums of r.v.s tends to a standard normal r.v.. That is, if $S_n = \sum_{i=1}^{n} X_i$, where X_i is i.i.d. with $EX_i = \mu$ and $V(X_i) = \sigma^2$, then the distribution $F_n(z)$ of

$$Z_n = \frac{S_n - ES_n}{\sqrt{V(S_n)}}$$

approaches $\mathcal{N}(0, 1) = F(z)$. However, this result does not give the information as to how large the approximation error $|F_n(z) - F(z)|$ is for a particular value of n. Information on the size of this error can be found from the Berry–Esseen theorem:

Theorem: Let $\{X_i\}$ be independent r.v.s such that $EX_i = \mu$, $V(X_i) = \sigma^2$ and $E|X_i - \mu|^3 = \mu_3 < \infty$. Then

$$\sup_z |F_n(z) - F(z)| \leq \frac{c}{\sqrt{n}} \frac{\mu_3}{\sigma^3},$$

where $c = 33/4$.

This theorem shows that the rate of convergence to normality is of the order of magnitude $O(n^{-1/2})$ (see the definitions O and o below).

For independent but not identically distributed r.v.s the Berry–Esseen result takes the form

$$\sup_{z} |F_n(z) - F(z)| \leq c \frac{\sum_1^n \mu_{3i}}{\left(\sum_1^n \sigma_i^2\right)^{3/2}}.$$

A disadvantage of the above approximation is that it does not provide guidance in choosing between asymptotically equivalent results. This leads to the concept of asymptotic expansions of the approximation errors. The idea behind an asymptotic expansion of the distribution function is that it can be expressed as

$$F_n(z) = F(z) + \frac{F_1(z)}{\sqrt{n}} + \frac{F_2(z)}{n} + \cdots,$$

where the first term is $F(z) \sim \mathcal{N}(0, 1)$ and $F_i(z)$ are some functions of z. Such expansions are known as an Edgeworth expansion or a Gram–Charlier type expansion. For details on these expansions, see Kendall and Stuart (1973), Phillips (1977), and Rothenberg (1984).

A.4   Order of Magnitudes (Small o and Large O)

Sometimes it is useful to have a measure of the order of magnitude of a particular sequence, say, $\{X_n\}$. The magnitude is determined by looking into the behavior of X_n for large n. The following definitions are useful in this context:

Definition 1: The sequence $\{X_n\}$ of real numbers is said to be at most of order n^k and is denoted by

$$X_n = O(n^k), \quad \text{if} \quad \frac{X_n}{n^k} \to c$$

as $n \to \infty$ for some constant $c > 0$. Further if $\{X_n\}$ is a sequence of r.v.s then

$$X_n = O_p(n^k) \quad \text{or} \quad O_{a.s.}(n^k)$$

if, as $n \to \infty$,

$$\frac{X_n}{n^k} - c_n \to 0 \quad \text{in prob.} \quad \text{or} \quad \text{a.s.,}$$

respectively, where c_n is a nonstochastic sequence. The $O_p(n^k)$, for example, represents at most of order n^k in probability.

Definition 2: The sequence $\{X_n\}$ of real numbers is said to be of smaller order than n^k and is denoted by

$$X_n = o(n^k), \quad \text{if} \quad \frac{X_n}{n^k} \to 0$$

as $n \to \infty$. Further if $\{X_n\}$ is stochastic then

$$X_n = o_p(n^k) \quad \text{or} \quad o_{\text{a.s.}}(n^k)$$

if

$$\frac{X_n}{n^k} \to 0 \quad \text{in prob. or a.s.}$$

In the above definitions k can take any real value (positive or negative). As an example consider a nonstochastic sequence

$$\{X_n\} = \frac{1}{n+4}. \tag{A.57}$$

It is easy to verify that for $k = -1$ in definition 1,

$$\frac{X_n}{n^{-1}} = \frac{n}{n+4} \to 1 \tag{A.58}$$

as $n \to \infty$. Thus $X_n = O(n^{-1}) = O(1/n)$.

The sequence $X_n = 1/(n+4)$ is also $o(1) = o(n^0)$. This is because, for $k=0$, using Definition 2, $X_n/n^0 = X_n = 1/n+4 \to 0$ as $n \to \infty$.

As another example, note that $X_n = \sum_{i=1}^{n} z_i^2 = O(n)$, where z_i is nonstochastic, if $\sum_1^n z_i^2/n \to c$ as $n \to \infty$. However, if z_i is such that $\sum_{i=1}^{n} z_i^2/n^3 \to c$ as $n \to \infty$ then $\sum_1^n z_i^2 = O(n^3)$. For example, if $z_i = i$, then $\sum_1^n z_i^2 = n(n+1)(2n+1)/6 = O(n^3)$; the reader should verify that $n+1 = O(n) = o(n^2)$; $e^{-n} = o(n^{-\lambda})$, $\lambda > 0$; $\log_e n = o(n^\lambda)$, $\lambda > 0$; $30n^2 + 20n = O(n^2) = o(n^3)$.

Now consider a stochastic sequence $\bar{X}_n = \frac{1}{n}\sum_{i=1}^{n} X_i$, where $EX_i = \mu$ and $V(X_i) = \sigma^2$. Note that, for $k = -1/2$ in Definition 1,

$$\frac{\bar{X}_n}{n^{-1/2}} = n^{1/2}\bar{X}_n. \tag{A.59}$$

But $n^{1/2}\bar{X}_n - n^{1/2}\mu$ is $O_p(1)$ by using Chebychev's inequality. Thus $\bar{X}_n - \mu = O_p(n^{-1/2})$. It also follows that $\bar{X}_n = \mu + o_p(1)$.

The small o and capital O satisfy the following properties.

If $X_n = O(n^k)$ and $Y_n = O(n^m)$ then

(i)	$X_n Y_n = O(n^{k+m}),$	
(ii)	$X_n^r = O(n^{rk}),$	(A.60)
(iii)	$X_n + Y_n = O(n^{k_o}), \quad k_0 = \max(k, m).$	

The same results hold for small o in place of capital O.

Further, if $X_n = O(n^k)$ but $Y_n = o(n^m)$, then

(i)	$X_n + Y_n = O(n^k),$	
(ii)	$X_n Y_n = o(n^{k+m}).$	(A.61)

A.5   Asymptotic Theory for Dependent Observations

In Sections A.1 to A.4 we gave asymptotic theory results for the case of i.i.d. random variables or independent r.v.s. Here we consider the case of dependent r.v.s. In this instance, the asymptotic theory is developed under different assumptions on the nature of dependence. Before doing so we note that, as before, (Ω, F, P) denotes a probability space. Further let $\{X_{ni}, i = 0, \pm 1, \ldots, n = 1, 2, \ldots\}$ be a double (triangular) array of random vectors on (Ω, F, P). In general it can take values 1 to k_n with $k_n \to \infty$ as $n \to \infty$. For the sake of simplicity in exposition we shall write $\{X_{ni}\}$ as $\{X_i\}$. Let $F_{n,j}^{j'} = F_j^{j'} = \sigma(X_j, \ldots, X_{j'})$ be the σ-field generated by $X_j, \ldots, X_{j'}$ for all $j \le j'$. For example, $F_{-\infty}^{j'}$ and $F_{j'+1}^{\infty}$ are the two σ-fields representing past and future values of Xs. Denoting $\|\cdot\|_q$ as the L^q norm, that is, $\|X_i\|_q = (E |X_i|^q)^{1/q}$, $X_i \in L_q$ if $\|X_i\|_q < \infty$, and observing that if f and g are measurable real-valued functions (see definitions in A.1.3), then cf, $f + g$, fg, and $|f|$ are also measurable. For a proof of the latter see Bartle (1966, Lemma 2.6).

Definition 1: A one-to-one transformation $T : \Omega \to \Omega$ defined on (Ω, F, P) is measurable provided $T^{-1}(F)$ is contained in F.

Note that when a T operates on a set (family) then it is understood to be operating on each element of a set (family). The definition implies that the transformation T is measurable provided that any set taken by the transformation (or its inverse) into F is itself a set in F. The transformation T maps a point of Ω, say $\omega = (\ldots, x_{t-1}, x_t, x_{t+1}, x_{t+2}, \ldots)$, into another point of Ω, say $\omega' = Tw = (\ldots, x_t, x_{t+1}, x_{t+2}, x_{t+3}, \ldots)$. This particular transformation is also known as the shift operator.

Definition 2: A transformation T from Ω to Ω is measure preserving if it is measurable and if $P(T^{-1}F^*) = P(F^*)$ for all $F^* \in F$.

Definition 3 (Strict Stationarity): A sequence $\{X_i\}$ is said to be stationary (strictly) if and only if the joint distribution of $X_{i_1}, \ldots, X_{i_n}$ has the same joint distribution of $X_{i_{1+\tau}} \ldots, X_{i_{n+\tau}}$ for all $i_1, \ldots, i_n$ and τ.

Definition 4 (Covariance Stationarity): A sequence $\{X_i\}$ is said to be covariance stationary if the $E(X_i) = \mu$ exists, $\mathrm{cov}(X_i, X_{i+\tau}) = \gamma(\tau)$ exists, and $\gamma(\tau) \to 0$ as $\tau \to \infty$.

Definition 3 implies that shifting the time origin by an amount τ has no effect on the joint distribution, that is, the distribution depends only on the intervals between $i_1, \ldots, i_n$. For example, if $i_1 = 1, i_2 = 2, \ldots, i_n = n$ then the distribution of X_1, X_2 should be the same as the distribution of $X_{1+\tau}, \ldots, X_{n+\tau}$. Further, if $n = 1$, it implies that the distribution of X_i must be the same for all i. Without this assumption it would be impossible to determine the n means and variances of X_i from a simple realization.

Strict stationarity itself is not enough to provide a law of large numbers and a central limit theorem. We need to impose restrictions on the nature of dependence or "memory" of the sequence. These are known as ergodicity and mixing conditions (restrictions). These conditions stem from the assumption that dependence between X_{i_1} and X_{i_2} needs to weaken as the distance $i_2 - i_1$ increases. For example, the dependence between a typical economic variable for $i_1 = 1988$ and $i_2 = 1989$ would be expected to be greater than when $i_1 = 1940$ and $i_2 = 1989$.

A.5.1 Ergodicity

Definition: Let $\{X_i\}$ be a stationary sequence and let T be a measure-preserving transformation on (Ω, F, P) such that $X_1(\omega) = X_1(\omega)$, $X_2(\omega) = X_1(T\omega)$, $X_3(\omega) = X_1(T^2\omega), \ldots, X_n(\omega) = X_1(T^{n-1}\omega)$ for all ω in Ω. Then $\{X_i\}$ is ergodic if and only if for any two events F_1 and $F_2 \in F$

$$\lim_{n \to \infty} n^{-1} \sum_{i=1}^{n} P\left(F_1 \cap T^i F_2\right) = P(F_1)P(F_2). \tag{A.62}$$

Note that $T^i F_2$ can be thought of as the event F_2 shifted i periods into the future, while, since T is measure preserving, $P(T^i F_2) = P(F_2)$. Thus ergodicity can be regarded as a form of "average asymptotic independence." In the case of a covariance stationary sequence $\{X_i\}$ such that $\text{cov}(X_i, X_{i+\tau}) = \gamma(\tau)$, asymptotic uncorrelatedness implies $\gamma(\tau) \to 0$ as $\tau \to \infty$. A weaker form of such a memory restriction is

$$\frac{1}{n} \sum_{\tau=1}^{n} \gamma(\tau) \to 0 \tag{A.63}$$

as $n \to \infty$. A sequence satisfying this is ergodic. When $\{X_i\}$ is Gaussian the two definitions of ergodicity are the same, since in this case uncorrelatedness implies dependence. However, this may not be true for non-Gaussian sequences. We now state a useful theorem.

Theorem: Let $g_i = g(X_i, X_{i+1}, \ldots)$, where $X_i \in R^q$ and g is a measurable function on R^q. Then

(i) If $\{X_i\}$ is stationary, g_i is strictly stationary.
(ii) If X_i is strictly stationary and ergodic, then g_i is strictly stationary and ergodic.

Theorem (Ergodic L.L.N.): Let $\{X_i\}$ be a stationary ergodic sequence with $EX_i = \mu < \infty$. Then

$$\bar{X}_n \xrightarrow{a.s.} \mu.$$

This theorem is for dependent but identically distributed r.v.s.

A.5.2 Mixing Sequences

To investigate the L.L.N. for dependent heterogeneous observations we need to replace the ergodicity condition with stronger conditions on the asymptotic dependence of the r.v.s involved. These conditions are known as *mixing conditions,* and the sequence $\{X_i\}$ satisfying these conditions constitutes a mixing sequence, see Bradley (1980b, 1980c, 1980d, 1981a). Roussas and Ioannides (1987), Ioannides and Roussas (1988), and Roussas (1988) have discussed four kinds of mixing sequences, which they refer to as ϕ_i-mixing ($i = 1, 2, 3.4$). Here we shall consider only the two best known and frequently used definitions of mixing sequences, which are referred to as α and ϕ mixing; these correspond to ϕ_2- and ϕ_4-mixing in Roussas and Ioannides (1987).

Before defining dependence measures we let $F^\ell_{-\infty}$ and $F^\infty_{\ell+\tau}$ be the two σ-fields of events $\sigma(\ldots, X_\ell)$ and $\sigma(X_{\ell+\tau}, \ldots, X_\infty)$ separated by τ periods. One can think of $F^\ell_{-\infty}$ as representing all information contained in the past of the sequence $\{X_i\}$ up to time period ℓ, whereas $F^\infty_{\ell+\tau}$ represents all the information contained in the future of the sequence $\{X_i\}$ from time $\ell + \tau$ on. The events belonging to $F^\ell_{-\infty}$ and $F^\infty_{\ell+\tau}$ are designated F_1, F_2, respectively, while the sup over F_1, F_2 represents the sup over $F_1 \in F^\ell_{-\infty}$ and $F_2 \in F^\infty_{\ell+\tau}$.

Definition: The uniform (ϕ) and strong (α) mixing coefficients for $\{X_i\}$ are

$$\phi_\tau = \sup_\ell \sup_{F_1, F_2} |P(F_1|F_2) - P(F_1)|,$$
$$\alpha_\tau = \sup_\ell \sup_{F_1, F_2} |P(F_1 \cap F_2) - P(F_1)P(F_2)|. \tag{A.64}$$

Both ϕ_τ and α_τ provide measures of the amount of dependence between events involving X_i separated by at least τ time periods. α_τ is nonincreasing in τ with $1 \geq \alpha_1 \geq \alpha_2$. Note that for $\{X_i\} = \{X_{ni}\}$ these coefficients are defined as $\phi^*_\tau = \sup_n \phi_\tau$ and $\alpha^*_\tau = \sup_n \alpha_\tau$.

Definition: The sequence $\{X_i\}$ is said to be uniform (ϕ) mixing and strong (α) mixing if

$$\phi_\tau \to 0 \tag{A.65}$$

and

$$\alpha_\tau \to 0 \qquad\qquad\qquad\qquad (A.66)$$

as $\tau \to \infty$, respectively.

In a mixing process therefore the distant future is virtually independent of the past and the present (and vice versa). The ϕ-mixing processes are due to Ibragimov (1962) and discussed in Billingsley (1968) whereas α-mixing processes were introduced by Rosenblatt (1956a). Trivial examples of mixing processes are independent processes for which $\phi_\tau = \alpha_\tau = 0$ for $\tau > 1$ and m-dependent processes for which $\phi_\tau = \alpha_\tau = 0$ for $\tau > m$. Note that a process is m-dependent if, for i_1 and i_2, X_{i_1} and X_{i_2} are independent for $|i_1 - i_2| > m$. For $i_1 = i$ and $i_2 = i + \tau$ it means X_i and $X_{i+\tau}$ are m-dependent for all $\tau > m$. For the Gaussian case, m-dependence can be checked by seeing whether $\text{cov}(X_i, X_{i+\tau}) = 0$ for $\tau > m$.

Note that the stationary Gaussian AR(1) process for X_i is also α-mixing since $\alpha_\tau \to 0$ as $\tau \to \infty$ (see Ibragimov and Linnik (1971)), but it is not ϕ-mixing since ϕ_τ does not approach 0 as $\tau \to \infty$. This is not surprising since the inequality

$$\phi_\tau \geq \alpha_\tau$$

follows by writing $P(F_1|F_2) - P(F_1) = [P(F_1 \cap F_2) - P(F_1)P(F_2)]/P(F_2)$ and noting that $0 < P(F_2) \leq 1$. Thus ϕ-mixing implies α-mixing but not vice versa.

We note here that the asymptotic independence implied by mixing is a stronger memory requirement than that of ergodicity. This is because, for a strictly stationary sequence, mixing implies ergodicity, that is, if $\alpha_\tau \to 0$ as $\tau \to \infty$, X_i is ergodic (Rosenblatt, 1978). Further, since ϕ-mixing implies α-mixing, a ϕ-mixing process is also ergodic. However, ergodic processes are not necessarily mixing processes.

In many applications, ϕ or α is required to approach zero at a certain rate. The following definition is useful in this context.

Definition: Let $\{\alpha_\tau\}$ be a sequence of nonnegative numbers. Then $\{\alpha_\tau\}$ is of size m if $\alpha_\tau = 0(\tau^{-\lambda})$ for some $\lambda > m$. The definition also holds for α_τ replaced by ϕ_τ. For the asymptotic properties of nonparametric estimators we often use the result that measurable functions of mixing processes are themselves mixing, provided the function depends on only a finite number of lagged values of the process. That is, unlike strictly stationary processes, measurable functions of the entire history of mixing processes are not necessarily mixing.

Lemma: Let g be a measurable function on R^{q+1} and $g_i = g(X_i, X_{i+1}, \ldots, X_{i+q})$. If the sequence $\{X_i\}$ is mixing such that $\phi_\tau(\alpha_\tau)$ is of size m, then the sequence g_i is also mixing with mixing coefficient $\phi_{\tau,g}(\alpha_{\tau,g})$ satisfying $\phi_{\tau,g}(\alpha_{\tau,g}) \leq \phi_{\tau-q,g}(\alpha_{\tau-q,g})$ for $\tau > q$, and with the same size m.

Proof: See White (1984) and Fan (1990c).   Q.E.D.

The above property is known as the transformation-preserving property of mixing processes. Apart from this property, the following inequalities involving expectations are also useful for asymptotic theory. Essentially these inequalities indicate that the covariance between two r.v.s measurable with respect to $F_{-\infty}^\ell$ and $F_{\ell+\tau}^\infty$ respectively is bounded by a proportion of a certain positive power of ϕ or α. Therefore, asymptotically, such r.v.s are uncorrelated.

Lemma: Let X_1 and X_2, respectively, be $F_{-\infty}^\ell$ measurable and $F_{\ell+\tau}^\infty$ measurable r.v.s such that:

(i) if $E\,|X_1|^p, E\,|X_2|^r < \infty$ for $p, r > 1$ with $1/p + 1/r = 1$ then

$$|E(X_1 X_2) - (EX_1)(EX_2)| \leq 2\phi_\tau^{1/p}\,\|X_1\|_p\,\|X_2\|_r,$$

(ii) if $E\,|X_1|^p, E\,|X_2|^q < \infty$ for $p, r > 1$ with $1/p + 1/r < 1$ then

$$|E(X_1 X_2) - (EX_1)(EX_2)| \leq 10\alpha_\tau^{1-(\frac{1}{p}+\frac{1}{r})}\,\|X_1\|_p\,\|X_2\|_r.$$

Proof: See Roussas and Ioannides (1987) or Hall and Heyde (1980).
Q.E.D.

There are other versions of this lemma, depending on whether one of the two r.v.s or both are bounded; see Hall and Heyde (1980). Different versions may lead to different conditions on the consistency of estimators. For nonparametric estimators the above lemma is commonly used; see Roussas (1988, 1989).

The next lemma indicates the result that the conditional expectation of a r.v. X, given the past up to ℓ, converges to the unconditional expectation as τ gets larger and larger.

Lemma: Suppose X is a ϕ- or α-mixing r.v. measurable with respect to $F_1 = F_{-\infty}^\ell$ and $1 \leq p \leq r \leq \infty$. Then

(i) $\|E(X|F_1) - EX\| \leq 2\phi^{1-\frac{1}{r}}\,\|X\|_r,$

(ii) $\|E(X|F_1) - EX\| \leq 2(2^{1/p} + 1)\alpha^{\frac{1}{p}-\frac{1}{r}}\,\|X\|_r.$

Proof: See McLeish (1975).   Q.E.D.

This lemma is also useful in proving the earlier lemma.

Now we provide probability inequalities related to ϕ- and α-mixing.

Collomb's (1984) Inequality (ϕ-Mixing) If $\{X_i\}$ is ϕ-mixing with $EX_i = 0$, $|X_i| \leq d$, $EX_i^2 \leq D$, and $E|X_i| \leq \delta$, then

$$P\left[\left|\sum_{i=1}^{n} X_i\right| > \epsilon\right] \leq e^{(3\sqrt{e}n\tau^{-1}\phi_\tau - \beta\epsilon + 6\beta^2 n(D+4\delta\Sigma_1^\tau \phi_i))},$$

where β is a real number and τ an integer satisfying $1 \leq \tau \leq n$ and $\beta\tau d \leq 1/4$. For additional probability inequalities about ϕ-mixing, see Bradley (1980a).

Carbon's (1983) Inequality (α-Mixing) If $\{X_i\}$ is α-mixing with $EX_i = 0$, $|X_i| \leq d$, and $EX_i^2 \leq D$, then

$$P\left(\left|\sum_{i=1}^{n} X_i\right| > \epsilon\right) \leq 2e^{-(\beta\epsilon + 6\beta^2 e(D+8d^2\Sigma_{i=1}^\tau \alpha_i)n}e^{2\sqrt{e}\beta_\tau^{2\tau/5n}}n\tau^{-1},$$

where β is a real number and τ an integer satisfying $q \leq \tau \leq n$ and $0 \leq \beta \leq (\tau de)/4$.

For further discussion on α-mixing see Bradley (1980a, 1981b) and Ahmad (1979). The above inequalities can be used to obtain strong consistency results for nonparametric estimators.

Now we turn to LLNs for mixing sequences for dependent but heterogeneous processes.

Theorem (McLeish): Let $\{X_i\}$ be a ϕ sequence of size $p = r/(2r-1)$ or an α sequence of size $p_0 = r/(r-1)$, $r > 1$, with $\mu_i = EX_i < \infty$. If for some δ, $0 < \delta \leq r$, $\sum_{i=1}^{\infty}(E|X_i - \mu_i|^{r+\delta}/i^{r+\delta})^{1/r} < \infty$, then

$$\bar{X}_n - \bar{\mu}_n \xrightarrow{a.s.} 0.$$

Proof: See McLeish (1975, Theorem 2.10). Q.E.D.

Note that if $\{X_i\}$ is such that $E|X_i|^{r+\delta} < D < \infty$ for some $\delta > 0$, and all i, then the condition of the above theorem is satisfied, and $\bar{X}_n - \bar{\mu}_n \xrightarrow{a.s.} 0$. Moreover, for a sequence with exponential memory decay, r is close to 1, and so the moment condition is not restrictive. However, for a sequence with longer memory, r is larger, and hence more restrictive moment conditions will be needed.

Central Limit Theorem: Let $\{X_i\}$ be a sequence such that either ϕ or α is of size $r/(r-1)$, $r > 1$ with $EX_i = \mu_i$, $V(X_i) = \sigma_i^2$, $\sigma_i^2 \neq 0$ and $E|X_i|^{2r} < D < \infty$ for all i. Define $\bar{\sigma}_{a,n}^2 = V\left(n^{-1/2}\sum_{i=a+1}^{a+n} X_i\right)$. If there exists

$0 < \bar{\sigma}^2 < \infty$ such that $\bar{\sigma}_{a,n}^2 \to \bar{\sigma}^2$ as $n \to \infty$ uniformly in a, then

$$\sqrt{n} \frac{(\bar{X}_n - \bar{\mu}_n)}{\bar{\sigma}_n} \xrightarrow{d} \mathcal{N}(0, 1).$$

Proof: See Serfling (1968) for ϕ-mixing and White and Domowitz (1984) for α-mixing. Q.E.D.

This theorem corresponds to the Liapounov central limit theorem in the independent case. The moment conditions are now stronger in recognition of the dependence in X_i. When $r = 1$, the condition here is the same as in the independent case.

A.5.3   Near-Epoch Dependent Sequences

As noted in the last section, one limitation of the mixing process is that measurable functions, say $g(X_i, X_{i+1}, \ldots, X_{i+\tau})$, of mixing processes are measurable when τ is finite but not necessarily when τ is infinite. For example, Andrews (1984) has shown that the $AR(1)$ process with Bernoulli (p) errors is neither a ϕ- nor an α-mixing process. However, it does belong to a wider class of sequences (processes) that are asymptotically uncorrelated and have enough structure for the LLN and functional central limit theorems (FCLT) to hold. This is the class of functions of mixing process or near-epoch dependent sequences (NEDS), with respect to mixing processes. The LLN for functions of mixing sequences, NEDS, is provided by Andrews (1988) and the corresponding FCLT by Woolridge and White (1988). Gallant and White (1988) extensively explore the NEDS for nonlinear dynamic models. NEDS processes have not been used much in the nonparametric literature.

Definition: The sequence $\{X_i\}$ is L^p–NEDS with respect to $\{g_i = g_{ni}\}$ for some $1 \le p \le 2$ if and only if $X_i \in L_p$ for all n, $i \in N$, and there exist constants $\mu_m \ge 0$, $m = 0, 1, \ldots$, with $\mu_m \downarrow 0$ and $d_{ni} = d_i > 0$ such that

$$\left\| X_i - E\left(X_i | F_{i-m}^{i+m}\right) \right\|_p \le \mu_m d_i.$$

An example of a NEDS process is $y_i = \theta y_{i-1} + \epsilon_i$, where ϵ_i is Bernoulli (p) with $P(\epsilon_i = a) = p$, $P(\epsilon_i = b) = 1 - p$, and a and b are finite numbers.

Unfortunately, functions of NEDS are not necessarily NEDS unless one restricts the class of functions in certain ways. One possible choice is the class of Lipschitz functions of order 1.

Lipschitz Function: Let f be a real valued function on R^q. It is a Lipschitz function of order 1 if the following inequality is satisfied:

$$|f(x) - f(y)| \le c \|x - y\|,$$

where x and y are two arbitrary points in R^q and $\|x - y\|$ is the norm of $x - y$, for example, $((x - y)'(x - y))^{1/2}$.

A concept that is often useful in asymptotic theory for NEDS is that of equicontinuity or Holder's continuity, defined as:

Definition (Equicontinuity): A sequence of real-valued functions $\{f_n(x)\}$ is said to be equicontinuous at x_0 if and only if for any $\epsilon > 0$, there exists a $\delta > 0$ such that $|x - x_0| < \delta$ implies $|f_n(x) - f_n(x_0)| < \epsilon$ for all $n \ge 1$.

A.5.4 Martingale Differences and Mixingales

Mcleish (1975), under moment restrictions, generalized the concept of NEDS with respect to ϕ- or α-mixing processes; such processes are called *mixingales*. Andrews (1988) extended the idea of mixingales to L^p-mixingales for some $1 \le p \le 2$ and derived the corresponding L.L.N., the case when $p = 2$ being McLeish's mixingale. However, a functional limit theorem is not available for mixingales and the transformation-preserving property holds only under a very restrictive class of transformations, which limits their application in practice. An L^p-mixingale is an asymptotic analogue of a martingale difference. Thus we first define this latter concept.

Definition: The sequence $\{X_i, F_i\}$ is a martingale difference sequence if it is measurable with respect to $F^i_{-\infty} = F_i \subset F$, and if

$$E(X_i|F_{i-1}) = 0 \quad \text{for all} \quad 2 \le i \le n.$$

Note that if $\{X_i, F_i\}$ is a martingale sequence then $EX_i = 0$.

Probability Inequality I (Azuma 1967) If $\{X_i\}$ is a martingale difference sequence and $|X_i| \le M$ a.s. then for all $\epsilon > 0$

$$P\left[\left|\sum_{i=1}^{n} X_i\right| > \epsilon\right] \le 2e^{-\epsilon^2/2nM^2}.$$

Probability Inequality II   If $\{X_i\}$ is a real-valued martingale differ-ence sequence and $|X_i| \leq M$ a.s. then for all integers $m > 0$ and all $\epsilon > 0$

$$P\left[\left|\sum_{i=1}^n (X_i - EX_i|F_{i-m})\right| > \epsilon\right] < 2me^{-\epsilon^2/2nm^2M^2}.$$

For a proof of this inequality see Gyorfi et al. (1989).

Next we note the following L.L.N. and central limit theorem for martingale sequences.

L.L.N. for Martingale Differences   Let $\{X_i, F_i\}$ be a martingale difference sequence. If for some $r \geq 1$, $\sum_{j=1}^{\infty} \left(E|X_j|^{2r}\right)/j^{1+r} < \infty$, then $\bar{X}_n \xrightarrow{a.s.} 0$.

Proof: See Stout (1974, pp. 154–155). Q.E.D.

A Liapounov-type central limit theorem follows.

Central Limit Theorem for Martingale Differences   Let $\{X_{ni}, F_{ni}\}$ be a martingale difference sequence such that $EX_{ni}^2 = \sigma_{ni}^2 \neq 0$ and $E|X_{ni}|^{2+\delta} < D < \infty$ for some $\delta > 0$ and all i. If $\bar{\sigma}_n^2 = \lim_{n\to\infty} n^{-1} \sum \sigma_{ni}^2 > \delta' > 0$ for all n sufficiently large and $n^{-1} \sum_{i=1}^n (X_{ni}^2 - \bar{\sigma}_n^2) \to \infty$, then $\sqrt{n}\bar{X}_n/\bar{\sigma} \xrightarrow{d} \mathcal{N}(0, 1)$.

For this and a Lindberg–Feller-type central limit theorem see White (1984).

Definition: The sequence $\{X_i, F_i\}$ is an L^p-mixingale if there exist nonnegative constants C_i, $i = 1, \ldots, n$ and $\psi_m = 0, 1, \ldots$ such that $\psi_m \downarrow 0$ as $m \to \infty$ and for all i

(i) $\|E(X_i|F_{i-m})\|_p \leq C_i\psi_m$

and

(ii) $\|X_i - E(X_i|F_{i+m})\|_p \leq C_i\psi_{m+1}$.

When $X_i = X_{ni}$ and $F_i = F_{ni}$ is a triangular array, C_i is replaced by C_{ni} in the above.

The constants $\{\psi_m\}$ are referred to as the L^p-mixingales numbers, and they reflect the degree of dependence of X_i on the past information F_{i-m}. When $m \to \infty$ the conditional expectation becomes the unconditional expectation.

For the L^p-mixingale sequence we can verify that

$$|EX_i| = |E(E(X_i|F_{i-m}))| \leq E|E(X_i|F_{i-m})|$$

$$\leq \|E(X_i|F_{i-m})\|_p \leq C_i\psi_m \to 0 \quad \text{as } m \to \infty.$$

Under certain conditions (Woolridge and White (1988)) functions of mixing sequences can be shown to be mixingale sequences. For some other properties and a L.L.N. for mixingales see Gyorfi et al. (1989).

A.5.5 Rosenblatt's (1970) Measure of Dependence β_n

Rosenblatt (1970) introduced a "dependence index" based simply on the difference between the bivariate density function and the product of univariate density functions. This is given by

$$\beta_n = \sup_{x,y} \sum_{i=1}^{n} |f_i(x, y) - f(x)f(y)|,$$

where $f_i(x, y)$ is the joint density of X_1 and $Y = X_{1+i}, i = 1, 2, \ldots$ (assumed finite for each i, x, y), and $f(x)$ is the marginal density of the stationary sequence $\{X_i\}, i = 1, 2, \ldots$. Note that for i.i.d. sequences $\beta_n = 0$; for sequences with high long range dependence β_n may tend to infinity; and in between β_n may converge to a finite limit. For details on β_n see Rosenblatt (1970) and Castellana and Leadbetter (1986).

A.5.6 Stochastic Equicontinuity

The concept of stochastic equicontinuity of an empirical process is very useful in developing the asymptotic normality results of semiparametric estimators. To define stochastic equicontinuity, consider $\{X_i, i = 1, 2, \ldots\}$ to be a sequence of random variables defined on a probability space, $X_i \in R^q$. Further let $m(X_i, \tau)$ be a class of R^k-valued functions defined on X, where τ is a vector-valued function belonging to an infinite-dimensional set $\Im$. The element τ may be represented by the nonparametric regression or density estimators that appear as a nuisance parameter estimator in the definition of a semiparametric estimator.

Now consider an empirical process:

$$\nu_n(\tau) = \frac{1}{\sqrt{n}} \sum_{1}^{n} (m(X_i, \tau) - Em(X_i, \tau))$$

$$= \sqrt{n} \left(\bar{m}_n(\cdot, \tau) - \bar{m}_n^*(\cdot, \tau) \right), \tag{A.67}$$

where $\bar{m}_n(\cdot, \tau) = n^{-1} \sum^n m(X_i, \tau)$ and $\bar{m}_n^*(\cdot, \tau) = E\bar{m}_n(\cdot, \tau)$. In many applications, $\sqrt{n}\bar{m}_n(\cdot, \tau)$ is a $k \times 1$ vector of normalized first-order conditions for a semiparametric estimator evaluated at the true value of the R^p-dimensional parameter vector $\theta = \theta_0$. The process $\nu_n(\tau)$ is said to be stochastically equicontinuous at τ if for all $\epsilon > 0$ and $\eta > 0$, there exists $\delta > 0$ such that

$$\lim_{n \to \infty} P \left(\sup_{\tau \in \mathfrak{I}, \rho_y(\tau, \tau_0) < \delta} |\nu_n(\tau) - \nu_n(\tau_0)| > n \right) < \epsilon$$

where the random variable in parentheses is measurable and $\rho_y(\tau, \tau_0)$ is a pseudo-metric such that $\rho_\tau(\tau, \tau_0) = 0$ does not necessarily imply that $\tau = \tau_0$. In this sense stochastic equicontinuity is a stochastic and asymptotic version of the definition of the continuity of a function. An equivalent definition of stochastic equicontinuity is that, for all $\hat{\tau}_n (n > 1)$ satisfying $\rho_\mathfrak{I}(\hat{\tau}, \tau_0) \xrightarrow{p} 0$, we have $\nu_n(\hat{\tau}_n) - \nu_n(\tau_0) \xrightarrow{p} 0$.

The above definitions of stochastic equicontinuity are from Andrews (1994); also see Billingsley (1968, p. 55).

The concept of stochastic equicontinuity provides weak convergence and asymptotic normality of $\nu_n(\tau)$. For example, from Pollard (1990), if $(\mathfrak{I}, \rho_y)$ is a totally bounded pseudo-metric space, ν_n is stochastically equicontinuous, and $\{(\nu_n(\tau_1), \ldots, \nu_n(\tau_L))'\}$ converges in distribution for all finite-dimensional vectors $(\tau_1, \ldots, \tau_L)'$ then $\nu_n(\cdot)$ converges weakly to a stochastic process on $\mathfrak{I}$ that has uniformly $\rho_\mathfrak{I}$-continuous sample paths.

Now we consider the asymptotic normality of the semiparametric estimators $\hat{\theta}$ that are a solution of the first-order condition

$$\frac{1}{\sqrt{n}} \sum_{i=1}^n m\,(X_i, \theta, \hat{\tau}) = \sqrt{n}\bar{m}_n(\theta, \hat{\tau}) = 0, \tag{A.68}$$

where θ is a R^p parameter vector and $\hat{\tau}$ is a preliminary nonparametric estimator of an infinite-dimensional parameter, for example a regression or density function. It follows from Andrews (1994) that if $\hat{\tau}$ is consistent for τ_0 with respect to pseudo-metric ρ_y, $\nu_n(\tau)$ is stochastically equicontinuous, and

$$\frac{1}{\sqrt{n}} \sum_{i=1}^n Em\,(X_i, \theta, \hat{\tau}) \xrightarrow{p} 0 \tag{A.69}$$

then

$$\sqrt{n}\left(\hat{\theta} - \theta_0\right) \xrightarrow{d} \mathcal{N}\left(0, M^{-1}S(M^{-1})'\right), \tag{A.70}$$

where $M = n^{-1} \sum^n E\left(\partial/\partial\theta'\right) m_i\,(\theta_0, \tau_0)$ as $n \to \infty$ and S is the asymptotic covariance matrix of $n^{-1/2} \sum^n m\,(X_i, \theta_0, \tau_0)$, that is, $S = V(\sqrt{n}\bar{m}_n\,(\theta_0, \tau_0))$ as $n \to \infty$. The proof follows by using element-by-element mean value expansion of $\sqrt{n}\bar{m}_n\left(\hat{\theta}, \hat{\tau}\right)$ around θ_0. This gives

$$0 = \sqrt{n}\bar{m}_n\left(\hat{\theta}_0, \hat{\tau}\right) = \sqrt{n}\bar{m}_n(\theta_0, \hat{\tau}) + \frac{\partial}{\partial\theta'}\bar{m}_n\left(\theta^*, \hat{\tau}\right)\sqrt{n}\left(\hat{\theta} - \theta_0\right), \tag{A.71}$$

where θ^* lies between $\hat\theta$ and θ_0. Under suitable conditions on $m_i(\theta, \tau) = m(X_i, \theta, \tau)$ one can show that

$$\frac{\partial}{\partial\theta'}\bar m_n(\theta^*, \hat\tau) = M + o_p(1). \tag{A.72}$$

Thus, for large n,

$$\sqrt{n}\left(\hat\theta - \theta_0\right) = \left(M^{-1} + o_p(1)\right)\sqrt{n}\bar m_n(\theta_0, \hat\tau) \tag{A.73}$$

$$\xrightarrow{d} M^{-1}\sqrt{n}\bar m_n(\theta_0, \tau_0) + M^{-1}\sqrt{n}\left(\bar m_n(\theta_0, \hat\tau)\right.$$
$$\left. - \bar m_n(\theta_0, \tau_0)\right). \tag{A.74}$$

But

$$\sqrt{n}(\bar m_n(\theta_0, \hat\tau) - \bar m_n(\theta_0, \tau_0)) = v_n(\hat\tau) - v_n(\tau_0) - \sqrt{n}\bar m_n^*(\theta_0, \hat\tau)$$

tends in probability to zero if $v_n(\tau)$ is stochastically equicontinuous. Hence the result in (A.70) follows under general conditions by a central limit theorem.

We observe that the condition in (A.69) is an asymptotic orthogonality condition between $\hat\theta$ and $\hat\tau$ that is analogous to the block diagonality of the information matrix in case of maximum likelihood estimation with finite-dimensioned τ.

Andrews (1994) also provides the sufficient conditions of stochastic equicontinuity for the classes of smooth functions $m_i(\cdot, \tau)$ and underlying random variables X_i that are strong mixing with $\sum_{j=1}^\infty \alpha_j < \infty$, where α_j is the strong mixing coefficient.

Andrews's MINPIN Estimators

The MINPIN estimators are defined as estimators that minimize a criterion function that may depend on a preliminary infinite-dimensional nuisance parameter estimator. Most of the parametric and semiparametric estimators can essentially be seen as the MINPIN estimator. To define the MINPIN estimator let $d\left(\bar m_n(\theta, \hat\tau), \hat\Omega\right)$ be a nonrandom, real-valued discrepancy function, for example $\bar m'\hat\Omega\bar m/2$, where $\hat\Omega$ is a preliminary nuisance parameter estimator. Then $\hat\theta$ is a MINPIN estimator of the p-dimensional vector θ if

$$d\left(\bar m_n(\hat\theta, \hat\tau), \hat\Omega\right) = \inf_\theta d\left(\bar m_n(\theta, \hat\tau), \hat\Omega\right). \tag{A.75}$$

We note that $\hat\Omega$ could be infinite dimensional, and often it is an estimated weight matrix. In the special case where $k = p$ we get $\hat\theta$ as obtained from (A.68). Examples of MINPIN estimators include the semiparametric estimators discussed in Chapter 5.

Now we look into the conditions for the normality of the MINPIN estimator $\hat\theta$. We make the following assumptions (Andrews, 1994):

(a) $\hat{\theta} \xrightarrow{P} \theta_0$, where θ_0 is an interior point.

(b) $P(\hat{\tau} \in \Im) \to 1$, $\hat{\tau} \xrightarrow{P} \tau_0$, and $\hat{\Omega} \xrightarrow{P} \Omega_0$.

(c) $\sqrt{n} \frac{\partial}{\partial m} d\left(\bar{m}_n^*(\theta_0, \hat{\tau}), \hat{\Omega}\right) \xrightarrow{P} 0$.

(d) $\{v_n(\tau)\}$ is stochastically equicontinuous.

(e) $\frac{\partial}{\partial m} d(m, \Omega)$ and $\frac{\partial^2}{\partial m \partial m'} d(m, \Omega)$ exist for all (m, τ) and are continuous at $(m, \gamma) = (m(\theta_0, \tau_0), \gamma_0)$.

(f) $m_i(\theta, \tau)$ is twice continuously differentiable for all θ and τ. $m_i(\theta, \tau)$ and $\frac{\partial}{\partial \theta'} m_i(\theta, \tau)$ satisfy uniform WLLNs. Further, both $m(\theta, \tau) = \lim n^{-1} \sum E m_i(\theta \tau)$ as $n \to \infty$ and M exist uniformly over θ and τ and are continuous at (θ_0, τ_0) with respect to some pseudo-metric for which $(\hat{\theta}, \hat{\tau}) \xrightarrow{P} (\theta_0, \tau_0)$. Also, $n^{-1} \sum^n E B_i < \infty$ as $n \to \infty$, where

$$B_i = \sup_{\theta, \tau} \left\| \frac{\partial^2}{\partial \theta \partial \theta'} m_i(\theta, \tau) \right\|.$$

(g) $M'DM$ is nonsingular, where $D = \frac{\partial^2}{\partial m \partial m'} d(m(\theta_0, \tau_0), \gamma_0)$.

Under these assumptions the MINPIN estimator $\hat{\theta}$ satisfies

$$\sqrt{n}\left(\hat{\theta} - \theta\right) \sim \mathcal{N}(0, V) \tag{A.76}$$

as $n \to \infty$, where

$$V = (M'DM)^{-1} M'DSDM(M'DM)^{-1}.$$

When $p = k$, V becomes $M^{-1} S (M^{-1})'$ as given in (A.70).

If $d(m, \Omega) = m' \Omega m / 2$ then the assumption g can be relaxed by dropping the condition on $E B_i$ and changing $m_i(\theta, \theta)$ to be differentiable only once.

A consistent estimator of V can be written as

$$\hat{V} = (\hat{M}'\hat{D}\hat{M})^{-1} \hat{M}'\hat{D}\hat{S}\hat{D}\hat{M}(\hat{M}'\hat{D}\hat{M})^{-1}, \tag{A.77}$$

where

$$\hat{D} = \frac{\partial^2}{\partial m \partial m'} d\left(\bar{m}_n(\hat{\theta}, \hat{\tau}), \hat{\Omega}\right), \quad \hat{M} = \frac{1}{n} \sum^n \frac{\partial}{\partial \theta'} m_i(\hat{\theta}, \hat{\tau}), \tag{A.78}$$

and

$$\hat{S} = \frac{1}{n} \sum^n m_i(\hat{\theta}, \hat{\tau}) m_i(\hat{\theta}, \hat{\tau})'. \tag{A.79}$$

The function $\hat{S}$ is consistent under a to g with $(\partial / \partial \theta') m_i(\theta, \tau)$ replaced by $m_i(\theta, \tau) m_i(\theta, \tau)'$. If $m_i(\theta, \tau)$ is not i.i.d. then the estimators $\hat{S}$ needs to be replaced by heteroskedastic and autocorrelation consistent covariance matrix estimators.

References

Abdulal, H. I. (1984), *On Density Estimation*, Ph.D. thesis, Colorado State University.

Abramson, I. S. (1982), "On Bandwidth Variation in Kernel Estimates – A Square Root Law," *Annals of Statistics*, 10, 1217–1223.

Afriat, S. (1967), "The Construction of Utility Functions from Expenditure Data," *International Economic Review*, 8, 67–77.

Ahmad, I. A. (1979), "Strong Consistency of Density Estimation by Orthogonal Series Methods for Dependent Variables with Applications," *Annals of the Institute of Statistical Mathematics*, 31, 279–288.

Ahmad, I. A. (1980), "Nonparametric Estimation of an Affinity Measure between Two Absolutely Continuous Distributions with Hypothesis Testing Applications," *Annals of the Institute of Statistical Mathematics*, 32, Part A, 223–240.

Ahmad, I. A. and Q. Li (1997a), "Testing Symmetry of an Unknown Density Function by Kernel Method," *Journal of Nonparametric Statistics*, 7, 279–293.

Ahmad, I. A. and Q. Li (1997b), "Testing Independence by Nonparametric Kernel Method," *Statistics and Probability Letters*, 34, 201–210.

Ahmad, I. A. and P. E. Lin (1976), "Nonparametric Sequential Estimation of a Multiple Regression Function," *Bulletin of Mathematical Statistics*, 17, 63–75.

Ahmad, I. A. and P. E. Lin (1984), "Fitting a Multiple Regression," *Journal of Statistical Planning and Inference*, 2, 163–176.

Ahmad, I. A. and A. Ullah (1988), Nonparametric Estimation of the p-th Order Derivative of a Regression Function, London, University of Western Ontario.

Ahmad, I. A. and G. Van Belle (1974), "Measuring Affinity of Distributions," in F. Proschan and R. J. Serfling (eds.), *Reliability and Biometry: Statistical Analysis of Lifelength*, Philadelphia, SIAM, 651–668.

Ahn, H. and J. L. Powell (1993), "Semiparametric Estimation of Censored Selection Models with a Nonparametric Selection Mechanism," *Journal of Econometrics*, 58, 3–29.

Ai, C. (1997), "A Semiparametric Maximum Likelihood Estimator," *Econometrica*, 65, 933–963.

Aigner, D. J., T. Amemiya, and D. Poirier (1976), "On the Estimation of Production Frontiers: Maximum Likelihood Estimation of the Parameters of a Discontinuous Density Function," *International Economic Review*, 17, 377–396.

Ait-Sahalia, Y. (1994), "The Delta Method for Nonparametric Kernel Functionals," manuscript, University of Chicago.

Ait-Sahalia, Y. (1996a), "Testing Continuous Time Models of the Spot Interest Rate," *Review of Financial Studies*, 2, 385–426.

Ait-Sahalia, Y. (1996b), "Nonparametric Pricing of Interest Rate Derivative Securities," *Econometrica*, 64, 527–560.

Akaike, H. (1974), "A New Look at the Statistical Model Identification," *IEEE Transactions on Automatic Control AC*, 19, 716–723.

Alessie, R., A. Lusardi, and T. Aldershof (1997), "Income and Wealth over the Life Cycle: Evidence from Panel Data," *Review of Income and Wealth*, 43, 1–31.

Altman, N. S. (1990), "Kernel Smoothing of Data with Correlated Errors," *Journal of the American Statistical Association*, 85, 749–759.

Altug, S. and P. A. Miller (1998), "The Effect of Work Experience on Female Wages and Labor Supply," *Review of Economic Studies*, 65, 45–48.

Amemiya, T. (1973), "Regression Analysis When the Dependent Variable is Truncated Normal," *Econometrica*, 41, 997–1016.

Amemiya, T. (1974), "The Non-Linear Two-stage Least-Squares Estimator," *Journal of Econometrics*, 2, 105–110.

Amemiya, T. (1975), "The Nonlinear Limited-Information Maximum-Likelihood Estimator and the Modified Nonlinear Two Stage Least Squares Estimator," *Journal of Econometrics*, 3, 375–386.

Amemiya, T. (1977), "The Maximum Likelihood and Nonlinear Three-Stage Least Squares Estimator in the General Nonlinear Simultaneous Equations Model," *Econometrica*, 45, 955–968.

Amemiya, T. (1981), "Qualitative Response Models: A Survey," *Journal of Economic Literature*, 19, 1483–1536.

Amemiya, T. (1983), "Nonlinear Regression Models," in Z. Griliches and M. D. Intriligator (eds.), *Handbook of Econometrics*, Amsterdam, North Holland, 334–389.

Amemiya, T. (1985), *Advanced Econometrics*, Cambridge, Harvard University Press.

Amemiya, T. and J. L. Powell (1981), "A Comparison of the Box-Cox Maximum Likelihood Estimator and the Non-Linear Two-Stage Least Squares Estimator," *Journal of Econometrics*, 17, 351–381.

Anderson, N. H., P. Hall, and D. M. Titterington (1994), "Two-Sample Test Statistics for Measuring Discrepancies between Two Multivariate Probability Density Functions Using Kernel-Based Density Estimates," *Journal of Multivariate Analysis*, 50, 41–54.

Andrews, D. W. K. (1984), "Non-Strong Mixing Autoregressive Processes," *Journal of Applied Probability*, 21, 930–934.

Andrews, D. W. K. (1988), "Law of Large Numbers for Dependent Non-Identically Distributed Random Variables," *Econometric Theory*, 4, 458–467.

Andrews, D. W. K. (1991a), "Asymptotic Normality of Series Estimators for Nonparametric and Semiparametric Regression Models," *Econometrica*, 59, 307–345.

Andrews, D. W. K. (1991b), "Heteroskedasticity and Autocorrelation Consistent Covariance Matrix Estimation," *Econometrica*, 59, 817–858.

Andrews, D. W. K. (1991c), "Asymptotic Optimality of Generalized C_L Cross-Validation, and Generalized Cross-Validation in Regression with Heteroskedastic Errors," *Journal of Econometrics*, 47, 359–377.

Andrews, D. W. K. (1991d), "An Empirical Process Central Limit Theorem for Dependent Non-Identically Distributed Random Variable," *Journal of Multivariate Analysis*, 38, 187–203.

Andrews, D. W. K. (1994), "Asymptotics for Semiparametric Econometric Models via Stochastic Equicontinuity," *Econometrica*, 62, 43–72.

Andrews, D. W. K. (1995), "Nonparametric Kernel Estimation for Semiparametric Models," *Econometric Theory*, 11, 560–596.

Andrews, D. W. K. (1997), "A Conditional Kolmogorov Test," *Econometrica*, 65, 1097–1128.

Andrews, D. W. K. and M. M. A. Schafgans (1998), "Semiparametric Estimation of the Intercept of a Sample Selection Model," *Review of Economic Studies*, 65, 497–517.

Andrews, D. W. K. and Y. J. Whang (1990), "Additive Interactive Regression Models: Circumvention of the Curse of Dimensionality," *Econometric Theory*, 6, 466–479.

Anglin, P. and R. Gencay (1996), "Semiparametric Estimation of a Hedonic Price Function," *Journal of Applied Econometrics*, 11, 633–648.

Appelbaum, E. and A. Ullah (1997), "Estimation of Moments and Production Decisions under Uncertainty," *Review of Economics and Statistics*, LXXIX, 631–637.

Arcones, M. and E. Giné (1992), "On the Bootstrap of M-Estimators and Other Statistical Functionals," in R. LePage and L. Billard (eds.), *Exploring the Limits of the Bootstrap*, Wiley, New York, 13–47.

Azuma, K. (1967), "Weighted Sums of Certain Dependent Random Variables," *Tôhoku Mathematical Journal*, 19, 357–367.

Bai, Z. D. and X. R. Chen (1987), "Necessary and Sufficient Conditions for the Convergence of Integrated and Mean-Integrated p-th Order Error of the Kernel Density Estimates," *Technical Report No. 87-06*, Center for Multivariate Analysis, University of Pittsburgh.

Barnett, W. A. and P. Yue (1988), "Semiparametric Estimation of the Asymptotically Ideal Model Demand System," in G. Rhodes and T. B. Fomby (ed.), *Nonparametric and Robust Inference Model, Advances in Econometrics*, 7, 229–251, JAI Press.

Barro, R. (1977), "Unanticipated Money Growth and Unemployment in the United States," *American Economic Review*, 67, 101–115.

Bartle, R. G. (1966), *The Elements of Integration*, New York, John Wiley.

Bartlett, M. S. (1963), "Statistical Estimation of Density Functions," *Sankhya*, A, 25, 245–254.

Basu, R. and A. Ullah (1992), "Chinese Earnings–Age Profile: A Nonparametric analysis," *Journal of International Trade and Economic Development*, 1, 151–165.

Bean, C. (1986), "The Estimation of 'Surprise' Models and the 'Surprise' Consumption Function," *Review of Economic Studies*, 53, 497–516.

Begun, J. M., W. J. Hall, W. Huang, and J. A. Wellner (1983), "Information and Asymptotic Efficiency in Parametric–Nonparametric Models," *Annals of Statistics*, 11, 432–452.

Benedetti, J. K. (1977), "On the Nonparametric Estimates of Regression Function," *Journal of the Royal Statistical Society*, Series B, 39, 248–253.

Bennett, G. (1962), "Probability Inequalities for Sums of Independent Random Variables," *Journal of the American Statistical Association*, 57, 33–45.

Bera, A. K. and C. M. Jarque (1981), "Efficient Tests for Normality, Homoscedasticity and Serial Independence of Regression Residuals: Monte Carlo Evidence," *Economics Letters*, 7, 313–318.

Bera, A. K. and P. T. Ng (1992), "Robust Tests for Heteroskedasticity and Autocorrelation Using Score Function," Faculty Working Paper 0171, *Bureau of Economic and Business Research*, University of Illinois.

Beran, R. (1976), "Adaptive Estimates for Autoregressive Processes," *Annals of the Institute of Statistical Mathematics*, 28, 77–89.

Berndt, E. R., B. M. Hall, R. E. Hall, and J. A. Hausman (1974), "Estimation and Inference in Nonlinear Structural Models," *Annals of Economic and Social Measurement*, 3, 653–666.

Berndt, E. R. and M. S. Khaled (1979), "Parametric Productivity Measurement and Choice among Flexible Functional Forms," *Journal of Political Economy*, 87, 1220–1245.

Berry, A. C. (1941), "The Accuracy of the Gaussian Approximation to the Sum of Independent Variates," *Transactions of the American Mathematical Society*, 49, 122–136.

Bertrand-Retali, M. (1978), "Convergence Uniforme d'un Estimateur de la Densité par la Méthode du Noyau," *Reveue Roumaine de Mathématiques Pures et Appliquées*, 23, 361–385.

Bhattacharya, P. K. (1967), "Estimation of a Probability Density Function and Its Derivatives," *Sankhya*, Series A, 29, 373–82.

Bhattacharya, P. K. and Y. P. Mack (1987), "Weak Convergence of k-NN Density and Regression Estimators with Varying k and Applications," *Annals of Statistics*, 15, 976–994.

Bickel, P. J. (1978), "Using Residuals Robustly I: Tests for Heteroscedasticity, Nonlinearity," *Annals of Statistics*, 6, 266–291.

Bickel, P. J. (1982), "On Adaptive Estimation," *Annals of Statistics*, 10, 647–671.

Bickel, P. J., C. A. J. Klaassen, Y. Ritov, and J. A. Wellner (1993), *Efficient and Adaptive Estimation for Semiparametric Models*, Baltimore, Johns Hopkins Press.

Bickel, P. J. and M. Rosenblatt (1973), "On Some Global Measures of the Deviations of Density Function Estimates," *Annals of Statistics*, 1, 1071–1095.

Bierens, H. J. (1981), *Robust Methods and Asymptotic Theory in Nonlinear Econometrics*, Lecture Notes in Economics and Mathematical Systems, Berlin, Springer-Verlag.

Bierens, H. J. (1982), "Consistent Model Specification Tests," *Journal of Econometrics*, 20, 105–134.

Bierens, H. J. (1983), "Uniform Consistency of Kernel Estimators of a Regression Function under Generalized Conditions," *Journal of the American Statistical Association*, 77, 699–707.

Bierens, H. J. (1987a), "Kernel Estimators of Regression Functions," Ch. 3 in T. F. Bewley (ed.), *Advances in Econometrics*, Cambridge University Press, Vol. I, 99–144.

Bierens, H. J. (1987b), "Convergence," *Research Report 19*, Free University, Amsterdam.

Bierens, H. J. (1990), "A Consistent Conditional Moment Test of Functional Form," *Econometrica*, 58, 1443–1458.

Bierens, H. J. and W. Ploberger (1997), "Asymptotic Theory of Integrated Conditional Moment Tests," *Econometrica*, 65, 1129–1151.

Bierens, H. J. and H. A. Pott-Buter (1990), "Specification of Household Engel Curves by Nonparametric Regression," *Econometric Reviews*, 9, 123–184.

Billingsley, P. (1968), *Convergence of Probability Measures*, New York, Wiley.

Boente, G. and R. Fraiman (1988), "Consistency of a Nonparametric Estimate of a Density Function for Dependent Variables," *Journal of Multivariate Analysis*, 25, 90–99.

Boneva, L. I., D. Kendall, and I. Stefanov (1970), "Spline Transformations: Three New Diagnostic Aids for the Statistical Data Analyst," *Journal of the Royal Statistical Society*, Series B, 32, 1–71.

Bossaerts, P., C. Hafner, and W. Härdle, (1996), "Foreign Exchange Rates Have Surprising Volatility," in P. M. Robinson and M. Rosenblatt (eds.), *Athens Conference on Applied Probability and Time Series*, Vol. II, New York, Springer, 55–72.

Bossaerts, P. and P. Hillion (1997), "Local Parametric Analysis of Hedging in Discrete Time," *Journal of Econometrics*, 81, 243–272.

Bowden, R. (1973), "The Theory of Parametric Identification," *Econometrica*, 41, 1069–1074.

Bowden, R. J. and D. A. Turkington (1981), "A Comparative Study of Instrumental Variables Estimators for Nonlinear Simultaneous Models," *Journal of the American Statistical Association*, 76, 988–995.

Bowman, A. W. (1984), "An Alternative Method of Cross-Validation for the Smoothing of Density Estimates," *Biometrika*, 71, 353–360.

Bowman, K. O. and L. R. Shenton (1975), "Omnibus Test Contours for Departures from Normality based on $\sqrt{b_1}$ and b_2," *Biometrika*, 62, 243–250.

Bradley, R. C. (1980a), "On the ϕ-Mixing Condition for Stationary Random Sequences," *Duke Mathematical Journal*, 47, 421–433.

Bradley, R. C. (1980b), "On the Strong Mixing and Weak Bernouilli Conditions," *Zeitschrift für Wahrscheinlichkeitstheorie und Verwandte Gabiet*, 51, 49–54.

Bradley, R. C. (1980c), "A Remark on the Central Limit Question for Dependent Random Variables," *Journal of Applied Probability*, 17, 94–101.

Bradley, R. C. (1980d), "A Note on Strong Mixing Conditions," *Annals of Probability*, 8, 636–638.

Bradley, R. C. (1981a), "A Sufficient Condition for Linear Growth of Variances in Stationary Random Sequences," *Proceedings of the American Mathematical Society*, 83, 586–593.

Bradley, R. C. (1981b), "Central Limit Theorems Under Weak Dependence," *Journal of Multivariate Analysis*, 11, 1–16.

Breiman, L. and J. Friedman (1985), "Estimating Optimal Transformations for Multiple Regression and Correlation," *Journal of the American Statistical Association*, 80, 580–619.

Breiman, L., W. Meisel, and E. Purcell (1977), "Variable Kernel Estimates of Multivariate Densities," *Technometrics*, 19, 135–144.

388   Nonparametric Econometrics

Breslaw, J. A. (1995), "Nonparametric Estimation of Welfare Changes," *Econometric Reviews*, 14, 163–182.

Breusch, T. S. and A. R. Pagan (1979), "A Simple Test for Heteroscedasticity and Random Coefficient Variation," *Econometrica*, 47, 1287–1294.

Breusch, T. S. and A. R. Pagan (1980), "The Lagrange Multiplier Test and Its Applications to Model Specification in Econometrics," *Review of Economic Studies*, 47, 239–253.

Brown, B. W. (1983), "The Identification Problem in Systems Nonlinear in the Variables," *Econometrica*, 51, 175–196.

Brown, B. W. and R. S. Mariano (1984), "Residual-Based Procedures for Prediction and Estimation in a Nonlinear Simultaneous System," *Econometrica*, 52, 321–343.

Buchinsky, M. (1994), "Changes in the US Wage Structure, 1963–1987: Application of Quantile Regression," *Econometrica*, 62, 405–458.

Buckley, J. and I. James (1979) "Linear Regression with Censored Data," *Biometrika*, 66, 429–436.

Budd, J. W. (1993), "Changing Food Prices and Rural Welfare: A Nonparametric Examination of the Côte d'Ivoire," *Economic Development and Cultural Change*, 41, 587–603.

Buja, A., T. Hastie, and R. Tibshirani (1989), "Linear Smoothers and Additive Models" (with discussion), *Annals of Statistics*, 17, 453–555.

Burbidge, J. B. and J. B. Davies (1994), "Household Data on Saving Behavior in Canada," in J. M. Poterba (ed.), *International Comparisons of Household Saving*, University of Chicago Press for the NBER, 11–56.

Burguete, J. F., A. R. Gallant, and G. Souza (1982), "On the Unification of the Asymptotic Theory of Nonlinear Econometric Models," *Econometric Reviews*, 1, 151–190.

Byron, R. P. and A. K. Bera (1983), "Least Squares Approximations to Unknown Regression Functions: A Comment," *International Economic Review*, 24, 255–260.

Cacoullos, T. (1966), "Estimation of a Multivariate Density," *Annals of the Institute of Statistical Mathematics*, 18, 179–189.

Carbon, M. (1983), "Inégalite de Bernstein pour les Processus Fortement Mélangeants, Non Nécessairement Stationnaires," *Comptes Rendus des Séances de l'Académie des Sciences*, Paris, I, 297, 303–306.

Carroll, R. J. (1982), "Adapting for Heteroscedasticity in Linear Models," *Annals of Statistics*, 10, 1224–1233.

Carroll, R. J. and W. Härdle (1988), "Symmetrized Nearest Neighbor Regression Estimates," *Letters in Probability and Statistics*, 7, 315–318.

Carroll, R. J. and D. Ruppert (1982), "Robust Estimation of Heteroskedastic Linear Models," *Annals of Statistics*, 10, 429–441.

Carroll, R. J. and D. Ruppert (1984), "Power Transformations When Fitting Theoretical Models to Data," *Journal of the American Statistical Association*, 79, 321–328.

Carroll, R. J. and D. Ruppert (1988), *Transformations and Weighting in Regression*, New York, Chapman and Hall.

Castellana, J. V. and M. R. Leadbetter (1986), "On Smooth Probability Density Estimation for Stationary Processes," *Stochastic Processes and Their Applications*, 21, 179–193.

Čencov, N. N. (1962), "Evaluation of an Unknown Distribution Density from Observations," *Soviet Mathematics*, 3, 1559–1562.

Chalfant, J. A. and A. R. Gallant (1985), "Estimating Substitution Elasticities with the Fourier Cost Function: Some Monte Carlo Results," *Journal of Econometrics*, 28, 205–222.

Chamberlain, G. (1984), "Comments to 'Adaptive Estimation of Non-Linear Regression Models'," *Econometric Reviews*, 3, 199–202.

Chamberlain, G. (1986), "Asymptotic Efficiency in Semiparametric Models with Censoring," *Journal of Econometrics*, 32, 189–218.

Chamberlain, G. (1987), "Asymptotic Efficiency in Estimation with Conditional Moment Restrictions," *Journal of Econometrics*, 34, 305–334.

Chen, R., W. Härdle, O. B. Linton, and E. Sevarance-Lossin (1996), "Nonparametric Estimation of Additive Separable Regression Models," *Statistical Theory and Computational Aspects of Smoothing*, Physica Verlag, 247–265.

Cheng, K. F. and P. E. Lin (1981), "Nonparametric Estimation of a Regression Function," *Zeitschrift für Wahrscheinlichkeitstheorie und Verwandte Gebiete*, 57, 223–233.

Chesher, A., T. Lancaster, and M. Irish (1985), "On Detecting the Failure of Distributional Assumptions," *Annales de l'INSEE*, 59/60, 7–44.

Choi, K. (1990), "The Semiparametric Estimation of the Sample Selection Model Using Series Expansion and the Propensity Score," manuscript, University of Chicago.

Chow, G. C. (1983), *Econometrics*, New York, McGraw-Hill.

Christensen, L., D. Jorgenson, and L. Lau (1973), "Transcendental Logarithmic Production Frontiers," *Review of Economics and Statistics*, 55, 28–45.

Chu, C. K. (1989), "Comparison of Two Kernel Estimators," manuscript, University of North Carolina.

Chu, C. K. and J. S. Marron (1991), "Choosing a Kernel Regression Estimator," *Statistical Science*, 6, 404–436.

Chung, K. L. (1974), *A Course in Probability Theory*, 2nd ed., New York, Academic Press.

Clark, R. M. (1980), "Calibration, Cross Validation and Carbon-14 II," *Journal of the Royal Statistical Society*, Series A, 143, 177–194.

Cleveland, W. S. (1979), "Robust Locally Weighted Regression and Smoothing Scatterplots," *Journal of the American Statistical Association*, 74, 829–836.

Cleveland, W. S., S. J. Devlin, and E. Grosse (1988), "Regression by Local Fitting," *Journal of Econometrics*, 37, 87–114.

Collomb, G. (1981), "Estimation Nonparamétrique de la Régression: Revue Bibliographique," *International Statistical Review*, 49, 75–93.

Collomb, G. (1984), "Propriétés de Convergence Presque Complète du Prédicteur à Noyau," *Zeitschrift für Wahrscheinlichkeitstheorie und Verwandte Gebiete*, 66, 441–460.

Conley, T. G. and D. W. Galenson (1994), "Quantile Regression Analysis of Censored Wealth Data," *Historical Studies*, 27, 149–165.

Copas, J. B. (1995), "Local Likelihood Based on Kernel Censoring," *Journal of the Royal Statistical Society*, Series B, 57, 221–235.

Cosslett, S. R. (1983), "Distribution-Free Maximum Likelihood Estimator of the Binary Choice Model," *Econometrica*, 51, 765–782.

Cosslett, S. R. (1987), "Efficiency Bounds for Distribution-Free Estimators of the Binary Choice and the Censored Regression Models," *Econometrica*, 55, 559–585.

Cosslett, S. R. (1991), "Semiparametric Estimation of a Regression Model with Sampling Selectivity," in W. A. Barnett, J. Powell, and G. E. Tauchen (eds.), *Nonparametric and Semiparametric Methods in Econometrics and Statistics*, New York, Cambridge University Press, 175–197.

Coulson, N. E. and R. P. Robins (1985), "Aggregate Economic Activity and the Variance of Inflation: Another Look," *Economics Letters*, 17, 71–75.

Cox, D. R. and D. V. Hinkley (1974), *Theoretical Statistics*, London, Chapman and Hall.

Cramér, H. (1974), *Mathematical Methods of Statistics*, Princeton, Princeton University Press.

Craven, P. and G. Wahba (1979), "Smoothing Noisy Data with Spline Functions," *Numerische Mathematik*, 31, 377–403.

Cristóbal, J. A., P. F. Roca, and W. G. Manteiga (1987), "A Class of Linear Regression Parameter Estimates Constructed by Nonparametric Estimation," *Annals of Statistics*, 15, 602–609.

Das, S. (1991), "A Semiparametric Structural Analysis of the Idling of Cement Kilns," *Journal of Econometrics*, 50, 235–256.

Daubechies, I. (1992), *Ten Lectures on Wavelets,* Philadelphia, SIAM.

Davis, K. B. (1975), "Mean Square Error Properties of Density Estimates," *Annals of Statistics*, 3, 1025–1030.

Davis, K. B. (1977), "Mean Integrated Square Error Properties of Density Estimates," *Annals of Statistics*, 5, 530–535.

Deaton, A. (1989), "Rice Prices and Income Distribution in Thailand: A Nonparametric Analysis," *Economic Journal*, 99, 1–37.

Deaton, A. (1997), *The Analysis of Household Surveys: Micro Econometric Analysis for Development Policy*, John Hopkins University Press for the World Bank, Maryland.

Deaton A. and S. Ng (1998), "Parametric and Nonparametric Approaches to Price and Tax Reforms," *Journal of the American Statistical Association*, 93, 900–909.

Deheuvels, P. (1974), "Conditions Nécessaires et Suffsantes de Convergerce Presque Sûre et Uniforme Presque Sûre des Estimateurs de la Densité," *Comptes Rendus Academie des Sciences de Paris*, Series A, 278, 1217–1220.

Deheuvels, P. (1977), "Estimation Nonparametrique de la Densite par Histogrammes Generalises," *Revue de Statistique Appliquee*, 35, 5–42.

Deheuvels, P. (1979), "Estimation Nonparametrique de la Densite Comptetenu d'Information sur le Support," *Revue de Statistique Appliquee*, 27, 47–68.

Delgado, M. A. (1992), "Semiparametric Generalized Least Squares in the Multivariate Nonlinear Regression Model," *Econometric Theory*, 8, 203–222.

Delgado, M. A., Q. Li, and T. Stengos (1996), "Nonparametric Specification Testing of Non-Nested Econometric Models," manuscript, Universidad Carlos III de Madrid.

Delgado, M. A. and J. Mora (1995), "Nonparametric and Semiparametric Estimation with Discrete Regressors," *Econometrica*, 63, 1477–1484.

Delgado, M. A. and J. Mora (1998), "Testing Non-Nested Semiparametric Models: An Application to Engel Curve Specification," *Journal of Applied Econometrics*, 13, 145–162.

Delgado, M. A. and T. Stengos (1994), "Semiparametric Specification Testing of Non-Nested Econometric Models," *Review of Economic Studies*, 61, 291–303.

Denby, L. (1986), "Smooth Regression Functions," *Statistical Research Report No. 26*, Bell Laboratories.

Devroye, L. P. (1978), "The Uniform Convergence of the Nadaraya–Watson Regression Function Estimate," *Canadian Journal of Statistics*, 6, 179–191.

Devroye, L. P. (1981), "On the Almost Everywhere Convergence of Nonparametric Regression Function Estimates," *Annals of Statistics*, 9, 1310–1319.

Devroye, L. P. (1983), "The Equivalence of Weak, Strong and Complete Convergence in L_1 for Kernel Density Estimates," *Annals of Statistics*, 11, 896–904.

Devroye, L. P. and L. Györfi (1985), *Nonparametric Density Estimation*, New York, Wiley.

Devroye, L. P. and T. J. Wagner (1979), "The L_1 Convergence of Kernel Density Estimates," *Annals of Statistics*, 7, 1136–1139.

Devroye, L. P. and T. J. Wagner (1980a), "On the L_1 Convergence of Kernel Estimators of Regression Functions with Applications in Discrimination," *Zeitschrift für Wahrscheinlichkeitstheorie und Verwandte Gabiet*, 51, 15–25.

Devroye, L. P. and T. J. Wagner (1980b), "Distribution Free Consistency Results in Nonparametric Discrimination and Regression Function Estimation," *Annals of Statistics*, 8, 231–239.

Devroye, L. P. and T. J. Wagner (1980c), "The Strong Uniform Consistency of Kernel Density Estimates," in P. R. Krishnaiah (ed.), *Multivariate Analysis*, Vol. 5, New York, North-Holland, 59–77.

Diebold, F. and J. Nason (1990), "Nonparametric Exchange Rate Prediction," *Journal of International Economics*, 28, 315–332.

Diewert, W. E. (1971), "An Application of the Shephard Duality Theorem: A Generalized Leontief Production Function," *Journal of Political Economy*, 79, 481–507.

Diewert, W. E. and C. Parkan (1978), "Tests for the Consistency of Consumer Data and Nonparametric Index Numbers," *Discussion Paper 78-27*, University of British Columbia.

Dinardo, J., N. M. Fortin, and T. Lemieux (1996), "Labor Market Institutions and the Distribution of Wages, 1973–1992: A Semiparametric Approach," *Econometrica*, 64, 5, 1001–1044.

Dodge, Y. (1986), "Some Difficulties Involving Nonparametric Estimation of a Density Function," *Journal of Official Statistics*, 2, 193–202.

Domowitz, I. and H. White (1982), "Misspecified Models with Dependent Observations," *Journal of Econometrics*, 20, 35–38.

Donald, S. G. and W. K. Newey (1994), "Series Estimation of Semilinear Models," *Journal of Multivariate Analysis*, 50, 30–40.

Doob, J. (1953), *Stochastic Processes*, New York, Wiley.

Drost, F. and C. Klassen (1997), "Efficient Estimation in Semiparametric GARCH Models," *Journal of Econometrics*, 81, 193–221.

Duin, R. P. W. (1976), "On the Choice of Smoothing Parameters for Parzen Estimators of Probability Density Function," *IEEE Transactions on Computers*, C-25, 1175–1179.

Duncan, G. M. (1986), "A Semiparametric Censored Regression Estimator," *Journal of Econometrics*, 32, 5–34.

Duncan, G. M. (1987), "A Simplified Approach to M-Estimation with Application to Two-Stage Estimators," *Journal of Econometrics*, 34, 373–389.

Durbin, J. (1970), "Testing for Serial Correlation in Least Squares Regression When Some of the Regressors Are Lagged Dependent Variables," *Econometrica*, 38, 410–421.

Eastwood, B. J. and A. R. Gallant (1991), "Adaptive Rules for Seminonparametric Estimators that Achieve Asymptotic Normality," *Econometric Theory*, 7, 307–340.

Edmunds, D. E. and V. B. Moscatelli (1977), "Fourier Approximation and Embeddings of Sobolev Spaces," *Dissertiones Mathematicae*, 145, 1–46.

Engle, R. F. (1982), "Autoregressive Conditional Heteroscedasticity with Estimates of the Variance of United Kingdom Inflation," *Econometrica*, 50, 987–1007.

Engle, R. F. (1984), "Wald, Likelihood Ratio and Lagrange Multiplier Tests in Econometrics," in Z. Griliches and M. D. Intriligator (eds.), *Handbook of Econometrics*, Vol. II, Amsterdam, North-Holland, 775–826.

Engle, R. F. and G. Gonzalez-Rivera (1991), "Semiparametric ARCH Models," *Journal of Business and Economic Statistics*, 9, 345–359.

Engle, R. F., C. W. J. Granger, J. Rice, and A. Weiss (1986), "Semiparametric Estimates of the Relation between Weather and Electricity Sales," *Journal of the American Statistical Association*, 81, 310–320.

Engle, R. F., D. M. Lilien, and R. P. Robins (1987), "Estimating Time Varying Risk Premia in the Term Structure: The ARCH-M Model," *Econometrica*, 55, 391–407.

Epanechnikov, V. A. (1969), "Nonparametric Estimates of a Multivariate Probability Density," *Theory of Probability and Applications*, 14, 153–158.

Epstein, L. G. and A. J. Yatchew (1985), "Nonparametric Hypothesis Testing Procedures and Applications to Demand Analysis," *Journal of Econometrics*, 30, 149–169.

Esseen, G. (1945), "Fourier Analysis of Distribution Functions. A Mathematical Study of the Laplace–Gaussian Law," *Acta Mathematica*, 77, 1–25.

Eubank, R. (1988), *Spline Smoothing and Nonparametric Regression*, New York, Dekker.

Eubank, R. L. and C. H. Spiegelman (1990), "Testing the Goodness-of-Fit of Linear Models via Nonparametric Regression Techniques," *Journal of the American Statistical Association*, 85, 387–392.

Fan, J. (1992), "Design Adaptive Nonparametric Regression," *Journal of the American Statistical Association*, 87, 998–1004.

Fan, J. (1993), "Local Linear Regression Smoothers and Their Minimax Efficiences," *Annals of Statistics*, 21, 196–216.

Fan, J. and I. Gijbels (1992), "Variable Bandwidth and Local Linear Regression Smoothers," *Annals of Statistics*, 20, 2008–2036.

Fan, J. and J. S. Marron (1992), "Comparison of Data-Driven Bandwidth Selectors," *Journal of the American Statistical Association*, 85, 66–72.

Fan, Y. (1990a), "Consistent Nonparametric Multiple Regression for Dependent Heterogeneous Processes: The Fixed Design Case," *The Journal of Multivariate Analysis*, 33, 72–88.

Fan, Y. (1990b), "A Direct Way to Formulate Indirect Estimators of Average Derivatives," manuscript, University of Windsor.

Fan, Y. (1990c), *Seemingly Unrelated Essays in Econometrics*, Ph.D. thesis, Unversity of Western Ontario.

Fan, Y. (1994), "Testing the Goodness-of-Fit of a Parametric Density Function by Kernel Method," *Econometric Theory*, 10, 316–356.

Fan, Y. (1995), "Goodness-of-Fit Tests for a Multivariate Distribution by the Empirical Characteristic Function," manuscript, University of Windsor.

Fan, Y. (1995), "Bootstrapping a Consistent Nonparametric Goodness-of-Fit Test," *Econometric Reviews*, 14, 367–382.

Fan, Y. and R. Gencay (1993), "Hypothesis Testing Based on Modified Nonparametric Estimation of an Affinity Measure between Two Distributions," *Journal of Nonparametric Statistics*, 2, 389–403.

Fan, Y. and R. Gencay (1995), "A Consistent Nonparametric Test of Symmetry in Linear Regression Models," *Journal of the American Statistical Association*, 90, 551–557.

Fan, Y. and Q. Li (1996a), "Consistent Model Specification Tests: Omitted Variables and Semiparametric Functional Forms," *Econometrica*, 64, 865–890.

Fan, Y. and Q. Li (1996b), "Consistent Model Specification Tests: Nonparametric Versus Bierens' Tests," manuscript, University of Windsor.

Fan, Y. and Q. Li (1996c), "Central Limit Theorem for Degenerate U-statistics of Absolutely Regular Process with Application to Model Specification Testing," Discussion Paper, No. 8, University of Guelph.

Fan, Y., Q. Li, and T. Stengos (1995), "Root-N-Consistent Semiparametric Regression with Conditionally Heteroskedastic Disturbances," *Journal of Quantitative Economics*, 11, 229–240.

Fan, Y. and Z. Liu (1997), "A Simple Test for a Parametric Single Index Model," *Journal of Quantitative Economics*, 13, 95–103.

Fan, Y. and A. Ullah (1996), "Asymptotic Normality of a Combined Regression Estimator," manuscript, University of Windsor.

Fan, Y. and A. Ullah (1999), "On Goodness-of-Fit Tests for Weakly Dependent Processes using Kernel Methods," *Journal of Nonparametric Statistics*, forthcoming.

Feller, W. (1968), *An Introduction to Probability Theory and Its Application*, Vol. I and II, New York, Wiley.

Fernandez, L. (1986), "Nonparametric Maximum Likelihood Estimation of Censored Regression Models," *Journal of Econometrics*, 32, 35–57.

Fisher, F. M. (1966), *The Identification Problem in Econometrics*, New York, McGraw-Hill.

Fix, E. and J. L. Hodges (1951), "Discriminatory Analysis, Nonparametric Estimation: Consistency Properties," *Report No. 4, Project No. 21-49-004*, USAF School of Aviation Medicine, Randolph Field, Texas.

Földes, A. (1981), "Strong Uniform Consistency of the Product Limit Estimator under Variable Censoring," *Zeitschrift für Wahrscheinlichkeitstheorie und Verwandte Gebiete*, 58, 95–107.

Friedman, J. H. (1985), "A Variable Span Smoother," *Technical Report LCS05*, Department of Statistics, Stanford University.

Friedman, J. H. and B. W. Silverman (1989), "Flexible Parsimonious Smoothing and Additive Modelling," *Technometrics*, 31, 3–21.

Friedman, J. H. and W. Stuetzle (1981), "Projection Pursuit Regression," *Journal of the American Statistical Association*, 76, 817–823.

Friedman, J. H. and J. W. Tukey (1974), "A Projection Pursuit Algorithm for Exploratory Data Analysis," *IEEE Transactions on Computers*, C-23, 881–890.

Fuller, W. A. (1976), *Introduction to Statistical Time Series*, New York, Wiley.

Gabler, S., F. Laisney, and M. Lechner (1993), "Seminonparametric Estimation of Binary Choice Models with an Application to Labor Force Participation," *Journal of Business and Economic Statistics*, 11, 61–80.

Gallant, A. R. (1981), "On the Bias in Flexible Functional Forms and an Essentially Unbiased Form: The Fourier Flexible Form," *Journal of Econometrics*, 15, 211–245.

Gallant, A. R. (1982), "Unbiased Determination of Production Technologies," *Journal of Econometrics*, 20, 285–323.

Gallant, A. R. (1987), "Identification and Consistency in Seminonparametric Regression," in T. F. Bewley (ed.), *Advances in Econometrics: Fifth World Congress Vol. 1*, Cambridge, Cambridge University Press, 145–170.

Gallant, A. R. and G. H. Golub (1984), "Imposing Curvature Restrictions on Flexible Functional Forms," *Journal of Econometrics*, 26, 295–321.

Gallant, A. R., D. Hsieh, and G. Tauchen (1991), "On Fitting a Recalcitrant Series: The Pound/Dollar Exchange Rate, 1974–83," in W. A. Barnett, J. Powell, and G. E. Tauchen (eds.), *Nonparametric and Semiparametric Methods in Econometrics and Statistics*, Cambridge, Cambridge University Press, 199–240.

Gallant, A. R. and D. W. Nychka (1987), "Seminonparametric Maximum Likelihood Estimation," *Econometrica*, 55, 363–390.

Gallant, A. R. and G. Tauchen (1989), "Semiparametric Estimation of Conditionally Constrained Heterogenous Processes: Asset Pricing Applications," *Econometrica*, 57, 1091–1120.

Gallant, A. R. and G. Tauchen (1992), "A Nonparametric Approach to Nonlinear Time Series Analysis: Estimation and Simulation," in D. Brillinger, P. Caines, J. Geweke, E. Parzer, M. Rosenblatt, and M. Taqqu (eds.), *New Direction in Time Series Analysis*, New York, Springer-Verlag, 71–91.

Gallant, A. R. and H. White (1988), *A Unified Theory of Estimation and Inference for Nonlinear Dynamic Models*, New York, Blackwell.

Gasser, T. and H. G. Müller (1979), "Kernel Estimation of Regression Functions," in T. Gasser and M. Rosenblatt (eds.), *Smoothing Techniques for Curve Estimation*, Lecture Notes in Mathematics, No. 757, Berlin, Springer-Verlag, 23–68.

Gasser, T. and H. G. Müller (1984), "Estimating Regression Functions and Their Derivatives by the Kernel Method," *Scandanavian Journal of Statistics*, 11, 171–185.

Gasser, T., H. G. Müller, and V. Mammitzsch (1985), "Kernels for Nonparametric Curve Estimation," *Journal of the Royal Statistical Society*, Series B, 47, 238–252.

Geman, S. and C. Hwang (1982), "Nonparametric Maximum Likelihood Estimation by the Method of Sieves," *Annals of Statistics*, 10, 401–414.

Georgiev, A. A. (1984), "Speed of Convergence in Nonparametric Kernel Estimation of Regression Function and Its Dervatives," *Annals of the Institute of Statistical Mathematics*, 36, 455–462.

Georgiev, A. A. (1988), "Consistent Nonparametric Multiple Regression: The Fixed Design Case," *Journal of Multivariate Analysis*, 25, 100–110.

Georgiev, A. A. and W. Greblicki (1986), "Nonparametric Function Recovering from Noisy Observations," *Journal of Statistical Planning and Inference*, 13, 1–14.

Gerfin, M. (1996), "Parametric and Semiparametric Estimation of the Binary Response Model of Labor Market Participation," *Journal of Applied Econometrics*, 11, 321–340.

Ghorai, J. K. and H. Rubin (1979), "Computational Procedures for Maximum Penalized Likelihood Estimate," *Journal of Statistical Computation and Simulation*, 10, 65–78.

Glad, I. K. (1998), "Parametrically Guided Nonparametric Regression," *Scandanivian Journal of Statistics*, 25, 649–668.

Godfrey, L. G. (1978), "Testing for Multiplicative Heteroskedasticity," *Journal of Econometrics*, 8, 227–236.

Gokhale, D. V., M. Rahman, and A. Ullah (1997), "A Note on Combining Parametric and Nonparametric Regression," *Communications in Statistics: Simulation and Computation*, 26, 519–529.

Goldfeld, S. M. and R. E. Quandt (1968), "Nonlinear Simultaneous Equations: Estimation and Prediction," *International Economic Review*, 9, 113–136.

González-Manteiga, W. and R. Cao-Abad (1993), "Testing the Hypothesis of a General Linear Model Using Nonparametric Regression Estimation," *Test*, 2, 161–188.

González-Rivera, G. and A. Ullah (1998), "Rao's Score Test with Nonparametric Density Estimators," *Journal of Statistical Planning and Inference*, forthcoming.

Good, I. J. and R. A. Gaskins (1971), "Nonparametric Roughness Penalties for Probability Densities," *Biometrika*, 58, 255–277.

Good, I. J. and R. A. Gaskins (1980), "Density Estimation and Bump-Hunting by the Penalized Likelihood Method Exemplified by Scattering and Meteorite Data," *Journal of the American Statistical Association*, 75, 42–73.

Gourieroux, C. and O. Scaillet (1994), "Estimation of the Term Structure from Bond Data," *Working Paper No. 9415*, CEPREMAP.

Gozalo, P. L. (1993), "A Consistent Model Specification Test for Nonparametric Estimation of Regression Function Models," *Econometric Theory*, 9, 451–477.

Gozalo, P. L. (1995), "Nonparametric Specification Testing with $\sqrt{n}$–Local Power and Bootstrap Critical Values," *Working Paper No. 95-21 R*, Brown University.

Gozalo, P. L. (1997), "Nonparametric Bootstrap Analysis with Application to Demographic Effects in Demand Functions" *Journal of Econometrics*, 81, 387–393.

Gozalo, P. L. and O. Linton (1994), "Local Nonlinear Least Squares Estimation Using Parametric Information Nonparametrically," *Discussion Paper No. 1075*, Cowles Foundation, Yale University.

Gozalo, P. L. and O. Linton (1995), "Using Parametric Information in Nonparametric Regression," *Working Paper No. 95-40*, Brown University.

Greblicki, W. and A. Krzyżak (1980), "Asymptotic Properties of Kernel Estimates of a Regression Function," *Journal of Statistical Planning and Inference*, 4, 81–90.

Greblicki, W., A. Krzyżak, and M. Pawlak (1984), "Distribution-Free Pointwise Consistency of Kernel Regression Estimate," *Annals of Statistics*, 12, 1570–1575.

Greblicki, W. and M. Pawlak (1987), "Necessary and Sufficient Consistency Conditions for a Recursive Kernel Regression Estimate," *Journal of Multivariate Analysis*, 23, 67–76.

Greene, W. H. (1997), *Econometric Analysis*, 3rd edition, Prentice-Hall, New Jersey.

Gronau, R. (1974), "The Effects of Children on the Housewife's Value of Time," *Journal of Political Economy*, 81, S168–S199.

Grund, B., P. Hall, and J. Marron (1994), "Loss and Risk in Smoothing Parameter Selection," *Journal of Nonparametric Statistics*, 4, 107–123.

Györfi, L. (1972), "Estimation of Probability Density and Optimal Decision Function in RKHS," in J. Gani, K. Sarkadi, and I. Vincze (eds.), *Progress in Statistics*, Amsterdam, North-Holland, 289–301.

Györfi, L. (1976), "An Upper Bound of Error Probabilities for Multi-Hypotheses Testing and Its Application in Adaptive Pattern Recognition," *Problems of Control and Information Theory*, 5, 449–457.

Györfi, L. (1978), "On the Rate of Convergence of Nearest Neighbour Rules," *IEEE Transactions on Information Theory*, IT-24, 509–512.

Györfi, L. (1981a), "The Rate of Convergence of K-NN Regression Estimates and Classification Rules," *IEEE Transactions on Information Theory*, IT-27, 362–364.

Györfi, L. (1981b), "Strong Consistent Density Estimate from Ergodic Sample," *Journal of Multivariate Analysis*, 11, 81–84.

Györfi, L. (1981c), "Recent Results on Nonparametric Regression Estimate and Multiple Classification," *Problems of Control and Information Theory*, 10, 43–52.

Györfi, L. (1987), "Density Estimation from Dependent Sample," in Y. Dodge (ed.), *Statistical Data Analysis Based on the L_1-Norm and Related Methods*, New York, North-Holland, 393–402.

Györfi, L., W. Härdle, P. Sarda, and P. Vieu, (1989), *Nonparametric Curve Estimation from Time Series*, New York, Springer-Verlag.

Hahn, J. (1995), "Bootstrapping Quantile Regression Estimators," *Econometric Theory*, 11, 105–121.

Hajek, J. (1970), "A Characterization of Limiting Distributions of Regular Estimates," *Zeitschrift für Wahrscheinlichkeitstheorie und Verwandte Gabiet*, 14, 323–330.

Hajek, J. and Z. Sidak (1967), *Theory of Rank Tests*, New York, Academic Press.

Hall, P. (1983), "Large Sample Optimality of Least Square Cross-Validation in Density Estimation," *Annals of Statistics*, 11, 1156–1174.

Hall, P. (1984), "Central Limit Theorem for Integrated Square Error of Multivariate Nonparametric Density Estimators," *Annals of Statistics*, 14, 1–16.

Hall, P. (1985), "Asymptotic Theory of Minimum Integrated Square Error for Multivariate Density Estimation," in P. R. Krishnaiah (ed.), *Proceedings of the Sixth International Symposium on Multivariate Analysis*, New York, North-Holland, 289–309.

Hall, P. (1987a), "On the Use of Compactly Supported Density Estimates in Problems of Discrimination," *Journal of Multivariate Analysis*, 23, 131–158.

Hall, P. (1987b), "On Kullback–Leibler Loss and Density Estimation," *Annals of Statistics*, 15, 1491–1519.

Hall, P. (1989), "On Projection Pursuit Regression," *Annals of Statistics*, 17, 573–588.

Hall, P. (1990), "On the Bias of Variable Bandwidth Curve Estimators," *Biometrika*, 77, 529–535.

Hall, P. (1992), "Effect of Bias Estimation on Coverage Accuracy of Bootstrap Confidence Intervals for a Probability Density," *Annals of Statistics*, 20, 675–694.

Hall, P. and J. Hart (1990), "Nonparametric Regression with Long-Range Dependence," *Stochastic Processes and Their Applications*, 36, 339–351.

Hall, P. and C. C. Heyde (1980), *Martingale Limit Theory and Its Application*, New York, Academic Press.

Hall, P. and J. L. Horowitz (1990), "Bandwidth Selection in Semiparametric Estimation of Censored Linear Regression Models," *Econometric Theory*, 6, 123–150.

Hall, P. and I. Johnstone (1992), "Empirical Functionals and Efficient Smoothing Parameter Selection," *Journal of the Royal Statistical Society*, Series B, 54, 475–530.

Hall, P. and J. S. Marron (1987), "On the Amount of Noise Inherent in Bandwidth Selection for a Kernel Density Estimator," *Annals of Statistics*, 15, 163–181.

Hall, P. and J. S. Marron (1991), "Lower Bounds for Bandwidth Selection in Density Estimation," *Probability Theory and Related Fields*, 90, 149–173.

Hall, P., P. Patil, and Y. K. Truong (1994), "On Wavelet Methods for Curve Estimation in Time Series," manuscript, Australian National University.

Hall, P., S. J. Sheather, M. C. Jones, and J. S. Marron (1991), "On Optimal Data-Based Bandwidth Selection in Kernel Density Estimation," *Biometrika*, 78, 263–269.

Hall, P., J. S. Marron, N. H. Neumann, and D. M. Titterington (1997), "Curve Estimation When the Design Density is Low," *Annals of Statistics*, 25, 756–770.

Hall, W. J. and J. A. Wellner (1980), "Confidence Bands for a Survival Curve from Censored Data," *Biometrika*, 67, 133–143.

Han, A. K. (1987), "Nonparametric Analysis of a Generalized Regression Model," *Journal of Econometrics*, 35, 303–316.

Hanoch, G. and M. Rothschild (1972), "Testing the Assumptions of Production Theory: A Nonparametric Approach," *Journal of Political Economy*, 80, 256–275.

Hansen, L. P. (1982), "Large Sample Properties of Generalized Method of Moments Estimators," *Econometrica*, 50, 1029–1054.

Härdle, W. (1984), "Robust Regression Function Estimation," *Journal of Multivariate Analysis*, 14, 169–180.

Härdle, W. (1990), *Applied Nonparametric Regression*, New York, Cambridge University Press.

Härdle, W. and A. Bowman (1988), "Bootstrapping in Nonparametric Regression: Local Adaptive Smoothing and Confidence Bounds," *Journal of the American Statistical Association*, 83, 102–110.

Härdle, W. and T. Gasser (1984), "Robust Nonparametric Function Fitting," *Journal of the Royal Statistical Society*, Series B, 46, 42–51.

Härdle, W. and T. Gasser (1985), "On Robust Kernel Estimation of Derivatives of Regression Functions," *Scandinavian Journal of Statistics*, 12, 233–240.

Härdle, W., P. Hall, and J. S. Marron (1988), "How Far Are Automatically Chosen Regression Smoothing Parameters from Their Optimum," *Journal of the American Statistical Association*, 83, 86–101.

Härdle, W., P. Hall, and J. S. Marron (1992), "Regression Smoothing Parameters that Are not Far from Their Optimum," *Journal of the American Statistical Association*, 87, 227–233.

Härdle, W., J. D. Hart, J. S. Marron, and A. B. Tsybakov (1992), "Bandwidth Choice for Average Derivative Estimation," *Journal of American Statistical Association*, 87, 218–233.

Härdle, W., W. Hildenbrand, and M. Jerison (1991), "Empirical Evidence of the Law of Demand," *Econometrica*, 59, 1525–1549.

Härdle, W. and M. Jerison (1991), "Cross Section Engel Curves Over Time," *Recherches Economiques de Louvain*, 57, 391–431.

Härdle, W. and O. Linton (1994), "Applied Nonparametric Methods," in D. McFadden and R. F. Engle (eds.), *The Handbook of Econometrics*, Vol. IV, New York, North Holland, 2295–2339.

Härdle, W. and E. Mammen (1993), "Comparing Nonparametric versus Parametric Regression Fits," *Annals of Statistics*, 21, 1926–1947.

Härdle, W. and J. S. Marron (1983), "Optimal Bandwidth Selection in Nonparametric Regression Function Estimation," *The Annals of Statistics*, 13, 1465–1481.

Härdle, W. and J. S. Marron (1988), "Bandwidth Choice for Density Derivatives," *Discussion Paper A-157*, University of Bonn.

Härdle, W. and T. M. Stoker (1989), "Investigating Smooth Multiple Regression by the Method of Average Derivatives," *Journal of the American Statistical Association*, 84, 986–995.

Härdle, W. and A. B. Tsybakov (1988), "Robust Nonparametric Regression with Simultaneous Scale Curve Estimation," *Annals of Statistics*, 16, 120–135.

Hastie, T. and C. Loader (1993), "Local Regression: Automatic Kernel Carpentry," *Statistical Science*, 8, 120–143.

Hastie, T. and R. Tibshirani (1986), "General Additive Models" (with discussion), *Statistical Science*, 1, 297–318.

Hastie, T. and R. Tibshirani (1990), *General Additive Models*, New York, Chapman and Hall.

Hausman, J. A. (1978), "Specification Tests in Econometrics," *Econometrica*, 46, 1251–1272.

Hausman, J. A., H. Ichimura, W. K. Newey, and J. L. Powell (1991), "Identification and Estimation of Polynomial Errors-in-Variables Models," *Journal of Econometrics*, 50, 273–295.

Hausman, J. A. and W. K. Newey (1995), "Nonparametric Estimation of Exact Consumer Surplus and Deadweight Loss," *Econometrica*, 63, 1445–1476.

Hausman, J. A., W. K. Newey, and J. L. Powell (1989), "Nonparametric and Semi-parametric Estimation of Errors-in-Variables Models," Department of Economics, Princeton University.

Heckman, J. J. (1974), "Shadow Prices, Market Wages, and Labor Supply," *Econometrica*, 42, 679–693.

Heckman, J. J. (1976), "The Common Structure of Statistical Models of Truncation, Sample Selection and Limited Dependent Variables and a Simple Estimator for Such Models," *Annals of Economic and Social Measurement*, 5, 475–492.

Heckman, J. J. (1990), "Varieties of Selection Bias," *American Economic Review*, 80, 313–318.

Heckman, J. and S. Polachek (1974), "Empirical Evidence on Functional Form of the Earnings–Schooling Relationship," *Journal of the American Statistical Association*, 69, 350–354.

Heckman, J. J. and R. Robb, Jr. (1985), "Alternative Methods for Evaluating the Impact of Interventions," in J. J. Heckman and B. Singer (eds.), *Longitudinal Analysis of Labor Market Data*, New York, Cambridge University Press, 156–245.

Herrmann, E., T. Gasser, and A. Kneip (1992), "Choice of Bandwidth for Kernel Regression when Residuals are Correlated," *Biometrika*, 79, 783–795.

Hidalgo, J. (1992), "Adaptive Estimation in Time Series Regression Models with Heteroskedasticity of Unknown Form," *Econometric Theory*, 8, 161–187.

Hjort, N. L. (1996), "Bayesian Approach to Semiparametric Density Estimation," in J. Berger, J. Beruardo, A. P. David, and A. F. M. Smith (eds.), *Proceedings of the Fifth Valencia International Meeting on Bayesian Statistics*, pp. 223–253, Oxford University Press.

Hjort, N. L. and I. K. Glad (1995), "Nonparametric Density Estimation with a Parametric Start," *Annals of Statistics*, 23, 882–904.

Hjort, N. L. and M. C. Jones (1996), "Locally Parametric Nonparametric Density Estimation," *Annals of Statistics*, 23, 882–904.

Hodrick, R. (1989), "Risk, Uncertainty and Exchange Rates," *Journal of Monetary Economics*, 23, 433–459.

Hoeffding, W. (1948), "A Class of Statistics with Asymptotically Normal Distribution," *Annals of Mathematical Statistics*, 19, 293–325.

Hoeffding, W. (1963), "Probability Inequalities for Sums of Bounded Random Variables," *Journal of American Statistical Association*, 58, 13–30.

Hong, Y. M. (1993), "Consistent Specification Testing Using Optimal Nonparametric Kernel Estimation," mimeo, Cornell University.

Hong, Y. M. and H. White (1995), "Consistent Specification Testing via Nonaprametric Series Regression," *Econometrica*, 63, 1133–1159.

Hong, Y. S. and A. R. Pagan (1988), "Some Simulation Studies of Nonparametric Estimators," *Empirical Economics*, 13, 251–266.

Honore, B. E., E. Kyriazidou, and C. Udry (1997), "Estimation of Type 3 Tobit Models Using Symmetric Trimming and Pairwise Comparisons," *Journal of Econometrics*, 76, 107–128.

Hoogstrate, A. J. (1994), "Nonparametric Regression with Integrated Processes," manuscript, University of Maastricht.

Horowitz, J. L. (1986), "A Distribution-Free Least Squares Estimator for Censored Linear Regression Models," *Journal of Econometrics*, 32, 59–84.

Horowitz, J. L. (1988a) "Semiparametric M-Estimation of Censored Linear Regression Models," in G. F. Rhodes and T. B. Fomby (eds.), *Advances in Econometrics*, 7, 45–83.

Horowitz, J. L. (1988b), "The Asymptotic Efficiency of Semiparametric Estimators for Censored Linear Regression Models," *Empirical Economics*, 13, 123–140.

Horowitz, J. L. (1992), "A Smoothed Maximum Score Estimator for the Binary Response Model," *Econometrica*, 60, 505–531.

Horowitz, J. L. (1993a), "Semiparametric Estimation of a Work-Trip Mode Choice Model," *Journal of Econometrics*, 58, 49–70.

Horowitz, J. L. (1993b), "Semiparametric and Nonparametric Estimation of Quantal Response Models," in G. S. Maddala, C. R. Rao, and H. D. Vinod (eds.), *Handbook of Statistics*, Vol. II, Amsterdam, Elsevier, 45–72.

Horowitz, J. L. and W. Härdle (1994), "Testing a Parametric Model Against a Semiparametric Alternative," *Econometric Theory*, 10, 821–848.

Horowitz, J. L. and W. Härdle (1996), "Direct Semiparametric Estimation of Single-Index Models with Discrete Covariates," *Journal of the American Statistical Association*, 91, 1632–1640.

Horowitz, J. L. and M. Markatov (1996), "Semiparametric Estimation of Regression Models for Panel Data," *The Review of Economic Studies*, 63, 145–168.

Horowitz, J. L. and G. R. Neumann (1987), "Semiparametric Estimation of Employment Duration Models," *Econometric Reviews*, 6, 5–40.

Horowitz, J. L. and G. R. Neumann (1989a), "Specification Testing in Censored Regression Models: Parametric and Semiparametric Methods," *Journal of Applied Econometrics*, 4, S61–S86.

Horowitz, J. L. and G. R. Neumann (1989b), "Computational and Statistical Efficiency of Semiparametric GLS Estimators," *Econometric Reviews*, 8, 223–225.

Hsieh, D. A. and C. F. Manski (1987), "Monte Carlo Evidence on Adaptive Maximum Likelihood Estimation of a Regression," *Annals of Statistics*, 15, 541–551.

Huber, P. J. (1964), "Robust Estimates of a Location Parameter," *Annals of Mathematical Statistics*, 35, 73–101.

Huber, P. J. (1967), "The Behavior of Maximum Likelihood Estimates Under Nonstandard Conditions," *Proceedings of the 5th Berkeley Symposium, Mathematical Statistics and Probability*, Vol. 1, University of California Press, 221–233.

Huber, P. J. (1973), "Robust Regression: Asymptotics, Conjectures and Monte Carlo," *Annals of Statistics*, 1, 799–821.

Huber, P. J. (1981), *Robust Statistics*, New York, Wiley.

Hutchison, J. M., A. W. Lo, and T. Poggio (1994), "A Nonparametric Approach to Pricing and Hedging Derivative Securities Via Learning Networks," *Journal of Finance*, 49, 851–889.

Ibragimov, I. A (1962), "Some Limit Theorems for Stationary Processes," *Theory of Probability and Its Application*, 7, 349–382.

Ibragimov, I. A. and Y. V. Linnik (1971), *Independent and Stationary Sequences of Variables*, Groningen, Wolters-Noordhoff.

Ichimura, H. (1993), "Semiparametric Least Squares (SLS) and Weighted SLS Estimation of Single-Index Models," *Journal of Econometrics*, 58, 71–120.

Ichimura, H. and L. Lee (1991), "Semiparametric Least Squares Estimation of Multiple Index Models: Single Equation Estimation," in W. A. Barnett, J. Powell, and G. E. Tauchen (eds.), *Nonparametric and Semiparametric Methods in Econometrics and Statistics*, Cambridge, UK, Cambridge University Press, 3–49.

Ioannides, D. and G. G. Roussas, (1988), "Probability Bounds for Sums in Triangular Arrays of Random Variables under Mixing Conditions," in K. Matusita (ed.),

Statistical Theory and Data Analysis II, Amsterdam, North Holland Publishers, 293–308.

Jennen-Steinmetz, C. and T. Gasser (1988), "A Unifying Approach to Nonparametric Regression Estimation," *Journal of the American Statistical Association*, 83, 1084–1089.

Jennrich, R. I. (1969), "Asymptotic Properties of Nonlinear Least Squares Estimates," *Annals of Mathematical Statistics*, 40, 633–643.

Johnson, N. L. and S. Kotz (1969), *Distributions in Statistics: Discrete Distributions*, New York, Wiley.

Johnson, N. L. and S. Kotz (1970), *Distributions in Statistics: Continuous Univariate Distributions*, New York, Wiley.

Johnson, N. L. and S. Kotz (1972), *Distributions in Statistics: Continuous Multivariate Distributions*, New York, Wiley.

Johnston, G. J. (1979), "Smooth Nonparametric Regression Analysis," Mimeo Series 1253, Institute of Statistics, Chapel Hill, University of North Carolina.

Johnston, G. J. (1982), "Probabilities of Maximal Deviations for Nonparametric Regression Function Estimates," *Journal of Multivariate Analysis*, 12, 402–414.

Johnston, J. (1984), *Econometric Methods*, 3rd edition, New York, McGraw-Hill.

Jones, M. C. (1991), "The Roles of ISE and MISE in Density Estimation," *Statistics and Probability Letters*, 12, 511–519.

Jorgenson, D. W. and J. J. Laffont (1974), "Efficient Estimation of Nonlinear Simultaneous Equations with Additive Disturbances," *Annals of Economics and Social Measurement*, 3, 615–640.

Judge, G. G., W. E. Griffiths, R. C. Hill, H. Lütkepohl, and T. C. Lee (1985), *The Theory and Practice of Econometrics*, New York, Wiley.

Judge, G. G. and T. A. Yancey (1986), *Improved Methods of Inference in Econometrics*, Amsterdam, North Holland.

Jung, Y. (1995), *Four Essays on Some Applications of Semiparametric Estimators in Econometrics*, unpublished doctoral thesis, University of Rochester.

Kaplan, E. L. and P. Meier (1958), "Nonparametric Estimation from Incomplete Observations," *Journal of the American Statistical Association*, 53, 457–481.

Kakwani, N. (1980), *Income Inequality and Poverty: Methods of Estimation and Policy Application*, New York, Oxford University Press.

Kearns, P. (1993), *Volatility and the Pricing of Interest Rate Derivatives Claims*, unpublished doctoral dissertation, University of Rochester.

Kelejian, H. (1971), "Two-Stage Least Squares and Econometric Systems Linear in Parameters but Nonlinear in Endogenous Variables," *Journal of the American Statistical Association*, 66, 373–374.

Kendall, M. G. and A. Stuart (1969), *The Advanced Theory of Statistics*, Vol. 1, 3rd Edition, London, Charles Griffin.

Kendall, M. G. and A. Stuart (1973), *The Advanced Theory of Statistics*, Vol. 2, 3rd Edition, London, Charles Griffin.

Kennan, J. K. (1985), "The Duration of Contract Strikes in U.S. Manufacturing," *Journal of Econometrics*, 28, 5–28.

Khanna, M., K. Mundra, and A. Ullah (1998), "Parametric and Semi-Parametric Estimation of the Effect of Firm Attributes on Efficiency: The Electricity Generating
Sector in India," Working Paper No. 17, University of California, Riverside.

Kim, J. and D. Pollard (1990), "Cube Root Asymptotics," *Annals of Statistics*, 18, 191–
219.

Klein, R. W. (1993), "Specification Tests for Binary Choice Models Based on Index
Quantiles," *Journal of Econometrics*, 59, 343–375.

Klein, R. W. (1994), "Correcting for Sample Selection Bias in a Service Choice/Usage
Model," manuscript, Bell Laboratories.

Klein, R. W. and R. H. Spady (1993), "An Efficient Semiparametric Estimator of Binary
Response Models," *Econometrica*, 61, 387–421.

Kneisner, T. and Q. Li (1996), "Semiparametric Panel Data Models with Dynamic Adjustment: Theoretical Considerations and Application to Labor Supply,"
manuscript, University of Guelph.

Koenker, R. (1982), "Robust Methods in Econometrics," *Econometric Reviews*, 1, 213–
255.

Koenker, R. and G. Bassett (1978), "Regression Quantiles," *Econometrica*, 46, 33–50.

Koenker, R. and G. Bassett (1982), "Robust Tests for Heteroscedasticity Based on Regression Quantiles," *Econometrica*, 50, 43–61.

Koenker, R., P. Ng, and S. Portnoy (1994), "Quantile Smoothing Splines," *Biometrika*,
81, 673–680.

Kreiss, J. P. (1987), "On Adaptive Estimation in Stationary ARMA Processes," *Annals
of Statistics*, 15, 112–133.

Kruskal, J. B. (1969), "Toward a Practical Method Which Helps Uncover the Structure
of a Set of Multivariate Observations by Finding the Linear Transformation Which
Optimizes a New Index of Conversation," in R. C. Milton and J. A. Nelder (eds.),
Statistical Computing, New York, Academic Press.

Krzyzak, A. and M. Pawlak (1984), "Distribution-Free Consistency of a Nonparametric
Kernel Regression Estimate and Classification," *IEEE Transactions on Information
Theory*, 30, 78–81.

Kuan, C. M. and H. White (1994), "Artificial Neural Networks: An Econometric Perspective," *Econometric Reviews*, 13, 1–91.

Lai, T. L. and Z. Ying (1988), "Consistency and Asymptotic Normality of Buckley–
James-Type Statistics in Regression Analysis of Censored or Truncated Data,"
Technical Report, Dept. of Statistics, Stanford University.

Lau, L. (1986), "Functional Forms in Econometric Model Building," in Z. Grilliches
and M. D. Intriligator (eds.), *Handbook of Econometrics*, Vol. 3, Ch. 26, New York,
North Holland, 1516–1566.

Lavergne, P. (1998), "An Equality Test across Nonparametric Regressions," manuscript,
INRA-ESR.

Lavergne, P. and Q. H. Vuong (1996), "Nonparametric Selection of Regressors: The
Nonnested Case," *Econometrica*, 64, 207–219.

LeCam, L. (1960), "Locally Asymptotically Normal Families of Distributions," *University of California, Publications in Statistics*, 3, 37–98.

Lee, B. J. (1992), "A Heteroskedasticity Test Robust to Conditional Mean Misspecification," *Econometrica*, 60, 159–171.

Lee, B. J. (1994), "Asymptotic Distribution of the Ullah-Type Specification Test Against the Nonparametric Alternative," *Journal of Quantitative Economics*, 10, 73–92.

Lee, D. K. C. (1988), "Semiparametric Analysis of the 'Surprise' Consumption Function," manuscript, London School of Economics.

Lee, L. F. (1982), "Some Approaches to the Correction of Selectivity Bias," *Review of Economic Studies*, 49, 355–372.

Lee, L. F. (1994), "Semiparametric Two-Stage Estimation of Sample Selection Models Subject to Tobit-Type Selection Rules," *Journal of Econometrics*, 61, 305–344.

Lee, L. F. (1995), "Semiparametric Maximum Likelihood Estimation of Polychotomous and Sequential Choice Models," *Journal of Econometrics*, 65, 381–428.

Lee, S. W. (1990), "Numerical Comparison of the Asymptotic Efficiency of the Semiparametric Estimator of the Sample Selection Model," manuscript, University of Rochester.

Lee, T. H., H. White, and C. W. J. Granger (1993), "Testing for Neglected Nonlinearity in Time Series Models: A Comparison of Neural Network Methods and Alternative Tests," *Journal of Econometrics*, 56, 269–290.

Leontief, W. (1947), "Introduction to a Theory of the Internal Structure of Functional Relationships," *Econometrica*, 15, 361–373.

Leurgans, S. (1982), "Asymptotic Distributions of Slope-of-Greatest-Convex-Minorant Estimators," *Annals of Statistics*, 10, 287–296.

Lewbel, A. (1991), "The Rank of Demand Systems: Theory and Nonparametric Estimation," *Econometrica*, 59, 711–730.

Lewbel, A. (1992), "Consistent Nonparametric Tests of Regression, Density or Derivative Constraints, with Applications," manuscript, Brandeis University.

Lewbel, A. (1993), "Nonparametric Estimation of Average Compensated Price Derivatives," manuscript, Brandeis University.

Lewbel, A. (1995), "Consistent Nonparametric Hypothesis Tests with an Application to Slutsky Symmetry," *Journal of Econometrics*, 67, 379–401.

Lewis, H. G. (1974), *Union Relative Wage Effects: A Survey*, Chicago, University of Chicago Press.

Li, K. C. (1987), "Asymptotic Optimality for C_p, C_L, Cross-validation and Generalized Cross-Validation: Discrete Index Set," *Annals of Statistics*, 15, 958–975.

Li, Q. (1996), "Nonparametric Testing of Closeness between Two Unknown Distribution Functions," *Econometric Reviews*, 15, 261–274.

Li, Q. (1997), "A Consistent Test for the Parametric Specification of the Distribution of a Regression Disturbance," manuscript, University of Guelph.

Li, Q., X. Lu, and A. Ullah (1996), "Estimating Average Derivative by Local Least Squares Method," manuscript, University of Guelph.

Li, Q. and S. Wang (1998), "A Simple Consistent Bootstrap Test for a Parametric Regression Function," *Journal of Econometrics*, 87, 145–165.

Lin, K. and H. Shu (1994), "Local Maximum Likelihood Estimation of a Disequilibrium Transition Model: The Case of Consumer Goods Market in China, 1954–1991," manuscript, Portland State University.

Linton, O. B. (1992), "Small Sample Properties of Adaptive GLS Estimators," manuscript, Nuffield College, Oxford.

Linton, O. B. (1993), "Adaptive Estimation in ARCH Models," *Econometric Theory*, 9, 539–569.

Linton, O. B. (1995), "Second Order Approximation in the Partially Linear Regression Model," *Econometrica*, 63, 1079–1113.

Linton, O. B. (1996a), "Edgeworth Approximation for MINPIN Estimators in Semiparametric Regression Models," *Econometric Theory*, 12, 30–60.

Linton, O. B. (1996b), "Second Order Approximation in a Linear Regression with Heteroscedasticity of Unknown Form," *Econometric Reviews*, 15, 1–32.

Linton, O. B. and P. L. Gozalo (1995), "A Nonparametric Test of Conditional Independence," manuscript, Brown University.

Linton, O. B. and P. L. Gozalo (1996), "Testing Additivity in Generalized Nonparametric Regression Models," manuscript, Yale University and Brown University.

Linton, O. B. and W. Härdle (1996), "Estimating Additive Regression Models with Known Links," *Biometrika*, 83, 529–540.

Linton, O. B. and J. P. Nielsen (1995), "A Kernel Method of Estimating Structured Nonparametric Regression Based on Marginal Integration," *Biometrika*, 82, 93–100.

Loader, C. R. (1993), "Local Likelihood Density Estimation," manuscript, AT&T Laboratories, Murray Hill.

Lofstgaarden, D. O. and C. P. Quesenberry (1965), "A Nonparametric Estimate of a Multivariate Density Function," *Annals of Mathematical Statistics*, 36, 1049–1051.

Mack, Y. P. (1981), "Local Properties of k-NN Regression Estimates," *SIAM Journal of Algebraic and Discrete Methods*, 2, 311–323.

Mack, Y. P. and H. Muller, (1989), "Derivative Estimation in Random-Design Nonparametric Regression," *Sankhya*, Series A, 51, 59–72.

Mack, Y. P. and B. W. Silverman (1982), "Weak and Strong Uniform Consistency of Kernel Regression Estimates," *Zeitschrift für Wahrscheinlichkeitstheorie und Verwandte Gebiete*, 61, 405–415.

Magee, L., J. B. Burbidge, and A. L. Robb (1991), "Computing Kernel-Smoothed Conditional Quantiles from Many Observations," *Journal of the American Statistical Association*, 86, 673–677.

Mallows, C. L. (1973), "Some Comments on Cp," *Technometrics*, 15, 661–675.

Maltz, C. (1974), "Estimation of k-th Derivative of a Distribution Function," *Annals of Statistics*, 2, 359–61.

Mammen E. (1992), *When Does Bootstrap Work: Asymptotic Results and Simulations*, Lecture Notes in Statistics, 77, Berlin, Springer-Verlago.

Mann, H. B. and A. Wald (1943), "On Stochastic Limit and Order Relationships," *Annals of Mathematical Statistics*, 14, 217–226.

Manski, C. F. (1975), "The Maximum Score Estimation of the Stochastic Utility Model of Choice," *Journal of Econometrics*, 3, 205–228.

Manski, C. F. (1984), "Adaptive Estimation of Non-Linear Regression Models," *Econometric Reviews*, 3, 145–194.

Manski, C. F. (1985), "Semiparametric Analysis of Discrete Response: Asymptotic Properties of the Maximum Score Estimator," *Journal of Econometrics*, 27, 313–334.

Manski, C. F. and T. S. Thompson (1988), "Operational Characteristics of Maximum Score Estimation," *Journal of Econometrics*, 32, 85–108.

Marron, J. S. (1987), "Partitioned Cross-Validation," *Econometric Reviews*, 6, 271–283.

Marron, J. S. (1988), "Automatic Smoothing Parameter Selection: A Survey," *Empirical Economics*, 13, 187–208.

Marron, J. S. and H. P. Schmitz (1992), "Simultaneous Density Estimation of Several Income Distributions," *Econometric Theory*, 8, 476–488.

Marron, J. S. and M. P. Wand (1992), "Exact Mean Integrated Squared Error," *Annals of Statistics*, 20, 712–736.

Matzkin, R. L. (1992), "Nonparametric and Distribution-Free Estimation of the Binary Threshold Crossing and the Binary Choice Models," *Econometrica*, 60, 239–270.

McAllister, P. H. and D. A. McManus (1993), "Resolving the Scale Efficiency Puzzle in Banking," *Journal of Banking and Finance*, 17, 389–405.

McCurdy, T. E. (1982), "Using Information on the Moments of the Disturbance to Increase the Efficiency of Estimation," manuscript, Stanford University.

McDonald, J. A. and A. B. Owen (1986), "Smoothing with Split Linear Fits," *Technometrics*, 28, 195–208.

McFadden, D. (1985), "Specification of Econometric Models," Presidential Address, Fifth World Congress of the Econometric Society.

McLeish, D. L. (1975), "A Maximal Inequality and Dependent Strong Laws," *Annals of Probability*, 3, 829–839.

McManus, D. A. (1994a), "The Nonparametric Translog with Application to Banking Scale and Scope Economies," *Proceedings of the Business and Economic Statistics Section*, American Statistical Association.

McManus, D. A. (1994b), "Making the Cobb–Douglas Functional Form an Efficient Nonparametric Estimator Through Localization," manuscript, Board of Governors of the Federal Reserve.

McMillan, J., A. Ullah, and H. D. Vinod (1989), "Estimation of the Shape of the Demand Curve by Nonparametric Kernel Methods," in B. Raj (ed.), *Advances in Econometrics and Modelling*, Boston, Kluwer Academic Publishers, 85–92.

Meier, P. (1975), "Estimation of a Distribution Function from Incomplete Observations," in J. Gani (ed.), *Perspectives in Probability and Statistics*, Applied Probability Trust, 67–87.

Melenberg, B. and A. Van Soest (1993), "Semi-Parametric Estimation of the Sample Selection Model," manuscript, Tilburg University.

Melenberg, B. and A. Van Soest (1996), "Parametric and Semiparametric Modelling of Vacation Expenditure," *Journal of Applied Econometrics*, 11, 59–76.

Meyer, Y. (1993), *Wavelets: Algorithms and Applications*, translated by R. D. Ryan, Philadelphia, SIAM.

Mincer, J. (1974), *Schooling, Experience and Earnings*, New York, Columbia University Press for the National Bureau of Economic Research.

Ming, X. (1993), "Semi-Parametric Maximum Likelihood Estimation of Discrete Choice Models," manuscript, Rice University.

Ming, X. and F. Vella (1994), "Semiparametric Estimation via Synthetic Fixed Effects," manuscript, Rice University.

Ming, X. and F. Vella (1995), "Semiparametric Instrumental Variables Estimation of the Sample Selection Model," manuscript, Rice University.

Mizrach, B. (1992), "Multivariate Nearest Neighbour Forecasts of EMS Exchange Rates," *Journal of Applied Econometrics*, 7, S151–S163.

Monahan, J. F. (1981), "Enumeration of Elementary Multi-Indexes for Multivariate Fourier Series," *Mimeograph Series No. 1338*, Institute of Statistics, North Carolina State University.

Moon, C. G. (1989), "A Monte Carlo Comparison of Semiparametric Tobit Estimators," *Journal of Applied Econometrics*, 4, 361–382.

Müller, H. G. (1987), "Weak and Universal Consistency of Moving Weighted Averages," *Periodica Mathematica Hungarica*, 18, 241–250.

Müller, H. G. (1988), *Nonparametric Regression Analysis of Longitudinal Data*, Berlin, Springer-Verlag.

Murphy, K. M. and F. Welch (1990), "Empirical Age–Earnings Profiles," *Journal of Labor Economics*, 8, 202–29.

Mustafi, C. K. (1978), "On the Asymptotic Distribution of the Estimates of the Derivatives of a Distribution Function," *SIAM Journal on Applied Mathematics*, 34, 73–77.

Nadaraya, É. A. (1964), "On Estimating Regression," *Theory of Probability and Its Applications*, 9, 141–142.

Nadaraya, É. A. (1965), "On Nonparametric Estimation of Density Functions and Regression Curves," *Theory of Probability and Its Applications*, 10, 186–190.

Nadaraya, É. A. (1970), "Remarks on Nonparametric Estimates for Density Functions and Regression Curves," *Theory of Probability and Its Applications*, 15, 134–137.

Newey, W. K. (1984), "A Method of Moments Interpretation of Sequential Estimators," *Economics Letters*, 14, 201–206.

Newey, W. K. (1985), "Maximum Likelihood Specification Testing and Conditional Moment Tests," *Econometrica*, 53, 1047–1070.

Newey, W. K. (1988), "Adaptive Estimation of Regression Models via Moment Restrictions," *Journal of Econometrics*, 38, 301–339.

Newey, W. K. (1989), "Locally Efficient, Residual Based Estimation of Nonlinear Simultaneous Equations," manuscript, M.I.T.

Newey, W. K. (1990a), "Semiparametric Efficiency Bounds," *Journal of Applied Econometrics*, 5, 99–135.

Newey, W. K. (1990b), "Efficient Instrumental Variables Estimation of Nonlinear Models," *Econometrica*, 58, 809–837.

Newey, W. K. (1991a), "Two-Step Series Estimation of Sample Selection Models," manuscript, M.I.T.

Newey, W. K. (1991b), "Consistency and Asymptotic Normality of Nonparametric Projection Estimators," *Working Paper No. 584*, Department of Economics, M.I.T.

Newey, W. K. (1991c), "Efficient Estimation of Tobit Models Under Conditional Symmetry," in W. A. Barnett, J. Powell, and G. E. Tauchen (eds.), *Nonparametric and Semiparametric Methods in Econometrics and Statistics*, Cambridge, Cambridge University Press, 291–336.

Newey, W. K. (1993a), "Efficiency Bounds for Some Semiparametric Selection Models," *Journal of Econometrics*, 58, 169–184.

Newey, W. K. (1993b), "Efficient Estimation of Models with Conditional Moment Restrictions," in G. S. Maddala, C. R. Rao, and H. D. Vinod (eds.), *Handbook of Statistics*, Vol 11, Amsterdam, North Holland, Elsevier Science Publishers, 419–454.

Newey, W. K. (1994a), "The Asymptotic Variance of Semiparametric Estimators," *Econometrica*, 62, 1349–1382.

Newey, W. K. (1994b), "Kernel Estimation of Partial Means and a General Variance Estimator," *Econometric Theory*, 10, 233–253.

Newey, W. K. (1994c), "Series Estimation of Regression Functionals," *Econometric Theory*, 10, 1–28.

Newey, W. K. (1997), "Convergence Rates and Asymptotic Normality of Series Estimators," *Journal of Econometrics*, 29, 147–168.

Newey, W. K. and J. L. Powell (1987), "Asymmetric Least Squares Estimation and Testing," *Econometrica*, 55, 819–847.

Newey, W. K. and J. L. Powell (1990a), "Nonparametric Instrumental Variables Estimation," manuscript, Princeton University.

Newey, W. K. and J. L. Powell (1990b), "Efficient Estimation of Linear and Type I Censored Regression Models under Conditional Quantile Restrictions," *Econometric Theory*, 6, 295–317.

Newey, W. K., J. L. Powell, and J. Walker (1990), "Semiparametric Estimation of Selection Models: Some Empirical Results," *American Economic Review Papers and Proceedings*, 80, 324–28.

Newey, W. K. and K. D. West (1987), "A Simple Positive Semi-Definite, Heteroskedasticity and Autocorrelation Consistent Covariance Matrix," *Econometrica*, 55, 703–708.

Nicol, C. J. (1993), "An Empirical Comparison of Nonparametric and Parametric Engel Functions," *Empirical Economics*, 18, 233–249.

Ng, P. (1995), "An Algorithm for Quantile Smoothing Splines," manuscript, University of Houston.

Ng, P. and J. L. Smith (1995), "The Elasticity of Demand for Gasoline: A Semiparametric Analysis," manuscript, University of Houston.

Noda, K. (1976), "Estimation of a Regression Function by the Parzen Kernel Type Density Estimators," *Annals of the Institute of Statistical Mathematics*, 128, 221–234.

Nolan, O. and D. Pollard (1987), "U-Processes: Rates of Convergence," *Annals of Statistics*, 15, 780–799.

Nychka, D., G. Wahba, S. Goldfarb, and T. Pugh (1984), "Cross-validated Spline Methods for the Estimation of Three-Dimensional Tumor Size Distributions from Observations on Two-Dimensional Cross-Sections," *Journal of the American Statistical Association*, 79, 832–846.

Olkin, I. and C. H. Spiegelman (1987), "A Semiparametric Approach to Density Estimation," *Journal of the American Statistical Association*, 82, 858–865.

O'Sullivan, F. (1986), "A Statistical Perspective on Ill-Posed Inverse Problems" (with discussion), *Statistical Science*, 1, 502–527.

Owen, A. B. (1987), *Nonparametric Conditional Estimation*, Ph.D. thesis, Stanford University.

Paarsch, H. J. (1984), "A Monte Carlo Comparison of Estimators for Censored Regression Models," *Journal of Econometrics*, 21, 197–213.

Pagan, A. R. (1984a), "Model Evaluation by Variable Addition," in D. F. Hendry and K. F. Wallis (eds.), *Econometrics and Quantitative Economics*, Oxford, Blackwell, 103–133.

Pagan, A. R. (1984b), "Econometric Issues in the Analysis of Regressions with Generated Regressors," *International Economic Review*, 25, 221–247.

Pagan, A. R. (1986), "Two Stage and Related Estimators and Their Applications," *Review of Economic Studies*, 53, 517–538.

Pagan, A. R. and A. D. Hall (1983), "Diagnostic Tests as Residual Analysis," *Econometric Reviews*, 2, 159–218.

Pagan, A. R. and Y. S. Hong (1991), "Nonparametric Estimation and the Risk Premium," in W. A. Barnett, J. Powell, and G. E. Tauchen (eds.), *Nonparametric and Semiparametric Methods in Econometrics and Statistics*, Cambridge, Cambridge University Press, 51–75.

Pagan, A. R. and Y. Jung (1993), "Understanding Some Failures of Some Instrumental Variable Estimators," manuscript, Australian National University.

Pagan, A. R. and G. W. Schwert (1990), "Alternative Models for Conditional Stock Volatility," *Journal of Econometrics*, 45, 267–290.

Pagan, A. R. and A. Ullah (1988), "The Econometric Analysis of Models with Risk Terms," *Journal of Applied Econometrics*, 3, 87–105.

Pagan, A. R. and F. Vella (1989), "Diagnostic Tests for Models Based on Individual Data: A Survey," *Journal of Applied Econometrics*, 4, S29–S59.

Pagan, A. R. and M. R. Wickens (1989), "A Survey of Some Recent Econometric Methods," *Economic Journal*, 99, 962–1025.

Park, B. U. and J. S. Marron (1990), "Comparison of Data-Driven Bandwidth Selectors," *Journal of the American Statistical Association*, 85, 66–72.

Parzen, E. (1962), "On Estimation of a Probability Density and Mode," *Annals of Mathematical Statistics*, 33, 1065–1076.

Parzen, E. (1979), "Nonparametric Statistical Data Modelling" (with discussion), *Journal of the American Statistical Association*, 74, 105–131.

Philipp, W. (1977), "A Functional Law of the Iterated Logarithm for Empirical Distribution Functions of Weakly Dependent Random Variables," *Annals of Probability*, 5, 319–350.

Phillips, P. C. B. (1977), "A General Theorem in the Theory of Asymptotic Expansions as Approximations to the Finite Sample Distributions of Econometric Estimators," *Econometrica*, 45, 1517–1534.

Phillips, P. C. B. (1991), "A Shortcut to LAD Estimator Asymptotics," *Econometric Theory*, 7, 450–463.

Phillips, P. C. B. and J. Y. Park (1998), "Nonstationary Density Estimation and Kernel Autoregression," Cowles Foundation Discussion Paper, no. 1181, Yale University.

Ploberger, W. and H. J. Bierens (1995), "Asymptotic Power of the Integrated Conditional Moment Test Against Large Local Alternatives," *Working Paper*, Southern Methodist University.

Pollard, D. (1985), "New Ways of Proving Central Limit Theorems," *Econometric Theory*, 295–313.

Pollard, D. (1990), "Empirical Processes: Theory and Applications," *CBMS Conference Series in Probability and Statistics, Vol. 2*, Hayward, California, Institute of Mathematical Statistics.

Pötscher, B. M. and I. R. Prucha (1989), "A Uniform Law of Large Numbers for Dependent and Heterogenous Data Processes," *Econometrica*, 57, 675–683.

Powell, J. L. (1984), "Least Absolute Deviations Estimation for the Censored Regression Model," *Journal of Econometrics*, 25, 303–325.

Powell, J. L. (1986a), "Censored Regression Quantiles," *Journal of Econometrics*, 32, 143–155.

Powell, J. L. (1986b), "Symmetrically Trimmed Least Squares Estimation for Tobit Models," *Econometrica*, 54, 1435–1460.

Powell, J. L. (1987), "Semiparametric Estimation of Bivariate Latent Variable Models," Working Paper No. 8704, University of Wisconsin.

Powell, J. L. (1991), "Estimation of Monotonic Regression Models under Quantile Restrictions," in W. A. Barnett, J. Powell, and G. E. Tauchen (eds.), *Nonparametric and Semiparametric Methods in Econometrics and Statistics*, New York, Cambridge University Press, 357–384.

Powell, J. L., J. H. Stock, and T. M. Stoker (1989), "Semiparametric Estimation of Index Coefficients," *Econometrica*, 57, 1403–1430.

Powell, J. L. and T. M. Stoker (1996), "Optimal Bandwidth Choice for Density-Weighted Averages," *Journal of Econometrics*, 75, 291–316.

Powell, M. J. D. (1981), *Approximation Theory and Methods*, New York, Cambridge University Press.

Prakasa-Rao, B. L. S. (1983), *Nonparametric Functional Estimation*, New York, Academic Press.

Prescott, D. M. and T. Stengos (1991), "Testing for Forecastible Non-Linear Dependence in Weekly Gold Rates of Return," manuscript, University of Guelph.

Priestley, M. B. and M. T. Chao (1972), "Nonparametric Function Fitting," *Journal of the Royal Statistical Society*, Series B, 34, 385–392.

Pritsker, M. (1998), "Nonparametric Density Estimation and Tests of Continuous-Time Interest Rate Models," *The Review of Financial Studies*, 11, 449–487.

Proença, I. (1993), "On the Performance of the H-H Test," manuscript, Center for Operations Research and Econometrics.

Pudney, S. (1993), "Income and Wealth Inequality and the Life Cycle: A Nonparametric Analysis for China," *Journal of Applied Econometrics*, 8, 249–276.

Quah, D. T. (1997), "Empirics for Growth and Distribution: Stratification, Polarization, and Convergence Clubs," *Journal of Economic Growth*, 2, 27–59.

Racine, J. S. and J. B. Smith (1991), "Nonparametric Estimation of Growth in Replenishable Resource Stocks," manuscript, York University, Canada.

Racine, J. (1997), "Consistent Significance Testing for Nonparametric Regression," *Journal of Business and Economic Statistics*, 15(3), 369–378.

Rahman, M., B. Arnold, D. G. Gokhale, and A. Ullah (1994), "Data-Based Smoothing Parameter in Kernel Density Estimation Using Exact MISE and Approximate MISE," manuscript, University of California at Riverside.

Ramanathan, R. (1989), *Introductory Econometrics with Applications*, San Diego, Harcourt Brace Jovanovich.

Rao, C. R. (1973), *Linear Statistical Inference and Its Applications*, New York, Wiley.

Ray, B. K. and R. S. Tsay (1997), "Bandwidth Selection for Kernel Regression with Long-Range Dependent Errors," *Biometrika*, 84, 791–802.

Reinsch, H. (1967), "Smoothing by Spline Functions," *Numerische Mathematik*, 10, 177–183.

Revesz, P. (1977), "How to Apply the Method of Stochastic Approximation in the Nonparametric Estimation of a Regression Function," *Mathematische Operationsforschung, Serie Statistics*, 8, 119–126.

Rice, J. (1984a), "Bandwidth Choice for Nonparametric Regression," *Annals of Statistics*, 12, 1215–1230.

Rice, J. (1984b), "Boundary Modification for Kernel Regression," *Communication in Statistics, Theory and Methods*, 13, 893–900.

Rilstone, P. (1987), *Nonparametric Partial Derivative Estimation*, Ph.D. thesis, University of Western Ontario.

Rilstone, P. (1989), "Semiparametric Instrumental Variables Estimation," manuscript, Laval University, revised.

Rilstone, P. (1991a), "Efficient Instrumental Variable Estimation of Nonlinear Dependent Process," manuscript, Laval University.

Rilstone, P. (1991b), "Nonparametric Hypothesis Testing with Parametric Rates of Convergence," *International Economic Review*, 32, 209–227.

Rilstone, P. (1991c), "Some Monte Carlo Evidence on the Relative Efficiency of Parametric and Semiparametric EGLS Estimators," *Journal of Business and Economic Statistics*, 9, 179–187.

Rilstone, P. (1992a), "Nonparametric Hypothesis Testing for Realistically Sized Samples," Research Report, Laval University.

Rilstone, P. (1992b), "Semiparametric IV Estimation with Parameter Dependent Instruments," *Econometric Theory*, 8, 403–406.

Rilstone, P. (1993), "Calculating the (Local) Semiparametric Efficiency Bounds for the Generated Regressors Problem," *Journal of Econometrics*, 56, 357–370.

Rilstone, P. and A. Ullah (1989), "Nonparametric Estimation of Response Coefficients," *Communications in Statistics, Theory and Methods*, 18, 2615–2627.

Robb, A. L., L. Magee, and J. B. Burbidge (1992), "Kernel Smoothed Consumption Age Quantiles," *Canadian Journal of Economics*, 25, 669–680.

Robinson, P. M. (1983), "Nonparametric Estimators for Time Series," *Journal of Time Series Analysis*, 4, 185–207.

Robinson, P. M. (1984), "Robust Nonparametric Autoregression," in J. Franke et al. (eds.), *Robust and Nonlinear Time Series Analysis*, Lecture Notes in Statistics, Vol. 26, Springer-Verlag, 247–255.

Robinson, P. M. (1986a), "On the Consistency and Finite Sample Properties of Nonparametric Kernel Time Series Regression, Autoregression and Density Estimators," *Annals of the Institute of Statistical Mathematics*, 38, 539–549.

Robinson, P. M. (1986b), "Nonparametric Estimation of Time Series Residuals," *Cahiers du C.E.R.O.*, 28, 197–202.

Robinson, P. M. (1987), "Asymptotically Efficient Estimation in the Presence of Heteroskedasticity of Unknown Form," *Econometrica*, 55, 875–891.

Robinson, P. M. (1988a), "Root−N-Consistent Semiparametric Regression," *Econometrica*, 56, 931–954.

Robinson, P. M. (1988b), "Adaptive Estimation of Heteroskedastic Econometric Models," *Discussion Paper No. R7*, London School of Economics.

Robinson, P. M. (1988c), "Semiparametric Econometrics: A Survey," *Journal of Applied Econometrics*, 3, 35–51.

Robinson, P. M. (1989), "Hypothesis Testing in Semiparametric and Nonparametric Models for Economic Time Series," *Review of Economic Studies*, 56, 511–534.

Robinson, P. M. (1991a), "Best Nonlinear Three-Stage Least Squares Estimation of Certain Econometric Models," *Econometrica*, 59, 755–786.

Robinson, P. M. (1991b), "Consistent Nonparametric Entropy-Based Testing," *Review of Economic Studies*, 58, 437–453.

Rodriguez, D. and T. M. Stoker (1993), "A Regression Test of Semiparametric Index Model Specification," manuscript, Sloan School of Management, M.I.T.

Roehrig, C. S. (1988), "Conditions for Identification in Nonparametric and Parametric Models," *Econometrica*, 56, 433–447.

Rose, R. L. (1978), *Nonparametric Estimation of Weights in Least-Squares Regression Analysis*, doctoral dissertation, University of California at Davis.

Rosenblatt, M. (1956a), "A Central Limit Theorem and a Strong Mixing Condition," *Proceedings of the National Academy of Sciences of the United States of America*, 42, 43–47.

Rosenblatt, M. (1956b), "Remarks on Some Nonparametric Estimates of a Density Function," *Annals of Mathematical Statistics*, 27, 642–669.

Rosenblatt, M. (1969), "Conditional Probability Density and Regression Estimators," in *Multivariate Analysis*, II, New York, Academic Press, 25–31.

Rosenblatt, M. (1970), "Density Estimates and Markov Sequences," in M. L. Puri (ed.), *Nonparametric Techniques in Statistical Inferences*, Cambridge, Cambridge University Press, 199–213.

Rosenblatt, M. (1975), "A Quadratic Measure of Deviation of Two-dimensional Density Estimates and a Test of Independence," *Annals of Statistics*, 3, 1–14.

Rosenblatt, M. (1978), "Dependence and Asymptotic Independence for Random Processes," in M. Rosenblatt (ed.), *Studies in Probability Theory*, Washington, DC, Mathematical Association of America, 24–25.

Rosenblatt, M. and B. E. Wahlen (1992), "A Nonparametric Measure of Independence under a Hypothesis of Independent Components," *Statistics and Probability Letters*, 15, 245–252.

Rothenberg, T. J. (1971), "Indentification in Parametric Models," *Econometrica*, 39, 577–592.

Rothenberg, T. J. (1984), "Approximating the Distribution of Econometric Estimators and Test Statistics," in Z. Griliches and M. D. Intriligator (eds.), *Handbook of Econometrics*, Vol. II, Amsterdam, North Holland, 15, 882–935.

Rothenberg, T. J. and C. T. Leenders (1964), "Efficient Estimation of Simultaneous Equation Systems," *Econometrica*, 32, 57–76.

Roussas, G. G. (1988), "A Moment Inequality of S_n, K_n for Triangular Arrays of Random Variables under Mixing Conditions, with Applications," in K. Matusita (ed.), *Statistical Theory and Data Analysis, II*, New York, North-Holland Publishers, 273–292.

Roussas, G. G. (1989), "Consistent Regression Estimation with Fixed Design Points under Dependent Conditions," *Statistics and Probability Letters*, 8, 235–243.

Roussas, G. G. and D. Ioannides (1987), "Moment Inequalities for Mixing Sequences of Random Variables," *Stochastic Analysis and Applications*, 5, 61–120.

Roy, A. D. (1951), "Some Thoughts on the Distribution of Earnings," *Oxford Economic Paper*, 3, 135–146.

Roy, N. (1997), *Nonparametric and Semiparametric Analysis of Panel Data Models: An Application to Calorie-Income Relation for Rural South India*, Ph.D. thesis, University of California, Riverside.

Royall, R. M. (1966), *A Class of Nonparametric Estimates of a Smooth Regression Function*, doctoral dissertation, Stanford University.

Royden, H. L. (1968), *Real Analysis*, London, MacMillan.

Rudemo, M. (1982), "Empirical Choice of Histograms and Kernel Density Estimators," *Scandinavian Journal of Statistics*, 9, 65–78.

Ruppert, D. and B. Aldershof (1989), "Transformations to Symmetry and Homoscedasticity," *Journal of the American Statistical Association*, 84, 437–446.

Ruppert, D. and R. J. Carroll (1981), "On Prediction and the Power Transformation Family," *Biometrika*, 68, 609–615.

Ruppert, D. and M. P. Wand (1994), "Multivariate Locally Weighted Least Squares Regression," *Annals of Statistics*, 22, 1346–1370.

Rust, R. T. (1988), "Flexible Regression," *Journal of Marketing Research*, 25, 10–24.

Rutkowski, L. (1985a), "Nonparametric Identification of Quasi-Stationary Systems," *Systems and Control Letters*, 6, 33–35.

Rutkowski, L. (1985b), "Real-Time Identification of Time-Varying System by Nonparametric Algorithms Based on Parzen Kernels," *International Journal of Systems Science*, 16, 1123–1130.

Ruud, P. A. (1983), "Sufficient Conditions for the Consistency of Maximum Likelihood Estimation Despite Misspecification of Distribution in Multinomial Discrete Choice Models," *Econometrica*, 51, 225–228.

Samiuddin, M. and G. M. El-Sayyad (1990), "On Nonparametric Kernel Density Estimates," *Biometrika*, 77, 865–874.

Samuelson, P. A. (1938), "A Note on the Pure Theory of Consumers Behaviour," *Economica*, 5, 61–71.

Sargan, J. D. (1958), "The Estimation of Economic Relationships Using Instrumental Variables," *Econometrica*, 26, 393–415.

Schoenberg, I. J. (1964), "Spline Function and the Problem of Graduation," *Mathematics*, 52, 947–950.

Schucany, W. R. and J. P. Summers (1977), "Improvement of Kernel Type Density Estimators," *Journal of the American Statistical Association*, 72, 420–423.

Schuster, E. F. (1969), "Estimation of a Probability Density Function and Its Derivatives," *Annals of Mathematical Statistics*, 40, 1187–95.

Schuster, E. F. (1970), "Note on Uniform Convergence of Density Estimates," *Annals of Mathematical Statistics*, 41, 1347–48.

Schuster, E. F. (1972), "Joint Asymptotic Distribution of the Estimated Regression Function at a Finite Number of Distinct Points," *Annals of Mathematical Statistics*, 43, 84–88.

Schuster, E. and S. Yakowitz (1979), "Contributions to the Theory of Nonparametric Regression, with Applications to System Identification," *Annals of Statistics*, 7, 139–149.

Schweppe, F. C. (1965), "Evaluation of Likelihood Functions for Gaussian Signals," *I.E.E.E. Transactions on Information Theory*, 11, 61–70.

Scott, D. W. (1979), "On Optimal and Data-Based Histograms," *Biometrika*, 66, 605–610.

Scott, D. W. (1986), "Choosing Smoothing Parameters for Density Estimators," in D. M. Allen (ed.), *Computer Science and Statistics: Proceedings of the 17th Symposium on the Interface*, New York, Elsevier Science Publishers, North Holland, 225–229.

Scott, D. W. and L. E. Factor (1981), "Monte Carlo Study of Three Data-Based Non-parametric Probability Density Estimators," *Journal of the American Statistical Association*, 76, 9–15.

Scott, D. W., R. A. Tapia, and J. R. Thompson (1980), "Nonparametric Probability Density Estimation by Discrete Maximum Penalized-Likelihood Criteria," *Annals of Statistics*, 8, 820–832.

Scott, D. W. and G. R. Terrell (1987), "Biased and Unbiased Cross-Validation in Density Estimation," *Journal of the American Statistical Association*, 82, 1131–1146.

Serfling, R. J. (1968), "Contributions to Central Limit Theory for Dependent Variables," *Annals of Mathematical Statistics*, 39, 1158–1175.

Serfling, R. J. (1980), *Approximation Theorems of Mathematical Statistics*, New York, Wiley.

Sheather, S. J. (1986), "An Improved Data-Based Algorithm for Choosing the Window Width When Estimating the Density at a Point," *Computational Statistics and Data Analysis*, 4, 61–65.

Sheather, S. J. and M. C. Jones (1991), "A Reliable Data Based Bandwidth Selection Method for Kernel Density Estimation," *Journal of the Royal Statistical Society*, Series B, 53, 683–690.

Sherman, R. P. (1993), "The Limiting Distribution of the Maximum Rank Correlation Estimator," *Econometrica*, 61, 123–137.

Shorack, G. R. and J. A. Wellner (1986), *Empirical Processes with Applications to Statistics*, New York, Wiley.

Silverman, B. W. (1978), "Weak and Strong Uniform Consistency of the Kernel Estimate of a Density and Its Derivatives," *Annals of Statistics*, 6, 177–184.

Silverman, B. W. (1980), "Density Estimation: Are Theoretical Results Useful in Practice?," in I. M. Chakravarti (eds.), *Asymptotic Theory of Statistical Tests and Estimation*, New York, Academic Press, 179–203.

Silverman, B. W. (1982), "On the Estimation of a Probability Density Function by the Maximum Penalized Likelihood Method," *Annals of Statistics*, 10, 795–810.

Silverman, B. W. (1984), "Spline Smoothing: The Equivalent Variable Kernel Method," *Annals of Statistics*, 12, 898–916.

Silverman, B. W. (1986), *Density Estimation for Statistics and Data Analysis*, New York, Chapman and Hall.

Singh, R. S. and D. S. Tracy (1970), "Strongly Consistent Estimators of k-th Order Regression Curves and Rates of Convergence" *Zeitschrift für Wahrscheinlichkeitstheorie und Verwandte Gabiet*, 40, 339–348.

Singh, R. S. and A. Ullah (1985), "Nonparametric Time Series Estimation of Joint DGP, Conditional DGP and Vector Autoregression," *Econometric Theory*, 1, 27–52, also erratum (1987), 547.

Singh, R. S. and A. Ullah (1986), "Nonparametric Recursive Estimation of a Multivariate, Marginal and Conditional DGP with an Application to Specification of Econometric Models," *Communications in Statistics, Theory and Methods*, 15, 3489–3513.

Singh, R. S., A. Ullah, and R. A. L. Carter (1987), "Nonparametric Inference in Econometrics: New Applications," in Ian B. MacNeill and G. J. Umphrey (eds.), *Time Series and Econometric Modelling, Vol. III*, Boston, D. Reidell, 253–278.

Smith, P. J. (1988), "Asymptotic Properties of Linear Regression Estimators under a Fixed Censorship Model," *Australian Journal of Statistics*, 30, 52–66.

Spanos, A. (1986), *Statistical Foundations of Econometric Modelling*, New York, Cambridge University Press.

Speckman, P. (1988), "Kernel Smoothing in Partial Linear Models," *Journal of the Royal Statistical Society*, Series B, 50, 413–446.

Staniswalis, J. G. (1989), "The Kernel Estimate of a Regression Function in Likelihood Based Models," *Journal of the American Statistical Association*, 84, 276–283.

Staniswalis, J. G. and T. A. Severini (1991), "Diagnostics for Assessing Regression Models," *Journal of the American Statistical Association*, 86, 684–692.

Steigerwald, D. (1993), "Efficient Estimation of Models with Conditional Heteroskedasticity," manuscript, University of California, Santa Barbara.

Stein, C. (1956), "Efficent Nonparametric Testing and Estimation," *Proceedings of the Third Berkeley Symposium on Mathematical Statistics and Probability*, Berkeley, University of California Press, 1, 187–196.

Stinchcombe, M. B. and H. White (1998), "Consistent Specification Testing with Nuisance Parameters Present Only under the Alternative," *Econometric Theory*, 14, 295–325.

Stock, J. H. (1989), "Nonparametric Policy Analysis," *Journal of the American Statistical Association*, 84, 567–575.

Stoker, T. M. (1986), "Consistent Estimation of Scaled Coefficients," *Econometrica*, 54, 1461–1481.

Stoker, T. M. (1989), "Tests of Additive Derivative Constraints," *Review of Economic Studies*, 56, 535–552.

Stoker, T. M. (1991), "Equivalence of Direct, Indirect and Slope Estimators of Average Derivatives," in W. A. Barnett, J. L. Powell, and G. E. Tauchen (eds.), *Nonparametric and Semiparametric Methods in Econometrics and Statistics*, New York, Cambridge University Press, 99–118.

Stoker, T. M. (1992), *Lectures on Semiparametric Econometrics*, Louvain-la-Neuve, CORE Foundation.

Stoker, T. M. (1993), "Smoothing Bias in Density Derivative Estimation," *Journal of the American Statistical Association*, 88, 855–863.

Stone, C. J. (1975), "Adaptive Maximum Likelihood of a Location Parameter," *Annals of Statistics*, 3, 267–284.

Stone, C. J. (1977), "Consistent Nonparametric Regression," *Annals of Statistics*, 5, 595–645.

Stone, C. J. (1980), "Optimal Convergence Rates for Nonparametric Estimators," *Annals of Statistics*, 8, 1348–1360.

Stone, C. J. (1984), "An Asymptotically Optimal Window Selection Rule for Kernel Density Estimates," *Annals of Statistics*, 12, 1285–97.

Stone, C. J. (1985), "Additive Regression and Other Nonparametric Models," *Annals of Statistics*, 13, 689–705.

Stout, W. F. (1974), *Almost Sure Convergence*, New York, Academic Press.

Stute, W. (1984), "Asymptotic Normality of Nearest Neighbor Regression Function Estimates," *The Annals of Statistics*, 12, 917–926.

Stützle, W. and Y. Mittal (1979), "Some Comments on the Asymptotic Behaviour of Robust Smoothers," in T. Gasser and M. Rosenblatt (eds.), *Smoothing Techniques for Curve Estimation*, No. 757, Heidelberg, Springer-Verlag, 191–195.

Subramanian, S. and A. Deaton (1996), "The Demand for Food and Calories, Further Evidence from India," *Journal of Political Economy*, 104, 133–162.

Szu, H. and R. Hartley (1987), "Fast Simulated Annealing," *Physics Letters*, A, 122, 157–162.

Takada, H., A. Ullah, and Y. Chen (1995), "Estimation of the SUR Model When the Error Covariance Matrix Is Singular: An Application to a Marketing Model," *Journal of Applied Statistics*, 22, 501–514.

Tapia, R. A. and J. R. Thompson (1977), *Nonparametric Probability Density Estimation*, Baltimore, Johns Hopkins University Press.

Tauchen, G. (1985), "Diagnostic Testing and Evaluation of Maximum Likelihood Models," *Journal of Econometrics*, 30, 415–443.

Tauchen, G. (1986), "Statistical Properties of Generalized Method of Moments Estimates of Utility Function Parameters Based on Financial Market Data," *Journal of Business and Economic Statistics*, 4, 397–415.

Taylor, J. M. G. (1985), "Power Transformations to Symmetry," *Biometrika*, 72, 145–152.

Theil, H. (1971), *Principles of Econometrics*, New York, Wiley.

Thompson, T. S. (1993), "Some Efficiency Bounds for Semiparametric Discrete Choice Models," *Journal of Econometrics*, 58, 257–274.

Tibshirani, R. (1984), *Local Likelihood Estimation*, Ph.D. thesis, Stanford University.

Titterington, D. M. (1985), "Common Structure of Smoothing Techniques in Statistics," *International Statistical Review*, 53, 141–170.

Tjøstheim, D. and B. Auestad (1994), "Nonparametric Identification of Nonlinear Time Series: Projections," *Journal of the American Statistical Association*, 89, 1398–1409.

Tobin, J. (1958), "Estimation of Relationships for Limited Dependent Variables," *Econometrica*, 26, 24–36.

Tsybakov, A. B. (1982), "Robust Estimates of a Function," *Problems of Information Transmission*, 18, 190–201.

Tukey, J. W. (1977), *Exploratory Data Analysis*, Reading, Massachusetts, Addison-Wesley.

Ullah, A. (1985), "Specification Analysis of Econometric Models," *Journal of Quantitative Economics*, 1, 187–209.

Ullah, A. (1988a), "Nonparametric Estimation and Hypothesis Testing in Econometric Models," *Empirical Economics*, 13, 223–249.

Ullah, A. (1988b), Nonparametric Estimation of Econometric Functionals, *Canadian Journal of Economics*, 21, 625–658.

Ullah, A. (1992), "The Exact Density of Nonparametric Regression Estimators: Fixed Design Case," *Communications in Statistics, Theory and Methods*, 21, 1251–1254.

Ullah, A. (1996), "Entropy, Divergence and Distance Measures with Econometric Applications," *Journal of Statistical Planning and Inference*, 49, 137–162.

Ullah, A. and K. Mundra (1998), "Semiparametric Panel Data Estimation: An Application to Immigrants Homelink Effect on U.S. Producer Trade Flows," Working Paper No. 15, University of California, Riverside.

Ullah, A. and J. Racine (1992), "Smooth Improved Estimators of Econometric Parameters," in W. E. Griffith et al. (eds.), *Readings in Econometric Theory and Practice*, New York, North Holland, 197–213.

Ullah, A. and N. Roy (1998), "Nonparametric and Semiparametric Econometrics of Panel Data," in A. Ullah and D. E. A. Giles (eds.), *Handbook of Applied Economic Statistics*, Marcel Dekker, Ch. 17, 579–604.

Ullah, A. and R. S. Singh (1989), "Estimation of a Probability Density Function with Applications to Nonparametric Inference in Econometrics," in B. Raj (ed.), *Advances in Econometrics and Modelling, Advanced Studies in Theoretical and Applied Econometrics*, Dordrecht, Kluwer Academic Publishers, 69–83.

Ullah, A., V. K. Srivastava, and R. Chandra (1983), "Properties of Shrinkage Estimators in Linear Regression When Disturbances Are not Normal," *Journal of Econometrics*, 21, 389–402.

Ullah, A. and H. D. Vinod (1988), "Nonparametric Kernel Estimation of Econometric Parameters," *Journal of Quantitative Economics*, 4, 81–87.

Ullah, A. and H. D. Vinod (1993), "General Nonparametric Regression Estimation and Testing in Econometrics," in G. S. Maddala, C. R. Rao, and H. D. Vinod (eds.), *Handbook of Statistics*, Vol. 11, Amsterdam, Elsevier Publishing Co., 85–116.

Van Ryzin, J. (1969), "On Strong Consistency of Density Estimates," *Annals of Mathematical Statistics*, 40, 1765–1772.

Van Ryzin, J. (1973), "A Histogram Method of Density Estimation," *Communications in Statistics*, 2, 493–506.

Varian, H. R. (1984), "The Nonparametric Approach to Production Analysis," *Econometrica*, 52, 579–598.

Varian, H. R. (1985), "Nonparametric Analysis of Optimizing Behaviour with Measurement Error," *Journal of Econometrics*, 30, 445–458.

Vieu, P. (1994), "Choice of Regressors in Nonparametric Estimation," *Computational Statistics and Data Analysis*, 17, 575–594.

Vinod, H. D. and A. Ullah (1981), *Recent Advances in Regression Methods*, New York, Marcel Dekker.

Vinod, H. D. and A. Ullah (1988), "Flexible Production Estimation by Nonparametric Kernel Estimators," in T. B. Fomby and G. F. Rhodes (eds.), *Advances in Econometrics: Nonparametric and Robust Statistical Inference*, Vol. 7, London, JAI Press, 139–160.

Vuong, Q. H. (1989), "Likelihood Ratio Tests for Model Selection and Non-Nested Hypotheses," *Econometrica*, 57, 307–333.

Wahba, G. (1979), "Smoothing and Ill-Posed Problems," in M. A. Goldberg (ed.), *Solution Methods for Integral Equations: Theory and Applications*, New York, Plenum, 183–194.

Wahba, G. (1985), "A Comparison of GCV and GML for Choosing the Smoothing Parameter in the Generalized Spline Smoothing Problem," *Annals of Statistics*, 13, 1378–1402.

Wahba, G. (1986), "Partial and Interaction Spline Models for the Semiparametric Estimation of Functions of Several Variables," in T. J. Boardman (ed.), *Computer Science and Statistics: Proceedings of the 18th Symposium on the Interface*, Washington, DC, American Statistical Association, 75–80.

Wales, T. J. and A. D. Woodland (1980), "Sample Selectivity and the Estimation of Labor Supply Functions," *International Economic Review*, 21, 437–468.

Wand, M. P. and M. C. Jones (1993), "Comparison of Smoothing Parameterizations in Bivariate Kernel Density Estimation," *Journal of the American Statistical Association*, 88, 520–528.

Wang, W. and M. Zhou (1995), "Iterative Least Squares Estimator of Binary Choice Models: A Semiparametric Approach," *Working Paper # E-180-95*, University of Kentucky.

Watson, G. S. (1964), "Smooth Regression Analysis," *Sankhya*, Series A, 26, 359–372.

Watson, G. S. and M. R. Leadbetter (1963), "On the Estimation of Probability Density, I," *Annals of Mathematical Statistics*, 34, 480–491.

Whang, Y. J. and D. W. K. Andrews (1993), "Tests of Specification for Parametric and Semiparametric Models," *Journal of Econometrics*, 57, 277–318.

Whistler, D. (1988), "Semiparametric ARCH Estimation of Intra-Daily Exchange Rate Volatility," manuscript, London School of Economics.

White, H. (1980a), "Using Least Squares to Approximate Unknown Regression Functions," *International Economic Review*, 21, 149–170.

White, H. (1980b), "A Heteroskedasticity-Consistent Covariance Matrix Estimator and a Direct Test for Heteroskedasticity," *Econometrica*, 48, 817–838.

White, H. (1982), "Instrumental Variables Estimation with Independent Observations," *Econometrica*, 50, 483–500.

White, H. (1984), *Asymptotic Theory for Econometricians*, Orlando, Academic Press Inc.

White, H. (1992), *Estimation, Inference and Specification Analysis* New York, Cambridge University Press.

White, H. and I. Domowitz (1984), "Nonlinear Regression with Dependent Observations," *Econometrica*, 52, 143–162.

White, H. and J. M. Wooldridge (1991), "Some Results on Sieve Estimation with Dependent Observations," in W. J. Barnett, J. Powell, and G. Tauchen (eds.), *Nonparametric and Semiparametric Methods in Econometrics and Statistics*, New York, Cambridge University Press, 459–493.

Whittaker, E. T. (1923), "On a New Method of Graduation," *Proceedings of the Edinburgh Mathematical Society*, 41, 63–75.

Wolverton, C. T. and T. J. Wagner (1969), "Asymptotically Optimal Discriminant Function for Pattern Classification," *IEEE Transactions on Information Theory*, IT-15, 258–265.

Woodroofe, M. (1970), "On Choosing a Delta Sequence," *Annals of Mathematical Statistics*, 41, 1665–1671.

Wooldridge, J. M. (1992), "A Test for Functional Form Against Nonparametric Alternatives," *Econometric Theory*, 8, 452–475.

Wooldridge, J. M. and H. White (1988), "Some Invariance Principle and Central Limit Theorems for Dependent Heterogeneous Processes," *Econometric Theory*, 4, 210–230.

Wulwick, N. J. and Y. P. Mack (1990), "A Kernel Regression of Phillips' Data," *Working Paper No. 40*, New York, Jerone Levy Economics Institute, Bard College.

Yamato, H. (1971), "Sequential Estimation of a Continuous Probability Function and Mode," *Bulletin of Mathematical Statistics*, 14, 1–12.

Yang, S. S. (1981), "Linear Function of Concomitants of Order Statistics with Application to Nonparametric Estimation of a Regression Function," *Journal of the American Statistical Association*, 76, 658–662.

Yatchew, A. J. (1992), "Nonparametric Regression Tests Based on Least Squares," *Econometric Theory*, 8, 435–451.

Zellner, A., D. S. Huang, and L. C. Chau (1965), "Further Analysis of the Short Run Consumption Function with Emphasis on the Role of Liquid Assets," *Econometrica*, 33, 571–581.

Zhao, L. and Z. Fang (1985), "Strong Convergence of Kernel Estimates of Nonparametric Regression Functions," *Chinese Annals of Mathematics*, Series B, 6, 147–155.

Zheng, J. X. (1993), "A Consistent Test of Conditional Parametric Distributions," manuscript, University of Texas, Austin.

Zheng, J. X. (1995), "A Specification Test of Conditional Parametric Distributions Using Kernel Estimation Methods," manuscript, University of Texas, Austin.

Zheng, J. X. (1996), "A Consistent Test of Functional Form via Nonparametric Estimation Techniques," *Journal of Econometrics*, 75, 263–290.

Zheng, J. X. (1999), "Specification Testing and Nonparametric Estimation of the Human Capital Model," in T. B. Fomby and R. C. Hill (eds.), *Advances in Econometrics: Applying Kernel and Nonparametric Estimation to Economic Topics*, 14, JAI Press.

Zhou, Z. (1993), *The Predictability of Stock Returns*, Ph.D. thesis, University of California, Riverside.

Index

420   **Index**